Communications
in Computer and Information Science   **674**

Commenced Publication in 2007
Founding and Former Series Editors:
Alfredo Cuzzocrea, Dominik Ślęzak, and Xiaokang Yang

More information about this series at http://www.springer.com/series/7899

Andrei V. Chugunov · Radomir Bolgov
Yury Kabanov · George Kampis
Maria Wimmer (Eds.)

Digital Transformation and Global Society

First International Conference, DTGS 2016
St. Petersburg, Russia, June 22–24, 2016
Revised Selected Papers

 Springer

Editors

Andrei V. Chugunov
ITMO University
St. Petersburg
Russia

Radomir Bolgov
Saint Petersburg State University
St. Petersburg
Russia

Yury Kabanov
National Research University Higher
  School of Economics
St. Petersburg
Russia

George Kampis
Eotvos University Budapest
Budapest
Hungary

Maria Wimmer
Universität Koblenz-Landau
Koblenz, Rheinland-Pfalz
Germany

ISSN 1865-0929   ISSN 1865-0937 (electronic)
Communications in Computer and Information Science
ISBN 978-3-319-49699-3   ISBN 978-3-319-49700-6 (eBook)
DOI 10.1007/978-3-319-49700-6

Library of Congress Control Number: 2016957855

Printed on acid-free paper

This Springer imprint is published by Springer Nature
The registered company is Springer International Publishing AG
The registered company address is: Gewerbestrasse 11, 6330 Cham, Switzerland

Preface

The world and society are becoming more and more complex thanks to the transformational power of digital information and communication technologies. Digital transformation changes all spheres of human activity and opens new horizons for innovation, development, and welfare. Yet it also poses new challenges for our society asking how we should react and adapt to the ongoing innovation, be it the emergence of new ways of political participation, education, and science, urban planning, and health care. For scholars, the process of digital transformation brings about a broad, multidisciplinary research agenda with plenty of puzzles to solve and questions to answer.

These were the issues we kept in mind when organizing the new international conference "Digital Transformation and Global Society" (DTGS 2016). It was held on June 22–24, 2016 in St. Petersburg, Russia. The conference was hosted by ITMO University and was also co-organized by the University of Amsterdam, the European University at Saint-Petersburg, and the e-Development Partnership in the north-west of Russia (PRIOR North-West).

The conference became a successor of another significant international event – the international joint conference "Internet and Modern Society" (IMS) held annually in St. Petersburg since 1998. It brings together researchers and experts from all over Russia and abroad to discuss a wide range of information society issues. The IMS conference has become a well-established forum recognized by academic scholars and practitioners for offering a great opportunity to collaborate in knowledge exchange. Building on this unique and long-lasting legacy, in 2016, IMS acquired a stronger international dimension under the DTGS umbrella – an Information Society Technology Week at ITMO University with the aim of attracting new international researchers and raising the quality of submitted papers.

The present volume contains the papers presented at DTGS 2016. We received 157 submissions; each of them was reviewed by at least three, and in some cases by four, international Program Committee members. The committee accepted 61 papers, with an acceptance rate of 39%. The papers in this volume attempt to describe the emerging digital transformation challenges and to offer research insights addressing these challenges from both social and technological perspectives.

The structure of this volume corresponds to the five DTGS 2016 tracks:

- eSociety, with issues regarding the mutual adaptation of technologies and sociopolitical systems. Owing to the large number of papers, the track was divided into two: E-Government and E-Participation, and New Social Media Studies.
- eKnowledge, devoted to the prospects, practices, and perils of the usage of new technologies in the sphere of knowledge-sharing and innovations in educational and academic activities.
- eCity, presenting the state of the art in the theory and practice of smart city technologies, municipal development and urban/rural planning and management.

- eHealth, bringing together scientists to discuss current trends the usage of ICTs in health care.
- eScience, encompassing questions of scientific development due to new technologies, big data research, and collaborations between social and technical fields of inquiry.

The conference started with the posters and ongoing research session. The best short papers are included in the volume along with the full papers from seven plenary sessions and workshops.

Two keynote reports were presented as well:

- Professor Peter Sloot (University of Amsterdam) presented an insightful report on "Complexity Science and the Internet of Things," explaining how the latter may help to understand complex systems, "from a biological cell... to millions of computer systems... to our society."
- Latif Ladid (University of Luxembourg), Founder and President of IPv6 Forum, shared his view on the future of the Internet and perspectives on the use of IPv6 in innovations, such as the Internet of Things, cloud computing, and smart cities.

We would like to thank all those who made this event possible and successful. We especially express our gratitude to all Program Committee members for their contribution to the high academic level of the event. We thank all the authors for presenting their excellent papers and also the session chairs, who led fruitful discussions. We are also grateful to all organizers, representatives of institutions, and hosts who contributed to the success of this conference. Finally, we are proud to attract a great team of scholars from different countries and disciplines and, as discussed at the conference, we will work further to sustain and expand the DTGS community through continuous research and collaboration. We believe that the DTGS has the potential to turn into a new important forum for fruitful academic discussion.

September 2016

Andrei V. Chugunov
Radomir Bolgov
Yury Kabanov
George Kampis
Maria Wimmer
Valeria Krzhizhanovskaya
Alexander V. Boukhanovsky

Organization

Organizing Committee

Alexander V. Boukhanovsky	ITMO University, Russia
Anna Bylyatdinova	ITMO University
Radomir Bolgov	St. Petersburg State University, Russia
Andrei V. Chugunov	ITMO University, Russia
Olga Dmitrova	ITMO University, Russia
Carlos Gerschenson	Universidad Nacional Autónoma de México, Mexico
	Massachusetts Institute of Technology, USA
Yury Kabanov	National Research University Higher School of Economics, Russia
	ITMO University, Russia
Valeria Krzhizhanovskaya	University of Amsterdam, The Netherlands
Marina Lebedeva	ITMO University, Russia
Peter M.A. Sloot	University of Amsterdam, The Netherlands
Diana West	European University at St. Petersburg, Russia

Session Chairs

Francisco Pacheco de Andrade	University of Minho, Portugal
Nikolay Butakov	ITMO University, Russia
Sergei Ivanov	ITMO University
George Kampis	Eötvös University, Hungary
Philipp Kazin	ITMO University, Russia
Fabian Kirstein	Fraunhofer FOKUS, Germany
Sotirios Koussouris	National Technical University of Athens, Greece
Yuri Misnikov	ITMO University, Russia
	eGovernance Academy, Estonia
Dessislava Petrova-Antonova	Sofia University, Bulgaria
Leonid Smorgunov	St. Petersburg State University, Russia
Lyudmila Vidiasova	ITMO University, Russia
Maria Wimmer	University Koblenz-Landau, Germany

Program Committee

Olusegun Agbabiaka	National eGovernment Strategies, Nigeria
Dimitris Alimisis	EDUMOTIVA-European Lab for Educational Technology, Greece
Luis Amaral	University of Minho, Portugal
Cornelia Amihalachioae	e-Government Center, Moldova
Arry Akhmad Arman	School of Electrical Engineering and Informatics of ITB, Indonesia
Mohammed Awad	American University of Ras al-Khaimah, United Arab Emirates
Johnstone Baguma	Toro Development Network (ToroDev), Uganda
Alexander Balthasar	Institute for State Organisation and Administrative Reform, A.F.C., Austria
Anna Bilyatdinova	ITMO University, Russia
Radomir Bolgov	Saint-Petersburg State University, Russia
Alexander Boukhanovsky	ITMO University, Russia
Mikhail Bundin	Lobachevski State University of Nizhni Novgorod, Russia
Olga Bychkova	European University at St. Petersburg, Russia
Sunil Choenni	Rotterdam University of Applied Sciences, The Netherlands
Andrei V. Chugunov	ITMO University, Russia
Cesar Alberto Collazos	University of Cauca, Colombia
Meghan Cook	University at Albany SUNY, USA
Vytautas Cyras	Vilnius University, Lithuania
Shefali Dash	National Informatics Centre, India
Francisco de Andrade	University of Minho, Portugal
Maria Esther Del Moral Perez	University of Oviedo, Spain
Olga Dmitrova	ITMO University, Russia
Sofia Dokuka	Higher School of Economics, Russia
Zuzana Dvořáková	Academy of Sciences of the Czech Republic, Czech Republic
Johanna Ekua Awotwi	Centre for e-Governance, Ghana
Joan Omololu Fabgule	University of Ilorin, Nigeria
Behnam Faghih	Shiraz University, Iran
Isabel Ferreira	University of Minho, Portugal
Pablo Fillottrani	Universidad Nacional del Sur, Argentina
Simon Fong	Department of Computer and Information Science University of Macau, SAR, China
Enrico Francesconi	National Research Council, Italy
Fernando Galindo	University of Zaragoza, Spain
Ramon Garcia	Center for Technology in Government, University at Albany, SUNY, USA
Despina Garyfallidou	Univerisity of Patras, Greece

Carlos Gershenson	Autonomous University of Mexico, Mexico
Paul Gibson	Le département Logiciels-Réseaux (LOR) Telecom Sud Paris, France
Christoph Glauser	Institute for Applied Argumentation Research, Switzerland
María Gonzalez	Universidad Nacional del Sur, Argentina
Elissaveta Gourova	Sofia University, Bulgaria
Dimitris Gouscos	University of Athens, Greece
Ronald Greenberg	Brown & Weinraub, PLLC, USA
Stefanos Gritzalis	University of the Aegean, Greece
Ahsan Habib	North East University Bangladesh, Bangladesh
Janusz Holyst	Warsaw University of Technology, Poland
Nikolina Hrustek	University of Zagreb, Croatia
Vigneswara Ilavarasan	Indian Institute of Technology New Delhi, India
Diana Ishmatova	APEC e-Government Research Center
Yury Kabanov	National Research University Higher School of Economics, Russia
Katerina Kabassi	TEI of the Ionian Islands, Greece ·
Christos Kalloniatis	University of the Aegean, Greece
Samia Kamal	Oxford Brookes University, UK
George Kampis	Budapest University, Hungary
Vitalina Karachay	ITMO University, Russia
Sergei Koltcov	National Research University Higher School of Economics, Russia
Olessia Koltsova	National Research University Higher School of Economics, Russia
Ah Lian Kor	Leeds Metropolitan University, UK
Valeria Krzhizhanovskaya	University of Amsterdam, The Netherlands
Akmaral Kuatbayeva	Shokan Ualikhanov Kokshetau State University, Kazakhstan
Subrata Kumar Dey	Independent University, Bangladesh
Sanjeev Kumar Katara	National Informatics Centre, India
Latif Ladid	University of Luxembourg, Luxembourg
David Lamas	Tallinn University, Estonia
Mike Lees	University of Amsterdam, The Netherlands
Christine Leitner	Center for Economics and Public Administration, Austria
Sandro Leuchter	Mannheim University of Applied Sciences, Germany
Claudia Linnhoff-Popien	Ludwig Maximilians University Munich, Germany
C.K. Lok	HKU, Hong Kong, SAR China
Francesco Longo	University of Messina, Italy
Latifa Mahdaoui	University of Science and Technology – Houari Boumediene, Algeria
Ignacio Marcovesshio	Universidad Nacional del Sur, Argentina
Aleksei Martynov	Lobachevski State University of Nizhni Novgorod, Russia

Fabro Steibel	Open Government Partnership in Brazil, Brazil
Meng Sun	Peking University, China
Alexander Sungurov	National Research University Higher School of Economics, Russia
Jirapon Sunkpho	Thammasat University, Thailand
Tamás Szádeczky	National University of Public Service, Hungary
Antonio Tavares	University of Minho, Portugal
Anas Tawileh	Systematics Consulting, Oman
Alice Trindade	Pólo Universitário da Ajuda, Portugal
Dmitrii Trutnev	ITMO University, Russia
Rita Tse Tan Sim	Macao Polytechnic Institute, China
Elpida Tzafestas	University of Athens, Greece
Mario Vacca	University of Rome, Italy
Natalia Vasilyeva	Saint Petersburg State University, Russia
Costas Vassilakis	University of the Peloponnese, Greece
Cyril Velikanov	Memorial Society, Moscow, Russia
Lyudmila Vidyasova	ITMO University, Russia
Wilfred Warioba	Commission for Human Rights and Good Governance, Tanzania
Diana West	European University at St. Petersburg, Russia
Hentie Wilson	University of South Africa, South Africa
Fang Chun Yang	Academy of e-Government, China
Sherali Zeadally	University of Kentucky, USA
Hans-Dieter Zimmermann	FHS St. Gallen University of Applied Sciences, Switzerland

Sponsors

The conference is sponsored by Russian Scientific Foundation Agreement # 14-21-00137 dated 15.08.2014 "Supercomputer Modeling of Critical Phenomena in Complex Social Systems."

Contents

eKnowledge: ICTs in Learning and Education Management

eCity: ICTs for Better Urban (Rural) Planning and Living

eHealth: ICTs in Healthcare

eScience: Big Data and Complex Calculations

eSociety: New Social Media Studies

The Phenomenon of the Virtual Youth Twitter-Community in the Discourses of Sociological Concepts and Self-representations

Veronika Shcheblanova[1(✉)], Elena Bogomiagkova[2], and Tatiana Semchenko[3]

[1] Saratov State Legal Academy, Saratov, Russia
vsheblanova@mail.ru
[2] St. Petersburg State University, St. Petersburg, Russia
e.bogomyagkova@spbu.ru
[3] National Research State University of Saratov, Saratov, Russia
semtatjanal@rambler.ru

Abstract. The article is devoted to the study of the phenomenon of the youth Twitter-community from two main perspectives. First, we analyze sociological theoretical and methodological concepts. Second, we interpret both the survey data provided by informants (N = 10; 2014–2015), residing in the city of Saratov and being popular within a given community, and the materials of the informants' Twitter-accounts. In our opinion this social network underlines the new trends of modernity better than others, successfully displays the person's inner world. According to the results of theoretical and methodological analysis, significant sociological discourse fields of the youth virtual communities were highlighted. The results of the collected interviews' analysis are provided.

Keywords: Virtual social networks · Youth twitter-community · Sociological discourses · Interview · Social functions of microblog · Activism in social networking websites · Microblog's privacy vs. publicity · Online diary · Trend designing · Popularity in microblog

1 Introduction

The article is based on the analysis of the phenomenon of the youth Twitter-community from both sociological concepts and results of empirical research. Results of empirical research are based on data from interviews with informants (N = 10; 2014–2015), residing in the city of Saratov and being popular within a given community, and on the materials of the informants' Twitter-accounts. Key concepts of the article include understanding of Twitter as a microbolog service and as a virtual community that brings people together for a definite purpose, acts in accordance with the rules and regulations, helps to transform social interactions and relationships. The results of the analysis of the youth Twitter-community members' self-representations are provided in the article. We are interested in how the youth perceive Twitter, use it, what meanings

© Springer International Publishing AG 2016
A.V. Chugunov et al. (Eds.): DTGS 2016, CCIS 674, pp. 3–13, 2016.
DOI: 10.1007/978-3-319-49700-6_1

and feelings arise in the processes of using Twitter. The purpose of this research was to analyze Twitter as a form of an on-line diary, networking in the designing trends and popularity and to consider Twitter as a popular resource and means to achieve popularity.

2   Sociological Discourses of Virtual Community: Functionality, Activity Monitoring, Collective Capital

Twitter represents a microblog, the part of the phenomenon of the Internet blog-golization. The flowering of blogs, live journals on the Internet started in the beginning of the two thousandth's, Twitter blossoming in Russia occurred in 2011. According to given regular research of active audience of social networks in Russia Twitter takes the third place (after "Vkontakte" and "Instagram") by the number of the "writing" authors. Number of active authors a little more than 1 million people here, and the audience of Twitter in November, 2015 has made 7,7 million people [9]. Indeed, "Facebook", "Vkontakte", "Odnoklassniki" have the so-called "personal profile" structure, which in many ways directs, prescribes what information and in which form to write. Twitter limits only the size of the tweet messages to 140 characters, but in all the other respects a person is free to do whatever he wants – to write about himself a lot or a little, to describe each action or to write once a month. Everyone has the right to read almost any user without confirmation, in contrast with other social networks. In a sociological perspective the authors identify two areas of blog analysis: one of them focuses on social networks, emerging in the blogosphere, and the other - on the social action [7] through the features of which the social structure is being studied. And we will address both of these areas.

"Social Network Sites exhibit wide popularity, high diffusion and an increasing number of features" [19: 3287]. A virtual community is a cyberspace having various Internet-based chat technologies, including discussion forums (discussion or bulletin board). It depends on social interaction among its members, who share interests, build relationships, create fantasies, and conduct transactions [13: 522]. Rheinghold, specializing in the study of social relations on the Internet, defined the virtual community as a kind of smart mobs, as "a social aggregation that emerges from the Internet when enough people carry on those public discussions long enough, with sufficient human feeling, to form webs of personal relationships in cyberspace" [16: 448]. Some other authors stress the fact that "trust is a key element in fostering the voluntary online cooperation between strangers seen in virtual communities" [17: 271]. In our research we hold to this very concept of the term "virtual community", considering the youth virtual Twitter-community as an association of the particular social network members related to a certain age and connected by the system of interactions.

The Twitter-community represents a part of the youth solidarity culture and, surely, affects it, and the culture in its turn has an effect on the community. But, despite the commonality of life-worlds of young people, derived from their membership in the same community as well, it is not solidarity only that defines the unity of views and opinions. Their "biographical situation integrated into the actually prevailing system of interests" [18: 133] is largely individual, but, nevertheless, it incorporates a lot of things common to all people, which are studied by each person in the process of socialization. This allows members of the youth Twitter-community to find common ground, organize discussions, meetings in real life. And the process of comprehension of the individual experience by each member of the community preconditions the difference in opinions, ways of thinking, contributes to the emergence of microgroups within the community on the basis of shared beliefs and interests.

The youth Twitter-community can be characterized as "public sphere" (the embodiment of communicative rationality) by Habermas as well [6: 72]. The key elements of publicity as recognized in the early works by Habermas are "open access, reliable sources of information, voluntary participation, rational argument and reasoning, the freedom to express opinions, the freedom to discuss matters of the state, the freedom to participate in the discussion outside institutional roles" [1: 111]. Communication in the youth Twitter-community meets almost all of these key elements and the very social network Twitter can be viewed as a sample of the mass media, which possesses freedom of speech and freedom of the press.

From the perspective of functionalism, the Twitter-community has a variety of functions, including functions of control, socialization, communication. Following Merton's distinction between explicit and latent functions, we note that the Twitter-community performs both explicit (the function of communication among people, the "rostrum" function for the expression of opinions, feelings) and latent functions (it is an agent of cyber-socialization, performs control function). The acquirement by an individual of certain knowledge, skills, norms and values occurs throughout life, but most intensively, this process is going on in the childhood and youth. Although members of the youth Twitter-community mainly talk about their daily activities or simply read "reports" of other users of what they have done for the day, still on Twitter, more than on any other social networks, it is common practice to read news feeds, repost events significant for the country and to discuss them. The youth Twitter-community can be described more as a "positive" agent of socialization, which is inferior in its influence to others, such as family, school. However, for some people cyber-socialization represents probably the main and one and the only type of socialization. For a large number of challenged people such cyber-socialization can be regarded as practically the only alternative to socialization in the conditions of real life-sustaining activity. In addition, some dysfunctions of the virtual youth Twitter-community can be mentioned. First, it is organization by means of the Twitter-community of any radical groups potentially dangerous for the society in general or for a specific group of people, in particular. Second, one can notice retreat of the youth Twitter-community members from the real life, excessive operating of a microblog, overshadowing other interests, dependence on this Web-site.

Problematization of the Twitter-community phenomenon from the point of view of integral concepts of modernity can reveal other peculiarities of the Twitter-community. So, based on the structuration theory by Giddens, one could claim that the members of the youth Twitter-community act in accordance with the stratification model of the actor, including the rationalization of action, reflexive monitoring of action and motivation of action. Operating a microblog means publishing "report" of their activities and also makes it possible to monitor the actions of other users, displayed in their profiles. Rationalization of action is "the capability to maintain a continuing 'theoretical understanding' of the grounds of their social activity" [5: 5]. Certainly, members of the youth Twitter-community are competent in their behavior, they are able to explain what they are doing and for what reasons, if another user has a question. Or they perform actions both within the Internet resource and beyond it that are socially approved and do not require explanation. The level of motivation in the form of conscious and unconscious desires are implicitly inherent in all people; respectively, both the young men and girls of the Twitter-community have a motivational component of behavior. For example, keeping their own profile is an unconsciously motivational action for them as it belongs to the scope of routine practices. However, if a user operates a microblog with a certain purpose (for example, describes visits to the best parties of the city), then his activity is motivated, focused on achieving status, popularity.

Besides the Twitter-community is a social-community field (Bourdieu), characterized by a predominance of social capital. Bourdieu and Wacquant define social capital as "the sum of the resources, actual or virtual, that accrue to an individual or a group by virtue of possessing a durable network of more or less institutionalized relationships of mutual acquaintance and recognition" [2: 14]. In other words, social capital depends on membership in a group. A number of studies have identified a robust relationship between the use of social network sites and positive outcomes such as social capital [21: 585].

It is important to note the role of social media in the information support of the society in emergency situations. Not so long ago, the term "'digital volunteers' appeared on the network, designating the people who cannot be on the site of the disaster physically, but they find important information and spread it through social media" [14: 143]. These "network volunteers" can be found in Twitter-community as well. Researchers Lenhart, Fox emphasize the fact that Twitter was used for the collection and dissemination of information during such events as fires in California in 2008, the recent elections in the United States, the terrorist attacks in Mumbai and even crash landing of Flight 1549 US Airways on the Hudson River. J. Krum, the ferry passenger, who was nearby took the picture of the plane using a mobile phone and made a post in Twitter [12].

A variety of the studied problematics connected with social network Twitter continues to increase. And in a number of last mentions about Twitter it would be desirable to note new research vectors and thematic, contextual finds. So results of recent regional sociological research "Influence of social networks on protest activity in Republic Mordovia" [20: 23] ascertain that audience of Twitter takes the second seat after "Odnoklassniki" among the most politized audiences of social networks (N = 379; quote and proportional sample; 2015). In turn, researcher Chen analyzes role of Twitter in the organization of revolutions in Egypt, where as soon as the local social crises had turned to political one, active use of Twitter has promptly passed in a political plane during these protests. The author does the important conclusion that "phenomenal mass character and popularity of public protest movement Occupy Wall Street were resulted from an effective utilization of social platforms Twitter which shaped an information background of protests and demonstrations" [3: 24]. It is necessary to mention and the dissertational research, devoted to a phenomenon of "tviplomatiya" or "using social network Twitter by politicians for realization of political and diplomatic problems" [4: 18]. In the given dissertation the analysis of discourses of accounts of presidents of Venezuela, Ecuador, Brazil in social network Twitter is spent, the role and possibilities of Twitter in presidential election is accented.

3 Instrumentality of Twitter: Privacy vs. Publicity

We investigate the representations of members of the virtual youth Twitter community. For this purpose, we analyze the following aspects: profiles on Twitter as a form of on-line diaries; the ratio of public and private information in the network space; demand for Twitter among young people; Twitter influence on the world of fashion design and trends; Twitter role in achieving popularity.

For the analysis of self-representations of the youth Twitter-community members, qualitative methods of data collection were selected, namely semi-structured interview [8]. Informants were selected through a "mediator" that is, in the very beginning we conducted the interview with one of those Twitter-community members whose account has been studied for 3 years, and who is one of the most active participants of this community. He is 18 years old, he has been keeping his microblog for a long time and he has many friends on Twitter. He advised us several other informants and some of them, in their turn, advised us to contact the other acquaintances of theirs who were users of Twitter too. Moreover, all the informants met some fundamental criteria – age 17–18 years, active blogging, experience of using Twitter is not less than 1.5 years, living in Saratov, the number of readers is more than 100 readers. A total of 10 interviews (5 – with girls, 5 – with boys, Table 1) were delivered. These interviews were analyzed using the interpretive approach [15]. To be precise, the following categorization of interview contents was used: functions and purposes of the use of microblogs by the community members; the prototype of Twitter; degree of dependence on this social network; taboo topics; gender differences in keeping of the account; universally valid questions; the most popular accounts; "significant others"; a microblog as a means on the way to fame and advantages of the popularity on the Web.

3.1 Twitter as a Form of an On-line Diary

A personal diary can be considered the prototype of Twitter, as well as of other blogs. The main difference between a personal diary and Twitter is the degree of publicity and openness, respectively. This fact has been noted by almost all the informants. However, such an opinion was expressed that on Twitter a person can be as open and sincere as in his personal diary (I 10). Perhaps the fact that the user does not realize who exactly will read the user's feed, removes many of the limitations of moral character from the author of online diary. That is why most of our interviewees admitted that they do not resort to self-censorship of their records: "I write everything whatever comes into my head" (I 8). Perhaps people create online diaries with the purpose of overcoming barriers in real communication, or even ignoring the rules, regulations specific to the live communication.

Table 1. List of used interviews

Interview	Information about respondents
Interview 1	Alex, 18 years old, student, working, Saratov, keeps Twitter 3 years, the number of readers - 144, active blogging - every day 10–12 tweets
Interview 2	Anton, 18 years old, student, Saratov, keeps Twitter 3 years, the number of readers - 261, active blogging - every day from 2–3 tweets
Interview 3	Artyom, 17 years, student, Saratov, keeps Twitter 1.5 years, the number of readers - 309, active blogging - every day 10–15 tweets
Interview 4	Vyacheslav, 17 years old, student, Saratov, keeps Twitter 3 years, the number of readers - 111, active blogging - every day 10 tweets
Interview 5	5 Diana, 18 years old, student, Saratov, keeps Twitter 2–2,5 years, the number of readers - 179, active blogging - every day 15–20 tweets
Interview 6	Ksenia, 17 years old, schoolgirl, Saratov, keeps Twitter 2.5 years, the number of readers - 313, active blogging - every day from 5 tweets
Interview 7	Lyubov, 18 years old, student, Saratov, keeps Twitter 3 years, the number of readers - 120, active blogging - every day from 5 tweets
Interview 8	Maria, 17 years old, schoolgirl, Saratov, keeps Twitter 2 years, the number of readers - 204, active blogging - every day from 10 tweets
Interview 9	Sergey, 18 years old, student, Saratov, keeps Twitter 1.5 years, the number of readers - 100, active blogging - every day 5–10 tweets
Interview 10	Julia, 18 years old, student, working, Saratov, keeps Twitter 2, 5–3 years, the number of readers - 480, active blogging - every day 15–20 tweets

Among taboo subjects that users do not touch upon in microblogs, the young men have the following: personal, sexual relations, family, conflicts. The girls said they would not touch particularly personal relations, but those users, who they read, often write about everything in great detail, and basically it is typical for girls. The young men also claimed that they write on general topics, about things that they are interested in, on politics. Kon believes that such gender differences in the operating of a microblog are quite predictable: "boys and young men discuss social and extrafamilial problems more often, while girls talk about their immediate environment" [10: 50]. Perhaps it is because of this that most girls would not want their parents to read their microblogs. Some guys, on the other hand, do not see anything wrong with that, "Let them read, I think they would be proud of me, since I am microblogging in an interesting way" (I 1).

We would also like to pay attention to the fact (based on observations of Twitter-accounts of our informants) that in self-representations of users-young men ethnically tinged information is used which sometimes demonstrates a negative attitude to the representatives of "Caucasian nationalities": "These wogs venture too far, aren't they tired from walking in "Triumph"? Red Moccasins are sold already" (02.13.2014); "When will you return to your homeland?"; "Filthy black (Caucasian wedding image with the words: "the rest of your life he will beat and humiliate you, have a nice wedding" is attached to it)" (03.10.2014). Quite a lot of posts are dedicated to the critical attitude of users towards romantic relationships between Russian girls and the "Caucasians": "girls, do not win Fatima's guy away from her, date with Russian guys

(the image with the words "Fatima also has Mohammed"" is attached (10.17.2013));
"any girl that is dating Caucasian is a wh**e" (04.15.2014), "girls, are you all right?
(the image of a T-shirt with the sign: "Caucasian girl" is attached (10.11.2013). Such
discourses probably reflect the aspirations of young men to emphasize their ethnicity as
an element of common identity with the girls as well as demarcation line with foreign
boys from the "Caucasian republics".

3.2 Networking in the Designing Trends and Popularity

As for the most widely read bloggers-celebrities, among them the interviewed people
mentioned S. Shurins, M. Galustyan, A. Navalny, A. Karimov and D. Belik. However,
most of the informants were of the opinion that these are not specific individuals whose
microblogs are the most widely read on Twitter, but "page-quotations": "a lot of people
read Koffboy, this is a guy who has 400 thousand subscribers. He posts on Twitter all the
news that is written in other public servers and also quotes from various sources" (I 4);
"There are such tweeters as "Chamber №6", "drunk twitter" where all sorts of quota-
tions are posted, so they are read almost by everybody" (I 10). Among the reasons why
people read the accounts listed, the community members identified the following: 1.
interest, fanaticism ("people read celebrities, because it is possible to communicate with
them in such a way, write to them, and it is likely that they will read and answer, you can
join the great" (I 9)); 2. feel the unity, the ability to be understood ("people read Twitters
"drunk tweet" and "Chamber №6" just to see some "life" tweet, tweet about themselves
and retweet" (I 10)).

In the formation of the fashion trends photos of the things (which a person wants to
have) posted on personal pages of a microblog play an important role. The more
frequently different people have an image of the same object, the clearer a trend
becomes, and the process of trend designing is going on. Among the members of the
youth Twitter-community the most popular were the photos of clothing and footwear
("they are very often posted, mostly by girls: I want to own such airmax and attach
photos of the desired sneakers. Or: "I got my clothes, going for it" (I 3). Often there are
tweets on automobile topics, sometimes posts dedicated to books, phones and tablets
appear to be relevant. But in connection with Instagram resource development informants indicated that photos of things are more often posted out there now: (I 5; I 6). If
the first event messages often appear on Twitter, the first images now appear in
Instagram feed. Despite this fact, all the informants were unanimous in their opinion
that fashion trends are distributed through Twitter. It becomes possible: firstly, through
the "pages of catwalk models when people watch the way they dress and start imi-
tating" (I 10); secondly, through the accounts of popular people ("twitter can spread the
fashion trends in technology, often they write here about all sorts of updates, gadgets,
novelties, famous people write and they are read by many subscribers"(I 2)); and,
thirdly, with the assistance of "pages of different clothing stores, where they post
garments, information on what is fashionable now and many people read it, use and
purchase" (I 4).

An important role in the formation of human personality is played by so-called
"significant others". As the results of interviews revealed, almost none of the

informants has people who he or she would like to bear a resemblance with. At the same time they all claimed that their friends have idols. This brought us to belief that the young men and girls just did not like such question formulation, as "Are there any popular people who you look up to in your life, whose appearance or character appeal to you?" Young people aged 17–18 years strive for individuality, and, probably they do not want to admit they want to be like someone else. All informants admitted that their friends write from time to time in microblogs about their favorite actors, musicians and other famous people. As it turned out, it is interesting for the majority of the participants of the youth community to read these posts, as it is "useful for the overall development" (I 4); "It's always interesting to know what my friends like" (I 6); "You learn something new about this person" (I 10) and "interesting to compare tastes" (I 7). Thus, even if indirectly, but "significant others" of friends still have influence on the personalities of young tweeter-users. A man exists in culture, and culture influences the person, socializing and adapting him to the changing realia of the outer world.

3.3   Demand for Twitter Among Young People: A Popular Resource and a Means to Achieve Popularity

Based on these interviews, we identified several reasons why microblogging has gained popularity among young people in recent years. In the first place by mentioning there turned to be the reason of "hipness" of this resource among young people, "perhaps because the friends of each other want to know if you are on twitter. If not, they are surprised how it is. All of us are using it" (I 5); "Herd mentality, I think. I signed up for this reason" (I 3). The second is the desire to be heard, "its popularity stems from the fact that young people want to share their problems and experiences, on Twitter they are looking for the opportunity to meet new people and the opportunity to discuss their problems, to find people who will support them" (I 2). Also, two other reasons were given: the opportunity of mobile access ("increase in popularity can be explained by the fact that a few years ago smart phones became more affordable, they can maintain good access to the Internet, and to live constantly on mobile platforms (mobile phones) is characteristic of the youth, there are more young people on Twitter" (I 4)) and a certain status ("the youth must be willing to feel successful, and such people are always in sight, always up to date" (I 1)). So that means Twitter is not only subject to fashion trends, but also it is a definite trend.

Today Twitter for the most part corresponds to the expectations of the youth group of users. It is evident from the results of interviews. All informants are generally satisfied with microblogging and its features, and either would not make any changes at all or would improve it just a little. Among the possible changes the following things are mentioned: "I would add music there" (I 10); "I would cancel volume restrictions" (I 3) or "I would add to the volume of messages 50 more characters" (I 4); « I would bring back the old design" (I 9). The desire of informants to introduce records in the microblogging interface has been traced throughout the interview. Changing of the volume of tweets has also been sometimes referred to by users during a conversation. However, this is far from everyday necessity. Informants remembered it only when it was necessary to place a long story or poem.

Let us move on to the question of how microblogging can help to "glorify" an ordinary person. The members of the virtual youth community were unanimous in belief that through Twitter a person can become popular if he wants to. However, just few specific examples were provided as a proof. But some individuals were named, for example, "that very Koffboy, who I have talked about" (I 4); "One man who lives in Novosibirsk, when I signed up for his page, he had 100 readers, and 2 years later there are 11,000 subscribers already" (I 1); "Some American, who gave daily advice to his son on Twitter, has collected hundreds of thousands of readers. Or all of Moscow hipsters, who have thousands of subscribers, are popular in their kind" (I 9). However, in order to have a lot of readers on Twitter it is not enough just to write about your life, you need to take care about the image, raise interesting themes or post original photos. According to Kurus and Artamonova, "the structure of the blog author's image can be divided into 2 parts: the direct image (appearance, speech, behavior, style of clothing) and indirect virtual image (the creative activity of the blogger performs the function of the image carrier in this case)" [11: 34]. So what is it necessary to write about in order to become popular? For example, a blogger can be "simple, honest" (I 8) and at the same time can write "about some commonplace things, about something that all people care about, share, about some life staff" (I 10). Or he can place something "relevant and new that people have not seen before so that they would like to discuss it" (I 1). But these must be people with a very good mentality "(I 5) or it is better not to try to attract all users but to "find your own audience and to write what will be interesting for it" (I 9).

It turned out that members of the youth Twitter-community are not very ambitious in matters of fame. The desire to have a lot of readers, be a well-known blogger is relevant not to all users, there are less than half of them. The rest relate to the possible popularity either indifferently or do not want it at all. The advantages of being famous in microblogging are seen by young men and girls as follows: "it is possible through your page to promote production, to advertise, get paid for it" (I 1), "there is always the opportunity to talk to someone" (I 4); "You may be noticed by a proper, influential person, you'll find useful connections" (I 5); "People would have recognized me in the street, have asked for autographs" (I 3).

4   Conclusions

The article deals with the significant discursive fields of virtual youth communities. Social networks, such as Twitter, are now used not only for social communication, but also they act as a means of dissemination of information of public interest, a way to demonstrate social activity and as an agent of socialization. Self-representations of young Twitter users living in Saratov have been studied. Microblog can be studied as a form of online diary, as its structure corresponds to such resources; the only difference is the restriction on the Twitter Posts volume. However, the microblogging still remains quite intimate compared to other social networks, and therefore you can notice the unique peculiarities of self-representations of the Twitter-community participants expressed in: the purposes of blogging (for the purpose of communication or as a diary); their theme filter choice (taboo subjects including personal relationships, family, religion); self-censorship of messages (the members of the youth Twitter-community do not use it); gender differences in the operating of a microblog (young men communicate more, but there are also more taboo subjects, girls write more about themselves, but sometimes in great intimate detail).

After examining the boundaries of personal and public spaces in the microblog, it is noted that the scope of personal space in the youth Twitter-community is rather undeveloped, because almost nobody uses personal messages of this resource. So Twitter is rather a publicity area, because young people register here, first of all, to reveal themselves, their potential and not to conceal something. We have found out that Twitter is a great mechanism of influence on consumer preferences of young people, on the design and fashion trends through the pages of famous people, popular bloggers, and representatives of the companies. The members of the youth Twitter-community themselves are not the least in spreading of fashion trends.

Also it is established that popularity of Twitter among young people is due to a number of reasons. Firstly, this online resource is the most famous microblogging service and differs significantly from other social networks, and as you know, something new always attracts attention, especially the attention of progressive groups of population. Secondly, to have a Twitter account is fashionable and it is approved by peers, and failure to use the microblogging is criticized. Thirdly, this social network allows, according to the informants, to be heard, share their problems and get support from peers. These are the features that keep the "tweeting" resource among the selected communication platforms. And if desired, the user can conquer not only the Internet, but also move to a new level, reaching the success and popularity in the real world.

References

1. Bodrunova, S.: The concept of public sphere and theory of mediacracy: the search for common ground. J. Sociol. Soc. Anthropol. **14**(1), 110–132 (2011)
2. Bourdieu, P., Wacquant, L.: An Invitation to Reflexive Sociology. University of Chicago Press, Chicago (1992)
3. Chen, D.: Social media in the solution of actual social and political problems. The Abstract of the Thesis for Degree of the Candidate of Political Sciences, St. Petersburg (2015)
4. Filatkina, G.: Communicative strategy in a political media discourse of presidents of Venezuela, Ecuador, Brazil (1999–2014). The Abstract of the Thesis for Degree of Candidate of Philology, Moscow (2015)
5. Giddens, A.: The Constitution of Society Outline of the Theory of Structuration. Polity Press, Cambridge, in association with Basil Blackwell, Oxford (1984)
6. Habermas, J.: Legitimation Crisis. Polity Press, Cambridge (1988)
7. Himelboim, I., McCreery, S., Smith, M.: Birds of a feather tweet together: integrating network and content analyses to examine cross-ideology exposure on Twitter. J. Comput.-Mediated Commun. **18**(2), 40–60 (2013). doi:10.1111/jcc4.12001
8. Irvine, A., Drew, P., Sainsbury, R.: Am I not answering your questions properly? Clarification, adequacy and responsiveness in semi-structured telephone and face-to-face interviews. Qual. Res. **13**(1), 87–106 (2013). doi:10.1177/1468794112439086
9. Komm, S.: Social Networks in Russia, Winter 2015–2016. The Figures, Trends, Forecasts (2015–2016). http://www.sostav.ru/blogs/112218/18945
10. Kon, I.: From an intimate diary to social networks. Psychol. Every Day **4**, 50–51 (2010)

11. Kurus, A., Artamonova, O.: Shaping the image of the blogger. In: Proceedings of the International Scientific-practical Conference "Actual Problems of Socio-economic Sciences and Humanities", pp. 33–37. PSU, Penza (2012)
12. Lenhart, A., Fox S.: Twitter and status updating. Pew Internet & American Life Project (2009). http://fortysouth.com/wp-content/uploads/2009/05/Twitter-and-status-updating.pdf
13. Lin, H.F.: Determinants of successful virtual communities: contributions from system characteristics and social factors. Inf. Manag. **45**(8), 522–527 (2008). doi:10.1016/j.im.2008.08.002
14. Morozova, E., Miroshnichenko, I.: Network community in emergencies: new opportunities for citizens and authorities. Policy **1**, 140–152 (2011)
15. Oliver, D., Serovich, J., Mason, T.: Constraints and opportunities with interview transcription: towards reflection in qualitative research. Soc. Forces **84**(2), 1273–1289 (2005). doi:10.1353/sof.2006.0023
16. Rheingold, H.: The Virtual Community: Homesteading on the Electronic Frontier. The MIT Press, Cambridge (2000)
17. Ridings, C., Gefen, D., Arinze, B.: Some antecedents and effects of trust in virtual communities. J. Strateg. Inf. Syst. **11**(3–4), 271–295 (2002). doi:10.1016/S0963-8687(02)00021-5
18. Schütz, A.: Selection: world Glowing with Sense. Rosspen, Moscow (2004)
19. Spiliotopoulos, T., Oakley, I.: Understanding motivations for Facebook use: usage metrics, network structure, and privacy. In: Proceedings of the SIGCHI Conference on Human Factors in Computing Systems, pp. 3287–3296. Paris, France (2013)
20. Ushkin, S.: Influence of virtual social networks on protest activity in the Russian society. The Abstract of the Thesis for Degree of the Candidate of Sociological Sciences, Saransk (2015)
21. Yoder, C., Stutzman, F.: Identifying social capital in the Facebook interface. In: Proceedings of CHI, pp. 585–588, Vancouver, BC, Canada. ACM (2011)

Russian Large Cities Authorities' Pages in Social Media: A Platform for Expert Communication?

Mikhail Karyagin[✉]

National Research University Higher School of Economics, Saint Petersburg, Russia
karyaginm@gmail.com

Abstract. The paper presents the results of empirical research aimed at analyzing the effectiveness of the social media usage by administrations of Russian cities. We use both qualitative and quantitative methods to assess the content of municipalities' SNS accounts, as well as ways of communication between public employees and citizens in the digital public policy sphere. It is argued that in the overwhelming majority of cases municipal authorities do not use the potential of SNS to contact with citizens, mainly because of lack of material adaptation, necessary recourses, as well as inability to adapt to the new information environment.

Keywords: Social networks · Social media · Internet · Municipal authorities · Russian cities

1 Introduction

In recent years the social networking sites (SNS), which are still called the new media, have stopped to be actually new. They have intervened in our life so deeply that are now an ordinary means of communication not only in private everyday life, but also in business communication.

The share of active Internet – users in Russia (those using the Net at least once a day) is now 53%, or 61,5 million people[1], and practically each user has an account in at least one SNS[2]. Moreover, each year the length of SNS usage sessions is increasing, according to the Romir Holding data, a Russian user spends about 143 min a day in social networks[3].

SNS today is an effective channel of communication, with the majority of citizens having access to them (to add, the Internet-penetration rate in large cities with the population over 100,000 is notably higher than the average of 53%). Hence, it can be said for

---

[1] Internet in Russia: Dynamics of Penetration. Spring 2015 [in Russian]. FOM, 12.08.2015, http://fom.ru/SMI-i-internet/12275.

[2] TNS Web Index [in Russian]. TNS, 01.03.2016, http://www.tns-global.ru/services/media/media-audience/internet/information/.

[3] How Much Time Do the Russians Spend in the Social Networks [in Russian]. The Village, 21.05.2015, http://www.the-village.ru/village/city/city/214995-sotsialnye-seti.

© Springer International Publishing AG 2016
A.V. Chugunov et al. (Eds.): DTGS 2016, CCIS 674, pp. 14–21, 2016.
DOI: 10.1007/978-3-319-49700-6_2

sure that the official accounts of public authorities may become a platform of interaction between public policy actors for decision-making on the municipal level.

Besides, it is necessary to take into account the global agenda: the Arab – spring and the so-called Twitter – revolutions phenomenon have raised the question of states' strategy towards the behavior in SNS. It has become obvious that it is impossible to ignore the new media, since the virtual processes going on there may have quite real consequences in political, economic and social areas.

The technique, developed and tested within the present research is unique and can be applied by researches from different countries, and the conceptual findings characterize the situation not only in the Russian segment of SNS, but encompass more general tendencies plausible for the whole area.

2 Research Design

The key question we were interested in during the research is whether cities administration accounts in popular SNS can be considered platforms for expert communication between the government and citizens. To answer this question we examined all municipalities in the Russian Federation and chose the cities with the constant population of 100, 000 and more (excluding Moscow, St. Petersburg and Sevastopol)[4]. First, it helped to indicate the research field. Secondly, the indicators of the Internet – penetration are higher in these cities, and therefore there are more opportunities for communication between public policy actors. As a result, we have chosen 166 municipalities under consideration, with the overall population of municipalities as many as 56,7 million people.

To verify a large number of municipal accounts in SNS, we analyzed official websites of big cities administrations on whether they have a link to their SNS – pages. It allowed us to include the official accounts only and eliminate those civic pages that deliberately or by chance had been arranged as official city administrations' accounts.

To specify the list of SNS under consideration, we used the Brand Analytics data to reveal the most popular SNS. According to the date, the most popular SNS in Russia are: Vkontakte, Odnoklassniki, Facebook, Moi Mir, LiveJournal, Instagram, Twitter.

After the formation of official accounts' list we gathered qualitative and quantitative indicators: number of subscribers, number of posts by the authorities in SNS, topic and content of published information, as well as design of a post in SNS.

3 Research Methods

In research we used the methods of qualitative and quantitative content-analysis of official websites of large cities administrations, as well as their SNS accounts, as well as the qualitative content – analysis of published information and users' activities on

---

[4] Population Count of Municipalities of the Russian Federation [in Russian]. Federal Service of Statistics, 06.08.2015, http://www.gks.ru/wps/wcm/connect/rosstat_main/rosstat/ru/statistics/publications/catalog/afc8ea004d56a39ab251f2bafc3a6fce.

SNS pages of the municipalities. Within the quantitative content - analysis the units of analysis were the links to the official accounts in SNS at the official web-sites of the municipalities. During the research we focused not only on quantitative characteristics, but also on the qualitative indicators:

– Adaptation of published materials to the peculiarities of a SNS;
– Tag usage;
– Topics and content of published information (news, entertainment, information materials);
– Links to official web-sites of municipal administrations;
– Interaction with the users in the commenting section and by personal messages;
– Informal style usage (humor and Internet – memes in posts).

We also used automated tools for gathering data (fanpage karma, Fake Followers by SocialBakers and Twitteraudit), which allowed to analyze the effectiveness of cities administration accounts' in Facebook and Twitter. We also ran several semi-structured interviews with public servants of those municipalities, which SNS accounts had appeared to be the most effective and popular, as well as conducted the overall survey of administrations' employees.

4 Why Do Public Authorities Need SNS?

Policy – making is becoming a more complex phenomenon nowadays. Even in hybrid political regimes with the shift to authoritarianism official organizations must follow the rules of game to legitimize political decisions. Considering the decision-making algorithm by Anderson and Dunn, one of the five steps is "confirmation of public decisions", which seems to be done more effective via modern communications technologies [5, 6].

Public policy space has a much more complex configuration of actors, than a public administration system. "Instead of one traditional actor – a state – we have the civil society represented by NGO leaders, as well as expert community related to science and systematic knowledge" [10].

To set the effective dialogue between the participants of discussion, a platform with equal access for all is needed. For this purpose web-recourses on the basis of official websites can be made, but technical development of such facilities requires a large amount of resources, which makes it irrational, especially in cities with no sufficient budget. The usage of ready and free platforms that provide opportunities for public discussion of important city problems, seems an easy and effective decision: "Information and communication infrastructure allows to regard public administration system not as a centralized hierarchy, but as a network organization of authority units, connected by horizontal unities, accountable and transparent to citizens" [8].

Despite the system motivators of SNS familiarization by public authorities, it is important to note individual motives [3] of executives. As one of our respondents notes, SNS reduce burden placed on divisions in charge of the official communication in a public authority. It is easy for administrations' employees to respond to citizens' questions and problems in SNS, rather than to deal with the document circulation under official inquires received by public authorities.

In the course of interviewing we found another interesting task solved by cities administrations' representatives by means of SNS: "Citizens in SNS are the same people we can meet on the streets. It is better to solve questions and problems in SNS, rather than see their consequences in reality aftermath. Sore points and problematic issues are seen well on the Internet". Other advantages the state gets by actively using SNS are described in detail in literature that can be easily found [7].

5 Why Do Citizens Need SNS?

State and municipalities' accounts in SNS do not only solve problems of government, but allows citizens getting a range of benefits, the key of which are the following:

(1) SNS are the instrument of controlling the government by citizens. In case of qualitative and effective administration of SNS account, civil activists, NGO and other public policy actors can expose control over the government's activities. This leads to the increase of public authorities' transparency [1].
(2) By means of SNS citizens can raise questions for discussion, i.e. to set agenda, which was confirmed empirically [4].
(3) SNS have e-democracy options [2], like online voting on important issues. It is clear that such instruments lack institutional power, and results of such voting do not have any official status, and hence, the obligatory character for the executive power, but the government can use the results of such polls and voting to consider public opinion in decision-making.
(4) Citizens and experts can participate in discussing strategic city issues, which allows the government making necessary corrections to the government policy. Generally, the representation of public bodies in SNS is a mutually beneficial process, in case of the correct maintenance of communication.

6 Research Results

According to our primary analysis of municipal administrations' websites, only 77 out of 166 cities with the population over 100,000 have their accounts in SNS, which forms 43,3%. The general amount of accounts in different SNS is 204, and the overall audience of these pages on date of the data gathering was 364,749 users. The distribution of accounts and audience in percentage is the following:

VK	OD	FB	TW	INST	YT	LJ
General Audience						
209403	10377	53415	56211	29625	5543	175
57,41%	2,84%	14,64%	15,41%	8,12%	1,52%	0,05%
Number of Accounts						
54	11	39	52	15	28	4
31,76%	6,47%	22,94%	30,59%	8,82%	16,47%	2,35%

To avoid the quantitative indicators being abstract figures, we connected them to cities' population count, as well as to indicators of SNS penetration in a region from Brand Analytics[5]. That was made to level cities with different population (from 100 thousand to 2 million).

The indicators of SNS penetration allow forming an assumption on a potential audience of official accounts according to the formula: (city population * SNS penetration in a region)/100. Accordingly, having defined potential audiences, it became possible to draw conclusions on effectiveness of public authorities in this area.

In the overwhelming majority of cases it was revealed, that the audience of SNS municipal authorities' accounts does not correspond to the level of SNS development in the regions. It means that public authorities pay inadequate attention to the problem, and the realization of potential is in average 17,48%. Twitter and Facebook are exceptions here, but it can be explained rather by low levels of these SNS' penetration rather than governments' activeness. For instance, penetration of Twitter in the North-Caucasian regions is about 1–2%.

Municipal SNS pages' administrators in the majority of cases do not adapt the content to the format of a SNS, meaning that press relaeases do not fit the audience of a SNS. For instance, the audience in Vkontakte is younger than the one of Facebook or Odnoklassniki[6], hence different language and communication style should be applied. Adaptation of materials is carried out only in 44,44% of account, in the rest of cases news from websites are simply copied and pasted to the SNS.

Twitter format assumes just 140 symbols to place the content in, but there we more often saw a simple placement of a link to the original source without any adaptation. The latter is done in 19,61% of cases only.

A widespread practice is the so-called cross-posting, when materials from one SNS are automatically transmitted to other ones, therefore, such automatization do not speak for the effectiveness of such accounts.

---

[5] Social Networking Sites Statistics [in Russian]. Brand Analytics, April 2016, http://br-analytics.ru/statistics/author.

[6] TNS Web Index [in Russian]. TNS 01.03.2016, http://www.tns-global.ru/services/media/media-audience/internet/information/.

The results of our research reveal the low engagement of users into the discussion of materials posted in municipal SNS pages. For instance, only 9 out of 54 pages in Vkontakte have discussions between users and group administrators (communication in other SNS is totally absent). The reasons for this low activity are the following:

- Poor adaptation of materials, which leads to lack of its comprehension and acceptance by the audience.
- Publication of information having no social significance. It is often the case when public authorities publish news on internal procedural activities (internal councils, meetings with neighboring municipalities' administration etc.)
- SNS accounts' administrators do not react to users' questions. Usually subscribers ask clarifying questions or give critical comments that draw no attention, and sometimes are deleted. We have carried out an experiment by commenting one publication about the mayor's statement on the official page of Lipetsk City Administration (https://vk.com/public60460495). As a result our comment has been deleted and our page has been banned.
- Unwillingness of state and municipal structures to adapt to the open format of social networks. This is the most popular answer by city administration representatives', according to our survey (25% of respondents).

Our research shows that municipal authorities usually choose Twitter as SNS, apparently assuming it to be the easiest to run. The problem however is that not all authorities adapt materials to the format of Twitter (usually it is just cross-posting), as well as they disregard the low popularity of micro-blogging in Russia. Hence the major part of the audience remains uncovered. Despite the fact that the number of SNS accounts in Vkontakte is comparable, they have much larger audiences and are more vivid in terms of communication quality.

In the context of resource constraints (9 out of 32 our respondents pointed out the problem of combining SNS administering with other responsibilities), the strategic choice of SNS for municipality will be defining.

7   Conclusions and Recommendations

The primary analysis has shown that the representation of the Russian authorities remains at the primitive stage. On the municipal level the development is carried out much slower, that on the federal one[7], due to the following reasons:

- The larger resource base of federal authorities. Federal executive bodies have human and financial resources that provide SNS development. Some pages of federal authorities are administered by outsourcing.

---

[7] Results of the Analysis of Representativeness of Federal Executive Authorities in Social Networking Sites, carried out by the author within the Infometer Project [in Russian]. Project center "Infometer" spring 2015, http://www.infometer.org/analitika/foiv_smm_2014, http://www.infometer.org/analitika/foiv_twitter_2015, http://www.infometer.org/analitika/foiv-v-instagram.

- The index of SNS penetration and the quality of the Internet connection is much better that in the regions of the Russian Federation.
- Attention of the Open Government[8] to federal authorities' SNS accounts is an additional stimulus for development, while there are no such indices for regions or municipalities.
- Human resources potential is much higher in federal authorities than in municipalities. Many municipal employees, according to our survey, have no skills to effectively manage SNS pages.

Unfortunately, 'municipal administrations' accounts in SNS cannot be considered platforms for public policy actors' effective communication in majority of cases. There are several positive examples in the cities of Irkutsk (http://vk.com/public95424720) and Achinsk (https://vk.com/nashach), but in general the accounts play the role of sounding out the newsfeed from official websites. The potential of SNS is not used fully, as information is important, but not the main advantage of Web 2.0. The latter is the opportunity to arrange feedback, but now this channel is used only in direction from the authority to the society.

In the course of research we considered factors that could have changed the situation. The process of municipal SNS accounts seems to be carried out in two directions: citizens should use cities' pages actively, while authorities should be more active in entering this new information space.

The demand makes the supply. It is crucial to subscribe to municipal administration pages, and follow the news more actively, as well as comment on publications and inquire additional information. Should a municipality do not have accounts in SNS, citizens must demand their creation. Civic activism promotes openness and transparency of authorities, which in turn stimulates their activity in these or those policy actions. The government must be more active in new technologies' usage. There is plenty of literature on social media at the moment, as well as free online-courses, that may help public servants. It is important to understand advantages the government can gain by using SNS.

References

1. Bertot, J.C., Jaeger, P.T., Grimes, J.M.: Using ICTs to create a culture of transparency: E-government and social media as openness and anti-corruption tools for societies. Government Information Quarterly. http://ac.els-cdn.com/S0740624X10000201/1-s2.0-S0740624X10000201-main.pdf?_tid=3ee9962e-f4b4-11e5-bfbc-00000aab0f02&acdnat=1459149249_84614ce4c14a4079eeef60d6038174a7
2. Breindl, Y.; Francq, P.: Can web 2.0 applications save e-democracy? A study of how new internet applications may enhance citizen participation in the political process online. Int. J. Electron. Democracy **1**(1) (2008). http://citeseerx.ist.psu.edu/viewdoc/download?doi=10.1.1.604.1117&rep=rep1&type=pdf

---

[8] Rating of Activity of Ministries and Authorities in Social Networks. [in Russian]. Open Government, 23.12.2014, http://open.gov.ru/events/5511187/.

3. Casebourne, J.: Why Motivation Matters in Public Sector Innovation (2014). https://www.nesta.org.uk/sites/default/files/why_motivation_matters_in_public_sector_innovation.pdf
4. Couldry, N.: New media for global citizens? The future of the digital divide debate. Brown J. World Aff. **14**, 249–261 (2007)
5. Dunn, W.: Public Policy Analysis: An Introduction, 3rd edn. Pearson Prentice Hall, Upper Saddle River (2004)
6. Anderson, J.: Public Policymaking: An Introduction. Longman, Boston (2003)
7. Margo, M.J.: A Review of Social Media Use in E-Government. MDPI - Open Access Publishing, 148–161 (2012). doi:10.3390/admsci2020148, www.mdpi.com/2076-3387/2/2/148/pdf
8. Miroshnichenko, I.V.: Network Landscape of Russian Public Policy. Prosveschenie – Yug, Krasnodar (2013). (in Russian)
9. Social Media in Government High-level Guidance. New Zealand Government Web Toolkit (2011). https://webtoolkit.govt.nz/files/Social-Media-in-Government-High-level-Guidance-final.pdf
10. Sungurov, A.Y.: Public policy as a field of interaction and decision – making process. In: Gorny, M.B., Sungurov, A.Y. (eds.) Public Policy – Norma, St. Petersburg (2005). (in Russian)

Common People in Media: Content Gaps as a Challenge for the Digital Media Professionals

Sergey G. Korkonosenko[✉] and Marina A. Berezhnaia

Saint Petersburg State University, St. Petersburg, Russia
{s.korkonosenko,m.a.berezhnaya}@spbu.ru

Abstract. According to authors' research, traditional media staff has lost sharp interest to ordinary people. Such a trend means a lack of interest to the mainstream everyday life which is represented in the common persons' lives. These content gaps should become a focus of attention for nontraditional media if they wish to develop the "people-to-people" model of communication in a new media environment. New social Internet projects challenge the traditional media routine. Thus, the digital media can gain an advantage in their competition with print and audiovisual channels.

Keywords: Media · Ordinary people · Content gaps · Media inequality

1 Introduction

Great actuality of the chosen theme was emphasized by known researchers: "The participation of ordinary people is fundamental to all … media"; at the same time, "there is almost nothing written about, and very little empirical research which examines, what use 'actual' ordinary people might make of them", particularly of online content [5, pp. 5–6]. This topic is closely linked with other classic areas of media studies, first of all the audience research, which also suffers today a lack of interest from scholars. Czech authors write that media audiences "were rendered almost invisible in the post-socialist study of media" while in fact it means the slackening of the study of "ordinary people and their cultures in general" [3, pp. 130–131]. Other observers add that "by contrast, it could be argued that journalism researchers have focused on 'studying up' or engaging in 'elite research' … by paying a disproportionate amount of attention to elite individuals, news organizations and texts" [6, p. 12]. Other words, the digital epoch in communications started with maintaining a dramatic difference between the illusory world of media and reality in both journalism practices and media studies.

To overcome the contradiction mentioned above the focused researches of relationship between common people and media practices would help. Our particular project on this direction contains few problem questions. First, can the ordinary man find an adequate image of himself? Second, how much he is satisfied with the portraying of him? Third, to what degree the online media compensate mainstream media's lack of attention to the common people' interests and needs? In fact, these

A.V. Chugunov et al. (Eds.): DTGS 2016, CCIS 674, pp. 22–25, 2016.
DOI: 10.1007/978-3-319-49700-6_3

questions closely relate to the competition for audience between traditional media and digital newcomers.

The article uses results of the project "Media discourses on material and ethnic gaps. A comparative study in St Petersburg and Stockholm", supported by the Foundation for Baltic and East European Studies, Sweden. The aim of the paper consists in answering on problems questions mentioned above as fully as possible in a small text. More detailed reporting on the project conditions and results may be found in the previously published work [2]. For the analysis few empirical methods were used. Among them there were: (1) a content analysis method which was specially applied for studying 3 regional newspapers and 4 TV programs; (2) an expert in-depth interview by the standard guide, of 1.5 – 2 h duration; the list of experts contained 9 persons including regional news journalists, regional Legislative Assembly deputies, and journalism researchers; (3) 4 focus groups which represented low/middle educated people, high educated persons, ethnic immigrants – permanent residents of St Petersburg, and poor Russian citizens.

Cecilia von Feilitzen and Peter Petrov from Södertörn University (Sweden) were the partners of us in the methodology working out as well as in the statistical data processing. In the paper we use primarily findings concerning the Russian media, with some references to Swedish data.

2 Findings and Analysis

The content analysis findings of Russian TV news and especially newspapers revealed that on a frequency of presence common persons visibly lose to non-common persons (Table 1). As Swedish analyzer writes, "celebrities come and go with astonishing rapidity in the media industry's constant and relentless quest for new talent" [4, p. 100]. But within our project Swedish media demonstrate rather soft disproportion, in comparison with Russian indicators. Such a divergence depends on traditional mental attitudes towards so-called exclusive figures. The project expert expressively described this national-cultural attribute of his compatriots: "…The authorities are not those who solve, but those who can help with the solution of problems… Unfortunately, we do not have what in the Europe is called a public service… For us the authorities are something sacral, not clearly whence appeared and obliged nothing to the population".

Table 1. Common and non-common persons in media

Media	Country	Number of relevant excerpts	Presence of persons	
			Common persons/%	Non-common persons/%
TV	Russia	537	420/78	470/86
	Sweden	251	215/86	83/33
Newspapers	Russia	658	223/34	511/68
	Sweden	435	381/88	112/26

It may be assumed that the level of the ordinary people presence in media depends on the preferable thematic spectrum. If so, there is a task to indicate certain topics, which need common citizens' participation along with other thematic subjects, within which journalists should search "non-common" comments and engage celebrities, officials, and experts. Among the 54 topics, included in the content analysis program, the leading group consisted of (TV/newspapers): Culture, in different dimensions (6%/15%), Crime and accidents (11%/5%), City planning and infrastructure (4%/8%), Reports about or with celebrities (4%/2%), Civic activities (4%/4%), Legislation (4%/3%), Child care and family issues (4%/1%), Traffic (3%/4%), and Living conditions (4/4). At least 3 of these topics imply the involvement of common people for a better presentation of the situation, namely Child care & family issues, Living conditions, and Civic activities. But some substantial and even painful aspects of routine everyday life (Youth, Elderly people, Handicap, Homeless persons, Food & cooking, Interior decoration & home furnishing, Travels & tourism, Consumer issues, etc.) do not attract much interest of regional media professionals.

One of the experts from media professionals confessed that journalists often become victims of stereotype approach while covering daily problems of certain social groups: "It is somehow strange to write that a grandmother or grandfather lives well, as well as people with disabilities. Elderly persons, pensioners, handicapped live badly; orphans after orphanages become criminals or commit suicide. In reality it is not always like that". There were rather contradictive experts' comments concerned the necessity of unfortunate people representation on TV: "A TV viewer prefers to watch either somebody like himself, or something unknown. Nobody wants to see anything causing disgust or irritation, or something troublesome". At the same time most of the project participants stressed, that "there is a gap, and that there is a tragic misunderstanding of how disadvantaged people live. Because of this there are very big problems".

Concerning happy ending stories, aimed at "the inspiration of people for life", as the expert-journalist formulated, they are not perceived by the audience in such a humanistic respect. One of the focus group debaters declared skeptically: "Due to the lack of objective information exchange between the top of society and common people, plenty of wrong decisions are taken, a wrong policy is conducted". Alternative agenda is being setting now in the new media. The civil net projects have started from charity and environmental fields, but nowadays they widen their activities using journalistic content, both amateur and professional one. Being busy with everyday peoples' issues, such projects attract target audiences integrated in their functioning, as the observers argue [1]. Among them Blue bucket society, Bloggers against trash, Zoopatrol, RosZHKH, etc. should be mentioned. Slogan presented on information portal "These things" (Takie dela) reveals much more perspective treatment of "happy end stories": "We want to become the success stories project. We will make every effort to every story and the problem described by us would be resolved successfully" [7]. Journalism associated with social activities acquires new features and creative formats, such as media documentary project Business of the life (Delo.Life) focused on social business.

3 Conclusions

The comprehensive research revealed the distances between everyday life and its media representation in the aspect of common people quantitative and qualitative presence in regional media content. Staying far from the ordinary people issues, traditional media risk losing a reflection of everyday life as an essential characteristic of journalism. Alternative journalistic practices based on social needs of people are developing in the Net and contribute new professional features and formats. Further progression of these trends is expected in the course of competition for the audience.

References

1. Frolova, T.I.: The identity discourse in Russian media: civil network projects. In: Vasilieva, V.V. (ed.) Proceedings of the 55th International Scientific Forum "Media in the Modern World - Petersburg Readings". School of Journalism and Mass Communications of St. Petersburg State University, St. Petersburg (2016). http://jf.spbu.ru/conference/6081/6088.html. (in Russian)
2. Korkonosenko, S.G., Berezhnaia, M.A.: Ordinary people in media: nowadays portrait and digital perspective. Int. J. Adv. Res. 4(6), 2118–2123 (2016)
3. Reifová, I., Pavlíčková, T.: Invisible audiences: structure and agency in post-socialist media studies. Mediální Studia II, 130–136 (2013)
4. Rübsamen, M.: Approaching celebrity – sketching an analytical framework. In: Trivundža, I. T., Carpentier, N., Nieminen, H., Pruulmann-Venerfeldt, P., Kilborn, R., Sundin, E., Olsson, T. (eds.) Critical Perspectives on the European Mediasphere. The Intellectual Work of the 2011 ECREA European Media and Communication Doctoral Summer School. Faculty of Social Sciences, pp. 95–104. Založba FDV, Ljubljana (2011)
5. Turner, G.: Ordinary People and the Media: The Demotic Turn. SAGE Publications Ltd., London (2010)
6. Wahl-Jorgensen, K., Hanitzsch, T. (eds.): The Handbook of Journalism Studies. Routledge, New York (2009)
7. We develop the philanthropy in Russia. http://takiedela.ru/about. (in Russian)

Online Social Activity in Latin America (Mexico, Chile and Uruguay) and Russia: Cross-National Research

Elena Brodovskaya[1], Anna Dombrovskaya[1(✉)], Aleksey Synyakov[1], and Irina Batanina[2]

[1] Social Computing Laboratory, Moscow State University for Education, Moscow, Russia
brodovskaya@inbox.ru, an-doc@yandex.ru, alekssin@gmail.com
[2] Institute for the Humanities, Tula State University, Tula, Russia
batanina@mail.ru

Abstract. The article is based on the cross-national analysis of the social behavior on the Internet. The authors identify the development coefficients of the Internet as a means of political empowerment, financial activity, consumer behavior and social communication in Russia and Latin America, including such countries as Mexico, Chile and Uruguay. The national databases of the mass poll in Russia, Mexico Chile and Uruguay comprise the empirical research base. The key results of the research reveal the differences in development of various Internet segments (functions) from county to country. Chile and Uruguay have the greatest values of Internet use for financial and consumer purposes, whereas Russia and Mexico have low values, however, the latter countries have greater values of Internet use for social, communication and entertainment activities.

Keywords: Internet-communication · Cross-national analysis · Online financial activity · Online consumer behavior · E-participation · Online civil activity · Online political subjectivity · Online entertainment activity

1 Introduction

Modern studies of Internet communication often focus on the problems of uneven development of various Internet segments or functions: informational, social, communicative, economic, and political. Therefore, it is important to maintain conditions for an equally intensive development of information and communication sectors as well as financial and consumer online opportunities and political functions of the global network.

Global network plays a significant role in developing and strengthening the democratic institutions. However, modern Internet technologies and telecommunication initiatives are often aimed at the acquisition of power, or the mobilization of protest activity, promoting social destabilization. Consequently, the development of Internet technologies aimed at the authority application for social welfare becomes a key research element. In this connection it is necessary to combat the low level of e-participation and create favorable conditions for the development of e-democracy in

© Springer International Publishing AG 2016
A.V. Chugunov et al. (Eds.): DTGS 2016, CCIS 674, pp. 26–34, 2016.
DOI: 10.1007/978-3-319-49700-6_4

the world. The research also analyses the use of ICT for improvement of citizens' social welfare in Russia and Latin America.

The research also provides value comparison of Russia and Latin America countries: the Russian Federation and Latin America countries have similar processes in the overall global context; Russia and Latin America countries have a fairly similar level of economic development, as measured per capita income; community development and strengthening of democratic institutions are relevant goals for Latin America and Russia.

The comparative analysis of political system and social development in Russia and in Latin America was conducted by T.E. Vorozheykina [26], J.G. Sumbatyan and V.T. Roshupkin [23].

The influence on the political state systems exerted by the Internet was thoroughly studied by R. Baeza-Yates [1], M. Bakardjieva [2], N.K. Baym [3], M. Castells [4], B. Danet [5], L.J. Gurak [7], C. Haythornthwaite, A.L. Nielsen [8], C. Kadushin [9], R. Kling, H. Rosenbaum and S. Sawyer [10], E. Kollock and E. Russell Braziel [11], K. Leetaru [13], P. Norris [19], O'Donnel S. Mamwaring and J.S. Valenzuela [20], M. Poster [21], H. Rheingold [22], B. Wellman [24]. S. Ward, R. Gibson and W. Lusoli [27], L.M. Weber, A. Loumakis and J. Bergman [29], J. Wynn [30].

The researchers studied the Internet impact on the development of democracy and democratic institutions; they also analyzed the possible application of Internet technologies for consolidation of democratic regimes.

The participation of Mexico, Uruguay and Chile in the World Internet Project determined their selection as case studies for comparative analysis with Russia. This condition allows the researchers to use the same methodology for the comparative analysis of the perception of the Internet as a means of political citizens' participation in the selected regions.

2 Methods

The study is based on the World Internet Project methodology [29]. Formalized interviews with citizens of selected countries allowed collecting data: Mexico had 2,000 respondents, Uruguay – 2,006 respondents, Chile – 741 and Russia – 1,600. The sampling is representative on gender, age and place of residence.

The model of analyses includes: the identifying of Involvement of the citizens in Russia, Uruguay, Mexico and Chile in the Internet communication and the impact of socio-demographic factors on the process, the calculation of the weighted average ratio of the online political, communicational, consumer and financial activity in Russia, Uruguay, Mexico and Chile: k-means cluster analysis of Internet-usage profiles in Russia, Uruguay, Mexico and Chile using SPSS for Windows 17.0.

3 Results

According to research the Internet involvement of Uruguayans is the highest among the selected countries (80.1%).

Approximately equal parts - two-thirds of the population - are Two-thirds of the population (approximately equal parts) is Internet users in Russia (67.6%), Mexico (64.6%) and Chile (63.0%). Gender, age and education are considered to be significant stratification factors hindering the Internet communication in Mexico. In this country, women, elderly people and respondents with a low educational level are more likely to be self-excluded from the Internet communication. In Uruguay, Chile and Russia, both men and women are actively using the global network, with the senior age and lack of qualification serving to some extent as barriers. However, Russia has the greatest digital division between generations (99,0% users among youth and 11,6% users among senior people). The low involvement of elderly Russians in Internet communication can be explained by their referring to traditional sources of information and communication channels, lack of equipment for the Internet connection and insufficient skills of Internet communication. Domineering of men on the Internet in Mexico can be explained by the lower level of education among women (25% of Mexican women have a university degree or college degree, opposed to 35% of Mexican men). Being a factor of Internet communication, the low level of education determines the lack of skills in using the Internet and low interest in the content of the global network.

The citizens' attitudes to the Internet opportunities are treated as effective tools, which ensure better understanding between the public and politicians, they also are considered to be key factors of social stability and conventional political behavior. According to the cross-national analysis, Russia is characterized by a more optimistic assessment of the global network as a means of getting information on the political decision-making processes [10]. The Russian depth interviews and the comparison of their results with those of the cluster analysis of Internet behavior have shown that a large proportion of the citizens in Russia are quite interested in political content online, moreover, they consider the opportunity to get information about political decisions and their reasons to be really meaningful.

The research results show that the respondents think that each user has the right to freely criticize the government online. The Uruguayans and Russians expressed complete unanimity on this issue. The average weighted of this variable in Uruguay and Russia amounted to 2.7 (4.0 at the maximum). This means that the global network is perceived by people, first of all, as a platform where they can express their views on policy and political decisions of authorities. The ability to discuss political solutions helps to stabilize the public sentiment, which is supported by the results of data matching cluster analysis of Internet behavior of Russians [14–18]. According to this comparative analysis, people who express their political views on the Internet feel satisfied with their activity follow the lines of conventional political behavior and refuse to protest either online or offline.

Unlike Uruguay where there are noticeable and intensive democratic processes, the Russian opposition and protest are not encouraged in the least. Depth interviews with Russians provided a different interpretation, according to which the basic model of political behavior of Russians in the global network is characterized by a positive attitude towards the current government. Thus, Russians can really feel safe in expressing all that they think about politics, since those views are quite constructive and positive towards the ruling regime. From this perspective, Uruguayans, while criticizing the government may not feel as safe as Russians who support the government.

The agreement with the statement «By using the Internet one can have more political power» means that citizens recognize the Internet as a means of implementing political activity and involvement in the political life of their state. In Mexico, this figure amounted to 2.0, in Uruguay - 2.1, d the highest level of agreement with this statement. On the one hand, these findings contradict the results of the distribution of the Uruguayans' responses to questions about whether they feel free and safe in expressing all their views on politics. On the other hand, this contradiction can be explained by the existence of various political Internet content, different Internet sites and platforms that Uruguayans perceived as ways of having more political power. Mexico can be characterized by the same situation: open criticism of political actors can be difficult because of institutional reasons; the relatively high degree of agreement with the statement «By using the Internet one can have more political power» can be explained by the developed system of political orientation of Internet resources. The Russians and Chileans perceive this statement in a different way. Their opinion about the Internet as a means of having more political power is much more skeptical. As for Russia, these figures can be explained after understanding the specifics of the political activity of Russians in the global network. It means "being aware of" political news and having the opportunity to discuss it on Internet forums. Thus, the Russians do not perceive the Internet as a real tool for empowerment, but only as a source of information about the country's political life and the way to express their views on what is happening in the state. Russians demonstrated the most skeptical attitude towards the chances of political empowerment in the process of Internet communication.

The values of the respondents' agreement with the statement «By using the Internet one can have more political power» are directly correlated with their attitudes to the statement «By using the Internet public officials will care more what people think» . These expressions imply that the global network enables citizens' real influence on management decisions and actions of officials. In Uruguay, Russia the degree of the agreement with this statement is the highest in comparison with similar values in other countries. According to in-depth interviews, it is a widespread belief among Russians that public opinion, expressed on the Internet, has some influence on the decisions and actions of politicians. The Russians believe that their opinions are regularly measured and taken into account by politicians (2, 2). In Chile, this indicator has the lowest value (1, 7), which indicates a rather reserved attitude towards the possibility of political influence through the Internet communication on the officials.

This conclusion is also confirmed by the number of the respondents who expressed their consent with the statement «Use of the Internet increases contact with people (online and offline) who share political views». This variable characteristic had the smallest numeric value (Mexico - 1.6, Russia - 0.5). These low levels may indicate that the respondents do not perceive the Internet as an important tool of communication with people who share the same political views. Moreover, the respondents do not consider such communication to be an important tool of influencing the government policy.

The statement «How much do you agree that Okay for people to express extreme ideas on the Internet» manifests the way the Internet users evaluate the global network as the space where they can express their attitudes to the actions of officials. Uruguayans are characterized by a relatively high coefficient-weighted average of this variable (2.2), whereas Russians do not agree with the statement (1.7). Thus, the

Uruguayans are quite consistent in their perception of the Internet as the space of free and open expression of any opinion, including extremist ones. Russians think that different opinions can be expressed in the global network; however, the freedom of speech on the Internet should exclude extremist opinions.

The citizens' activity in online financial investment is very low in the selected countries. The smallest value of the average weighted rate is typical for Mexico, where the vast majority of users never practiced investment through the Internet. In Russia and Chile this experience a little wider, but in general it also has a low representation of this Internet practice. Although, the issue was not included in the questionnaire in Uruguay, experts believe that the practice of online investing in Uruguay as well as in the other countries is not common either.

These low values of the indicator can point out to several circumstances: the lack of trust to the online investment; the lack of investment opportunities for the majority of the population of the selected countries; the low level of Internet development infrastructure for the implementation of such practices.

This practice is relatively common in Uruguay to Chile and twice less intensively used in Mexico and Russia. Such relatively low levels can be attributed to citizens' distrust to online transactions, as well as insufficient competencies of online banking.

The analyzed countries are characterized by considerable differentiation in the values of this variable. In Mexico this practice is not very common, it is a little more intense in Uruguay and Russia, whereas Chileans perform online payments quite frequently. It should be emphasized that about a fifth of Chilean citizens pay their bills every month online. This can be explained by a well-developed technical infrastructure of such payments, the citizens find these operations safe and they developed necessary competencies of online payment. Obviously, these factors are rather weaker in Mexico, Uruguay and Russia.

Information search for products and services are generally more common practice in the selected countries than financial transactions online. This reveals a more positive attitude to information search in comparison with the willingness to perform any financial transactions on the Internet. Uruguayans take the leading position in this practice, while the citizens in Chile, Mexico and Russia are slightly less active. The data comparison of two previous indicators leads to the conclusion that the Uruguayans are much more focused on getting information online, but they show a very low rate of online shopping, which is even lower than among the Chilean citizens who less actively search for information about goods or services. This tendency is typical for all the selected countries, where Internet information is in greater demand than online shopping. There may several reasons for this tendency: distrust to the goods and services that are ordered online, the low online offer in the analyzed countries. In particular, Russia has a very high cost of product delivery and a long period of delivery.

The analysis of online financial and consumer activity in Mexico, Chile, Uruguay and Russia shows relatively low citizens' activity in these countries to use the Internet data. This practice is more developed in Chile and Uruguay, it is less developed in Russia and it is the least common in Mexico. The distribution of profiles of Internet use in the selected countries provides the explanation of the collected data.

The frequency of e-mailing in the selected countries has the highest values of all type of Internet-communication. Uruguay has the highest e-mail activity of citizens;

Russia and Mexico have lower indicators, with Chile having the lowest level. This variable indicates that citizens use the Internet primarily for social interaction. E-mailing is the most convenient way of messaging, even more preferable than phone calls and chatting.

The average rates of all the components variables show the same trend in all the selected countries. The perception of the Internet as a means of political empowerment has the greatest value. Thus, Mexicans, Chileans, Uruguayans and Russians in general, appreciate the opportunity of their political participation. However, the variables used in the World Internet Project questionnaire, allow only finding out the attitudes to these opportunities, but they do not allow measuring the citizens' attitude towards the global network as a means of electronic participation.

Least mastered by citizens of selected countries is a component of the financial and consumer activity online. Thus in Uruguay value of this coefficient is relatively high. The main reason for that is a relatively high level of confidence in the Uruguayans to the Internet. For comparison - in Uruguay Internet rely totally on the two values ("absolutely reliable" and "mostly reliable") 41.6% of users, while at the same time in Russia and Chile, the figure is less than a third of respondents. The combination of low-intensity use of the Internet as a tool for financial and consumer activity and a relatively high level of trust to the Internet in Mexico can be attributed to the focus on Mexicans certain Internet content that is not related to economic activity. Confirmation of this hypothesis is provided by data clustering Internet usage in selected countries profiles.

Uruguay and Chile are characterized by a relatively large spread of cluster users who actively use all opportunities of the global network (11,3% of Uruguayans and 9,6% of Chileans). This explains the relatively higher figures of Uruguay and Chile in the intensity of online financial and consumer activity, as well as relatively high values of the other variables analyzed. In Russia and Mexico, the dominant profile of Internet use is oriented on an entertainment Internet-content (41,8% of Mexicans and 33,4% of Russians). This explains the relatively lower intensity of the citizens of these countries to use the financial capability and consumer activity online, and much more intensive use of social and communication opportunities. Noteworthy is the similarity in the distribution of the cluster "moderate and pragmatic" in Chile (12,4% of citizens) and Uruguay (12,0% of nation) - the number of this profile in these countries, on average, three times higher than in Mexico (1,9% of population) and RF (4,4% of Russians). It shows the relationship between the user shares, oriented to the benefit and entertainment on the Internet: the more the country "to entertain a global network", the less the "Internet pragmatists". This relationship may also explain the somewhat high rates of Chile and Uruguay in the application of these features of the Internet, as the implementation of online financial and consumer activity.

4 Discussion

The research allowed carrying out a comparison of the two axes: a cross-national and structural. Cross-national analysis allowed comparing the country's level of development of the Internet infrastructure conditions and facilities for the use of citizens of different Capability of the global network. Structural analysis of the set of priorities in the use of various Internet features. At the same time, used the World Internet Project methodology had some limitations. The political component contained variables that reflect no real practice of using the Internet as a means of realizing political subjectivity, and only the people's attitude to these possibilities of the Internet. However, this ratio may indirectly indicate behavioral attitudes in the sphere of application of the global network as a mean of political empowerment.

Comparison of the intensity of use of the various possibilities of the Internet carried out as leading experts in the field of Internet communications Chile professor of the Pontifical Catholic University in Santiago, Sergio Godoy [6]. His results generally correlate to the data of our study - set a much more intensive use of communications and information capabilities of the global network, as well as the relatively low level of social trust in the network. Sergio Godoy argues that significant scientific and practical task is to equalize the level of development of the various possibilities of the Internet and increase the level of social trust in networks and Internet content. This measure, in our opinion, will provide and increase the intensity of the use of financial opportunities, consumer activity and the implementation of political participation in the network.

5   Conclusion

The study showed that the most advanced features of the Internet, the intensity of the citizens of Mexico, Chile, Uruguay and Russia; it is possible to obtain information and social communication. Quite significant for users of all countries studied are political functions of the global network, associated with electronic participation of citizens. The least popular in Mexico, Chile, Uruguay and Russia are the possibilities of online financial and consumer activity. A significant impediment to balanced development in all spheres of the global network is a low level of user confidence in the Internet My Content and interoperability via the Internet.

The creation of conditions for improving the well-being of individuals and social groups with a global network require overcoming the problems identified.

6   Research Perspectives

Important research perspective is the revising the World Internet Project methodology. It seems very significant to add the indicators reflecting the experience of the citizen's e-participation (including political and civil participation). This will improve the scale of matching degree of intensity of use of political, economic, social and communication functions and justify the universal method of studying the degree of development of the Internet as a means of political empowerment, as a tool for financial and consumer activity, and as a channel of social communication for the implementation of cross-national analysis.

Acknowledgments. Research was financed by the Ministry of Education and Science of the Russian Federation within realization of the state task "Detection of regularities of interrelation of development of political systems and Internet communication" for 2014–2016. Code of the state task 2816.

References

1. Baeza-Yates, R., Ribeiro-Neto, B.: Modern Information Retrieval. Addison-Wesley, New York (1999)
2. Bakardjieva, M.: Internet Society: the Internet in Everyday Life. Sage Publications Ltd., London (2005)
3. Baym, N.K.: Finding the quality in qualitative internet research. In: Silver, D., Massanari, A. (eds.) Critical Cyberculture Studies, pp. 79–87. University Press, New York (2006)
4. Castells, M.: Communication Power. Oxford university press, Oxford (2009)
5. Danet, B., Herring, S.C.: The Multilingual Internet: Language, Culture, and Communication Online. Oxford University Press, New York (2009)
6. Godoy, S.E.: Who owns the worlds media?, pp. 641–674. Oxford University Press, Chile (2016)
7. Gurak, L.J.: Cyberliteracy: Navigating the Internet with Awareness. Yale University Press, New Haven (2001)
8. Haythornthwaite, C., Nielsen, A.L.: Revisiting computer-mediated communication for work, community and learning. In: Gaskenbach, J. (ed.) Psychology and the Internet: Intrapersonal, Interpersonal and Transpersonal Implications, 2nd edn, pp. 167–186. Academic Press, San Diego (2006)
9. Kadushin, C.: Understanding Social Networks: Theories, Concepts and Findings. Oxford University Press, New York (2011)
10. Kling, R., Rosenbaum, H., Sawyer, S.: Understanding and Communicating Social Informatics: A Framework for Studying and Teaching the Human Contexts of Information and Communication Technologies. Information Today, Inc., Medford (2005)
11. Kollock, E., Russell Braziel, E.: How not to build an online market: the sociology of market microstructure. In: Thye, S.R., Lawler, E.J. (eds.) Social Psychology of the Workplace: Advances in Group Processes, vol. 23, pp. 283–306. Elsevier Science, New York (2006)
12. Lee, C., Chang, K., Berry, F.S.: Testing the development and diffusion of e-government and e-democracy: a global perspective. Public Adm. Rev. 71(3), 444–454 (2011). doi:10.1111/j.1540-6210.2011.02228.x
13. Leetaru, K.: Data Mining Methods for the Content Analyst: An Introduction to the Computational Analysis of Content. Routledge, New York (2011)
14. Nechaev, V., Brodovskaya, E., Dombrovskaya, A.: Perception of political subjectivity on the Internet: results of the cross-national cluster analysis in the USA, United Kingdom, Mexico, Sweden, Russia, China, The Republic of South Africa. 031-ASS Asian Soc. Sci. Can. 7(11), 269–277 (2014). doi:10.5539/ass.v11n7p269
15. Nechaev, V., Brodovskaya, E., Dombrovskaya, A.: The national profiles of Internet-communication: the results of cross-national cluster analysis. Eur. J. Sci. Theol. 3(11), 125–130 (2015)
16. Nechaev, V., Brodovskaya, E., Dombrovskaya, A.: Spiritual orientations of Russians in the era of the Internet (the results of national sociological research). Eur. J. Sci. Theol. 3(11), 225–236 (2014)
17. Nechaev, V., Brodovskaya, E., Dombrovskaya, A.: The Internet - cultures and e-democracy in Russia and the United States: results of a cross - national study. On the Way to a Stable World: Security and Sustainable Development A Collection of Scientific Papers (San Diego, USA, 2015), pp. 68–73. Global Partnership on Development of Scientific Cooperation, LLC (2015)
18. Nechaev, V., Brodovskaya, E., Kaira, Yu., Dombrovskaya, A.: Classification of Russian Internet users: preliminary results of cluster analysis. Life Sci. J. 11(12), 330–335 (2014)

19. Norris, P.: Digital Divide: Civic Engagement, Information Poverty, and the Internet Worldwide. University Press, Cambridge (2001)
20. O'Donnel, G.: Transitions, continuities and paradoxes. In: Mamwaring, S., O'Donnel, G., Valenzuela, J.S. (eds.) Issues in Democratic Consolidation: The New South American Democracies in Comparative Perspective. University of Notre Dame, Notre Dame (1992)
21. Poster, M.: Cyberdemocracy: Internet and the Public Sphere – Internet Culture. Routledge, New York (1997)
22. Rheingold, H.: The Great Equalizer. Whole Earth Review, New York, pp. 4–11 (1991)
23. Sumbatyan, J.G., Roshupkin, V.T.: The role of the army in the political life of Latin American countries. Lat. Am. **1**, 76–89 (1999)
24. Wellman, B., Haythornthwaite, C. (eds.): The Internet in Everyday Life. Wiley-Blackwell, Oxford (2002)
25. The Research World Wide Web Foundation: A rating of development of the Internet in the countries of the world in 2014. Center of humanitarian technologies 05 February 2015. http://gtmarket.ru/news/2015/02/05/7084
26. Vorozheykina, T.E.: Democracy and economic reform. Experience of the comparative analysis of Russian and Latin America (2014). http://ecsocman.hse.ru/data/743/679/1219/014Vorozhejkina.pdf
27. Ward, S., Gibson, R., Lusoli, W.: Online participation and mobilization in Britain: hype, hope and reality. Parliamentary Aff. **56**, 24–42 (2003)
28. Weber, L.M., Loumakis, A., Bergman, J.: Who participates and why? An analysis of citizens on the Internet and the mass public. Soc. Sci. Comput. Rev. **21**, 652–668 (2003)
29. World Internet Project (2016). http://www.worldinternetproject.net
30. Wynn, J.: Digital sociology: emergent technologies in the field and the classroom. Sociol. Forum **24**(2), 448–456 (2009)

Social Media Impact on the Transformation of Imaginary Political Characters in Russian Youth Culture

Andrei Ulianovskii, Vadim Golubev, Olga Filatova$^{(\boxtimes)}$,
and Aleksey Smirnov

St. Petersburg State University, St. Petersburg, Russia
ullianav@gmail.com, vadimgol@gmail.com,
filatovo@gmail.com, darapti@mail.ru

Abstract. The paper discusses the role of emotionally significant political images in Russian youth culture. The study covers the period between 2006 and 2012, during which Russia saw not only a political and economic transition, but also dramatic changes in communication technology. The 6-stage research included two waves of testing in 2006 and 2012, with 179 respondents selected for the final stage of the survey. Respondents were aged 17 to 24 years old.

Keywords: Imaginary political characters · Youth values · Cultural studies · Political culture · Social media

1 Introduction

Currently, new media are playing an increasingly important part in political image making. As part of this, we see signs of a comparatively new phenomenon: people demonstrate an active interest in imaginary worlds and their entities. The trend began to emerge in the first five years of the third millennium. Published in 2006, the groundbreaking book, *The 101 Most Influential People Who Never Lived* by Karlan, D. et al. [13] describes fictional characters who have had a great influence on the lives of Americans. The top list of these creatures includes the Marlboro Man, Big Brother, King Arthur, Santa Claus, Hamlet, and Frankenstein's Monster. Imaginary characters have occupied television, art, folklore, business, etc. These characters promote their own values and lifestyles, which have become part of the agenda in public administration and contemporary politics.

Social media demonstrated dramatic growth in Russia between 2006 and 2012. Internet became faster to the point that it allowed people to watch English-language TV series on their smartphones, exchange links to dynamic content, and create humorous photo collages with various characters. Our study demonstrates that this combination of software and hardware developments made a great impact on viewer content and, consequently, on young peoples' values [25].

The purpose of this study is to identify emotional and value aspects of imaginary political characters as reflected Russian youth culture. We are interested in understanding how political meaning models, which prevailed in youth culture during the

© Springer International Publishing AG 2016
A.V. Chugunov et al. (Eds.): DTGS 2016, CCIS 674, pp. 35–44, 2016.
DOI: 10.1007/978-3-319-49700-6_5

last years of the Soviet Union (young people, who were 17–24 years old in 2005–2006, had been born in the USSR), have been replaced by new models of political values in post-Soviet Russia (young people, who were 17–24 years old in 2011–2012, had been born after the collapse of the Soviet Union). The study aimed to identify and describe transformations of imaginary political characters in the youth culture of the last Soviet generation and that of the first post-Soviet generation. The study was carried out in two waves, in 2006 and 2012.

We believe that there is a significant difference between the political culture of those who were born in Russia and those who were born in the USSR. The reason is the nature of media (classical electronic media vs digital media) and the context of cultural socialisation.

2 Literature Review

Our survey of literature has yielded the following conclusions:

(1) Political aspects of the traditional electronic and print media are well studied by both sociologists and political science scholars such as Lasswell, H., Lipmann, W., and Lazarsfeld, P. [14, 17, 19] who focus on the crucial role of media in modern society.
(2) There is an extensive body of research in social media and other ways of digital communication [4, 7, 9, 15, 24, 25]. Many media studies discuss *format* as a mechanism of producing online media texts as part of convergent media production process. They view *format* as a way to express social reality [10, 12, 16].
(3) Research of imaginary characters in politics and political mythology can be found in [1–3, 8, 18, 23]. Formalists Propp V., Jakobson R. laid the foundation for a structural understanding of classical mythology [11, 21].
(4) Bottici C., Esch J. provide a theoretical framework of the imaginary as a combination of historical knowledge, current culture, and political myth-making [1, 2, 6]. Danilov M., Persson E. & Petersson B. focus on different aspects media impact in post-Soviet countries [5, 20].
(5) Advertising and public relations research [22] focuses on the social myth aspects of the media. In order to create successful projects in the fields of political PR and public administration, one should be able to integrate political mythology into humanities, media format, contemporary art and folklore. In relation to characters, this idea means dropping semantic boundaries between the fictional and the real.

3 Research Methodology

Imaginary characters or images are defined as spontaneously recalled emotionally significant animate objects of a shared reality in the entire specter of their manifestations (beliefs, values, looks, speech patterns, behavior, talents, and lifestyle). These objects originate in, and transformed by, the media rather than are personal imagination.

The method used in this study is based on the concept of respondents identifying and describing imaginary characters through their stream of consciousness, which is embodied in the creative process of drawing and writing. This method has successfully been used in brand identification studies. It enables to poll hundreds of people and collect as much information as can be collected through in-depth interviews.

The research included St Petersburg social sciences and humanities students aged 19 to 27 years old. We selected 179 participants for the second stage in both waves of the study. To be selected, students had to have strong creative motivation, an ability to draw and write, and hold imaginary characters in their minds at the same time. In the study, respondents identified and described imaginary characters by drawing and writing about them.

The study consisted of two main stages broken into sub-stages [24, p. 125]: selecting test participants and involving them in the process of gathering and identifying imaginary characters. At the second stage, test participants responded to a short questionnaire that included naming several imaginary characters and drawing sketches of them. In 2006, the final part of the test involved 52 scriptwriters and 13 illustrators, in 2012–79 scriptwriters and 35 illustrators. The result was a table of imaginary characters, which included 240 characters in 2006 and 336 in 2012.

Our choice of respondents was based on the following reasons. Firstly, our assumption was that the above ability was the result of many years of academic selection. Secondly, by virtue of their future professional activity (journalism and social and commercial communication) our respondents were likely to make the most impact on society. Thirdly, these students represented virtually every Russian region since they had been accepted on the basis of the Russia-wide Uniform State Examination results. Finally, this study was designed as a pilot qualitative study of 18-23-year-old Russians. Rather than being an extrapolation from the part to the whole (philosophical semantics), it was a pilot, rough version of the whole (sociological semantics of a measure of representativeness of a general population in the sampling).

4 Emotionally Significant Political Images in the 2006–2012 Research Data

This paper covers exclusively the political aspects of the research. A full description of the study can be found in Russian [24, 25]. Table 1 presents a comparison of the 2006 and 2012 research data.

Table 1. Imaginary political characters in Russian media

Compared parameter	2006	2012
Imaginary characters (total number)	240	336
Imaginary political characters (number/percentage)	25/10, 4	7/2, 1
Nationality-related characters (number)	7	1
Political concepts (number)	8	4
Politicians (number)	0	1
American characters (number)	3	0
Historical persons (number)	7	1

In 2006, respondents mentioned seven nationality-related characters or groups (an Englishman, an American, Germans, a Russian, a Finn, a Frenchman, and a Chukchi), eight political images (Big Brother, Paper Tiger, Stormy Petrel, Dove of Peace, Motherland, The Soviet Hero, Democracy, and Freedom), three images associated with United States politics (Uncle Sam, the Democratic Donkey, and the Republican Elephant), and seven historical persons (Vasily Ivanovich Chapaev, Ivan the Terrible, Peter the Great, Rasputin, Grandpa Lenin, Vovochka (Lenin as a teenager), and Che Guevara).

In 2012, respondents mentioned just nine imaginary political characters. They include seven political images (Big Brother, MedvePut (formed by a combination of the two family names: MEDVEdev and PUTin), Putin Is a Mushroom, Tandem, Powerful People of the World, Friendship of Nations, The Great Chief), one historical person (Stalin), and one politician (Zhirinovsky).

Below are participants' descriptions of some imaginary characters and images. The described characters were chosen collectively while the illustrations and the descriptions of fictional characters belong to individual authors. Most descriptions are given in reduced form in this paper.

Big Brother (2006). "George Orwell was the first to introduce the concept of Big Brother in the dystopia, *1984*, in 1949. Big Brother seems to be a scientist, who watches all members of society. Everything Big Brother says is the law! He was released into the telecommunication space by way of a reality show. It is worth mentioning that Big Brother himself became the father of this form of TV entertainment. The show is broadcast in more than 30 countries. Big Brother does not have any personal characteristics; he is a kind of abstract image. Yet people tend to visualize the image as a real person. It would be fair to suppose that Russians mainly associate Big Brother with the KGB. A lot of Russian scientists hypothesize about how events in Russia could develop if they took the path described in *1984*."

The Soviet Hero (2006). "It is necessary to differentiate between an act of real human sacrifice for high values and the cultivating of a hyperbolical image of this social existence created by propaganda, which is based on the double standards of the propagandists. The Soviet Hero as a character had great importance for Soviet citizens for a long time. Contemporary Russia is the cultural successor of the Soviet Union, therefore the image of the Soviet Hero retains much of its original value and is still perceived as a symbol of heroism, a symbol of devotion to patriotic ideas and courage.

This image is also one of the main literary characters of the Soviet period, notably in the works of Maxim Gorky. At first, Gorky used zoomorphic forms to build the image of a Soviet hero (*Song of the Falcon* and *The Stormy Petrel*), but then he switched to the anthropomorphic images (Pavel Vlasov in the novel, *Mother*)".

The image has the following main personality traits: (1) personal enthusiasm; (2) a special combination of honesty and a desire to denounce; (3) special fanatical exaltation; (4) unbending will; (5) devotion to the ideals of communism; (6) pursuit of justice; (7) self-sacrifice, the abandonment of personal things for the sake of a Great cause. The character of the Soviet Hero still has its significance as the perfect embodiment of the idea of serving others and devotion to the Motherland.

Uncle Sam (2006). "Everyone has seen Uncle Sam, that old man wearing a star-spangled top hat, a red tie, and a blue jacket; always looking at us and pointing his finger. But the image of this guy is not the portrait of a real person named Sam. The expression 'Uncle Sam' was associated with the U.S. Government for the first time during the War of 1812 between the British Empire and the United States. Samuel Wilson (1766–1854), a supplier of meat to the U.S. Army from Troy (NY), shipped the meat in barrels with big letters 'US' written across, which meant 'The United States'. But an Irish watchman thought that this acronym stood for the supplier's name, and read it as 'Uncle Sam Wilson'."

The Great Chief (2012). "It is the image of the Supreme commander of the Indians in the USA, a true leader. He is trying to protect the honor of his nation that has been fighting for its rights against Columbus with his Columbians for so long that it's too late to apologize. It's well known that Indians had begun growing corn long before Khrushchev knew about it. They took the courage to pass it as gold and so deceived naïve Yanks. It is easy to guess that popcorn was invented by Indians to lure Americans to cinemas, while the indigenous people were winning back their land. The custom of smoking was his doing as well, but no one cares about it today. While the Grand Chief lit his pipe and watched brainwashed Americans, who just ate popcorn and watched Hollywood masterpieces, he did not notice that there had appeared more dangerous enemies in his way – cowboys. The fight between the cowboys and the Indians was savage…

Meanwhile, Americans decide to deliver their best agent directly into the hands of the Great Chief to strike him in his heart. They believed that a mock anthropologist would be able to kill the Great Chief and destroy Indian morale. But the leader felt it. He managed to fill the pipe with something more interesting (forbidden) than tobacco and to undermine the morale of the enemy. So that's where Carlos Castaneda came from! The plan of the leader was successful: now Americans read Castaneda, looking for deep truth in his works, and forget about the long war."

Stalin (2012). "Stalin was involved in criminal affairs, but his pseudonym helped him to escape responsibility (however, he had spent some time in prison during his youth). He was a political and military leader of the USSR. He issued a "Not a single step back" decree. He arranged executions and murders of army commanders and lots of Soviet citizens. Stalin died on 1 March 1953 from cerebral hemorrhage. Soon after that Stalin's cult of personality was eradicated, and, later, Joseph Stalin became a popular media character, well known for his paranoid charisma and a passion for puffing a pipe filled with unknown stuff."

Tandem (2012). "This word acquired a new meaning in March 2008 after the election of Dmitry Medvedev to the post of the President of Russia. The term refers to the close collaboration of President Dmitry Medvedev and Prime Minister Vladimir Putin. We can see incredible rapport and understanding between them with rare exceptions in some controversial issues (for example, their opinions concerning the events that took place in Libya in spring 2011, the investigation of the Domodedovo airport terrorist attack, or the trial of Mikhail Khodorkovsky and Platon Lebedev). This understanding enables them to act and make decisions together."

Fig. 1. MedvePut, the name of an imaginary character that was formed by the combination of the two family names of MEDVEdev and PUTin, 2012.

MedvePut (2012). "Common MedvePut is the rarest species of the Russian fauna listed in the "Red Book of the IMF". Sanctity of species is enshrined in the Constitution. Special characteristics: fanatical love to the Apple Inc. products, hence people close to it call it by the endearing nickname of Ipaddy. Specimens tend to be found in the vertical of power, but it does not neglect horizontals either. It is often seen in the lobbies of the Kremlin, but its favorite places there are the seats of the President and the Prime Minister. There is a hypothesis that MedvePut is the product of a scientific experiment; its cells were taken from our country's top officials.

The creature is vicious, emotionally unstable and prone to tyranny; it masks imperial ambitions with a love for democratic rules. Probably, it wants to conquer the world, but this information has no documentary evidence yet. It takes after Putin and Medvedev equally. Usually, MedvePut has an evil grin on its face" (see Fig. 1).

Putin Is a Mushroom (2012). "How can we explain the current political situation in Russia? People have refused to express their will and delegated it to the government and the authorities. Maybe the whole country eats mushrooms and simply does not understand anything at all? It is hard to understand the behavior of Russians, so, perhaps, we can find the explanation in less logical places, for example, in mushrooms. Let mushrooms be everywhere. Not only those that are edible, but also those that govern the entire mankind. This is some form of mental illness.

People eat mushrooms; people pick up mushrooms; people are managed by mushrooms; and people are mushrooms. Well, who else could it be that took such deep roots in the Kremlin? A mushroom, of course. And the Kremlin is its mycelium. There is a documentary called 'The Mould'; it was shown on a Russian central TV channel a few years ago. It said that mould 'is able to take over a tremendous mass of people and change the course of history. If it declares war on us, we will have no chance to survive'. So, we have found out who and what mushroom is, no comments are needed. What is left to do is to learn to live with the idea that you are a citizen in the country,

Fig. 2. Putin is a mushroom, 2012.

Fig. 3. Zhirinovsky, the leader of the Liberal Democratic Party of Russia (one of four major political parties in Russia), 2012.

where power over you belongs to mushrooms. Who knows, maybe you are a mushroom too" (see Fig. 2.)

Zhirinovsky (2012). "Vladimir Zhirinovsky was born on 25 April, 1946 in Alma-Ata. This political character is familiar to us as a meme, a joke, and most importantly a Member of Parliament. Moreover, he ran for presidency a couple of times. Zhirinovsky gained popularity during the 1990 TV debates, when he was the first to impress the electorate with his ability to start arguments turning into fights. The next generation of Russians should also be ready to get to know him: he once said that he wanted to clone himself in the nearest future; this, in his opinion, would be 'a benefit to the nation'. Definitely an unpredictable and unique character" (see Fig. 3).

Friendship of Nations (2012). "This concept was mentioned for the first time during the Soviet era. It means that the various nations within a country and abroad should cooperate with each other. The aim of this 'project' was the expansion of socialist society and the triumph of communist ideology. Nowadays, the project 'Friendship of Nations' still lives in Russian hearts. We can say that today the Friendship of Nations weaves together three basic ideas: the friendship of people within a state, the friendship between Russian people and migrants from southern countries, and, of course, the friendship with representatives of Western civilization.

But what is the difference? Still, many 'real' Russians, called neo-Nazis (in whose veins, in truth, no one knows what blood flows), make fun of some northern nations and show apparent hostility to southern ones. As far as the attitude of 'Russians' to people from the Central Asian republics of the former Soviet Union, one can hardly even talk about mutual understanding, let alone friendship."

5   Conclusions

Several conclusions follow from the study:

1. The comparison of two waves of the study shows a significant decline in the interest in political characters in general. In 2006 there were 25 imaginary political characters, which constitutes 10,4% of total characters. In 2012, the participants identified only 7 imaginary political characters or 2,1% of 336 characters. It demonstrates that politics occupied a negligible part in the life of the first post-Soviet generation. Young people showed indifference to politics, political power and political authorities. It was outside the interest of young intellectuals.

2. By 2012, political jokes - an important and influential horizontal communication channel in Russia – had been almost destroyed by the Internet, particularly by Internet memes. There was a clear reduction of young people's education level, especially in the fields of history and literature. Verbal culture of political communication had been replaced by visual communication throughout the Internet and social networks. In 2006, the tradition of political jokes was represented by seven ethnic characters. Today, as Maksim Danilov notes, there is a trend to abuse political power in social media [5]. Interestingly, Ivan the Terrible as the czar and the character of a Soviet popular comedy, became a popular Internet meme: "Ivan the Terrible kills...".

3. The Internet gave Russian young people access to English-language TV shows. Between 2011 and 2015, almost all English-language TV series, which people had only been able to watch online, were shown on regular TV. These serials included a variety of likeable negative characters. The more young people liked anti-heroes, the more they showed tolerance to ugly manifestations of political power.

4. By 2012, characters related to US politics had been replaced by characters from American TV series. There was no ideology any more. There were no political myths of self-identification any longer. In 2006, Russian youth had been more domestically oriented and politically engaged, while in 2012 they were more

internationally oriented and less politically engaged. In 2012, foreign policy had totally left young people's area of interest.

5. The following were characteristics of a successful Russian political leader in the eyes of young Russians in 2012: It is a male. He has a traditional sexual orientation. He is well-built and attractive. His behavior is principled and logical. He represents a big idea or concept. This image has come out of television politics and become part of modern Internet folklore via social networks. For example, Zhirinovsky is known as a showman; in the context of the study, he is a close neighbor with such characters as Dr. House, Iron Man, Cinderella, and Ivan the Fool.

6. There still were vestigial elements of Soviet ideology ("Mother Russia", "The Soviet Hero", "The October Revolution and Heroes of the Revolution") in the descriptions of political characters in 2006. These parts of Soviet ideology showed the strongest vitality in Russian youth culture.

6   Further Research Avenues

The current study analyses data collected before the dramatic change of power in Ukraine and the subsequent changes in Russian foreign and domestic policy. A third wave of our research in 2018 could give us unique empirical data for further studies of young people's attitudes to Russia's transition from a traditional free market economy and a western-type democratic political system to a new political model as reflected in the world of fictional characters.

We need to verify the statement that the current political authorities had lost an exalted status in the eyes of Russian youth and now look monstrous. Also, we need to verify empirical data about youth's acceptance of war as an ideology and its esthetization.

A more advanced research methodology is required to assess the role of social media in the perception change and to assign the change to social media.

References

1. Bottici, C.: A Philosophy of Political Myth. Cambridge University Press, Cambridge (2007)
2. Bottici, C.: Myths of Europe: a theoretical approach. J. Educ. Media Mem. Soc. **1**(2), 9–33 (2007)
3. Cassirer, E.: The Myth of the State. Greenwood Press, New York (1979)
4. Chugunov, A., Filatova, O., Misnikov, Y.: Online discourse as a microdemocracy tool: towards new discursive epistemics for policy deliberation. In: ICEGOV 2016 Proceedings of the 8th International Conference on Theory and Practice of Electronic Governance, pp. 40–49. ACM, New York (2016). doi:10.1145/2910019.2910100
5. Danilov, M.: Fol'klornye obrazy v predstavlenii socialno-gumanitarnoi intelligenzii nachala XXI veka. In: Ulianovskii, A. V. (ed.) Vymyshlennye sushchestva epokhi massmedia: Rossiia, XXI vek. Volna 2012. St. Petersburg: Svoe Izdatelstvo, pp. 200–208 (2013)
6. Esch, J.: Legitimizing the 'War on Terror': political myth in official-level rhetoric. Polit. Psychol. **31**(3), 357–391 (2010)

7. Evans, D.: Social Media Marketing: An Hour a Day. Symbex, Indianapolis (2008)
8. Flood, C.G.: Political Myth: A Theoretical Introduction. Garland Pub. Inc., New York (1996)
9. Halligan, B., Shan, D.: Inbound Marketing: Get Found Using Google, Social Media, and Blogs. Wiley, New York (2009)
10. Ilchenco, S.N.: The dualism of the internet in modern media: pros and cons. In: Proceedings of the 1st Annual Conference. Sovremennye SMI v kontexte informacionnyh tehnologii (The St. Petersburg State University of Technology and Design, St. Petersburg, Russia, 9–10 April 2014) (2015)
11. Jakobson, R.: Selected Writings, vol. 8. 's-Gravenhage, Mouton (1988)
12. Kardinskaya, S.V.: The boundary "us/them" in the structure of a media text. In: Proceedings of the 1st Annual Conference. Sovremennye SMI v kontexte informacionnyh tehnologii (St. Petersburg State University of Tecnology and Design, The St. Petersburg, The Russia, 9–10 April 2014) (2015)
13. Karlan, D., Lazar, A., Salter, J.: The 101 Most Influential People Who Never Lived: How Characters of Fiction, Myth, Legends, Television, and Movies Have Shaped Our Society, Changed Our Behavior, and Set the Course of History. William Morrow (2006)
14. Katz, E., Lazarsfeld, P.F.: Personal Influence: The Part Played by People in the Flow of Mass Communication. Free Press, Glencoe (1955)
15. Kaushik, A.: Web Analytics 2.0: The Art of Online Accountability and Science of Customer Centricity. Sybex, Alameda (2009)
16. Kim, M.N.: The production of media in a converge of mass media. In: Proceedings of the 1st Annual Conference. Sovremennye SMI v kontexte informacionnyh tehnologii (St. Petersburg State University of Tecnology and Design, St. Petersburg, Russia, 9–10 April 2014) (2015)
17. Lasswell, H.: The Structure and Function of Communication in Society. The Process and Effects of Mass Communication, Chicago (1971)
18. Lieberman, S., Gray, T.: The role of political myth in the international conflict over genetically modified foods and crops. Eur. Environ. J. Eur. Environ. Policy 17(6), 376–386 (2007)
19. Lippman, W.: Public Opinion. Harcourt, Brace and Company, New York (1922)
20. Persson, E., Petersson, B.: Political mythmaking and the 2014 winter olympics in Sochi: Olympism and the Russian great power myth. East Eur. Polit. 30(2), 192–209 (2014)
21. Propp, V.: Morphology of the Folktale. L.: Academia (1928)
22. Runduzzo, Sal: The Myth Makers. Probus publishing, Cambridge (1995)
23. Qualman, E.: Socialnomics: How Social Media Transforms the Way We Live and Do Business. Wiley, New York (2009)
24. Ulianovskii, A.V.: Vymyshlennye sushchestva epokhi massmedia: Rossiia, XXI vek. Knizhnyi Dom, St. Petersburg (2008)
25. Ulianovskii, A.V. (ed.): Vymyshlennye sushchestva epokhi massmedia: Rossiia, XXI vek. Volna 2012. Svoe Izdatelstvo, St. Petersburg (2013)

"Soviet" in the Space of Social Networks: A Form of Political Reflection

Natalya Mishankina and Nadezhda Zilberman[✉]

Tomsk State University, Tomsk, Russia
n1999@rambler.ru, zilberman@ido.tsu.ru

Abstract. In this article we review the understanding of the "Soviet" phenomenon by social network users. The scope of our analysis includes social networks that are most often used by Russian citizens: Vkontakte, Odnoklassniki and Facebook. In the course of the research, there were used methods of content analysis and linguistic analysis. Techniques of semantic and textual analysis were applied to the analysis of certain types of text: titles, slogans, descriptions of groups and user comments. Content analysis method was used to identify the key semantic categories (topics) that are relevant to users of social networks. The analysis of the information placed in groups (communities) in social networks shows a significant difference in understanding of the investigated phenomenon.

Keywords: Online communication · Social networks · Online communities · Political reflection · The Soviet Union

1 Introduction

The notion of online communication occupies the minds of researchers more and more as an active and rapidly developing phenomenon [1]. The space of the computer communications is conceptualized as an open communicative environment with specific conditions of communication with a large number of participants. Accordingly, the processes that take place in modern society and the life of an individual, as a representative of this society, are embodied in a new communication format and subjected to transformations [2, 3, 7].

The environment of online communications represents an opportunity to study social (including verbal) behavior in new communicative conditions [7]. The transformation of social norms is possible through particular discursive parameters of communication on the Internet: (1) dual chronotope, i.e. each communicant is in two chronotopes – real and virtual, the latter is common to the communicants, the real one is communicatively reduced, although it may influence the course of communication; (2) anonymity: the physical side of communicants is hidden from direct observation – a speaker is present in the form of a virtual equivalent – a sign of personality, modeled by the communicant [7]. The last parameter creates a much greater sense of social freedom and promotes a more open statement of the socio-political views [5, 6, 8].

© Springer International Publishing AG 2016
A.V. Chugunov et al. (Eds.): DTGS 2016, CCIS 674, pp. 45–50, 2016.
DOI: 10.1007/978-3-319-49700-6_6

In modern public and private life of Russians more and more attention is paid to the phenomenon of "Soviet". It appears that this is for two reasons. First, the national community overcame that minimum temporary, historical "distance", when anger and rejection in relation to the previous political system gave way to attempt to see it closer. The generation that was born and developed in a completely different cultural environment grew up having a natural interest in the ways of the world order and, primarily, in which their parents lived. The Russian society appeared in cultural and historical situations requiring reflection, first of all, to restore cultural and historical ties, to form of the cultural-historical identity for a new generation of Russians. Therefore, the interest in the phenomenon of the Soviet in a historical and cultural perspective is formed, from our point of view, a completely natural, spontaneous way as an attempt of cultural and historical identity. The second reason is socio-political changes taking place in the life of a modern Russian. Earlier we considered these processes in the field of virtual discourse on the material of the forums, where forms and the facts of life during the "Soviet" system were actively discussed [4], in this paper, we turn to the analysis of reflection forms of this phenomenon in social networks.

2   Reflection in the Groups of Social Networks

2.1   Material and Study Procedure

The scope of our analysis includes social networks that are most often used by Russian citizens: Vkontakte, Odnoklassniki and Facebook. In the study we examined the groups dedicated to the discussion of the "Soviet" phenomenon in social networks. In the course of the research, there were used methods of content analysis and linguistic analysis. Techniques of semantic and textual analysis were applied to the analysis of certain types of text: titles, slogans, descriptions of groups and user comments. Content analysis method was used to identify the key semantic categories (topics) that are relevant to users of social networks. Quantitative analysis of verbal units that represent certain semantic categories (topics), led to the qualitative conclusion about the interest of the users to the phenomenon of the "Soviet". The immediate material analysis were texts posted in the news of the social network group. The selection of text posts the most large groups devoted to the phenomenon of the Soviet was made for each social network, based on linguistic analysis. We chose the topics for the analysis, in which the number of posts exceeded 100, indicating the interest of the participants. The total number of selected subjects was more than 10 thousand posts (hereafter taken as 100%).

2.2   Results

2.2.1   Characteristics of "Soviet" Groups in Social Networks

At the first stage of analysis, a number of communicative spaces (groups) were revealed in the framework of these social networks dedicated to the phenomenon of the Soviet. Through search systems, queries were typed, aimed at the identification of the thematic groups associated with the notion of "Soviet": "Soviet Union", "USSR". There was formed a query associated with the name of the major political leader of the Soviet Union – "Stalin". Odnoklassniki is the leader among the number of resources associated with the memory of the Soviet, which is quite understandable from the point of view of age composition of network users. However, Vkontakte social network shows a significant number of the studied thematic groups, which supports the hypothesis of the search for identity among the youth. The meaningful analysis of the identified resources demonstrated a significant difference of the discussed issues from earlier results based on the material of forums [4]. The main difference is a significant dominance of political issues. The materials of the forums show that the basic problem is the evaluation of the phenomena of the Soviet reality: negative with respect to the family-raising and types of family interaction, everyday life and ways of the household organization, the principles of grooming, education, politics and power. The positive assessment focuses on the Soviet gastronomy, the rationality of housekeeping, principles of socialization, culture in the aspect of innovative aesthetics [4].

2.2.2   Group in Vkontakte Social Network

The material for the analysis was the posts in the discussion of the "SOVIET_ UNION_IN_OUR_HEARTS" group. Most of the discussions are on political topics (about 71% of posts). The following countries and regions that are referenced directly in the titles of topics came in sight of the participants: the USSR, Russia, Ukraine, Belarus, Germany, the USA, China, North Korea, Japan, South Korea, Libya and Caucasus (general category). The most discussed country is Ukraine (4%). The discussion of countries often takes place in the context of military topics. It should be noted that the topics that are somehow related to the concept of war, containing such lexemes as *war, weapon, armed, army, battle*, etc. take about 10%. In the framework of the political subject, there are discussed the ideology of communism and socialism (3%), the Communist Party of the Russian Federation and the United Russia (2%), elections (2%, overall negative assessment of the events). A large number of topics (31%) touch upon the personalities of politicians. Individual topics concerning Vladimir Putin (13%), I. Stalin (11%) and Vladimir Lenin (3%) are open for discussion; there are also separate topics about M. Gorbachev, N. Khrushchev, Zyuganov, Kolchak.

In addition to political topics, science/education/philosophy (4%), religion (4%) culture (2%), sports, demographic problems, health care, economic problems (less than 1%) are also discussed. In most topics, modern Russia is opposed to the USSR (4%). Reflection of the past through the culture is presented not so wide, only 0.7% of certain topics are dedicated to the Soviet cinema and animation. The participants consider the possibility of return of the Soviet political system, which is reflected in the following topics (10%). As a rule, the participants consider revolution as a way for the revival of this regime. Interestingly, along with such plans, the group has sections devoted to thoughts about the future, which mainly relate to the future of Russia (1%). However personal aspects of life are not discussed, the future takes its way across the country or the world, but not the individual.

2.2.3   Group in Odnoklassniki Social Network

Users of Odnoklassniki social network, in contrast, are focused largely on socio-cultural aspects. What is more, posts in the news feed are, as a rule, graphics: photos, demotivators, etc. The text component of the post is accompanying remark and comments from the participants of a discussion. By the number of reposts and comments (100 posts on the social group the wall is 100%), the most relevant topics are those related to the facts of social inequality (34%), the Soviet way of life and the world of artifacts (incl. gastronomy (16%), the Soviet childhood and school (15%), the Soviet cinema (15%). However, this feed contains obviously advertising material, for example, advertising of cosmetic products (10%). It is curious that the feed has almost equal number of posts (3%), dedicated to Soviet cosmonauts and religious artifacts – images of icons with a call to repost for better living conditions.

In this communicative space, there is also the obvious juxtaposition of modern Russia and the Soviet Union, but social and ethical norms of life are opposed. Modern Russia is perceived as immoral in relation to the Soviet Union – the space of love and friendship. However, during the discussions of the individual positions (we considered those with more than 100 comments), there are lively discussions related to the evaluation of the facts of Soviet life. Despite the positive beginning, the topic of ethnic relations is unfolding as a discussion of contemporary political relations between former Soviet republics and Ukraine is in the center of it. It is revealed in the discussions of complex issues relating to the understanding of the Soviet as a social and as a political system. In addition, as in the case with users of Vkontakte social network, it is clear that for the members of groups in Odnoklassniki Soviet topics are closely connected with the modern state of Russia, they are comprehended through the prism of modern negative events.

2.2.4   Group in Facebook Social Network

Communities devoted to understanding of the Soviet phenomenon by Facebook users primarily consider the USSR as cultural space – 42% of the information in the news feed is devoted to cultural content – Soviet films, television, and art in general (100 posts on the social group the wall is 100%). 17% of posts contain information about important world events, achievements of the Soviet people. It should be noted that in groups of this social network, the posts dedicated to the artifact world of the Soviet are very rare, primarily, there is information about personalities: actors, writers, scientists, military, etc. who created the reputation of the Soviet state. However, directly in the news feed, messages about current political events (12%) are posted, associated with the actions of the president, the comprehension of political events etc. In addition, the commenting is done in a much more restrained manner compared to other social networks. And probably due to the fact that the area of culture is perceived as more holistic and unambiguous, the discussions rarely pass into debates, interlocutors usually agree in the evaluation of the event.

3   Conclusion

The study of forms of reflection of the Soviet phenomenon in Vkontakte, Odnoklassniki and Facebook social networks showed that the reflection concerning the past political system is expressed in the form of active discussion of various aspects of the Soviet. The users of different social networks conceptualize these manifestations in different ways. On the one hand, we observe an obvious similarity between users of Vkontakte and Odnoklassniki in active reflection – they form a lot of communicative spaces for a discussion. Facebook users are less active in this respect – the number of created communities is much less. At the same time, in a meaningful aspect, the members of the Vkontakte groups are rather concentrated on the problems of contemporary policy and issues related to the Soviet become an occasion for intensive discussions about the problems of the modern world. The users of Odnoklassniki are focused on nostalgia for the material world and the world of their childhood. In this community, the problems of modern social inequality are comprehended especially crucially, there is a constant comparison with the social structure of the Soviet Union. The users of Facebook, on the contrary, are aimed at the socio-cultural sector – most of the information is formed by the texts about culturally significant events and persons. The obtained results allow to draw a conclusion about a significant difference of reflection of the modern user of social networks from participants in similar discussions on the forums: in the spotlight of social network users, there are socio-political and socio-cultural issues. It is possible to trace the differences in the phenomena evaluation: as a rule, Soviet culture, education, the social structure of society, gastronomy are evaluated positively, but the same phenomena of contemporary reality have a negative assessment. As a political system the Soviet is conceptualized primarily from the perspective of the integrity and importance in global politics. The users of social networks, sometimes covertly, sometimes quite openly, declare the illegality of the collapse of the Soviet Union, about the negative consequences for all objects of the former Soviet Empire and announce intentions on its reconstruction.

References

1. Bell, D. (ed.): Cybercultures: Critical Concepts in Media and Cultural Studies: Cyberculture, Cyberpolitics, Cybersociety, vol. 3. Routledge, London (2008). 471 pages
2. Maximova, O.B.: Social aspects of Internet communication: virtual community and communication personality. Bull. Peoples' Friendship Univ. Russia. Ser. Sociol. **1**, 24–33 (2011). Publishing House of Peoples' Friendship University of Russia, Moscow
3. Mirloy, L., Gordon, M.: Sociolinguistics: Method and Interpretation. Blackwell Publishing, Oxford (2003). 261 pages
4. Mishankina, N.A.: Motherland or Sovok? Reflection of the "Soviet" life style in virtual discourse. In: Rezanova, Z.I. (ed.) Nostalgia for the Soviet, pp. 126–139. Publishing House of Tomsk State University, Tomsk (2011)
5. Diaghileva, N.S., Zhuravleva, L.A.: The essence of sociocultural identity of young people in the environment of online communications. Bull. Chelyabinsk State Univ. **42**, 152–153 (2009). Publishing House of Chelyabinsk State University, Chelyabinsk

6. Kalimullin, D.D.: The space of Internet communications as a tolerant environment. Bull. Kazan State Univ. Cult. Arts **1**, 135–138 (2009). Publishing House of Kazan State University of Culture and Arts, Kazan

7. Mishankina, N.A.: Social norms in Internet communication: sociolinguistic aspect. In: Mozhaeva, G.V. (ed.) Humanitarian informatics, vol. 7, pp. 72–78. Publishing House of Tomsk State University, Tomsk (2013)

8. Morozova, O.N.: Political Internet communication: its role, functions and forms. In: Chudinov, A.P. (ed.) Political Linguistics, vol. 1, pp. 156–161. Publishing House of Ural State Pedagogical University, Yekaterinburg (2011)

9. Social Networks in Russia: Figures, trends and forecasts. In: Brand Analytics: Monitoring and Analysis System of the Brand in Social Media and Mass Media, Spring 2015. http://br-analytics.ru/blog/socialnye-seti-v-rossii-vesna-2015-cifry-trendy-prognozy

Towards the Improvement of Sociological Studies Processes Through Social Networking and ICT(s)

Fantazi Abdelouaheb[✉] and Latifa Mahdaoui

KMEELEA Team, RIIMA Laboratory, Computer Science Department,
University of Science and Technologies "Houari Boumédiène", PB #32, El-Alia,
16111 Bab-Ezzouar, Algiers, Algeria
abdelouahebfantazi@gmail.com, lmahdaoui@usthb.dz

Abstract. The field of sociology became a science with the introduction of methodological and mathematical tools to study and analyze the sociological phenomena. On the other side, the invasion of ICT in all areas force to a review of the methodological processes of sociology studies for an efficient use of technologies and to improve the quality level of the sampling, the conduct of investigations and more rapid delivery of results. Indeed, a social phenomenon is characterized by an unpredictable cycle and the results are in a risk of subjectivity. This paper is intended as a fairly exhaustive study of currents that have influenced the process of sociological studies analyzing different aspects. We then move to a proposed hybrid life cycle and functional architecture of what would be a cooperative sociology system combining various technologies such as social networks and geographical information systems. We call that "geographic sociology system".

Keywords: ICT · Geographical sociology · Method of analysis · Quantitative and qualitative method · Social networking · Sociology phenomena · Sociological information system · Cooperation · Social inquiry

1 Introduction

Nowadays, the influence of the technology of information and communication on the set of the word societies is very significant. This significance is interpreted in the digital importance of the technophiles that make an inventory of (invented) the last years on the international scale. In front of this dramatic advance of the new technologies, each activity sector tries to be accordingly redefined. In case it is recognized that ICT influence significantly the economic dimensions, sociology is not away from this tendency.

With the coming of these technologies of information and communication, including the motors leading to profound changes in analyzing methods of social phenomena. Their major effect is to propose a new process of dynamic analysis of change linked to a growing complexity.

This document aims at analyzing complex relations that experiment the method of analysis and spatial dynamics of sociological phenomena bred by the technology of information and communication (ICT) which is not exploited so far; it is certainly early

© Springer International Publishing AG 2016
A.V. Chugunov et al. (Eds.): DTGS 2016, CCIS 674, pp. 51–63, 2016.
DOI: 10.1007/978-3-319-49700-6_7

to conclude about the question. The same for the geography of sociological phenomena, it would be possible to stand out clearly methods of analysis when ICT and GIS would meet a level of diffusion sufficiently important so as the spatial dimension can be really visible. It is then possible to set an analogy between the method of analysis (quantitative, qualitative or hybrid) and the geographic paradox of the sociological phenomena propagation. If the ICT present intrinsic characteristics of decentralization, it cannot find a counterpart in the geographic sociology that diffuse in the set of sciences and technology of sociology and train the reorganizations.

Technologies of information and communication, including the motors leading to profound changes in analyzing methods of social phenomena which their main effect is to suggest a new process of a dynamic analysis of change linked to a growing complexity. On the hand, decision makers and analysts and researchers benefited from facilities in term of performances, interactivity, simplicity or personalization. On the other hand, to our knowledge, sociology would arrange new tools which help in deploying a will of innovation never seen so far.

We mean by geographic sociology all social data linked to an entity localized by geographic data. The sociological phenomenon has a double dimension, a geographic nature in the true meaning of the term and a doctrinal or ideal content.

2   State of the Art

2.1   Literature Review

In literature, other types related to methods of analysis of sociological phenomena are treated by:

Philippe Cibois [15] presented a book in which he aims at giving to creator of the survey some ways to understand methods which allowed him, using the available software, to realize the despoliation of the efficient survey (quest). The used strategy to put into action methods of analysis and respect the situation of incertitude of the start and not to impose a method that forces results in a sense or another, but that let emergence of any eventual surprises. To this end, the process of analysis will be characterized by the use of a concept of the variable interest: each survey is made when we are in face of a phenomenon which we want to realize. This focus determines one or many 'variables of interest' which we want to be realizable. The suggested method spots the questions of the survey which is linked to the variable interest. To this end, the PEM, the percentage of maximal gap allowed doing this work.

Michel Mercier and Anne De Muelenaere [14] presented methods of analysis in groups which are based on hermeneutics approach according to the vision of Paul Ricoeur [16] on the conflict of interpretations. From the observations of the already experienced by different actors, the divergences and convergences of the interpretations are identified and experienced. The objective then is to articulate the individual comprehensions and the explanatory methods in a new comprehension issued from the confrontations within a group of analysis.

A theoretical reflection is built to allow realizing the coherence of convergences and analyzing the remaining divergences. This step is based on the social change.

The theoretical work brings the change of action which itself modifies the theory that explains the operated change. This method is developed and applied in different social environments in different research centers. Actually, it is applied in a European Equal [7] to the problematic of network and social representation in the accompaniment of the employment of weakened persons.

Maria Mercanti-Guérin [12] is an article in the analysis of social networks (ARS) is described as a new methodology of studies of online communities. In order to bring into a better comprehension of the ARS, previous synthesis of research was suggested. It details the techniques of data collection, structural measures used (density, centrality, structural gaps…), networks' properties; existent soft works in the marketing of online commonalities mentioned. A particular accent is carried on the empirical applications and the future developments of this new field. Different suggested attempts of work related to methods of analysis of sociological phenomena which are based particularly on the subject of qualitative and quantitative methods. This turns its specific methods to the context explain/comprehend. We think that the tilt of the method of analysis of sociological phenomenon in the digital era will be a true revolution carried by the use of ICT. Sociology will dispose new methods of analysis; it will allow the deployment of a will of innovation never seen so far and after that will identify new axes of research.

2.2   Steps of Sociological Study

Two persons, considered as central because of their report specific and essential for the theoretical elaboration, will mark this step of the constitution of the new scientific discipline.

Explain (find the exterior determinants of the social phenomena) [9] or understand (find interior motifs of a social conduct.) [13], represent an ancient debate which seems, nowadays, a little outdated in sociology.

The opposition explains/understands the social facts are structured in the history of sociology, mainly between Durkheim and Weber who polarize to the extreme these two social visions between the objective explanations on one hand and the subjective comprehension on the other. But this classical opposition made largely cured to poster a detriment occasionally to the comprehension of the social world.

The Holistic Step. A holistic approach is an approach, which considers the social structures, which influence and explain the individual conduct. Durkheim's sociology raised from a holistic approach.

The Individualist Step. An individualist step, which considers, by contrast, that the collective phenomenon are the results of actions, of belief or individual attitude. The Weberian sociology is raised from an individualist approach.

The registration of sociology in the scientific domain implies, further, the resort to systematic methods of empirical investigation.

Two great types of methods, which correspond to two great types of data: the quantitative and qualitative methods.

According to [1]: "quantitative and qualitative techniques are occasionally opposed to the point that the upholders of the former are frequently fervent contemnors of seconds and vice versa". Yet these techniques can be complementary, mainly when it treat subjects sparsely tackled.

Away from make both approaches impermeable one to the other, the fact that they return to the two domains of intelligentability based their complementarities.

The qualitative methods are rich of instructions in the exploratory phase of the quantitative survey. They can serve to elaborate the questionnaire more in their problematic issues than in its formulation.

In some cases, it can for a part of the population concerned by the quantitative survey not to be questioned either because of it supposition in the borderline of the survey field or it is more difficult in reparation. It can be interesting to complete the quantitative survey by series of observation interviews targeted nearby a complementary paradigm.

Even if it is possible it guarantee its representative statistics, this step helps enriching the work of statistics.

The qualitative methods are rich of instructions in the exploratory phase of the quantitative survey. They can serve to elaborate the questionnaire more in their problematic issues than in its formulation.

In some cases, it can for a part of the population concerned by the quantitative survey not to be questioned either because of it supposition in the borderline of the survey field or it is more difficult in reparation. It can be interesting to complete the quantitative survey by series of observation interviews targeted nearby a complementary paradigm.

Even if it is possible it guarantees its representative statistics, this step helps enrich the work of statistics.

The qualitative methods help in coding the open questions. They can show limits of categorization, which perform the investigators when they situate their surveys.

The interviews can allow verifying the coherence between the answers of certain closed questions of the questionnaire and the content of a discourse collected posterior on the same theme. The comparison allows at a time to better understand opinions of the questioned person and evaluate the quality of the retrospective questioning.

Dispose at the time questionnaires and tests for the same target population allow performing a crossed reading of quantitative and qualitative results. The quantitative results allow exploring the systems of representation (constructed thoughts) and the social practices (experiences) which cannot be fully apprehended in the frame of a quantitative questionnaire.

The data of framing allow grasping specifies of persons answering an interview. They also allow defining specifies of their conduct.

Results of a survey can suggest quests; bring hypotheses including treatment and validation depending on a qualitative step.

The quantitative and qualitative methods seem then complementary. The choice of one method depends on the object of research and questions that look for answers to the questions of thee researcher. In some cases, the linkage of quantitative and qualitative methods allows understanding more completely phenomena in which each method can grasp only certain aspects.

The qualitative methods and the quantitative methods answer in two ways to apprehend what is real, two modes of 'intelligibility', and two bodies of methods. Qualitative and quantitative researches are coherent sets of methods oriented for the former on the setting of evidence of the singular aspects of the phenomenon and for the latter on the regular aspects.

Each of these alternatives induces an adapted methodology of research, characterized by a system of information, methods of data and results' validation and principles of generalization advancing the 'scientificity' of analysis [6].

The Sequencing of the Qualitative and Quantitative Approaches. The complementary of the intelligibility domains, which reflect the two approaches, is mobilized to guide and enrich the process of research. The step is sequential; the qualitative and quantitative studies follows one the other in a cycle (Fig. 1) in a way to reinforce the concepts, the hypothesis and the results of research.

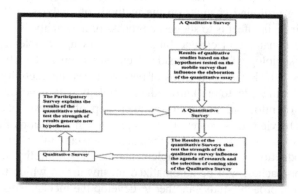

Fig. 1. Combination of qualitative and quantitative in a research cycle: [17]

3   Problematic

Many articles have handled the quantitative and qualitative methods subject. Similarly, others have developed new methods like the hybrids ones.

Nevertheless, the objectivity of the analysis results remains one of the biggest shortcoming of these methods. The latter is related to several factors:

- The subjectivity and the impartiality of the individual who is leading the sociological phenomenon.
- The slowness in terms of time affects the results whatever the analysis method used.
- The huge vivacity.
- The sociological phenomenon is often correlated to other sociological and economic phenomena.
- The social and economic incidences of the sociological phenomena.

- The decision makers indicate growing requirements in terms of performances, qualities and urgencies. According to the social dimension, they need to make quick decisions as possible as they can to encourage or fight the sociological phenomena.

4   Towards a Methodology of Sociological Studies by the USE of ICTs

4.1   The Suggested Model of Life Cycle

The previous section allowed us to free the different necessary concepts and notions for the accomplishment of this work. Our interest is carried particularly on the combination of the qualitative and the quantitative studies during the research to counter the phenomenon of the scholar loss with socioeconomic and sociopolitical traits.

Technologies of information and communication, which will be the engines (motors), inducing profound changes on the methods of analysis of the sociological phenomena. Their main effect is to suggest a process of new analysis, which takes into consideration the dynamics of change linked to a growing complexity, which is an important trait in sociology. On the one side, decision makers and analysts will benefit from the facilities, which can be in terms of performances, interactivity, simplicity or personalization. On the side, to our knowledge, sociology will dispose new tools.

In the sense of information system, another step of analysis of a sociological phenomenon can be viewed as process that can lead the intervention of a set of actors, which cooperate to assure better results to explain/understand this phenomenon.

With the introduction of ICT, the complementary of 'intelligibility' domains, which expel the two approaches, will be automatized meanwhile in which the information circulate from an approach (study) another to develop the mechanisms (processes) to optimize the flow of analysis.

At the Level of the Execution of the Survey Itself. Concerning the first level; we inspire from Fig. 1 (Combination of qualitative and quantitative studies during the research cycle), the life cycle of the process is summed up in six (06) essential as illustrated in Fig. 2:

The qualitative study preliminary conducted to a quantitative analysis registered the social representations of the phenomenon in conceptual frame of research. It participates, as a consequence, in the definition of the pertinent variables and the hypotheses to be tested, the adequate stratification: it guides, therefore, the elaboration of the questionnaire.

The quantitative study allows confirming or affirm certain results in the measure where they can be translated in hypotheses statistically refutable. The letters will therefore potentially extrapolated, the quantitative study conducted on larger sample, are sometimes representative.

Downstream from the quantitative analysis, the qualitative provides possibilities of interpretation richer turning the results significant. Indeed, the qualitative analysis set cause relations where the quantitative study perceives correlations; it can participate in

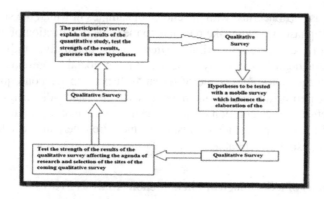

Fig. 2. Life cycle of an analysis of a sociological phenomenon

the explanation of unexpected results. It also allows testing the pertinence of the results and precise or reorient hypotheses of research.

At the level of investigation, to the selection of the sample in which the survey will be realized.

In this paragraph, our interest is carried on the use of technologies of Social Networking. We want to apply technologies, which show their evidence in the detection of communities in the social networks; these communities will be employed as indicated in the title identically samples in which the survey will be executed. Accordingly, a great deal of research works will focus on this subject. Two examples are:

- Traces of use of research engines on the web [4],
- Exchange traces of resources in the pair networks' a pair [18],
- Interactions in the social networks online as Facebook, twitter and Linked in [3],
- The prediction of links on the social networks [11],
- Community Detection in Networks: The leader-Follower Algorithm [8],
- Community detection in the great graphs of interactions (multiplexes) [10].

The life cycle of this process is summed up in three phases as it is illustrated in Fig. 3:

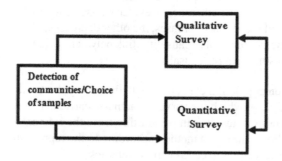

Fig. 3. Life cycle of hybrid analysis combined in the choice of community selection

The first phase is concerned with the choice of samples in which the survey will be realized (in this phase, we can make recourse to the tools of detection of communities in the context of social networks online). After that, the qualitative study preliminary conducted has a quantitative analysis registered the social representations of the phenomenon in the conceptual frame of research. It participates consequently in the definition of the pertinent variables and hypotheses to be tested, adequate stratification; it guides, therefore, the elaboration of questionnaire. After that, the quantitative study allows confirming or affirm certain results, in the measure where they can be translated in hypotheses statistically refutable.

4.2 Meta-model of a Sociological Phenomenon Analysis Process

In order to allow a better comprehension of different manipulated concepts, we present some basic definitions and notions of sociology [5].
    Concepts of methods of quantitative and qualitative analysis are:

Survey. Series of predefined questions on a particular theme based on a great number of persons. This method allows producing numbered data on studied phenomenon. The questions are standardized: they are the same questions asked, in the same order to all persons questioned. They can carry on the base of simple factual information (age, professional category; etc…), on the same practices, or also on the representations, values, beliefs of the questioned persons. It is frequently about closed questions.

Dependent/Independent Variables. A dependent variable is a variable that we are in search to explain and which corresponds in general to a theme of the survey (ex. vote, practices, clothing practices, leisure…). An independent variable is an explanatory variable in which we illustrate the explanation of the evolution of the dependent variable. In sociology, the independent variables match frequently some social characteristics of individuals: sex, age, category, professional…

Correlation. A particular relation observed between two variables, which can be positive or negative. A correlation is positive when the two variables evolve in the same sense (when one increases, the other increases also). It is negative when the two variables evolve in the opposed sense (one increases, the other decreases). The existence of correlation can submit the existence of a 'causality' link between variables, but the correlation is not necessarily a synonym of 'causality'.

Sample. On a given population concerned with the survey theme, the sample goes with the part of population on which the survey is actually carried. The sampling represents the procedure that constitutes the sample starting from the reference population. It can be unreliable or follows the quota method according to the representative sample of the studied population according to certain characteristics.

Closed/Open Questions. The open questions are questions that a person can answer freely. The closed questions are questions where the interviewer suggests a list of pre-formulated answers, and then the requested person must choose any answer. The open questions allow to have spontaneous answers more rich and more developed. On the contrary, they are difficult to be exploited in the quantitative treatment sphere. The closed questions, which have a quantitative exploitation, don't allow the interviewed person to give spontaneous answers. But, he is given answers that are not necessarily corresponding to his situation.

Field. The field goes hand in hand with the study object of the researcher, considered for its strictly empirical dimension (not problematic). This expression is especially used in qualitative surveys. «Making the field», «being in the field» designate the moments when the researcher is in direct contact with his study object (taking notes or an interviewing).

Interview. A sociological interview is a verbal interaction between the researcher and his requested person, in an explicit objective of a sociological study, on a precise theme that is related to this study. The questions asked by the researcher should be open questions that expect free and developed answers from the interviewee.

Observation. It is a survey method in which the researcher observes while he is in the field studying the social phenomena. Observations can be punctual, for instance when they talk about a precise event (manifestation). They can be also long and can involve a more consequent appointment of the researcher who stands permanently on his observation field (ex. A several years survey of a particular street).

Field Book. The field book is an essential support of the collection of data and the researcher thinking. This book represents the principal mark of the work of the survey. This is where the researcher registers the collected data in the end of each observation session. Methodological thinking can be added to the data, tracks of sociological analysis, and more subjective thinking of the researcher in his field report.

The question is: «does the analysis method suggested in the previous paragraph represent a cooperative information system?» The answer is 'Yes' because of followings:

- We have actors that accomplish roles and tasks.
- These roles take action in the procedures (or processes).
- These actors will cooperate via a platform that would be provided with technological tools.

We can notice that all the necessary elements of the conception and the modelization of the cooperative information system for gather.

We are particularly interested in the combination of the qualitative and quantitative studies during a research cycle to fight school wastage phenomenon, which has a socioeconomic character.

According to the «Petit Larousse» dictionary; school wastage means the progressive loss and the decrease.

Hence, the school wastage means the progressive loss of learners during their educational cycle. This loss bands the set of exclusions decided by the teachers' council for the following reasons: bad results, bad behavior, decided abandons by the learner and/or his parents because of a social or an economic motive. The school wastage is a waste of equipment's for both; the educational system and the whole society. It is interpreted in terms of problems of repetition and/or study abandon. It is a premature release of a part of the school learners in a syllabus.

In the industrialized and the third world countries the academic performance is a matter of correctness, for, it is an integrating part of education, which is a social pertinence subject.

The influential actors entering into interaction with the learner during his learning process; the teacher, the parents and the society, are responsible for the learner failure or success. The teacher, the knowledge and the learner is the first triptych in the teaching process. The success or the failure of transmitting any knowledge depends on the dynamism of the relation between the protagonists of this triangle.

The educational entity, the learner and the parents are the triptych that sets the parental attitude and their socioeconomic conditions against the educational process of their off springs.

The learner, the knowledge and the society; this triptych is influenced by the psycho social and the psycho-pedagogical factors. The society is the reference point of all knowledge.

The learner, the parents and the society; this point is a complementary element of the previous one because it deals with parental preoccupations against the society and its children.

We can notice that three groups of actors are involved in the school wastage phenomenon analysis process; the decision makers, the population (administrators, teachers, students and their parents) and the analysts. The cooperation links can be found on different levels and various objectives.

The meta-model will have the essential concepts of the automatic analysis process.

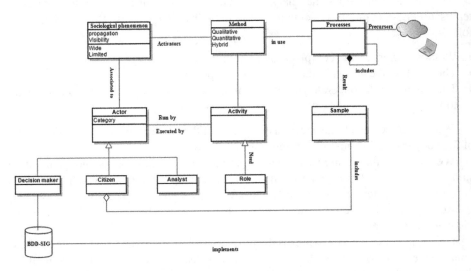

Fig. 4. Analysis process of a sociological phenomenon

The following diagram abstracts the analysis processes of a sociological phenomenon using computing tools (Fig. 4):

5 An Example: The School Wastage (Repetition)

This phase will generate the instances of models and carry their execution after the implementation of the different aspects of the process model.

We have to bear in mind that the objective of this work is not to resolve or find solutions for sociological phenomena, but our interest is the projection of the analysis method in the domain of technologies. An analysis method can be seen as a cooperative information system that can involve a set of actors cooperating between each other in order to guarantee the best method to analyze the school wastage phenomenon.

In order to experiment our meta-model we were interested in a model suggested by the report in [2] to highlight the repetition and the abandon case in Algeria in 2014, thus its evolution since 1962. This model has 5 analytic dimensions.

5.1 Used Methodology

The methodological approach suggested is first based on the results of the quantitative analysis of the non-schooling. These results allow identifying categories of non-schooling according to the age, the gender and the region. The quantitative characterization of the non-schooling allows evaluating the scale of the phenomenon comparing with the occurring schooling offer. The appreciation of the scale of the non-schooling according to the place, region, gender and age allows distinguishing the population groups more affected by this phenomenon.

These categories are faced to an analysis of the schooling demand according to the demographic database to shape the cover of the educational system related to the socioeconomic characteristics of the children out of school (category «place»).

A particular attention is paid to the repeaters and different factors of the repetition on both levels; primary and middle.

The following diagram abstracts the analysis process using computing tools (Fig. 5):

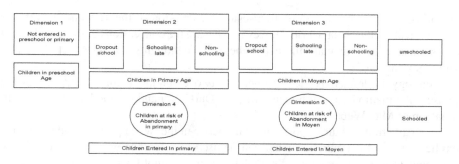

Fig. 5. Model of five dimensions

The dimension 1 is about children of 5 years old in the preparatory cycle considering the children at the age of school but yet they are always out institutions of preparatory learning.

The dimensions 2 and 3 give requirement about the non-schooling in the Primary and Middle cycles. These estimations are based on the formulas provided by the general methodological frame of the «OOSCI» which use the indicators to calculate the number of children out of schools.

The dimensions 4 and 5 provide a probabilistic estimation of risk of school failure for both cycles; Primary and Middle. These estimations are based on the formulas provided by the general methodological frame of the «OOSCI» which use the indicators to calculate the number of children out of schools.

The following diagram shows the relationships and correlation between the implied activities and roles. It's about a functional architecture which describes the target system (Fig. 6):

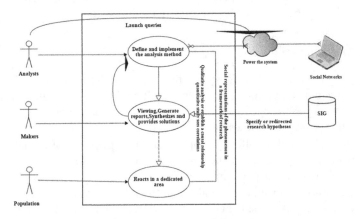

Fig. 6. Functional architecture of a research cycle

6   Conclusion

Like all other sciences, sociology focuses on the creation of theories and hypotheses then their tests in the social world. However, what are the conceptions of the social world and its causality that can make these hypotheses? The thoughts of this subject of the way that the approach of

Sociology is defined is clearly released, two essential distinguished modes are opposed; the methodological holism of Emile Durkheim and the methodological individualism of Max Weber.

The distinction and the opposition set up between the two approach modes just like «explication» and «comprehension», can be used as reference point to formalize the sociological theory and practice. We think that using technology notions in sociological phenomena analysis methods allow avoiding ambiguity (explain/understand) (a notion appeared in literature years ago). To bring to light such an idea by the analysts and decision makers with technology tools is a possible thing.

In order to experiment the suggested meta-model, we were particularly interested in the combination of qualitative and quantitative studies during a research cycle to fight the school wastage phenomenon which has a socioeconomic character. The suggested diagram will show the relationships and the correlation between the implied activities and roles.

References

1. Couvreur, A., Lehuede, F.: Essai de comparaison de méthodes quantitatives et qualitatives a partir d'un exemple: le passage a l'euro vécu par les consommateurs, France (2002)
2. Algérie rapport national sur les enfants non scolarisés, Alger (2014)
3. Archambault, A., Grudin, J.: Les interactions dans les réseaux sociaux en-ligne, comme facebook, twitter ou encore LinkedIn (2012)
4. Baeza-Yates, R., Kanawati, R.: Web Traces of use of search engines on the web (2007)
5. Barbusse, B., Glaymann, D.: Introduction à la sociologie, Vanves: Foucher; De Singly, F. (1992). L'enquête et ses méthodes: le questionnaire, Paris: Nathan (2004)
6. Claire, G.-D.: The combination of qualitative and quantitative analysis for a study of Malagasy rural poverty dynamics. Savings and Finance. University Montesquieu Bordeaux IV, France (2006)
7. Couty, P.: La vérité doit être construite. Cahiers de l'O.R.S.T.O.M. (Organisme de Recherche Scientifique et Technique d'Outre Mer), Série Sciences Humaines, Institut de Recherche pour le Développement (IRD), Paris, vol. 20, no. 1, pp. 5–15 (1984)
8. Shah, D., Zaman, T.: Community Detection in Networks: The Leader-Follower Algorithm (2010)
9. Durkheim, E.: Règles de la méthode sociologique (1895)
10. Kanawati, R.: Detection of communities in large graphs of multiplexes interactions (2010)
11. Kanawati, R., Rouveirol, C.: Prediction links in social networks topological approaches. Summer School Web Intelligence (2009)
12. Mercanti-Guérin, M.: Analyse des réseaux sociaux et communautés en ligne: quelles applications en marketing. Université d'Evry Val d'Essonne, France
13. Weber, M.: Economie et société (1921)
14. Mercier, M., De Muelenaere, A.: La méthode d'analyse en groupe: Application à la problématique de la mise à l'emploi des personnes fragilisées. Université de Namur (2007)
15. Cibois, P.: Les méthodes d'analyse d'enquêtes, Paris (2007)
16. Ricoeur, P.: De l'interprétation. Seuil, Paris (1965)
17. Robb, C.M.: Can the Poor Influence Policy: Participatory Poverty. World Bank, États-Unis (1999)
18. Shahabi, C., Kashani, F.B., Aidouni, F.: Les traces d'échanges de ressources sur des réseaux pair à pair (2009)

Communications in Cyberspace: Designs Features

Olga F. Guchinskaia[✉] and Irina I. Tolstikova

ITMO University, Saint Petersburg, Russia
guchinskaya@corp.ifmo.ru, tolstikova_irina@mail.ru

Abstract. The intensive development of cyberspace regarding the requirements of developing and improving the quality of communication, requires the emergence of some new tools in order to form (certain) communication strategies. In this article the authors describe the various aspects of building an effective communication strategy in cyberspace.

The research purpose was to explore a set of design tools for effective communication strategies in cyberspace. The authors propose a new approach to assessing the prospects of development of cyberspace based on the research presented in the works of D. Burt, A. Kleiner, J.P. Nicholas, et al.

As a result, the following research identified key features common to all online resources: a lack of emphasis on building effective communication strategies of online resources (web-sites, web-pages, networking communities) for interaction with users. This reduces the effectiveness of communication, and poses the problem of low satisfaction within society regarding the results of the interaction with the online resource. Low efficiency is manifested in the form of reduced financial stability of the resource, its popularity with users and decreased satisfaction in communication. For increasing the level of effectiveness of communications in the cyberspace the authors suggest a set of tools that allow you to perform data analysis to assess the effectiveness of engagement strategies, as well as to undertake measures to improve the characteristics of the resource, and adjust its "behavior" with a view to an increase of efficiency.

Keywords: Cyberspace · Cybersphere · Communications · Communication strategy · Communicative processes · Network researches

1 Development of Cyberspace as a New Environment

Globalization's impact on society's development is reflected in the trends of the further formation and development of cyberspace as a new habitat of human activities, which are an integral part of communicative processes. As evidence of the development and growing importance of cyberspace in modern society there are official data documenting a large increase in the volume of services in the info-communication sphere in the last 10 years.

An increasing number of objects and processes within society's activities are being transformed, "flowing" in the Internet environment.

There are various aspects of building effective communication strategies in cyberspace. The researches of cyberspace permit us to understand the goals of participants in

A.V. Chugunov et al. (Eds.): DTGS 2016, CCIS 674, pp. 64–71, 2016.
DOI: 10.1007/978-3-319-49700-6_8

communication processes. The purpose of their communication makes it possible to build the most effective strategies to achieve the best results, and therefore positively affect all spheres of public life.

Contemporary conditions are contributed to by constant use of information technologies and new methods of communication, as well as by cybersphere development. The transformation of social life occurs in electronic digital era conditions which are reflected in political, socio-cultural, economic, and other processes. International cooperation imposes increasingly high requirements on the level of multicultural literacy, which is based on the understanding that diversity is an objective feature of world culture. The influence of the interpenetration of international cultures on the development of society is reflected in the trends of continued growth and development of cyberspace as a new habitat of the individual, an integral part of which are the continuous communicative processes.

Tasks that were solved by the authors to achieve the objectives in the study of these processes are as follows:

1. To consider the theoretical basis, current status, trends and prospects of the development of cyberspace as a communicative sphere in which to offer a conceptually new approach to the assessment of prospects of developing cyber-space at both a local and a global level.
2. Explore the features, capabilities, and vision for funds for the development of socio-cultural interaction in cyberspace, and the existing design principles of communication strategies in the information environment.
3. To recommend a set of tools for analysis and design of an effective communication strategy in cyberspace.

The theory of a post-industrial (informational) society is the basis of the research of cyberspace and of the processes occurring within it. The founders of the originating society, its origin and development, are the political scientists, sociologists and futurologists D. Bell, M. Porat, Y. Masuda, M. Castells and etc. [1, 5, 6, 15, 18].

A number of Russian scientists proposed tools and methods of the information society and processes of interaction in virtual space. More applied in nature are the works of T.V. Ershova, Y.E. Hohlov, S.B. Shaposhnik, Chugunov V.A., Bershadskaya L., D. Trutnev, G.Y. Misnikov, I.I. Tolstikova, M.I. Shubinskii, A.S. Bikkulov and etc., which analyse the perspectives of practical realisation of those or other theoretical models of the information society and using social research in virtual space [2, 3, 7, 9, 16, 20, 23–25].

Currently researches of Internet communications and social networks should be based on an interdisciplinary approach using sociological, psychological, marketing and management tools, because such approaches do not contradict each other, rather they are complementary [11, 12, 17, 19, 21, 22].

Modeling the new socio-cultural environment constitutes an objective reality, which implements social, cultural and communicative practices.

The development of information and communication technologies (ICT) is the basis for stable economic growth of the country. Despite the difficult economic situation in the Russian market the activity of companies in the infocommunication sphere is growing, while their market share is over 16%. According to the FAS Russia, over the last 10 years the number of ICT companies increased in 300 times.

Field research of cyberspace and its development allow us to predict the impact of future changes in real life within society and different directions of its activities on the formation of relations and communications in the cybersphere.

D. Burt, A. Kleiner, J.P. Nicholas, K. Sullivan, M. Graham, S.A. Hale, and M. Stephens [4, 10], devoted to the study and forecasting of levels of informatisation, evaluation of quantitative indicators, adoption of information and communication technologies in public life in different countries, proposed a new approach to the assessment of the prospects for the development of cyberspace, which is consistent with the concept of the information society, proposed by W.J. Martin. [14].

In our study we propose to use a systematic approach based on the combination and interaction of the following groups of factors that determine the development of information society: macroeconomic, socio-demographic and technological.

Figure 1 shows the expected changes in the number of ICT users in the world and presents a comparative chart of the ratio of levels and perspective of the pace of informatisation in some 10 countries around the world. The investigated countries were divided in four groups. The first one includes countries that have already (data of 2015) observed the high level of penetration of information and communication technologies in public. It included Germany and Japan, where already the percentage of informatisation of the society is close to 100%. The second group includes countries such as Russia, USA, France, Brazil: the potential in them (the prospects) of information to be determined by is at the level of 20–25%. The third group includes China, India and Nigeria, where today's level of computerisation was less than 70% relative to the forecast values by 2025.

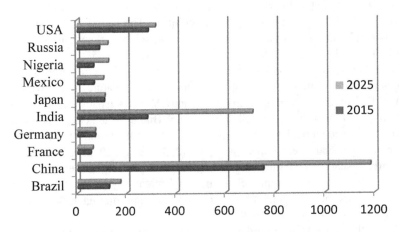

Fig. 1. The prospects of increasing the number of Internet users in 2025 compared with situation in 2015 (Source: DUP 2013/02/18)

Development of open and mobile technologies [8, 13] provide the effectiveness of communication in the sphere of decisions of social problems of citizens. They provide not only convenience, but also give substantial savings in time and financial resources.

Thus, use of mobile devices increases the effectiveness of the authorities in the field of social service not less than 45%.

The use of mobile services, ensuring the interaction of citizens with the government to resolve various issues of the population in the social-cultural sphere in a city with a population of about 4.5 million people (for example in one of the developed countries) provides the total time savings of about 500,000 h a year, equivalent to 11.3 million USD per year. Cooperation of authorities and citizens in dealing with the many issues of public importance, the transition from E-government to Mobile Government contributes to the growth of efficiency of the work of authorities. And the advancement of mobile technology is the most important factor of intensification of development of communication in cyberspace.

In conditions of continuous qualitative change, development, growth in the number of objects in cyberspace, technical and content improvement of the interactions between the creation of a set of instruments, combine to create an effective communicative strategy that is manifested in an increase of the degree of satisfaction with the process and the result of communication, reducing the time taken to achieve the goals of communication.

2 Prospects of Development of Social Communications in Cyberspace

The development of information and computer technologies have had a considerable influence on the practice of interpersonal communication, dissemination of scientific and socially important information. It indicates successful implementation of human-human-interaction. Network technology and online communities characterise the current stage of development of society, and are key to establishing higher democratic standards.

The role of the Internet is reduced to mediating multifunction communication. It is an anthropogenic intermediate object that is physically placed between the subjects of interaction.

As the number of Internet users increases, the importance of social network grows. It also reveals many problems associated with the identification of the person in these communities, social practices, and normative values and social controls over them. The occurrence of such problems requires close attention of researchers of processes and objects in Internet space.

The networks of the Internet community reflect traditionally established structures of social and cultural life and constitute a special socio-cultural space.

Due to the that network proved itself as a new level of existence the role of social networks in the communicative space of modern society turned into a kind of global social relations coordination center based on new ways of modeling objective reality and regulatory and communication processes in social systems, in order to meet personal and group communication needs.

On one hand, social processes of information and culture create new opportunities and forms of communication between representatives of different cultures. On the other hand they may demonstrate their destructiveness.

3   Effectiveness of Communication Processes and Strategies in Cyberspace

The differences of a cultural, social or ethnic nature which exist in intercultural communication can be overcome through the application of socially useful knowledge and experience. For the overcoming of cross-cultural barriers, misunderstandings and conflict situations, different forms of intercultural communication competence were developed, as well as special training in this area.

Communication is an integral part of human interaction with different subjects and objects in cyberspace, such as different Internet resources. The research examined approaches and tools for developing communication strategies to justify selection of methods for its creation. The main condition for the effectiveness of intercultural communication is the search for patterns and practices of mutual understanding, dialogue-based interaction, and forming tolerant attitudes toward the culture of communication partners. All of this requires a high degree of intercultural competence, which is necessary for the adaptation to different cultural conditions for successful and effective intercultural communication, joint activities and cooperation, and is understood as sociocultural indicators. The main barriers that reduce the efficiency of interactions are the differences of cognitive schemes used by different cultures (especially language and nonverbal systems and elements of social consciousness). The main condition for the effectiveness of inter-cultural communication is the search for patterns and practices of mutual understanding, dialogue-based interaction, and forming tolerant attitudes to the culture of communication partners. All of this requires a degree of intercultural competence, understood as a socio-cultural trait necessary for its adaptation to different culture conditions for successful and effective inter-cultural communication, joint activities and cooperation. Internet communications researchers have expressed different opinions about what kind of communication can be considered effective. As an indicator of the communication effectiveness for commercial Internet resources is attainment primarily the commercial effect, but for the objects of social and cultural sphere of cyberspace as assessing the effectiveness of the most acceptable methods are the evaluating the ratio of goals and results.

As possible targets of communication in cyberspace, there are the following aspects:

1. Creating a positive perception of the Internet resource by users.
2. Giving information about the web resource to the target audience.
3. Urging users of the Internet resource to specific actions, leading to an expected effect.

Among the expected effects from the implementation of a new communication strategy in conditions are the following:

1. Practical and utilitarian.
2. The strengthening of certain positions, such as raising the status, financial results, etc.
3. Cognitive and informational.
4. Reducing the interaction's time by improving its effectiveness.
5. Ethical involves the growth of responsibility for the communication by all participants in the process, and enhances the socio-cultural level of communication.
6. Aesthetic – high level of usability in the interaction.

7. Emotional – the emotional satisfaction from the results of the interaction.

It remains an open problem of unification and further improve the approaches to the protection of communications objects in different networks (ranging from individual users to different Internet resources) from cybercrime because security is an important factor for the effective of communication in cyberspace.

Building an effective communication strategy in cyberspace is important for any Internet resources, such as social networks, media, personal, information or commercial Internet resources, and a user interaction is determined by the possibility to implement its functions, aims and objectives by means of ICT technologies. In conditions of tough competition, a carefully designed programme of building of communications with the user of the resource often plays a decisive role. The lack of communication strategy or a superficial approach to its development can pose a threat to the further development of the online resource. Information and communication technologies are the source and means of influence on the target audience. For the development and promotion of an Internet resource, increasing its rank in the network, as well as increase demand and awareness among actual and potential users, it is possible to use different methods of promotion. Let's note that for the development and implementation of training programs as experts resource developers, and for users, it is convenient to use such educational resources and technology as: e-Learning, MOOC, on-line webinars etc.

In order to design effective communication strategies there are following techniques:

1. Contextual advertising usage in popular search engines.
2. Results of SEO analysis.
3. Creation and promotion of a community social network.
4. The development of subject resources for marketing purposes (blogs, forums, media).
5. Interaction's partnerships between different Internet resources.
6. Distribution of printed leaflets, brochures, other advertising techniques, advertising and the media.
7. Training programs of competence development in Internet.
8. Create opportunities for user training resources.
9. The development of tools to learn about the activities of the resource's character-istics and the results of its functioning.
10. Newsletter of actual and potential users.

The list of tools in the integrated approach allows for the analysis of the level of effectiveness of communication strategies in future, to improve the effectiveness of communication and the performance of the Internet resource.

4   Conclusion

Network communication as a universal socio-cultural mechanism, as a result of the genesis and functioning of culture in relation to social parameters, determines the current stage of societal development. This can be defined as an information and communication society, and cyberspace is a universal place for communication. On the one hand, the Internet community network is a continuation and a new dimension of traditional sociocultural structures. On the other hand they represent a particular sociocultural space: by transforming the existing social reality, a new aspect to everyday life develops. In other words, a new sociocultural space is being modeled as an objective reality, in which social, cultural and communicative practices manifest themselves in a transparent way. One special feature when entering into a cultural field through a virtual information space is its temporality. It is determined by the duration of the communication session. It can also identify the temporality of cultural self-identification, the possibility to "leave" an alien culture. But a multiple virtual crossing of cultural boundaries can also create a stable association with a foreign culture and lead to leaving one's own culture. But this session-based immersion allows people to attain a state of multiculturalism, visiting different cultural worlds. The reality of the information society creates fundamentally new forms of human interaction. If these were simply extrapolated from the virtual world to traditional schemes and laws they would cause mistrust.

Internet technology is not just a tool to use. It involves processes that should be further developed. The authors plan to study in detail the participants' views of cyber-communications about the level of effectiveness of communication strategy; development and validation of methodology for the design of effective communication in cyberspace, and give a description of conditions for its implementation. Consideration of processes of formation of cyberspace in the context of globalization, the theoretical rationale and definition of practical approaches to the establishment and development of effective communication strategies in cyberspace aimed at improving human interaction with a variety of information resources of cyberspace. In future work the authors plan more detailed study of the development of communication strategies, including creating policies for specific objects of cyberspace, the conduct of monitoring for research the different characteristics of human interaction with network resources.

References

1. Bell, D.: The Coming of Post-industrial Society: Experience of Social Forecasting. Academy, Moscow (2004). 788 pages (in Russian)
2. Bershadskaya, L., Chugunov, A., Trutnev, D.: Information society development in Russia: measuring progress and gaps. In: 2014 Conference on Electronic Governance and Open Society: Challenges in Eurasia (EGOSE 2014), pp. 7–13. ACM, New York (2014). doi: 10.1145/2729104.2729122
3. Bikkulov, A.S., Chugunov, A.V.: The Network Approach in Social Science: Modeling of Social and Economic Processes and Researching in Social Networks. Textbook. ITMO University, St. Petersburg (2013). 124 pages (in Russian)
4. Burt, D., Kleiner, A., Nicholas, J.P., Sullivan, K.: Cyberspace-2025: today's decisions, tomorrow's terrain. In: Navigating the Future of Cybersecurity Policy, vol. 06, p. 47 (2014)
5. Castells, M.: The information age: economy, society and culture. In: Shkaratan, O.I. (ed.) National Research University Higher School of Economics, Moscow (2000). 608 pages (in Russian)
6. Castells, M., Fernandez-Ardevol, M., et al.: Mobile Communication and Society: A Global Perspective. MIT Press, Cambridge (2007). 331 pages
7. Chugunov, A.V.: Information Society Development: Theories, Concepts and Programs: A Training Manual. St. Petersburg state University, St. Petersburg (2007). 101 pages (in Russian)

8. Eggers, D.W., Jaffe, J.: Gov on the Go: Boosting Public Sector Productivity by Going Mobile. Deloitte Development LLC, 18 Feb 2013. 40 pages

9. Ershova, T., Hohlov, Y., Shaposnik, S.B.: Spatial and social aspects of the digital divide in Russia. In: Andreasson, K. (ed.) Digital Divides: the New Challenges and Opportunities of e-Inclusion, pp. 79–106. CRC Press, Boca Raton (2015)

10. Graham, M., Hale, S.A., Stephens, M.: Map Concept Derived from Geographies of the World's Knowledge. Convoco! Edition, London (2011). 29 pages

11. Guchinskaia, O.F., Dashinimaeva, E.B.: Communication Strategy: Features of the Formation in Modern Cyberspace. Sci. Forum Siberia 1, 125–128 (2015). (in Russian)

12. Guchinskaia, O.F., Kudryavtseva, M.V.: The electronic distance technologies using as a tool of open education in the Russian Federation. In: Proceedings of the XVIII Conference of Information Society: Education, Science, Culture and Technology of the Future, pp. 72–81. ITMO University, St. Petersburg (2014) (in Russian)

13. Kumar, H.: Could cyberspace turn into empty space? In: South China Morning Post, 09 Aug 2014. http://www.scmp.com/comment/insight-opinion/article/1569545/could-cyberspace-turn-empty-space

14. Martin, W.J.: The information society (abstract). In: Vinogradov, V.A., et al. (eds.) Theory and Practice of the General Value of Scientific Information, vol. 3, pp. 115–123. Academy of Sciences of the USSR, Moscow (1990) (in Russian)

15. Masuda, Y.: The Information Society as Post-industrial Society. World Future Society, Washington, D.C. (1981). 171 pages

16. Misnikov, Y.G., Chugunov, A.V.: E-participation in EEU: the conceptualization of monitoring studies in the context of the un goals for sustainable development. Eurasian Law J. 1(92), 314–318 (2016). (in Russian)

17. Orlov, R.A.: The Organization of Information Impact the Hidden Methods of Marketing. Innov. Inf. Commun. Technol. 1, 633–635 (2014). (in Russian)

18. Porat, M.U.: The Information Economy: Definition and Measurement. U.S. Dept. of Commerce, Office of Telecommunications, Washington (1977). 249 pages

19. Shelomentsev, V.V.: Internet and modern information technology in marketing research. Acad. Bull. 2(20), 104–106 (2012). (in Russian)

20. The index of readiness of Russian regions to the information society 2013–2014. Analysis of information inequality in Russian regions. In: Ershova, T., Hohlov, Y., Shaposnik, S.B. (eds.) Information Society Development Institute, Moscow (2015). 534 pages (in Russian)

21. Tkachenko, E.V.: Communicative activities in virtual communities. Theory Pract. Soc. Dev. 16, 199–201 (2015). (in Russian)

22. Tolstikova, I.I.: Cultural studies of cyberspace and social interaction in the internet. In: Information Resources of Russia, No. 6(136), pp. 22–26 (2013). (in Russian). http://elibrary.ru/item.asp?id=20862471

23. Tolstikova, I.I., Shubinskii, M.I.: Museum's website as a significant tool: case of the Baltic-Sea region. In: Multi Conference of Computer Science and Information Systems: Proceedings of the International Conferences: ICT, Society and Human Beings, pp. 313–318 (2014)

24. Tolstikova, I., Shubinskiy, M., Nizomutdinov, B.: Hospital websites as a tool of health service. In: Proceedings of International Conference on Electronic Governance and Open Society: Challenges in Eurasia (EGOSE), pp. 136–142. ITMO University, St. Petersburg (2015)

25. Welsh, A., Lavoie, J.A.: E-Business' risks: an examination of risk-taking, online disclosiveness and cyberstalking victimization. Cyberpsychology J. Psychosoc. Res. Cyberspace 6(1) (2012). art. 4. doi:10.5817/CP2012-1-4. http://www.cyberpsychology.eu/view.php?cisloclanku=2012051301&article=4

Towards Computer Game Research Area in Russia

Olga Sergeyeva[1,2(✉)], Olga Kononova[3], Ekaterina Orekh[1,2],
and Marina Kudriavtceva[3]

[1] St. Petersburg State University, SPbSU, St. Petersburg, Russia
{sergeyeva.olga, ek.orech}@mail.ru
[2] The Sociological Institute of the Russian Academy of Sciences,
St. Petersburg, Russia
[3] St. Petersburg National Research University of Information Technologies,
Mechanics and Optics, ITMO University, St. Petersburg, Russia
kononolg@yandex.ru, mvkudriavtceva@corp.ifmo.ru

Abstract. Computer games are the new research theme for social scientists and humanitarians with increased interest over the past 10–15 years. To evaluate the dynamics of research interest to the different thematic aspects of computer games expansion we made the review of the Russian scientific journals for the period 2005–2016 by the e-Library «Humanitariana» having the function of a flexible thematic full-text search. This information system is developed at the ITMO University. We used the methods of frequency-oriented search. We analyzed material of articles (N = 601) which were placed on the portal e-LIBRARY (http://elibrary.ru/).

We based on the idea that the language of scientific publications as well as the mass media language is included in the formation of the "agenda-setting". Scientific agenda manifested in the fact that the importance of certain issues, ideas, approaches were determined by the frequency of their reference in journal publications. It creates a set of scientific topics that are understood as the most important by research community.

Firstly, our results allow to see "top concepts" or "hot zone" as a set of burning issues reflecting the specificity of texts devoted to computer games. Secondly, we identified meaningful groups and analyzed their composition in denotative and connotative aspects in the set of top concepts. Third, we examined the dynamics of the use of terms for years, such as "addiction", "child", "teenager", "education", it helps to interpret the development of computer games research subject. In conclusion we discussed lack in area of Russian computer games studies.

Keywords: Computer games · Scientific review · Content analysis · Russian scientific journals

1 Introduction

Computer games often called video games is the research theme that has been considered by social scientists and humanitarians with the increasing interest over the past 10–15 years. As any new scientific field the computer games research is

© Springer International Publishing AG 2016
A.V. Chugunov et al. (Eds.): DTGS 2016, CCIS 674, pp. 72–81, 2016.
DOI: 10.1007/978-3-319-49700-6_9

institutionalized and presents itself to academic community mainly through publications in the scientific journals. Scientific periodical press is the way that is the most efficiently compared with the scientific monographs.

The question that is raised with the increasing numbers of publications on this topic is how to analyze the existing empirical and theoretical knowledge about computer games in the social sciences and humanities such as psychology, education theory, sociology, economics, law, political science, philology, philosophy, cultural studies. What is the conceptual system of the new interdisciplinary scientific field? What is the volume of annual publications, and if there is any dynamics? Partly these questions can be answered with the quantified analysis of texts or the content analysis of scientific articles devoted to computer games. We write "partly" because for a comprehensive evaluation it is necessary to use a full set of bibliometrics, for example, analysis of authors and researches in this field, citations, the dynamics of subject headings, etc.

In accordance with the interest to development of computer games research as a scientific field our aim was: to make a quantified review of the leading trends in the Russian scientific journals of social and humanitarian profile taking into account the dynamics of the decade (from 2005 to 2015). We assume this aim has a scientific novelty as in the existing Russian papers on various aspects of computer games the contribution of Russian authors is analyzed very briefly, usually through a mere listing up the names with reference to the works of the relevant subject which is devoted to the publication [e.g. 1, 2]. A detailed review and analysis of the research trends is given only in relation to foreign theories of game studies [11]. In contrast we are trying to show the agenda of domestic computer games research on the basis of the frequency of use in the Russian scientific articles of certain concepts. Agenda demonstrates the importance of some of the issues, ideas, approaches, compared with others which are not articulated. According to the agenda a set of research topics that are understood by the academic community as important can be seen.

2   Research Methodology

2.1   Sampling

We have analyzed the articles that are placed on the Russian information-analytical portal eLIBRARY (http://elibrary.ru). For the formation documents set we entered the keyword "computer games" in the form of the advanced search limiting the search for articles in journals and conference proceedings as well as years of publication from 2005 to 2015.

It should be added that the search was conducted in February 2016. In the future, the number of relevant documents will be other, as the number of publications placed on the portal eLIBRARY is constantly growing. We saved 601 full-text documents which are related to the social sciences and humanities. These documents have been imported into the information system «Humanitariana» for content analysis.

2.2   Processing the Data

We used electronic library information system «Humanitariana» with the function of thematic full-text search. This information system is developed at the ITMO University. Its function is optimization of information search for educational and research processes. Before start using the information system «Humanitariana» full-text documents (in this case, 601 articles in Russian language) should be loaded into it. After loading the texts it is possible to formulate our distinct requests to information system.

We used the methods of frequency-oriented search which, in fact, is a computerized content analysis. The frequency-oriented search is targeted to construction of ranked list of terms (nouns) and thus the explication of semantic features that characterize one document or large digital archive.

The information system «Humanitariana» supports two types of frequency-oriented search:

- an absolute frequency search, the result of which is a frequency-ranked list of nouns (in the Nom., sing.) included in the search area resources;
- a relative frequency search, the result of which is frequency-ranked list of nouns included only in those passages which contain the user-specified term.

The results of frequency-oriented search are "terminogramms". Terminogram is a complex of units of analysis (or table of terms) which contains information about the absolute (in numbers) and relative (in ‰, ppm) frequency of terms used in texts.

After making a frequency-oriented search by means of «Humanitariana» we were able to assess such content analytical indicators of the Russian scientific articles about computer games as:

- the most commonly used terms (it is the answer to the question "what topics are there...?");
- "top-50" or the occurrence of terms in which we are interested in accounted range (it is the answer to the question "is there anything on targeted topic?");
- connections of the most commonly used terms with other words (it is the answer to the question "what is a semantic context of the key topics?").

3   Results

One of the main results of the quantitative analysis of articles about computer games is the identification of publications growth. We note two periods of fundamental increase in the number of articles: the first is the transition between 2008 and 2009, the second is the development between 2013 and 2015 years. In the first period there was more than double growth in the publications flow during the year. In the second period we can see twofold increase, but for two years, that has not been so striking (Fig. 1).

Definition of a "hot zone" consisting of a set of relevant terms which reflect the specificity of scientific texts about computer games is the result of quantitative analysis of articles too. The basic numerical characteristic of the concepts/terms is the amount of its usage among all texts. We have obtained the list of the most commonly used terms

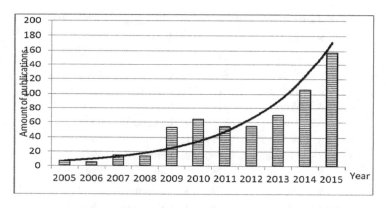

Fig. 1. The number of publications by years (exponential trend)

outlining the lexical frames of research field. We reserved 50 terms (top-50). Top-50 allows to concentrate on the specifics of meaning and to find the sense groups within the top do not disperse attention to the whole detected list. The example of termino-gram is given in Table 1.

Analysis of meaning of terms gave the opportunity to identify six theme groups (Table 2). Each group brings together the terms the essence of which is a particular manifestation of the general phenomenon that has been introduced into the name of the group. We call theme group of terms a paradigm (as it is usual in linguistics and semiotics) having in mind that this is a general system for constituent elements. All elements of a paradigm have some similarities allowing them to be one system. Thus, the top of terms from scientific articles about computer games are presented by the vocabulary of the following paradigms:

(1) paradigm of social subjects (individuals and institutions),
(2) paradigm of activity types,
(3) paradigm of behavior,
(4) paradigm of space and time,
(5) paradigm of culture,
(6) paradigm of technology.

In addition to description of frequency of terms used in all samples we show their occurrence on an annual basis. In this case the regularity of using a particular term and the differences in frequency from year to year are becoming evident. For example, Table 3 shows the characteristics of the terms referred by us to the paradigm of "social subjects". It is clear that children/child and teenagers appeared in the scientific literature about computer games not immediately, the general concept "gamer" was the first. The most balanced usage of the term (without big variations) refers to the word child. All other names of social actors were mentioned in the articles uneven, they were used more often, some less.

Comparison of the dynamics of terms usage expressed graphically demonstrates the coincidence or discrepancy in the functioning of the concepts. We received information

Table 1. «Top 50» terms on the scientific articles (2005–2015)

№[a]	Term	N[b]	№[a]	Term	N[b]
1	Children	2475	26	People	1005
2	Work	2341	27	Reality	1000
3	Teaching	2279	28	Culture	992
4	World	2173	29	Science	980
5	Time	2118	30	Language	954
6	People	1999	31	Personality	917
7	Technology	1990	32	Behavior	914
8	Group	1765	33	Link	841
9	Image	1745	34	Environment	840
10	Player	1642	35	Experience	831
11	Teen	1619	36	Russia	823
12	Education	1447	37	School	816
13	Dependence	1437	38	Case	782
14	Life	1385	39	Influence	778
15	Child	1375	40	Job	767
16	Action	1325	41	Role	763
17	Knowledge	1322	42	The rule	763
18	Student	1315	43	Space	736
19	Solution	1269	44	Management	731
20	The word	1250	45	Lesson	728
21	The situation	1127	46	Skill	722
22	Attitude	1121	47	Help	722
23	Internet	1101	48	University	716
24	Information	1026	49	Interest	703
25	Age	1021	50	Student	687

The place of the term in «Top 50»; [b]the number of occurrences of the term in on the scientific document collections

illustrating "life lines" of the terms which can help us to estimate their co-presence in articles (Fig. 2).

Contextual associations of terms (that is, their location in the same paragraph) show us some "semantic shadows" which help to explain more precisely (compared to the top 50) the thematic focus of scientific publications.

Connection between "teenager–game–addiction" and "education–game–technology" has been constant in the texts over time (from 2008 to 2015). The discovery of this context helps to determine the leading psychological and pedagogical topics in the publications of Russian researchers.

Table 2. The theme groups in «top 50» (2005–2015)

Social subjects		Activity	Behavior
Individual	Institutions		
Children	Science	Work	Addiction
People	School	Teaching	Attitude
Group	University	Education	Action
Gaymer		Management	Experience
Teenager		Lesson	Influence
Child		Solution	Skill
Student		Help	Interest
People			
Personality			
Student			

Space and time (chronotop)	Culture	Technology
World	Image	Technology
Time	Knowledge	Internet
Life	Word	
Situation	Information	
Reality	Language	
Environment		
Russia		
Case		
Space		

Table 3. Dynamics of usage of terms "social subjects" (2006–2015)

Terms	2006	2007	2008	2009	2010
Children			6,36 (2)	2,58 (9)	4,52 (2)
Gamer[a]	1,20 (47)		3,07 (21)	1,60 (27)	1,53 (45)
People			2,21 (49)	1,49 (34)	1,75 (30)
Child			2,36 (45)	1,91 (20)	2,08 (20)
Teenager			3,93 (11)	1,22 (49)	1,67 (37)
Student		23,2 (8)			
People		10,67 (43)	4,57 (6)	2,4 (12)	1,7 (34)

Terms	2011	2012	2013	2014	2015
Children	2,41 (13)	2,69 (29)	3,91 (6)	5,08 (2)	4,11 (5)
Gamer	1,50 (42)	3,95 (9)	3,60 (7)	2,52 (20)	3,17 (13)
People				2,10 (39)	
Child	1,43 (46)	2,27 (37)	1,90 (23)	2,01 (42)	2,59 (18)
Teenager	2,15 (18)	3,64 (12)	1,86 (27)	3,11 (14)	3,26 (12)
Student	1,59 (35)	3,25 (18)			2,03 (42)
People	2,41 (14)	4,51 (6)	1,88 (28)	4,46 (5)	3,32 (11)

In the boxes there is a number of occurrences of the term per source (in brackets there is a place of the frequency of the term in the sample)

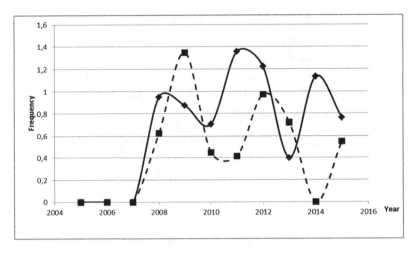

Fig. 2. Dynamics of the terms "addiction" and "reality" (dotted line)

4   Discussion

In this article we have considered the socio-humanitarian scientific articles dealt with computer games which were written by Russian authors and published from 2005 to 2015 years through the lens of content analysis. It becomes clear due to the quantitative analysis with the information system "Humanitariana" to what extend the number of publications has risen. From exclusive research topic computer game research is turning into an interdisciplinary scientific area.

The context of academic reality in which we see an increasing trend of game research is characterized, for example, by establishing and operating such organizations as: Laboratory of Computer Game Studies (it is a division of Media Philosophy Research Center, St. Petersburg) [7]; Moscow Game Center (it is developing on the basis of the Philosophy Faculty of Moscow State University) [8]; portal GameStudies.ru [4]. There are conferences that are organized based on those topics (recent event [10]). There are many examples of PhD theses (examples of works from different disciplines [5, 6, 9]). This means that the exponential growth of scientific articles reflects the institutionalization of the Russian researchers community in computer game area.

The most frequent terms tell us what attracts the attention of researchers. The scientific agenda becomes more understandable if to combine the terms through expert way into theme groups. Thus we identify social subjects, activities, characteristics of behavior, culture and technology, time-space features. We found that leading social subjects in the discourse of the articles are children and teenagers (Tables 1 and 2). But gamer was initially the generalized concept that appeared in articles about computer games. We can see the differentiation of umbrella term by age since 2008 only (Table 3). The scholars vocabulary showing the age differentiation of gamers identifies the formation of subject field of research, namely, it is the focus on children's and teenagers' aspects of computer games practices.

Outlining the theme "children and computer games" is due, as we suppose, to our shared cultural logic of understanding games as the main component of the children's everyday life or as a basic condition for socialization. The appearance of the games on the screen has become a challenge for the adult world in general and, in particular, for the world of adult researchers. Judging from the "hot" terms of terminogramm the challenge from media innovation has been accepted by researchers who have responded to it, primarily, through the understanding of the computer games potential in education and teaching. Our data demonstrate that these activities are being the subject of discussion now, and school and universities, also referring to the frequently used terms, make the complete picture of the academic agenda. It turns out that scientific texts about computer games objectify pedagogical-psychological perspective: games - children/teenagers - teaching - school/university. While developing and proving this conclusion we note the discovered contextual relationship between terms education-game technology (Table 4) which also shows a significant elaboration of topic relating to the computerization of school and university practices.

Table 4. Contextual associations of the terms "teenager" and "education"

2008–2012			2013–2015		
Word	*Q*[a]	*F*[b]	*Word*	*Q*[a]	*F*[b]
Teenager					
Game	377	10.5	Game	982	16.0
Addiction	135	3.75	Addiction	235	15.8
Group	129	3.59	Children	180	2.92
Computer	99	2.75	Development	160	2.60
Level	96	2.67	Life	137	2.23
2008–2012			2013–2015		
Word	*Q*[a]	*F*[b]	*Word*	*Q*[a]	*F*[b]
Education					
Game	376	11.9	Game	617	8.31
Teaching	191	6.07	Technology	283	3.81
Technology	87	2.76	Teaching	269	3.62
Process	82	2.61	Development	257	3.46

[a]Quantity; [b]Frequency

Let's remember also that we recorded a jump in scientific publications of computer games targeted research in 2009. Considering leading the theme of games as technology included in education we think that the dramatic increase in the number of articles depended on the computerization of schools [3]. Teachers who became actively involved in discussion influenced on more than twofold expansion of the articles flow.

Taking into account the semantic line teenager-game-addiction (Table 4) we offer to consider, if a problematisation of teenager's experience of computer games is not overly alarmist? Of course, the problem of computer addiction needs a scientific analysis, but in our opinion, recurring topic "game - dependence" indicates a specific and rather biased view on computer games. There is a stereotypical way of formulation of scientific questions in relation to game experience. Association between computer game and addiction reflects partly our cultural fears of advanced technology.

Our results confirm environmental interpretation of computer games which is reproducible by scientific language. Spatio-Temporal vocabulary (reality, space, habitat) from the top-50 shows the strength of the border which divides our world into real and virtual for some time now. Computer games embody the image of another reality and game practice looks like a form of escapism.

We believe one of the important outcomes of the quantitative study of the national scientific content is identifying the least-developed aspects in thematic areas of socio-humanitarian studies of computer games. Family vocabulary - parents, grand-parents, intergenerational relations - in connection with computer games are beyond the terminogramm and thus outside the main research interest of Russian authors. Gender game practices and the theme of adult gamers are poorly covered too.

5 Conclusion

The flow of Russian socio-humanitarian publications about the games is growing. Our results have allowed to introduce "thematic hot zone" as a set of burning terms reflecting the specificity of texts devoted to computer games. These data help to fix not only the language of computer game studies, but also the scientific agenda of the new direction.

Agenda that was established over ten years (2005–2015) is characterized by understanding of computer games as a phenomenon associated primarily with the period of childhood and adolescent development. Priority is given to the integration of computer games into school and university education and understanding their role in the learning technology. Observed dynamics in the research subject is related to the approval of addiction issue that happened approximately in 2007–2008.

As the theme "children-games-education" dominates it should be thought about limited attention to adult gamers and computer game expansion in family, law, finance, art. Certainly, all these topics are in Russian scientific publications, but the psychological and pedagogical discourse prevails. Multi-disciplinary review of scientific journals provides an incentive for a substantiation of relevance of scientific research about the computer games which should appear in the near future.

Acknowledgements. The reported study was funded by RFBR according to the research project "Scientific methods in research of computer game experience" №. 16-06-00368.

References

1. Belousov, A.D.: Priznaki i prediktory vysokoy uvlechennosti nesovershennoletnikh komp'yuternymi igrami [Characteristics and predictors of teenager obsession with computer games]. Prikladnaya yuridicheskaya psikhologiya [Applied juridical psychology] **1**, 164–173 (2011)

2. Belyantsev, A.E., Gershteyn, I.Z.: Obraz strany cherez komp'yuternuyu igru: istoriko-politicheskiy aspect [The image of the country through a computer game: historical-political aspect]. Vestnik Nizhegorodskogo universiteta im. N.I. Lobachevskogo [Bulletin of the Nizhny Novgorod University named after N. Lobachevsky] **6**, 279–283 (2010)

3. Federal'naya tselevaya programma "Razvitie edinoy obrazovatel'noy informatsionnoy sredy (2001–2005 gody)" [The Federal target program "Development of United educational information environment (2001–2005)"]. Moscow: The government of the Russian Federation. http://www.ict.edu.ru/lib/index.php?id_res=3352/

4. GameStudies.ru. http://gamestudies.ru/

5. Garipov, L.F.: Formirovanie kul'tury dosuga mladshikh shkol'nikov v protsesse komp'yuternykh igr: dis. … kand. ped. nauk [The creation of a culture of leisure of younger schoolchildren in the process of computer games: Ph.D. thesis]. Sholokhov Moscow State University for Humanities, Moscow (2015, unpublished)

6. Gutman, I.E.: Komp'yuternye virtual'nye igry: dis…. kand. filos. nauk. [Computer virtual games: Ph.D. thesis]. Saint Petersburg State University, St. Petersburg (2009, unpublished)

7. Media Philosophy Research Center. O proekte "Laboratoriya issledovaniya komp'yuternykh igr" [About the project "Laboratory of computer game studies"]. http://mediaphilosophy.ru/liki/about/

8. Moscow Game Center. https://vk.com/moscowgamecenter/

9. Omel'chenko, N.V.: Lichnostnye osobennosti igrayushchikh v komp'yuternye igry: dis…. kand. psikhol. nauk [Personal characteristics of computer games players: Ph.D. thesis]. Kuban State University, Krasnodar (2011, unpublished)

10. Sankt-Peterburgskiy gosudarstvennyy universitet, yuridicheskiy fakul'tet. Mezhdunarodnaya nauchno-prakticheskaya konferentsiya "Pravovoe regulirovanie komp'yuternykh igr: problemy teorii i praktiki", 30 sentyabrya 2015 [International scientific-practical conference "Legal regulation of computer games: issues of theory and practice", 30 September 2015]. http://law.spbu.ru/aboutfaculty/video/conferences/15-09-30/aaf54d39-1bfe-47b0-aa40-ed4961850d06.aspx/

11. Vertushinskiy, A.S.: To play game studies press the START button. Logos **25**(1), 41–60 (2015)

eSociety: eGovernment and eParticipation: Perspectives on ICTs in Public Administration and Democracy

E-Government Development Factors: Evidence from the Russian Regions

Yury Kabanov[✉] and Alexander Sungurov

National Research University Higher School of Economics, St. Petersburg, Russia
{ykabanov,asungurov}@hse.ru

Abstract. The paper aims at revealing factors influencing the development of e-government in the Russian regions. Based mainly on the innovation diffusion concept we run quantitative analysis, testing the significance of political, technological, socio-economic and administrative variables. Our study shows that the diffusion of e-government itself was to a large extent the result of a vertical influence of the federal government, however, disproportions of e-government performance can better be explained by internal characteristics of the regions. We argue that the key predictors for a more mature e-government are relatively democratic political regime, technological advancement, bureaucracy effectiveness and investment in ICT. The explanatory model could best be expanded by case studies focused on agency rather than the structure.

Keywords: Electronic government · Russian regions · Diffusion of innovations · Performance factors · Quantitative methods · Regression analysis

1 Introduction

The process of e-government implementation in Russia already has quite a long history, although it is still far from being successfully accomplished in terms of institutions and practices [6]. When thinking of the reasons for e-government failure in Russia, scholars usually place an emphasis on the agency, e.g. the role of government, public bureaucracy and its inability to adapt to new rules of the game, as well as on citizens' demands [30]. This approach makes a great contribution to our understanding of e-government from the actors' viewpoint, as emphasized by Meijer and Bekkers [19]. However, there are few attempts to place the Russian case in the explanation paradigm so far, i.e. the one that helps to build some general patterns [19].

Another rationale of the paper is to unveil the possible ways e-government in Russia can be enhanced. The apparent growth point is at regional level. Municipalities in Russia do not have enough resources, and national government is too distant from people and demonstrates unstable attention to the issue, so regional authorities seem to be at the forefront of e-services provision. Understanding the factors that foster or hinder the regional effort is therefore of high topicality. The paper is structured as follows. First, we present a literature review on the factors of e-government development and the theories they are grounded in. The second part is devoted to the role of federal authorities

A.V. Chugunov et al. (Eds.): DTGS 2016, CCIS 674, pp. 85–95, 2016.
DOI: 10.1007/978-3-319-49700-6_10

in regional e-government development that should be considered an important limitation of the further analysis. Thirdly, we conduct empirical quantitative research, describe its design, variables and proxies and present the results of the analysis as well as the interpretation. In conclusion we sum up the key findings.

2   E-Government Development Factors: A Review

In her influential work on the digital divide, Norris attempted to reveal some general patterns of virtual political system elements, including e-government. Her main hypotheses derive from three groups of theories: developmental, technological and democratisation, i.e. the performance of public electronic tools might be explained by socioeconomic conditions (human capital), technology advancement (Internet spread) and political conditions (democracy) [21, pp. 105–108]. As the only significant factor of e-governance rise in her analysis was the population online, she concludes that public administrators "have taken to the Internet in societies leading the digital revolution" [21, pp. 123–128]. Although the explanatory models have been sophisticated over time, the topicality of technological, socio-economic and political variables remain the same.

One of the most popular concepts in explaining e-government is the diffusion of innovations [19, p. 238]. Originally developed by Rogers [25], it was further expanded by Berry and Berry. They have argued that there might be two general strategies to explain policy adoption. One is the internal determinants model that relies on specific characteristics of recipient actors, the other – diffusion models – are based on communication between actors and comprise of (1) national interaction model, (2) regional diffusion model, (3) leader-laggard models, (4) vertical influence models, as well as a group of internal determinants models that rely on internal characteristics of recipients rather than on communication factors [4]. These models aim at understanding the pattern of policy diffusion, as well as its key determinants.

Lee et al have found the importance of diffusion factors. According to their results, diffusion mechanisms (learning, political norms, competition and citizen pressures) are important for an e-government worldwide tour. They have shown that e-government maturity is significantly correlated with human capital and Internet users, government transparency and participation in international organisations [17].

Nevertheless, although international communication and issue salience may be important in policy adoption, they by no means guarantee successful implementation on their own. A meta – analysis by Zhang et al. shows the relevance of internal characteristics, indicating that the key factors of e-government diffusion and performance seem to fall into three categories: technological factors (ICT), organizational factors (agency, bureaucracy and leadership) and environmental factors (from institutions and culture to city size) [33]. Quality of government and state capacity is another important predictor. Several works emphasize that effective bureaucracy, freedom from corruption, state investment in IT, etc., contribute to e-government success [2, 9, 13].

Political determinants, namely the political regime, seem to be controversial in explaining e-government performance. Several works underline the rising irrelevance of democracy in this context from the 2000s to the present day [28]. Authoritarian countries are actively adopting e-government and even e-participation tools, and their willingness to do it depends on their linkage with globalisation, state capacity and ability to retain democratisation effects of new technologies. If considering all countries in a sample however, the democratic effect is still positive though fading away [3, 15].

In sum, on the national level this perspective of e-government development explanation is linked with four general aspects: technological development, human capital, government institutions and capacity, and political characteristics.

Studies on regions or municipalities within a nation generally support the robustness of global appraisals. Regional diffusion can be facilitated through strong institutions, wealth and income, education [29], strong political leadership and network communication [32], as well as citizens' demands [27].

Our previous research devoted to Russian regional e-governments was quite in line with the abovementioned findings. The key outcome of their statistical testing is that e-government performance (but not the decision to implement) is mostly due to inherently regional characteristics rather than financial or organisational support of national authorities. The latter is playing a key role in promoting e-government, as we will further elaborate, but such vertical influence is quite the same among regions and cannot explain the variance [16]. However, the relative importance of internal variables is yet to be specified.

The task of this paper is hence twofold. We first explain the diffusion pattern of regional e-governments in Russia. Secondly, we test four hypotheses that derive from the literature:

- *Technological hypothesis.* e-Government performance is the result of technological advancement, namely, Internet diffusion.
- *Developmental hypothesis.* The more developed a region is in social and economic terms, the better are its results in e-government performance.
- *Political hypothesis.* Regions with a relatively more democratic political regime will be more successful in developing e-government.
- *Bureaucracy Effectiveness hypothesis.* In regions with relatively efficient public administration there is a better-developed e-government.

3 E-Government in Russian Regions: Origins and State-of-the-Art

To trace the pattern of e-government diffusion in Russian one needs to understand two peculiarities of the national government's decision-making. As Bershadskaya et al. argue, first, it is a "vertical of power" with its purely administrative top-down policy implementation. Secondly, the strongest motivation to implement e-services is the objective to be higher in international rankings [5]. That makes no exception for Russia from other non-democracies that strive for higher ranks in international indices in order to keep international status and raise legitimacy [3, 15, 28]. Practically all spurts in e-government policy may be linked to either the international milieu (Okinawa Charter 2000, World Summit on Information Society 2003–2005, Open Data Charter 2013) or quest for legitimacy, especially in electoral periods 2007–2008 and 2011–2012.

These two features of Russian national policy strongly affect regional e-governments. The administrative system allows making regions follow unified regulations proposed by the federal authorities, regardless their resources and capacities to meet the requirements. At the same time, in case there is no credible commitment by regional authorities, the regional policy dynamics will resemble the central one with its ups and downs.

For quite a long period of time this was not the case. During the first period of e-government implementation that started in 2002 with the adoption of the federal program "Electronic Russia" regions were quite independent, as they were only invited to participate in the program [11]. By 2005 about 35 regions had participated in co-financing of the program [7], but in general those with a lack of resources and low democracy level were reluctant to change [18].

The launch of administrative reform in Russia became an impetus for a more coherent policy. Since 2006 we can trace a trend of a top-down e-government implementation, or vertical influence diffusion pattern. The possible mechanisms of it are (1) political, or discursive, (2) legal, (3) organisational and (4) financial influence.

The first one is connected with strong leadership of high-ranked officials, president and prime minister. It was particularly clear in the case of Medvedev (2008–2012) who showed interest in new IT as a means for image and legitimacy building [20] and demanded that regions be more active in e-government implementation [31].

The second mechanism is the legal dimension. In 2006 the Russian government adopted the Regional Informatisation Concept, aiming at "providing the smoothing of regional Informatisation tempo and level", connecting federal and subnational levels and providing standards and typical decisions for regions [24]. The E-Government Concept was further developed to underline the "information unity of the country" [8]. This course has now continued in a new Concept of Regional Informatisation 2014 [23]. Despite strategic documents aimed at vertical policy implementations there are also federal laws and other norms that oblige regions to meet national requirements, e.g. Federal Law on Government and Municipal Services adopted in 2010 [10].

The third way to influence regional e-governments is organisational decisions, for instance, to appoint Rostelecom, the largest telecommunication company with a strong government presence, a single national operator of the Russian e-government. Although the right to choose remained, key market positions and federal support left little space for maneuvering and not taking Rostelecom's off-the-shelf solutions [14].

In the case of financial support, in 2012 the Russian government launched a grant competition program for co-financing the most successful regional e-government projects [26]. It is too early to draw conclusions about the outcomes, but the program seems to make regions follow federal requirements, as the evaluation of e-government success is conducted by federal criteria.

The facts mentioned above speak well for the vertical influence model of e-government diffusion in Russia. Although regions may go far beyond the compulsory programme, it is the federal government that provides the basis for e-services. The costs of not following requirements are too high for regions, even if they have no incentives to adopt innovation.

The similarities of institutional design have not eliminated the problem of disparities in regional e-government performance. According to the Index of Russian Regions E-Readiness a large gap between the most and the least developed remains (see Fig. 1). Another measurement, conducted by Bershadskaya et al using UNDESA methodology in 2014, reveals that online services index of subnational e-government web-sites ranges from 0,00 to 0,93. At the same time, regional websites are less developed than federal ones [1].

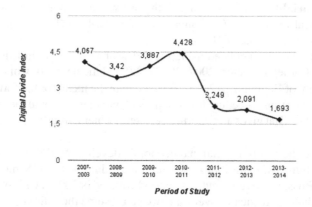

Fig. 1. Regional digital divide, ICT in regional and municipal authorities. (Source: Index of Russian Regions E-Readiness, http://eregion.ru/en/information-inequality-regions)

If the federal government is the key player in e-government diffusion by creating institutions (norms), as well as positive and negative incentives, regional factors and dynamics seem to be a clue for these disproportions and need to be uncovered.

4   Factors of E-Government Performance: An Empirical Analysis

4.1   Research Design

To test the hypotheses we use the method of multiple linear regression (ordinary least squares). The research period generally covers the period of 2007–2014. However there are certain problems with collecting quantitative data in the case of the Russian regions. First, both dependent and independent variables lack data for some periods and/or regions. Secondly, some data (especially e-government measurements) can be biased in some cases. That is why we employ data covering the available periods and calculate the mean. That can to some extent smooth the problems and provide a more objective view.

Dependent Variable. The dependent variable – EGOV – measures the state of regional e-government development. We use data from the Index of Russian Regions E-Readiness that is conducted on a biennial basis. The sub-index we use – ICT in Regional and Municipal Authorities – is formed by combining statistics on ICT usage and penetration, as well as expert estimates on web-sites' quality, and this value ranges from 0 to 1.

The period covered is 2007–2014, the only case excluded is the Chechen Republic, as there are no data available. Descriptive statistics of EGOV are presented in Table 1.

Table 1. Descriptive statistics of dependent variable (EGOV). Source: authors' calculations.

N	Min	Max	Mean	Std. Deviation
82	,23	,63	,4071	,06606

Independent Variables. In accordance with our hypotheses we use four independent variables: political regime (REG), human capital (HUM), ICT development (TECH) and bureaucratic effectiveness (BUR).

Data for the first are calculated using the Index of Democracy in Russian Regions by the Moscow Carnegie Center (2007–2012) [22] and the new Index of democracy by the Higher School of Economics (2015). We calculate the mean for the former one, then run the z-standardisation procedure for both indices and then compute the mean between two measurements. That gives an opportunity to see a general trend in a region's political development.

To determine the level of social and economic development of the regions we use data from the Human Capital Index measured according to the UN methodology by UNDP and the Russian Government. The period covered is 2006–2011, but as this indicator does not change drastically over time, we can assume the estimate is applicable to the present period as well.

ICT development, or in other words, population online, is measured using statistics from the Rosstat (Federal Service of State Statistics, gks.ru) on the percentile of people having the Internet – access in the region. The data cover the period of 2010–2014. This measurement helps to understand the overall ability of the region to develop ICT infrastructure, as well as grasp the possible citizens' demand from the regional government to innovate.

Finally, to analyse the effectiveness of the regional government we use the data from Rosstat, measuring the quantity of civil servants per 1000 economically active citizens. This proxy helps to understand the level of regional bureaucratisation: the higher the number of bureaucrats, the stronger and more rigid to innovations the regional authority is. On the contrary, a more mobile apparatus will be more efficient in terms of cost reduction and institutional change.

Table 2. Descriptive statistics of the independent variables. **Source**: Authors' calculations

Variable	N	Min	Max	Mean	Std. Deviation
REG	82	−2,09	2,30	,0038	,87726
HUM	83	,73	,93	,8022	,02898
TECH	81	23,46	72,76	53,1089	8,12230
BUR	82	10,28	70,05	27,1280	10,34180

Descriptive statistics for independent variables are presented in Table 2. It is important to note that independent variables are to a certain degree interconnected (see Table 3). For instance, human capital strongly correlates with bureaucracy effectiveness, as well as with the spread of the Internet. It seems that while some regions have higher values in all variables, the others fall behind in all categories. Although correlation coefficients are relatively low, we check our regression models for multicollinearity, taking the confidence level of variance inflation factor (VIF) as VIF < 4.0.

Table 3. Correlation analysis of independent variables (Pearson's Correlation). Source: Authors' calculations

	REG	HUM	TECH	BUR
REG	-	,298(***)	,301(***)	−,276(**)
HUM	,298(***)	-	,473(***)	−,489(***)
TECH	,301(***)	,473(***)	–	−,199
BUR	−,276(**)	−,489(***)	−,199	-

Notes: ***- Significance at the 0.01 level; **- Significance at the 0.05 level.

Control Variables. We also use several control variables. The first one - CITY - denotes the percentage of a region's inhabitants living in urban areas (it is believed that cities are more easily provided with the Internet, etc.). The second variable – SPEND – measures the volume of spending on ICT, software and hardware made by all organisations, as this correlates highly with e-government development [16]. By this variable we consider the amount of the financial resources allocated to the development of ICT infrastructure and electronic tools. Both variables are taken from Rosstat for the period of 2007–2013.

4.2 Analysis and Interpretation

The results of the regression analysis are shown in Table 4. All models presented there meet some basic assumptions like the absence of multicollinearity, autocorrelation and heteroscedasticity.

Table 4. Regression analysis results (Dependent Variable – EGOV). Source: Authors' calculations

Models	Standardized Beta – coefficients				
Variables	M1	M2	M3	M4	M5
REG	,275**	,245**	,247**	,221	,249**
HUM	,251*	,138	0,41	,037	-
TECH	,415***	,426***	,383***	,361***	,394***
BUR	-	−,259**	−,229*	−,220	−,241**
CITY	-	-	-	,081	-
SPEND	-	-	,247*	,233	,260**
Adjusted R square	**,481**	**,530**	**,568**	**,566**	**,573**
St. Error	,68945	,656207	,628731	,629944	,625199

Note: ***- significance at the 0.01 level; **- significance at the 0.05 level; * - significance at the 0.1 level

The results show no significance of the human capital regarding the development of e-government. Despite a significant correlation of EGOV and HUM (,539**), this effect is weakened when adding other variables. It seems that correlation does not mean causality in this case: both the performance of the regional e-government and the level of socio-economic development might stem from another factor, mainly from the efficiency of bureaucracy. Apparently we cannot regard the human capital in a certain region as a driver for democratisation and technological development [21, p. 108].

It turns out that the level of technological diffusion is the best predictor of e-government. Russian regions continue to face visible disparities in connection to the Web, online population, speed and cost of Internet access. We argue that this factor affects e-government in several ways. First, the level of technological development either facilitates or hinders the possibilities of the regional authorities to build an e-government infrastructure within the allocated resources. Secondly, a demand for better eservices is more likely to come from the growing online population. In the regions with low Internet penetration neither the government nor the citizens have incentives to develop e-government beyond the minimal federal requirements.

The political hypothesis is quite plausible as well. In more democratic regions we may expect a more sophisticated and citizen-oriented e-government. Even if e-services per se do not pose a threat to incumbents, the enhancement of e-government towards openness and e-participation (which is also a federal trend) may seem hazardous and hence need to be restrained. When a regional political regime leaves space for discussions and public engagement in policy-making, the demand for better services may be taken into account with higher probability.

Despite some exogenous factors, we should bear in mind that e-government development is also a technical task, the daily routine of low- and middle-level executives. Hence the bureaucratic effectiveness is also one of the e-government development predictors. The regression models show that the more bureaucratised the region is, the lower the results of e-government performance are. When the apparatus is huge, and hence stronger, it is able to resist innovations and to transform technologies to suit its needs [12]. Furthermore it is harder for the large bureaucratic structure to be provided with all the necessary equipment and training, which again freezes the existing patterns of functioning.

We should also note that the control variable – SPEND – is also an important factor for e-government development. The more resources are concentrated in the IT sector of government and business, the better are the chances for high e-government performance. It is since some regions literally lack finances to invest in e-government, and because of the development of IT in business, for instance, that may put pressure on the regional government for better performance in the area.

All significant factors are combined in Model 5 (see Table 4). This model explains about 57% of the sample, i.e. more than a half of the regions. The analysis has proved three hypotheses plausible: Technological, Political and Bureaucracy Effectiveness, as well as has revealed another important dimension of financial resources' significance. In sum, we may expect a better e-government performance in those regions that are relatively democratic, technologically advanced, with effective bureaucratic structures and higher investment in ICT.

5 Conclusion

The findings of the research may be summarised as following:

- The case of the Russian regions seems to be quite in accordance with the previous studies concentrated on other nations and regions within nations. It is the evidence that there are general tendencies of e-government diffusion and development predicted by political, technological and institutional factors. Hence these theories may be applied to Russian regions to improve e-government performance.
- Despite Russia being a federal state, the central government plays a key role in e-government diffusion. The vertical influence (political, legal, organisational and financial) has created an incentives-costs structure that makes regional authorities comply with the federal requirements, even if there is a lack of motivation to innovate among regional actors. This creates a situation where all regions have similar institutional design of e-government but highly diverge in its performance.
- The regression analysis has shown that the key predictors of e-government success in Russian regions are political development (democratic regime), technological advancement (Internet), bureaucracy effectiveness and the level of ICT spending. The most important factor is the technological one, as regions still face the problem of the digital divide.
- Despite the robustness of models presented further research is needed, first, in order to find other factors to enhance the explanatory power of models, secondly, to employ qualitative methods to reveal peculiarities of regional internal dynamics.

Acknowledgements. The paper was prepared within the framework of the Academic Fund Program at the National Research University Higher School of Economics (HSE) in 2016 (grant №. 16-05-0059) and supported within the framework of a subsidy granted to the HSE by the Government of the Russian Federation for the implementation of the Global Competitiveness Program.

References

1. Abdrakhmanova, M.M., Chugunov, A., Trutnev, D., Bershadskaya, L.: A framework for evaluating online services and e-participation tools: un methodology application to Russian regions. In: Tambouris, E., et al. (eds.). Innovation and the Public Sector - 2015, Vol. 22. Electronic Government and Electronic Participation. Joint Proceedings of Ongoing Research, Ph.D. Papers, Posters and Workshops of IFIP EGOV and ePart 2015, pp. 253–260 (2015). doi:10.3233/978-1-61499-570-8-2532015
2. Aladwani, A.: Corruption as a source of e-Government projects failure in developing countries: a theoretical exposition. Int. J. Inf. Manag. **36**(1), 105–112 (2016). doi:10.1016/j.ijinfomgt.2015.10.005
3. Åström, J., Karlsson, M., Linde, J., Pirannejad, A.: Understanding the rise of e-participation in non-democracies: domestic and international factors. Gov. Inf. Q. **29**(2), 142–150 (2012)
4. Berry, F.S., Berry, W.D.: Innovation and diffusion models in policy research. In: Sabatier, P., Weible, C. (eds.) Theories of the Policy Process, pp. 223–260. Westview Press, Boulder (1999)

5. Bershadskaya, L., Chugunov, A., Trutnev, D.: e-Government in Russia: is or seems? In: Proceedings of the 6th International Conference on Theory and Practice of Electronic Governance (NY, USA, 22–25 October 2012), ICEGOV 2012, pp. 79–82. ACM, New York (2012). doi:10.1145/2463728.2463747

6. Bershadskaya, L., Chugunov, A., Trutnev, D.: Information society development in Russia: measuring progress and gaps. In: Proceedings of the 2014 Conference on Electronic Governance and Open Society: Challenges in Eurasia (St. Petersburg, Russia, November 18–20 2014), EGOSE 2014, pp. 7–13. ACM, New York (2014). doi:http://dl.acm.org/citation.cfm?doid=2729104.2729122

7. CNews Analytics. IT in State Authorities in Russia – 2005 (2005). http://www.cnews.ru/reviews/free/gov2005/part17/index2.shtml. (in Russian)

8. Concept of E-Government Formation in the Russian Federation until 2010 (2008). http://www.consultant.ru/document/cons_doc_LAW_86005. (in Russian)

9. Domnguez, L., Sanchez, I., Gallego, I.: Determining factors of e-government development: a worldwide national approach. Int. Publ. Manag. J. **14**(2), 218–248 (2011). doi:10.1080/10967494.2011.597152

10. Federal Law of the Russian Federation On Organization of Government and Municipal Services Delivery (2010). http://www.consultant.ru/document/cons_doc_LAW_103023. (in Russian)

11. Federal Targeted Program "Electronic Russia (2002–2010)". http://www.minsvyaz.ru/ru/activity/programs/6/. (in Russian)

12. Fountain, J.: Building the Virtual State: Information Technology and Institutional Change. Brookings Institution Press, Washington, D.C (2004)

13. Gulati, G., Williams, C., Yates, D.: Predictors of on-line services and e-participation: a cross-national comparison. Gov. Inf. Q. **31**(4), 526–533 (2014). doi:10.1016/j.giq.2014.07.005

14. Igor Tschegolev urged regions to use Rostelecom's off-the-shelf solutions (2010). http://egov.ifmo.ru/news_egov/news_10_10_28-4. (in Russian)

15. Kabanov, Y.: Electronic Authoritarianism": E-Participation Institute in Non-Democratic Countries. Politeia, forthcoming (2016). (in Russian)

16. Kabanov, Y., Sungurov, A.: Regional e-governments in Russia: institutional and resource constraints. In: State and Citizens in Electronic Environment: Theories and Technologies of Research, pp. 61–72. ITMO University, St. Petersburg (2015). http://openbooks.ifmo.ru/ru/file/2219/2219.pdf. (in Russian)

17. Lee, C., Chang, K., Berry, F.S.: Testing the development and diffusion of e-government and e-democracy: a global perspective. Publ. Adm. Rev. **71**(3), 444–454 (2011). doi:10.1111/j.1540-6210.2011.02228.x

18. McHenry, W., Borisov, A.: E-government and democracy in Russia. Commun. Assoc. Inf. Syst. **17**(1), 1064–1123 (2006)

19. Meijer, A., Bekkers, V.: A metatheory of e-government: creating some order in a fragmented research field. Gov. Inf. Q. **32**(3), 237–245 (2015). doi:10.1016/j.giq.2015.04.006

20. Nocetti, J.: Digital Kremlin: Power and the Internet in Russia, no. 59. IFRI. Russie. NEI. Visions (2011)

21. Norris, P.: Digital divide: Civic Engagement, Information Poverty, and the Internet Worldwide. Cambridge University Press, New York (2001)

22. Petrov, N., Titkov, A.: Rating of Democracy by Moscow Carnegie Center: 10 Years in Service. Moscow Carnegie Center, Moscow (2014). (in Russian)

23. Regional Informatisation Concept of the Russian Federation (2014). http://government.ru/media/files/Ea8O35fPr3I.pdf. (in Russian)

24. Regional Informatisation Concept of the Russian Federation until 2010 (2006). http://www.inforegion.ru/ru/main/goverment/reg_inform_concept/reg_inform_concept_text/. (in Russian)
25. Rogers, E.M.: Diffusion of Innovations. Free Press, New York (1995)
26. Russian Government Decision On Rules of Distribution and Provision of Subsidies from Federal Budget to Regional Budgets on Support of Projects, Aimed at Information Society Development in Russian Regions (2012). http://government.consultant.ru/page.aspx?1614736. (in Russian)
27. Singh, M., Sarkar, P., Dissanayake, D., Pittachayawa, S.: Diffusion of e-government services in Australia: citizens' perspectives. In: Proceedings of ECIS 2008, Paper 197 (2008). http://aisel.aisnet.org/ecis2008/197
28. Stier, S.: Political determinants of e-government performance revisited: comparing democracies and autocracies. Gov. Inf. Q. **32**(3), 270–278 (2015). doi:10.1016/j.giq.2015.05.004
29. Tolbert, C., Mossberger, K., McNeal, R.: Institutions, policy innovation, and e-government in the American States. Publ. Adm. Rev. **68**(3), 549–563 (2008). doi:10.1111/j.1540-6210.2008.00890.x
30. Trakhtenberg, A.: Electronic state services from the government's and citizens' standpoint. In: Proceedings of the 2015 2nd International Conference on Electronic Governance and Open Society: Challenges in Eurasia (St. Petersburg, Russia, 24–25 November 2015), EGOSE 2015, pp. 89–96. ACM. New York (2015). doi:http://dl.acm.org/citation.cfm?doid=2846012.2846047
31. Verbatim report of the joint meeting of council on information society development (Moscow, Russia, 23 December 2009). http://kremlin.ru/events/president/transcripts/6443. (in Russian)
32. Yun, H.J., Opheim, C.: Building on success: the diffusion of e-government in the American States. Electron. J. E-Gov. **8**(1), 71–82 (2010)
33. Zhang, H., Xu, X., Xiao, J.: Diffusion of e-government : a literature review and directions for future directions. Gov. Inf. Q. **31**(4), 631–636 (2014). doi:10.1016/j.giq.2013.10.013

Digital Transformation: Is Public Sector Following the Enterprise 2.0 Paradigm?

Panagiotis Kokkinakos[(✉)], Ourania Markaki, Sotirios Koussouris, and John Psarras

National Technical University of Athens,
Heroon Polytechniou 9, 15780 Zografou, Greece
{pkokkinakos,omarkaki,skous,john}@epu.ntua.gr

Abstract. Among the most important, and certainly most promising, trends of the last decade is this of digitization. Organizations, and mainly businesses, of various profiles invest lots of money and effort in order to digitize processes, products and offerings. The paper at hand aims to investigate whether the same applies to the public sector as well. A pair of carefully selected indicators (namely Digital Adoption Index and Digital Evolution Index) are applied to a selected sample of countries (namely Germany, Greece, Russia, Spain and United Kingdom) in order for interesting results to be derived.

Keywords: Digitalization · Digitization · Enterprise 2.0 · Indicators · Metrics · Policy making · Government · Public sector transformation

1 Introduction

It can be taken for granted that state of the art technologies, like cloud-based services, mobile computing, social software, data analytics etc., revolutionize the every-day operations of modern organizations in every possible level and way. It is thus expected that Digital Transformation lately constitutes one of the prevalent terms around the World Wide Web; many companies and individuals try to define and discuss the exact notion of digital transformation. A concise, yet representative definition is provided by Altimeter Group, stating that digital transformation is "the realignment of, or new investment in, technology and business models to more effectively engage digital customers at every touchpoint in the customer experience lifecycle" [23].

Many concepts of various natures and levels exist that are considered to play an important role in the digital transformation procedure of any modern business, regardless of the organization's domain of activity in most of the cases. Indicatively, yet not exhaustively, one can recognize: Digital Supply Chain [2, 4]; Application Integration [12]; Mobility Management [17]; Knowledge Work Automation [21]; e-Service Design [26]; Digital Artefact [22, 28].

In this context, it is particularly interesting to identify and report the latest developments that enterprises appear to have in the aforementioned axes, as enterprises always constitute the driving force of such innovations. Given this analysis, the digitization status of the public sector will be compared to the one of the entrepreneurial world,

© Springer International Publishing AG 2016
A.V. Chugunov et al. (Eds.): DTGS 2016, CCIS 674, pp. 96–105, 2016.
DOI: 10.1007/978-3-319-49700-6_11

through comparing proper indicators and metrics. Thus, the paper at hand is structured as follows. The current section serves as an introduction, followed by a state of the art analysis of digital transformation in enterprises (Sect. 2). Section 3 performs a comparative analysis between the digitization status of the entrepreneurial world and the digitization status of the public sector, focusing (from the geographic perspective) on European cases. Section 4 provides the results of the comparative analysis, followed by a related discussion and conclusions (Sect. 5).

2   Digital Transformation in Enterprises

2.1   The Concept of Digital Enterprise

Nowadays, a vast majority of enterprises and businesses around the globe utilize digital technology in various different forms and at least in a small percentage of their activities [20]. The digital economy itself is growing at 7 times the rate of the rest economy [8]. However, a digital enterprise is a subcategory of entrepreneurship, and creating or becoming a digital enterprise is a truly challenging and complex task [15].

It's indicative that a plethora of definitions of the digital enterprise is available [7, 16]. Moreover, there is an active discussion relevant to what are the most important/defining aspects of a digital enterprise [11, 18]. Many relevant analyses tend to include notions such as: Digital Marketplace/ Economy/Value Chain; Digital Leadership/Strategy; Digital Skills, Capabilities and Infrastructure; Digital Culture and Mentality. Figure 1 presents a relevant analysis from Accenture, showing the different steps for a company towards its digitization.

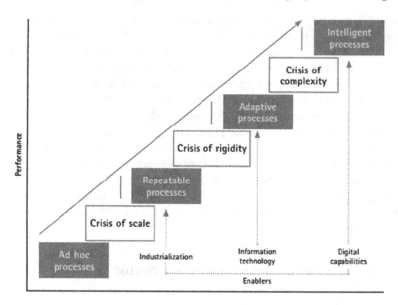

Fig. 1. The path to intelligent digital process [24]

In addition, studies exist that try to distinguish various phases of the digital enterprise, using as categorization criteria the digital capabilities of the organization and the level of their integration. A relevant analysis by Deloitte is depicted in Fig. 2.

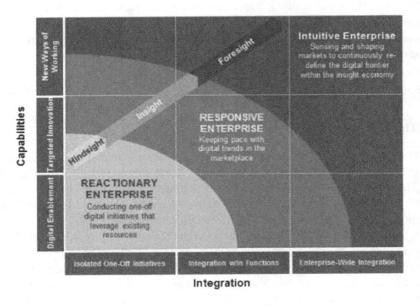

Fig. 2. The intuitive enterprise [6]

Capgemini, trying to capture as many aspects of digital transformation as possible, has proposed a digital transformation framework as well [14]. However, one could wonder whether creating (or becoming) a digital enterprise is worth the investment, both from the time and from the monetary cost perspectives. Capgemini claim that digitization matters in every industry, as digital maturity comes with revenue generation, greater profitability and higher market valuations [3]. Being a digital enterprise is considered to be a competitive advantage itself [13]. Benchmarking of the digital maturity of the entrepreneurial landscape is available [19]. All countries members of the European Union are implementing (or have implemented initiatives) that are (either strongly or weakly) related to the digital transformation of enterprises. Indicative examples could include the "Promoting innovative IT take up in SMEs" in Denmark and the "Mission for digital economy" in France [9]. In the pan-European landscape initiatives such as the Digital Agenda, the FI-PPP and the Collective Awareness Platforms can be reported as indicative [8].

3   Digital Transformation in the Public Sector

3.1   Background

The digital era is not only driving innovation in the enterprise sector, but seems also to influence developments in the public sector as well. Governments around the world are in the midst of a historic (and frequently wrenching) transformation as they abandon analogue operating models in favor of their digital counterparts. As most studies of global scope point out though [1, 10, 25] governments are at very different stages in their journey of digital transformation. In fact, a recent study by Deloitte [10] identifies three levels of maturity with regard to governments' digital transformation; whereas it acknowledges a set of five factors that shape the path to digital transformation: strategy, leadership, workforce skills, digital culture, and user focus (Fig. 3).

	Early	Developing	Maturing
Strategy	Aimed at cost reduction	Aimed at improving customer experience and decision making	Aimed at fundamental transformation of processes
Leadership	Lacks awareness and skills	Digitally aware	Digitally sophisticated
Workforce development	Insufficient investment	Moderate investment	Adequate investment
User focus	Absent	Gaining traction	"Central" to digital transformation
Culture	Risk averse; disintegrated	Risk tolerant; accommodates innovation and collaboration	Risk receptive; fosters innovation and collaboration

Fig. 3. Characteristics of a digitally maturing public organization [10]

In this context, it is interesting to investigate how the public sector progresses towards digital transformation and whether an overall economy's course towards digitization is further affected by its particular characteristics.

3.2 Methodological Framework

Nowadays, dedicated metrics and indicators constitute the most popular way of depicting and evaluating a country's performance in various thematic areas. Thus, in order to perform the desired analysis, the authors focused on selecting a set of representative indicators, issued by credible and well-respected organizations. These indicators were collected and visualized for each of the countries that constitute the application sample of the paper and the respective results were compared in order to draw interesting conclusions. This methodology, slightly adapted, is based on the guidelines set by the Policy Compass[1] project, aiming to develop methods and tools that facilitate more factual, evidence-based, transparent and accountable policy evaluation and analysis. The following figure provides a visualized overview of the paper's methodology, followed by a short, yet comprehensive, elaboration on each corresponding step (Fig. 4).

Fig. 4. Methodological framework

---

[1] http://policycompass.eu/.

As a first step, a set of appropriate indicators that relate to digital transformation was sought. The identification and selection of the most appropriate ones for the needs of the paper was based on a set of specific criteria. First of all, the indicators had to be open, in order to ensure transparency. Thus, only indicators whose mathematical formulas and basic calculation data were freely accessible have been taken into consideration. Secondly, credibility played also an important role. As such, only indicators coming from trusted, well-known and well-respected sources (e.g. OECD, Eurostat, European Central Bank, World Bank etc.) were considered candidates. Moreover, availability of results for the region under investigation constituted an on-off criterion. Both consequent and recent calculation results were sought for; only indicators that were diachronically available up to the latest years were taken into consideration.

Upon selecting the appropriate indicators, the second step of the methodology was to select the countries that were to be analyzed. In addition, and closely related to the previous step, the authors selected countries that instantiations of the selected indicators were diachronically and up to the latest years available. The third step consists of the data import and visualization for each of the selected indicators and country. Finally, the last step of the methodology is the comparison of the results derived in the previous step, in order to identify and report possible associations, contradictions etc.

3.3 Selected Indicators

In an attempt to discuss the fundamental questions raised in this paper and to provide quantitative evidence on digital transformation progress, the authors have employed two relevant indicators, i.e. the Digital Adoption Index (DAI)[2] and the Digital Evolution Index (DEI)[3].

The Digital Adoption Index has been defined by the World Bank, as a measure of the digital technology diffusion across three segments of the economy, namely businesses, people and governments [27]. DAI reflects the extent to which digital technologies are available and adopted by all they key agents in an economy, thus providing a more comprehensive picture of technology spread than other ICT indices, whereas it is constructed using actual data, thereby being more robust compared to indicators that are based on perception surveys. In this respect, it is addressed to policy makers, who can use it to benchmark countries and to design nuanced digital strategies with differentiating policies to promote digital adoption across different user groups.

The Digital Adoption Index is in fact a composite index, comprising of three sectoral sub-indices covering businesses, people, and governments, with each sub-index assigned an equal weight. The authors have focused in particular on the Business and Government DAI sub-indexes, the former being calculated the simple average of the normalized values of the percentage of businesses with websites, the number of secure servers per million residents, download speed (Kbps), and 3G coverage in the country, and the latter being respectively computed as the simple average of core administrative systems, online public services, and digital identification indices.

---

[2] http://www.digitaladoptionindex.org/?w=780&h=608.
[3] http://fletcher.tufts.edu/eBiz/Index.

On the other hand, the Digital Evolution Index [5], an indicator created by The Fletcher School, in collaboration with MasterCard Worldwide[4] and DataCash[5], analyses the key underlying drivers (and barriers), i.e. demand conditions, supply conditions, institutional environment and innovation and change that govern a country's evolution into a digital economy. To this end, these drivers are further divided into 12 components, measured in turn using a set of 83 indicators. The indicator's rationale is based on the fact that digital evolution is not governed by just one, to or few silver bullets such as technology, government regulation, consumer behavior or fulfilment networks; instead digital readiness is the result of the interplay of several factors.

The aforementioned DAI components are used to benchmark the performance of the public sector in terms of digital transformation against that of the enterprise sector, whereas the DEI is applied to provide a more comprehensive outlook of the digital trajectory of economies across time.

3.4 Selected Countries

For the needs of this paper, five countries (Germany, Greece, the Russian Federation, Spain and United Kingdom) have been indicatively selected and analyzed. Germany has been selected as it is a country that traditionally promotes innovation and can be considered as leader in the field of public sector digital transformation. The same applies for the United Kingdom, which also ranks second (after Germany) in the list of European countries, ordered by GDP. Spain and Greece, on the other side are two Mediterranean countries, the first one ranking fourth in terms of geographical area and the second one, being one of the smaller (both in terms of geographical area and GDP) European countries, both though bearing the specificity that they have been affected by the recent economic crisis. What all these four countries have in common is the fact that they develop and implement their digital transformation policies in line with the EU directions. On the other hand, the Russian Federation is a federal semi-presidential republic that spans two continents and is worth analysing, as it is a country that enacts and follows its own policies in this respect.

4   Application and Results

Figure 5 depicts the latest measured values of the government DAI component against that of the respective business component. Surprisingly, in 3 out of the 5 countries considered, namely Germany, Russia and Spain, digital technology diffusion in the business sector is found to be well below than the government sector, whereas only in Greece and the United Kingdom the business sector is preceded.

This leads prima facie to the assumption that despite the fact that government bodies are often hampered by cultures, processes, and skill sets that are out of step with the current technologically advanced era, the public sector may well be at the forefront of

---

[4] https://www.mastercard.us/en-us.html.
[5] https://www.datacash.com/.

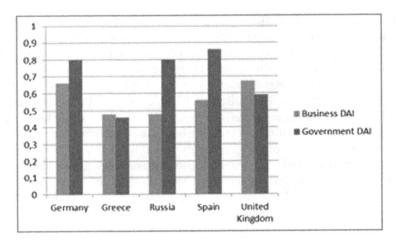

Fig. 5. Digital Adoption Index business and government rankings

technological transformations, given that it is also the carrier of strategic developments and the one to pull the strings with regard to any amendments necessary in the legal framework with regard to the adoption and use of new technological trends. This assumption may actually be true; nevertheless a more careful consideration of the individual parameters that are used for the calculation of the DAI indicates that while for the Government component of the index these represent core digital transformation features that are necessary for the modernization of the public sector towards this direction, thus providing a more accurate view of the former's digitization status, when it comes to the Business sub-index these concern basic infrastructure elements that do not necessarily depict the enterprise 2.0 paradigm at its full scale.

Indeed, with the exception of the business websites' parameter, which can be tracked down to the individual enterprise level, these are mostly associated with each country's ICT infrastructure, which provides the basis for undertaking further business digital transformation steps, and are not able to capture the specific and more sophisticated digitization initiatives that may be undertaken by enterprises. On the contrary, the components of the DAI Government sub-index are more representative, as they are further analyzed into a series of more specific aspects, such as the range of services accessed, the digital signature functionality and the card features in the case of the digital identification parameter or the specific types of systems (e.g. financial management information, human resources, e-tax, e-customs, e-procurement systems) involved in that of the core administrative systems' component. It is further interesting that the values of the DAI present a greater dispersion for the government sector, a fact which indicates that the actual performance of the former in respect to digitization has to be analyzed and assessed in all cases taking into account factors, such as strategic design and leadership commitment. Thereupon, digital transformation overall seems to be dependent upon the particular characteristics of each economy. This claim is better reflected in Fig. 6, where the Digital Evolution Index is illustrated for the selected countries for a period of years from 2008 to 2013. At this point, attention should be drawn to the fact that DEI offers a more complete picture with regard to a country's evolution towards digitization.

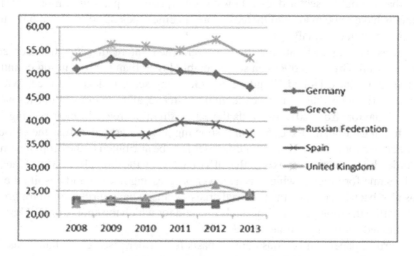

Fig. 6. Digital Evolution Index (2008–2013)

The results indicate that Germany and the United Kingdom are the ones to progress better, as expected, Spain's course of evolution is a more moderate one, while Greece and the Russian Federation have a quite comparable track of evolution. In the same report by [2], Germany and United Kingdom are characterized as stall-out or slowly receding countries that have to further promote innovation and reinforce efforts to seek markets beyond domestic borders, Greece and the Russian Federation are slowly advancing countries that face significant opportunities as well as challenges, whereas Spain is caught somewhere in the middle.

5   Discussion, Conclusions and Future Work

Taking as granted that the shift towards digitized processes and offerings is nowadays a core quality of modern and competitive enterprises, the analysis presented within the paper at hand targeted towards investigating whether the public sector follows the same paradigm or lags behind in terms of digitization.

Towards this direction, from the plethora of relevant available indicators and metrics, the authors selected the Digital Adoption Index (DAI) and Digital Evolution Index (DEI) as the most suitable for the needs of the aforementioned analysis. The focus from the first index was on comparing the scoring between the private and public sector, while the latter was utilized for examining the diachronic scoring (for six consequent years). The necessary data for these two indexes were collected for five case studies; namely Germany, Greece, Russia, Spain and United Kingdom.

Regarding the Digital Adoption Index, the results were particularly interesting. The figures evinced that the public sector does not only keep up with the private one in terms of digitization, but in three (out of the five) cases leads the race. Especially in the cases of Russia and Spain, the Government DAI is significantly higher than the one of the business. Nevertheless, the nature of the indicators used suggests that in order to be able to state that the public sector does follow the enterprise 2.0 paradigm, more informed judgements have to be made and thereby more specific types of information have to be taken into account and analyzed.

As far as the Digital Evolution Index is concerned, interesting insights accrued as well. First of all, Greece and Russia score notably lower than the remaining countries; along the same lines, United Kingdom and Germany seem to lead the race. What is equally remarkable is that with the exception of Greece, all remaining countries have a common behavior; from 2012 onwards there is a slight decrease in their scoring. The truth is that in general, digital evolution is showing positive growth across the globe, so such a decrease for most of the former countries is to be attributed to the drop of demand (as recorded by the respective axis of the DEI), caused by the Great Recession. The case is not the same for Greece, which, as a slower progressing market and despite the fact that has also been affected by the financial crisis, seems to have further room for growth (at least within the time period of the analysis), and for which the course of DEI has thus to be evaluated for a longer time period.

The current paper can be considered a basis for further research and analysis. The conducted work can definitely be broadened in order to include as many cases (i.e. countries) as desired; actually, the same analysis can be performed for any geographical area, on the sole condition that the necessary data are open and credible. Further, the inclusion of more related indicators and metrics would also allow for more sophisticated analysis (e.g. correlation among metrics, noting of unexpected phenomena etc.). Last but not least, it is interesting to update the paper's results over time; by including the latest indicators and data in the analysis, the analyst can acquire an effective realtime grasp on the course of the comparison between the digitization of the public and the business sector.

Acknowledgements. The research leading to these results has been supported by the EC FP7 under the projects "Policy Compass" Grant Agreement No. 612133, "FutureEnterprise" Grant Agreement No. 611948, and "SONNETS" Grant Agreement No. 692868.

References

1. Accenture: Digital government pathways to delivering public services for the future. http://nstore.accenture.com/acn_com/Accenture-Digital-Government-Pathways-to-Delivering-Public-Services-for-the-Future.pdf
2. Accenture Strategy: The digital supply network: a new paradigm for supply chain management (2014)
3. Capgemini Consulting: The digital advantage: how digital leaders outperform their peers in every industry (2012)
4. Capgemini Consulting: Digital transformation of supply chains (2011)
5. Chakravorti, B., Tunnard, C., Chaturvedi, R.V.: Digital planet: readying for the rise of the e-Consumer (2014). http://fletcher.tufts.edu/eBiz/Index
6. Deloitte: The intuitive enterprise (2014). http://www2.deloitte.com/us/en/pages/consulting/articles/the-intuitive-enterprise.html#. Accessed 1 Mar 2016

7. Digital Naiv: A definition of a digital business (2014). http://digitalnaiv.com/2014/09/12/en-a-definition-of-a-digital-business/. Accessed 1 Mar 2016

8. EC: Digital agenda 2020 (2014). http://ec.europa.eu/digital-agenda/

9. EC: Factories of the future (2014). http://ec.europa.eu/research/industrial_technologies/factories-of-the-future_en.html

10. Eggers, W.D., Bellman, J.: The journey to government's digital transformation. Deloitte University Press. http://dupress.com/articles/digital-transformation-in-government/

11. Emergent Enterprise: 7 defining aspects of a digital enterprise (2014). http://emergent enterprise.com/?p=87. Accessed 1 Mar 2016

12. Fenner, J.: Enterprise application integration techniques. http://www.cs.ucl.ac.uk/staff/ucacwxe/lectures/3C05-02-03/aswe21-essay.pdf. Accessed Sept 2011

13. Fenwick, N.: How to achieve competitive advantage through digital business (2013). http://www.cio.co.uk/insight/enterprise-apps/how-achieve-competitive-advantage-through-digital-business/?page=1. Accessed 1 Mar 2016

14. Fitzgerald, M., Kruschwitz, N, Bonnet, D., Welch, M.: Embracing Digital Technology. Capgemini Consulting (2013)

15. Future of CIO: Three characteristics of digital enterprise (2011). http://futureofcio.blogspot.gr/2013/06/three-characteristics-of-digital.html. Accessed 1 Mar 2016

16. Gartner: Digital business 2014. http://www.gartner.com/technology/research/digital-business/. Accessed 1 Mar 2016

17. Gartner: Enterprise mobility and its impact on IT (2012). https://www.gartner.com/doc/1985016/enterprise-mobility-impact-it. Accessed 1 Mar 2016

18. i-SCOOP: Can you survive the age of integration and collaboration? (2015) http://www.i-scoop.eu/can-survive-age-integration-collaboration/. Accessed 1 Mar 2016

19. Lloyds Bank (in association with Accenture): Benchmarking the digital maturity of small and medium-sized enterprises and charities in the UK (2014)

20. McKinsey: The digital enterprise (2013). http://www.mckinsey.com/insights/business_technology/the_digital_enterprise. Accessed 1 Mar 2016

21. McKinsey & Company: Disruptive technologies: advances that will transform life, business, and the global economy (2013)

22. Rethinking ICT: Digital artefacts (2015). https://rethinkingict.wikispaces.com/Digital+Artefacts

23. Solis, B., Lieb, R., Szymanski, J.: The 2014 State of Digital Transformation. Altimeter Group (2014)

24. Thomas, J.R., Kass, A., Davarzani, L.: From Looking Digital to Being Digital: The Impact of Technology on the Future of Work. Accenture (2014)

25. UN, E-Government Survey 2014. https://publicadministration.un.org/egovkb/Portals/egovkb/Documents/un/2014-Survey/E-Gov_Complete_Survey-2014.pdf

26. Wikipedia: Service design (2015). http://en.wikipedia.org/wiki/Service_design

27. World Bank: Digital dividends – world development report 2016. http://www.worldbank.org/en/publication/wdr2016)

28. Yoo, Y., Boland Jr., R.J., Lyytinen, K., Majchrzak, A.: Organizing for innovation in the digitized world. Organ. Sci. **23**(5), 1398–1408 (2016)

Information Technologies as an Instrument to Administrate Added Value Tax

Lada Koroleva[1(✉)] and Ariadna Aleksandrova[2(✉)]

[1] 74, Kuibysheva 10, St. Petersburg, Russia
klada69@mail.ru
[2] 153, Svetlanovsky pr. 72/1, St. Petersburg, Russia
aariadna@mail.ru

Abstract. This paper discusses the functions of value added tax, shortcomings of value added tax levying in Russian taxing practice, it also justifies the necessity of transition to the new electronic system of tax administration. Main attention is paid to issues of comprehensive tax administration modernization on the basis of information technologies, description of the innovations and advantages of the new system that came into use in 2015.

Keywords: Information technologies · Electronic administration of value added tax · Modernization of the tax administration architecture

1   Introduction

According to International Monetary fund (2004), more than 70% of the world's population now live in the countries applying VAT, and VAT makes up approximately a quarter of total government revenue [14]. Therefore, the common strategic goal of tax administration in all countries is increasing the efficiency of VAT collection.

E-government in the taxation field can hardly be considered only as a technological solution allowing to optimize the state tax service performance. The mission of electronic tax administration is to ensure growth and stability of the national budget.

It should also include such an important target of the e-government as economic crime elimination and improvement of relations between economic agents within the framework of economic security enhancement.

The transition to electronic documents is a global trend aimed at national legislation harmonization with regard to electronic invoices. It took the European Union countries about 10 years to develop a mechanism of electronic tax administration. Compared with the countries that use the electronic tax administration system, in Russia this process is still in its infancy. To date, in Russia the legal framework for the electronic document submission and electronic invoices exchange has already been established, with a number of pilot projects successfully carried out.

The analysis of statistical data has shown that VAT has always constituted the greatest share of the federal budget tax revenues. VAT share in total tax revenue exceeds 45% [9]. In the past 10 years the size of VAT revenues to the Russian budget has been

© Springer International Publishing AG 2016
A.V. Chugunov et al. (Eds.): DTGS 2016, CCIS 674, pp. 106–122, 2016.
DOI: 10.1007/978-3-319-49700-6_12

growing. In the last five years, its share in GDP has remained at the level of 5.5–6%. In 2004 VAT revenues to the Russian budget amounted to 2,5 billion and in 2014 they totaled 3,81 billion. Given this tax role in the current tax revenue structure, one should not underestimate the problem of VAT collection. Thus it should be considered as a strategically important issue for the implementation of economic and social programs in Russia.

Various aspects of VAT tax administration are determined by its importance for the budget and difficulties of VAT taxation processes. Tax administration in its organizational aspect is aimed at increasing efficiency and optimizing taxation processes, while the purpose of financial aspect is ensuring complete collection of tax payments to the state budget.

The main idea of the transition to electronic administration is consolidation and integration of information resources and establishment of unified super-large data warehouse. The use of information and analytical systems as an effective management tool facilitates the achievement of higher efficiency target of the Federal Tax Service.

The Russian theory of tax administration was actively developed in 2000–2007, now its basic conceptual issues are considered as well established. At the same time, the problem of practical increase of VAT administration efficiency requires further scientific development due to the complexity of this tax calculation mechanism and its special status in the Russian Federation tax system.

The new AIS system based on electronic forms of document flows was the subject of a number of Russian articles that describe the purpose and advantages of the new electronic system [13, 23] as well as the reasons why it is difficult to quickly put it into practice [10].

In this paper, we conducted a comprehensive study that includes history of the transition to the new information technologies in VAT administration within the framework of the tax administration architecture modernization, as well as VAT economic and administrative aspects.

2 Information Technologies as a Response to the Tax Problems

The necessity of reforming the VAT system and its technical modernization are caused by some well-known economic and management problems. The former include the problems of VAT refunds and justifications for the tax deduction, the existence of opportunities for evading VAT on imports, illegal tax refund from the budget in the cases of false export, using various illegal tax minimization schemes. The latter group includes administrative efficiency problems, such as a lack of integration and harmonization of administrative components, the high cost and complexity of administration processes.

The introduction of a modern legislative framework for taxation, coupled with automation in enforcement and a focus on taxpayer services; the formalization of business processes and operating procedures; the integration of different tax departments into a single tax authority, with integrated IT systems are the key challenges faced by the tax administration in Egypt [5].

The main challenge facing Bosnia and Herzegovina in the late 1990s and early 2000s was to improve administration and compliance, which means the integration of isolated tax authorities into a single system, providing archiving and monitoring [5].

The biggest challenge facing Norwegian Tax Administration is the efficient management and exploitation of the data. Improving compliance by taxpayers is the most serious problem for the Ministry of Taxes of Azerbaijan Republic [17]. The biggest challenge facing Norwegian Tax Administration is the efficient management and exploitation of the data. Improving compliance by taxpayers is the most serious problem for the Ministry of Taxes of Azerbaijan Republic [17]. Creating the department of analysis of tax crimes and tax debt in 2015–2016 [6] on the reform of the tax control system in Azerbaijan was a response to this problem.

The role of tax audit determines its consideration as a separate sphere of administration in tax risk management on the national level. Tax risk issues are equally relevant to all administrations, and, therefore, play an important role in the architecture and creation of information systems. We can see that the management of tax risk in today's automated tax systems requires including other types of risk – information risks. See [18] items relating to technological issues, namely information security of data, customer relationship management and channel management, increasing on-line taxpayer services are put on a par with functional and strategic tasks facing the modern Tax Administration.

Despite national differences in tax systems and issues emphasized in the research, a central theme can be well defined which has been the most urgent in the last two decades. This is modernization of tax systems based on information technology, carried out by the tax authorities of different countries.

Conducting pilot projects for the implementation of technologies in the tax area as reported in various sources [4, 14] and the results confirm the role of technology as an important component of the reform of tax systems providing the effect of policy and legislative changes.

No matter what problem is put forward by the specialists and managers of tax services as the main one to date, its solution is always associated with the need to solve the issues of technological information management.

3   Electronic VAT Administration in Dealing with Tax Revenue Problems

3.1   Advantages of E-administration

The end user of goods, work or services pays the seller a tax for the total value of the purchased product. But the budget starts to receive this amount prior to the final process implementation, because everyone who is involved in production of goods, works or services at different stages of the end product creation pays VAT to the budget for the cost of purchased raw materials, works or services required for production.

Accordance between the buyer's right to obtain a VAT deduction and the seller's obligation to pay this tax to the budget is a "specular" principle of VAT operation.

Administrating of VAT is a laborious process that takes at least half working time. Tax authorities tend to strengthen control over this tax, because VAT is one of the most corrupted taxes. This is due to the VAT refunding procedure described above. Advantages of electronic circulation of paperless invoices and source documents for taxpayers are determined by the fact that they allow to cut costs and optimize business processes. Electronic invoices and source documents circulation for the tax authorities will improve the quality and efficiency of data collection, and besides, it will accelerate the administrative checks. A whole procedure increases the efficiency of the value added tax (VAT).

Main advantages of the electronic document include the following [12]:

- centralized and systematic documents storage;
- cost reduction of paper invoices' printing, storage and mailing;
- unified procedures for document drafting and processing (registration, approval, etc.);
- reduced time for documents delivery, registration and approval;
- faster documents signing;
- possibility to perform any online operations with documents: searching, downloading, printing, collation, deviation, and tracking their motion;
- quick documents search;
- audit user access to documents.

3.2 Shortcomings of the Russian Value Added Taxation

In other countries when using the offset method, a company transfers to the budget only a difference between the two VAT amounts. In Russia, the taxing offset is called "tax deduction" and is implemented as a tax refund from the budget which has already been paid to the supplier by the taxpayer. The main problem of the Russia VAT collection practices is that the return goes to taxpayers's accounts as "live" money, while the world practice widely uses offset method.

Changes in tax legislation, as well as the taxpayer's desire to minimize tax payments led to the fact that the tax deduction amount is growing faster than the VAT revenue amount. As a result, currently the fiscal capacity of value added tax is not fully implemented.

In Russia the added value share in GDP is increasing, while VAT refund amount compared to the accrued tax amount is very high. Therefore, in fact, the real VAT share in the gross value added is more than 2 times lower than it should be according 18% rate. The high level of VAT refunds is caused by several factors such as the increase in material costs per unit of production, changes in tax legislation, labor intensive tax collection mechanism. The widespread use of criminal schemes to avoid VAT is another reason. This results in a shortfall in large-scale state tax amounts. According to the tax authorities' estimation, unwarranted deductions cause annual budget losses up to one third of VAT revenues, while VAT refund on export operations growth exceeds the exports growth.

The state is losing hundreds of billions of rubles as a result of un-scrupulous taxpayers activities, with tax revenue being much lower than it would be expected. Thus, while in 2010, taxpayers received 88% of the tax amount on their accounts in 2014 they received 93.7% [9].

If this trend continues, the VAT amount which is charged to the budget may be equal to deduction sums. It is the case, when to spend taxation processes is not profitable. For example, for St. Petersburg safe performance of the VAT deduction is equal to 90.40% from the accrued VAT [13].

Curves in Fig. 1 show dynamics of charged VAT and actual VAT paid to the budget. This diagram was created by the authors according to FTS data [22].

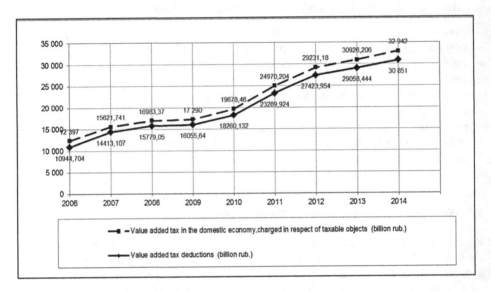

Fig. 1.   Assessed value added tax, and the actual VAT paid to the budget

In order to analyze the relationship between the gross added value, the estimated VAT and real income from VAT for the Russian Federation budget we collected the statistical information of FTS data [22]. Figure 2 shows the growth of all indicators in 2006–2014.

The proportions between the amount of VAT accrued and VAT entered in the budget within the considered period have not changed. In 2014 the amount of charged VAT was 62.4% of the gross added value, while this percentage in 2008 was 80%. The gap between the gross value added and the accrued VAT over 9 years increased. Income from the tax amount actually received in the budget is on average 6–8% of GVA.

Taking into account that the VAT rate is 18%, we can say that there is potential for increasing VAT revenues.

The graph in Fig. 2 shows stable relation between tax deduction and the tax amount assessed in 2006–2014. By 2015, the situation has not changed, so it is clear that a fundamentally new architecture of VAT control and new process technologies are required. A more complete assessment of new technologies impact will be possible with the new FTS data after 2016. In the future, we can expect not only financial implications but also cost reduction effect in business processes.

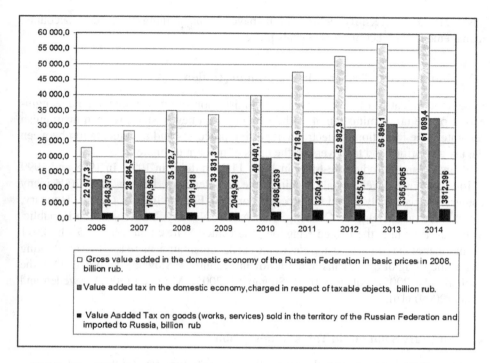

Fig. 2. The GVA dynamics, VAT output, federal budget income from VAT, billion rub

4   Modern Tax Administration Systems: Structure and Software Products

4.1   New Structural Changes in the Modern Taxation

In literature, [5, 18] we can see some common logic in the description of tax administration system. The core tax system is the central system in a tax administration. IT support of tax administration functions is applied within the central tax system.

According reference [18] Tax Administration Framework is a complex of three components: Core Tax Processing System, E-Tax Administration, Compliance Management. Compliance components - Collection, Audit, Fraud Detection, Legal Software solutions from different vendors - constitute the technical framework of the tax administration.

E-Tax Administration is implemented using the Web Portal, and E-Tax Self Services. Tax Web Portal provides taxpayers with E-Tax Self Services, which involve Registration, Filing, Payment, Compliance, Self Audit, Taxpayer Service, Research Policy. E-Tax Self Services serve as tools for processes such as Registration, Returns, Remittances. E-Data Store includes two types of data: Authoritative Taxpayer Account Data and Compliance Data Warehouse.

Different information technologies correspond to the different functions of the tax administration, for example, processing registration filings and issuing taxpayer identification numbers, monitoring compliance, validating and processing returns and payments, audit (identify delinquent taxpayers), maintaining taxpayer's accounts, management of objections and appeals process.

4.2   E-filing – New Tendency in Tax Administration

In the modernization of the national tax administration systems along with the reengineering of the tax administration as the structure of a new system, we can distinguish separately the transition to electronic reporting processes and documentation between the tax authorities and taxpayers on the basis of modern technologies.

New Zeland introduced e-filing in 1992. Finland did it in 1997. In 1998 and 1999 e-filing was introduced in Italy, Spain, Chile and Denmark. During 2000–2004 many countries successively joined the process: Portugal, France, Ireland, Greece, Hungary, Korea, Australia, Belgium, Canada, South Africa, Norway, Mexico, Czech Republic, Slovenia, Romania, the United Kingdom, the United States. Later, in 2005 - by 2011 the number of the countries using electronic tax documentation increased due to adopting electronic filing of documents in the following countries: Slovak Republic (2005), the Netherlands (2005), Poland (2006), Singapore (2005), Morocco (2007), Sweden and Israel (2009) [16].

4.3   Software Solutions in Tax Administration

There are three types of technologies for the administration: tax point solutions, standalone solutions, and enterprise-level solutions. Tax point solutions generally include "manual" work processes and user-friendly interface, so they can serve as a starting point for some users. These include ONESOURCE® Workflow Manager and CORPTAX® WorkSpace.

They provide a good starting point for some users, as they have a friendly user interface. Standalone solutions, such as Global 360, MetaStorm, Lombardi, Pegasystems®, Savvion® typically address particular capabilities and can plug into just about any environment [11].

Enterprise-level solutions are designed to process management. Oracle® Workflow is intended for modeling, automation, and continuous improvement capabilities. SAP® NetWeaver, TM includes role-based workflow inside the ERP system. In general, the base product, SAP NetWeaver is positioned to the consumer as a service-oriented integration platform.

Modernization has become the current trend for many national taxation systems. More and more countries are pursuing a comprehensive restructuring of the tax authorities, using information technology tools.

Many countries are using products from software vendors for tax administration. For example, Namibia, Zambia, Saudi Arabic, Morocco and Egypt, Botswana, Rwanda and Ethiopia implement product e-ris and its previous versions of Chinese company Bull-e-ris.info.

Twenty countries on three continents and the Caribbean use SIGTAS (Standard Integrated Government Tax Administration System) of Canadian company CRC Sogema. Jordan, Philippines, Mongolia, Ghana, Guyana use "TRIPS" for VAT administration, developed by Crown Agents. TRIPS is considered more of a portable solution that COTS (a Commercial Off The Shelf System). COTS is a product of Oracle, a global enterprise software company. About 15 US states, 3 Canadian provinces and Trinidad and Tobago use GenTax. It is a product of US company "Fast enterprices". GenTax is a complete integrated tax processing software package designed to tax administration. New Zealand, Denmark, Kentucky and Vermont use OETPM69, a product designed by Oracle. 13 state departments in India and Uganda use TRM70 by SAP [5].

Thus, it is obvious that the market of information programs for tax administration is well developed, and a lot of different technologies turn into the available tools for different functional tasks at all tax management levels.

5   The Practice of Applying New Technologies in Tax Administration in Russia

5.1   Improved Approaches to Tax Administration Before 2015

Back in September 2004, the Government decided on the introduction of an electronic invoices mechanism. However, the VAT control mechanism was not implemented until 2015.

From January to June 2009, a pilot project to create invoices generation in the electronic system was successfully tested.

In 2011, the Russian Federal Tax Service set a goal of creating a new automated system in which all tax administration data are stored and processed in a federal repository. The new generation system has been called the Automated Information System "Tax-3". Automated monitoring system "VAT ASC-2" is VAT automated cameral control based on the tax returns analysis. Since 2013, the automated control system "VAT ASC" was launched, while "VAT ASC-2" was introduced into service in 2015 year. This allows the use of risk management and focuses on taxpayers within the red danger zone. The Federal Tax Service has introduced 55 risk criteria, which are incorporated into the software control system. The criteria are not disclosed, so as not to allow taxpayers to outwit control.

A single software product had to combine information resources not only of Control Department, but also of Research Department, Cameral Control Department, Transaction Pricing Department.

Cameral Control Department works with an automatic control system of VAT reimbursement ("VAT ASC-2"). Research Department engages tax monitoring based on the industry's average indicators. The main function of Transaction Pricing Department is to analyze transactions data. Information Environment Protection deals with preventing information leaks and unauthorized activities with information in AIS "Tax-3", which are protected by information security systems. All reports on VAT (and, hence, all invoices) fall into a nationwide database. The program compares the data on each transaction in the goods movement chain. The system shows the inspectors "tax discrepancies", operations on which taxpayers already received deductions, but have not paid VAT.

Trial AIS "Tax-3" operation showed that the full-scale launch of AIS "Tax-3" in the commercial operation was not possible to start immediately. This was caused by two main reasons. Firstly, the existing infrastructure of Federal Data Center was not ready to meet all system needs. Secondly, the inspection databases were not ready for transfer to transactional and analytical segments [20].

Due to these reasons, the project management group of the Federal Tax Service gradually began to introduce some subsystems of AIS "Tax-3" simultaneously continuing the operation of the others.

5.2   New Principles of Tax Administration

Tax authority's modernization includes various components:

– financial transparency and easy tax reporting;
– clear tax laws;
– full automation of operation processes;
– information exchange between tax authorities and taxpayers.

Now tax-payers are required to submit digitally purchases ledgers and sales in form of declarations that will be merged into a single database of about 15 billion documents. Now all companies must regularly provide declarations data concerning each invoice. All information is stored in "Big data" system. Automation of tax administration processes in the new architecture required business process re-engineering in the department. As a result, functions that require an interactive user interaction with the system and taxpayers that are performed as interactive services and «tax machine» functions were transferred to the Federal Data Center.

Interaction with taxpayers is provided by "My Account" service. Interdepartmental electronic interaction is provided by the interagency electronic interaction system and the public services portal. Thus, tax authorities' load is significantly reduced. Access control to system functionality and access control to the system data are information protection tools. The «Tax-3» system includes 2 levels: workplaces where the application is installed and Federal Data Service. The application updating at sites is carried out automatically.

Figure 3 shows how the VAT administration processes architecture has changed (the drawing based on the presentation "The modernization project of the tax authorities" of Russian Federal Tax Service [21].

Federal Tax Service monitors tax legislation implementation of the Russian Federation. FTS has a branched structure consisting of the following components:

• Federal Tax Service central office;
• Interregional Inspection of federal districts and specialized interregional inspectorates;
• 82 control subjects by Federal Tax Service of the Russian Federation;
• about 1,500 regional, urban and interdistrict tax inspections.

FTS provides information exchange with various ministries and departments of the Russian Federation, local authorities, as well as both individual taxpayers and legal

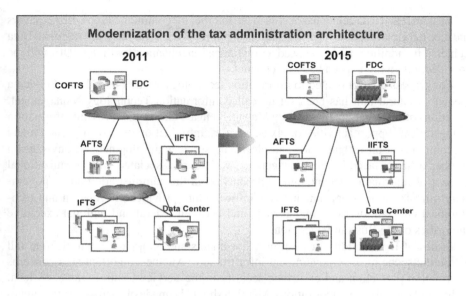

Fig. 3. Modernization of the tax administration architecture

entities. FTS has one of the most powerful information systems among public institutions. It includes over 50,000 computers, over 6,000 servers, a single multi-service network.

Given the existing systemic problems in information activities development of the tax authorities, it was decided to establish an automated information system of data processing centers (DPCs), which should serve for data collection, storage, processing and dissemination.

The following levels can be described as a part of each data center:

1. The premises and its engineering systems (power supply, air conditioning, fire alarm and protection, access control and video surveillance, structured cabling system).
2. Terminal equipment telecommunication channels that combine data centers into a single system.
3. Local Area Network.
4. Storage Area Network (SAN).
5. Computing equipment (servers, workstations).
6. Peripheral equipment (scanners, printers, machines).
7. System software.
8. Control and security system.

Explanations: COFTS – The central office of Federal Tax Service;
FDC – Federal Data Center; AFTS – Administration of Federal Tax Service;
IIFNS – Interregional inspection of Federal Tax Service of the Russian Federation for a centralized data processing;
FNS – Inspectorate of Federal Tax Service;
Data Center – data processing center.

Besides, each data center has access to the Internet for communication with taxpayers and tax data publication on FNS sites. To improve the reliability all regional Data Centers, in addition to high-speed communication channels with FTSDC will be provided with a high-speed back-up channel.

For process control related to information technology in the Federal Tax Service a special structural unit has been set up called Information Technology Management. Functions of Information Technology Management are aimed at improving information and technical support activities of tax authorities, introduction of new information and telecommunication technologies and electronic services development. It envisages a number of tasks faced by the management, which are associated with organizational process of information technologies introduction in the administration and e-government infrastructure establishment. This infrastructure provides information and technological cooperation as an interagency, and between federal and regional executive authorities of the Russian Federation.

Issues of legal validity of electronic documents and recipients' identification fall within the scope of the e-government infrastructure. Another important area concerns information protection and electronic security in the Service Central Office, its local bodies and subordinate organizations. Mention should be made of such security arrangements as supervision of cryptographic information protection, access to operation with encryption techniques and algorithms, issuance and registration of key documentation, as well as information security control at all stages: creation, storage, processing, and transmission [1].

Improved management system will make a clear movement in the VAT chain from the producer to the end consumer, and thus eradicate "ephemeral" company schemes. Taxpayers will be faced with a new challenge of responsibility for their information accuracy and timely declarations submission to the tax office.

Another problem concerns a requirement to respond quickly to regulatory authorities' requests. The following elements form the basis of the new VAT administration mechanism:

– ACS software VAT 3;
– electronic data storage;
– on-the-spot control interregional inspectorate directly subordinate to Russia's Federal Tax Service, whose function is to identify inconsistencies in VAT declarations.

Information comes from taxpayers in form of records from purchases and sales ledgers and invoices registration as part of tax returns followed by tax inspectors identification of unproven deductions. Residues are considered unproven in the event that the taxpayer does not file a VAT return, or accounts do not reflect the relevant market information about the transactions.

5.3 New Technologies of Electronic VAT Administration of Russian Federation

Unified Data Center (Big Data) in Dubna (near Moscow) was opened on May 27, 2015.

Big Data technology consists of a series of approaches, tools and methods for handling huge volume of structured and unstructured data. This is a new solutions class developed in the late 2000s called Business Intelligence. Big Data's paradigm defines three main types of tasks:

- data storage and management with volume of hundreds of terabytes or petabytes which cannot be processed by conventional databases;
- organization of unstructured information consisting of text, images, video and other types of data;
- analysis and analytical reports generation to design predictive models [7].

BI technologies are designed to handle large volumes of unstructured data for business intelligence purposes. The BI main task is handling large amounts of data and simulation of various options' outcome for the decision-making activities. Business Intelligence Technology Series is designed to translate source data into a usable form. In the first place, this series includes parallel processing means for large-scale vaguely structured data, including this solution NoSQL, MapReduce algorithms category, the Hadoop project.

NoSQL is a term designating a number of approaches to database storage implementation, significantly different from the models used in conventional relational database data access by means of SQL.

MapReduce is a programming distributed computing model provided by Google that is used for parallel computing on very large, multiple petabytes data sets in computer clusters. Hadoop is a set of tools, libraries, and frameworks for programs development and running on clusters of hundreds or thousands of nodes, which is freely available. It was created as a result of the project Apache Software Foundation Fund.

"Apache Hadoop" software library is a framework that allows you to distribute data sets on computer clusters by using a simple programming model. It is designed to expand from single servers to thousands of machines. The library itself is intended for failure detection and processing at the application level without resorting to the hardware to ensure high data availability.

It is used for the implementation of search and contextual mechanisms of many overloaded websites including Yahoo and Facebook. It is considered to be one of the basic Big Data technologies. A lot of new projects and technologies that have been created within the framework of the Hadoop project later have become independent products.

It should be noted that FNS project is one of the examples of successful experience in implementing such projects on the emerging Big Data market in Russia. "Tinkoff Credit Systems" can be cited as another example of a company that uses Big Data technology [8].

Unified Data Center based on the application of these technologies for tax administration takes a few seconds to detect unscrupulous taxpayers who are evading VAT. Now you do not need to consolidate regional reports, they are automatically shipped to the federal file and stored on servers in Dubna. Unified Data Center enables to see the real picture online. These documents are stored for 5 years, and then they will be sent to an archive file with invoices stored there forever.

Companies are divided into risk groups indicated by different colors: green companies have a low risk level mark, companies with yellow and red indicators are high and highest risk sources. The number of "red" companies fell from 4% to 1%. Yellow companies account for about 50%. Big business is almost all "green". Corrupt officials also will not be able to hide from Big Data all-seeing eye, as the computer software automatically sends a signal to check performing agencies [8].

In the new architecture of the taxation system a large role is played by the cloud computing. The cloud computing model allows access to information and resources of one computer from any location connected to the network. The main function of cloud computing is to meet the needs of users in remote processing without intermediaries. The use of cloud computing in business processes began in 2006. "Amazon" company introduced the web services architecture that provides customers with access to remote computing processes.

6   The Effect of the Use of Administration Technologies

The new version of VAT automated control system demonstrated its first operation results: every tenth organization in Russia was found to have numerous inconsistencies in tax reporting. As planned by the tax authorities, the next step to apply Big Data technology will concern automatic generation of requests on discrepancies between the company's operations and its contractors [2].

The system identifies all gaps in the VAT payment chain, analyzes invoices tax declarations and reveals contradictions between taxpayers' invoices. The observed discrepancies serve a ground for tax audit performance.

According to the Tax Code, the seller is obliged to put the invoice to the buyer in transaction. The buyer can register the invoice in the purchase ledger. The seller, in his turn, registers the invoice in sales ledger. In the VAT return it is necessary to show the amount of tax payable, and the deduction calculated on the basis of purchase and sales ledgers. Since 2015 for audit it is necessary to include these documents into a declaration. This information is included in a declaration in form of separate application files, in the stipulated format. When companies do not provide clarifications for the revealed differences to tax authorities, they are refused VAT deduction reception. According to the Russian Federal Tax Service site, after the new tax system introduction they already processed 1.4 million VAT declarations in the 1st quarter 2015 and found errors in declarations of 46 million taxpayers. Discrepancies were identified in the automatic mode, thereafter requirements for clarification were sent to taxpayers. During one year the system has identified discrepancies in the documentation reports in 10% of Russian companies [3].

The first results did not take long to appear: in the period 2011–2014 revenue growth in real terms amounted to 116.8%, while the GDP did to 110%. In 2015, this trend has continued and real revenues growth rate amounted to 103.9%. According to the calculations of Russian Federal Tax Service additional revenue through improved tax administration amounted to a quarter of the total increase in tax revenues.

7   The Difficulties and Challenges to Solve

The first problem is the necessity to choice the operator. Representatives of medium and large businesses in Telecommunications and Mass Media field with a valid license can act as trusted FTS operators in Russia [2]:

1. The Federal Service for Supervision of Communications, Information Technology and Mass Communications are entered to provide telematics communication services;
2. The Federal Service for Technical and Export Control (FSTEC Russia) provide information technical protection;
    Federal Security Service (FSS of Russia) is given the right:
    - to provide data encryption;
    - to carry out activities for cryptographic devices dissemination;
    - to service cryptographic hardware.

Before signing a contract with the operator, taxpayers should check the operator's interface and information support for document exchange with contractors. The compatibility of the accounting program with the operator's system is also an essential issue as it will determine the cost of electronic document management in the organization. Currently organizations that use the "1C" program can send an electronic document with a single click. However, this is possible only under the following conditions:

1. Work with a certified operator who acts as an intermediary between buyers and sellers.
2. Application of "1C: Enterprise 8" program (SCP Buhkorp, Trade Management), including:
    - "Enterprise Accounting 8.0" (starting with version 2.0.35.5);
    - "Enterprise Accounting 8 CORP" (starting with version 2.0.35.5);
    - "Management of Manufacturing Enterprise 8.0" (starting with version 1.3.25.1);
    - "Integrated Automation 8" (starting with version 1.1.21.1).

This implies that the process of transition to electronic administration requires the use of automation in accounting firms management.

The second problem [2] concerns electronic document signatures. Exchange between encrypted documents guarantees confidentiality. Electronic digital signature (EDS) ensures signatory identification and transmitted documents integrity. Advanced electronic signature verification key that consists of a unique characters sequence is used to enhance protection. Certificate of electronic signature verification key is a document confirming the right to use the electronic signature verification key. The key can be both in paper and electronic form.

The third problem concerns difficulties faced by multi-branch companies that have to combine several databases into a single VAT report for shipment to the Federal Tax Service. Currently, not all organizations keep their records with appropriate software allowing to do everything automatically, thus without common mechanisms it is expensive in terms of time consumption and human resources.

The fourth problem concerns the question of whether taxpayers can make claims for any amounts of unpaid VAT or some limit should be set on these amounts. It is obvious that additional VAT charging in the amount of less than several tens of thousands is just not cost-effective.

8   Conclusion

The study has revealed all the typical trends for improving tax systems of various countries including e-filing, development of services for the taxpayer, integration of regional services, creating a single repository of data in digital form, control automation. The data collected gives an idea of the wide geographical range of the ongoing changes and of the common problems of tax administration in the world. The paper shows the dependence of the development of information technologies of functional elements in the tax systems and their improvement objectives and identifies the major software products for tax management purposes.

The main results of this study are as follows:

– consideration of the VAT importance for the Russian economy as an important source of revenues and an object of structurally complex processes of its calculation;
– economic analysis of the Russian practice of value added tax and its the specific shortcomings;
– a proved necessity of the modernization of the tax administration system, which has recently started in Russia;
– identification of the key areas of modernization of tax administration;
– consideration of the main technologies underlying the principles of the new system and the mechanism of ACS-3;
– description of the major changes in the architecture of the new administrative system;
– identification of the main problems of the new system.

The main task facing the government at the present stage is the creation of an effective monitoring system for the receipt of taxes. Control is the key function in tax administration and the efficiency of tax control depends primarily on the improvement of tax administration technologies.

What novelty does the new management system provide in order to improve the efficiency of tax administration? Automation of key operational and management processes has been carried out and process standards have been introduced. Inspections on the centralized data processing of data have been formed on the interregional level. In the context of modernization, automation during the desk audit Tax Service of Russia unified standard control relationships between indicators of taxpayers declared and received from external organizations have been developed. Tax Service has reported some positive changes that took place in 2015: reduction of revenue losses from VAT and a reduction of tax fraud and criminal schemes for refunds, increasing tax revenues and an increase in the flow rate of the tax revenue to the budget. Planned changes in the system of tax administration are not possible without further improvement of information systems, enhancing scientific and technological capabilities, the establishment of appropriate information technology to improve the efficiency of the tax administration system that provides full receipt of payments to the budgets of all levels.

Acknowledgments. Our thanks to ITMO University for the support.

References

1. Belyaev, A.I.: Modern information technologies in the work of the tax authorities. The Moscow Tax Institute. https://yandex.ru/search/?text=nalogi.ru%E2%80%BAranh%2F9%2Fsit.doc&lr=2&clid=2186620
2. Chesnokov, S.V: The introduction of electronic document management in Russian companies. Accountant and Law, N 1 (2015). http://base.consultant.ru/cons/cgi/online.cgi?req=doc;base=PBI;n=132117
3. Chief Accountant. http://www.glavbukh.ru/cnews
4. Garcia, A.A.: The immediate supply of information system. In: Self-service for Tax Administration. IOTA (2016). https://www.iota-tax.org/sites/default/files/pub/self_service/index.html
5. Jimenez, G., Mac an tSionnaigh, N., Kamenov, A.: Information technology for tax administration. In: USAID's Leadership in Public Financial Management. https://yandex.ru/search/?text=pdf.usaid.gov%E2%80%BApdf_docs%2Fpnaea485.pdf&lr=2&clid=2186620
6. Intra-European Organisation of Tax Administrations (IOTA). https://www.iota-tax.org/news/reforms-tax-system-republic-azerbaijan
7. Ipinform.ru. http://ipinform.ru/news/edinyj-centr
8. Kiseleva, I.: Pros and cons of the use of electronic document. Financial Newspaper. http://fingazeta.ru/discuss/50127/
9. Nice Finances. http://www.nicefinances.ru/ereads-766-1.html
10. Novitskaya, E.: Information technologies and their development in the field of taxation and the tax authorities on the transition of the AIS «Tax-3». Econ. Sci. Sci. Alm **7**(9), 160–163 (2015)
11. Role Based Workflow Modeling. IEEE Xplore Conference: IEEE International Conference on Systems, Man and Cybernetics, SMC 2006, vol. 6 (2006). doi:10.1109/ICSMC.2006.385072. https://www.researchgate.net/publication/4262935_Role_Based_Workflow_Modeling
12. PSYERA: Humanities legal portal. http://psyera.ru/6528/sushchnost-i-znachenie-nds
13. Savinova, T.: Development of information support systems of the tax authorities at the present stage. Sci. Soc. Ser. Finan. Credit **3**(18), 65–71 (2014)
14. Abay, S.T.: Assessment on the implementation of value-added tax (VAT) in Mekelle City Administration. Int. J. Sci. Res. (IJSR) **4**, 459–467 (2013). ISSN 2319–7064 (Online). Index Copernicus Value: 6.14. http://www.ijsr.net/
15. Strazdaite, A.: E-services for Taxpayers – Making Tax Complaince Obligations Simpler and Faster/Self-service for Tax Administration. IOTA (2016). https://www.iota-tax.org/sites/default/files/pub/self_service/index.html
16. Tax Administration 2015: Comparative Information on OECD and Other Advanced and Emerging Economies. doi:10.1787/tax_admin-2015-7-en. http://www.oecd.org/ctp/tax-administration-23077727.htm
17. Tax Tribune: Magazine of the Intra-European Organization of Tax Administrations, Issue 34 (2016) https://www.iota-tax.org/

18. Lutes, T.: Global trends in revenue administration. In: Meeting Economic Challenges and Tax System Modernization Goals. Forum on Tax Administration: Taxpayer Services Sub-group. Siem Reap: Asia Tax Forum, October 2010. https://yandex.ru/search/?text=tax.gov.kh %E2%80%BAatf%2Ffiles%2F1%20-%20Terence%20Lutes.pdf&lr=2&clid=2186620
19. The website of Accounting Center in St. Petersburg. http://www.spbbu.ru/actual/izmenenija-po-nds-v-2015-godu.html
20. The website nanalog.ru: Popularly about taxes and taxation. http://nanalog.ru/
21. The website of Research Computing Center of the Federal Tax Service. https://www.gnivc.ru/html/ais3.ppt
22. The website of the Federal Tax Service. https://www.nalog.ru/rn77/news/activities
23. Vinnichenko, T.: Information systems for tax service of Russia. Modern trends in education and science. In: Sat: Scientific Tr. Materials International Scientific-Practical Conference, Tambov, Part 13, 28 November 2014, pp. 23–24 (2014)

How Traditional Banks Should Work in Smart City

Marina Makarchenko[1(✉)], Sofiia Nerkararian[2(✉)], and Irina A. Shmeleva[3(✉)]

[1] Department of Production Management and Technology Transfer,
ITMO University, St. Petersburg, Russia
makarchenko68@mail.ru
[2] ITMO University, St. Petersburg, Russia
sofiianerkararyan@gmail.com
[3] Institute of Design and Urban Studies, ITMO University, St. Petersburg, Russia
i_a_shmeleva@corp.ifmo.ru

Abstract. Smart and sustainable cities use information and communication technologies to improve quality of life. Smart economy and digitalization of banking are the core issues of this trend. New technologies are profoundly changing the strategic context of the financial business and communication by changing customers' attitude and expectations, the nature of competition and business conduct. The progress of ICT services all over the world is different and is underdeveloped in some countries and continents. The paper will present insights from various studies and explore the future banking landscape. The behavior and financial needs of millennials will be examined. The arguments supporting the idea that digital transformation of banks is an imperative for survival and thriving in smart cities will be presented. The ICT transformation of Deutche Bank, Raiffisen Bank, Hana-Bank and Bank Group "Otkrities" will be analyzed. Recommendations for the Russian bank smart transformation will be discussed.

Keywords: Smart city · Digitization · Digital age · NFC (near field communication) · Biometric recognition · Mobile banking · Fintechs · Change process

1 Introduction

The concept of a smart city is a broad one: in urban planning and architecture it is a set of strategies aimed at optimization and innovation of public services, physical infrastructure of cities through the use of new communication technologies, mobility, environment and energy efficiency [6, 12]. According to the Group on Smart and Sustainable Cities "A smart and sustainable city is an innovative city that uses information and communication technologies (ICTs) and other means to improve quality of life, efficiency or urban operations and services, and competitiveness, while ensuring that it meets the needs of present and future generations with respect to economic, social, environmental as well as cultural aspects" [8]. As Staffans and Horelli (2014) indicate, there is an on-going debate between the followers of top-down technocratic approach adopted by multinational corporations, several governments and political decision makers all over the world and a bottom-up approach supported mainly by academics

© Springer International Publishing AG 2016
A.V. Chugunov et al. (Eds.): DTGS 2016, CCIS 674, pp. 123–134, 2016.
DOI: 10.1007/978-3-319-49700-6_13

and community with a "multidimensional vision of the smart city as a sustainable and livable community" [13]. As indicated by the authors, a smart cities agenda is a core issues now for the global ICT companies such as IBM and CISCO, for emerging economies of Asia and Latin America and for European Union as well. Smart Cities are promoted by the Europe 2020 strategy and through research funding. From a European perspective, the dimensions of smart cities are: Smart People, Smart Governance, Smart Mobility, Smart Environment, Smart Living and Smart Economy [13].

As HABITAT III report indicates [9], the rise of knowledge economy in North America and Europe is driven by new ICT services that gives the opportunities to e-Government, e-Governance and e-Participation. All around the world, knowledge and digital economy stimulated economic development in various aspects including banking and retail. The progress in ICT services in various parts of the world is different and in some countries and continents they are underdeveloped.

Economists argue that a city can be called smart, when investment in communications infrastructure ensure sustainable economic development, high quality of life and wise management of natural resources, while meeting the needs of citizens, enterprises and institutions. The concept of a smart city is based primarily on efficiency, which in turn is based on business management, integration of ICT and the active participation of citizens. This implies a new type of governance with genuine citizen involvement in public policy [11].

The case of Italian Trento Smart City strategy [15] also supports these arguments and indicates the list of stakeholders to be involved that along with Municipalities, Active citizens associations, Business companies, University research centers include Lending institutions and Banks.

Due to the US Financial Crisis and the Global Recession of 2008, the bank regulation has been tightened, so banks have been forced to change their business model having a significant amount of costs/revenue pressure. Achieving a whole new level of efficiency on the one hand and presenting new growth on the other was impossible without new trends in ICT in banking management. Today the level of banks digitalization is different in different countries [3]. Most banks in Russia today except several most advanced still use the models of 15–20 years ago that influence their competitive ability, resilience and flexibility. Today banks in Russia use the ICT and solutions adopted worldwide more than develop unique and client oriented solutions.

The demographic forecast [10] states that in 2020 along with the increasing urbanization, millennial generation cohort born after 1980 will constitute a half of the global work force. The millennial generation represents a new type of consumers, a tech-savvy citizen, that require a brand new customer experience, that demonstrated behavior and fundamental differences in the choice of products and services in ICT field.

This argument supports our hypothesis that banks digitalization will be one of the drivers of the transformation of the traditional city towards the smart city.

The trend for the banks to transform through the application of modern ICT is not currently covered in scientific literature. It could be found inside the analytical report of different banks such as Deutche Bank in Germany, FBA and Raiffeisen's Bank in Austria, Hana-Bank in South Korea, National Bank of India but it's difficult to come across such analytical report for Russian Banks.

The goal of our study was to systematize the analytical information on the trends and processes of innovative banking services in smart cities oriented towards the future generations. The data presented in this study has never been systematized and displayed before as a set of applied knowledge, this fact therefore makes this study innovative and represents a particular value to all banking industry that want to succeed in the future.

The results and recommendation based on this study could be used by the Russian banks especially by the Bank Group "Otkrytie" – the fourth private bank group in Russia oriented to be the leader of transformations on the market.

2 Smart Economy

2.1 Digitization Changes Economy

The present economic activity is becoming increasingly digital, having an effect at the macroeconomic scale. Digitization is changing the way we interact with each other and how we handle our personal data. Overall, the importance of ICT is growing in all business sectors. If companies fail to adapt to digital structural change today, they will be forced out of the market tomorrow. Technology changes the way people behave and interact in their everyday life. Information of all kind is easy to find as never before - from proprietary big data to social networks and public open data sources. Smart mobile devices make that information available instantly to billions of users around the world. However, it is not only the volume of information traffic that is rising, but also the number of internet users. Finally, it becomes increasingly important to learn how to use this data professionally and efficiently. Today the information represents a genuine economic good, while personal data in particular has an increasing economic value. The ethical aspects of using such data present an additional challenge.

The Deutsche Bank researchers consider structural change to be the core issue of digitalization that can be presented as a pattern of several steps:

The first step can be named the new Internet–based consumption. Along with it, technological progress generates new media usage and adaptation of new technologies to the daily life of consumers.

The second step can be considered as a replacement of the established ICT processes with the modern intelligent software solutions and algorithms.

The need in the third step appears when sales and profits are shrinking and traditional business models are threatened.

The next step indicates that competition is rising and new market players are growing their market share while traditional players shrink their presence. Then laggards introduce adjustment processes and cost-intensive reforms.

And finally, the last step is visible when the financial market players enter and establish themselves on the market and have their first profits [7].

According to Deutsche Bank analytics, two aspects of digital business evolution could be considered. The first one is an optimization opportunity. It can be understood as transformation, optimization and consolidation of existing resources. This approach can bring cost-reduction and increased agility.

The second aspect is a new business opportunity that is focused on reinvention through development of new services and business models valuable to the customer. This approach brings innovation and new revenues.

As this analysis shows, most banks and companies are focused only on the first aspect, which could not be considered a true digitalization. The true digitization is oriented towards changing the business approach as a whole, and, in particular, the relationship between customer value and company revenue [7].

2.2 New Type of Consumer

A new type of consumer is the main driver for digitization along with emerging technologies. The tech-savvy consumer is coming to the stage as a result of demographic change. Today European and North American consumers prefer to deal with socially responsible companies that care for the environment (e.g. those which use recyclable materials). At the same time they want to participate and even influence some business-processes of the companies. Some banks, for example, suggest on-line surveys to their clients' seeking their feedback on existing or potential products or ask their opinion on new credit card design.

The behavior and preferences of millennium generation will shape the future of banking, as well as the relationship between a bank and a customer. The following trends are defined responding to the demand by the millennials: mobile apps, fast payments (such as NFC –near field communication), transformed branches, paperless banking, confidentiality of personal data and use of secure systems (such as biometrics recognition that replaces passwords and PINs – personal identification number), user–friendly design and simplicity. Accenture study states that 94% of millennials are active users of online banking, 72% are active users of mobile banking, 39% would consider using a branchless digital bank, compared to just 16% for those clients over 55 years old [14].

Traditional branches with fixed opening hours are becoming less and less popular for all customers. They increasingly use their smart phones to pay for things, exchange opinions or look for recommendations from other users. They also execute routine banking transactions online, while visiting banks' branches less often than ever before [5].

According to Global Survey 2014 on mobility and the state of customer loyalty to banking customers in 18 of 22 conducted more than 50% of their banking interactions through digital channels. Mobile is the most used banking channel in 13 of 22 countries and accounts for 30% of all interactions worldwide. Mobile aps usage rose by 19% last year and online usage via computers dropped down 3% last year. More than half of customers used both digital and physical channels such as branches and call centers. Customers use several channels to research and buy banking products. In the US 47% of customers consulted their bank website, 37% applied for recommendations to the bank employees.

In 2015 Bain conducted global survey and asked 115,000 customers in different countries which banking channels they prefer, it turned out that mobile apps or online services prevailed over branch, ATM or phone experience [4].

3   Banks Going Digital: Exploring Challenges and Opportunities

Going digital in smart city bank is not an option but an imperative. The branch providing transactional services is not enough for smart city citizens – they want new products and services in digital form. While stepping out of their comfort zones on the way to multi-channel, client-centric and digital-centric models, banks will experience a number of challenges both from their internal and external environment.

3.1   Increased Competition and the Emergence of New Competitors

According to North America Consumer Digital Banking Survey, competitive landscape in banking today is far from what we saw twenty or ten years ago. "Banks with new value propositions (ethical, social, etc.) are providing alternatives to traditional banks' products and services as well as an engaging customer experience. Furthermore, banks will no longer fight for customers against other retail banks" [14].

The arrival of new entrants is favored by the regulatory changes that simplify the entrance to the banking industry. Combined with the digital revolution, this trend has created a fertile ground for innovation and creation of purely digital tech-savvy players, so called Fin Techs. According to study by Oracle, by 2020 Fin Techs will be a major threat for the banks worldwide; as social media networks (29%), telecoms companies (29%) and retailers (22%) are to become their serious competitors. Moreover, by 2020 new banks (57%) and alternative payment method providers (56%) will be a greater competitive threat to them than other traditional retail banks (40%) [3] (Fig. 1).

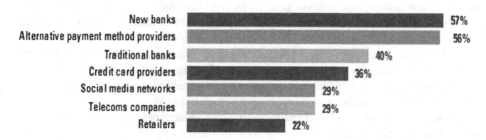

Fig. 1. Direct competitors by 2020 (2015) Banking is Changing… with or without Banks. Response to the Millennials/ A Research Report by Oracle Financial Services Global Business Unit (2015). http://oracledigitalbank.com/resources/pdf/DBOF_Industry_Research_Report.pdf

Companies like Square or PayPal are already providing customers with easy and secure payment or loan services. Entrants from other industries such as Amazon, Facebook or Aliexpress are leveraging their customer knowledge to create and deliver new value by combining financial and non-financial services. The rise of crowdfunding, peer-2-peer lending and other similar initiatives led by players such as eToro, Kickstarter, Zopa or Funding Circle kills the intermediation and addresses customers directly [2]. While these various entrants will not necessarily replace banks, they are becoming a serious concern for banking industry. They shift customer expectations, bring new products, business models, and advanced customer knowledge (e-commerce players or retailers). They also benefit from the absence of legacy systems, they are fully digital agile institutions with previously young employees and often young leaders. In their turn banks have unique advantages of their own, e.g. they have a more fundamental view of customer data as well as a solid experience in risk management [1]. In this light, a dialogue and partnership might be a better option than opposition and finally might result in a solution mutually beneficial for all market players.

3.2 New Customer Behavior and Expectations

As Digital Banking Survey shows "today's banking customers are looking for proximity, agility and speed from a financial service provider". The explanation comes from the statement that for the largest demographic cohort, born after 1980, instant communication, social networks, one-click purchases and 24-hour delivery is their natural environment and they prefer service that can provide all of this. [14].

Concerning the Bank services the expectations of this generation include anticipating their needs, not bombarding them with product offerings, no surprises in term of fees, personalized services on demand, transparent and simple products. Customers that are better informed compare offers across different platforms, including social media and financial aggregators [3].

The children of millennials will be even more agile with technology and will learn using smartphones before they start school.

The North American Consumer Digital Banking Survey shows that there are, however two services that are on top of customers wish list today: payments via mobile devices and real-time view across channels. Beyond this, there are other desired digital initiatives, such as digital advisory services, real-time spend analytics, location-driven services and comparison services. The customers want to know how much money they spent this month, how can they optimize spending and investments, what offers are available in their vicinity right now? Accenture study states that 67% of millennials want help in managing their finances and are interested in their bank to be more proactive, compared with 31% of clients who are over 55 years old [14].

These advisory services would provide an added value, creating a customer-centric bank interaction model. It is evident that bank in a smart city cannot be just a provider of financial products; it should be a "universe unit" serving also as an advisor, a value aggregator and an access facilitator.

3.3 Failure to Commit to Digitization

Despite recognizing the importance of digitization, the banking market is lagging behind especially in financial technologies and when it comes to real-time services. According to the Oracle digital study, market lag, location driven services and real-time analytics are the most problematic areas that stop them from being attractive for customer. The results of the survey based on two main questions: "Thinking about digitized customer engagement, how important would you say each of the following will be in order to be a successful bank in five years' time?" and "What is your organization's current status in relation to each of the following developments?" are presented in a Table 1.

Table 1. Digitized customer engagement. Banking is changing … with or without the banks. Response to the millennials. Financial services, (2015) http://oracledigitalbank.com/resources/pdf/DBOF_Industry_Research_Report.pdf

	Important	**Current** capability	Market lag
Mobile device payments	94%	44%	-50%
Market Lag	92%	24%	
Real-time analytics	90%	30%	-60%
Digital advisory service	83%	28%	-55%
Location-driven services	82%	19%	-63%
Offers via social media	78%	34%	-44%
Comparison services based on financial profile	76%	28%	-48%
Social media account management	72%	14%	-58%
Gamification	72%	15%	-57%
Digital personal assistant	67%	12%	-55%

Furthermore, within the challenge of overcoming legacy systems, nearly all banks (88%) see it as a barrier against multichannel digitization. Among other serious barriers are high cost of implementation and lack of appropriate technology in the organization (Fig. 2).

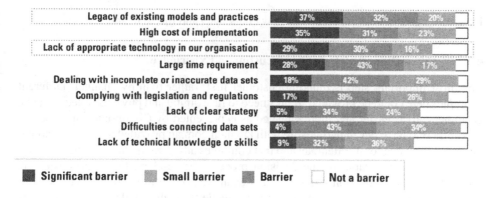

Fig. 2. Barriers to omni-channel customer engagement Banking is Changing… with or without Banks. Response to the Millennials/ A Research Report by Oracle Financial Services Global Business Unit (2015). http://oracledigitalbank.com/resources/pdf/DBOF_Industry_Research_Report.pdf

Market lag is derived from the difference between the banks current capability in delivering a variety of services and the perceived importance in meeting customer demand for these capabilities. One of the main reasons why banks are lagging is because currently they have a bank-centric relationship with their customer. It is crucial that they start now to gain better knowledge of their customers: how they spend their money, where they go on holiday, and what car do they drive and which is the closest restaurant to their residence. However, having the data is not enough. To make the data really work banks not only need to change fundamentally their underlying operation processes but introduce a cultural change. The role of the latter cannot be underestimated. Employees and CEOs should become real ambassadors of digitalization, shift their mindset to forward-thinking, more curious, open to risk- and- learn approach.

3.4   Smart Early Warning Solutions Against NPAs

Speaking about digitization we must also address the issues of non- performing assets (NPAs).

Having integrated data from different channels, a bank can provide better credit rating to improve NPAs. The implementation of so-called early warning solutions (EWS) can definitely change the way and the speed of loan classification. The EWS not only can handle data in less time, but are also capable of timely signaling a change in consumer preferences and links.

Integrated with a bank's customer management systems and enabled through the bank's database and analytics solutions the robot will perform qualitative and quantitative analysis and define a risk profile. This technology will be particularly valuable in the emerging markets where the share of NPAs is higher.

4   Discussion

How can banks evolve to meet these new challenges and thrive in smart city?

4.1   Create a Differentiated Digital Customer-Experience

The most important step is thinking customer first, rather than by channel. Different examples here could be provided. Banks need to fuse digital and physical assets to make customers' lives easier and more engaged as is presented by Commonwealth Bank of Australia (CBA). CBA in partnership with Domain.com.au provided an exciting home-buying experience for its client: an app that combines advisory service, mortgage application online and a rapid online decision process with e-alerts that keep customers updated on their application status. Another example is the transfer funds to the vendor and mortgage balance management that is available through mobile, online and ATM channel. The Hana Bank in South Korea offers the full-service bank in a smartphone, the so called Hana N mobile platform, which combines an integrated money management and monitoring system working entirely online, NFC payments technology in different stores, the location-based offers and the ability to borrow for larger purchases while in the store. These solutions require cooperation of IT, marketing, product groups, along with the CEO's sponsorship [4].

Building a great customer journey requires commitment and collaboration of all employees and the CEO's sponsorship: it means rethinking the traditional banking with clients in mind. But customers trust will come as a reward. To trust their banks customers need to feel that banks are acting in their interests – common banking practices such as deposit rates that reset after a certain time go against this, while the ability to design your own mortgage or investment is in line with this thinking. Banks will benefit significantly if they take a leadership role also in educating customers making it a part of sales process.

4.2 Build an Omnichannel Distribution

To succeed in "anything, anytime, anywhere" automated formats are essential. Innovations and investments in smart banking technologies should be made now to make it more attractive for customers tomorrow. The mobile experience is becoming a crucial aspect of digital strategy that banks must address. Just to roll out mobile apps is not enough; there is a need of a better coordination across channels and seamless channel connection.

The branch network must undergo a substantial change. New branch formats such as self-service kiosks or the full-service flagship stores that incorporate digital technologies should replace traditional branches. "Banks might consider cutting the number of branch tellers in favor of relationship adviser roles. As technology develops, smart ATMs, in-branch tablets, video teller machines could potentially replace tellers" [5]. Raiffeisen's flagship branch in Zurich, for example, offers a robotic retrieval system for a 24 h access to safe-deposit boxes, while Intesa Sangallo have launched Superflash branches across Italy targeting customers aged 18 to 35, and rather than a bank it looks like a lounge café that hosts special events and attracts young public with its contemporary design, a spacious self-service area, large tables with video terminal for financial consultations, video walls, instead of posters, offering documentaries and advertising. State bank of India (SBI) has launched two types of branches: In Touch and In Touch Lite: where a visitors can open an account through the use of machines and get a personalized debit card (with his name and photograph on it) in under 12 min. Together with this service a client can find a "gamification" table to plan his investments and expenses, a "dream wall" for instant loans approval as well as a remote advisor through video conferencing.

For customer loyalty purposes, when designing their branches, oriented for the future banks apply for the findings of behavioral science and use modeling techniques, geodemographic data and geomapping software to improve decisions about building their networks [5].

4.3 Overhaul the Technology Platform

The experts mostly state that a corresponding IT transformation must support a business transformation. Today some services might be available online and through mobile, but for some services in some countries customers still have to go to a branch. According to the experts overview adding digital just as a channel to an existing legacy infrastructure will be not sustainable in the future. A few core characteristics of IT infrastructure transformation are needed, including customer communication real-time processing engine, risk management and cyber security solutions. The innovations can include storage technologies, joined-up customer data systems, data analytics, modern core systems, technology that supports one-and-done processes. According to Bain &

Company experts "building new infrastructure is expensive but its prioritization will establish a robust technical foundation for digitalization" [5].

4.4 Fund the Transformation

Apparently, all market players understand the importance of investments in digitization, but often funding represents a major challenge to management. Not all banks have a dedicated budget for a digital change, and many do not understand the full cost of it. According to Bain & Company Customers Digital Report banks use different strategies for digital transformation. Some of them as freeing up funds by simplifying their products, processes, organization structure and systems or limiting themselves by introducing separate digital projects and pilots do not directly accelerate the digital transformation. As consultants suggest in order to accomplish the change over a number of years in the future the importance of investing cannot be underestimated or postponed [5].

4.5 Organize to Speed up Innovation and Change

Along with investments in technology investments in human capital are needed. There is a growing talent mismatch as companies are trying to both change personnel behavior and find new talents in areas that cannot be automated. Such areas include digital skills like those of artificial-intelligence programmers or data scientists, digital marketers and strategists who can think creatively about new business designs. And finally, a new type of CEO is required, the one who forges the digital transformation internally and externally and ensures that the whole organization is ready to digest new technologies, that IT and marketing can deliver solutions to clients, and that a brand new and the best practices are in place.

An culture of openness should be promoted. Training and internal communication must involve everyone, including departments not directly impacted by digital.

The bank overcoming digital transformation needs to follow common innovation requirements that need to be adopted by senior management and at all levels of employees and partners and include freedom to test new ideas and freedom of sharing feedback. "Common innovation requirements, such as freedom to test new ideas and tolerance of failure must be adopted and sponsored by senior management, as well as a practice of sharing feedback among employees of all level and partners [4]".

Furthermore, remuneration approach also needs to be changed. Currently, compensation for branch managers depends heavily on his/her sales; with the development of branchless and fully digitals services that approach creates a conflict in the organization.

Finally, the relatively slow culture of traditional banks needs an accelerant to keep pace with digital innovations. Forward-looking banks may also benefit from partnering with digital companies and start-ups or create their own R&D innovation centers, separated from the core business, to do research on innovations.

5 Conclusion

Banking will change faster over the next years than in the most recent decades. Russian banks will need to follow the world trend for smart technologies not to be outsiders. The perspectives of the smart banking in Russia could be seen in the case of the bank Group "Otkrytie" that is one of the biggest private banking group that includes three Banks and have a fourth position among the banking groups of the Russian Federation. Reliability of this Banking Group is proved by the International Rating Agencies as Standart & Poors and Moody. This banking group is one of the most advanced for the optimization of the bank managing processes based on IC Technologies. We can apply the results of our analysis to this banking group organizing them in 3 units: (1) already used in the bank group "Otkrytie"; (2) planned to be implemented; (3) being in a "waiting list".

The first unit includes two decisions. The first one is the design of the own virtual bank platform or attracting the partner with already developed platform. The "Otkrytie" bank group made its decision to invite the partner with the well developed platform and the client data base.

The second decision concerned the development of the mobile banking and education for their clients. The updates of this application as usual give the client new opportunities and are accompanied by the new option with customer education and help service.

The second unit (planned to be implemented) consists of two recommendations: first, to change format for self-service system through the office-kiosk. According to this solution the number of operation cashiers will be replaced by the increased number of consultants ready to help clients in multifunctional one window service; second – to organize the "reconstruction fund" for all divisions' integration.

The third unit (being in a waiting list) includes two recommendations: implementation of the biometrical identification that will give the competitive advantage for security reasons to the bank. And the last solution could be the permanent monitoring of the geodemographic data (Big Data) that will support the decisions for opening the new bank offices or the new bank machines launches.

There is no other way of banking service modernization in a smart city as extinction of the ordinary branches and replacing them by apps for mobile devices, designing of the core database centers enabling banks to create attractive and useful financial services attractive to millennials and future generation: from online payment solutions and advisory services to deposit-taking through online banking and other modern financial software.

References

1. Abdou, H., English, J., Adewunmi, P.: An investigation of risk management practices in electronic banking: the case of the UK banks. Banks Bank Syst. **9**(3) (2014). http://eprints.hud.ac.uk/21250/
2. Andrieux, D.: Banking in the digital age. Sopra banking software (2013) http://www.soprabanking.com/docs/librariesprovider17/sopra-bankingsoftware/white-paper—banking-in-the-digital-age.pdf?sfvrsn=0

3. Banking is Changing… with or without Banks. Response to the Millennials/ A Research Report by Oracle Financial Services Global Business Unit (2015). http://oracledigitalbank.com/resources/pdf/DBOF_Industry_Research_Report.pdf

4. Customer Behavior and Loyalty in Retail Banking (2015). http://www.bain.com/bank-loyalty-interactive/

5. Customer Loyalty in Retail Banking: Global Edition, December 2014. http://www.bain.com/publications/articles/customer-loyalty-in-retail-banking-2014-global.aspx

6. Demitri, M.: Smart city: smart cities, digital and inclusive. But what are they really? http://www.marcodemitri.it/smart-city-citta-intelligenti/

7. Fintech – the digital (r)evolution in the financial sector. Current issue Digital economy and structural changes. Deutsche Bank (2014). https://www.dbresearch.com/PROD/DBR_INTERNET_ENPROD/PROD0000000000345837.pdf

8. Focus Group on Smart Sustainable Cities. http://www.itu.int/en/ITU-T/focusgroups/ssc/Pages/default.aspx

9. Habitat III Regional Report on Housing and Urban Development for the UNECE Region Towards a City-Focused People-Oriented and Integrated Approach to the New Urban Agenda. http://www.unece.org/fileadmin/DAM/hlm/projects/HIII_Regional_Report/HABITAT_111_Regional_Report_for_UNECE_Region_-_draft_8.0_-_14_march.pdf

10. Millennials at Work: Reshaping the Workplace. http://www.pwc.com/m1/en/services/consulting/documents/millennials-at-work.pdf

11. Seisdedos, G.: The road to smart city in bit. In: Monografico, vol. 188, pp. 35–37 (2002). http://www.coit.es/publicaciones/bit/bit188/monograficoseisdedos.pdf

12. Smart cities for sustainable development. FUB. http://www.fub.it/node/2218

13. Staffans, A., Horelli, L.: Expanded urban planning as a vehicle for understanding and shaping smart, liveable cities. J. Community Inform. **10**(3) (2014). http://ci-journal.net/index.php/ciej/about

14. The Digital Disruption in Banking, 2014 North America Consumer Digital Banking Survey. https://www.accenture.com/us-en/~/media/Accenture/Conversion-Assets/DotCom/Documents/Global/PDF/Industries_5/Accenture-2014-NAConsumer-Digital-Banking-Survey.pdf

15. The IEEE Smart Cities Initiative. http://smartcities.ieee.org/core-cities.html

The Comparison of Governmental and Non-governmental E-Participation Tools Functioning at a City-Level in Russia

Lyudmila Vidiasova[✉] and Ekaterina Mikhaylova

ITMO University, Saint Petersburg, Russia
bershadskaya.lyudmila@gmail.com,
ek.mikhailova@mail.ru

Abstract. The paper examines different types of e-participation tools functioning in Russia. This research presents a part of a complex scientific sociological project focused on determination of the critical factors which influence the e-participation development in Russia. This paper reflects the results of a comparative study of e-participation portals functioning with a special attention to its nature: government and non-government.

The authors made an attempt to find the effectiveness of Saint Petersburg portals' work with the use of an automated information system. The research hypothesis stated that individuals and their groups could be more productive in e-participation tools development.

The research results showed the difference in activities on each portal as well as an expected fate of e-petitions. The research hypothesis was partly confirmed. The first practice of citizens' electronic collaboration was linked with an initiative platform "Beautiful Saint Petersburg". At the same time a governmental portal "Our Petersburg" also demonstrated a high-level of citizens' interest and involvement. The research also showed comparatively common citizens' activity in different city districts.

The study revealed that Saint Petersburg example is an illustration of authorities' orientation to the citizens' needs. The development of e-participation platforms of both types had found a positive feedback from the citizens from the very beginning of its operation.

Keywords: E-participation · E-democracy · Comparative analysis · Institutional functions

1 Introduction

In the last 14 years a sustainable growth of positive assessments of the authorities in the Russian citizens has been detected. For instance, the results of sociological surveys in Russia showed that positive assessment has been highly increased in relation to the President (from 54% in 2001 to 71% now), the Government (from 31% to 49%) the State Duma (from 12% to 28%), Army (44% in 2001 and 55% today) and the Church (47% in 2001, 48% -now) [4].

© Springer International Publishing AG 2016
A.V. Chugunov et al. (Eds.): DTGS 2016, CCIS 674, pp. 135–144, 2016.
DOI: 10.1007/978-3-319-49700-6_14

E-participation technologies have been actively developed over the last decade in Russia. According to some experts' estimates, the scale of electronic platforms and services offer is much higher than the demand for them (even taking into account that such tools promise considerable benefits from their use like saving time, money, extra channels of communication with citizens). The practice of those countries that have already actively used e-participation tools (Estonia, Singapore, United Kingdom, and others) shows the efficiency and effectiveness of their application.

The social contract between government and society presupposes the quite clear procedures and methods of cooperation. In today's society there are some dynamic imbalances often associated with high citizens' expectations from the state. In situations when these expectations are not met, the citizens express a negative evaluation in relation to the authorities' actions. In such situation e-participation tool could improve the situation to adjust their estimates and expectations to the decision-makers.

This research presents a part of a complex scientific sociological project focused on determination of the critical factors which influence on the e-participation development in Russia. This paper reflects the results of a comparative study of e-participation portals functioning with a special attention to its nature: governmental and non-governmental. This orientation was determined by the research hypothesis about the influence on governmental/non-governmental form of the tool on citizens' attitudes and willingness to use such resources.

2   State of the Art

The world research practice counts a significant number of different research projects focused on e-participation. We can state that e-participation phenomenon has been studied by separating into specific components.

For instance, e-participation channels have been distinguished by S. Alathur and colleagues [2] as the following: ICT development to unite citizens and create online education communities; ICT use for group conversations and discussions; ICT use to attract supporters and/or voters; social media for voting and polls; economic forums and e-business; knowledge sharing platforms; and networks as monitoring systems.

A classic study by Macintosh and Whyte towards an evaluation framework for eParticipation [9] tested the applicability of methods measuring democratic (representation, engagement, transparency, conflict and consensus, political equality, community control), project (engaging with wider audience, obtaining better informed opinion, enabling more in-depth consultation, cost effective analysis of contribution, providing feedback to citizens), and socio-technical (social, acceptability, usefulness, usability) criteria. A case study of eParticipation evaluation for four local authorities, semi-structured interview, phone interview, observation, project documentation analysis, web-server analysis made the base for research analysis. This research underlined the importance of multi-method approach, and the complexity domain needed to be developed.

E-participation categories (e-participation activities, e-participation actors, e-participation effects, contextual factors and e-participation evaluation) have been identified by R. Medaglia through the publication analysis [10].

The detection of e-participation level through institutional and technological determinants has been developed in the works of Jho and Song [6]. This study revealed a direct correlation between technology (online population) and e-participation. The democracy level also showed a positive impact on e-participation, technology played a decisive role while the variable of political institutions was rejected statistically.

Evaluating websites from a public value perspective in Turkey [7] assessed public value created through participation online using the standard criteria (content, usability, quality), and public value indicators (accessibility, citizen engagement, transparency, responsiveness, dialog, balancing of interests). The researchers noticed the fact that the most websites had a high rate according to standard criteria and the low rate for the public value development.

The study of e-participation in Germany by Schroetera and colleagues [15] tested the value of public participation by analyzing inclusiveness, information exchange and learning, and the influence on political decision. Semi-structured interviews, qualitative research, document analysis were put into research practice. The study revealed eight dimensions of participation process: expectancy, transparency, acceptance, fairness, effectiveness, and efficiency, own impact, satisfaction.

However the attempts of creating a framework for measurement in this field have not been fully described. The UN developed a unified methodology for an e-participation index, including assessment of e-information, e-consultation and e-decision-making [16]. This index is used now for cross-countries assessment in e-participation development. Some researchers has been concentrated on information aspect of transparency and accountability of websites and tools [12], the other referred to participation in general and different methods of participation [14, 17]. We could found that evaluations of e-participation were rare [5, 8, 18] and emerging frameworks were inconsistent [1].

Referring to the practical life, where people currently participate in decision-making of a municipal competency, the researchers underlines the need to study e-participation at the local level [3, 13]. In this research work the authors tried to make a contribution in the scientific field regarding e-participation development at the local level.

3   Research Methodology

The research methodology was based on neoinstitutional approach [11] assuming an important role of non-government structures in the social order establishment. The research hypothesis stated that individuals and their groups could be more productive in e-participation tools development, and they are able to organize the community in the field of the common needs and interests and solve the arising issues. That's way the authors selected two types of e-participation tools for the analysis: the governmental and non-governmental ones.

3.1 Research Objects

We have determined Saint Petersburg as an example of a city level analysis and found the illustration to governmental and non-governmental e-participation practices.

The 'Beautiful Petersburg' (http://xn–80accfiasjf8cghbfut2k.xn–p1ai/about) – was created in 2012 by St. Petersburg volunteers with the purpose to improve the city. This portal was selected as an example of non-governmental e-participation tool. This portal gives an opportunity to publish a complaint, to create an account, to select a category and subcategory, to describe the problem and propose a solution. The site has a link to similar sites in other regions (Cherepovets, Moscow, Nizhny Tagil, Vologda, Leningrad, Irkutsk region, and so on).

The "Our Petersburg" (http://gorod.gov.spb.ru) was developed in 2014 under the initiative of St. Petersburg Governor to create conditions for an effective dialogue between citizens and authorities. On the portal each user can get information about the objects of urban infrastructure, report about urban problems and monitor the progress of its' decision. The mechanism of publication is quite simple – it's enough to create the complaint and describe a problem. The availability of the photos "before" and "after" solutions is a distinctive feature of the portal.

3.2 Automated Monitoring System

For the research purposes an automated monitoring system for e-participation portal evaluation has been developed at ITMO University. The monitoring system was designed to collect information on the dynamics of voting on e-participation portals This data was used for the further analysis, filtering, navigation and display in order to monitor the changes in the intensity of voting on different topics and categories.

Various methods of data collection from e-participation portals are applied in the monitoring system. The first way - is to use the API (application programming interface) of the site to obtain information, and the second - is the use data parsing of the source code (Fig. 1).

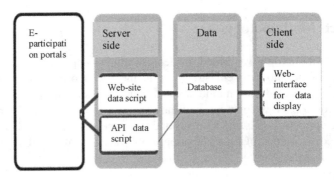

Fig. 1. Architecture of the monitoring system for e-participation portals' evaluation

Currently the system is connected to the following portals: "Russian public initiative", "Beautiful Petersburg" and "Our St. Petersburg."

3.3 Indicators for Analysis

During the research we have measured the following indicators on a governmental and a non-governmental portal in accordance with neo-institutional focus:

- formal and non-formal rules of interaction,
- dynamics of petition publication,
- representation of Saint Petersburg districts,
- status requests of citizens' treatments,
- solution of the problems and satisfaction.

Using these indicators allowed finding the evidences for proving governmental and non-governmental influence on e-participation development.

4 Findings

Beautiful St. Petersburg was developed with an aim to make the city more comfortable and convenient for people's lives. It was a volunteer movement of active individuals by its nature. The objective of the movement is quite simple: to teach people simple and effective ways to impact on the quality of the urban environment. The portals' activity is addressed to beautification, roads, housing and communal services. Our Petersburg portal was developed 2 years later and appeared as an illustration to the common governmental policy on openness and citizens' involvement.

The regulatory framework that supports the work of both resources is a federal law 02.05.2006 N 59- "On the order of consideration of citizens' applications in the Russian Federation', which obliges civil servants to consider appeals and give an answer within 30 days. So, both resources have a common framework for G2C collaboration. At the same time Our Petersburg pretends to look wider than the official framework claims in the filed of a time-period needed for the problem solution. For instance, the possible faster ways of assessing the claim is declared on the web-portal.

The authors analyzed the dynamics and status of citizens' requests on the platforms. According to a comparative character of the study the researchers looked on data separated by districts and per months of the year, and figured out how each platform affected on problem solving and satisfaction of applicants. We took into consideration a one-year period, representing the 2015 year.

During the studied period the number of applications on "Our Petersburg" was a little bit higher and reached 62 thousand. "Beautiful St. Petersburg", in opposite, collected almost 53 thousand treatments.

Saint Petersburg is a big megapolis divided into 18 districts. The charts below show the distribution of citizens' requests by city district. Kalininskiy, Centralniy, Primorskiy, Vyborgskiy, Nevskiy and Krasnoselsky districts became the leaders on the number of requests on the platform "Beautiful Petersburg" in 2015 (Fig. 2).

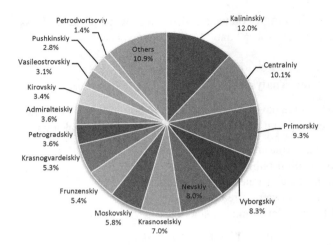

Fig. 2. A number of requests by city district on "Beautiful Petersburg" platform

Petrodvortsoviy, Nevskiy, Centralniy, Admiralteyskiy and Kalininskiy districts are among the leaders on the platform "Our Petersburg" in 2015 (Fig. 3). Thus, on both platforms citizens of the Kalininskiy, Centralniy and Nevsky districts were the most active. Moskovskiy and Frunzenskiy districts showed relatively closed values on both portals. It was detected that citizens from Petrodvorets most actively used "Our Petersburg", but "Beautiful Petersburg" was not quite popular among them.

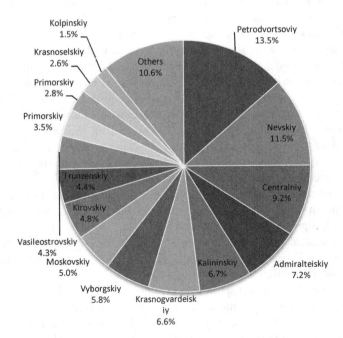

Fig. 3. A number of requests by city district on "Our Petersburg" platform

The findings lead to the conclusion that the most active citizens in 2015 represented the three districts of the city: Kalininskiy, Centralniy and Nevsky. The maximum activity on the sites in terms of the period is significantly different: the second quarter of 2015 for "Beautiful Petersburg" and the end of the year for "Our Petersburg".

Based on an analysis of quite different (in the classification of both platforms) problems in requests, we could assume that "Beautiful Petersburg" users were concentrated mostly on the problems with parking in wrong places, roads (such as holes in the road) – it is about 28,5% of applications, and littered areas and garbage – almost 17% of requests. Unfortunately, the automated system didn't not allow building visual graphs of all subjects queries on the platform, "Beautiful Petersburg", and the authors were manually analyzed subjects.

At the same time, the most popular problems reflected in requests on "Our Petersburg" were about territory landscaping (56,1%), but problems about the renovation of different objects is no so popular as it was on "Beautiful Petersburg". Thus, topics of citizens' treatments were associated mostly with landscaping and infrastructure of the city, and applicants were particularly interested in receiving feedback from the authorities and solving problems in this field.

The monthly activity analytics showed the peak of number of application on "Beautiful Petersburg" in March 2015, and on "Our Petersburg" - December 2015. These data clearly presented in the tables below (Tables 1 and 2).

Table 1. The distribution of treatments' status at "Our Petersburg", absolute values, by month

Status/month	Under consideration	Response received	Satisfied
01.2015	0	132	198
02.2015	0	228	499
03.2015	199	524	984
04.2015	222	1020	1218
05.2015	285	958	1303
06.2015	559	1123	1853
07.2015	468	1049	2045
08.2015	466	885	2567
09.2015	478	1615	2232
10.2015	660	1462	2657
11.2015	1655	1665	2675
12.2015	1687	2682	3561

It is important to compare the distribution of the received status requests. In particular, the status of request "response received" is significantly different on the considered sources: on "Our Petersburg" 29.9% of the requests belonged to this category, but on the platform "Beautiful Petersburg" it is only 9.2% of the total number of requests.

Also it is relevant to compare the proportion of requests that received the status "problem solved" and "problem is partially solved" on "Beautiful Petersburg" and the status "satisfied" on "Our Petersburg". Thus, 8.8% of requests with problems on

Table 2. The distribution of treatments' status at "Beautiful Petersburg", absolute values, by month.

Status/month	Not sent	Sent	Rejected	Solved	Partially solved
01.2015	152	1599	138	248	49
02.2015	173	2201	150	286	69
03.2015	458	5033	330	519	113
04.2015	441	4316	279	437	76
05.2015	515	3932	272	350	59
06.2015	755	2959	190	301	64
07.2015	345	3194	216	302	62
08.2015	309	2960	194	249	50
09.2015	374	3480	184	194	31
10.2015	392	3046	111	158	39
11.2015	350	3151	159	143	26
12.2015	308	2332	131	99	0

"Beautiful Petersburg" in 2015 had the status of solved or partially solved problems. At the same time, the proportion of status "satisfied" on platform "Our Petersburg" significantly higher - 47.5%.

It should be underlined that a satisfaction criterion on the sites is rather subjective, due to the fact that a citizen should prove his personal satisfaction by posting it in a special message on the portal. At the same time this option is not compulsory, and the citizens' not often pay such attention to publish their gratitude. However the issue could be solved and the citizen could be satisfied without posting it on a web-site. So, we can conclude that this option could be a filter for a feedback from citizens but doesn't reflect a level of proposed solutions.

The study citizens' treatments statuses gave an indication of the effectiveness of problem-solving depending on the platform. The study revealed that the proportion of requests that received a response on "Our Petersburg" was more than 3 times higher than on "Beautiful Petersburg" in 2015.

The same trend was observed with the status of problem-solving: the proportion of satisfied requests on "Our Petersburg" was almost half of all received issues. At the time, less than 10% of the problems derived from requests on the site "Beautiful Petersburg" were solved or partially solved. From the standpoint of requests' subject matter, the study revealed that the target audience of the platform "Our Petersburg" was more interested in questions of land improvement, while, on the platform "Beautiful Petersburg" city residents sent most queries containing requests for repair or beautification.

5   Conclusions

The research revealed that e-participation tools have been actively used by the citizens of Saint Petersburg. The research hypothesis was partly confirmed. The first practice of citizens' electronic collaboration was linked with an initiative platform "Beautiful Saint

Petersburg". A group of activists managed to rally citizens around the urban environment and to achieve its improvement.

At the same time a governmental portal, created as "a fashion trend" of government's openness, also demonstrated a high-level of citizens' interest and involvement. This fact brings us to the idea that the citizens were not absolutely satisfied with the existed work of "Beautiful Saint Petersburg" at the moment of a governmental web-site creation. That could be a reason for giving a preference to a governmental e-participation tool in 2015.

The research showed comparatively common citizens' activity in different city districts. Traditionally, the oldest districts (like Centralniy and Nevsky) received a lot of attention on the both portals. These areas often suffer from the roofs' floods in winter, and the buildings in such districts need the restoration. In addition, spatial planning doesn't still solve the problem of parking at these locations. In this way the residents are trying to use all channels of communication with the authorities to solve the urgent problems.

The study revealed that Saint Petersburg example is an illustration of authorities' adjustment to the needs of citizens. In particular, the establishment of government e-participation platforms is perceived by citizens as effective tools for the openness policy implementation. From this regards, we can talk about a transformation of public institutions' roles and functions according to the needs of civil society.

In such situations, when the government cannot stay indifferent to the citizens' treatments, it is necessary to analyze and predict changes in these tools in subsequent periods. In our view the most promising areas for further research are the following:

- the development of e-participation tools classification;
- identification of factors affecting the development of each tool;
- making forecasts about reaching the solution by different types of petitions, treatments and application.

The authors are going to continue the research work in this direction and develop the monitoring system in accordance with research tasks.

Acknowledgements. This work was conducted with support of the Grant of the President of the Russian Federation to young scientists №MK-5953.2016.6 "The research of e-participation tools development factors in Russian Federation".

References

1. Aichholzer, G., Allhutter, D.: Evaluation perspectives and key criteria in eParticipation. In: Proceedings of 6th Eastern European eGovernment Days, 23–25 April 2008, Prague, Oesterreichische Computer Gesellschaft (2008)
2. Alathur, S., Vigneswara, I., Gupta, M.P.: Citizen empowerment and participation in e-democracy: Indian context. In: Proceedings of the 5th International Conference on Theory and Practice of Electronic Governance, pp. 11–19 (2011)

3. Brody, S.D., Zahran, S., Grover, H., Vedliz, A.: A spatial analysis of local climate change policy in the United States: risks, stress, and opportunity. Landscape Urban Plan **87**(1), 33–41 (2008)
4. Citizens trust to social institutions in Russia, Levada-Center research (2015). http://izvestia.ru/news/592638
5. Janssen, D., Kies, R.: Online forums and deliberative democracy. Acta Polit. **40**, 317–335 (2005)
6. Jho, W., Song, K.: Institutional and technological determinants of civil e-Participation: solo or duet? Gov. Inf. Q. **32**, 488–495 (2015)
7. Karkin, N., Janssen, M.: Evaluating websites from a public value perspective: a review of Turkish local government websites. Int. J. Inf. Manag. **34**, 351–363 (2014)
8. Kubicek, H., Lippa, B., Westholm, H.: Medienmix in der lokalen Demokratie. Die Integration von Online-Elementen in Verfahren der Bürgerbeteiligung, Final report to the HansBöckler-Foundation, Bremen (2007). http://www.ifib.de/projektedetail.html?id_projekt=135&detail=Medienmix%20in%20der%20lokalen%20Demokratie
9. Macintosh, A., Whyte, A.: Towards an evaluation framework for eParticipation. Transf. Gov. People Process Policy **2**(1), 16–30 (2008)
10. Medaglia, R.: eParticipation research: moving characterization forward (2006–2011). Gov. Inf. Q. **29**, 346–360 (2012)
11. Nort, D.: Institutions, Institutional Change, and Economic Performance. Cambridge University Press, Cambridge (1990)
12. Pina, V., Torres, L., Royo, S.: Are ICTs improving transparency and accountability in the EU regional and local governments? an empirical study. Public Adm. **85**(2), 449–472 (2007)
13. Portney, K.: Taking Sustainable Cities Seriously: Economic Development, the Environment, and Quality of Life in American Cities, 2nd edn. The MIT Press, Cambridge (2013)
14. Rowe, G., Frewer, L.J.: Evaluating public-participation exercises: a research agenda. Sci. Technol. Hum. Values **29**(4), 512–557 (2004)
15. Schroetera, R., Scheel, O., Renn. O., Schweizer. P.: Testing the value of public participation in Germany: theory, operationalization and a case study on the evaluation of participation. Energ. Res. Soc. Sci. (2015). http://dx.doi.org/10.1016/j.erss.2015.12.013
16. UN E-Government Survey (2014). http://unpan3.un.org/egovkb/Reports/UN-E-Government-Survey-2014
17. Warburton, D., Willson, R., Rainbow, E.: Making a difference: a guide to evaluating public participation in central government (2007). http://www.involve.org.uk/evaluation/Making%20a%20Differece%20-%20A%20guide%20to%20evaluating%20public%20participation%20in%20centralgovernment.pdf
18. Winkler, R.: e-Participation in comparison and contrast: online debates at the EU's platform 'Your Voice in Europe'. In: Proceedings of the 3rd International Conference on e-Government, University of Quebec at Montreal, Canada, 26–28 September 2007, Academic Conferences International, pp. 238–248 (2007)

The Applicability of International Techniques for E-Participation Assessment in the Russian Context

Lyudmila Vidiasova[✉]

ITMO University, Saint Petersburg, Russia
bershadskaya.lyudmila@gmail.com

Abstract. The paper presents a review on existed approaches to e-participation assessment with the focus on indicators and proposed metrics. A research on the applicability of international tools for e-participation evaluation to the Russian context has been conducted.

The focus of the analysis was concentrated on the Russian legislator documents that determine e-participation development. Based on the normative base study, a comprehensive research of international techniques for assessing the progress in this sphere has been developed. The researchers determine 10 spheres to be evaluated in accordance with stated goals and targets, and 5 international tools for e-participation evaluation reflecting different specific of the research phenomenon.

The research revealed the necessity of two kinds of innovations. The first one reflects the demand to develop a clear detailed strategic document describing e-participation targets, prospects and orientations. The second one is connected with the development of a monitoring system for e-participation evaluation adequate for the Russian context.

Keywords: E-participation · Evaluation · Monitoring · Effectiveness · Assessment · Regulations

1 Introduction

The world focus on breaking any barriers through new technologies usage has been spread significantly into a governmental sphere. Such terms as "open government", "open society", "e-participation of the citizens" reflect this modern trend and tend to be universal for the world communities. In this regards official authorities, political and social scientists pay a special attention to achievement a great progress in this field by providing different state programs, plans and other strategic documents. This activity also raises an important issue of a proper evaluation framework for measuring such progress and making governmental policy better.

The experience of e-participation tools in Russia is quite new. The experts consider its' active dissemination since 2012 year. Among the most popular tools being already developed in Russia are the Russian e-petition portal "Russian Public Initiative" (https://www.roi.ru), portals Change.org, Online Petition, Demokrator Ru, Our view, Alter Russia, as well as different platforms of citizens' complaints and urban issues like Angry

© Springer International Publishing AG 2016
A.V. Chugunov et al. (Eds.): DTGS 2016, CCIS 674, pp. 145–154, 2016.
DOI: 10.1007/978-3-319-49700-6_15

citizen, Beautiful Petersburg, Our Petersburg, Our city- Moscow etc. In general, the situation in this area can be described as sufficiently diffuse pattern having no systematization and mechanisms of assessment.

This paper reflects a practical idea to match the regulatory base and strategic goals of e-participation development in Russia with international techniques for its evaluation trying to estimate its completeness and applicability for usage in Russia.

2 Literature Review

In contemporary scientific literature we could find quite an impressive collection of different studies in the field of e-participation, its forms and methods. Alathur and colleagues have identified several existed forms (channels) of e-participation [2]: ICT development to unite citizens and create online education communities; ICT use for group conversations and discussions; ICT use to attract supporters and/or voters; social media for voting and polls; economic forums and e-business; knowledge sharing platforms; and networks as monitoring systems. His classification gathered almost every action in one way or another connected with participation. R. Medaglia analyzed publications on e-participation topic, identifying the following complex of the involved parts: activities actors, effects, contextual factors and evaluation [10]. Different researchers underlined a great role of institutional factors [6] and governmental form [19] in well-functioning of such a complex.

The 5 levels of participation (eInforming, eConsulting, eDiscussion, eParticipation, eEmpowerment) have been selected for another evaluation framework by Ter'an and Drobnjak [16]. The authors assessed web-presence, media diversity, synchronous and asynchronous communication channels and used modeling as the main research tool. This approach showed the benefits Web 2.0 network. The framework proposed in this work allowed a quantitative evaluation of different e-participation projects. The results of the evaluation showed the lack of the following technologies usage: Web 2.0, Web 3.0, audio, video, interactive video, and synchronous communication channels.

However the attempts of creating a framework for measurement in this field have not been fully described. The UN developed a unified methodology for an e-participation index, including assessment of e-information, e-consultation and e-decision-making [17]. This index is used now for cross-countries assessment in e-participation development.

A classic study by Macintosh and Whyte towards an evaluation framework for e-participation [8] tested the applicability of methods measuring democratic (representation, engagement, transparency, conflict and consensus, political equality, community control), project (engaging with wider audience, obtaining better informed opinion, enabling more in-depth consultation, cost effective analysis of contribution, providing feedback to citizens), and socio-technical (social, acceptability, usefulness, usability) criteria. A case study of e-participation evaluation for four local authorities, semi-structured interview, phone interview, observation, project documentation analysis, web-server analysis made the base for research analysis. This research underlined the importance of multi-method approach, and the complexity domain needed to be developed.

A complex approach has been developed in UNDESA and was called METEP (Measuring and Evaluating e-Participation) [9]. The METEP aim is the measurement of e-participation in different socio-economic conditions. The research indicators are separated into a political block (legal framework, organizational framework, modalities, channels, outreach measures), and a social block (e-decision-making, e-consultation, e-information), technical block (open data and open government, social media, mobility). Using the official statistic data, expert poll and questionnaire this monitoring proposes to evaluate good, satisfactory, certain, marginal or no progress at all. This approach is well-balanced and good for measurement the progress and making comparison between countries, regions, municipalities.

The study of e-participation in Germany by Schroetera and colleagues [12] tested the value of public participation by analyzing inclusiveness, information exchange and learning, and the influence on political decision. Semi-structured interviews, qualitative research, document analysis were put into research practice. The study revealed 8 dimensions of participation process: expectancy, transparency, acceptance, fairness, effectiveness, and efficiency, own impact, satisfaction.

The composite index assessing the completeness and quality of feedback for electronic participation procedures by Yakimets et al. [18] measures the governmental informational resources through such indicators as completeness of feedback opportunities (% of tools available at site) and feedback quality (informativeness, usability, simplicity). This techniques has been applied in Russia, using governmental web-sites' sites binary rating scale and expert poll conduction. The proposed methodology gives an opportunity for cross-country comparisons on the fullness of feedback; and provides site analysis of a single e-government.

Mathematical modeling of political stability proposed by Akhremeko [1] is also used for rating the relative effectiveness of both countries and regions within countries, as well as municipalities. The efficiency of decision-making is the main focus of this study. For the purpose of monitoring such indicators as budget costs, the level of social welfare and productivity (the ratio of costs and benefits) are evaluated. The researchers have deal with official statistics, economy analysis, and use MaxDEA 5.214 for results' counting. According to the approach, budgetary costs are considered as input, the level of welfare as an output (including life expectancy, crime, unemployment, and so on for each area). Output efficiency shows what proportion of potentially possible in the given-conditions the outcome the decision-making really achieves. Input efficiency shows how decision-making reduces costs while maintaining the current result.

Evaluating websites from a public value perspective in Turkey [7] assessed public value created through participation online using the standard criteria (content, usability, quality), and public value indicators (accessibility, citizen engagement, transparency, responsiveness, dialog, balancing of interests). They applied web-site assessment, systematical scanning approach, extensive search of journals, automated tests of web sites (using SortSite 4.7.564.0, Xenu's Link Sleuth 1.3.8, CSS validations of Turkish MM websites, Web Accessibility Inspector 5.11). The researchers noticed the fact that the most websites had a high rate according to standard criteria and the low rate for the public value development.

In addition to all the above mentioned indicators, a series of important risks should be taken into account: costs caused by web 2.0 and (direct costs, development of new services, additional staff, data management, indirect human costs, limited participation of users, indirect organizational costs, loss of control over the system, professional education and training of personnel, introduction of a new organizational policy), and the associated risks (political, legal, technical, social, weak social media policy, data ownership, information, freedom, reputation, critical reviews, digital divide) [13].

A review of the scientific research allowed underlining the lack of studies focusing on the assessment methodology for measuring e-participation impacts. We have found several examples in the foreign practice being already applied to e-participation assessment. These techniques have been selected for the analysis of its' applicability to the Russian context.

3   Research Framework

In this study, we proceeded from the logic of the institutional approach. A classic institutionalism applied a descriptive and inductive approach to legal norms, as well as formalized management issues in this area [4]. In the study of e-participation it's important to pay attention to the western best practices already achieved and being measured in the recent years. That's why we took into consideration the regulatory base defining the aims and objectives of e-government and e-participation development in Russia. The assessment of the stated goals and objectives achievement has been also selected as a key focus for the research.

The research analysis was concentrated on the following directions:

- regulatory documents analysis regarding e-participation development,
- analysis of e-participation evaluation techniques from international and the Russian practice,
- comparison of correspondence the tools for measurement progress in Russian.

The Fig. 1 presents the logic of a research process moving by different steps of analysis.

Fig. 1. Research methodology to find the applicability of international techniques for e-participation evaluation in the Russian context

From the analysis of the Russian legislation base we have not revealed the documents related to e-participation directly. But we revealed some strategic documents, federal law and a presidential decree that touched e-participation topic in terms of e-communication between citizens, business and government.

From the literature review we have selected the following techniques allowing evaluating e-participation in the most common sense:

– E-Participation Index by United Nations [17],
– Framework for e-participation evaluation by Macintosh and Whyte [8],
– Measuring and Evaluating e-Participation (METEP) by UNDESA [9],
– Testing the value of e-participation by Schroetera and colleagues [12],
– Evaluating websites from a public value perspective by Karkin and Janssen [7].

Comparing the distinctive features of the techniques with target indicators (reflected in the regulations), we have conducted a study on the possibility of using the international tools methodologies to assess e-participation progress in Russia.

4   Findings

The authors applied the document analysis method for detection the majority of the findings related to the study. The regulation documents have been accessed from the open sources, the description of e-participation tools have been published in the scientific articles and analytical reports.

4.1   Regulatory Documents Analysis

Presidential Decree "On the Main Direction of Improving Governance". The President of the Russian Federation decree "On the main directions of governance improvement" №601 from 07.05.2012 [11] the most fully covers the e-participation issues. It provides the development of the following initiatives:

– a platform for bills discussions within 60 days period,
– "Russian public initiative" as an e-petition portal development,
– open data active publishing,
– developing the mechanisms for citizens' assessment of the authorities and its' efficiency,
– enhancing citizens and business participation in control on government actions,
– development of judicial decisions placement system and broadcasts hearings.

The key efficiency indicators for such activities development include the level of citizens' satisfaction with online services, the percentage of citizens with ability to get online services, the percentage of citizens who receive online services, reducing the time in the queue when contacting authorities.

State Program "Information Society". The state program "Information Society" (2011–2012) [14] has been developed for the clear establishment of goals and tasks, as well as the financing for all the initiatives connected with them. The key efficiency indicators described in the program are the following:

- position of the Russian Federation in the international ranking on the IT development index;
- the percentage of citizens who use mechanism for obtaining public and municipal services in electronic form;
- reduction of the population that does not use "Internet" and telecommunications network for security reasons;
- the degree of differentiation of the Russian regions on the integral indicators of information development;
- the proportion of households with access to the Internet.

There is a special sub-program related to e-governance called "Information State". From the perspective of such sub-program, the main focus is concentrated on such indicators as sharing of electronic documents between public authorities in the overall volume of interdepartmental document, the use of high-speed Internet in the authorities, the use of e-signature, the use of e-passports among citizens.

Systematic Project of E-government in Russia. The Systematic approach of e-government in Russia [15] was developed in 2016 by the Ministry of Telecom and Mass Communications of the Russian Federation and pretended to be a strategic document reflecting e-government scenario development. Actually this document focuses not just on e-government but contain the development of partnerships between government, civil society and business. This fact means different types of citizens' involvement into decision-making, which is really close to e-participation concept.

The main principles of this document include the following aspects:

- user orientation,
- efficiency (social and economic) through optimization of administrative processes, citizens' involvement, open G2C dialogue support,
- inclusiveness,
- security and confidence,
- flexibility and adaptability,
- orientation on data,
- continuity.

This document provides an orientation to transformational scenario of development, implying an idea of reducing the costs from governmental functions and involving the civil society.

By preparing this document the Ministry intends to provide services for the processes of civilian control and examination support, as well as the implementation of a national inspector functions, activities of professional and expert communities. The establishment of systems to ensure participation of civil society and business in the development, adoption and implementation of state and municipal decisions also refers to the current tasks. The efficiency indicators are described as the following: the level of citizens' satisfaction with e-government services, the proportion of e-services among other types of services, reduction in the average cost of providing public services, a part of citizens who use e-government services for interaction.

Federal Law "On the Order of Citizens' Requests Consideration". The federal law 59 "On the order debated the requests of citizens of the Russian Federation" from 21.04.2006 (the latest edition from 18.07.2012 №19-P) [3] regulates the implementation of the constitutionally enshrined rights of citizens to appeal to the state and municipal authorities.

This document guarantees the right to make an individual or a collective request. Article 4 of this document describes the electronic method as one of the equally ways of citizens' treatments. According to this law, all requests must necessarily be examined by the authorities within 30 days. The cases of information about violations of migration legislation are the exceptions (20 days period). The document determines the following types of treatments: a proposal, a statement and a complaint.

4.2 Summary of the Goals and Target Indicators

The provided overview of the selected documents has set a list of objects which were compulsory traits of e-participation development according to the established institutional framework. Analysis of regulations allowed grouping the following phenomena that were in the focus of e-participation development in Russian:

- Channels of e-participation,
- Administrative level of usage,
- Citizens assessment and satisfaction,
- Citizens' engagement (enhancing the level of e-participation),
- Statistical and infrastructure indicators, technology usage,
- Opening governmental data,
- Security and confidence,
- Assessment of different types of e-participation,
- Social and economic efficiency.

Consideration of these parts is reflected in the effectiveness indicators of government programs and plans. These phenomena were put under the analysis of applicability the international techniques to the Russian context.

4.3 Analysis of the Methods' Applicability for Russia

A careful study on the Russian targeted topics presence in the international tools for e-participation assessment has been provided. All of the mentioned goals, targets and indicators have been reflected by authors into 10 dimensions:

- channels (variety of communication types, portals, chats, e-voting etc.),
- administration level (programs and targets, governmental resolutions and actions),
- citizens' satisfaction (level of perception and attitudes),

- engagement (real involvement in e-participation processes, registration on portals, votes etc.),
- technology (IT infrastructure and services),
- Open data (sharing public data with a wider audience),
- security (safety channels, confidentiality),
- e-participation types (feedback forms, e-petitions, claims, e-voting and its' usage),
- economic effects (costs and benefits from e-participation development),
- social impacts, public value (social transformation through e-participation tools' usage, political and citizens' activity, influence on decision-making, level of civic advocacy).

The results of the techniques' applicability analysis are presented in Table 1.

Table 1. The applicability of international e-participation evaluation tools to the Russian stated targets

Dimensions	EPI	Macintosh & Whyte	METEP	Testing value	Websites evaluation
Channels	V		V		
Admin. level		V	V		
Citizens satisfaction		V		V	
Engagement			V		V
Technology	V	V	V	V	V
Open data	V		V		
Security					
EPART types	V	V	V		
Economic effects		V		V	
Social impacts, public value		V		V	V

Conformity assessment was carried out on the basis of a detailed analysis of the techniques and the methods that were used in an each tool. For instance, the EPI methodology stated the assessment of citizens' feedback, but really didn't count engagement or satisfaction, due to the selected instrument- web-presence identification. According to the research results, we could conclude that none of the international techniques had covered all of the targeted e-participation areas. The technological and statistical side was the most popular among the studied tools. The research also revealed an interest to public values evaluation.

Citizens' engagement and satisfaction have been observed only in 2 techniques. Open Data technologies detection has been covered in the United Nations tools appropriate for a national scale assessment. The observed economic effects lead mostly to the costs reduction which partly reflects the Russian targets from that side.

Administrative level has been partly analyzed in the observed tools but usually it included the management style and organization, but not the use of e-documents or e-signatures.

Different types of e-participation through separation to the practical cases or wider categories like e-consultation or e-decision-making have been presented in three techniques but in a completely different manner. Security side was not covered at all. According to official statistics, approximately 10 % of citizens who didn't use the Internet in Russia did it in such manner because there were unsatisfied with the security level.

5 Conclusions

A comprehensive analysis showed a necessity to develop the strategic document defining the principles of e-participation development in Russia. The current regulations consider e-participation as an additional part of e-government concept. These laws and programs are focused on governmental online services mostly and doesn't draw the perspectives for citizens' involvement into decision-making and policy modeling, as well as its' measurement.

The conducted research revealed two international techniques, which covered the majority of indicators targeted in the official documents: METEP and Macintosh & Whyte framework. We consider that these tools from conceptualization side could be applied for the analysis in the Russian context with addition of missed spheres.

Several years ago Gil-Garcia and Pardo [5] highlighted the need to use to a multi-method approach to research and evaluate the digital government. We support this point a view and believe that it could be applied in the field of e-participation assessment with a purpose to create a special technique correlating with federal targets but also reflecting all sides of the researched phenomenon.

We see the solution of such contradiction in the development of monitoring system for e-participation performance assessment. We could determine the following features of this system:

- be based on the interconnected indicators,
- be balanced and reflect the goals and objectives of key documents,
- should establish a cause-effect relationship of the results of project implementation and spent resources,
- should upgrade the existing disparate tools (statistical monitoring, reporting authorities, public polls) traditionally used for measuring the progress in e-government,
- should develop a data collection and processing system,
- should result into a model of e-participation efficiency.

The positive experience of such monitoring system development could be translated to other countries. The development of a monitoring system could make a significant impact into the interpretation and forecasting of e-participation development.

Acknowledgements. This work was conducted with support of the Grant of the President of the Russian Federation to young scientists №MK-5953.2016.6 "The research of e-participation tools development factors in Russian Federation".

References

1. Akhremenko, A.S.: A dynamic approach to the mathematical modeling of political stability. Polit. Stud. **3**, 105–112 (2009)
2. Alathur, S., Vigneswara, I., Gupta, M.P.: Citizen empowerment and participation in e-democracy: Indian context. Proceedings of the 5th International Conference on Theory and Practice of Electronic Governance, pp. 11–19 (2011)
3. Federal law №59 "On the order debated the requests of citizens of the Russian Federation" from 21.04.2006 (2006)
4. Friedrich, C.J.: Constitutional Government and Democracy: Theory and Practice in Europe and America. Ginn, Boston (1950)
5. Gil-Garcia, R., Pardo, T.: Multi-method approaches to digital government research: value lessons and implementation challenges. In: Proceedings of the 39th Annual Hawaii International Conference of System Sciences (HICSS-39) (2006)
6. Jho, W., Song, K.: Institutional and technological determinants of civil e-Participation: solo or duet? Gov. Inf. Q. **32**, 488–495 (2015)
7. Karkin, N., Janssen, M.: Evaluating websites from a public value perspective: a review of Turkish local government websites. Int. J. Inf. Manag. **34**, 351–363 (2014)
8. Macintosh, A., Whyte, A.: Towards an evaluation framework for e-Participation. Transf. Gov. People Process Policy **2**(1), 16–30 (2008)
9. Measuring and Evaluating e-Participation (METEP): Assessment of Readiness at the Country Level. UNDESA Working Paper (2013). http://workspace.unpan.org/sites/Internet/Documents/METEP%20framework_18%20Jul_MOST%20LATEST%20Version.pdf
10. Medaglia, R.: eParticipation research: moving characterization forward (2006–2011). Gov. Inf. Q. **29**, 346–360 (2012)
11. Presidential decree of the Russian Federation № 601 "On the main directions of governance improvement" from 07.05.2012 (2012)
12. Schroetera, R., Scheel, O., Renn, O., Schweizer, P.: Testing the value of public participation in Germany: theory, operationalization and a case study on the evaluation of participation. Energ. Res. Soc. Sci. (2015). doi:10.1016/j.erss.2015.12.013
13. Sivarajah, U., Irani, Z., Weerakkody, V.: Evaluating the use impact of Web 2.0 technologies in local government. Gov. Inf. Q. **32**, 473–487 (2015)
14. State Program "Information Society" (2011–2010). The Russian government regulation №313 from 13.04.2014 (2014)
15. Systematic project of e-Government in Russia. Ministry of Telecom and Mass Communication (2016)
16. Ter'an, L., Drobnjak, A.: An evaluation framework for eParticipation: the VAAs case study. Int. Scholary Sci. Res. Innov. **7**(1), 77–85 (2013)
17. UN E-Government Survey (2014). http://unpan3.un.org/egovkb/Reports/UN-E-Government-Survey-2014
18. Yakimets, V.N., Leonova, M.V.: The composite index assessing the effectiveness of information resources feedback of the Russian federal authorities. In: Proceedings of "Internet and modern society conference", IMS 2007, pp. 217–220 (2007)
19. Zheng, Y., Schachter, H.L., Holzer, M.: The impact of government from e-participation: a study of New Jersey municipalities. Gov. Inf. Q. **31**, 653–659 (2014)

Synergy for Digital Transformation: Person's Multiple Roles and Subject Domains Integration

Evgeny Zinder[✉] and Irina Yunatova

FOSTAS Foundation, Moscow, St. Petersburg, Russian Federation
{ezinder,to}@fostas.ru

Abstract. This paper describes the model of citizens and more generally any person engagement in Digital Transformation processes. Essential barriers that governments, business and people face and should be ready to overcome in the Digital Era are examined. The two-level model of person involvement in the Digital Transformation based on an increase in person's motivation for acquiring additional competences and participation in the Transformation is suggested. This motivation is ensured by the synergy of person's multiple roles and subject domains integration. Successful methods and practices in areas of integrated using information about children's healthcare and education in Russia, the UK, and Canada are presented in evidence of possibility to gain valuable synergy achieved even at the first level of involvement. The schematic chart of the person's Private Virtual Workplace and interactions in the Digital Society is presented for the second level of person involvement model realization.

Keywords: Digital Society · Digital transformation · E-government · Involvement · Participation · Engagement · Synergy · Subject domains integration · Citizen · Multiple roles · Private Virtual Workplace

1 Introduction

Despite the multiplicity of technological novelties and recipes for their implementation in business, public governance, and private life, real Digital Transformation (DT) is taking much longer and facing more difficulties than it has been expected. A common approach to DT consists of creative innovations based on Information and Communication Technology (ICT). However, innovation activities are carried out by people; therefore, the authors argue that factual and wide DT development can only be reached by engaging ordinary people in innovative usage of ICT.

This paper presents the research that actually started in 2013 after the authors developed a specific model for professional competencies in ICT and other domains that are necessary for Digital Transformation [1]. The normalized competencies model took into consideration not only knowledge and skills, but also the person's attitude and other personal traits, as well as these components interconnections. What is important, personal traits constituting "attitude" [1] that are primarily defined by the person's motivation appeared to be the most meaningful. At the next stage, we explored new competencies and other digital characteristics of employees and whole enterprises in the

© Springer International Publishing AG 2016
A.V. Chugunov et al. (Eds.): DTGS 2016, CCIS 674, pp. 155–168, 2016.
DOI: 10.1007/978-3-319-49700-6_16

context of new integral paradigm of enterprise engineering for Digital Era [2]. Application of our methods in ICT companies described in [2] confirmed that strong motivation is a winning component ensuring the person's successful acquisition of digital knowledge and skills and their effective utilizing. It was also demonstrated in that research that high level of DT can be achieved not only by new ICT capabilities, but also by their creative integration with old ones.

According to abovementioned, the general purpose of the current research is the analysis of the essential barriers and problems in DT and defining ways to allow overcoming the most significant barriers hindering wide engagement of people and enterprises in DT. The first goal of the research is bringing forward hypotheses concerning a general model of people involvement in DT aimed at implementation of the model in various DT sectors and subject domains. The second goal is justifying this model feasibility for significant particular subject domains concerning such regular activities of people that motivate them to acquire novel competencies and to carry out new digital tasks. The third goal is forming such primary characteristics of Private Virtual Workplace (PVW) architecture for every person and such incorporating PVW in the common information environment of Digital Society that would enable every person to fully participate in DT in various subject domains and their combinations.

The rest of the paper is structured as follows. Section 2 presents the related works in this area and the research background including analysis of problems encountered during the initial and modern endeavors directed at digital transformation in business and public areas. Section 3 proposes a system of hypotheses and a two-level model aiming at expanding people engagement in DT and extending DT to a greater number of people and subject domains. Section 4 provides justification of the suggested hypotheses with regard to joining two particular subject domains for the first level of person involvement. Section 5 presents the additional capabilities recommended by external experts participating in the research. Besides, the transition to the second level of people involvement is presented there including new information architecture of citizens' personal data and their PVW in the global information environment. Finally, Sect. 6 summaries the primary findings and conclusions as well as suggests directions of future works.

2 Initial and Modern Endeavors of Digital Transformation: Background and Some Problems

2.1 DT Interpretation. First Endeavors and Problems

Digital Transformation is now commonly interpreted as such usage of ICT, when not trivial automation is performed, but fundamentally new capabilities are created in business, public government, and in people's and society life, as mentioned by Allan Martin [3, p. 173]. Leena Rantala and Juha Suoranta highlight in [4, p. 105] the requirement of radical nature of DT. They mention in particular that the eEurope 2002 Action Plan strives to ensure full employment through "a radical transformation of the economy and skills to match the opportunities of the new economy". Such a plan considers education and training as crucial means to meet mentioned challenges; however, motivation as a determinant factor is not addressed there.

What is significant, similar radical endeavors have had considerable history. Michael Hammer in [5] described this task for business 26 years ago when he evaluated "automation" as a wrong tradition and brought forward a goal of revolutionary changes basing on a radical Business Process Reengineering (BPR) with creative ICT usage. BPR proved promising, but it engendered a lot of criticism due to the problems accompanying its application. The reason often originated from using "BPR" term for "compulsory Digital Transformation" followed by dismissing half the staff and the necessity to use computers much more intensively by the rest of the staff. Before long, a revolutionary BPR version began being replaced by somewhat "softer" approaches, and in [6], for instance, continuous improvement and incremental approaches were mentioned. Problems caused by human factors were named among the main reasons of this kind of DT failure, and overloading the staff with new functions together with inadequate inner motivation for performing these functions was one of these problems. So, similar barriers first emerged more than 25 years ago, and now they are showing up again. Lessons should be at last learnt, and adequate measures should be taken.

Addressing e-government and civil society, it is necessary to mention that the goals of DT of the government, business, and whole society in Digital Era were considered in the very first e-government programs. For instance, Fang [7, p. 3] sets the goal to ensure "citizen participation in government, enhancing communications and facilitating democratic processes" in 2002 and to plan bidirectional interactions showed in Fig. 1. Thus, about 15 years ago the necessity of citizen participation and of partnership relations shown in Fig. 1 was determined. However, the barriers for participation and partnership still exist and will be discussed later on. Besides, the necessity of e-government users' collaboration in Russian Federation was introduced by one of the authors in [8], but this collaboration has been realized only on a small scale yet.

2.2 DT in the Modern Society and Actual Problems

In the modern society, DT is realized on the new spiral turn of its life, but the truth is that not everything is going smoothly. In fact, some problems generated by the human factor became even more meaningful at this stage of transformation development.

Many authors have been lately viewing a human factor and culture as the main barriers to changes. For instance, the MIT/CC research claims that "A major cultural issue is related to changes in jobs due to automation or information empowerment" [9, p. 38]. Similarly, according to the HBS report [10], "Cultural resistance to change" and "Lack of digital leadership" are viewed as the most essential barriers to digital business development for companies belonging to the "LAGGARDS" category [10, p. 4] which is one of the main categories-of-interest in our research.

One important instance of such a cultural issue is essential conservatism degree in relation to transformation in such an industry as education where ICT are primarily demanded in the context of the traditional classroom [11]. Besides, conservative people behavior is perceived as an essential hindering factor by many authors. In particular, [12] cites the evaluation given in [13] "Never underestimate the fondness of people and organizations for the status quo". Another meaningful issue is that people who are to be

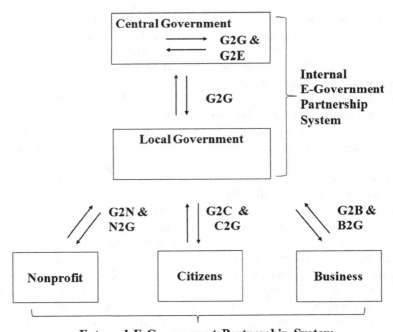

Fig. 1. An early schematic system of participants and their interactions for E-Government models (Based on [7], p. 10)

involved in DT are "busy people with short attention spans, who have a lot to get done and who can always reach for email" according to the analysis in [14] quoting [13].

At the same time, the results presented in [10] demonstrate that specifying the main reasons for DT barriers require essential revision. In particular, the graph in Fig. 7 [10, p. 7] demonstrates that respondents from different industries admit that acquiring "digital knowledge is a high priority" for their function heads. At the same time, the graph in Fig. 9 [10, p. 10] shows that primary barriers for acquiring digital knowledge are specified as the following: "We don't have the right forums in place" (45% responses) and "They're too busy" (34% responses). In our opinion, both barriers could be eliminated if employees were highly motivated and demonstrated appropriate level of personal traits constituting "attitude" in their actual competencies. Thus, motivation appears the main driver of successful person involvement in DT.

It is necessary to point out that abovementioned evaluation of the situation is relevant both for DT in business and for participation in public digital governance.

Perspective on government DT is described in the global UN report [15] which highlights the necessity of a deeper transformation based on people engagement, participation and online collaboration of the citizens, government, and businesses. For implementing such collaboration, significant transformation in cultural sphere is required: « transform mind-sets and build a culture of collaboration, transparency and accountability » [15, p. 77]. The report points out that such a transformation must be based on strictly exercised principles, including, for example, Easy Access and Citizen-centric ones, which will provide a convenient framework and methodology tools for a citizen.

Besides, the report particularly mentions that such a transformation is hindered by the existing situation when "citizens tend to think of government as a kind of vending machine. They put in taxes and get out services that governments provide" [15, p. 161], and the idea of Government as a Platform (GaaP) is suggested instead. In the same paragraph it is noted that "the platform metaphor means that government provides a system in place to deliver services not by governments alone, but also by citizens and others" [15, p. 161]. The conducted and presented above analysis confirms that the idea of GaaP is fruitful but not sufficient enough for enabling wide citizen participation. It is important that UN report notes that citizens should have motivation for their efforts needed for active e-participation, and that "citizens who depend on public services have strong motivation to contribute to their design and implementation; however, appropriate mechanisms are needed to adequately channel citizens' views, opinions and to involve them in the design and delivery of services" [15, p. 88]. This can be interpreted as setting up a research area for exploring and designing such mechanisms.

As for the source of motivation, it is only said there that "Motivating engagement depends more on a sense of belonging to a political community with shared traditions and values" [15, pp. 6–7]. In our opinion, such understanding of motivation sources is not satisfactory, as it cannot serve as a mechanism of practical realization of wide involvement in performing more complicated activities than in Twitter or Instagram and even in digital voting. Analyzing requirements for sources and level of motivation, it should be taken into account that in simple cases GaaP suggests to the end user tailoring ready-to-use functions and information content according to his/her needs. In more advanced cases, the end user will be able to utilize GaaP as a kind of "workbench" or "workshop" with convenient tools for orchestrating necessary services and functions and assembling information structures.

For differentiating various levels of participation, the UN report uses a three-level model "that moves from more "passive" to "active" engagement with people" [15, p. 62]. Although this model is applicable for ranking participation development in different countries, it is not suitable for our goals as it does not aim at enabling citizen motivation and mechanisms of transforming motivation into participation.

3   Digital Transformation and Our Hypotheses

All abovementioned presents sufficient background for specifying our research area aiming at practical methods for involving people in DT. The conducted analysis showed that providing high motivation to a person is the highest priority, and supplying him/her with convenient tools for Self Service mode acting is also essential. Then people and enterprises including those from LAGGARDS category will be able to overcome barriers on the way of digital knowledge and skills acquisition as well as to perform additional works in the information environment of Digital Society. Basing on this, we formulate our hypotheses suggesting specific principles and the model of wide people involvement in DT.

3.1   Our Hypotheses

The authors believe that deep engagement of a significant number of people in Digital Transformation in the areas of business and public governance is possible in the nearest future if they have their high inner motivation to do some new and not easy activities, and moreover, often in collaboration with other actors. High motivation can be achieved if a person has vitally important tasks as a stimulus for changing their attitude and acquiring skills for doing new activities in Self Service mode.

More specifically, high level of motivation must be based on the ground that a citizen will get new invaluable capabilities that cannot be gained (or can be gained with a lot of efforts) by separately using services and information from different sources. The value of these capabilities should be generated by a synergetic effect of integrating and joined using information and services received from different sources and subject domains. Successful person involvement can be realized first of all in those domains and necessary activities where a person has to solve vitally important problems under time pressure, and has easy-to-use tools at his/her disposal.

In this publication, we specifically use citizen participation in Digital Transformation as an example for justifying the feasibility of our suggestions. This is essential, as in interactions G2B, B2B, and G2G the main actor is also a person, and most often that is a citizen. That is the reason why we consider the logic of analysis and conclusions of this research applicable also in DT of business, government, non-profit organization, and their interactions.

Considering all above mentioned, the authors formulated the hypothesis of the effectiveness of a two-level involvement model.

We assume that it is hardly possible to enable the necessary degree of involvement in digital governance or digital business in one-step procedure. The first reason is that the way towards deeper and wider participation in governance and DT includes a set of complicated issues and components. The person needs relevant competencies, tools for co-working, appropriate legislation etc. The second reason is that there is always the first step, and the first step should be observable, manageable, doable, and valuable. Realizing that, the two-level model was suggested.

The First Level of Involvement Model. At the first level, a person is engaged in dealing with only the government and public organizations (hospitals, universities, kindergartens, police, libraries, social support centers etc.), and he/she is involved by the government in the delivery of services to him-/herself, in Self Service mode. The person uses existing and emerging services based on GaaP for joined using services and information of the government and other public organizations in his/her own self-interests. The citizen can gain many new « first level » capabilities, but he/she is restricted by limits set by the government. Even the first level of this model brings such essential person engagement that can support the first and second levels of a UN three-level participation model.

The Second Level of Involvement Model. At the second level, the person is already better prepared and trained and might be hoped to be able to participate in much wider interactions with the greater number of partners, namely, with government as a whole, commercial business, nonprofit organizations, other citizens etc. Besides, he/she is able to use more information sources for combining, developing, and delivery of the services necessary for him-/herself. The person interacts with all stakeholders on equal terms, independently determining his/her PVW content and expanding it in Self Service mode. Realization of the second level of the model provides such engagement that can support all three levels of the UN participation model.

4 Capabilities Analysis and Hypotheses Justification

Methodology of the research is based on common architectural approach and Enterprise Architecture as a professional discipline in the area of multi-aspect analysis and synthesis which are applicable in very large socio-technical systems. In accordance with general principles of Enterprise Architecture, we take into account human factors, motivation aspect, culture, information, and processes of integration of all abovementioned, as well as the progress of DT in the historical aspect. We used secondary data analysis as an important particular method for proving our hypotheses. We also started with secondary data analysis for defining background of all the research. Besides, we used principles and rules of Delphi method for expert estimation of value and feasibilities of our suggestions and recommendations. Finally, we applied the method of high level information architecture design for synthesizing the global information environment of Digital Society.

4.1 Justification of Getting Synergy from Joining Subject Domains

During the research, the authors analyzed a capability for services and information in G2C and B2C interaction classes to generate valuable synergy for high motivation and to become highly demanded. For this purpose, we examined existence of such subject domains and services that are vitally important for many people.

For instance, one of the problems researched was the question of whether the citizen can obtain a synergetic effect by analyzing information about his/her child's education and healthcare in an integrated style for overall children progress.

One of the positive answers to the mentioned question is presented by the message in [16] stating that Leeds city in the UK has set up a program for integrating, and «children and families now experience one service, supporting their health, social care and early educational needs» . Benefit is also gained "from an innovative approach which will enable people to access their information online", notes the above mentioned message.

Another example given in [17] presents a valuable positive response for more extreme situations as a method of integral work with children with special needs and their parents as it is described in Handbook for Parents published in Manitoba, Canada.

An example addressed to healthy children's parents is given in [18], and it refers to Saint Petersburg Sport & Health University approach for organizing initial girls' preparation in the rhythmic gymnastics area. It utilizes an integrated approach for "general developmental, health-improving, educational, and training tasks in the musical-motor training for girls aged 6–7 years".

Thereby, we have obtained sufficient justification of our hypothesis that information integration in healthcare and education spheres proves being innovatively effective and having a significant synergetic effect, for children and their parents in particular.

Besides, we have got justification that:

- maintaining this effect requires informational and methodical support of parents' activities in different ways, including access to all information online and individual ways for small groups of users and certain families;
- the effect is reinforced when other services in the sphere of social support, trainings, and others are added to the set of integrated functions.

4.2 Analysis of the Feasibility of Synergy Development at the First Level of Involvement

It was assumed that the first level of citizen involvement must be achieved with relatively low expenses for additional ICT development. Thus, already existing electronic services that the citizen can get or is already getting from the government and other public organizations should constitute the basis of the first level of engagement.

We also relied on the fact that many organizations already provide the citizens and other people with information and functions for dealing with them, in particular, using PVW. It was revealed that services for making appointments with the doctors at hospitals and other medical centers are rather popular and widely used, for instance, in Saint Petersburg [19]. Services enabling parents' access to the relevant actual information about children's educational process at school, such as "Electronic diary" [20], appeared to be also widely used in Russia. In the healthcare, business is nowadays providing the service known as Patient's PVW and some capabilities for the patient to operate with it in Self Service mode. For instance, Internet service [21] provides inhabitants of Saint Petersburg and other Russian cities with the capability for storing diagnostic tests results, viewing them online, even in the mobile mode, and informing the patient via email.

To reach the goals of his/her child's education and healthcare progress, the citizen should have a usable set of facilities as tools for integrated processing of information from various domains and for supporting his/her further activities in addition to existing services and information resources. Consequently, the list should be extendable and include at least the following options:

- get access to their child's PVW in accordance with the effective law;
- get and accumulate records and electronic documents from any organizations (hospitals, pharmacies, universities, sport camps, and others) and add new ones at his/her discretion (such as doctors' opinions initially received not in the digital format, child's awards and like);

- establish various types of links between records, documents, and events from the different subject domains;
- view records (documents) in various ways (in chronological order, in the order determined by causal relations, etc.);
- get reminders and recommendations as well as help in establishing connections with organizations from a personal electronic assistant (not a mandatory component in the very beginning);
- provide third parties (for instance, such as doctors, teachers, or some relatives) with the limited access to the child's PVW.

4.3 Expert Feedback and Additional Recommendations for the First Level of Engagement

The hypotheses and abovementioned justification were tested in an expert evaluation conducted in a group of selected experts from Russia (Moscow, Saint Petersburg, Novosibirsk), the USA, the Netherlands, Montenegro and Israel using main rules of Delphi method. The method was enriched with some techniques of web-based Delphi for organizing the evaluation process with the geographically distributed experts.

We selected 14 experts willing to share their vision of the problem and their own evaluation of our proposals. Our volunteers were well-educated with a degree in one of such areas as ICT, economics, physics, bioengineering, and others. We selected ladies having children and possibly grandchildren and having actively participated in all educational, sport, and healthcare activities with their children.

After conducting two rounds of collecting experts' individual responses, the general consensus evaluation of synergetic effect and its ability to motivate people's involvement in collaboration was achieved. This consensus evaluation confirmed:

- high value of the activity mode integrating various information resources from various subject domains described above;
- feasibility of organizing such kind of work;
- potential personal readiness to carry out such work.

The experts noticed that a significant useful effect will be already obtained even if only all the documents and records about children were properly stored thus avoiding their loss which often happens because of parents' time deficit.

Besides, the experts enriched our proposals with valuable additions among which the main ones are:

- to expand capabilities to work not only with own children's PVW, but also with PVW of other people under the person's wardship (for instance, the person's parents);
- to add to the child's PVW an opportunity for integrated work with information in the person's own PVW; for instance, for revealing and monitoring links between mother's and child's health;
- to ensure the highest possible level of information security for PVW;
- to expand communications between PVW and educational institutions by adding information exchange about the whole educational program and its changes as well

as about the child's limitations or disabilities, other circumstances, and parent's suggestions;

- to include "Portfolio" section in the child's PVW and fill it during the whole period of education;
- to include "Health Passport" in the child's PVW as a mandatory section which will enable planning actions for maintaining the child's health or for responsible and authorized admission to participation in events assuming some advanced physical load after reaching him the age of 18;
- to ensure the personal information usefulness and validity when the person or/and the child changes residence.

The experts confirmed that well-organized help in the integrated work might be more important than many other specific goals often formulated for e-government.

5 Discussion of the First Level of Involvement and of Transition to the Second Level

5.1 Discussion of the First Level

The expert group participants' suggestions not only justified our proposals, but they also demonstrated that:

- specific solution of many problems depends on changes in federal and local legislation as well as on generally accepted ethic norms;
- really convenient and rich PVW becomes a big independent value for the citizen (another person), and this PVW is becoming inherently less connected with the government, another "leading" organization, or an association of organizations;
- defining such PVW, the structure, formats and semantics of the stored data requires development and guaranteed compliance with the group of specific standards connected with the standards in related subject domains (for instance with the standards for "Electronic medical history", "Electronic diary" and others).

It is important that even if a person interacts only with e-government and works in their PVW, he/she needs to have an opportunity to perform different roles, such as a citizen, a legitimate representative of a citizen, enterprise representative, etc. In all these roles, the person acts as the same individual and uses his/her main personal information. It is very important for our goals that legal utilizing of various roles' information and these roles' authorizations and obligations can enhance opportunities to increase described above high citizens' motivation and synergetic effect. This is necessary even at the first level of involvement in Digital Transformations. In addition, the person obtains his/her own integral multirole profile.

5.2 Discussion of the Transition to the Second Level

Charts similar to those presented in Fig. 1 demonstrate some valuable points and have still been used. However, they are inadequate for Society Digital Transformation

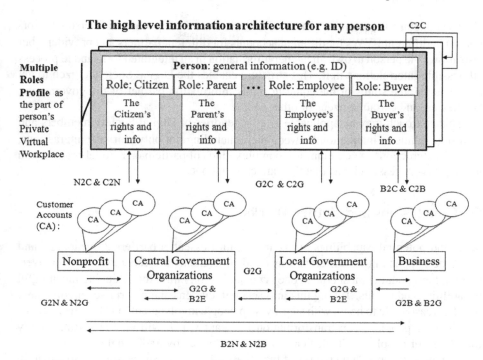

Fig. 2. The advisable schematic chart of the person's/customer's Private Virtual Workplace and its integration in the Digital Society environment

problems as these charts might be misleading for e-governance development. One reason for this is that the chart does not reflect "Citizen-centric" principle and consequential conclusions (the chart might be rather called "Government-centric"). What is important, PVW becomes an independent value for the person, only partly and on equal rights related with the government as well as with a big number of other organizations, which can include banks, transportation, trade and other companies.

Current state of affairs forces the citizen to have many accounts with different services providers as their customer. Some providers associate these accounts with customer's PVW that they offer to the person. Sometimes such an offer is optional, and sometimes it might be mandatory, but in any case the person's information is divided among many providers, is not fully controlled by the person, and is not suited for integrated processing. All this prevents getting a valuable synergetic effect necessary for person involvement in DT. That is the reason why we conclude that in order to be successfully involved in DT, the person should have an opportunity to fully control integrated storing and processing all the information about the history of all his interactions with all his/her contact people and organizations, as the owner. This transformation of information environment will enable the growth of synergy effects in the future. E-government in this framework is only one of the person's partners, and often not the major one. The general chart of the advisable architecture of such person's PVW and interactions in the Digital Society is presented in Fig. 2.

The structure shown in Fig. 2 not only allows to avoid duplication of personal information in different PVWs for different accounts for different partners and providers, but also allows the person to own all his/her information in an integrated form and to process all possible interrelations in it. This structure enables the Digital Society citizen to get a new status, the status of the equal in rights information partner of the government, businesses, and certain citizens or other people.

This approach may be applicable to all categories of Digital Society members and to various kinds of interaction between them including not only pairwise interactions, but also interactions in communities, complex kinds of participants' collaboration, and in business-processes chains that they are carrying out.

6 Conclusions and Future Works

Ideas and potential capabilities of DT met against essential barriers 25 years ago and the same happens now. Different ways and instruments are recommended for overcoming them, but the most crucial one is people's motivation for achieving meaningful capabilities and results. Taking this into account, citizens and enterprises involvement in DT is reasonable to begin with step-by-step people involvement in DT in the interests of the same people. Such transformation is meant which will enable getting vitally important for people results that can hardly be achieved by traditional methods.

The authors formulated the set of hypotheses describing successful involvement in DT and defined a feasible two-level model of people involvement in DT. The model is based on raising people's motivation by getting a valuable for them synergetic effect from joined using services and information from various sources and subject domains. At the first level of involvement, integrated usage is restricted by services and information received from e-government and public organizations. At the second level of involvement, integrated using services and information received in the global information environment of Digital Society is considered. Realization of the two-level involvement model can support all three levels of the UN participation model.

Various examples of methods and practices in joined using information about children's healthcare and education in Russia, the UK, and Canada proved valuable synergy achieved even at the first level of involvement. These practices can be widely spread by concerned parents having appropriate information and services within their PVW. These conclusions were confirmed by consensual evaluation by the experts from Russia, Israel, the USA, Montenegro, and the Netherlands. Recommendations for the set of necessary diverse facilities or tools that might make the suggested approach valuable and feasible were formulated.

The authors suggested high-level architecture of the global information environment and a specific way of including person's PVW in the architecture. Such architecture enables a person to integrate all the roles he/she performs in this information environment and be an equal in rights with all the organizations and other people in Digital Society.

The authors believe that only the described or a similar approach seems appropriate for consideration in the full-blown Digital Transformation Era.

It is reasonable to conduct further researches in the following directions:

- exploration and justification of industries and work processes where the two-level model of involvement can be applied for getting a valuable synergetic effect for wider people engagement in DT for business change and development;
- exploration and justification of e-government's role and ability to support the suggested architecture of the person's Private Virtual Workplace and its integration in common information environment of Digital Society.

Acknowledgements. This paper uses some results of research in the areas of new paradigm of enterprise engineering and architecture of information environment supported by Russian Foundation for Basic Research – RFBR under grants №. 13-07-00917 (during 2013 – 2014) and №. 16-07-01062 (during 2016).

We are grateful to the Universities that invited us to deliver educational courses in which we addressed perspectives for e-governance and enterprises architectures. Those establishments were IBS Academy, MISIS University, ITMO University, and Novosibirsk University of Economics and Management.

We want to pay special thanks to Yuriy F. Telnov (MESI University), Vladimir A. Sukhomlin (MSU), Andrey V. Chugunov (ITMO e-Government Technologies Centre), and Mikhail R. Kogalovskiy (ACM SIGMOD Moscow Chapter) for invitations to present at their conferences and seminars where we had an opportunity to professionally discuss our research.

References

1. Zinder, E.Z., Yunatova, I.G.: Conceptual framework, models, and methods of knowledge acquisition and management for competency management in various areas. In: Klinov, P., Mouromtsev, D. (eds.) KESW 2013. CCIS, vol. 394, pp. 228–241. Springer, Heidelberg (2013). doi:10.1007/978-3-642-41360-5_18. Print ISBN 978-3-642-41359-9, Online ISBN 978-3-642-41360-5. http://dx.doi.org/10.1007/978-3-642-41360-5_18

2. Guzik, S.V., Zinder, E.Z., Yunatova, I.G.: New enterprise engineering paradigm and work process – performers' competencies alignment (in Russian). In: 16th Conference "Enterprise Engineering & Knowledge Management", pp. 90–100. MESI, Moscow (2013)

3. Martin, A.: Digital literacy and the digital society. In: Lankshear, C., Knobel, M. (eds.) Digital literacies: concepts, policies and practices, vol. 30, pp. 151–176. Peter Lang, New York (2008). ISBN 978-1-4331-0168-7. http://researchonline.jcu.edu.au/27788/1/27788_Lankshear_and_Knobel_2008.pdf

4. Rantala, L., Suoranta, J.: The paper "digital literacy policies in the EU — inclusive partnership as the final stage of governmentality?". In: Lankshear, C., Knobel, M. (eds.) Digital Literacies: Concepts, Policies and Practices, vol. 30, pp. 91–117. Peter Lang, New York (2008). ISBN 978-1-4331-0168-7. http://researchonline.jcu.edu.au/27788/1/27788_Lankshear_and_Knobel_2008.pdf

5. Hammer M.: Reengineering work: don't automate, obliterate. In: Harvard Business Review (July–August), pp. 104–112 (1990). https://hbr.org/1990/07/reengineering-work-dont-automate-obliterate

6. Malhotra, Y.: Business process redesign: an overview. IEEE Eng. Manag. Rev. **26**(3) (1998). http://www.kmbook.com/bpr.htm

7. Fang, Z.: E-Government in digital era: concept, practice, and development. Int. J. Comput. Internet Manag. **10**(2), 1–22 (2002). http://unpan1.un.org/intradoc/groups/public/documents/apcity/unpan016377.pdf, http://www.ijcim.th.org/past_editions/2002V10N2/article1.pdf

8. Drozhzhinov, V.I., Zinder, E.Z. (eds.): Electronic Government: Guidelines for Russian Federation (in Russian). Eco-Trends (with E-Government Competence Center of American Chamber of Commerce in Russia and FOSTAS Foundation Support), Moscow (2004)

9. Digital Transformation: a roadmap for billion-dollar organizations. MIT Center for Digital Business and Capgemini Consulting (2011). http://ebooks.fr.capgemini-consulting.com/Digital-Transformation-Enquete/MIT-CC_report_lowres.pdf

10. Driving Digital Transformation: New Skills for Leaders, New Role for the CIO. A Harvard Business Review Analytic Services Report. Harvard Business School Publishing (2015). https://hbr.org/resources/pdfs/comm/RedHat/RedHatReportMay2015.pdf

11. Global Digital Economy – E-Health, E-Education and E-Government Trends. Paul Budde Communication Pty Ltd. (2015). http://www.marketresearchreports.com/paul-budde-communication-pty-ltd/global-digital-economy-e-health-e-education-and-e-government-trends

12. Biro, M.M.: Meet the Top 30 Social Salespeople in the World. Forbes Media (2014). http://www.forbes.com/sites/travisbradberry/2016/07/14/stress-literally-shrinks-your-brain-7-ways-to-reverse-the-damage/#21b79a8163de

13. McAfee, A.: Enterprise 2.0: new collaborative tools for your organization's toughest challenges. Harvard Business Press, Copyrighted Material, 232 P (2009). ISBN 978-1-4221-2587-8. https://www.amazon.com/Enterprise-2-0-Collaborative-Organizations-Challenges/dp/1422125874/ref=sr_1_1?s=books&ie=UTF8&qid=1469120116&sr=1-1&keywords=9781422125878

14. Lavenda, D.: People and Culture are the Biggest Barriers to Digital Transformation. Fast Company Inc. (2011). http://www.fastcompany.com/1796912/people-and-culture-are-biggest-barriers-digital-transformation

15. E-Government for the future we want. In: United Nations E-Government Survey 2014. United Nations, New York (2014). ISBN 978-92-1-123198-4, e-ISBN 978-92-1-056425-0. https://publicadministration.un.org/egovkb/en-us/Reports/UN-E-Government-Survey-2014

16. Integration pioneers leading the way for health and care reform. Press release from: UK Department of Health (2013). https://www.gov.uk/government/news/integration-pioneers-leading-the-way-for-health-and-care-reform–2

17. Working Together. A Handbook for Parents of Children with Special Needs in School (2004). http://www.edu.gov.mb.ca/k12/specedu/parent/pdf/workingtogether.pdf

18. Adrova, E.V., Fomina, N.A.: Integrated solution of general developmental, health-improving, educational, and training tasks in the process of musical-motor training for girls aged 6–7 years at the initial preparation stage of rhythmic gymnastics (in Russian). In: Lesgafta, P.F. (ed.) Uchenye zapiski universiteta imeni, no. 12 (94) pp. 7–11 (2012). doi:10.5930/issn.1994-4683.2012.12.94. http://lesgaft-notes.spb.ru/files/12-94-2012/p7-11.pdf

19. Official portal for making medical appointments in St. Petersburg (in Russian). https://gorzdrav.spb.ru/

20. "Electronic Diary" in Saint Petersburg (in Russian). http://petersburgedu.ru/dnevnik

21. Diagnostic Treatment Centre of the International Institute of Biological Systems. http://ldc.ru/en

Legal Perspective to be Forgotten in Russia and Freedom of Information

Mikhail Bundin[✉] and Aleksei Martynov

Lobachevsky State University of Nizhny Novgorod (UNN), Nizhny Novgorod, Russia
mbundin@mail.ru, avm@unn.ru

Abstract. The decision of the European Court of Justice (ECJ) in the case Google Spain (2014) has provoked continuous debates about the existence and the content of the so-called 'the right to be forgotten'. Many recent works contain different approaches to the idea and the rationale of such a legal concept in the framework of already existing and more well-known privacy rights as 'right to oblivion', 'right to erasure', etc. Nonetheless, the idea quickly has captured the minds of scholars and practitioners over the world. Russia has also followed the European initiative and adopted in 2015 similar provisions with entry into force on 1 January 2016. The paper seeks to evaluate probable consequences and risks for information society, access to information and principle of transparency in Russia. The inappropriate use of the right may affect seriously freedom of information and hide potentially crucial information from the general public.

Keywords: Privacy · Right to be forgotten · Personal data protection · Freedom of information

1 Introduction

Recent years show a great attention to the problems of Data Protection and Privacy in the Internet. One of the most debated issue here is the rationale and content of 'the right to be forgotten' that had been included in the new General Data Protection Regulation (GDPR)[1] text and ECJ practice. The ECJ ruling in Google Spain SL v. Agencia Española de Protección de Datos (AEPD)[2] intensified greatly discussions and was named quickly as establishing 'the right to be forgotten' for the whole European Union (EU). The Court clearly stated that an individual had the right to request to be delisted from search engine's result if the information was no more relevant. Only on the first day after the decision entered into force Google had received about 12 000 requests based on this ground trying to stop providing links to the undesirable information. According to the statistics, in the beginning of 2016 Google has already received more than 400 thousands

---

[1] Regulation (EU) 2016/679, http://eur-lex.europa.eu/legal-content/EN/TXT/PDF/?uri=CELEX:32016R0679&from=EN.

[2] JUDGMENT OF THE COURT (Grand Chamber) 13 May 2014, http://curia.europa.eu/juris/document/document.jsf?docid=152065&doclang=EN.

© Springer International Publishing AG 2016
A.V. Chugunov et al. (Eds.): DTGS 2016, CCIS 674, pp. 169–179, 2016.
DOI: 10.1007/978-3-319-49700-6_17

of requests and checked more than 1400 thousands of URL-addresses with more than 40 % of which were deleted[3].

The tendency has also affected Russian Government, which in July 2015 adopted a new law introducing similar provisions to 'the right to be forgotten'[4]. This legal initiative was cautiously met by the Internet community and scholars. Furious debates about its mere existence and rationale for Russian law and practice are still raging. It seems to be the right time to think over about the Russian Government decision's consequences to information society and to find the real place for the new right. This paper does not seek to critique arguments invoked in support or against the new law provisions but to help understanding its nature and to presume probable changes for Russian personal data and Internet market regulation and that is more crucial for access to information and principle of transparency.

2   The Right to be Forgotten's Origins

The right to be forgotten is now in the center of continuous debates not only in Europe. Its origin, nature and content are still being interpreted in different ways. The most important issue here is a place of the right to be forgotten among privacy rights. Sometimes there is certain misunderstanding in comparing it with some already existing theoretical concepts and privacy rights.

2.1   The Right to Oblivion (Droit á L'Oublie)

Some scholars and practitioners differently regard the nature of the right to oblivion. Most of them treat it like an European (French) concept – 'droit á l'oublie' that represents in general limits to media activities, forbidding press and TV to make public aspects of personal life mostly with a huge negative connotation that were the object of public interest in the past. There are series of court decisions not only in Europe but also in USA concerning people trying to stop making public the information about their unlawful or immoral activities in the past in order to help them start living with a 'clean slate'. Usually it was the case of ex-criminals with expired criminal record or ex-prostitutes [9]. This right is originally dedicated to prevent intervention in their private life by public media.

---

[3] European privacy requests for search removals, https://www.google.com/transparencyreport/removals/europeprivacy/.

[4] Federal Law of Russian Federation #264FZ 13 July 2015, http://www.rg.ru/2015/07/16/informacia-dok.html.

2.2 The Right to Erasure or Blocking, the Right to Object

These rights mentioned in art. 12 (right to erasure and blocking) and art. 14 (right to object) of the Directive 95/46/EC[5] are closely connected with the data protection. They enable an individual to stop his data unlawful use by a data controller. Those rights are closely connected with the idea that data subject has the right to control data processing including the right to demand their blocking, erasure or to object their processing by a controller [1]. The recently adopted GDPR also contains the right to erasure in art. 17 together with 'the right to forgotten'[6].

2.3 The Right to be Forgotten

The ECJ Decision in Google Spain v. AEPD became one of ground breaking judgments of recent years. Some of scholars presume it to be a certain shift in the balance between fundamental rights – the right to privacy and the freedom of expression and information [11]. Wide public as well as a large number of academics in Europe and Russia hurried to name it as introducing a new right – 'the right to be forgotten' [5]. This time the ECJ has enlarged the scope of the Directive 95/46/EC and applied it to searching engines treating them as data controllers. There is no need to describe here all the details of the proceeding or its influence on EU practice, but some details should be underlined for better understanding of the state of things:

- The Court clearly stated that search engines, even non-EU companies with sales and marketing subsidiaries inside EU, are subject to the European Data Protection law;
- Search engines should be treated as data controllers of the personal data that appear in their results and cannot rely on legitimate interest – the public interest in having access to the relevant information;
- Individuals can send a request to search engine to disable links to third party's page which come up against searches using their names even the information is accurate and lawfully published. The individual should prove that information is no longer being processed lawfully on the ground that it is inadequate, irrelevant or excessive to the original purpose for which it was processed in the light of the time, which has passed since that processing started.

Those three points let draw to the conclusion that the new concept as of about something between the right to oblivion (droit á l'oublie) and right to erasure and blocking. Regardless the close connection between them, this case represents an originally new concept based on the same idea as data protection – the right of an individual to control his data processing by third parties and treating personal data as part of his identity.

---

[5] Directive 95/46/EC of the European Parliament and of the Council of 24 October 1995 on the protection of individuals with regard to the processing of personal data and on the free movement of such data 1995, http://ec.europa.eu/justice/policies/privacy/docs/95-46-ce/dir1995-46_part1_en.pdf.

[6] Regulation (EU) 2016/679, http://eur-lex.europa.eu/legal-content/EN/TXT/PDF/?uri=CELEX:32016R0679&from=EN.

2.4   The Right to be 'Forgotten', 'Deindexing' or 'Delisting'?

New concept was very quickly absorbed by EU legislation and practice. Recently appeared GDPR also contains the new right but this time the right to be forgotten is outlined as a part of the right to erasure and a remedy to stop further public online dissemination of the personal data erased on a reasonable ground. In this case, the data controller that has made the personal data public shall take reasonable steps, taking account of available technology and cost of implementation, to inform other controllers processing the data of a data subject's request to erase any links to, copy or replication of them[7]. As to compare it with the ECJ Decision in Google Spain v. AEPD it seems like a different concept.

The latter illustrates obviously that even in European practice the origin, content and implementation of the 'right to be forgotten' is still being debated mainly for three reasons.

1. The new right is applied to the searching engines that do not make public the information themselves and provide only links to them;
2. The information is lawfully disseminated or published by third parties in the Internet but regarded by data subject as undesirable, inadequate or irrelevant;
3. The data subject's request is limited to the non-indexing of information or to not providing links to it.

Those arguments make think of a new right as different from "oblivion" or "forgetting". Some publications show a certain rethinking of the ECJ Decision in order to focus on its main consequence – a right of an individual to request non-indexing or de-indexing of the information, which concerns his private life. The French Data Protection Authority (La Commission Nationale de l'Informatique et des Libertés (CNIL)) named the new right as 'a right to delisting' (le droit au déréférencement)[8]. Surely, the usage of terms the right to oblivion or the right to be forgotten (droit a l'oublie) could produce a certain misunderstanding as French law and practice has been operating such a term in its original meaning connected with mass media activities and described here above. Moreover, some Brazilian scholars also prefer to name this right as the right to de-indexing (direito à desindexação) [8].

Regardless the discussion about the true term, the new right is being implemented and has enough of supporters among politicians, academics and general public as well as critics.

---

[7] Art. 17, Sect. 2, Regulation (EU) 2016/679, http://eur-lex.europa.eu/legal-content/EN/TXT/PDF/?uri=CELEX:32016R0679&from=EN.

[8] Right to delisting: Google informal appeal rejected, http://www.cnil.fr/english/news-and-events/news/article/right-to-delisting-google-informal-appeal-rejected.

3   The Right to be Forgotten in Russia

3.1   Data Protection System in Russia and the Right to Erasure and Blocking

Russia has come a long way towards its current data protection system. The first data protection bill announced in 1995[9] and introduced in State Duma in 1997 was quickly abandoned regardless a great support expressed by a panel of Council of Europe experts and a group of Russian scholars[10]. It had not meant an absolute lack of any regulation of the personal data processing this period. Some provisions of the Federal Labor Code, the Law on Information and the Administrative Code contained a few rules for data protection limited to their simple recognition as a confidential information which disclosure was liable under the law. In other words, before the adoption of the Federal law on Personal Data in 2006[11], Russia had not had any coherent regulation for data protection. Only after 2013 when the Law fully entered into force and Russian request for ratification of Council of Europe Convention #108 was accepted by the Depositary, Russian Federation had joined the club of countries with appropriate data protection system[12]. From the beginning, while creating its regulation for data protection Russia had taken as an example not only the Convention #108 but mostly Directive 95/46/EC[13]. That explains why the Russian data protection legislation is very close to the text of the Directive. The Federal Data Protection Law contains the large part of provisions of European Data Protection System as well as the rights of the data subject including the right to erasure and blocking in case of their unlawful use. Its article 14 clearly states - "the data subject shall have the right to demand from the operator clarification of his/her personal data, their blocking or deleting if the data are incomplete, outdated, inaccurate, illegally obtained or are not necessary for the declared purpose of processing, and also to take measures provided by law to protect his/her rights".

3.2   The Law on the 'Right to be Forgotten'

The adoption of a new Federal Law on 13 July 2015 introducing the right of an individual to require from a searching engine to stop indexing or providing links to false or irrelevant information produced a certain misunderstanding for some reasons. Firstly, the law did not amend the Federal Law on Personal Data but the Federal Law on Information that makes think of it generally as of another restriction to the right to information or

---

[9] Federal Law on Information, Informatization and Protection of Information #24FZ 20 February 1995, http://docs.cntd.ru/document/9010486.

[10] Bill #17844-3 1997, http://www.lawmix.ru/lawprojects/67047.

[11] Federal Law on Personal Data #152 27 July 2006, http://base.consultant.ru/cons/CGI/online.cgi?req=doc;base=LAW;n=61801.

[12] Chart of signatures and ratifications of Treaty 108, http://www.coe.int/en/web/conventions/full-list/-/conventions/treaty/108/signatures?p_auth=tafNJ8i9.

[13] Directive 95/46/EC of the European Parliament and of the Council of 24 October 1995 on the protection of individuals with regard to the processing of personal data and on the freemovement of such data, http://ec.europa.eu/justice/policies/privacy/docs/95-46-ce/dir1995-46_part1_en.pdf.

the freedom of information. Secondly, from the very beginning the new initiative was announced as a "Law on the right to be forgotten" [3, 4].

The law generally includes some new provisions – amendments to the Federal Law on Information. Firstly, it introduces the new term "searching engine" and a new article 10.3 on owner's (operator's) of searching engine obligations. According to the definition "searching engines" could be any "information system performing on user's request search in the Internet of information of particular content and providing the user with information about the index page of the site in the Internet (links) to access to the information…".

The article 10.3 has a rather detailed set of obligations of the searching engine's owner. The general obligation is stated as follows: "The operator of a search engine, providing advertising on the territory of Russia,…. shall be obliged to stop issuing information about the index page of the site in the Internet (the link), allowing access to information about the individual (the applicant) that is disseminated in violation of the legislation of the Russian Federation, false, irrelevant or obsolete for the applicant by subsequent events or his/her actions, except information about events, containing the signs of criminal acts, the deadlines of criminal responsibility for which has not expired, and information about crimes committed by a citizen, when the period of conviction is not expired".

The search engine upon receipt of a request of an applicant shall stop indexing the information (providing links to) within 10 business days or send a refusal notification that may be challenged in court. The operator shall have a right to ask the applicant to clarify the request or send him a copy of his identity documents. The request should contain: identification data (surname, name, patronymic, passport data, contact information; information about the applicant, issuance of links to which are to be terminated; URL address of the index page of a site; the grounds for termination of the issuance of the links by search engine; the applicant's consent for processing of his/her personal data.

3.3 Russia and EU Practice

There is a certain discrepancy in implementation of the right to be forgotten in Russia and EU practice. Generally, those differences could be summarized in two main and crucial points.

1. In Europe, an individual's request to remove links should be based only on his name-search results with an explanation of why the content was "inadequate, irrelevant or no longer relevant". Under Russian law an applicant wouldn't have to provide specific hyperlinks — but merely to point out what information he wants deleted. The latter do not facilitate the implementation of the right, especially from a technical point of view.
2. The Russian law does not contain any exception to the right, enlarging its scope even to the information where a great public interest is involved or about public figures. In Europe, the search engine operators have to delist URLs only if there is no

preponderant public interest in having access to the information and public figures are generally deprived of such a right.

4 What Right to be Forgotten Means for Privacy and Freedom of Information

4.1 ECJ Ruling and Information Society's Concerns in Europe

It is clear that the right to be forgotten represents potentially a strong and effective legal mechanism for protecting individuals' privacy in digital era. Its core element is in recognition of an individual's freedom to control information about him. It is beyond any doubt that a person should have a right to start living with a clean slate, especially when the criminal record is expired or he was acquitted. For example, EU Commissioner Viviane Reding described the ECJ ruling in Google Spain v AEPD as "a clear victory for the protection of personal data of Europeans" [13]. This point of view received a great support throughout Europe and its rationale is clearly understandable.

Nevertheless, the implementation of such a right could possibly affect freedom of information and transparency that are the most important elements of information society. An increasing number of requests to Google and probably to other searching engines makes reconsider the consequences of delisting information from online search. Furthermore, a potential misuse of the right to be forgotten to hide important information from the society should be also kept in mind while considering the existing practice.

This issue was strongly debated in Great Britain and was named by some MPs as "a draconian attack on free speech and transparency, totally at odds with Britain's liberal tradition" [2]. Open Rights Group also expressed significant concern about the consequences to online free speech that may follow the ECJ ruling[14].

The present situation with the implementation of the right to be forgotten by Google also evoked a great concern from a large number of scholars and practitioners in Europe. In May 2015, a large group of 80 academics published an open letter [7] to Google asking to make its delisting policies and decision-making processes more transparent to the public and data protection authorities. They name the existing mechanism "a silent and opaque process, with very little public process or understanding of delisting".

Within a day or two of the ECJ ruling, already the stories were coming out about pedophiles, politicians and general practitioners wanting to use the right to be forgotten to delete their Internet stories – a sort of rewriting of history that the term 'right to be forgotten' evokes, but that the decision in its nature does not provide for [14]. In this case, a vast majority of academics and politicians spoked against such a use of the right arguing that it did not concern public figures or information of a great social value.

All this statements are true but whether it is for Google to decide if the information is "irrelevant", "inadequate or no longer relevant"? That question could not be easily answered. In their letter, academics clearly admitted not only the necessity of transparency in delisting information but also the necessity of a public or a data protection

---

[14] ECJ Google Spain Ruling Raises Concerns for Online Free Speech, https://www.openrightsgroup.org/press/releases/ecj-google-spain-ruling-raises-concerns-for-online-free-speech.

authority's control other the process of delisting in order to find an appropriate balance between individual privacy and public discourse interests.

4.2 Debates in Russia and Recent Practice

Unexpected haste with the adoption of the new law on "the right to be forgotten" has only fomented debates on the problem. The officially expressed opinion mostly showed great support to the idea of protecting individuals online providing them with a right to control processing personal information by search engines [12].

The Internet community, network and search engines operators had no much time for its debating or a possibility to be involved seriously in its preparation and adoption. The famous Russian searching engine - Yandex named the new governmental initiative as "oblivion to the right to search"[15] for the following reasons:

1. The Law will complicate or make impossible the search of important and accurate information;
2. The proposed mechanism opens up the possibility for many abuses and does not require any justification or confirmation, just a single complaint. It is very convenient to achieve a variety of purposes, for example, to conceal information about fraud schemes or hinder competitors;
3. The law suggests for search engines to decide whether the information relevant and true - the function usually referred to the courts or law enforcement agencies. If the search engine refuses this role, she faces a constant fines or litigation;
4. The law does not take into account technical peculiarities of disseminating information on the Internet and the principles of search engines.

Other Russian searching engines like Rambler also said against the law implementation sometimes basing their claim that "deindexing" represents a service that should be a "paid" one[16].

Russian scholars seems to be also rather pessimistic about the new law provisions comparing them with the EU practice. Evidently, Russia created the right to be forgotten as *sui generis* right failing to account for the right of the general public to find and access information online [10].

Regardless the general anathema to the new provisions, searching engines were ready for its implementation and introduced a new application form for requests to exclude information from search results (under "the right to be forgotten") till 1 January 2016[17]. According to the statistics published by Yandex on 25 March 2015 it processed about 3600 requests from 1348 users and satisfied only 27 % of them[18]. The search engine explained such a huge number of refusals by the failure to check the accuracy of

---

[15] 'Oblivion to the right to search', https://yandex.ru/blog/company/96625/.

[16] Search engines reacted to the bill on "right to be forgotten" on the Internet, http://lenta.ru/news/2015/05/29/searchanswer/.

[17] Yandex "Right to be Forgotten" Form, https://yandex.ru/support/zout_abuse/troubleshooting/oblivion.xml; Mail.ru "Right to be Forgotten" Form, https://go.mail.ru/support/oblivion.

[18] Yandex blog, https://yandex.ru/blog/company/o-primenenii-zakona-o-prave-na-zabvenie.

information or a legality of its publication online. Yandex claimed that in most of the cases it simply has no legal means to fulfil it. Other search engine – Mail.Ru Group revealed similar statistics and satisfied only 20 % from 2000 users' requests to him[19].

Courts and legal practice is still rather shy in implementing right to be forgotten and only a few cases could be named, but some of them evoke again the question of misbalance of a new legislation with the freedom of information. Since February 2016 in the Internet there had been few publications involving right to be forgotten claimed by ex-state officials suspected of different crimes as well as public figures[20].

5 Conclusion

The new European initiative launched by the decision of ICJ seems to be a very wary ground and would have certainly serious consequences for Internet companies in Russia. The generally suggested term of the 'right to be forgotten' is also capable to worsen the matter. Some scholars deny the new term considering it as a specific case of the right to erasure or blocking of personal data. The suggestion on regarding it as a right to 'deindexing' or 'delisting' seems to be more prospective in this case and reflects better the reality and more close to another concept recently suggested by some scholars 'the idea of the right to control' [6].

The idea that citizens in Russia will obtain soon a clear and coherent mechanism to protect their online privacy and stop search engines providing links to inappropriate, inaccurate or unlawfully disseminated personal information seems to be also a prospective one. At the same time, the law contains some contestable and ambiguous provisions especially concerning the cases where the public interest is involved. Surely, the individual's right to delist information from the web search results should have more clear regulation and coherent restrictions.

The most suggested amendments here should be as follows:

1. Clear and comprehensive restrictions to the right to be forgotten. Special attention should be made to the public figures, information of great public value and especially to the governmental information subject to obligatory disclosure (e.g., information on public servants' income).
2. The law should also consider the rights of data protection authorities, civil society, individuals, webmasters and other subjects to object delisting information and to be informed about search engines policies in implementing of the right to be forgotten.
3. Search engines are to provide and publish more information about their delisting procedure and policy not limiting to the general information about a number of requests and simple results of their processing. The society should have the right to know: detailed information about categories of requests/requesters (what sort of

---

[19] Who Uses the "Right to Be Forgotten" in Russia, http://www.furfur.me/furfur/changes/changes/218309-pravo-na-zabvenie.

[20] Received the first lawsuits demanding the implementation of the law on the "right to be forgotten", http://b-online.ru/cyberlaws/5362-postupili-pervye-sudovye-iski-s-trebovaniem-vypolneniya-zakona-o-prave-na-zabvenie.html.

information asked to be delisting, are the requesters public figures, etc.); reasons for denial or acceptance of delisting, source of information (social media, official public records), where the webmaster was informed about delisting or not, etc.

Thus the Russian attempt to create similar provision with the EU that even in Europe sometimes have a limited support and are still debated seems to be rather 'ambiguous' and to some extend is regarded by scholars and practitioners in a pessimistic way. Nevertheless, it should be admitted that rights and freedoms as well as the right to privacy evolves constantly and gives birth to new concepts and ideas aimed to protect individuals in the digital era. The new concept "the right to be forgotten" or to be more precise "the right to be delisted" or is at least worth debating as a concept to evaluate the existing status quo in protecting privacy and personal data not only in Russia but in the world. As in other similar cases, the new right is capable to shift the existing balance between privacy rights and freedom of information that is to be reconsidered in the nearest future.

References

1. Ausloos, J.: The 'right to be forgotten' – worth remembering? Comput. Law Secur. Rev. 28(2), 143–152 (2012). doi:10.1016/j.clsr.2012.01.006
2. Doughty, S.: Europe grants the 'right to be forgotten online': EU court will force Google to remove people's personal data from search results on request. The Daily Mail, 13 May 2014. http://www.dailymail.co.uk/sciencetech/article-2626998/The-right-forgotten-EU-court-rule s-Google-remove-personal-data-search-results-request.html
3. Egorkin, S.: Right to be forgotten'. "Zakon.ru", 12 June 2015. https://zakon.ru/blog/ 2015/6/12/pravo_na_zabvenie
4. Sullivan, D.: Russian parliament approves "right to be forgotten" In: Search Engines. Search Engine Land, 3 July 2015. http://searchengineland.com/russia-right-to-forget-224466
5. Floridy, L.: The right to be forgotten – the road ahead, The Guardian, 8 October 2014. http:// www.theguardian.com/technology/2014/oct/08/the-right-to-be-forgotten-the-road-ahead
6. Qc, F.G., Berova, N.: The rule of law online: Treating data like the sale of goods: lessons for the internet from OECD and CISG and sacking Google as the regulator. Comput. Law Secur. Rev. 30(5), 465–481 (2014). doi:10.1016/j.clsr.2014.07.005
7. Kiss, J.: Dear Google: open letter from 80 academics on 'right to be forgotten. The Guardian, 14 May 2015. http://www.theguardian.com/technology/2015/may/14/deargoogleopenletter from80academicsonrighttobeforgotten
8. Luceno, C.: Direito à Desindexação. Direito, Tecnologia e Sociedade da Informação, 9 December 2014. http://claudiokilla.com.br/blog/direito+a+desindexacao-22
9. Mantelero, A.: The EU proposal for a general data protection regulation and the roots of the 'right to be forgotten'. Comput. Law Secur Rev. 29, 229–235 (2013). doi:10.1016/j.clsr. 2013.06.002
10. Nurullaev, R.: The right to be forgotten in the European Union and Russia: comparison and criticism, HSE Working paper (2015). https://www.hse.ru/pubs/share/direct/document/ 162072260
11. Rees, C., Heywood, D.: The 'right to be forgotten' or the 'principle that has been remembered'. Comput. Law Secur. Rev. 30(5), 574–578 (2014). doi:10.1016/j.clsr.2014.07.002
12. Shadrina, T.: 'Roskomnadzor supported the introduction in Russia of right to be forgotten', Rossiyskaya gazeta, 18 June 2015. http://www.rg.ru/2015/06/18/zabvenie-site.html

13. Timberk, C., Birnbaum, M.: In Google case, E.U. court says people are entitled to control their own online histories. The Washington Post, 13 May 2014. https://www.washing tonpost.com/business/technology/eu-court-people-entitled-to-control-own-online-histories/ 2014/05/13/8e4495d6-dabf-11e3-8009-71de85b9c527_story.html
14. Wakefield, J.: Politician and paedophile ask Google to be forgotten. BBC News, 14 May 2014. http://www.bbc.com/news/technology-27423527

How to Measure the Digital Diplomacy Efficiency: Problems and Constraints

Radomir Bolgov[✉], Sergey Bogdanovich, Vatanyar Yag'ya, and Marina Ermolina

St. Petersburg State University, St. Petersburg, Russia
rbolgov@yandex.ru, lacelestespb@gmail.com, usfmo@rambler.ru,
ermolinama@gmail.com

Abstract. The paper provides preliminary results of the comparative overview of e-participation projects development within the e-governance institutional structure in the Eurasian Economic Union (EAEU) member-states. The authors analyze (1) Legal base on e-governance and e-participation; (2) E-governance institutions and stuff; (3) Participation instruments of public engagement. In future the authors plan to elaborate the methodology of e-participation processes monitoring in the countries of the EAEU, and to examine the issue of e-governance institutions effectiveness in the EAEU region.

The purpose of research is to identify the challenges and opportunities of government's digital diplomacy effectiveness assessment. The authors review the up-to-date studies of digital diplomacy effectiveness assessment, generalize the international experience in the evaluation and practical implementation of digital diplomacy, as well as develop the proposals on indicators and criteria of digital diplomacy effectiveness assessment. The authors consider the effectiveness of digital diplomacy on three different levels: the level of information delivered to foreign audience, the level of influence, and the level of interaction with the foreign audience.

The authors find out that foreign policy strategies of leading powers do not contain references to the criteria for digital diplomacy effectiveness, with the exception of the United States. Therefore, the authors have attempted to develop such criteria and constraints that need to be discussed.

Keywords: Social media · Digital diplomacy · Influence on audience · Effectiveness assessment · Evaluation

1 Introduction

Digital diplomacy is understood by most researchers as the presence of diplomats (and diplomacy agencies) in social media in order to establish and maintain relations with foreign public. However diplomats and agencies may be responsible only for the implementation of the official course of the country's government, and global politics requires participation of non- governmental actors who can join forces with the government for the achievement of common goals. Therefore, along with the public accounts, it's worth to consider the accounts of news media (distributed information from the accounts of

© Springer International Publishing AG 2016
A.V. Chugunov et al. (Eds.): DTGS 2016, CCIS 674, pp. 180–188, 2016.
DOI: 10.1007/978-3-319-49700-6_18

the government), commercial and non-profit organizations, expert communities, academic institutions, well-known personalities (personal accounts of politicians and public figures).

In order to separate digital diplomacy from propaganda and other means of online communication we define only social networks posts (comments, multimedia files attached) of accounts openly linking themselves with the abovementioned policy actors, as elements of digital diplomacy.

Effectiveness can be defined as the achievement of goals in relation to the resources used. Therefore, the key component is a political goal (national interest), which will be implemented by digital diplomacy. Of course, the effects of digital and public diplomacy are not always obvious. Governments do not always understand the cost of paying off any digital diplomacy. At the moment, there are quite a few studies, expert reports, official documents published by ministries, for assessing the effectiveness of digital diplomacy.

The purpose of research is to identify the challenges and opportunities of government's digital diplomacy effectiveness assessment.

Objectives of the study:

- Review the up-to-date studies of digital diplomacy effectiveness assessment.
- Generalize the international experience in the evaluation and practical implementation of digital diplomacy.
- Develop the proposals on indicators and criteria of digital diplomacy effectiveness assessment.

2 Theoretical Framework and Research Material

The authors analyzed the foreign policy strategy of leading states (the US, the UK, France, the PRC, and Russia). However they turned out to do not contain references to the criteria for digital diplomacy effectiveness, with the exception of the United States. Therefore, the authors have attempted to develop such criteria and constraints that need to be discussed.

According to most researchers, there are two models of public diplomacy (and digital diplomacy as part of it) – competition-oriented and cooperation-oriented. John Robert Kelley distinguishes three models (levels) - information, influence and involvement in the dialogue [5]. According to Joseph Nye, there are the following models - regular relationship (interpretation of national and foreign policy), strategic communications (in order to influence the opinion on certain topics), and long-term relationships (building trust and reciprocity) [7]. So the question about the compatibility of these models arises. On the one hand, awareness and influence levels can be united in interests defending model (competition). In our view, this is not correctly because just presenting the facts (without any interpretation) and respond to the events is enough to inform the public. However the influence model includes the manipulative effect in the presentation of facts and the rise of public issues without being tied to past events that is not possible by simply informing.

Therefore, we assess the digital diplomacy effectiveness on three different levels: at the level of information delivered to foreign audience, the level of influence and level of interaction with the foreign audience.

3   Literature Review

Earlier, the topic that is close to the definition of methods for assessing the digital diplomacy (use of social media in public diplomacy), was studied by the following researchers.

Eric Abdullatif [1] evaluates the effectiveness of public engagement campaigns by Rapid Assessment Procedures, RAP. The technique itself is a combination of various methods of public opinion research (surveys, focus groups, interviews) and methods of communication between researchers and society. Public participation helps researchers to understand the phenomenon under study in a broad social context (political, economic, cultural and other reasons of their attitude to the program) and to bring recommendations to improve the effectiveness of the studied campaigns. The RAP technique is used under the time constraints, when it is not possible to spend time on your own full research. The author saw the objective of study as a RAP technique application to research the effectiveness of public engagement on the case of USAID campaign in the Horn of Africa in 2011. Using Google data (including Google Blogs) the authors analyzed the comments on the topic of USAID, dividing users into categories, depending on their relationship to the effectiveness of the program (by active enthusiasts to skeptics and rejecters). Next, the researchers identified the social context of users opinions (situation in the US 2011–2012 is characterized by tough cost-cutting budget and presidential campaign of 2012), and developed a communication strategy taking into account the social context (which became clear from the arguments cited in the posts for each category of respondents). The disadvantages of the method of RAP include fuzzy social stratification of the respondents: it is not always possible to identify which social, gender, age, racial group is the author of the post), biases of data (in the process of data selection the piece of information is inevitably eliminated, and with regard to social media there is a problem of unequal access of different social groups to social media), and countering the influence of the chosen strategy (along with our strategy counter-strategy of opponents will be present in the debate).

Maïté Kersaint [6] argues that social media do not provide a reliable source of political power, as the content of different actors is contradictory. In addition, the use of social media in the foreign policy practice (as a flexible, scalable and enduring tool) is faced with a static structure of the foreign ministries. The complexity of evaluating the effectiveness lies in the fact that the criteria that would be useful in the evaluation of social media (such as the impact) is not clearly defined. It is difficult to assess and raise questions from a scientific point of view [6]. On this basis, the author proposes multi-methodology which includes the Historical Institutionalism, Content Analysis and Guided Exploratory Interview. Research institutes reveal how actors behave in world politics and which existing institutions (formal and informal) affect the behavior [6]. It explains the combination of interests and events leading up to this or that decision, and also allows learning about the inter-countries differences in decision-making and political lines in relation to certain countries. A content analysis of the US, Germany, and the UK embassies posts in Facebook and Twitter from September 30, 2011 to December 17, 2011, during the conflict over the Tobin tax, indicates whether digital diplomacy ("public diplomacy 2.0") is used to support the position of the country during the conflict and whether it reflects the ideological foundations of the foreign policy of the compares countries. Interviews of diplomats, employees of public diplomacy institutions, experts on international relations and social media help to identify previously unknown details and to outline the general strategic lines of countries' behavior with regards to the studied issues [6]. However, interviews have significant drawbacks – from the subjectivity of the respondents to the ambiguity of their responses and social context.

Michael Egner in his dissertation [2] examines the public diplomacy campaign, held in the United States for support of military campaign in Iraq in 2003. To determine the effectiveness of the programs and make recommendations for their improvement Egner took advantage by frame analysis. The author adheres to the definition of Robert Entman, according to which the framing is a choice of some aspects of perceived reality with a view to update them in the communication message for a particular formulation ("definition") of the problem, determining the causal link, moral assessment, and recommendations to solve the problem. It is necessary to audit messages (posts, voice or any other type of communication), breaking them in frames (signals or arguments that reflect some aspect of the message, such as the moral side of the issue or economic benefit), i.e. to allocate messages with political, economic, cultural, or military subjects. On this basis, public diplomacy should be viewed as a coordinated system that produces and distributes certain frames to find understanding and support policies.

Frame Analysis is perfect for the "debriefing", when it is necessary to understand why a public diplomacy campaign was rejected or simply unperceived by the audience. Also, the frame analysis successfully solves the problem of improving the senses and reasoning used in the communication with foreign audiences. However, the frame analysis poorly adapted to the rapidly changing politics where the information field is being deformed every day under the influence of competing states and other political actors. If this occurs, the frame analysis applied in the middle of the "battle for the minds," threatens the loss of time and transition of initiative in the hands of an opponent.

4   Legal Framework Review

Publications and legislation of explored countries do not provide a clear answer to the question of digital diplomacy effectiveness assessment.

U.S. Department of State IT Strategic Plan 2011–2013 [3] offers as an indicator the level of internal and external usage of social media and collaboration tools (number of users and volume of use, user surveys of perceived value), i.e. the measurement of the number of participants and their activity. Also, the plan contains such an indicator as a level of centralization and standardization of diplomatic data, i.e. the creation of an integrated system of digital diplomacy campaigning, which would coordinate the activities of all participating bodies of the Department of State and possibly non-governmental actors, so that they do not contradict each other and carry out activities on time.

The IT Strategic Plan 2014–2016 [4] has already mentioned criteria for evaluation of mobile and digital diplomacy: the number of users/devices/access points/applications, i.e. platforms prepared to influence. The new criteria include the engagement with U.S. citizens and businesses, foreign publics, governments, and businesses. Later, the information is analyzed for the importance of foreign audiences, and analytic tools to enhance the value of information to the foreign affairs community are developed. However, it does not specify the means by which this should be done. It presented a general algorithm: preparing the infrastructure for digital diplomacy campaign; campaigning; counting the number of people involved; and analyzing the errors.

The document "Assessing US Public Diplomacy" [9] offers the following methods: audit of existing institutions and programs, focus groups (including the collection and analysis of public data) and expert surveys. The document also outlines the key issues on which the above-mentioned surveys are conducted: the dissemination of information, understanding/misunderstanding of US policy, the impact of US on the foreign audiences. Thus, the effectiveness of digital diplomacy should be tied to individual campaigns (short-term - at the level of influence, and long-term - at the level of strategic cooperation). Moreover it is necessary to measure, whether the campaign achieved success.

Program Assessment Rating Tool, PART, developed by Office of Management and Budget of Administration of the President George W. Bush, involves consideration of all the activities of the Department of State' public diplomacy in four categories: "purpose and structure" (transparency of purposes and specification of results), "strategic planning" (priority), "program management" (needs of funds) and "result" (degree of elaboration of the final result). Each of the four categories are graded from 0 to 100, after which the program is graded as "effective," "adequate," "ineffective" or "no result" (if the program does not have clear indicators of satisfaction).

Another strategy is called Advancing Public Diplomacy Impact (APDI) and carried out by a survey of elites (politicians, media professionals and NGOs, artists, scientists) who participated in the programs of public diplomacy (mainly exchange programs), and who did not participate in them, for understanding the policies and values of the United States and their approval by audience. APDI consistently shows that the attitude to the US of respondents, who participated in the program, is more favorable, but the assessment of the dynamics of the attitude to the United States and the reasons for participation in the programs is a daunting task for the technique.

5   Results of Research

The effectiveness of digital diplomacy can be considered on three different levels: the level of information delivered to foreign audience, the level of influence, and the level of interaction with the foreign audience.

5.1 Information Level

At the Information level the goal is the number of the informed people (P). It is possible even to quantify. We are putting the number of official accounts and count the number of subscribers in different social networks (we must consider very top ones for explored country). In the simplest case, we can count the number of subscribers (F gov) on the accounts of diplomats and departments (P = F gov). However, we must remember that not only the state, but also non-governmental actors may be interested in informing. Therefore it is better to consider the audience (number of subscribers) of all accounts (F gov + F nongov), given the reposters audience (since we are interested in a simple dissemination of information, we take into account bots as well if they have the real subscribers).

P = F gov + F repost + F nongov.

Then we can enter a value such as the coverage of posts in social network (number of users who see this or that post in the news, K). It differs from network to network and depends on the number of subscribers of the page, for example, the average value for Facebook, K fb = 3% [10]. Other social networks do not provide data on the coverage of posts.

Then, having the coverage values for each social network we can count the number of notified people as the amount of coverage of every social network users. The coverage of the audience depends on the number of subscribers: the less number of subscribers of page, the higher percentage of people you can reach. For each group with a certain number of subscribers we can find the average rate. For instance, for pages with the number of subscribers about 1 thousand the average coverage is 22% of the fans for the post. Pages with the more than 100 thousand fans reach on average only 6, 6% [8] - K1 for accounts with more than 100 000 subscribers, K2 for accounts with 50–100 000 subscribers, K3 for 10–50 000 subscribers, etc. Then, for each social network we should count P fb = F1/K1 + F2/K2 +... + Fn/Kn.

A common index for all the social networks is equal to

P = P fb + P twitter + P youtube +....

It should be noted that the person can be signed on the account of the department (company, NGO) in several social networks at once. So it makes sense to consider the same person several times.

5.2 Influence Level

Influence implies the existence of a certain political goal, which is to be achieved with the influence on the audience. It is almost impossible to directly affect the decision-making by the political leader (or group of leaders/experts) with only digital (public) diplomacy. Rather, it will be possible to influence the public, but this process is not a single day and it is extremely difficult to quantify its effectiveness.

Judging by a particular public opinion influence campaign (without considering the further attitude to decision-making person), the effectiveness of digital diplomacy can be evaluated on a scale of "all or nothing": whether a decision acceptable to us was adopted or not. We can assess the benefits and potential risks of the decision. They are often asymmetrical, so we can not always give a quantitative estimate. And if you take into account the public's future attitude to the decision-makers, then surveys at the beginning and end of the campaign would be most effective tool. Then it would be possible to evaluate the effectiveness of digital diplomacy by the amount of resources spent on the campaign.

We can count the shift in public opinion and divide the amount spent on the campaign by this shift. Then we get a number, meaning how much money we spent per audience convinced. However, first, not all surveys can be trusted, but we can not always to carry out an own survey. Second, the importance of the issue can vary greatly for the audience and for us who campaign. The multi-billion dollar defense contract which we want to get ourselves may leave most of the population indifferent.

Third (and most important), the campaign of digital diplomacy is not isolated from the whole information campaign (including public diplomacy, rumors, information and psychological impact). In turn, opinion polls reflect the general mood in society resulting from the use of entire spectrum of information impact tools, not only through official accounts on social networks. The question is how do you know which part of the campaign has the most effect - the official accounts or rumors and propaganda?

It seems that you need to collect the entire amount of information, the meaning of which supports the objectives of the campaign, and to allocate from it the portion of the data that refer to the official accounts and to their non-government supporters. Then we count the percentage, occupied in the general information. If the information on official accounts is circulated better than the rest of propaganda, it is most effective tool. But not more, because even a competent digital diplomacy alone would not save the poor information influence.

If it occurs, the surest method of evaluating the effectiveness of digital diplomacy is a periodic opinion poll with clarification of responses. For such surveys we can trace how much and for what reasons the motivation of society changes in thinking about solutions. What part of society use information resulting from digital diplomacy, what - form the rumors, what - from the other sources. Semantic and syntactic analysis of the responses would reveal the origin of the information. And from this it will be possible to determine the most popular sources of information.

Another way could be a survey with indication of opinion leaders (who you trust to when discussing this issue). But in a hostile environment to the initiator of the campaign, you can count a large number of non-response to this question.

5.3   Interaction with the International Audience

This level involves long-term periodic opinion polls on the subject of perception of our country and our values.

We can identify the success factors necessary for evaluation. They can be grouped into the following units:

- Adequate distribution of resources (some part of the campaign budget should go on its evaluation);
- The study of the target audience;

- Setting a clear, practical and measurable objectives for programs and institutions of public diplomacy;
- Independent assessment of the nature (hiring outside contractors who understand the goals and process of public diplomacy) and the building of the training system;
- "Appraisement of Appraisers" [2] (development of clear tender conditions for evaluating companies, if the appraisement is outsourced);
- Appraisers need to know that their work will be considered and will be integrated in the planning of future campaigns;
- Data collection should be suitable for any goal;
- A system of rewards for those who leave feedback on the campaigns should be developed;
- Evaluation results should be open for the public (if they are not secret) in order to attract the attention of the authorities and the sponsors.

The evaluation criteria should reflect an understanding of the digital diplomacy concept by government. Each government should develop criteria for evaluating the programs of digital diplomacy.

6   Conclusions and Future Work

The complexity of the public diplomacy effectiveness assessment is not only in the fact that we need to know what to assess (separate campaigns, taken together, or all activities), but also in how to assess - by process or by results; by qualitative or quantitative indicators; by intermediate or final results.

Further steps could be more detailed elaboration of proposals on indicators and criteria of digital diplomacy effectiveness evaluation, and development of a conceptual model of a comprehensive assessment of the digital diplomacy effectiveness. Also in the future the authors plan to analyze the interviews of experts and public opinion, media publications, global rankings. However there are few international rankings, evaluating the effectiveness of digital diplomacy, in particular, e-Diplomacy Index, Soft Power 30.

References

1. Abdulateef, E.: USAID's First Public Engagement Campaign: Measuring Public Engagement. Glob. Media J. **21**, 1–8 (2012). http://www.globalmediajournal.com/open-access/usaids-first-public-engagement-campaign-measuring-public-engagement.pdf
2. Egner, M.: Between Slogans and Solutions. A Frame-Based Assessment Methodology for Public Diplomacy. Pardee RAND Graduate School (2010)
3. IT Strategic Plan 2011–2013 Fiscal Years. U.S. Department of State. http://www.state.gov/m/irm/rls/c39428.htm
4. IT Strategic Plan 2014–2016 Fiscal Years. U.S. Department of State. http://www.state.gov/documents/organization/220034.pdf
5. Kelley, J.R.: Between 'take-offs' and 'crash landings': situational aspects of public diplomacy. In: Snow, N., Taylor, P.M. (eds.) Routledge Handbook of Public Diplomacy, pp. 72–85, Routledge, New York (2009)

6. Kersaint, M.: Exploring Public Diplomacy 2.0. A Comparison of German and U.S. Digital Public Diplomacy in Theory and Practice. Ph.D. Dissertation. Faculty for Cultural Studies, European University Viadrina Frankfurt (2014)
7. Nye, Jr., J.: Soft Power: The Means to Success in World Politics (2004)
8. Post can see only 16% of the fans? The truth about the coverage on Facebook, 28 March 2013. (in Russia). http://www.likeni.ru/analytics/pravda-pro-okhvat-v-facebook/
9. The US Advisory Commission on Public Diplomacy (2010). http://www.state.gov/documents/organization/149966.pdf
10. Zuckerberg should know better In: Lenta.ru, 31 December 2013. (in Russian). http://lenta.ru/articles/2013/12/31/facepaper/

Enhancing Municipal Decision-Making Through an Intelligent Conflict Support System

Marco Gomes[1]($\boxtimes$), Francisco Andrade[2]($\boxtimes$), and Paulo Novais[1]($\boxtimes$)

[1] Department of Informatics, Algoritmi Center,
University of Minho, Braga, Portugal
{marcogomes,pjon}@di.uminho.pt
[2] Law School, University of Minho, Braga, Portugal
fandrade@direito.uminho.pt

Abstract. Most conflict scholars, practitioners, and parties dedicated to the thematic of conflict agree that alternative means of solving and managing conflicts other than the traditional court system offers an efficient and cost-effective way to manage and resolve conflicts. However in the area of conflicts involving municipalities, the use of these alternative means and, in particular, early intelligent decision-support systems is not common. Therefore, we propose to deliver an intelligent environment capable of assisting elected and non-elected municipal officials in managing conflict. To develop this proposal, we present a brief review about how the conflict is handled in a digital environment. Further, the system's requirements and a conceptual framework to facilitate information gathering are depicted. Through a proof of concept, we also expose that our approach to handling conflict can be integrated into a generic municipal decision-making process in a viable and feasible way.

Keywords: Intelligent systems · Conflict management · Computer modeling in municipal decision-making · E-government

1 Introduction

Is all conflict dysfunctional and harmful? No. Conflict itself is neither inherently good nor inherently bad. Assuming this understanding, it turns out that engaging in conflict can have positive or adverse effects on relationships and organizations. In fact, it may yield either positive or negative consequences depending almost exclusively upon the way how conflict is handled. In order to better manage conflict, one can stand that acknowledging that is a step further in efficiently navigating and ultimately resolving conflict in personal and professional relationships. This kind of knowledge can be (and should be) applied in organizations, namely in public institutions such as municipalities. One of the problems of municipalities being at the frontline of solving today's local complex problems in such areas as budgets, education, land use, environment, economic development, among others issues, has been the absence of proper instruments to managing the degree of complexity of that problems. Problems that nowadays

© Springer International Publishing AG 2016
A.V. Chugunov et al. (Eds.): DTGS 2016, CCIS 674, pp. 189–204, 2016.
DOI: 10.1007/978-3-319-49700-6_19

demands levels of expertise and resources that exceed their capacity of handling it. Naturally, this type of situations creates a stressful environment within the municipality and lead to conflict among stakeholders groups [6]. Conflicts are, in fact, a part of the public life. For this reason, municipal authorities must provide to their officials conflict resolution skills and tools capable of being able to settle differences that arise within the institution and in the relationship with the citizen. It can be assumed that unmanaged or improperly managed conflict can reduce government efficiency, can cause financial and non-financial losses to municipalities and local communities, and demoralize public managers, among other impacts. The public entities must aim at improving the quality and pace of public service by developing and adopting new and alternative ways of managing and resolving conflicts. Admittedly, most conflict scholars, practitioners, and parties dedicated to the thematic of conflict agree that alternative means of solving and managing conflicts (other than the traditional court system) offers are an efficient and cost-effective way to manage and resolve conflicts. However in the field of conflicts involving municipalities, the use of these alternative means and, in particular, new intelligent decision-support systems is not common. In order to create the best possible conditions to manage conflict, so the municipalities can go forward independently to assist the conflict itself, this work presents an intelligent system designed to help the Municipalities to overcome the challenges of conventional conflict. To do so, in this work we present several approaches that range from novel methods to instruments and techniques dedicated to clarifying interests, identifying tradeoffs, recognizing party satisfaction and generating optimal solutions. In other words, it is our primary objective to deliver an intelligent environment capable of assisting elected and non-elected municipal officials in managing conflict and designing effective conflict resolution strategies that can be applied to areas of work within the municipality. Also, it is our goal to help municipalities to promote public confidence in local government by providing efficient and innovative leadership and support to municipal organizations by encouraging an intelligent self-directed conflict resolution and management through the intersection of Artificial Intelligence applications with alternative means of solving and managing conflicts. Despite of the conflict literature, it is recognized that the following terms may be associated with different scales of impacts and intensities, the terms "conflict", "dispute", "conflict resolution", and "conflict management", in this section and throughout this study, are used interchangeably. The remainder of this paper is structured into six sections. Section 2 draws on recent research to conceptualize the characteristics of a municipal decision-making process under an e-government vision. Section 3 presents the concept of conflict used in the study and introduces the how to handle it. Section 4 presents the case analysis with a particular focus on an intelligent system point of view in modeling municipal conflict management. Section 5 discusses a case scenario and the impacts made by the application of the proposed model of an intelligent conflict support to municipal decision-making process. Section 6 details the main conclusions drawn from this study.

2   Conceptualizing Municipal Decision-Making Under E-government Vision

Roughly speaking, the municipal (local) governments are, in essence, a form of public administration designed to deliver services and to administer a limited range of public policies within a geographical area. Their institutions and terminology can vary significantly between countries, but all share a common aspect: they are the (or near to) lowest tier of administration of the public organizational structure. Being at the "lowest tier" of the organizational structure, this form of public administration plays a pivotal role in balancing some upwards administrative functions and public service provisions. To be accomplished, the municipal government has to involve the development of partnerships between top-down government initiatives and bottom-up local institutions and policies. Furthermore, to convey these purposes while acting as a service organization and a political institution, the municipality must properly handle the citizens' and inhabitants' expectations with their institutional lines of decision-making and planning practices. Finding and maintaining this delicate balance can lead to complex situations involving many issues. Indeed, many of the municipal problems come from the complexity embedded in the processes of transforming political and community choices into desired actions and outcomes. More than ever, complex problems need intelligent decisions. To address this challenge, this work presents an approach to design an intelligent conflict support system to assist municipal decision makers. Its primary goal is to facilitate effective analysis and solution of specific conflict-related problems.

In recent years, academic and governmental attempts to adopt strategies enhancing municipal decision-making processes have faced significant challenges. One of them is how to improve what governments do when confronted with a conflict and how municipalities and stakeholders can develop unique and cooperative solutions to address the specific needs of the community? Obviously, there are no definite answers to this question. However, confronting these challenges directly can be a means to turn these difficulties into new opportunities. However, the opportunities can be partially found: (1) first, by analyzing how information age is, indeed, changing the way people work, learn, spend their free time and interact with government institutions; (2) second, by incorporating important contributions that are emerging from the progress in the intersection of Information and communication technologies (ICT) with government. Namely in e-government implementation and e-government reforms (successful strategies, pioneering practices and innovative approaches) that aim to make governments transparent and responsive to the needs of their citizens [15]. In this regard it is important to refer the main principles of the administrative procedure, including [2], and it is the case in Portugal, the principles of legality, good administration, collaboration with citizens, participation and also, concerning the electronic administration, the principles of availability, access, integrity, authenticity, confidentiality, preservation and security of information (Portuguese Code of Administrative Procedure - CPA, articles 3, 5, 11, 12 and 14) all this resulting in an acceptance of the main principle of open administration (article 17 Portuguese CPA).

Nevertheless, the electronic government concept cannot be reduced just to an integration of ICTs in government. Rather since its inception in 2003, the United Nations[1] have conceived a conceptual framework that adopted a holistic view of e-government development resting on three important dimensions: (i) the availability of online services, (ii) telecommunication infrastructure and (iii) human capacity. Taking into account this methodological framework, this work will carefully adapt its dimensions to reflect an innovative approach to tackling challenges evolving the development of a municipal conflict support system. In this support system, having access to important knowledge, will determine what the municipal official decide to do. For this, the platform developed provides a systematic way of supporting the process of decision-making.

This process has been generically represented in seven steps by Carrel et al. [5] Goal statement, problem identification, and search for alternatives, evaluation of the alternatives, rational choice of the best alternative, implementation, and control and evaluation. Mintzberg [12] divided strategic decision process into three phases: Problem identification, development of the solution and selection of the best alternative. These phases consist of different routines. In the identification phase, the problem is identified (decision recognition routine), and resources are given to the decision-making (diagnosis routine). In the development phase, the solutions for the problem are searched (search routine) or created (design routine). In the selection phase the alternatives are chosen (screen routine), evaluated (evaluation-choice routine) and the decision is authorized (authorization routine). Based on these descriptions, simplified decision-process is presented (adapted from Saarelainen et al. [14]). Applying the aforementioned strategic decision process to the proposed system:

- Identification Phase: After gathering information, it should be applied a theoretical framework to identify, organize, and depict relevant conflict aspects (dimensions). By analyzing key features of conflict situation, an evaluation of the more appropriate methods and techniques to deal with the current conflict must be performed.
- Development Phase: After perceiving a significant adverse change in the context of interaction the manager is required to intervene. The system will do so by adapting strategies (e.g. making a pause, suggesting solutions, using arguments to influence the participants). We propose the development of algorithms for the generation of solutions and strategies that can alleviate this effort and allow the manager to focus on other issues. To do it, the process of generating solutions can be implemented in an abstract way, given that the specific rules for the domain are provided that allow for valid and meaningful solutions to be created.
- Authorization Phase: Authorization will be a typically binary process, acceptance or rejection of the solution. In particular cases, conditional acceptance

---

[1] Visit: https://publicadministration.un.org/egovkb/Reports/UN-E-Government-Survey-2014.

can occur leading to a recycling of the solution presented through the development phase with every attempt made to overcome the parties' objections. Depending on the chosen method of conflict resolution, the parties or the conflict manager will decide whether the current solution or approach is the most appropriate. For instance, according to Zeleznikow[2], to be effective, a comprehensive system to support conflict management should encourage parties to start with negotiation. If negotiation does not settle the dispute, the process can progress to mediation and finally recommendation or arbitration, until the dispute is resolved or failure to resolve the conflict is reported.

3 The Conflict Process and How It Is Handled in a Digital Environment

There are many approaches in the literature to describe the nature of the conflict phenomena. Though definitions vary, conflict is consistently viewed as a sequential, dynamic process. In other words, it is accepted that conflicts do not just erupt; rather they develop through various stages and tend to follow a pattern, despite the fact that, in the beginning, conflict may be perceived as a state or situation. Recognizing and delineating the different dynamics occurring at each stage of a conflict can be useful to a better understanding and addressing the dynamics of conflict. Further, conflicts can develop in stages and consequently may involve many different responses as the conflict proceeds. People involved may develop various strategies, solutions or behaviors to deal with the conflict. In fact, the style of dealing with a conflict must be seen as having a preponderant role in the outcome of a conflict resolution process, especially in those where parties interact directly (e.g. negotiation, mediation). Moreover, there are several styles of behavior by which conflict can be handled and, depending upon the situation, one style may be more suitable than other. Eventually, it is acceptable to state that the outcome will largely depend on the conflict resolution style of each party and the interaction of the styles of the parties. Different approaches may be followed to formalize how the conflict is handled strategically or contingently. The process of conflict resolution is a continuous process in which actors are always working to create the conditions that discourage dysfunctional conflict and encourage "win-win" solutions. In a more technical sense, conflict management refers to a broad range of tools used to predict, prevent and respond to conflict. A conflict resolution strategy involves a combination of these types of tools. In this work, a conceptual framework will take into account the methods and techniques used to deal will conflict.

Taking the advantage of the resources made available by the newest Information and Communications Technologies (ICT), new generations of platforms, to support the conflict handling, have highlighted the utilization of a more autonomous and efficient use of technical tools. Throughout the years, these systems have been significantly empowered by a range of technologies and methodologies that intersect different fields of knowledge such as Artificial Intelligence,

---

[2] Visit: http://www.mediate.com/pdf/lodder_zeleznikow.pdf.

Mathematics or Philosophy. Thus, the paradigm in which reactive communication tools are used by parties to share information have changed to an immersive, intelligent environment [1] which proactively supports the lifecycle of the conflict resolution mechanism with relevant knowledge. Evidently computational systems that implement the cognitive capabilities of a Human expert are not easy to accomplish, especially if we include the ability to perceive the emotions and desires of the parties involved. Indeed, many works have focused on the support of managing activities to resolve conflicts [7]. Two general ways have been employed to express and manage conflict issues:

- Mathematical model-based systems: which are generally based on game theory and economic behavior, where a vast majority of developed systems have utilized quantitative models, such as multi-criteria decision making, conflict analysis, group decision theory, multi-objective linear programming and fuzzy arithmetic to search for an efficient solution based on the negotiation criteria and preferences provided by the users;
- Heuristics model-based systems: which are developed using Artificial Intelligence techniques to model the strategic behavior of the negotiating parties. For instance, systems using knowledge-based systems to model the impact of decisions on competitive negotiations, and model and simulate possible negotiating positions.

Given the broad range of possibilities, it should be clear that there is no universally best approach or technique. Following these models, a review of the literature is presented with the aim of identifying the models, technologies, and failures that a conflict support system can accommodate in a digital environment. When analyzing the current literature, it is concluded that projects targeting the aforementioned particular issues are nearly non-existent. In fact, regardless of the extensive research in social and organizational sciences that address these issues, remarkable advances in computer sciences are still scarce.

4 Environment and Context to Model Municipal Conflict Management: From an Intelligent Perspective

Conflict management is also about creating conflict in the right environment. It can be seen as an ongoing process in which stakeholders continuously work to create the conditions that discourage dysfunctional conflict and encourage conflict resolution processes that facilitate beneficial outcomes. In a practical view, it can consist of a vast array of tools used to anticipate, prevent and react to conflicts. A successful strategy to deal with the conflict must involve a combination of these types of tools with the capability of generally accessing contextual factors and social clues. Previous works suggested that having this sort of information may improve the effectiveness of selecting the most situationally appropriate conflict handling response. Taking into account the relevance of the environment and context in which conflict is being managed, this section tries to analyze the relationship between conflict issues and how it can be addressed in and by digital means. Furthermore, attempts to uncover the most suitable technologies that can response to the challenge of gathering, analyzing and transforming into meaningful content the raw contextual and behavioral data, are abundant in conflict situations.

In summary, the primary objective is to identify the baseline artifacts and to outline the prominent issues involved in the development of such technological framework. In other words, the intent is to design a practical framework capable of acquiring and providing context and behavioral information about the participants of a conflict situation and about the situation itself. To do it, this kind of framework must encompass the determination of the existence or not of a conflict, its characterization and nature, the generation of possible arguments/proposals and the closure of the process. In order to implement a framework able to comprise this kind of information, this work will follow an approach in line with the concept of Intelligent Environment, in which an intelligent environment supports the conflict management platform with context information.

4.1   Modelling Conflict in Municipal Decision-Making Process

Following the work of David Elliott [8], it is suggested that Municipalities are involved in five forms of conflict:

- inter-governmental conflict conflict with another municipality, the Province, or local authority. In these conflicts both sides use public money to fund the dispute;
- contractual conflicts disputes over contracts between the municipality and the provider of goods or services. Disputes over the construction of municipal buildings is one example;
- employment disputes disputes between the municipality and a union related to a collective agreement, or employment contracts with management or non-unionized employees;
- public policy conflict conflict about a municipal decision or a policy the municipality should adopt. Land use planning disputes are an example of public policy conflict;
- disputes about municipal administration complaints by residents or businesses about the administration of municipal functions;
- disputes over provisions of goods and/or services conflicts between the municipality and the provider of goods or services.

Moreover, David Elliot in this work [8] makes an important statement regarding the complexity surrounding the way the municipalities handles with conflict:

> *Vast amounts of time and human and financial resources are spent in dealing with conflictual situations. In fact, planning in advance to avoid conflict, or managing conflict when it arises, is a large part of the function of every municipal government. It only makes sense to make sure the conflict resolution systems used by municipalities are efficient, economic, and produce sound results (in accordance with the main principle*

of good administration, such as it is recognized by Portuguese CPA article 5). Unfortunately, many systems fail on all three counts - they are expensive, inefficient, and often produce questionable results. With tighter government funding and greater concern over the expenditure of public money at all levels of government, municipalities must look at the ways they go about resolving disputes are they as efficient, economical, and sensible as they should be?

Some interesting initiatives are taking place in USA[3] and Australia[4] municipalities. They are answering this question by offering to its citizens a set of alternative means of dispute resolution. Despite this initiatives are achieving satisfying results, they still rely on traditional processes of resolution and conflict management tearing apart the benefits of the intersection with ICT for better managing and resolving disputes. It happens partly because traditional approaches to conflict management are inefficient and do not conveniently exploit the new technologies of communication and information. In this work, it was identified that one of the major faults is the failure to consider the context information and the conduct of the parties, inaccessible in the current municipal management information systems in digital environments. Concerning this matter, this section consists in trying to answer this question by choosing the most suitable technologies for the development of the technological framework that can acquire and provide context and social information about the participants in a conflict situation. The framework will encompass the determination of the existence or not of a conflict, its characterization and nature, the generation of possible arguments/proposals and the closure of the process. This work will follow an approach in line with the concept of IEs, in which an intelligent environment supports the conflict management platform with context information. In the following sections, the literature review is presented, establishing the current state of the art and identifying its main drawbacks.

In this section, the relationship between conflict and ICTs was analyzed. It was also explored the challenges that individuals face in using online technology for collaboration and conflict mediation purposes. It can be concluded that developments in ICTs have played a critical role in exacerbating and/or resolving conflicts [11]. It was also shown how recent AI innovations can facilitate knowledge acquisition, network building, and the analysis and presentation of conflict-related data. Indeed, some online-specific techniques have been developed to take advantage of the new technology; these include automated negotiation (without human intervention) and negotiation support systems. Meanwhile, regarding the review of literature in previous sections, the main drawbacks of current approaches can thus be summarized:

– The need for a rigorous conflict resolution instrument that measures conflict behavior rather than the self-report instruments;
– Acquisition of information is performed in rudimentary ways, without support;

---

[3] Visit: http://www.mass.gov/courts/programs/adr/.
[4] Visit: http://www.municipalaffairs.alberta.ca/mdrs.

- Current trend continues to focus mainly on the development of technological tools, leaving aside important issues that are present in traditional dispute resolution processes;
- Ongoing conflict handling systems have no autonomy and still rely primarily on the human.

The use of AI and more particularly Ambient Intelligence techniques can help to suppress these gaps. This work considers that a Conflict Management intelligent environment should be envisioned as a virtual space in which disputants have a variety of conflict resolution tools at their disposal. Participants or managers can select any tool they consider appropriate for the resolution of their conflict and use the tools in any order or manner they desire, or they can be guided through the process. It is also planned that the process of decision-making should be enriched with relevant knowledge. In the following sections it is presented a scratch of an intelligent system designed to assist parties to overcome the challenges of conventional negotiation through a range of analytical tools to clarify interests, identify tradeoffs, recognize party satisfaction and generate optimal solutions. In this context, it must be pointed out that the use of ICT and AmI applications and new technologies are not entirely risk-free. In any online medium, communications and data may be intercepted, monitored, altered, accessed, downloaded or even destroyed. However, this can be mitigated and minimized through encryption technologies, firewalls and passwords, as well as privacy enhancing technologies to ensure that information about parties remains confidential and secure. Issues of Identity Management and Data Protection must be considered [13].

4.2   Requirements for an Intelligent Conflict Support System

The pivotal phase of conflict consists in dealing with the actual conflict. Simply speaking, it is the phase in which disputants attempt to cope and manage conflict. From a technological point of view, the pretended system should support the decision-making process. Support is characterized by, among other things, facilitating access to information such as the handling style of the parties or their levels of stress. To do it, several main functionalities must be considered and developed:

Select the Stakeholders. The first logic step is to define the stakeholders. These may include human specialists (e.g. mediators, arbitrators, and law experts), the parties and system agents with specific tasks. This first step, therefore, depends on the specific details of each implementation scenario. In other words, the selection will depend on the nature of human experts as also on factors like the part of the law addressed or the conflict methodology (e.g. mediation, negotiation, arbitration).

Development of a Service-Oriented Architecture. The framework to support the process should focus on workflows, enhancing the communication between the parties. And for the collection and the providing of information for the manager. The most suitable way of guaranteeing these requirements is, in our opinion, to underpin the architecture under a service-oriented approach.

Generation of Arguments/Solutions. The focus should be on the development of algorithms for automatic generation of arguments or solutions. The main objective is to provide the platform the capability of intelligently generating arguments that the parties (or the manager) can use to influence the behavior of the participants. Built on previous work, it is suggested the use of evolutionary algorithms for the generation of solutions and their utility, supporting the manager in one of the hardest tasks in negotiation.

Incorporation of Machine Learning. The main objective is to research and apply machine-learning algorithms that can contribute to an automated or semiautomated improvement of some aspects of the framework. Moreover, the framework should also collect statistical information on the success or failure of the strategies followed. In doing this, it will improve the system's overall performance since successful strategies for similar cases will be preferred over the other.

4.3   Predicting and Classifying Human Behavior

The development of such a framework will result in a set of services or functionalities that will support the work of the manager and improve parties' commitment to the resolution process. The underlying idea is to release the participants from processual issues so that they can dedicate more time to more complex issues. Suggested by Galitsky [9] the following sequence of problems needs to be solved for predicting and classifying human behavior using a conflict management system:

- Discover how to reconstruct behavior patterns from the intelligent environment sensory/interaction data. Galitsky [9] stands that it turns out that communicative actions and their subjects are essential elements of behavior discourse;
- Construct a formal language to represent communicative actions. Finding attributes of communicative actions so that similarity between them can be defined. Analyzing how the mental space is "covered" by communicative activities, and forming a substitution matrix for them to measure similarity, can be a way of doing it.
- Build a way to extract information from a natural language for communicative actions and their subjects and parameters (which is significantly harder due to implicit references to these subjects in natural language);
- Observe that the sequence of behavior patterns can be packaged as a scenario. Defining a scenario as a graph including communicative actions and interaction

between their subjects, based on causal links and relations for argumentation seems a possible method of dealing with this;
– Define relationships between scenarios via sub-graphs, with respective operations on vertices and arcs. Define similarity between scenarios based on graphs and similarities between individual communicative actions;
– Build a machine learning framework and select a particular learning approach well suited to operate with scenario graphs. Evaluate whether concept learning is an adequate approach.

4.4   An Intelligent Conflict Support Environment

The proposed system is a conceptual framework which can be implemented as a computer-based support system to assist municipal decision-making in managing conflict in real-life environments. The designed system comprises several components needed for underpinning an intelligent environment that could be sensitive and responsive to both parties of a conflict management process (See Fig. 1). Each component of the system will be briefly explained in the following lines.

Data Collection. Information from physical sensors, called low-level context and acquired without any further interpretation, can be meaningless. So, to alleviate this problem, a high-level context information must be derived from

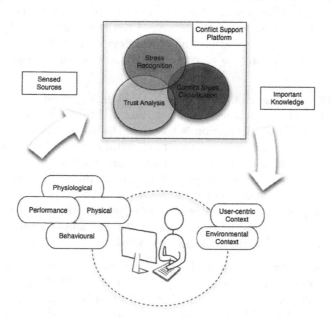

Fig. 1. Conceptual Framework for collecting transforming and presenting important knowledge to conflict's manager.

raw sensor values. The idea is to abstract from low-level context by creating a new model layer that gets sensor perceptions as input and generates or triggers a system. This will be done through a specification process when high-level information is recognized, i.e., sensor perceptions are aggregated and associated with a human-defined information label using classification techniques.

Feature Extraction. The extraction of illustrative features from sensor data is the core of the high-level information model construction. In this stage, the features handled by the system are extracted from multiple sensor observations and combined into a single concatenated feature vector which is introduced into the approaches as mentioned earlier and generates or triggers system actions based on template methods.

Classification Processes. To integrate all the multimodal evidence it was chosen a decision level integration strategy. Examples of decision level fusion methods used include weighted decision methods and machine learning techniques. This component unites all the processes that deal with the data level integration of the contextual and behavioral data gathered from the available sensors.

Stress Recognition: The level of stress is of the utmost importance in conflict resolution and is correlated with the conflict resolution style and the level of escalation of the conflict. For estimating the stress level of the participants, it was adapted/incorporated non-invasive methods, built on previous work [10, 16] in which it was successfully measured the effects of stress by analyzing the interaction patterns of users with handheld devices, considering features such as touch intensity, acceleration of gestures, the amount of movement or touch duration.

Trust Analysis: For the analysis of trust in this kind of scenarios, it is suggested the use of AI techniques that use a trust data model to collect and evaluate relevant information. This information is based on the assumption that observable trust between two entities (parties) results in certain typical behaviors. Namely, we assume the proposition that trust results in characteristic interaction behavior patterns that are statistically different from random interaction in a computerized conflict and negotiation management system. The measure of trust will be based on the application of a mathematical algorithm to measure the parties' interactions, obeying to the following postulates: (1) longer interactions imply less trust; (2) more interactions suggest less trust.

Conflict Styles Classification: To classify the conflict style, the proposals must be analyzed regarding their utility. In each stage of the negotiation, the parties' proposals are analyzed according to their utility value and a range of possible outcomes defined by the values of the worst alternative to a negotiated agreement (WATNA) and best alternative to a negotiated agreement (BATNA) of each party [3]. This approach uses a mathematical model [4] that classifies a party's conflict style considering the range of possible outcomes, the values of WATNA and BATNA as boundaries, and the utility of the proposal.

5   Municipal Service Delivery Proof of Concept

Due to the novelty of this work, the proof of concept was chosen to demonstrate the applicability of the concepts of conflict management enhanced by intelligent environments. Employing this method, it was aimed to prove the viability and feasibility of innovative concepts through prototypes and demonstrations of features. In this case, the proof was designed to demonstrate the functionality of the previously depicted system by implementing a rough technological prototype in a testbed environment. Therefore, a small experiment was set up in which we tried to estimate all the relevant aspects in a conflict situation that occur in a sensory rich municipal environment (where contextual modalities were monitored). Twenty-five individuals participated, both female and male, aged between 21 and 44 years old. In that sense, a web based simulation game was designed to simulate a scenario in which a municipality needs to perform a service contract (an agreement between a municipality and a service provider) to guarantee the repairs and maintenance of municipal equipment. Each party has to achieve a desired result in the negotiation, in other words, the negotiation outcome was to be a win/win situation for both sides. The objectives and the persona (the roles) for each party are described as:

- Municipal Official - this person plays the role of assisting the municipality during decision-making to accurately decide which service providers are the most suitable to provide a particular service on behalf of a municipality within a specific budget. He receives information to make a service contract in which he must ensure the repairs and maintenance of municipal electronic equipment on a short-term basis (only one year) within the allocated budget (1200 Euro or less);
- Service Provider he represents a private company commercial agent that provides repairs and maintenance of electronic equipment. He was not the only supplier of this kind of services. For his company to stay in business, he needed to sell 10000 Euro or more per service contract, knowing that prices of this sort of services can vary greatly depending on the local and the particular situation. If he did not achieve this, he would go bankrupt.

Regarding the conflict styles analysis, the ZOPA (Zone Of Possible Agreement) was bounded by the BATNA (10000 Euro) and WATNA (12000 Euro) values. The range of possible agreement was 2000, but the parties were not aware of this detail. The rst step of the experiment was to give randomly to the participants one of the predetermined roles. After the participants had started to interact, the next step was the monitoring of the individuals' interaction with the web-based simulation game. The data was provided by the system's monitoring process, which was customized to collect and treat the interaction data (see Sect. 4.4) allowing the analysis of the described features. Due to the limited number of available sensors in the experiment, some of the features were not considered. The features considered were the following: context features (analysis of the parties' actions such as the number of parties' proposals), behavioral features (e.g. conflict styles used during the negotiation), performance features (e.g. accuracy and response - time span between the beginning and the end of user's responses to the conflict resolution demands). Afterwards, in order to transform the extracted features into relevant information the classification processes (presented in Sect. 4.3) were used.

After the experiment has been performed, the first step was to run some analysis to compare the sets of data under study. The analysis shows that there is an apparent difference between the groups regarding the negotiation styles exhibited during the game. It is important to recall that participants were asked to negotiate a favorable deal in a competitive scenario. Meanwhile, we can also conclude from the outcomes that these are meaningless in the statistical sense due to the small sample size used in the current study. Some caution must be taken when interpreting the results. Also, the participants were recruited from a particular population (from our university) - a population that may limit the generalization of the results. Admittedly, the participants of the experiment may not be representative of negotiation parties in general. Consequently, we are unable to demonstrate the causality of the variables conclusively. However, we can stand that the results were approximately in line with the ones obtained in previous experiences. From the data collected, it can be concluded that most of the time the parties used an aggressive style, whether under stress or calm scenarios. The analysis shows that there is an apparent difference between the data set regarding the negotiation styles exhibited during the game. Similarly, but now concerning the roles played by participants, we conclude that the service providers were much more competitive than municipal officials while those were principally collaborative. Nevertheless, it is shown that when participants have a significant trust relationship they are more likely to transform it into a win/win situation. Finally, the proof of concept demonstrates how the platform enables the parties and managers to make more informed conflict-related decisions.

6   Conclusion

We aimed at first to deliver an intelligent environment capable of assisting elected and non-elected municipal officials in managing conflict. An experiment was designed to validate and to provide an understanding of the difficulties to technically and algorithmically capturing and computing conflict-related information in an intelligent environment. Concerning this matter, the tests were conducted to assure the system's performance and usability. They were interpreted and evaluated based on the conceptual framework and on the functional requirements defined earlier. It can be concluded that we don't notice any significant problems and, taking into account that this is an ongoing work, the fulfilment of most of the requirements defined earlier was achieved. Meanwhile, the experience gained through the observation of the outcomes points out that a more comprehensive and in-depth study to provide theoretical and technological advances should be developed. Secondly, from the results we conclude that this approach seems to us a valid path to help municipalities to promote public confidence in local government by giving them relevant information (such as parties' conflict styles) for taking well-grounded decisions. By providing efficient and innovative support to local government this work pretends to encourage the creation of better conditions to manage conflicts, so that the municipalities can go forward independently to manage the conflict themselves.

Acknowledgements. This work has been supported by COMPETE: POCI-01-0145-FEDER-007043 and FCT - Fundação para a Ciência e a Tecnologia (Portuguese Foundation for Science and Technology) within the Project Scope UID/CEC/00319/2013.

References

1. Aarts, E., Grotenhuis, F.: Ambient intelligence 2.0: towards synergetic prosperity. J. Ambient Intell. Smart Environ. **3**, 3–11 (2011)
2. Andrade, F., Novais, P., Machado, J., Neves, J.: Contracting agents: legal personality and representation. Artif. Intell. Law **15**(4), 357–373 (2007). http://dx.doi.org/10.1007/s10506-007-9046-0
3. Andrade, F., Novais, P., Carneiro, D., Zeleznikow, J., Neves, J.: Using BATNAs and WATNAs in online dispute resolution. In: Nakakoji, K., Murakami, Y., McCready, E. (eds.) JSAI-isAI 2009. LNCS (LNAI), vol. 6284, pp. 5–18. Springer, Heidelberg (2010). doi:10.1007/978-3-642-14888-0_2
4. Carneiro, D., Gomes, M., Novais, P., Neves, J.: Developing dynamic conflict resolution models based on the interpretation of personal conflict styles. In: Antunes, L., Pinto, H.S. (eds.) EPIA 2011. LNCS (LNAI), vol. 7026, pp. 44–58. Springer, Heidelberg (2011). doi:10.1007/978-3-642-24769-9_4
5. Carrell, M.R., Jennings, D.F., Heavrin, C.: Fundamentals of Organizational Behavior. Prentice Hall, Upper Saddle River (1997)
6. Maximum Out of Pocket Collaboration: Legislative study: Massachusetts municipal conflict resolution needs assessment, final report. Technical report, University of Massachusetts Boston (2016)
7. Cooper, S., Taleb-Bendiab, A.: CONCENSUS: multi-party negotiation support for conflict resolution in concurrent engineering design. J. Intell. Manuf. **9**(2), 155–159 (1998)
8. Elliott, D.C.: Creative collaboration: a sudden outbreak of common sense? (1994). https://books.google.pt/books?id=PsVWGwAACAAJ
9. Galitsky, B., de la Rosa, J.L.: Concept-based learning of human behavior for customer relationship management. Inf. Sci. **181**(10), 2016–2035 (2011). http://www.sciencedirect.com/science/article/pii/S0020025510004007
10. Gomes, M., Oliveira, T., Carneiro, D., Novais, P., Neves, J.: Studying the effects of stress on negotiation behavior. Cybern. Syst. **45**(3), 279–291 (2014)
11. Lodder, A.R., Zeleznikow, J.: Enhanced Dispute Resolution Through the Use of Information Technology. Cambridge University Press, Cambridge (2010)
12. Mintzberg, H., Raisinghani, D., Theoret, A.: The structure of unstructured decision processes. Adm. Sci. Q. **21**, 246–275 (1976)
13. Olsen, T., Mahler, T.: Identity management and data protection law: risk, responsibility and compliance in 'Circles of Trust'. Comput. Law Secur. Rep. Part I **23**, 415–426 (2007). (Sects. 1 and 2)

14. Saarelainen, M.M., Koskinen, J., Ahonen, J.J., Kankaanpaa, I., Sivula, H., Lintinen, H., Juutilainen, P., Tilus, T.: Group decision-making processes in industrial software evolution. In: 2007 International Conference on Software Engineering Advances, ICSEA 2007, p. 78 (2007)
15. Seifert, J.W., Chung, J.: Using e-government to reinforce government-citizen relationships: comparing government reform in the United States and China. Soc. Sci. Comput. Rev. **27**(1), 3–23 (2008)
16. Novais, P., Carneiro, D., Gomes, M., Neves, J.: The Relationship between Stress and Conflict Handling Style in an ODR Environment. In: Motomura, Y., Butler, A., Bekki, D. (eds.) JSAI-isAI 2012. LNCS (LNAI), vol. 7856, pp. 125–140. Springer, Heidelberg (2013). doi:10.1007/978-3-642-39931-2_10

E-Participation Projects Development in the E-Governance Institutional Structure of the Eurasian Economic Union's Countries: Comparative Overview

Radomir Bolgov[1]([⊠]) and Vitalina Karachay[2]

[1] St. Petersburg State University, St. Petersburg, Russia
rbolgov@yandex.ru
[2] E-Governance Center, ITMO University, St. Petersburg, Russia
karachay@egov-center.ru

Abstract. The paper provides preliminary results of the comparative overview of e-participation projects development within the e-governance institutional structure in the Eurasian Economic Union (EAEU) member-states. The authors analyze (1) Legal base on e-governance and e-participation; (2) E-governance institutions and stuff; (3) Participation instruments of public engagement. In future the authors plan to elaborate the methodology of e-participation processes monitoring in the countries of the EAEU, and to examine the issue of e-governance institutions effectiveness in the EAEU region.

Keywords: Electronic governance · Electronic participation · Information and communication technologies (ICT) · Institutional structure · Citizen engagement · Eurasian Economic Union (EAEU) · Eurasian integration

1 Introduction

December 21, 2015 the decision about establishment of new direction in the framework of Eurasian Economic Commission (EEC) Collegium's activity – internal markets, informatization, information and communication technologies (ICT) – was adopted at the supreme Eurasian economic council. The decision came into effect from the February, 2016.

Karine Minosyan (Armenia) was adopted as responsible for the issues of informatization, ICT, information interaction, and functioning the internal markets. Thus, the importance of forming the common digital agenda was stressed by members of the EAEU [17].

Implementation and development of e-participation instruments let to involve different groups of citizens in public policy and facilitate creation of new effective forms of interactions between citizens and state via creation of bilateral exchange of information.

© Springer International Publishing AG 2016
A.V. Chugunov et al. (Eds.): DTGS 2016, CCIS 674, pp. 205–218, 2016.
DOI: 10.1007/978-3-319-49700-6_20

Thereby, the perspective research direction is analysis of opportunities and perspectives of e-services providing e-cooperation between citizens and public authorities, assessment of new modern mechanisms of feedback, determination of high demand services via analysis of corresponding petitions.

It is worthy to note that e-governance technologies may be used not only for creation of the investment attraction of the regions and country, and improvement of quality of life, but also for achievement of goals of successful integration and advanced development. Thus, it is important to explore the national specifics of information technologies implementation and elaborate the recommendations for common e-governance development in the Eurasian region.

The purpose of the paper is analyzing the current state of e-participation projects development in EAEU member-states within the e-governance institutional structure.

2   Literature Review

The issue of e-governance development at post-Soviet countries, including the countries of EAEU, is considered as key component of the Information Society. According to the researches, the main obstacle for the development of Information Society in transitive countries is a low level of democracy [2], a low level of economic development [3]. E-Governance development in the EAEU countries is analyzed by D. Marushka and M. Ablameyko [9], G. Junusbekova [7], T. Pardo and E. Styrin [12].

The legal aspects of Information Society development in EAEU and the comparative analysis of e-governance implementation in the member-states of the Eurasian Economic Union is developed in the papers of V. Karachay and R. Bolgov [5, 8]. The issue of measurement and evaluation of socio-economic and political effects of e-governance, including the e-participation and open data effects are studied by Y. Misnikov [11]. The question of smart cross-border e-governance systems and applications is studied in the paper of A. Sideridis et al. [15]. The perspectives and approaches of electronic identification of citizens are analyzed in [4].

However, despite of the development of different aspects of the topic of e-governance development in the Eurasian region, there is a lack of complex comparative researches concerning the issues of e-participation projects within the frameworks of e-governance institutional structure in the countries of EAEU. Thus, the current research is aimed of fill the gap in this field.

3   Methodology

This study presents preliminary results of the comparative overview of the e-participation projects development in the e-governance institutional structure of the EAEU member-states. For conducting the research, we use a method of structural analysis of politics [16], which allows analyzing the different levels of e-governance decision-making system as a certain political structure, consisting of the elements and relationships between them.

For studying the e-participation projects development in the member-states of the EAEU, we analyze (1) Legal base on e-governance and e-participation; (2). E-Governance institutions and stuff; (3) Participation instruments of public engagement (in particular, by the example of e-government portals research).

Moreover, following by the framework for Measuring and Evaluating e-Participation (METEP), elaborated by the UNDESA's Division for Public Administration and Development Management (DPADM), for studying the promotion of the successful e-participation technologies in the EAEU countries, we aimed at the reaching of such objectives: determinate the eliminating barriers for participatory policy making; studying the effective public engagement tools; analyzing capacities for evaluating e-participation progress [10].

4   UN E-Participation Index of the EAEU Countries

E-participation instruments implementation may influence the nature of government, make it more transparent and more under controlled for publicity. Moreover, e-governance mechanisms development may facilitate the widening of the opportunities for citizens participation in public policy.

The level of ICT-development and e-governance instruments' maturity may be partially characterized by the position of the concrete state in the international ratings of e-government development. United Nation (UN) e-Government Development Index is counted for every country by averaging the results of three indexes: the level of e-services development, infrastructure, and human capital. Thereto, the e-participation index is rated separately, results of which influence the e-government development rate. The e-participation index was aimed at evaluation the level of cooperation between the state and the citizens with the use of Web 2.0 instruments, including the blogs, social networks, and mobile communication. The special attention was focused on that fact that citizens' interactions must be constantly conducted, but not only during the election campaign.

The Fig. 1, demonstrates the dynamics of the positions of the countries of Eurasian Economic Union (Armenia, Belarus, Kazakhstan, Kyrgyzstan, and Russia) in UN e-Participation Development Index [18]. Thus, it is worth to note the considerable progress of Russian (from 86th position in 2010 to 30th in 2014) and Armenia (from 135th position in 2010 to 59th in 2014). Generally, the positive dynamics of these EAEU countries in current e-government development rating is determined by improvement the positions of Russia and Armenia on the components of e-services development and the level of ICT-infrastructure development.

In particular, such growth in the position of Russia become possible because of ICT sector development and e-governance infrastructure development, including the government web-site development and active presentation the interest of Russian Federation in the frameworks of cooperation with the international organizations. The main advantage became the creation of Common Portal of State Services [1].

Generally, it is worth to note that the e-government actively develop in Russia during last several years. The part of participants that got e-services in 2014 passed 35 %. From

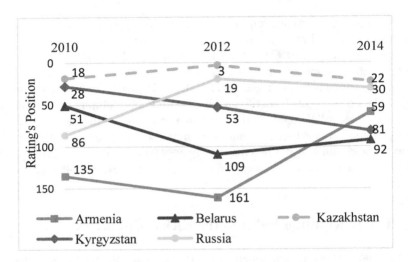

Fig. 1. The dynamics of EAEU Countries' positions in the UN e-participation Index

the beginning of 2015 it was counted 28, 8 million visits of Common Portal of State Services, totally from the moment of its launching the users visited it 205 million times. Daily average of visits for indicated period is about 200 thousand. For the first five months 2015 the users applied at the portal 6, 5 million of federal services, 256 thousand of regional services, and 278 thousand of municipal services [13].

Thus, despite on the positive dynamics of some member-states of EAEU (Armenia, Kazakhstan, Russia) in UN e-Participation Index, it is worth to note that the citizens of the member-states of the Eurasian Economic Union are rather the passive recipients of public services than co-authors of public values. Therefore, the public policy must be focused on citizens' inclusion to the decision-making process.

5   E-Participation Project's Development Within E-Governance Institutional Framework in Eurasian Economic Union

With the aim of analysis the e-participation projects development in EAEU countries within the e-governance institutional infrastructure the legislation base on e-governance, the responsible institutions, and the correspondent participation technologies of public engagement were examined.

5.1   Legal Base on E-Governance

The legislative on Information Society development defines the establishment and the implementation of the e-governance, including the e-participation in EAEU. The normative formalizing of e-governance and e-participation development will let to create effective instruments of citizens engagement in public policy and decision-making process.

E-governance Legislation Development in Armenia. The main legislative acts on the e-governance in Armenia are: Conception of the Information Technology Domain Development (August 28, 2008); the Law on e-Communication; Law on E-Documents and E-Signature (December 14, 2004); Conception on E-Administration System's Development in Republic Armenia.

It is worth noting that the legislation on e-governance development in Armenia is needed to be enriched. For example, some legislative acts have lost their power as the Conception E-Community Development (February 25, 2010). Thus, the e-participation initiatives must be supported by the correspondent legislation. Only in that way it would be possible to consider the real social participation in public policy via usage of ICT-instruments.

E-governance Legislation Development in Belarus. The main legislative acts on the e-governance in Belarus are: Strategy on Information Society Development till 2015 (adopted in 2010); National Program on Advanced Development in ICT Domain (March 28, 2011); resolution of the Council of Minister of the Republic of Belarus on Basic e-Services (February 10, 2012); President Decree on Some Issues of information Society Development in Belarus Republic (November 8, 2012); Law on the E-Document and E-Signature (December 28, 2009); Law on information, Informatization, and Information Protection (November 10, 2008); 'Electronic Belarus' (2002).

However, despite of the considerable legislation base on e-governance in Belarus, the main problem in e-governance implementation consists in forming urgent conceptual and legislation base for development of electronic cooperation between citizens and state. Moreover, it is worth to formalize legislatively the terms 'e-government', 'e-service', elaborate the law draft on citizens access to public information.

E-governance Legislation Development in Kazakhstan. The main legislative acts on the e-governance in Kazakhstan are: Law on Informatizaion (January 11, 2007); Law on Making Alterations and Amendments to Some Legislation Acts on 'e-Government' and 'Mobile Government' Issues (July, 2014); Law on Informatization; Law on Electronic Documents and Electronic Signature; State Program 'Information Kazakhstan - 2020'.

Thus, the e-governance development in Kazakhstan is supported by the substantial normative base. However, the main problem in e-governance implementation is consists in lack of critical mass of citizens who are ready to use e-governance services. Thereto, the citizens are not interested in participating in e-governance projects and initiatives.

E-governance Legislation Development in Kyrgyzstan. The main normative documents on e-governance development in Kyrgyzstan are the Program of ICT Development (November 8, 2001); National Strategy 'ICT for Kyrgyz Republic Development' (2002); Law on Informatization (1999); Program on e-Government Development (2013–2017).

It is worth noting that Kyrgyzstan is at the primary stage of e-governance development. The e-governance projects implementation will be regulated by the National Program 'Electronic Kyrgyzstan 2020–2025'. Within the framework of this program the necessary ICT-infrastructure will be created, the public services are planned to be delivered in electronic format.

E-governance Legislation Development in Russia. The main legislative acts on the e-governance in Russia are: Strategy of the Information Society Development in Russia (February 7, 2008); State Program of Russian Federation 'Information Society' (2011–2020) (October 20, 2010); the Federal Law № 210-FZ 'On the Organization of the State and Municipal e-Service Delivering' (July 27, 2010); the Decree of the President of the Russian Federation № 601 (May 7, 2012) 'On the Main Directions of Improvement the Public Administration System'.

It is significant that within the Russian legislation framework the main key-terms, priorities, and goals of Information Society are determined, the responsible persons form the implementation of the realization the corresponding policy are appointed ('competence zones'). However, often e-governance projects development in Russia is conducting out of frameworks of corresponding strategies and programs without guiding the main priorities and goals.

Based on the findings of the analysis of Information Society legislation in Armenia, Belarus, Kazakhstan, Kyrgyzstan and Russia, there are no Information Society Development Strategies in Kazakhstan and Armenia (as an independent document, like those that exist in Russia, Kyrgyzstan, and Belarus). Whereas taking into consideration the centralization of power and low level of the development of civil society in Kazakhstan and Armenia, it is reasonable to suggest that in condition of presence of the Strategies the level of development of the Information Society could be much better then without it.

The Programs on the Information Society development in EAEU countries are similar by objectives (create conditions for accelerated development of ICT services to facilitate the development of the Information Society, including provision of public e-services etc.) and priorities (modern ICT infrastructure, the efficiency of public administration, socio-economic and cultural development, development of the national information space, adoption of the e-government, overcoming the digital divide etc.). All the countries have the agencies responsible for the implementation of the Programs that raises the reliability of its implementation [5].

With the aim analysis of the priorities of Information Society development in EAEU countries, the corresponding programs and strategies were examined. In case of the element is present in strategy, we marked it 'S', in case of presence the element in the national Program we marked it by 'P'.

Table 1. Priorities of information society development (from EAEU Countries' strategies and programs)

Priorities	EAEU Countries				
	Armenia	Belarus	Kazakhstan	Kyrgyzstan	Russia
e-Government	S	S, P	P	S	S, P
e-Education		S, P			
e-Health		S, P			S
ICT infrastructure	S	S	P	S	S
Information security	S	P		S	S

Table 1, demonstrates that e-government and ICT infrastructure development are identified as priorities almost in all the Programs and Strategies. At the same time, such important components of Information Society as e-identification and registration of citizens as well as ICT in the civil society are not mentioned in the Programs and Strategies of these countries, except Kyrgyzstan.

Thus, based on analysis of legislation on e-governance in the countries of EAEU, it is worth to note common features. In particular, all the countries have the common priorities for development – communications, ICT, digital signature, e-government, information security. These priorities are formalized in the corresponding national programs and strategies. However, the issues of e-commerce, e-participation instruments development, e-learning etc. are out of legislative base [5].

5.2   E-Governance Institutions and Stuff

E-Governance Institutions and Stuff in Armenia. The main public authorities responsible on e-governance development in Armenia are:

- Ministry of Transport and Communication (Responsible for elaboration and implementation of the public policy in the field of communication and informatization in Armenia and facilitates the market environment creation in the sphere of telecommunication).
- Ministry of Economics (Responsible for economic public policy implementation in Armenia; attracts the investments for innovation enterprises; supports the IT-industrials; facilitates the regional cooperation).
- Commission on Public Services Regulations (Responsible for licensing in Republic of Armenia).

The ICT implementation and the creation of modern information and communication infrastructure are the priority directions of government's activity in Armenia. More than 60 % of population in Armenia uses the data transmission services.

E-Governance Institutions and Stuff in Belarus. The main responsible bodies on e-governance development in Republic of Belarus are Ministry of Communication and Informatization (Department of Informatization); Department on Information Systems Exploitation "National Center of e-Services"; Research initiative e-Belarus.org; Institute of Applied Program Systems; Association 'Infopark'.

It is worth noting that at the current moment the e-governance in Belarus is still not become an instrument for cooperation between the state and the citizens. The e-governance institutions development as well as the development of the corresponding legal base is needed to be completed.

E-Governance Institutions and Stuff in Kazakhstan. The main responsible bodies on e-governance development in Republic of Kazakhstan are Ministry on Investments and Development (Committee on Communication, Informatization, and Information); National Operator in the Field of Information Technologies of the Republic Kazakhstan 'National Information Technologies'; Center of the E-Government Competences;

National Information and Communication Holding Company 'Zerde'; Company 'National Information Technologies' (the national operator of the Republic Kazakhstan in the domain of information technologies); National Company 'Kazsatnet' (responsible executor for Single transport environment of public authorities of the Republic of Kazakhstan); 'Center of E-Commerce' (single operator in state electronic procurements); 'Kazcontent' (responsible for forming of the national segment of global international network Internet in Kazakhstan, including the network information resources development, It infrastructure organization; stimulation of the investment and innovative activity in IT-sphere); 'National Processing center'; 'National University of Information Technologies', 'Lincompany' (conducts the commerce researches); Department on Informatization and Information Resources Protection of the Administration of the President.

Despite on creation of the substantial technological base for e-governance projects' development, the particularity of e-governance development in Kazakhstan consists in that the most large-scale projects on e-governance implementation were realized by international IT-Companies.

E-Governance Institutions and Stuff in Kyrgyzstan. The main responsible bodies on e-governance development in Kyrgyz Republic are Ministry of Transport and Communication (the Center of ICT Development); E-governance Center of the Kyrgyz Republic Government (till 2015); Council on ICT (under the President of Kyrgyzstan) is responsible for coordination activity on determination and elaboration of the strategic directions on informatization, telecommunication, and modern ICT application; Public Information Center under the President Administration (facilitates the reinforcement of the transparency and accountability of public authorities activity to the civil society; delivers the official public information to citizens); 'Soros-Kyrgyzstan' Foundation (responsible for elaboration and the implementation of the instruments on local governments activity); ICT Development Foundation; Public Foundation 'Information Promotion'; Civil Initiative 'Internet Policies'; 'Kyrgyztelecom' (the National operator of e-government); Association of Communication's Operators; Association of the Professionals of the ICT Sphere.

Accordingly to the government's agenda, it is planned to implode the 68 public authorities into common electronic network till 2016. It is planned to complete the necessary ICT infrastructure and accomplish the transition of public services into the electronic format till 2025.

E-Governance Institutions and Stuff in Russia. The main body responsible for e-governance development and implementation in Russia is the Ministry of Telecom and Mass Communications of the Russian Federation (the e-Government Development Department). The Department is responsible for the regional informatization; for providing e-services for citizens and business; for e-government infrastructure development etc.

The Department of the Informatization Coordination of the Ministry of Telecom and Mass Communications of the Russian Federation is responsible for the methodical support of the public authorities on ICT and regional informatization. Furthermore, the

Ministry of Telecom and Mass Communications of the Russian Federation has a lot of coordinative and consultative bodies such as the Government commission on federal communication and technical issues of informatization; the Expert council on cloud computing; the Governmental commission on communications; Council on regional informatization; Expert council on IT development; Consultative council on e-governance development etc.

Besides, the Department of the state regulation in economy of the Ministry of the economic development of the Russian Federation is responsible, in particular, for state policy and legislation regulation on the issues of raising the quality of government e-services and information government systems; provides the functioning of the Russian Open Data portal data.gov.ru etc.

The functions of control and supervision of the mass-media (including electronic), IT and personal data processing are realized by the Federal service for supervision of communications, information technology, and mass media ("Roskomnadzor").

The Committee on Information Policy, Information Technologies and Communication of State Duma of the Russian Federation is responsible for legislative regulation on information technologies and mass-communications. The Department of IT and communications of the Government of the Russian Federation is responsible for development and implementation of the e-governance projects. Besides, the Temporary commission on the Information Society development of the Federal Council of the Russian Federation is functioning for providing the legislative regulation in the domain of Information Society development in Russia.

For the implementation of the "Open Government" in Russia there are some bodies responsible for its realization: the Department of the Government of Russian Federation on formation of the Open Government system and the Government commission on the coordination of Open Government activities (the head of the Commission is the Prime Minister of Russia). Besides, the Prime Minister of the Russia is also responsible for usage ICT for improving the quality of life and the entrepreneurship conditions, thus he is a head of the corresponding government commission.

Open Government in Russia is considered as a system of mechanisms and principles providing effective interactions between the state and society, high quality of the adopted balanced decisions in the conditions of increasing the dynamics of social and economic processes in Russia. Open Government ensures involvement of the non-profit and business organizations into the decision-making process. The main priorities of Open Government in Russia are increase of information openness of public authorities; providing the Open Data by public authorities; ensuring the transparency and accountability of the state costs and investments; providing the effective system of public control.

Thus, it is worth to summarize that the common feature in e-governance institutional infrastructure in all the countries of the Eurasian Economic Union is the existence of variety of institutions responsible for e-governance development. The difficulty of a great number of these institutions causes the duplication of functions and the dissipation of the responsibility in e-governance projects implementation.

Therefore, with the aim of refining the existent e-governance institutional structure in EAEU member-states, making it more efficient, it must to be transformed.

5.3   Participation Services of Public Engagement

E-governance development provides not only increase of the effectiveness of the functioning the public authorities, but also forming the effecting interactions between the citizens and government; improvement of the citizens access to public information; citizens engagement into policy-making, thus, effective electronic governance is the priority of the state development that facilitates providing the transparency and accountability of the public authorities [8, p. 64].

Based on the methodology of UN E-Participation Index Research, the e-government portals of every member-state of EAEU were examined: 'Electronic Government of the Republic of Armenia' (e-gov.am); 'Unified Portal of E-Services'(http://portal.gov.by – Belarus); 'Public Services and Information Online' (http://egov.kz/wps/portal/index? lang=ru – Kazakhstan); 'E-Petition Portal to Public Authorities of Kyrgyzstan for Citizens' (http://www.kattar.kg/), Common Government Services Portal of Russian Federation (https://www.gosuslugi.ru/). As the Common E-Government Portal of Kyrgyzstan is under the development the 'E-Petition Portal to Public Authorities of Kyrgyzstan for Citizens' was examined.

Such issues as presence of archive information (budget, legislation etc.) and data bases on education, healthcare, labor, environment, finance, social maintenance; number of portal's languages; social networks functions; e-consultation mechanisms on 6 issues: education, healthcare, finance, labor, environment, social maintenance; public opinion instrument (online forums, instruments for e-petitions, e-surveys, e-voting ets.); e-decision making instruments were selected for analysis (Table 2).

Table 2. Analysis of E-government portals of the EAEU member-states

Examined issues	EAEU Member-States' e-Government Portals				
	Armenia e-gov.am	Belarus http:// portal.gov.by	Kazakhstan http:// egov.kz/wp s/portal/ index? lang=ru	Kyrgyzstan http:// www.kattar.kg/	Russia https:// www.gosu slugi.ru/
Archive information and data bases	+	+	+	−	+
Number of portal's languages	2	3	3	2	4
Social networks functions	−	−	+	−	−
E-consultation mechanisms	+	+ −	+	+	+
Public opinion instrument	−	−	+	+	−
E-decision making instruments	−	−	−	−	−

Based on the analysis of e-government portals of the EAEU member-states, it is possible to conclude that almost all the web-sites (except the portal of Kyrgyzstan) contain the archive information and data bases on education, healthcare, labor, environment, finance, social maintenance. Moreover, the information at the all portals is presented at least in two languages (all the portals (except the portal of Kyrgyzstan) have English as the official language, thus the information is accessible for foreign citizens also). Besides, it is possible to get the e-consultations at all the portals (at the Belarus' portal we checked the marks '+' and '−', because on some issues the website gives only the possibility to address over the telephone).

However, the instruments for e-decisions making are absent at all the portals. Moreover, most of portals do not contain the mechanisms for getting the public opinion.

Thus, unfortunately, the e-government portals in member-states of EAEU do not operate as the instruments of public engagement.

It is worth noting that in all the countries of the Eurasian Economic Union the e-participation services progressively develop. The citizens can send the inquiry, voice the opinion, or get the consultation by means of corresponding portals (for example, 'My City' Belarus; 'RosYama', 'RosZhKH', 'Angry Citizen', public platforms for e-petitions and e-voting 'Russian Public Initiative' (RPI), 'Petitions247.com', 'Change.org', 'OnlinePetition', 'Democrator.ru' etc. (Russia); 'Information Initiative' Foundation, petitions' platform 'KzHета' (Kazakhstan); Global Network Community - Petitions' Portal 'Avaaz.org', 'GoPetition' etc.).

Nevertheless, contemporary electronic participation instruments in the countries of EAEU are aimed at provision the electronic interaction between citizens and state, however, currently it is reasonable to state the declared goals and objectives of some e-services (including, for example, public platforms for e-petitions and e-voting « Russian Public Initiative ») are not supported by its functional properties.

According to the researches of the Project on e-Services Development 'Transactional e-Governance Development in Armenia', the number of e-governance services users barely reaches 5 %. Moreover, 95 % of respondents declare about absence of the necessity of interaction with public authorities via modern ICT [6]. Thus, on the scale of ICT infrastructure development, the citizens' interest in getting e-public services is not improving.

Therefore, for effective development of e-governance mechanisms of e-participation in EAEU member-states it is necessary to develop the corresponding legislation, raise the citizens' literacy in the sphere of digital media, including via the increasing the awareness of publicity concerning the e-participation initiatives, engage the formal and informal e-participation institutions for citizens' involvement into the public policy (for example, social networks, crowdsourcing, mobile services), develop the official government portals as platforms for information cooperation etc. [14].

6 Conclusions and Future Work

The e-governance implementation in the countries of the Eurasian Economic union supposes not only the raise of effectiveness of public administration, but also the development of effective interactions between the state and the citizens; improvement of the citizen's access to information and public services; promotion the citizens participation in public decision-making (i.e. concerning the principles of socially inclusive governance), thus the issue of e-participation is an important and urgent component of Information Society, it facilitates the promotion of public accountability and transparency.

Based on comparative analysis of e-participation projects' development within the e-governance institutional structure of EAEU countries, it is worth noting that modern electronic participation instruments in the countries of EAEU are poorly developed. Despite on its aim is the provision of the electronic interaction between citizens and state, however, currently it is reasonable to state the declared goals and objectives of some e-services and initiatives are not supported by its functional properties.

Analysis of the legislation on e-governance of Armenia, Belarus, Kazakhstan, Kyrgyzstan, and Russia reveled similarity of the approaches of these countries to the Information Society development. Strategies, Programs and Laws marked similar goals, they have similar titles. They were adopted at about the same time. However, the corresponding legislative base is needed to be enriched (in particular, it is recommended to develop and normatively formalize some issues - e-commerce, e-learning etc.). This may encourage cooperation and integration in the information field. However, it is possible to assert that the development of e-governance in member-states of EAEU is contradictory, non-universal, not always coordinated with the main strategies and programs. Whereas, it should be linked with the strategic goals and priorities. Consequently, the barriers in effective e-governance development and its institutional immaturity influence the general development of e-governance in EAEU. Thus, at the current moment it is difficult to effectively encourage cooperation and integration in the region.

As the result of the research, it is concluded that there are a lot of institutions responsible for e-governance development in EAEU countries. The difficulty of a great number of these institutions causes the duplication of functions and the dissipation of the responsibility in e-governance projects (including the e-participation projects) implementation.

The issue for future research is might be the matter of determining the institutional maturity of e-governance development in EAEU member-states. This issue is rather contradictory. It might be connected with the lack of the corresponding researches in this domain. At the same time, there is no univalent definition of the institutional maturity and the principle of its assessing, that makes the issue debatable and needs more researches.

Moreover, it is planned to study in future researches the e-participation influence to the integration processes in the Eurasian region. Based on the results of this analysis, it is planned to elaborate the optimal e-governance model with aim of further Eurasian integration development and sustainable development of the Eurasian region.

Acknowledgments. The research was conducted with the support of Russian Foundation for Humanities, Grant №. 15-03-00715.

References

1. Aksyonov, A.: International ICT-development ratings (Mezhdunarodnye reitingi urovnya razvitiya ICT). http://d-russia.ru/mezhdunarodnye-rejtingi-urovnya-razvitiya-ikt.html
2. Astrom, J., Karlsson, M., Linde, J., Pirannejad, A.: Understanding the rise of e-participation in nondemocracies: domestic and international factors. Gov. Inf. Q. **29**(2), 142–150 (2012)
3. Bershadskaya, L., Chugunov, A., Dzhusupova, Z.: Understanding e-government development barriers in CIS countries and exploring mechanisms for regional cooperation. In: 2nd Joint International Conference on Electronic Government and the Information Systems Perspective, and International Conference on Electronic Democracy, pp. 87–101 (2013)
4. Bolgov, R., Chugunov, A., Filatova, O., Misnikov, Y.: Electronic identification of citizens: comparing perspectives and approaches. In: Proceedings of 8th International Conference on Theory and Practice of Electronic Governance (ICEGOV 2014), October 27–30, 2014, Guimarães, Portugal, pp. 484–485. ACM Press, New York (2014)
5. Bolgov, R., Karachay, V., Zinovieva, E.: Information society development in eurasian economic union countries: legal aspects. In: ACM International Conference Proceeding Series, 8th International Conference on Theory and Practice of Electronic Governance (ICEGOV 2014), pp. 387–390, October 27–30, 2014, Guimarães, Portugal. ACM Press, New York (2014)
6. E-Governance Development in Armenia. http://ega.ee/project/e-governance-development-in-armenia/
7. Junusbekova, G.A.: Electronic government in Republic of Kazakhstan as a way to improve state government system. Life Sci. J. **10**(4), 1353–1360 (2013)
8. Karachay, V., Bolgov, R.: An overview of the e-governance development in the Eurasian Economic Union (EAEU) countries: the case of Russia. electronic governance and open society: challenges in Eurasia. In: Proceedings of the International Conference, EGOSE 2015, 24–25 November, 2015, pp. 59–65 (2015)
9. Marushka, D., Ablameyko, M.: Belarus and the baltic states: comparison study on e-government development results. In: 7th International Conference on Theory and Practice of Electronic Governance, ICEGOV 2013, pp. 382–383 (2013)
10. Measuring and Evaluating e-Participation (METEP): Assessment of Readiness at the Country Level. http://workspace.unpan.org/sites/Internet/Documents/METEP%20framework_18%20Jul_MOST%20LATEST%20Version.pdf
11. Misnikov, Y.: E-Participation as a process and practice: What METEP can measure, why and how? UNDESA (2013). http://workspace.unpan.org/sites/Internet/Documents/UNPAN90456.pdf
12. Pardo, T., Styrin, E.: Digital government implementation: a comparative study in USA and Russia. In: 16th Americas Conference on Information Systems, AMCIS 2010, vol. 5, pp. 3815–3824 (2010)
13. Russia and Kyrgyzstan will activate the cooperation in the sphere of electronic government (Rossiya i Kirgiziya Aktiviziruyut Sotrudnichestvo v Oblasti Electronnogo Pravitelstva). http://minsvyaz.ru/ru/events/33432/
14. Sedikin, M.A.: e-Participation as dialog between the state and the citizens (Electronnoye Uchastie kak Dialog Vlasti I Obschestve). In: Discussion (Discussia), vol. 1 (№. 31), January 2013. http://www.journal-discussion.ru/publication.php?id=204
15. Sideridis, A.B., Protopappas, L., Tsiafoulis, S., Pimenidis, E.: Smart cross-border e-gov systems and applications. In: Communications in Computer and Information Science, vol. 570, pp. 151–165 (2015)
16. The Challenges of Theories on Democracy. Elaboration over new Trends in Transitology. Boulder, NY (2000)

17. The Chiefs of EAEU Member-States Ratified New Structure of EEC Collegium (Glavy EAES Utverdili Noviy Sostav Kollegii EEC). http://www.eurasiancommission.org/ru/nae/news/Pages/22-12-2015-5.aspx
18. UN E-Government Survey 2014. https://publicadministration.un.org/egovkb/en-us/Reports/UN-E-Government-Survey-2014

Resurgence of Co-operative Banks Through BI Tools

I.P.S. Sethi and O.P. Gupta$^{(\boxtimes)}$

National Informatics Centre, A Block, CGO Complex, Delhi, India
{sethi, op.gupta}@nic.in

Abstract. Reserve Bank of India (RBI) and Indian government focuses on financial inclusion as the foundation for inclusive growth. Around 2/3rd of the Indian population falls under the rural category and majority of it is currently not part of the mainstream banking. Rural India contributes a lot to country economy. In this regard, there is a long felt need to have systemic approach to leverage advances in technology to enhance effectiveness of rural cooperative credit structures, particularly delivery of payments and credits to rural citizens on various social sector schemes.

While the commercial banking system is taking steps to extend its reach to rural areas, there is a need to develop innovative solutions to provide access to people in rural areas so as to help them get efficient and reliable payment and banking services near to them.

To meet financial inclusion objectives, National Informatics Centre (NIC) has developed a Cooperative Core Banking Solution (CCBS) to serve the needs of the rural India to make availability of efficient and reliable payments and banking services closer at their doorsteps.

Keywords: Co-operative core banking solution · CCBS · Business intelligence · NABARD

1 Introduction

In India, Co-operative Banks are working for more than hundred years and are considered as one of the important financial institutions in the country. Co-operative Banks in India are registered under the Co-operative Societies Act and are regulated by Reserve Bank of India. The major contributions of these banks are mostly in rural areas where they play the most vital role in rural financing and micro financing. The major strengths of co-operative banks are their easy local reach, transparent interaction with the customers and their efficient services to common people.

Cooperative Credit Structure prevalent in India is bifurcated into Short Term Cooperative Credit Structure (STCCS) & the Long Term Cooperative Credit Structure (LTCCS).

The STCCS is a 3 tier structure comprising State Cooperative Banks (SCBs), District Central Co-operative Banks (DCCBs) & Primary Agriculture Cooperative Society (PACS). The LTCCS is a 2 tier structure comprising State Land Development

A.V. Chugunov et al. (Eds.): DTGS 2016, CCIS 674, pp. 219–231, 2016.
DOI: 10.1007/978-3-319-49700-6_21

Banks (SLDBs/SCARDB) & Primary Land Development Banks (PLDBs/PCARDB) & Financial Institutions/Corporation at National/State level (FIs) (Fig. 1).

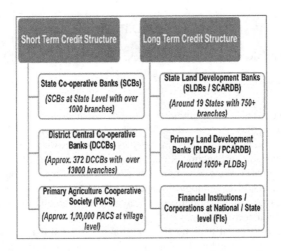

Fig. 1. Main page of CCBS application for operations

2 Co-operative Core Banking Solution (CCBS)

To overcome the challenges faced by cooperative banks, and make financial inclusion a reality, NIC has developed a specific web based Banking Software for this sector with the name Co-operative Core Banking Solution (CCBS) which is offered as 'Software as a Service' (SaaS) to the banks and is hosted at National Data Centre of NIC (Fig. 2).

Fig. 2. CCBS portal

CCBS is developed to provide basic banking as well as financial inclusion support. The main objective behind development of CCBS by NIC is to serve the poorest of the poor by furthering basic banking facility in the rural areas of the country.

CCBS plays a vital role in financial inclusion, a primary agenda of Government of India and National Bank for Agriculture and Rural Development (NABARD) for the upliftment of rural masses of India. CCBS is designed so as to enable the Agricultural Societies at the Village level to disburse all the social sector related Government fund (DBT, MGNREGA, Old Age Pension etc.) distribution to the targeted beneficiaries at the doorstep. It facilitates easy monitoring of fund disbursement and day to day position of fund distribution under these heads known at the apex level.

The CCBS as a product is customized for the Short term as well as Long term credit structure to cater to their requirements.

CCBS aims to provide a common interface for all the category of banks (Fig. 3).

Fig. 3. CCBS interfaces

3   CCBS Architecture

3.1   Logical Architecture

An architecture overview diagram at an enterprise level of the CCBS is depicted in CCBS Architecture. These entities located on the different geographical locations will access the CCBS portal system using internet and/or intranet connectivity under secured environment. These subsystems are logically separated without any virtualization of hardware system except they are co- located at the same Data Centre.

There are four main components in the architecture of CCBS (Fig. 4):

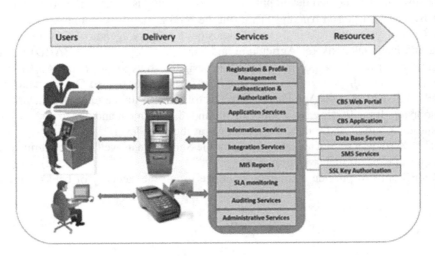

Fig. 4. CCBS interfaces

Users. The users of CBS portal are the cooperative bank employees who can access this application from their respective branch only.
Delivery. The branch user can access the application through a computer installed in the branch of bank.

Services

- Authentication & Authorization
- Application Services
- Information Services
- Integration Services
- MIS Reports
- Auditing Services
- Administrative Services

Resources

- CBS Web Portal
- CBS Application & Data Base Server
- SMS Services
- SSL Key Authorization

3.2   Technical Architecture

The CCBS application is hosted at the NIC's Data Centre. The application data flow for CCBS is as below (Fig. 5):

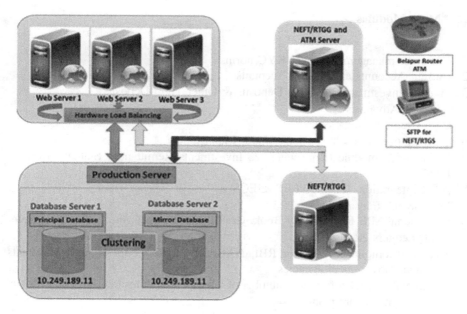

Fig. 5. Technical architecture

Technology Used in CCBS

- Technology: Microsoft .net Framework 4.5 with WCF
- Database Server: Microsoft SQL Server 2012 Enterprise Edition
- Web Server: Internet Information Services (IIS) Manager 8.0
- Reporting Server: Microsoft SQL Server 2012 Reporting Services
- System Software: Windows Server 2012
- Language Used: C#

4   Features of CCBS

4.1   Innovative Features of CCBS

1. Service oriented architecture (SOA) to provide interoperability with other e-Governance applications
2. Use of cloud computing infrastructure – hosted at National Data Centre, Shastri Park
3. Integration among all three layers of co-operative banking i.e. State, District & PACS level for monitoring & reporting
4. Standardized approach to adopt common accounting system upto PACS level
5. Inter-Bank transactions and Inter-Branch (between two different locations) transactions, simple and single click interest calculation and bank closing activity
6. Capability to handle Direct Benefit transfers through PACS level

4.2   Main Modules

1. Customer management as per KYC norms
2. Current Accounts and Saving Accounts
3. Fixed/Reinvestment/Recurring Deposits & Other Term Deposits
4. Loans & Advances
5. Cash Credit & Advances
6. Clearing operations & Lockers, Shares Management
7. Head Office module (Borrowings & Investments Remittances Statuary Reserve Fund)
8. ATM integration, RTGS, NEFT & ECS
9. Inter branch transactions
10. Operational MIS Reports-Day Book, Cash Book, Balance Sheet, Voucher, Statement, Ledgers etc.
11. Statutory/Compliance MIS for RBI, NABARD, State Cooperative Departments and other Government agencies
12. To strengthen CCBS further, a number of advanced modules like, Treasury, Social Sector Payments are planned

5   Benefits of CCBS

5.1   Benefits for Customers

1. KYC compliant customer management to reduce duplication and fraud situations
2. Account operation from any of the branch of the bank.
3. Account statement to customers
4. Printed Passbook/FD certificate
5. NEFT/RTGS fund transfer facility
6. SMS alert for all transactions enhancing comfort &security
7. Transfer of payments like cash subsidy, MGNREGA payments etc. directly in beneficiary's accounts
8. Accurate and timely application of interest on deposits & loans
9. Realization of cheque in less time
10. CCBS enabled with ATM machines thereby facilitating the customers to draw money 24*7 without any manual intervention
11. Benefits for Bank Management

5.2   Infrastructure and Customer Service

1. No need to set up and maintain 24*7 infrastructure.
2. Data Security under secured domain of GOI
3. Adaption of RBI/NABARD policy without any financial implication

4. Reduced Customer Service Cycle time
5. Faster and error free Audit of Bank/Branch

Online Monitoring for Bank/Branch

1. Facilitates monitoring of Agricultural/Non-agricultural loans and advances including KCC/SHG/Medium Term Loan
2. Facilitates monitoring of stocks (Fertilizers/Seeds/Pesticides) which may in turn be a key input for deciding subsidy
3. Facilitates Bank to measure financial health of their branches in terms of Asset and Liabilities of branch and in turn Bank
4. Accurate MIS and timely compliance of report & returns to the statutory body of the respective bank

6 Business Intelligence Tools

For the banks to indicate viability of transactions and help in planning of banks future growth, Business Intelligence (BI) tools are being used by the banks.

BI is related to the analysis of fast growth of the banking industry in India. In order to stay competitive, banks in India are taking the data analytics route and BI data can help the banks to maximize revenues and reduce costs.

There are dashboards being maintained by the banks to monitor the following parameters:

- A/c Statistics
- Transaction Status
- Cash Position
- Health Meter
- Account opened in last three months

The dashboard view of Meghalaya Co-operative Apex Bank (MCAB) is provided as below (Fig. 6):

The dashboard view of Delhi Finance Corporation (DFC) is provided as below:

The various advantages of BI tools are enlisted as below:

1. Provide insight into the past, current and future state of the bank,
2. Provide information on a daily basis and help quick turnaround by not depending on periodic reporting cycle,
3. Place financial information in the hands of the people empowering them to improve quality of key decisions,
4. Allow operational managers more time to analyze numbers, perform profitability and margin analysis,
5. Provide quick insight using drill down features into performance problems,
6. Help study the cause and effect of major new products and pricing policies.

The following types of analysis would be available under CCBS using Business Intelligence tools:

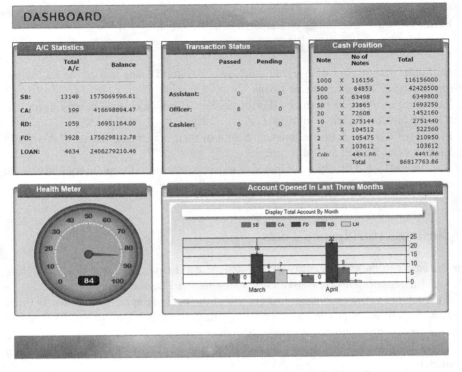

Fig. 6. Meghalaya Co-operative Apex Bank dashboard

6.1   Historical Analysis (Time-Series)

The Historical Analysis would help to gain visibility into business of the bank. Services and net income can be analyzed by the bank in order to increase profitability.

Modules of Historical Analysis (Time-Series).   It can include following type of analysis:

1. Profit ratio from previous to current financial year (To Gain visibility into their business operations to increase profitability and improve products/services)
2. Net income can be analyzed by revenue vs. expenditure comparison.

Benefits of Historical Analysis (Time-Series)

1. *Analyze organizational data.* Banks can improve and streamline operational efficiencies to better develop customer service programs.
2. *Improve operational efficiencies and boost profits.* Banks can reduce ongoing costs, and maximize existing resources and expertise, by analyzing operational processes and activities.

6.2   Overview Operations: Fixed Deposit

Using the Overview operations analysis, the operation of important products of bank like fixed deposits can be monitored.

Modules of Overview operations: Loans & Fixed Deposit

- Branch wise analysis for Accounts Added, Pending Applications and EMI unpaid
- Deep Dive KPI analytics for Fixed Deposits
- Analyze Fixed Deposits Branch wise and Product Wise
- Monitor Branch wise Interest paid
- Exception Alert for Fixed Deposits performance branch wise

Benefits of Overview Operations: Loans & Fixed Deposit

1. Helps in accurately estimating the risk of customer loans based on:

   - The financial assets and earning capacity of the borrower
   - Bank's prevailing economic climate

2. MoM and YoY analysis of maturity of FD and New FDs application can help bank to improve investment and loan sanctions.

6.3   Branch Performance Analysis

The Branch Performance Analysis would help to measure overall branch performance of the bank by analyzing number of customers added, EMI collected, total fixed deposit value (Fig. 7).

Branch Performace Analysis

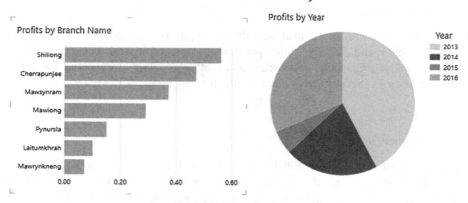

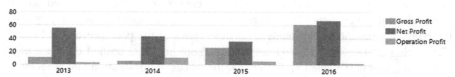

Fig. 7. Branch performance analysis dashboard

Modules of Branch Performance Analysis

1. Identify top-bottom performing branches by Loans Overdue
2. Branch wise performance in terms of customer added, loans sanctioned, EMI collected
3. Identify top-bottom branches with respect to Fixed Deposits value

Benefits of Branch Performance Analysis

1. Performance of each branch can be analysed by comparing GPM (Gross Profit Margin), Net Profit Margin (NPM) and Operation Profit Margin (OPM) of different branches by YoY wise.
2. Net Profits Ratio for last 3–4 Years among all branches can monitored at a glance.
3. Number of account opened vs. account closed charts can be viewed.

6.4 Trend Analysis

The Trend Analysis would help the banks to analyze trend by comparing Demand vs. Collection, Sanctioned vs. Disbursed etc.

Modules of Trend Analysis

1. Identify trend for Non-Performing Assets
2. Identify trend for Product wise Loans issued
3. Identify trend for Demand vs. Collection
4. Identify trend for Loan Approval Lead time
5. Identify trend for Sanction Loan vs. Disbursed
6. MoM & YoY Trend Analysis for Loans

Benefits of Trend Analysis

1. Trend Analysis will help in analysing the future profits by comparing pending dues and collection and identifying non-performing assets of all branches in a month.
2. Trend Analysis can help in securing money flow by monitoring trend for Sanctioned Loan vs. Security over a period of time.

6.5 Customer $360°$

Whenever a customer interacts with the bank, it is vital that the richness of information available on that customer informs and guides the processes that will help to maximize their experience, while simultaneously making the interaction as effective and efficient as possible. This includes everything from avoiding repetition or re-keying of information, to viewing customer history, establishing context and initiating desired actions.

360° view of the customer leads to better service to the customer as well as growth of the bank. A true 360° view needs to include views of the past, present and future.

Delivering on the 360° view is not simply about having a unified database of all activity, but rather being able to pull together the pieces of information that are relevant for a specific customer and specific interaction into an intuitive workspace for the agent or the customer.

Modules of Customer 360°. In terms of specific information, the 360° view should feed into all customer interactions, including those that relate to self-service, but a good example is that moment in the call center, at the start of a conversation, when the bank staff has just established the caller's identity. With a 360° view, this identity is used to **generate a rich picture of the customer in real time** and give the bank staff an instant snapshot regarding the background to the call. This snapshot should include:

- **Identity:** name, location, gender, age
- **Current activity:** NEFT, RTGS, ATM Transactions, Branch Transactions
- **History:** processes of all account holder transactions, cases across all lines of business and channels
- **Value:** Total Deposits, Total Advances

Benefits of Customer 360°

- Improve customer satisfaction through understanding and transparency: Banks can further increase customer satisfaction ratings by proactively harnessing data to give clients superior insight into their individual transitional operations, allowing them to more effectively management their finances by having:
  - Real-time understanding of payments
  - Real-time understating of receipts
- This will enable customers to easily manage finances by tracking and analyzing their spending and earning patterns. In addition, analysis of customer point-of-contact data can helps institutions understand customer sentiment and behaviours in order to:
  - Effectively and efficiently satisfy customer needs and demands
  - Win-over competitors customers

7 Implementation of CCBS

CCBS has been developed so as to minimize the cost and ensure better Return on Investment (ROI). Banks/PACS do not have to invest funds for the creation of Data Centre, Disaster Recovery site etc. and maintenance thereof. CCBS is designed in a way that all the Government fund distribution can be easily monitored and day-to-day position is known at the apex level.

7.1 Implementation Status

State Cooperative Banks (SCBs). All 49 branches including a head office of Meghalaya Cooperative Apex Bank (MCAB), a SCB, are in core banking environment. CCBS at MCAB provides the ATM and NEFT/RTGS facility RuPay credit card facility has been started for KCC account holders and DBTL (Direct Benefit Transfer for LPG) for LPG customers having account in bank is enabled. PoS facility has been started to be used for conducting transactions with any Merchant Bank. PMJJBY/PMSBY module of CCBS is under implementation. The total number of customers of MCAB is 7, 04,259. Approx. 18,500 ATM Cards have been issued till date. Average number of daily vouchers in year 2015 is 15,695.

District Central Co-operative Banks (DCCBs). All 61 branches including a head office of DCCB Raipur, are operational in core banking environment. NEFT/RTGS, DBTL & ATM services are in operation. The PMJJBY/PMSBY module of CCBS is under implementation.

Primary Agriculture Cooperative Society (PACS). Rajasthan government has awarded the work of computerization for 750 PACS under Phase-I. 30 PACS are operational under 14 DCCBs and have been made online for doing the transaction. Trainings have been conducted for all the PAC managers. Computerization of 5 PACs in West Godavari district of Andhra Pradesh has been started. Implementation is in pipeline at Meghalaya and Chhattisgarh states.

Punjab State Cooperative Agricultural Development Bank (PSCADB). Implementation of customized CCBS at 89 Branches of Punjab State Cooperative Agricultural Development Bank is in progress. 53 primary units are performing day to day operations. This bank is engaged in providing loan/advances for Long Term and fall under Long Term Cooperative Credit Structure (LTCCS).

Financial Institutions/Corporations at National/State level (FIs). Implementation and customization of CCBS for head office and three branches of Delhi Financial Corporation is in progress. Automation process of National Scheduled Castes Finance and Development Corporation (NSFDC) has been initiated.

Treasury Banks. Exploring State Bank of Sikkim for banking as well as treasury operations.

7.2   Financial Inclusion Support

CCBS developed by NIC provides the following financial inclusion support:

1. DBTL (Direct Beneficiary Transfer) support
2. Inclusion of the schemes like Pradhan Mantri Suraksha Bima Yojana **(PMSBY)** Scheme, Pradhan Mantri Jeevan Jyoti Bima Yojana **(PMJJBY)** Scheme and Pradhan Mantri Jan-Dhan Yojana **(PMJDY)**
3. Interface with Bank on Move **(BoM)** and Point of Sale **(PoS)**
4. Better monitoring of agriculture and non-agriculture loans
5. Support for cash less Dhan-Kharidi in Chhattisgarh
6. SMS alerts for every transactions on registered mobile numbers

8   Awards and Recognition

NIC-CCBS project has been appreciated with several awards like 6th eNorth East Award 2016, SecureIT 2015 Award, CSI-Nihilent e-Governance Award 2014 and SKOCH 2014 Merit of Excellence (Fig. 8).

Fig. 8. CCBS project awards & recognition

Acknowledgments. The authors express their gratitude to Dr. B.K. Gairola, then DG NIC, for proactively supporting the Co-operative Core Banking Solution (CCBS) initiative of NIC. The authors also acknowledge the valuable suggestions and ideas of Mr. Y.K. Sharma, then DDG NIC, for conceptualizing the project and focusing the Department's attention on developing CCBS application.

References

1. Government initiative for automation of co-operative banks structure through core banking solution. Presented and published at the Proceedings of the 8th International Conference on Theory and Practice of Electronic Governance, ICEGOV 2014, pp. 478–479, October 2014
2. Microsoft SQL Server 2008 R2 Customer Solution Case Study – Co-operative Core Banking Solution (CCBS) Modernizes Infrastructure, Empowers Small, Rural Co-operative Banks, February 2014
3. Empowering Co-operative Institutions through Core Banking Solution: 16th National e-Governance Conference on e-Governance, February 2013

From Public Administration Reform
to E-Government: Russian Path to Digital Public Services

Leonid Smorgunov[✉]

St. Petersburg State University, Universitetskaya nab., 7/9, St. Petersburg 199034, Russia
l.smorgunov@spbu.ru

Abstract. World perspectives of digital governance are directed by the idea of turn from services to the value of services and co-production. This idea transforms understanding of the relations between the government, businesses, and citizens. All of that attaches importance to the monitoring of service policy and policy feedback. Recent trends in Russian administrative reform (2006–2010) and in implementation of e-government (2009–2015) show some evidence of adopting connected d-governance perspectives here. Three main points could be mentioned: (1) feedback in the regulation of government monitoring of effectiveness; (2) citizen participation in the process of service standardization; (3) multi-functional centers, governmental service portals, and e-consultation on federal and regional levels of e-government. Some tensions and limits accompany these trends.

Keywords: Connected d-Governance · Value of services · Russian administrative reform · e-Government · Service portals

1 Introduction

The public administration system in Russia, which was formed in 1990th, had no complete character. The crash of the USSR (decommunization, desovietization of government, struggle for state of law), privatization and the transition to a market economy, and the building of a federal state influenced public administration. The problems associated with a market economy, democratic consolidation and centralization of power, rights and law, private property and justice, stability and development, openness before the world, national identity, and so on are related to the problems of what public administration will be and what government policy will be implemented. The situation changed after the economic crisis of 1998. Governmental weaknesses and the need for the politico-administrative reform have become apparent. Putin's Presidency (2000–2008) was a period of transition from a 'privatized' state to a state autonomy including the formation of government capacities for effective activities. Civil service (2002), administrative (2003) and budget (2004) reforms were directed to these purposes. An evaluation system was formed step by step during the process of these transformations. New impulse for that has been given by the Medvedev's Presidency (2008–2012), especially in the adoption of e-government initiatives in Russian public administration. For

© Springer International Publishing AG 2016
A.V. Chugunov et al. (Eds.): DTGS 2016, CCIS 674, pp. 232–246, 2016.
DOI: 10.1007/978-3-319-49700-6_22

this reason the administrative reform which was scheduled to finish in 2008 has been prolonged until 2010. Though Russia has many peculiarities in politico-administrative system, many influences from foreign experiences and governmentality are obvious here. Recent Russian administrative reform (two stages: 2003–2005 and 2006–2010) has been heavily influenced by New Public Management ideology. Government budget transformation was characterized by the transition to result budget management and civil officers' reform was oriented to efficiency and competition. But there are some evidences of new directions here. They are associated with public service delivery. Particularly intensive process of development of e-services is starting to develop since 2012. At the state level, a series of important documents that bind administrative transformation with the development of electronic services. The general condition and prospects of development of electronic services can be found in the recently (2016) adopted for public discussion the governmental project of e-government development until 2020 [20]. This trend has many peculiarities of transition to d-governance and citizens oriented public service delivery.

The processes of improving public services for businesses and citizens have intensified in recent years in Russia. It could be said world perspectives of digital governance and public services have become apparent. These perspectives are directed by the idea of a shift from services to the citizen's oriented services. This idea transforms understanding of the relations between government, businesses and citizens. All of that attaches importance to monitoring of services policy and policy feedback. In recent years the development of a combination of e-government and administrative transformations (based on NPM ideology in general) resulted into new conceptual base for improvement of service delivery, on the one hand. 'Connected governance' is the new name for this conception. "Connected governance is aimed at improving cooperation between government agencies, deepening consultation and engagement with citizens, and allowing for a greater involvement with multi-stakeholders regionally and internationally" [23: XIV]. On the other hand, 'connected governance' conception is penetrated by the idea of 'public value management'. The latter is the result of the intellectual transition from traditional Public administration (PA) to Customer relationship management (CRM) as newest variation of NPM, and then to Public value management (PVM) [7, 15, 19]. Traditional PA propagated a government-oriented approach to public service delivery. As a whole citizens were considered as simple consumers. Consumerist approach was criticized as economically ineffective for service delivery in public sphere. At the first stage the critic of consumerist approach was in the limits of NPM. Consumer rhetoric was changed on customer rhetoric [7, 12, 15]. Citizens were considered as influential customers. The concept of customer orientation in public administration, as Schedler and Summermatter (2007) describe, has seen a high in debated in literature since the early 1990s. It influenced on public administration in general and of e-government policy in particular. Programs of introduction of the electronic government in the 1990s and later were guided mainly by the ideology of New Public Management with its basic goal «to make the government effective and cheap». Appreciably it meant that using electronic government would make it possible to deliver the public services to citizens and business most effectively and less costly. Especially this emphasis is presented in works of an initial stage of movement for the electronic government. So, Dun Tepskott - one of defenders of the given idea in 1995 in his book «Digital economy» writes that ICTs «not only … reduce the costs of government, but also radically transform the way government programs are delivered and the very nature of governance. Internetworked government can overcome the barriers of time and distance to perform the business of government and give people public information and services, when and where they will want» [21: 163, cite on: 2: 276]. Problems of the intragovernmental coordination and information processes are concerned with orientation to economy of resources reached in managerial process [6]. Even elements of electronic democracy (electronic voting, consultations) were estimated appreciably by economic criteria [14]. In many countries the prompt use of the governmental portals for delivery of the greatest quantity of services was considered as primary goal of introduction of the electronic government. But it has appeared that the customer approach to the electronic government has many flaws, as well as a whole ideology of new public management. Anybody did not specially challenge the electronic services; it was a question that this customer emphasis is obviously not enough when possibilities of new ICTs and the Internet are considered.

So, the problem of citizen engagement into process of service delivery has appeared, and possible services through Internet began to be discussed in qualitative and public manner. Naturally, this process contained the complexities and problems [1]. Many critics consider governmental functions on the delivery of services and governmental relations with citizens through a sociopolitical prism. Andrew Chedvik and Christopher May specify the limited character of the relationship between the government and citizens when the latter act as "clients" of the state. «ICTs will enhance the delivery of services with more accurately targeted communication of citizen requests and faster responses, but the democratic possibilities of such communications are generally ignored, they write. At the center of managerial model is a presumption that change is incremental. While ICTs may represent both challenges and opportunities for the practice of governments (their interaction with the domestic economy and, more widely, civil society), their basic operational logic remains unaltered» [2: 277–278]. Jaeger also speaks about publicness of services, advantage of the information and technical abilities of the electronic state since all it is carried out in a certain social context, is subject to public opinion and interaction of the government with a society [5: 703]. Researches of public administration and the electronic government, therefore, should leave from focus on its modern customer idea to study what the government does and intends to do in a society. Radical position into this critic was occupied by Camilla Stivers who writes: "To be sure, a great deal has been written and discussed about the transformation of citizen to customer. But in the new governance, the contest between market thinking and citizen thinking is a very unequal one. Even though advocated of 'good governance', particularly on the international level, call for political renewal and participation, democracy is treated as a tool for the maintenance of market freedom, not as an end in itself" [18: 1096].

This critic of customer approach to public administration and e-government pushes forward the concept of public service delivery. For the subject of this paper the main concern is the transformation from the services to value of services. Inside the concept of 'public value management' this transition means that "public value is more than a summation of the individual preferences of the users or producers of public services.

The judgment of what is public value is collectively built through deliberation involving elected and appointed government officials and key stakeholders. The achievement of public value, in turn, depends on actions chosen in a reflexive manner from a range of intervention options that rely extensively on building and maintenance networks of provision" [19: 42]. Consequently collaborative approach to e-governance demonstrates new character of the relations between government and citizens and other users of public services: "An integral part of successful e-government around the world implies the provision of an effective platform of e-participation. Citizen involvement in public poli-cymaking is requiring governments to engage in multi-stakeholder citizen engagement" [23: 8].

Some important characteristics could be stressed if we pay attention to idea of 'value of services':

- The value of services for the citizens.
- Efficient, responsive, and tailored government.
- Citizen participation in public policy and service policy.
- Collaborative strategy of interactions between government and citizens.
- Feed-back relations in service delivery.
- Flexibility of service use, combination of traditional and new channels for service delivering.

New tendency is related to digital governance and co-production of the public services using digital equipment [8, 11, 16]. "We see digital government as the optimal use of electronic channels of communication and engagement to improve citizen satisfaction in service delivery, enhance economic competitiveness, forge new levels of engagement and trust, and increase productivity of public services" (Digital Government: www.accenture.com). User orientation in public service delivery means (OECD ideas):

- Design services with a focus on the user, rather than the office (co-selection).
- Take into account the difference between the user's request and its real need.
- Take into account the real context of life of the user service (space and time).
- Personalize services with a high degree of personalization instead of typing.
- Ensure the sharing of data and Internet resources to provide services (co-production).

Last trends in Russian administrative reform (2006–2010) give some evidences of adopting of connected governance and digital services perspectives here. The intensification of the implementation of e-services in 2012 led to a new understanding of the interaction between citizens and government and to assessment of its effectiveness. Some main points could be mentioned: (1) Russia administrative reform: from institutional transformations to improving access to public services delivery; (2) feedback in the regulation of government monitoring of effectiveness; (3) the process of services standardization and citizen participation; (4) multi-functional centers, governmental service portals, and e-consultation on federal and regional levels of e-government. Some tensions and limits accompany these trends.

2   Russia Administrative Reform: From Institutional Transformations to Improving Public Services Delivery

Three reforms – civil service reform (2002), administrative reform (2003), and budget reform (2004) – advanced the executive system in Russia to the next stage of administrative transformations. All these reforms were under the influence of the New Public Management ideology and were conducted by the 'liberals' from the Ministry of Economic Development and Commerce (in Russian, MERT – Ministerstvo Economicheskogo Razvitiya i Torgovli). Though these reforms were ambivalent and were sometimes criticized for inconsistency, they played an important role as the base for the second stage of administrative reform (2006–2010). NPM ideas came in Russia from Western experience of administrative reforms through diffusion rather than through elaboration of real needs and based conditions of Russian reform. Nevertheless a desire to implement NPM and practice of NPM reform (though very narrow) created a psychological atmosphere for further development. That is why the second stage of administrative transformations in Russia tried to combine NPM with public governance imperatives and new e-governance trends.

It is necessary to mention, that the administrative reform and the budgetary reform preceded the formation of the basic purposes and directions of public service reform. The administrative reform (2003) is concentrated on functional and structural improvements. The budgetary reform (2004) focused on a transition to a method of financing of activities by their results. Therefore, especially at the second stage (2006–2010) a number of the purposes which are connected with the process of stimulating administrative activity on the basis of a competition, estimations of quality and productivity of activity have been included here. The concept of the second stage of administrative reform (2006–2010) essentially does not change its general orientation, but includes some significant additional components - management by results, standardization of the state services and elaboration of administrative regulations, anticorruption measures, efficiency of interaction of the executives and a society, modernization of the informational system. The second stage of reform is focused on the implementation of these policies on subjects of the Russian Federation.

Certainly, when estimating administrative reform as a whole, it is necessary to explain, that it is a combination of elements of three administrative ideologies. First, undoubtedly, it concerns to the idea of rational bureaucracy, i.e. to a formation of administrative structures, subordinated to rational functioning on the basis of the laws and rules. This direction is connected with the struggle against informal norms in administrative activity, and aspires to achieve more organization, order, accountability, control, and unity in governance.

The second direction was stimulated by the New Public Management, whose ideology is based on the recognition of opportunity to use business-management mechanisms in public administration. Here the Russian reform uses only some elements, such as an evaluation of activity by results, result budgeting, consumer oriented public services, elements of a competition among the suppliers of the public services, a competitive system of hiring in civil service. The third direction includes ideas of democratic governance which in the general form are presented by a principle of governmental transparency and responsibility before a civil society.

Basically, the Russian administrative reform concerning a combination of various methodological models of public administration – the bureaucratic organization, economic neoinstitutionalism and theories of network management – does not differ from the general orientation of administrative reform in other countries after the crisis of universal models of New Public Management [3]. In the United States today the experts have started talking about lacks of both - minimalist approach to the state (neoconservatism) and positivistic one (NPM). They discuss the pragmatic approach focused on political ends – to overcome break in ability of the state to operate in new conditions of internal and a world policy. Such state is named here 'neoadministrative' which includes many organizations, activity, cultures, and intentions, taken from various theoretical constructions [4]. Johan Olsen – the Norwegian researcher of public administration and one of the pioneers of neoinstitutionalism – fixes a variety of national administrative reforms and speaks about necessity of the updated approach to the theory of bureaucracy under conditions of a combination of the bureaucratic organization, efficient control and network democratic participation [10: 16]. The given pluralism of the conceptual attitudes concerning administrative reform in Russia (and not only here), testifies to more complex representations of the modern state, than are incorporated in the 'holist' approach to the government.

The problem of the governmental functions is at the center of Russian administrative reform on the first stage. It is known, that the Governmental commission on the implementation of administrative reform 5634 functions are analyzed, of them 1468 are recognized as superfluous, 263 as redundant, and 868 functions are demanded to change. At the second stage the regulation of functions remains the primary problem of reform.

Reform of public service also is subordinated to the effective realization of governmental functions. The functional approach is clear, and governmental functions are good to regulate. But, as a matter of fact, the Russian administrative reform concerning functions and their realizations contains three reforms (with a different degree of elaboration): reform of the state administration, management reform of a state ownership, and management reform of delivering public services.

Development of public services also provided the concept of e-government services, which was approved by Decree № 2516-r of the Government of the Russian Federation, December 25, 2013. The above measures are steps for the implementation of the President's decree № 601 dated May 7, 2012, according to which by 2018 it is necessary to increase the share of citizens who use the mechanism for obtaining public and municipal services in electronic form up to 70%. The level of satisfaction of citizens' quality of public and municipal services should reach the level of 90%.

These three reforms then there is a clear accent on three components. (1) On the administrative state with ideas of a lawful state and rational bureaucracy. (2) On the state-proprietor defined by the economic approach to management of the property, by a principle of an evaluation of administrative activity by results, and rational use of budgetary funds. (3) On the state of delivering public services where attitudes on quality and efficiency are important.

The official ideology of Russian administrative reform and special program for e-government do not contain the concepts of 'public value management', 'connected governance' and 'value of services' accordingly. However some trends relate to them. The different aspects of citizen participation may be found into the system of policy evaluation, standardization of government functions and of delivery of public services, into idea and practices of multifunctional centers and governmental portals.

3   Feedback in the Regulation of Government Monitoring of Effectiveness

In recent years the evaluation of government efficiency is originated from the budgetary reform which established the budgeting focused on result (in Russian BOR – budszetirovanie, orientirovannoe na resultat). This system has been introduced by the RF Governmental directive in 22 May, 2004. On 28 June, 2007 by the Decree of the President of the Russian Federation the new system and the list of parameters for an efficiency evaluation of the regional executives was formed. On April 28, 2008, by the Decree of the President, the system of parameters for an efficiency evaluation of local government activities for city districts and municipal areas was determined. On February 9 and March 28, 2008 the Government of the Russian Federation made changes to the Concept of administrative reform and postponed of its implementation from 2008 till 2010. Thus the questions regarding the increase of efficiency of executive activity were of primary concern.

Currently, the improvement of public administration efficiency and quality assessment system is conducted in four main areas:

1. Development of the Unified State Automated Information System "Governance".
2. Reforming the system of public councils.
3. Development and implementation of indicators of the effectiveness and efficiency of public authorities and civil servants.
4. Anti-Corruption, the identification and subsequent elimination of the causes and conditions of corruption occurrence.

It is necessary to say the Russian system of efficiency evaluation has some elements of feedback. The basic feedback mechanism in this official system is public opinion polls on satisfaction of public services or activity of the executives by the citizens. By the Presidential decrees and the Government resolutions (2007, 2008, 2012) such public opinions polls must be an important part of evaluating processes. The second element of feedback is the system of public chambers (and councils) that was introduced on the different levels of state power, including federal and regional authorities. In the center there is the Public Chamber of the RF (see: www.oprf.ru) that consists from 126 deputies. The Chamber was formed by the Federal Law "On the Public Chamber of the Russian Federation" (2005). According to the Federal law the Public chamber consists of forty two citizens of the Russian Federation confirmed by the President of the Russian Federation, forty two representatives of the all-Russian public associations and forty two representatives of inter-regional and regional public associations. The Public Chamber of the Russian Federation provides interactions between citizens, public associations and federal public authorities, between public authorities of the subjects of the Russian Federation and local governments. The main concerns of these interactions are the requirements and interests of citizens, protection of their rights and freedom, the rights of civil associations which are connected to policy-making and to public control over activity of federal enforcement authorities, enforcement authorities of subjects of the Russian Federation and local governments. It assists realization of a government policy in the field of maintenance of human rights [17]. Different executive bodies constructed the consultative councils (soviets) and expert groups for improving decision-making and control over activity of several departments.

Currently, the work on implementation of public assessments of governmental activities is in accordance with the Resolution of the Russian Government dated 12 December, 2012 № 1284 "On the evaluation by the citizens of the effectiveness of heads of territorial bodies of federal executive bodies (their divisions), taking into account the quality of their public services, and the application of the results of this assessment as a basis for a decision on early termination of the respective leaders of their duties ". The collection of opinions of citizens is carried out after the receipt of public service results by using the following mechanisms: sending SMS messages of public services recipients to assess the quality of the services, a survey through electronic terminals or other devices located directly in the field of public services (including MFC), the survey through a dedicated resource on the Internet - site "Your control» (www.vashkon-trol.ru), as well as on a single portal of public and municipal services.

Citizens can assess the quality of government services by criteria such as waiting time, friendly staff, comfortable environment, the availability of information on how to obtain services and others.

On the level of subjects of the Russian Federation the evaluation of executive's activity by criteria of social and economic development is indirect and doesn't say about a role of administrative activity in this process. In system of criteria the differentiation of estimations of the structures which are carrying out the general policy and management, and the structures which are carrying out the public services is poorly examined.

As the result, the developed system of evaluating the efficiency of activity of executive bodies has no stimulating influence on the activity of civil servants.

Secondly, the system of efficiency evaluation has an internal character as a whole. In the given system there is no «an external instance of evaluation». Such external evaluating institutions could be the financial bodies of the state (the Central Bank, for example), independent estimated agencies, expert centers and groups or research groups. The potential of a civil society is now involved in this process actively.

In this connection it is possible to note, that often evaluation's result will suffer from the aspiration of executives to present their businesses in a positive light. Attraction of experts for evaluation using budgets on research work of corresponding departments does not solve the problem of objectivity and completeness, especially, as to direct estimations of executive's activity. Instead of efficiency they evaluate the general social and economic situation or the general parameters of activity. But new channels of assessment play positive role in joint learning citizens and authorities how to improve public service delivery.

4   The Process of Services Standardization and Citizen Participation

In 2008–2009 the concentrated activities on development of administrative regulations (in Russian 'reglaments') regarding the execution of various functions and the rendering services to the population were executed both by federal and regional bodies of government. The administrative regulations developed, approved and registered by the Ministry of Justice were totaled at 350. On the federal level 550 regulations were prepared, on the regional level approximately 35000 were.

As a matter of fact, the administrative regulations are a step-by-step, algorithmic description of the optimized process of execution of function or service delivery, including criteria of decision-making and the detailed characteristic of an end result in the form of the execution standard. Within the description of administrative process at each of its stages duties of the executors, necessary documents and payments are specified. These regulations are opened for the citizens. As A. Klimenko and A Szulin rightly stressed, "thanks to creation of administrative regulations the civil society has an opportunity for the first time to glance in the bureaucratic machinery remaining until recently absolutely closed, which at its discretion expands its powers, treats results of the activity. The openness of regulations provides unprecedented level of a transparency of bureaucracy. However opening in this connection possibilities are still insufficiently realized and demanded not only a civil society, but also the bureaucracy" [9: 124].

Administrative regulations have allowed solving problems of ordering of activity in management and rendering of services to the population, increasing the control over corresponding activity, reducing costs and increasing the quality of administrative activity and of delivered public services.

The study of use of administrative regulations nevertheless is not sufficient for a system evaluation of their efficiency. Having the certain positive effect a number of new problems and restrictions in administrative activity and in delivering services to the population are observed by agencies of the government also. There is a problem of a redundancy of administrative procedures. Though administrative regulations as a whole do a control system and delivery services more ordered and certain, they also strengthen its rigidity and slowness. Regulations are aimed at increasing the degree of predictability of activity of civil servants; however they do not consider the frequency that opportunities of extraordinary circumstances arise in spheres of administrative activity and delivering services to concrete users.

The degree of optimization of execution of the state functions and granting the public services requires updating. Really, administrative regulations raise an opportunity to control administrative activity and delivering services. However, first, it is frequently unclear who is responsible for the execution of concrete actions, secondly, as civil servants often say, the set of detailed instructions and the norms contained in rules, complicate the external control over corresponding actions. New problems arise in questions of integration of actions of various departments and officials when a function or service is interdepartmental or the decision of a question in case of arising disagreements is required.

Development and acceptance of administrative regulations is sometimes carried out with public hearings or public examination. Especially these are obvious on the regional and municipal levels. This is one of the mechanisms of feedback between the authorities and the citizens. But this is very rare procedure. Hence, many questions of optimization of activity, criteria of efficiency of delivering services and legitimizing administrative regulations remain unresolved. The state regulates own activity, guided by its understanding of standards and qualities. However a comparison of the administrative regulations with real practices of service delivering lets the citizens establishes the claim for the authorities and controls their activity.

5 Multifunctional Centers (MFC)

Realizing the idea of 'one window' for improvement of public service delivery the Russian government became to intensify creation of the Multifunctional Centers in different regions of the country in 2007. Now (2015) in Russian regions there are about 2700 MFC. Network of the "one open windows" - it is 12 thousand points across the country, of which about 2700 are complete multifunctional centers and still about 10 thousand is geographically separate units in small towns. Coverage of the MFC system is 94.2% of the population. Total in 2015 56 million services were provided by MFC. MFC is some kind of the intermediary between citizen and the state during delivery of public services. Citizens can address here practically any public service, having handed only the minimum list of the basic documents. All necessary additional information is requested without participation of citizen on the basis of the intensive interaction between various bodies of federal, regional and municipal authority.

The centers do not substitute the governmental bodies - the ministries and departments, does not carry out for them the duties ordered to it. The Multifunctional centers only organize interaction between all participants of service delivery on the base of administrative regulations. MFC network currently communicates with departmental systems through the System of interdepartmental electronic interaction (SIEI), but does not allow the provision of public services in one channel mode. The SIEI is a functional element of the e-government infrastructure, providing mainly the interaction of bodies of state power and local self-government within the framework provided in electronic form of public service delivery processes. Currently the SIEI connects to all the basic state information resources and organizations that provide public services. Total to the System of interdepartmental electronic interaction is connected about 12 thousand organizations, the number of transactions carried out with its help, grows rapidly - 1.8 billion in 2013 and 4.3 billion in 2014 [20: 6–7].

Primary goals of MFC are: conducting personal reception of citizens and formation of statements for the services in the presence of citizens on a principle of "one window"; gathering of documents for the citizens necessary for decision-making on delivery (refusal delivery) of the public services, by means of interaction with executive powers of the government and other organizations which are carrying out preparation of corresponding documents and data; formation of a full package of documents and data in electronic form and their transfer together with the statement of the citizen in an executive office of the government responsible for decision-making on delivery of the public service; monitoring of delivery of the public services by responsible executive bodies and informing of citizens about their inquiries and stages of delivery of the public services; the organization of reception of results of the public services from responsible bodies and delivery of ready results to applicants.

6   Governmental Portals (GP) of the Public Services

The Russian system of portals for delivering public services became to form last years. The year 2009 was very intensive in this concern. Now every subject of the RF has the governmental internet portal for public services. 15 December 2009 the Federal Governmental Portal of public cervices was opened (www.gosuslugi.ru). The Federal Governmental Portal of public services should provide a uniform point of access for citizens to the corresponding public services given by public authorities, to give to citizens and the organizations the uniform interface of access to the governmental information and to reception of the public services with possibility of transition to the Internet site of the authority responsible for granting of concrete state service or to an Internet portal of public authorities of the subject of the Russian Federation (a regional portal of the public services). At the beginning it provided only informational services, but in 2010 full transfer in an electronic form of 10 most significant public services was realized. Among them the following services were provided - filling of forms for registration of identification documents (passports, driver's licenses), various children's grants, and filling of receipts for payment of penalties for infringement of traffic rules. Now this portal has named in 'the Single portal of public and municipal services' (SPPMS). In 2015 the number of electronic services is increased to 655 federal and 2360 regional and municipal public services. New version of the SPPMS (2016) became more simple and mobile for the users. Now public services mobile application can be downloaded to smartphone and user can receive government services.

In 2015 the number of Russians registered in the Unified System of identification and authentication (USIA), increased on 7 million. Currently (January, 2016), in the system almost 23,4 million people are registered. According to a report of the Boston Consulting Group on the digital development of regions lagging behind from Moscow declined over the past five years, from 2.6 to 1.35 times ([14]; compare also Table 1 and below). The leaders in the use of this system are the Primorsky kray with 41% of population, the Khanty-Mansi Autonomous Okrug - Yugra - 36%, Tyumen oblast - 34%, Kaliningrad oblast - 34%, and Yamalo-Nenets Autonomous Okrug - 29%. The significant increase in the number of federal services ordered by the users in the portal can be mentioned: for the first ten months of 2015 users have ordered the services in electronic form 24.3 million times against 12.3 million for the same period in 2014. Increase in the number of the regional services is 275% in comparison with the same period in 2014 (from 213 thousand to 799 thousand). Municipal services showed an increase of 63% - from 296 thousand to 482 thousand.

Table 1. Ranking of using the portal of public services by region

Subject of the RF	Population	Users of the federal portal	% of the population
Moscow	11 977 988	679 800	5,7
Moscow oblast	7 050 557	444 200	6,3
Sverdlovskaya oblast	4 316 852	313 100	7,3
Primorsky kray	1 947 500	294 100	15,1
Samarskaya oblast	3 213 717	226 000	7
St. Petersburg	5 028 313	189 900	3,8
Tuemenskaya oblast	3 511 457	163 700	4,7
Khanty-Mansiysk authonomy	1 583 851	159 400	10,1
Rostovskaya oblast	4 254 763	129 800	3,1
Irkutskaya oblast	2 422 078	123 400	5,1
Khabarovsky kray	1 342 128	116 200	8,7
Altaysky kray	2 399 070	102500	4,3
Kaliningrad oblast	954 978	100 400	10,5
Novosibirsk oblast	2 709 836	96 500	3,6
Krasnodarsky oblast	5 332 252	91 900	1,7
Arkhangelskaya oblast	1 202 543	90 200	7,5
Bashkortostan Republic	4 061 546	90 100	2,2
Niszegorodskaya oblast	3 291 095	90 000	2,7
Omskaya oblast	1 974 361	86 800	4,4
Amurskaya oblast	816 992	84 800	10,4

Source: Data of Ministry of Telecom and Mass Communications, 2013

Accordingly to the conception of the GPs in Russia the system of portals of the public services is considered as a productive and effective means of delivering the public services from the point of view both authorities and citizens. For citizens first of all it is a uniform source of the actual, full, consistent and exact information on the public services, and also possibility of reception of the public services on a principle of "one window». For the executives and the their organizations GP is a factor of perfection of a control system in the field of productivity and efficiency of delivering the public services, and also the mechanism of the organization of interdepartmental interaction and most effective utilization of an information resources.

The purposes of the GPs are:

- Increase of an information openness and transparency of activity of the executives and the Government of the Russian Federation;
- Increase of awareness of citizens and the organizations about delivering ser-vices and executed functions of the authorities;

- Increase of convenience and comfort (decrease of financial and time expenses) for the citizens and for the legal bodies at reception of the state and municipal services according to the requirements fixed in administrative regulations of corresponding service (function);
- Increase of efficiency of an interdepartmental information exchange and in-teraction of the governmental departments regarding providing and delivering the public services and executions of the public functions by different authorities.

In 2014 The Ministry of Telecom and Mass Communications of the Russian Federation has defined short number of the Center unified portal of public services for user support. Now, using the phone number "115" Russian citizens will be able to get technical support on the portal of public services, to find out the status of the passage of his statement, address or schedule interested state or municipal enterprise. Unified support staff will also help citizens to solve the problems associated with the passage of registration on the portal of public services.

According to the results of monitoring the level of Russian Ministry of Economic Development citizen satisfaction with the quality of services is growing and it reached 81.2% in 2014 (the share of citizens who assessed the quality providing state and municipal services as "very good" or "rather good"; to "very good" quality is appreciated 28.4% of users). The level of satisfaction with electronic services provided through a single portal of public and municipal services and the official websites of federal agencies power is higher and respectively 87.5% and 84.7% of the citizens who use them [20: 5–6].

7 Conclusion

The important condition of overcoming the inefficiency with the least losses is ability of the state to be responsible. Certainly, responsibility is provided by the institutions - economic, political, legal, and moral. In not smaller degree it is provided by an internal ethos of responsible behavior for carried out governmental activities. For the government the responsible behavior is extremely significant. In last years a number of measures of the economic, politico-legal and moral plans for increase of responsibility of public authorities and civil servants were used. However still rupture between requirement of a society for the responsible state and level of its realization actually is not overcome. An indicator of this rupture is the data of polls which testify to low level of trust of the population in public authorities. During the administrative reform such measures like service standardization, monitoring of governmental efficiency, multifunctional centers, governmental portals for services and information, and so on put a base for change of this situation. More intensive participation of the citizens in policy-making and into evaluation of public services and governmental activities can radically transform public trust in the government and ability of the state to be responsible.

References

1. Atkinson, R., Leigh, A.: Customer-oriented e-government: can we ever get there? In: Gurtin, G., Sommer, M., Vis-Sommer, V. (eds.) The World of E-Government. Haworth Press, Binghampton (2003)
2. Chadwick, A., May, C.: Interaction between states and citizens in the age of the internet: "e-Government" in the United States, Britain, and the European Union. Gov. Int. J. Policy Adm. Inst. **16**, 271–300 (2003). doi:10.1111/1468-0491.00216
3. Dunleavy, P., Margetts, H., Bastow, S., Tinkler, J.: New public management is dead – long live digital-era governance. J. Public Adm. Res. Theor. **16**, 467–494 (2006). doi:10.1093/jopart/mui057
4. Durant, R.: Whither the neoadministrative state? Toward a polity-centered theory of administrative reform. J. Public Adm. Res. Theor. **10**, 79–109 (2000)
5. Jaeger, P.: Deliberative democracy and the conceptual foundations of electronic government. Gov. Inf. Q. **22**, 702–719 (2005)
6. Kaczorowski, W. (ed.): Connected Government: Thoughts Leaders: Essays from Innovators. Premium Publishing, London (2004)
7. King, S.: Citizens as customers: exploring the future of CRM in UK local government. Gov. Inf. Q. **24**, 47–63 (2007)
8. Klein, S.: Government digital service: the best startup in Europe we can't invest in. Gardian, 15 November 2013
9. Klimenko, A.V., Szulin, A.B.: Vserossiysky monitoring vnedreniya administrativnyh reglamentov. In: Voprocy gosudarstvennogo i munitsipalnogo upravleniya, N 1 (2009). (The All-Russia Monitoring of Introduction of the Administrative Regulations)
10. Olsen, J.: Maybe it is time to rediscover bureaucracy. J. Public Adm. Res. Theor. **16**, 1–24 (2006). doi:10.1093/jopart/mui027
11. O'Reilly, T.: Government as platform. In: Lathrop, D., Ruma, L. (eds.) Open Government. Creative Commons, San Francisco (2010)
12. Pang, G.M.L., Norris, R.: Applying customer relationship management (CRM) to government. J. Gov. Finan. Manag. **51**, 40–45 (2002)
13. Russia online? Catch cannot be left behind. The Report of the Boston Consulting Group, June 2016
14. Sheridan, W., Riley, T.: Comparing e-Government vs. e-Governance. In: eGov Monitor. Commonwealth Center for e-Governance, 3 July 2006, http://www.egovmonitor.com/node/6556
15. Schedler, K., Summermatter, L.: Customer orientation in electronic government: motives and effects. Gov. Inf. Q. **24**, 291–311 (2007)
16. Scherer, S., Wimmer, V., Strykowski, S.: Social government: a concept supporting communities in co-creation and co-production of public services. In: Proceedings of the 16th Annual International Conference on Digital Government Research, pp. 204–209. ACM, New York (2015)
17. Smorgunov, L.: Institutional learning for government-society relations: Russian case of 'Open Government'. In: Proceedings of the 2014 Conference on Electronic Governance and Open Society: Challenges in Eurasia, EGOSE 2014, pp. 101–108. ACM, New York (2014) doi: 10.1145/2729104.2729117
18. Stivers, C.: The ontology of public space: grounding governance in social reality. ABS. **52**, 1095–1108 (2009). doi:10.1177/0002764208327677
19. Stoker, G.: Public value management: a new narrative for networked governance? ARPA. **36**, 41–57 (2006). doi:10.1177/0275074005282583

20. Systemny proekt elektronnogo pravitelstva Rossiyskoy Federatcii 2020. Minkomsviaz. (System project of e-government in Russian Federation). http://minsvyaz.ru/ru/events/34763
21. Tapscott, D.: The Digital Economy: Promise and Peril in the Age of Networked Intelligence. McGraw-Hill, New York (1995)
22. Verheijen, T., Coombes, D. (eds.): Innovations in Public Management: Perspectives from East and West Europe. Edward Elgar, Cheltenham-Northampton (1998)
23. United Nations e-Government Survey: From e-Government to Connected Governance. UN, New York (2008)

E-Government in Russia: Meeting Growing Demand in the Era of Budget Constraints

Elena Dobrolyubova[1(✉)] and Oleg Alexandrov[2]

[1] Russian Academy of National Economy and Public Administration, Moscow, Russia
dobrolyubova@inbox.ru
[2] CEFC Group, Moscow, Russia
aleksandrov@cefc.ru

Abstract. Rapid improvements in access to ICT in Russia result in increased demand for e-government services. The citizens using electronic means to apply for and receive the results of public services demonstrate higher satisfaction with quality of public service delivery, compared to those who use traditional in-person application procedures. However, both statistical and sociological data analyzed in the article suggest that the share of public services actually delivered in electronic form is still low (about 3.2% of Russian citizens managed to receive the administrative public services in electronic form in 2015). To reduce the gap in e-services development with OECD countries in the current budget constraints, there is a need to reallocate ICT resources along the key priority public functions and services and to turn e-government tools from being a cost item to becoming a factor of budget savings. To achieve such results, it is expedient to introduce the practice of measuring and monitoring service delivery transaction costs and to use cost-effectiveness as one of the key factor guiding the decision-making process on ICT investments.

Keywords: Public services · Municipal services · e-government · e-services · Transaction cost · Optimization · Efficiency · Public expenditures

1 Introduction

After demonstrating some spectacular results in building information society and e-government in the early 2010s, Russia is facing difficulties in further improvement of the country's position in international ICT ratings. While the overall ranking in Network Readiness Index has improved (in 2015, Russia ranked the 41st compared to the 50th position in 2014 and the 80th position in 2010) [31], the progress seems to be more on the infrastructure side, while the environment and impact issues are lagging behind. Based on the 2015 ITU assessment [12], Russia ranks the 45th in ICT Development Index (with the best recent result being the 38th rank in 2013). Despite the overall position on E-government development index has remained stable in 2012–2014 (with Russia ranking the 27th) [29], it would be difficult to sustain this achievement for a long time without significant development and expansion of e-government services in Russia.

© Springer International Publishing AG 2016
A.V. Chugunov et al. (Eds.): DTGS 2016, CCIS 674, pp. 247–257, 2016.
DOI: 10.1007/978-3-319-49700-6_23

These recent evaluations suggest that Russia is unlikely to meet the ambitious targets set out in the *Information Society Development Strategy* which supposed that Russia would rank among the best 20 economies in the world in terms of the information society development by 2015 [24]. Moreover, sustaining the current level of e-government development as the country's competitive advantage calls for a new strategic approach oriented at reducing the existing gaps in ICT use indices in Russia as compared to the most ICT-advanced economies [5].

Designing such strategic vision should both take into account the international trends and the country's context. The recent recommendation on developing digital government strategies issued by the OECD Council [19] emphasizes the need to integrate digital government initiatives into public administration reforms and create the conditions for adopting cost-effective solutions driven more by the demand for services and e-participation on the part of the citizens rather than by the government itself.

2 Objective, Scope, and Methodology of the Paper

2.1 Literature Review

International academic and practitioner literature demonstrates a consensus that the demand for e-government should assume a central role in developing and implementing digital strategies (see for example [19, 22, 23]). Quite a number of studies have been recently conducted to evaluate the factors affecting the e-services uptake both in developed and developing economies, see [3, 10, 30]; however, the emphasis is still being placed on evaluating and therefore addressing more the supply side rather than the demand side both in Russia [26] and in other countries [25].

Though implementing e-government is often seen as a means for bringing cost-effective solutions to the public administration [6, 13, 14], at the initial stage of implementation the costs may significantly outweigh the benefits [7]. While a number of methods have been recently proposed in academic literature for conducting cost-benefit analysis of ICT investments [21] and e-services in particular (see [4, 15]), finding a practical approach to improving cost-efficiency and cost-effectiveness in implementing e-government strategies is still an important issue both in Russia and abroad.

Therefore, to contribute to the new e-government strategy, there is a need to assess both the demand for and supply of e-services in Russia, with special attention to the current resource constraints and the ways to overcome them.

2.2 Objective and Scope

The objective of this paper is to assess both the demand for and supply of e-services in Russia, and to develop proposals on improving public service delivery in the context of the current fiscal constraints.

The key hypothesis of the paper is that the allocation of the federal budget ICT resources for e-government (including e-services delivery) is not optimal and does not take into account the demand for e-services in Russia.

The paper is limited to the federal public services and, therefore, funding of ICT investments from the federal budget only. This limitation is justified both by the lack of consolidated data on sub-national public services and the funding allocated to such services, and by the fact that the federal level services account for about two thirds of all administrative public services rendered in Russia.

The research is built on a broad range of data sources, including official statistics, outcomes of sociological surveys, and the data on federal budget execution. Where possible, we used international statistics and publications of international organizations for comparison purposes.

3   Retaining the Positions: Key Challenges

3.1   The Demand Side: Public E-Services

For the past five years, citizen preparedness for electronic interaction with the public sector as well as the demand for such interaction has grown significantly. More than two thirds of Russian households are now connected to Internet (compared to 41.3% in 2010), while the total number of Internet users has reached 77 million. Over 80% of Russian businesses in 2014 had broadband connection to Internet (in 2010–56.7%). For the past five years, the share of households using Internet for booking goods and services and for searching information of public authorities has doubled. Better access to ICT creates higher demand for e-services: by the end of 2015, some 22.5 million citizens were registered at the Single Public Services Portal (SPSP, www.gosuslugi.ru). Given the total number for the Internet users, the prospective demand for e-services is about three times higher.

This conclusion is also supported by the outcomes of sociological surveys. For example, the results of a series of surveys conducted by the Russian Academy of the National Economy and Public Administration (RANEPA) in 2011–2015 aimed at measuring citizen perceptions of public service delivery demonstrate that the extent of public awareness about the SPSP has increased in 2011–2015 from 20.7% of respondents [21] to 68.9%[1]. The share of the respondents who use this resource has grown by 1.3 times for the past year and reached 17.2%.

There is significant variation in the SPSP use depending on disability: only some 4.7% of the respondents with disability used the portal resources, while the usage level among the respondents without disability was much higher (18.0%). This variation is partially explained by the lower extent of awareness about the SPSP among the disabled. However, such trend signals possible digital exclusion of the persons with disability from e-government processes. This is an important issue as for this group personal

---

[1] The survey was conducted in October 2015 in 77 Russian regions. The total sample comprised 10,000 adult citizens who had applied for administrative public services in 2015; the statistical error is 1.3% Survey methodology and is available in [32]. It should be noted that the subject of the surveys included only administrative public services rendered by public authorities (such as registering state property or a business, filing tax returns, etc.), while education, health services and the like were not included into the survey.

interaction with public authorities may require more efforts than for the citizens without disability.

Most of the respondents (68.4%) used the SPSP for information purposes, and not for application or receipt of the service result (Fig. 1). Only 18.5% of the respondents who used the SPSP (or 3.2% of the total sample) actually obtained the service result electronically through the portal.

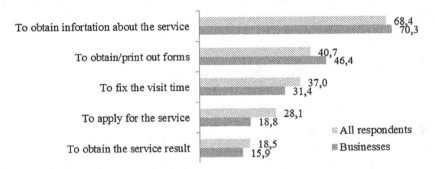

Fig. 1. Use of the SPSP in 2015 by objective (% of the respondents who used the portal)

While the frequency in SPSP use among businesses is higher than among the citizens applying for administrative public services for their own needs (30.2% vs. 16.1% of respondents in respective groups), the share of businesses obtaining the service results from the portal is lower than average (Fig. 1). Thus, Russia is significantly lagging behind the OECD countries in terms of e-services utilization where, on average, 48.6% of individuals and 83% of businesses used Internet to interact with public authorities, 32.8% of individuals and 77.9% of businesses sent filled forms to public authorities via Internet in 2014 [18].

Noteworthy, the respondents using the SPSP demonstrate higher satisfaction with the quality of service delivery. 87.7% of the respondents who used the SPSP at least for information purposes rate the quality of the public service delivery as 'good' or 'very good' compared to 83.8% on average. The satisfaction rate among the respondents who obtained the result of the public service electronically reached 92.8%.

Thus, the empirical data suggests that the demand for public services provided electronically is growing, and e-services have positive impact on citizen perceptions of public service delivery. To meet this demand, the spectrum of public services rendered electronically should be significantly broadened (together with possible utilization of other means, such as self-service kiosks [1]). So far, the menu of the e-services available does not match the public expectations.

3.2   The Supply Side: Fiscal Constraints

On the supply side, the fiscal constraints for the Russian federal budget are currently stricter than in 2008 when the *Information Society Development Strategy* was approved or in 2011, when the implementation of the state program *Information Society in the*

Russian Federation (2011–2020) started. While by OECD standards, the ICT-related expenditures of the Russian central government are not very high (84.6 bln. RUR or about 0.6% of total federal budget spending in 2015, which is comparable to such countries as Portugal and Belgium but is significantly below the budget in Australia, Canada, the US, and New Zealand) [17], there is a room for improvement both in terms of selecting the spending priorities and coordination.

The nominal amount of ICT expenditures from the federal budget remained roughly stable in 2012–2015 after the significant increase in 2012 (Fig. 2).

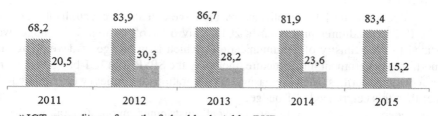

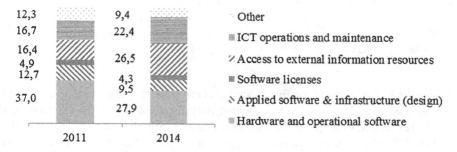

Fig. 2. ICT Expenditures from the Federal Budget in Russia in 2011–2015 Source: author calculations based on Federal Treasury data

However, given more than twofold devaluation of the national currency in 2014–2015 and significant share of imports on the Russian IT market, in real terms the ICT expenditures from the federal budget have decreased.

The structure of these expenditures has also changed. In 2014, the key components of the federal ICT expenditures included hardware and operational software (27.9%), access to external resources (26.5%), and ICT operations and maintenance (22.4%). As compared to the allocation of the federal budget ICT expenditures in 2011, there is an overall trend of decreased investment in hardware, software design, and infrastructure.

Fig. 3. Structure of federal budget ICT expenditures, % of total (Note: expenditures on ICT security are not accounted for separately and form a part of costs related to ICT infrastructure investment, hardware and software development as well as software licenses). Source: author calculations based on Federal Treasury data (www.roskazna.ru).

At the same time, the expenditures on connection services (access to external information resources), operations, and maintenance have been growing (Fig. 3).

Such changes in the cost structure imply that the scope of new ICT investment, including designing new IT systems for delivering e-services and introducing e-service delivery options in the new fields (i.e. for the new services), has been shrinking. The government has less and less room for maneuver in terms of funding new initiatives as it has to support and maintain the solutions introduced for the past years. Therefore, there is a clear need to centralize and concentrate these scarce resources on the highest priority areas.

The situation is further complicated by the large extent of decentralization of the federal ICT expenditures in Russia. In 2015, only 6.1% of the total ICT budget was allocated to the Ministry of Communications, which is in charge of developing and supporting e-government infrastructure, including the SPSP. The ICT budgets of some other federal authorities (such as treasury, tax, migration authorities) were significantly higher than this centralized ICT budget.

The federal ICT expenditures are unevenly distributed among federal authorities both in terms of functions they perform and in terms of their staff number. There is no correlation between the ICT spending and the number of public services provided or the applications for public services received in electronic format (Table 1).

Table 1. ICT budgets and number of transactions in selected federal authorities (Sources: author calculations based on the data published by Federal Treasury, Rosstat).

Federal executive body	ICT expenditures, mln. RUR		Number of services requested (2013)	Applications filed electronically, % of total (2013)	ICT expenditures in 2015 per 1 e- application, RUR
	2014	2015			
Federal registration service	3129.8	3283.9	44332032	10.2	726.6
Federal tax service	10677.6	8548.0	213028018	84.3	47.6
Federal migration service	4048.9	5895.9	73184627	2.5	3199.3
Ministry of interior	10838.1	7306.2	63510720	11.2	1030.4

Thus, the ICT budgets of the five federal executive bodies performing over 70% of total business inspections in 2015 accounted only for some 14.6% of the total ICT expenditures. The ICT budgets of the four federal executive bodies engaged in delivering more than 50% of administrative public services and receiving over 60% of all requests for e-services accounted for only 30% of the total federal budget ICT spending.

The ICT budgets do not correlate with the number of staff in these bodies, either. ICT expenditures per staff member in these federal bodies vary from 30.9 to 104 thousand RUR. Such variations may impact the capacity of the federal authorities both to deliver e-services and to engage in other e-participation formats.

Overall, the priority areas for e-government spending (general e-government infrastructure, supporting the core control and public service delivery functions, including revenue administration) account for about 56.6% of total ICT expenditures. The rest of the ICT expenditures potentially represent a source for possible savings and resource mobilization.

4 Developing E-Government Under Fiscal Constraints

The federal budget ICT spending analysis suggests the need for concentration of the federal budget resources both in terms of supporting priority e-government instruments (including the SPSP) and developing e-services and e-interaction applications in the areas which involve most individuals and businesses and, hence, could generate significant impact in terms of the future savings. Some centralization of ICT costs could also help to prevent development of parallel IT systems with similar (or partially similar) functionality and unclear impact for the public at large.

However, in our opinion, pure concentration and partial reallocation of the existing resources can be a short-term solution. In the medium term, more sustainable approaches which could turn the current ICT expenditures into the future budget savings are required. Achieving this objective would allow for funding e-government development from the savings generated in terms of operational costs, including payroll. Such approach has been implemented in the UK, where transition of all government e-services entailing at least 10,000 transactions per year to electronic format with at least 82% of transactions processed digitally is expected to yield annual savings estimated between 1.7 and 1.8 billion pounds [27]. Similar effects were calculated in New Zealand where the transaction cost of a telephone application to tax authorities was estimated 1.5 times lower than an in-person transaction [16].

Achieving systemic economies of scale from implementation of e-services calls for addressing a number of challenges both of administrative and technological nature. On the administrative side, there is a need for measuring and monitoring transaction costs, broadening the scope of public services which are presented in e-format, and reducing labor costs for processing e-services within the public administration. On the technology side, it is expedient to ensure ICT security, support new formats of public service delivery, such as broadening mobile formats and adopting e-services to the needs of persons with disabilities. While fully appreciating the need for these technological advancements for improving the e-service uptake, in this paper we will focus more on the administrative factors potentially generating budget savings.

Firstly, there is a need for measuring and monitoring public service transaction costs which should be factored in public authorities' performance framework. This is a challenge both in Russia and in the OECD countries where a recent open data survey revealed only one country where such measurement is mandatory (Mexico) and 11 countries where estimation of transaction costs is taking place from time to time [20].

One of the best examples of such practices is publishing the data on transaction costs on the UK public service performance portal [28]. As of March 2016, the dashboards presented on the portal contained performance data (such as the number of transactions, transaction costs, digital take-up, and client satisfaction) for more than 800 public services.

The data available to-date does not allow to measure unit costs per service, transaction, or function in Russia. Some expert evaluations suggest that transition to e-services only by 3 federal executive authorities could generate annual savings of at least 3.5 bln. RUR mostly in terms on savings on payroll and office support costs [2]. From our viewpoint, though measuring transaction costs does incur some methodological problems, this approach helps to keep the focus on using ICT as an important instrument for raising government efficiency. This would form the basis for creating saving targets for implementation of IT systems (in terms of reducing transaction costs, number of staff, etc.) and integrating these targets into the overall performance frameworks used for the budget planning.

Secondly, reducing transaction costs calls for full service digitalization. Partial transition to e-service delivery (when only some administrative procedures, such as fixing the appointment time, are performed electronically) does not result in significant economies of scale as it does not reduce the number of in-person applications for public services. Therefore, it is preferable that the most in-demand services are provided without personal application at any stage. Such formats are already successfully implemented by the Federal Tax Service where a taxpayer may apply and receive settlement of accounts without a personal visit to the inspectorate. In 2014, some 79.6% taxpayers had access to this e-service [9]. The recent EU benchmarking data shows that over 50% of public services in the EU are either fully automated or fully available online, while less than 20% of public services are available only offline. A large menu of the e-services available has a positive impact on the share of citizens preferring e- and m-services which has reached 48% [8].

Special attention should be paid to the needs of vulnerable social groups, including the persons with disabilities. In Russia, the accessibility of e-services to the persons with disabilities is not a subject of the regular monitoring [11], despite the recently approved requirements to web accessibility. Providing e-services to the persons with disability would, inter alia, promote cost savings, especially in the public bodies engaged with processing of welfare payments and providing other social services.

Thirdly, there is a need to automate the processes of data exchange among various government information systems, as the current practice of manual interagency data requests is costly. Automating these requests using the personal identification data collected at the time of registration on the SPSP is another option for reducing the e-services transaction costs.

Reducing transaction costs entails a risk of opposition from federal authorities interested in keeping the current staff levels. Addressing this risk calls for stronger coordination of ICT policy implementation and budget planning processes.

5   Conclusions

Russia is facing a challenge of meeting the growing demand for e-services (and e-government at large) with decreasing resources available. To meet this challenge there is a need to go beyond across-the-board budget cuts. The existing data confirms that the current allocation of the federal ICT budget funds is not proportionate to the number of e-services rendered or the number of e-service application received.

Improving cost-effectiveness in public service delivery should become an important and measurable target for the ICT investment, integrated in the overall performance framework. To implement this approach, we propose to introduce the practice for measuring transaction costs.

In the short term, there is a need to concentrate the existing resources on transforming the most in-demand services into electronic format, so as to achieve savings from the decreased transaction costs. Linking ICT development with the potential demand (both for e-services and also for some control functions) is critical for implementing cost-effective solutions. Actual cost reduction (as well as citizen satisfaction) should become an important performance indicator for these ICT investments. In the medium term, mobilizing the savings from the reduced transaction costs would serve as a sustainable source for further digital government developing, expanding the menu of e-services, and automating G2C, G2B, and G2G interactions.

References

1. Aleksandrov, O.V., Dobrolyubova, E.I.: Public service delivery through automated self-service kiosks: international experience and prospects for implementation in Russia. In: Proceedings of the 2nd International Conference on Electronic Governance and Open Society: Challenges in Eurasia (EGOSE 2015), pp. 205–210. ACM, New York (2015). doi: 10.1145/2846012.2846048
2. Aleksandrov, O.V., Dobrolyubova, E.I., Klochkova, E.N., Yuzhakov, V.N.: Optimizacija bjudzhetnyh rashodov v sfere gosudarstvennogo upravlenija. [Optimization of budget expenditures in public administration]. MESI, Moscow (2014). (in Russian)
3. Alshawi, S., Alalwany, H.: E-government evaluation: citizen's perspective in developing countries. Inform. Technol. Dev. 15(3), 193–208 (2009)
4. Andersen, K.V., Medaglia, R.: E-government front-end services: administrative and citizen cost-benefits. In: Wimmer, M.A., Scholl, H.J., Ferro, E. (eds.) EGOV 2008. LNCS, vol. 5184, pp. 148–159. Springer, Heidelberg (2008). doi:10.1007/978-3-540-85204-9_13
5. Bershadskaya, L., Chugunov, A., Trutnev, D.: Information society development in Russia: measuring progress and gaps. In: Proceedings of the 2014 Conference on Electronic Governance and Open Society: Challenges in Eurasia, EGOSE 2014, pp. 7–13. ACM, New York (2014)
6. Butler, T., Hackney, R.: Breaking the iron law: implementing cost effective, green ICT in the UK public sector. In: Proceedings of the 20th European Conference on Information Systems, ECIS 2012, Barcelona (2012)
7. Elsas, A.: Economic benchmarking of E-government. In.: Managing Information in the Digital Economy: Issues and Solutions, pp. 405–407. IBIMA, Bonn (2006)

8. European Commission. Digital Market. Digital Economy and Society. https://ec.europa.eu/digital-single-market/en/download-scoreboard-reports
9. Federal Tax Service. Statistics and Analytics. https://www.nalog.ru/rn77/related_activities/statistics_and_analytics/effectiveness/#t8. (in Russian)
10. Gatautis, R., Vitkauskaite, E.: E-government services: creating value through services' quality. In: Yannacopoulos, D., Manolitzas, P., Matsatsinis, N., Grigoroudis, E. (eds.) Evaluating Websites and Web Services: Interdisciplinary Perspectives on User Satisfaction, Information Science Reference, Hershey, pp. 42–59 (2014). doi: 10.4018/978-1-4666-5129-6.ch003
11. Improving Public Administration. Administrative Reform Portal. http://www.itu.int/wsis/docs/geneva/official/dop.html (in Russian)
12. International Telecommunications Union. http://www.itu.int/en/ITU-D/Statistics/Documents/publications/misr2015/MISR2015-w5.pdf
13. Jayashree, S., Marthandan, G.: Government to E-government to E-society. J. Appl. Sci. **10**(19), 2205–2210 (2010)
14. Milakovich, M.E.: Digital Governance: New Technologies for Improving Public Service and Participation. Routledge, New York (2012). doi:10.4324/9780203815991
15. Muñoz, L.A., Sánchez, R.G.: Implementation of e-government and reforms in public administrations in crisis periods: a scientometrics approach. In: Public Affairs and Administration: Concepts, Methodologies, Tools, and Applications, pp. 2028–2045. IRMA (2015)
16. New Zealand Controller and Auditor General. Inland Revenue Department: Making it easy to comply. http://www.oag.govt.nz/2011/making-it-easy-to-comply/docs/ird-making-it-easy-to-comply.pdf/view
17. OECD. Government at a Glance 2013. OECD Publishing, Paris (2013). doi:http://dx.doi.org/10.1787/gov_glance-2013-en
18. OECD. Government at a Glance 2015. OECD Publishing, Paris (2015). doi:http://dx.doi.org/10.1787/gov_glance-2015-en
19. OECD. Recommendation of the Council on Digital Government Strategies. Adopted by the OECD Council on 15 July 2014. http://www.oecd.org/gov/digital-government/Recommendation-digital-government-strategies.pdf
20. OECD Survey on Digital Government Performance 2014. http://qdd.oecd.org/subject.aspx?Subject=6C3F11AF-875E-4469-9C9E-AF93EE384796
21. Palka, W., Yigitel, G., Jurisch, M.C., Wolf, P., Krcmar, H.: Basic approaches for the evaluation of IT-investments in E-government: a literature review. In: Wimmer, M., Janssen, M., Macintosh, A., Scholl, H., Tambouris, E. (eds.) Lecture Notes in Informatics (LNI), Proceedings - Series of the Gesellschaft Fur Informatik (GI), P-221, pp. 27–34. Gesellschaft für Informatik, Bonn (2013)
22. Persaud, A., Persaud, P.: Rethinking E-government adoption: a user-centered model. In: Public Affairs and Administration: Concepts, Methodologies, Tools, and Applications, Chap. 2, pp. 657–676. IRMA (2015)
23. Qian, H.: Global perspectives on E-governance: from government-driven to citizen-centric public service delivery. In: ACM International Conference Proceeding Series, October 2010, pp. 1–8. ACM, New York (2010)
24. Sadovnikova, N.A., Klochkova, E.N., Dobrolyubova, E.I., Alexandrov, O.V.: Basic trends of information society development in Russia compared to world's leading countries. Int. Rev. Manag. Mark. **5**, 18–29 (2015)

25. Singh, S.: E-government considerations: a focus on South Africa. In: Public Affairs and Administration: Concepts, Methodologies, Tools, and Applications, Chap. 1, pp. 329–366. IRMA (2015)

26. Styrin, E., Dmitrieva, N.: Information services quality measurement: Russian federal authorities example. In: Proceedings of the 2nd International Conference "Electronic Governance and Open Society: Challenges in Eurasia" (EGOSE 2015), pp. 228–231. ACM, New York (2015)

27. UK Government. Digital Efficiency report, 6 November 2012. https://www.gov.uk/government/publications/digital-efficiency-report/digital-efficiency-report#savings-from-digitising-transactional-services

28. UK Government Performance. https://www.gov.uk/performance

29. United Nations. United Nations E-Government Survey (2014). https://publicadministration.un.org/egovkb/Portals/egovkb/Documents/un/2014-Survey/E-Gov_Complete_Survey-2014.pdf

30. Wang, H.-J., Lo, J.: Determinants of citizens' intent to use government websites in Taiwan. Inf. Dev. 29(2), 123–137 (2013). doi:10.1177/0266666912453835

31. World Economic Forum. Global Technology Information report 2015 (2015). http://reports.weforum.org/global-information-technology-report-2015/

32. Yuzhakov, V.N., Dobrolyubova, E.I., Pokida, A.N., Zybunovskaya, N.V.: Udovletvorennost grazhdan kachestvom predostavlenia administrativnych gosudarstvennyh i municipalnych uslug [Citizen Satisfaction with Quality of Administrative Public and Municipal Services]. Delo Publishing, Moscow (2015). (in Russian)

Direct Democracy: Prospects for the Use of Information Technology

Roman Amelin[1(✉)], Sergey Channov[2], and Tatyana Polyakova[3]

[1] National Research Saratov State University named after N.G. Chernyshevsky,
83 Astrakhanskaya Street, Saratov 410012, Russia
ame-roman@yandex.ru
[2] The Russian Presidental Academy of National Economy and Public Administration,
23/25 Sobornaya St., Saratov 410031, Russia
[3] Institute of State and Law Russian Academy of Sciences, 10 Znamenka St.,
Moscow 119019, Russia

Abstract. This paper dwells on the potential of information technology to ensure the mechanisms of direct democracy. The authors defend the thesis that modern information technologies provide all the necessary tools and the "building blocks" for direct participation of citizens in state affairs management. The authors analyze the strengths and weaknesses of direct democracy, considering the advantages of direct democracy forms to the representative one in today's society. The prospects and the possibility of implementation of the relevant institutions in the Russian Federation in accordance to Russian legislation are evaluated. The authors conclude that objectively there is a need for some institutions of direct participation of citizens in state affairs management (in particular, e-referendum) and offer to start working on introduction of relevant amendments to the legislation.

Keywords: E-democracy · Direct democracy · E-voting · E-referendum · Digital certification · Open data · Information and telecommunication infrastructure · The law on the referendum · State information systems

1 Introduction

The Constitution declares the Russian Federation a democratic legal state. According to Part. 1, Art. 3 of the Constitution of the Russian Federation, the only source of power in the Russian Federation is its multinational people. The people exercise their power directly and through bodies of state and local governments. Analysis of the Constitution and current legislation demonstrates that the real power in the country is carried out not by the people directly, but mostly by various authorities. Thus, democracy in the Russian Federation is not direct, but indirect (representative).

In general, this system of power and control is normal for most modern states. How A. Yugov indicates, "right of representative democracy takes a dominant position in the system of legal capacity of public authorities" [40, p. 30]. Direct democracy in public administration, of course, also takes place, but the circle of issues solved with the help

© Springer International Publishing AG 2016
A.V. Chugunov et al. (Eds.): DTGS 2016, CCIS 674, pp. 258–268, 2016.
DOI: 10.1007/978-3-319-49700-6_24

of its tools (elections, referendums, assemblies, etc.) is relatively small, although their importance is undeniable.

Direct democracy as the main way of solving problems of national importance existed only in a few states for all periods of historical development of humankind. Among the first ones here, of course, we can recall the ancient Greek city-states. It is to them we owe the appearance of the term democracy (δῆμος — "people" and κράτ — "power"). The political system of Athens in the VI century BC and some other Greek city-states can be defined by using the concept of "direct democracy". As noted by V. Fadeev, the main feature of Athenian democracy — direct participation of the sovereign demos in managing state affairs that was achieved by permanent functioning of the National Assembly responsible for all critical issues of life in the city-state. Personal involvement in the exercise of political functions was considered essential for the good political life and the only guarantee of freedom [11, p. 77].

However, the organization of public administration using only the mechanisms of direct democracy is impossible in most modern states for several reasons, first of all, for organizational ones. The specificity of the ancient Greek city-states was a small size and a relatively small population. It gave a real opportunity to direct account the views of all citizens. The same can be said about many other democracies, particularly democracies of the Veche of Novgorod and Pskov.

Modern states (with rare exceptions) have incomparably larger territory and population. Under such conditions, democratic mechanisms cannot be implemented directly, and require the formation of representative bodies and, as a consequence, the representative (indirect) democracy.

However, the current stage of development of information technology creates new opportunities in this area.

The purpose of this study is to analyze the current state and prospects of using new information technologies to implement forms of direct democracy in modern society.

Our study draws heavily on the works [19, 25, 33], which examined the benefits and controversies of direct democracy in the modern world. A very deep literature review on this issue, see [20]. Numerous approaches to the implementation of concept model and tools of e-democracy was considered in [9, 35, 37]. A deep comparison of the different models of e-democracy presented in [24]. The issues of implementation of e-government is deeply considered in [4, 32].

The study used proven methods of scientific knowledge. Methods of formal logic (description, comparison, classification, analysis and synthesis, etc.) allowed us to conduct the study and comparison of various information technologies that can be used in the implementation of forms of direct democracy. In addition, the use of these methods made it possible to conduct a study of existing legislation for compliance with the implementation of direct democracy in the Russian Federation. Historical-legal method allowed us to study the evolution of democratic forms in different countries at different stages of their development and to prove the new opportunities offered by modern information technology. The system-structural method provided a study of the use of information technology in the implementation of forms of direct democracy in the Russian Federation as a systemic phenomenon, allowed the identification of their core elements and objectively existing relations between them.

2   The Possibilities of Modern IT for the Purpose of Direct Democracy

1. The development of electronic voting technology and algorithms. Electronic voting should conform to the basic principles of electoral law. The principles of electoral law is a condition of its acceptance and implementation. Their adherence on elections makes these elections the people's will [31]. In particular, the vote should be (a) general, (b) secret, and (c) equal. Equality means that no vote can be counted twice and each citizen is able to make sure that his vote was counted according to his will [2]. Some time ago, the most serious problem was the simultaneous provision of the principles of secrecy and equality (verifiable) of electronic voting. Similarly, for a long time the idea of digital cash cannot be implemented technically because of the conflict between the two major properties: anonymity and uncopiabilty (inability to pay twice with the same "digital money"). The achievements of modern cryptography have enabled us to resolve these contradictions. The creation of Bitcoins has clearly proved it. Analogous algorithms and protocols have appeared in the field of e-voting. Let us mention, for example, algorithms He-Su [29], Pushscan (system of secret and checkable voting with ballots) [28] etc. Experts (including Russian) regularly propose new algorithms [39].

2. The digital identification of the citizen (including the procedures of direct democracy, in which anonymity is not required or even desirable, for example, public debate) can be introduced and implemented in many different ways now. Among them there are proven, mathematically robust and based on existing infrastructure ones – the use of digital signatures and other cryptographic algorithms – and quite exotic ones, such as algorithms for digital biometric identity identification (e.g., keyboard handwriting) [18]. Smart cards are widely used for identification purposes (digital passportization). In the Russian Federation, a large-scale project on universal electronic cards introduction was planned. They were supposed to serve as a means of identifying the citizen and his means of payment in the sphere of providing state and municipal services [1]. The project has been criticized (in particular, because of the idea of combining two different instruments with a completely different threat models on one carrier) and finally faced with insurmountable organizational and financial difficulties. At the same time, in Estonia, e-passports are valid since 2002, and the acceptance of applications for e-citizenship was opened since 2015. The entire population of Spain and Belgium has a card with an electronic identifier since 2009.

We should not ignore the side effects of a real implementation of such a tool. This is an opportunity for enhanced control of users' actions in the digital environment and eliminating the Internet anonymity. In conditions of the centralized state, concerned with the protection of its sovereignty – this scenario is much more probable than the scope of direct democracy expansion.

3. Open data provide the opportunity to use state (public) information resources to citizens and organizations, including the establishment of important public services (Federal and local). The main problem in Russia is not so much in technological difficulties, but in the lack of user confidence in open data stability To start the add-on mass serviçes on public data on civil initiative, a guarantee from the state that the data will be updated regularly, maintained, preserve compatibility with the current format is required. Where there is trust of users, we can see impressive examples [14]. Among the Russian regions, we note the experience of the Ulyanovsk region, as reflected in the report at the conference on electronic global society EGOSE'2015 [30].

4. Infrastructure of access to information and communication technologies (primarily the Internet), is currently well developed in all democratic countries. The Russian Federation has high rates of public access to the infrastructure. The report of The Boston Consulting Group in 2014 represented the country rating "index of electronic interference". Russia demonstrates good results for the infrastructure index, although occupies the 11th place from the end for industry indicators (business development obstacles on the Internet) [13]. These results have been achieved in the process of implementation of the federal laws on the organization of providing public and municipal services (2010) and on ensuring access to information about the activity of state bodies and local self-government (2009). Some families (and even, perhaps, some municipalities), do not have the access to the Internet. But we are confident enough to say that every adult citizen who has the minimum necessary qualities to participate in the management of state affairs (civic engagement, the intellectual level, the absence of constraints imposed by the court sentence, etc.), has a real opportunity to use the access infrastructure and the right to participate in managing state affairs.

Some government information systems allow citizens to receive directly and impart information related to the management of their affairs.

It should be noted that the state automated system "Elections" was created and has been operating for nearly 20 years in Russia. It is a complex distributed tool for determining the voting results, the processing of ballots and other objectives. Federal Law "On the State Automated System "Elections" provides a legal basis for the application of this system.

Most state information systems in Russia, including those based on federal laws, designed for the tasks of state accounting and control [3]:

- State Information system of Migration Control,
- Uniform Federal Automated Information System of Data on Displays of Films in Cinema Halls,
- Unified State Information System of Transport Security,
- The Federal Database of Genomic Information Data,
- Unified State Information System of Accounting of Wood and Deals with it, etc.
  Some of state information systems provide access to certain information:
- Unified Federal Register of Tour Operators,
- Federal Register of Apostilles,
- Unified Information System of Notaries,
- Federal Public Information System of Territorial Planning,
- System of Public Information Support in the Field of Agriculture,
- System of Public Information Support in the Field of Trade Activity, etc.

However, state information systems for the organization of information interaction of citizens and organizations with the state and with each other, have appeared in recent years. In addition to the Portal of State and Municipal Services it is worth mentioning the Information-analytical System "Working in Russia", which contains information on job opportunities, employers, job vacancies and vacancies, job seekers, etc. It is planned that in 2017 every citizen will have access to a personal account in the state information system for management of housing and communal services.

5. *Online communication systems* provide society and the business with the necessary information and organize two-way communication between public institutions, businesses and citizens. The appearance of the appropriate tools and services (e-mail, social networks, online conferences, discussion groups, chat rooms) allowed to talk about e-democracy once. Today it is part of everyday life. Residents of the city Innopolis in Tatarstan Republic are involved in solving local issues using the communication program "Telegram".

Awareness of the citizens is a necessary requirement for their participation in the management of state affairs. The availability of online communication tools, the development of network media removed the state monopoly on the media, created a technical possibility of obtaining a sufficiently complete and current information on any issue. Although, of course, the cultural aspect remains (the availability of the necessary skills and qualities required for the search and selection of high-quality information).

Open data, online communication systems and technology infrastructure make it possible to implement the concept of "e-government", which is currently implementing around the world. E-government is the way of information provision and public service delivery to citizens, businesses, other branches of the government and public officials, in which the personal interaction between the state and the applicant is minimized and information technology is used as much as possible. It is a system of electronic document management of governance, based on the automation of administrative processes across the country. Its goal is a significant increase in the efficiency of public administration and the reduction of social communications costs for each member of society.

Thus, now there is a real technical possibility to take into account the views of all citizens (voters) of a particular state without excessively high costs in each case. Of course, the implementation of such a system is expensive, but its maintenance and operation will be cheaper than, for example, the costs of elections and referend in the traditional way.

3 Direct Democracy: Advantages and Prospects

Of course, the potential use of new information technologies for the realization of various democratic procedures did not go beyond the attention of both scientists and government officials. Back in 2010, Russian President Dmitry Medvedev said directly: "I am absolutely sure that era of the return to a certain extent from representative democracy to direct democracy, the Internet democracy is coming" [23].

Indeed, direct democracy has a distinct advantage over representative one. It allows to consider directly the will of citizens of the state, not their representatives. Representatives often have interests separated from the interests of the majority. The formation of representative bodies of power functioning on a permanent long-term basis, in spite of their democratic nature, entails the appearance of groups of people who are "professional managers". They are often close to other power structures, business elites, etc., than to their constituents. This is reflected in their decisions. Quite naturally, the population reasonably criticizes the activities of such representative bodies. Suffice it is to recall the State Duma of the Russian Federation received for its often contentious legislative activity the nickname "mad printer" [7, 21].

At the same time, we believe that a complete rejection of representative democracy is no longer possible, at least in the near future neither in the Russian Federation nor in any other state. Challenges that modern government faces, are immeasurably more complex than those that were solved in the ancient Greek policies, or in the Veche republics. It is necessary to have a significant level of expertise for decision making. Furthermore, direct democracy requires from its subjects to devote significant time to the implementation of official procedures and the performance of various duties [8]. All of this highlights the need for professionalism in the management of a modern state not only in the executive and judicial authorities, but also in the legislative sphere.

In addition, it should be noted that the representative bodies of modern states often make decisions that are very unpopular, but necessary for the national good. "Society has never been just a collection of its members, like that the public interest is not merely the sum of individual interests. Interests of the individual and collective interests are an objective reality, which develops according to the laws of dialectics" [10].

Therefore, we should not idealize the direct democracy. Providing to all citizens of the state real possibility of making decisions on all governance issues will lead to its prosperity – not just naive, but dangerous delusion. On the contrary, in this situation there is a risk of transition of democracy in ochlocracy. History knows many examples when a more democratic state has lost historic competition to more authoritarian one, with a strong central government, precisely because of the inability of the authorities and the decision makers to go beyond their private, parochial interests [15, 26, 34].

Debate on the four "old" questions of direct democracy is still far from complete. Those questions are [19]:

- *Are voters competent?* "It is widely believed that there is a mismatch between the requirements of democracy and most people's ability to meet these requirements. If this mismatch is too prevalent, then effective self-governance is impossible. The democratic dilemma is that the people who are called upon to make reasoned choices may not be capable of doing so".
- *What role does money play?* "Money helps defeat initiatives, but it doesn't do much to help them pass. This makes sense, given voters' baseline preference to stick with the status quo. Spending by business groups is far less effective than spending by public interest groups". Convincing voters that an initiative represents an actual improvement over the status quo requires more than money: it requires endorsements (i.e. cues for voters) from well-known groups/individuals and volunteers".

- *How does direct democracy affect policy?* Even if voters get something passed, they rely on the legislators (who did not pass the initiative themselves, apparently) to implement it.
- *Does direct democracy benefit the many or the few?*

Therefore, it seems, in the transition to the massive use of information technology in the implementation of democratic procedures, to the "e-democracy", it is necessary to conduct not a complete rejection of indirect democracy, but on a much larger than at present, the use of procedures for the direct account of public opinion on a variety of issues.

4   "E-democracy". the Modern Stage

Today "e-democracy" means firstly, "the electronic submission of the democratic process" [38]. Basically, it is the use of forms of electronic voting in elections at various levels, online campaigns, online advocacy, use of electronic media for the dissemination of political information, and others [17, p. 43].

Many of these forms are already widely used in the Russian Federation (hearings in the State Duma of public initiatives that have collected at least 100 thousand votes of citizens, public discussion of draft laws and regulations, etc.). Presidential Department on the application of information technologies and the development of e-democracy, created in 2012. It is engaged in the implementation of these measures.

Authorities are very interested in the acting feedback mechanism with the citizens. Portal "Active Citizen" function in Moscow since 2014. This is a platform for electronic referendums. Its goal is to get citizens' views on various urban issues. Should the speed limit on the Boulevard Ring to be increased? As it is necessary to arrange well the New Arbat? "Active Citizen" polls are divided into three categories: city-wide, sectoral and district. Citizens receive bonus points for active participation in the polls. Bonus points can be redeemed for rewards. For example, theater tickets, travel tickets, souvenirs and parking meter. 10% of people in the capital are taking part in the polls.

However, these mechanisms from the standpoint of the development of direct e-democracy in the Russian Federation, are considered to be no more than half-measures, as they are not binding. As a result, the authorities in most cases ignore citizens' opinion on the discussed draft laws; community initiatives are rejected by the expert working group (and have not reached the representative bodies) etc. [16].

It devalues the value of e-participation tools. The low level of public confidence in the government and the information provided by the public authorities, forms a skeptical attitude to political participation as such. Meanwhile, studies of political activity on the Internet shows the people's attitude towards traditional forms of participation duplicates attitude towards traditional models [12].

In this regard, we believe that e-democracy should be developed mainly by way of introduction of mandatory forms of direct democracy. Electronic referendum is the main one.

At present, Russian law allows referendums at the federal, regional and local levels. However, in fact referendum in the Russian Federation is carried out very rarely, in exceptional cases. At the federal level, referendums are not conducted after the adoption of the Constitution. In addition to purely political reasons, we can see the reason in the great complexity of the referendum by conventional methods and, accordingly, the high cost of them. It is quite natural that Russian law on the referendum stipulates the possibility of carrying out a number of conditions, which are very difficult to observe in practice. For example, the procedure of initiation of a federal referendum directly by citizens is so complex that it is possible more in theory than in practice.

Information technology allows not only significantly reduce the cost of the referendums of various levels, but also significantly simplify the implementation of initiatives. The referendum as part of e-democracy could well become an operative mechanism of solving a variety of problems by Russian people directly. In this case, an electronic referendum will allow the government to get really objective answers to these questions, which can no longer be ignored.

In connection with the latter it is impossible to recall survey conducted in 2015 in the Republic of Crimea and Sevastopol on the electricity supply of the peninsula. The survey covered a little more than 3,000 inhabitants of these regions. 93.2% of respondents were not willing to enter into a contract with the Ukrainian side for the supply of electricity in the Crimea and Sevastopol, if it is stated that these subjects are part of Ukraine [27]. Note that, electronic referendum technology would allow to obtain the opinion of all the inhabitants almost as quickly, but the legal significance of the results would be much higher. In addition, an electronic referendum allows making a decision in compliance with the principle of anonymity, which cannot be achieved by telephone surveys. In situations like the above, the importance of the principle of anonymity is extremely large.

As part of the development of forms of direct electronic democracy development of e-voting systems in elections at all levels of government also seems promising. It appears that this would at least partly overcome one of the major ills of Russian elections - low voter turnout. It is significant that such proposals are now being discussed in other states [22].

5 Conclusions and Prospects

Of course, a comprehensive implementation of electronic procedures for the referendum, as well as other elements of e-democracy is not a question of tomorrow and, even, not the day after tomorrow. As M. Vaskova notes, a number of factors complicate the functioning of e-government with the elements of e-democracy in Russia. The most important are:

1. There is no legal regulation in many areas of the electronic state.
2. There are no qualitative characteristics of the subject of e-democracy [36].

V. Belov notes a number of conditions necessary for the spread of e-democracy: the involvement of citizens, citizens' confidence, the impact on the state, the formation of an expert network of e-democracy, and others [5, p. 136]. Direct e-democracy is the next step. It requires additional terms and solving additional issues.

The main problems of the development of e-democracy are similar to problems of foresight and crowdsourcing, which include false test results, reflecting the massive mythology that has developed in the community. As a result, decisions are shifted to the level of less-educated part of the population [6].

The solution of these problems cannot be momentary, but now the program of transition to a truly direct e-democracy designed for the next decade could be planned.

Of course, the implementation of the transition to the use of information technologies in the form of a binding nature of direct democracy, which were discussed in this article, will require, in addition to the organizational and technical aspects, changes in the current legislation. In particular, the procedure of referendum initiation should be significantly simplified.

For example, the Federal constitutional law "On referendum of the Russian Federation" stipulates that the initiative to hold a referendum of the Russian Federation holds:

(1) not less than two million Russian citizens, eligible to participate in the referendum, on condition that in the territory of one subject of the Russian Federation or outside the Russian Federation is a place of residence not more than 50 thousand of them;

(2) the Constitutional Assembly in the case provided for by part 3 of article 135 of the Constitution of the Russian Federation;

(3) the Federal state authorities in cases stipulated by international Treaty of the Russian Federation and Federal constitutional law.

It is clear that the initiative for a referendum of the Russian Federation citizens is extremely difficult, requires significant organizational efforts.

In the case of migration to a referendum of the Russian Federation in electronic form, the number of votes of citizens acting with the initiative can be painlessly reduced several times since the referendum will not require such complex measures and financial costs as it is now. At the same time, even the preservation of the threshold of two million votes will allow to implement the initiative of holding referendums more often when collecting the required number of votes will be done in electronic form. Practice shows that hundreds of thousands of votes for various initiatives can be collected electronically in a relatively short time.

Similar approaches in the formation of the requirements of the initiative can be applied to regional and local referendums.

At the same time, in our opinion, the existing bans on the holding of referendums on certain issues need to be kept for the reasons described above.

The authors are currently working on specific suggestions for the Russian legislation improvement in terms of an electronic referendum possibility.

References

1. Amelin, R.: On the relationship of legal and technological tools in the provision of public and municipal services in electronic form. In: Proceedings of the Conference on Right of Access to Information: Possibilities and Limitations in the Digital Environment, St. Petersburg, Issue 2, pp. 234–237 (2011)

2. Amelin, R.: The constitutional principles of electoral law in the development of automated information systems. In: Proceedings of the Conference on Constitutional Reading, Saratov, pp. 176–179 (2008)

3. Amelin, R., Channov, S.: State information systems in e-government in the Russian Federation: problems of legal regulation. In: Proceedings of the 2nd International Conference on Electronic Governance and Open Society: Challenges in Eurasia (EGOSE 2015), St. Petersburg, Russian Federation, 24–25, November, pp. 129–132. ACM, New York (2015)
4. Anttiroiko, A.: Electronic Government: Concepts, Methodologies, Tools, and Applications: Concepts, Methodologies, Tools, and Applications. IGI Global, Hershey (2008)
5. Belov, V.G.: E-democracy in modern Russia. Values Meanings **4**, 129–138 (2012)
6. Belousov, D.R., Solncev, O.G., Hromov, M.U.: Building a long-term scientific and technological forecast for Russia by the "Foresight". Probl. Forecast. **1**, 18–32 (2008)
7. Bocharova, S.: How do you annoy. https://lenta.ru/articles/2013/03/22/printer/
8. Buzeskul, V.P.: History of the Athenian democracy, St. Petersburg (2003)
9. Chadwick, A.: Web 2.0: new challenges for the study of e-democracy in an era of informational exuberance. ISJLP **5**, 9 (2008)
10. Ebzeev, B.S.: Russian constitution – 20 years old: state, democracy, identity through the prism of practical constitutionalism. Const. Justice Mag. **6**, 32 (2013)
11. Fadeev, V.I.: At the root of popular representation: political ideas and practices of ancient democracy. Const. Municipal Law **11**, 77–83 (2013)
12. Fossato, F., Lloyd, J.: The Web that Failed: How Opposition Politics and Independent Initiatives are Failing on the Internet in Russia. Reuters Institute for the Study of Journalism. University of Oxford (2008). http://reutersinstitute.politics.ox.ac.uk/fileadmin/documents/Publications/The_Web_that_Failed.pdf
13. Greasing the Wheels of the Internet Economy. https://www.bcgperspectivescom/content/articles/digital_economy_telecommunications_greasing_wheels_internet_economy/?chapter=3
14. Gurin, J.: Open Data Now: The Secret to Hot Startups, Smart Investing, Savvy Marketing, and Fast Innovation. McGraw-Hill Education, New York (2014)
15. Gvarliani, T.E., Vidishcheva, E.V., Rassolov, I.M.: The development of agriculture and trade relations in the caucasus in the early 20th century. BYLYE GODY **38**(4), 1039–1046 (2015)
16. Ivanov, M.: ROI reduce the subscription threshold (2013). http://kommersant.ru/doc/2897532
17. Kuryachaya, M.M.: E-democracy as a challenge to the modern legal policy. Const. Municipal Law **1**, 41–44 (2013)
18. Landeh, D.V., Furashev, V.N.: About digital identification. In: Public Information and Computer Integrated Technologies, Kharkiv, issue 34, pp. 127–135 (2007)
19. Lupia, A., Matsusaka, J.: Direct democracy: new approaches to old questions. Annu. Rev. Polit. Sci. **7**, 463–482 (2004). doi:10.1146/annurev.polisci.7.012003.104730
20. Maduz, L.: Direct democracy. Living Rev. Democracy **2**, 1–17 (2010)
21. Muratov, D.: These two laws together give a stunning effect. http://www.alebedev.ru/media/9399.html
22. Online-out. How to increase the turnout of young voters in elections. http://news.bigmir.net/ukraine/948578-Onlain-vihod-Kak-povisit-yavky-molodih-izbiratelei-na-viborah
23. Opening remarks at a meeting with activists of the All-Russian political party "United Russia". http://www.kremlin.ru/events/president/transcripts/7896
24. Päivärinta, T., Sæbø, Ø.: Models of E-Democracy. Communications of the Association for Information Systems **17** (2006). http://aisel.aisnet.org/cais/vol17/iss1/37. Article 37
25. Pallinger, Z.T., Kaufmann, B., Marxer, W., Schiller, T. (eds.): Direct Democracy in Europe: Developments and Prospects. VS Verlag für Sozialwissenschaften|Springer Fachmedien Wiesbaden GmbH, Wiesbaden (2007). doi:10.1007/978-3-531-90579-2
26. Penskoj, V.: Great gunshot revolution, Moscow (2010)

27. Petrov, V.: Crimeans voted against the contract with Ukraine for electricity. http://rg.ru/2016/01/01/krim-opros-site.html
28. Popoveniuc, S., Hosp, B.: An introduction to punchscan. In: VSRW 2006 (2006)
29. Qi, H., Zhongmin, S.: A new practical secure e-voting scheme. In: Proceedings of SEC 1998 (1998)
30. Riabushko, A.: Open data initiative to challenge the demand side problem. In: Proceedings of the 2nd International Conference on Electronic Governance and Open Society: Challenges in Eurasia (EGOSE 2015), St. Petersburg, Russian Federation, 24–25 November, pp. 10–16. ACM, New York (2015)
31. Rybakov, A.V.: Suffrage and electoral systems. Socio-political magazine **2**, 113–122 (1998)
32. Sahu, G.P.: E-government development and diffusion: inhibitors and facilitators of digital democracy: inhibitors and facilitators of digital democracy. IGI Global, Hershey (2009)
33. Surowiecki, J.: The Wisdom of Crowds: Why the Many are Smarter than the Few and How Collective Wisdom Shapes Business, Economies. Societies and Nations. Anchor Books, New York (2004)
34. Tymovskij, M., Kenevich, Y.A., Holycer, E.: History of Poland, Moscow (2004)
35. Ulrich, M.: E-Democracy: Public Online Engagement by the European Commission. VDM Publishing, Saarbrücken (2007)
36. Vaskova, M.G.: Problems of formation and implementation of e-democracy in the electronic state. Russ. Law J. **4**, 47–50 (2010)
37. Vedel, T.: The idea of electronic democracy: origins, visions and questions. Parliamentary Aff. **59**(2), 226–235 (2006)
38. Von Lucke J., Reinermann H.: Speyerer Definition von Electronic Government (2004). http://foev.dhv-speyer.de/ruvii
39. Yarkova, O.N., Osipova, A.A.: Secure electronic voting system based on cryptographic algorithms. Bull. Ural Fed. District Secur. Field Inf. 2, 9–15 (2014)
40. Yugov, A.A.: The right of the public authorities as the exclusive right of the people to power. Const. Municipal Law **9**, 28–33 (2012)

Digitalization and Evolution of Civic Engagement: New Ways of Participation in Public Policy

Alexander Sokolov[1(✉)] and Anton Verevkin[2]

[1] Demidov Yaroslavl State University, Yaroslavl, Russia
alex8119@mail.ru
[2] Regional Social and Political Research Foundation, Yaroslavl, Russia
verevkin.anton@gmail.com

Abstract. The current stage in development of Russian civil society bears the appearance of new forms of expression and realization of the interests of society. Terms of civic activity in Russia are associated primarily with increased activity of NGOs, the growth of social movements and networked civic movements and development of Internet technologies. Networked movement uses the principles of equality, resource interaction, voluntary participation, developing in the geography of their activities and number of participating citizens. The Internet provides new forms of civic engagement. Civic engagement appears on the Internet via web portals and sites, civic applications and social networking, crowdsourcing and crowdfunding platforms. Social networks and online applications provide significant opportunities for communication, transmission of information, resources, research, and become a really effective tool for horizontal relationships and connections in the community. Large-scale protests and civic companies are formed with the help of networks. Internet resources allow operatively spread information about activities and events, help to effectively mobilize members of civil activity.

Keywords: Public policy · Civic activism · Civil action · Civic engagement · Crowdsourcing · Social activism

1 Introduction

Trust decline to the traditional governmental institutions can be observed in modern Russia, resulting in increasing citizens' shift to other forms of their interests' expression. Groups of initiative citizens are formed around socially important problems. Their activities can be global (as in the case of some environmental, human rights and other organizations) and local. A common feature of these movements is, first, the desire to draw public attention to the chosen topic. A feature of this work is an active use of the Internet.

Internet use in the construction of public associations is natural, since a significant part of their activists are young people. This category of citizens more than any others uses the possibilities of the Internet and finds it convenient to use it in various fields.

© Springer International Publishing AG 2016
A.V. Chugunov et al. (Eds.): DTGS 2016, CCIS 674, pp. 269–274, 2016.
DOI: 10.1007/978-3-319-49700-6_25

In this regard, the fundamental importance is the availability and the degree of Internet penetration in various spheres of individual citizen's life.

2 Digital Methods of Civic Action Organization

The development of the Internet as a new space of communication and organization of political campaigns have been actively studied in political science. These studies can be divided into several groups:

- The study of the Internet as a network space (M. Castells [5], Y. Kaifeng and E. Bergrud [14]);
- The study of the impact of Internet technologies and Internet activity on the democratization and election campaigns (C.G. Reddick [10], V. Carty [4]);
- Study of the features of communication and discourse on the Internet (B. Warnick, D.S. Heineman [13], E. Downey and M. Jones [6]);
- Study of the role of social networks in collective action (Bekkers V., Beunders H., Edwards A., Moody R. [1], Earl J. and Kimport K. [7]).

All activities aimed at mobilizing citizens are carried out through technology. It is necessary to point the current trend of "e-mobilization" formation. In another way, it is called online, electronic mobilization or kiberaktivizm.

As D. Mercea points out, activists are using social networks (sites) that allow building political communication, and quickly organizing collective action, which is based on digital technologies [8]. The researcher notes that the formation of a collective identity and trust between the participants of the communication becomes crucially important within the process of mobilization.

The use of new multimedia applications, such as e-mail and Web sites can help mobilize new activists in social movements, thereby enhancing those movements [12].

The problem of building trust in the collective action, organized through social networks, can be solved via two of their main characteristics. The first is the selectivity of the groups' participants' formation process in social networks allowing them to include only loyal individuals [3]. The second is the personalization of the activity in the collective action [2].

3 New Forms of Citizen Participation in Russia

With the increasing popularity of the Internet and social networks, it has become a tool for self-organization of citizens. Proof of this are various associations of independent observers "For Fair Elections", which include the association "SONAR", project "Citizen Observer", "RosVybory", "Voice", "Russian Free Elections Fund", "Alliance of independent observers", "the SMS -CIK". This mass appearance of observers was caused by protest moods increased after the elections to the State Duma of the VI convocation, in December 2011. In addition, in March 2012, all polling stations were equipped with web-cameras, through which everyone could watch the online broadcast of all that was happening on the CIK.

Different platforms, allowing signing a petition in support of any initiative are actively developing. Change.org has become a popular service for on-line petitions. On Change.org people from all around the world begin their civil campaign, find supporters and together with those who make decisions, carry out important changes for them. More than 138 million people from 196 countries have participated in various civic campaigns. This allowed to make 16 600 victories in 196 countries.

Change.org is widely used in Russia.

Another type of service for civil activity on the Internet is crowdfunding platforms. They allow people to collect the necessary financial resources for organization and implementation of civil campaigns.

Since August 2012 more than 850 projects have collected more than 180 million rubles on Boomstarter (https://boomstarter.ru/). As of November 2015 data showed that 100 new projects had been registering on Boomstarter every day. Since June 2012 more than 381 million rubles have been collected for more than 2,500 projects on Planeta.ru.

Another unusual social phenomenon gaining popularity is crowdsourcing: people come together to perform certain tasks for a small fee or completely for free. Formation and widespread of crowdsourcing mechanism can be explained, first, by the ability of society to its self-organization and rational allocation of resources. Internet development has played an important role in the development of crowdsourcing projects. A striking example of such projects is "Rospil". It began operating in December 2011. Now it is a key example of the mainstream online communities within the framework of anti-corruption activities. The purpose of the project is to monitor budget funds expenses in the area of public procurement. In May 2012, "Rospil" made a statement about the fraud detected in the amount of 4.5 bln. rubles. Legal advisors of the project submitted 108 complaints to the Federal Antimonopoly Service of the Russian Federation, 68 of which have been officially recognized [9]. In 2014, the project has identified 133 auction with signs of cartel [1]. According to the results of other crowdsourcing project - "Rosyama" 19,347 pits were patched on the roads.

An important feature is the distribution of crowdfunding technology in socio-political activities. A characteristic feature of crowdfunding is that it becomes popular due to development and mass spread of the Internet. Gradually, Russia accumulates experience in organizing and carrying out crowdfunding campaigns to support various initiatives and programs of action. At this stage in the Russian socio-political practice, several major campaigns to raise funds for political projects were implemented [11]. All of them were connected with the so-called activity of non-systemic political forces (Table 1).

Crowdfunding serves for the society as a mutually beneficial mechanism of building relationships in the contemporary socio-cultural conditions. Having a deal with personal funds of citizens, it forms a consistent, responsible attitude of people to their preferences as well as builds new channels of vertical and horizontal communication. Crowdfunding provides relevant to the technological agenda ways of civil activity manifestations. Thus, the development of crowdfunding is one of the most promising factors for the formation of civil society in Russia.

Table 1. Crowdfunding projects in Russia

	Fundraising term	Number of contributors	Collected amount	Number of subscribers in the blog
«RosPil»	2.02.2011– 29.02.2012 387 days	13790 people – 4.05.2011	8 773 367 rub.	About 50000
«Putin. Corruption»	28.03.2011– 28.04.2011 30 days	2000 people	1 838 209 rub.	About 11000
Meeting "For Fair Elections" December 24, 2011	18.12.2011– 22.12.2011 4 days	4000 people	4 000 000 rub.	–
Leonid Volkov campaign	26.09.2011– 26.11.2011 62 days	361 people	832 850 rub.	About 5000
«RosPil» 2, 2012	19.12.2012 – 1.04.2013 100 days	8250 people	11 005 119 rub.	About 50000
MHG: Lyudmila Alekseeva	25.11.2012 – 11.12.2012 17 days	No data	2 500 000 rub. (only part - individual donations)	–
Khimki: Evgenia Chirikova	28.08.2012 – 12.10.2012 46 days	No data; approx - a few hundred people	500 000 rub.	About 2600
Pussy Riot	14.03.2012 – 10.03.2012 360 days	No data	3 000 000 rub.	–

4   Conclusion

Summing up the observations and conclusions presented above, we can make a series of statements about how the civic mobilization is changing in the new environment and what is happening within it.

Despite the indirect nature of interaction, digital technology and the environment of social media not only exacerbate the problem of building trust, but also contribute to its establishment. Digitalization significantly reduces the time it takes for people to start trusting each other. People quickly become allies due to successful experience of interaction, and therefore faster start to trust each other. No need for personal meetings and a full-time communication reduces the risks associated with the problem of communication "face to face". On the other hand, this leads to the risk of manipulation of citizens through social media.

Digitization also opens up the boundaries between cities, regions, countries and continents and gives civic activists tools with which even the local problem can become global, be agenda of the international negotiations, or government. In this regard, it is important to note that, on the one hand, digital technologies contribute to the formation of identity. However, on the other hand, we can observe such phenomenon as "solidarity", considered as the presence of a person on any matter or issue a certain point of view, similar to the views of uncertain group of other people who have no connection with each other. This may erase social, class and ideological boundaries. In a situation where the agenda changes rapidly every day, largely due to the instantaneous dissemination of information through social networks, solidarity comes to the fore, and often begins affecting the mobilization of people stronger than identity.

An equally important feature of how digitalization affects the civic mobilization is substantially lower costs of participation. Digitalization means not only reduction of transaction costs related to the search and analysis of information and decision-making based on them, but also reduction of cost of resources (time, money, health, etc.) for inclusion in civic activity. Mobilization now not only means access to meetings and demonstrations or collecting signatures on the streets, but also signing petitions online, making actual topics via top posts in social networks, and it is directly appeals to the authorities and business widely represented in social networks. It is a positive change, even if it carries a number of risks. Accessibility and ease of participation in civic campaigns on social media may reduce the attractiveness of participation in offline-mobilization, which is often necessary to solve local problems, such as housing and communal problems, yards, children's garden etc., where territorial identity is crucial, while the possibility of forming solidarity is low. In other words, Internet mobilization cannot completely replace the traditional forms of civic participation, but at the same time, it significantly reduces the motivation of citizens to participate in the offline-activity.

It is important to note that we can talk on truly notable successes of Internet mobilization only if them occur in the developed democratic political systems, where public opinion and civil society are important in decision-making, regardless of where it is expressed: on the street or on the Internet. Therefore it is necessary to note limited nature of the Internet mobilization, because it requires serious transformation of the political system and political culture of the country in order to make it replace offline-activity.

Acknowledgments. The research is sponsored by the Ministry of Education. Project №. 1127 "Legal and socio-political aspects of civic activism in contemporary Russia".

References

1. Bekkers, V., Beunders, H., Edwards, A., Moody, R.: New media, micromobilization, and political agenda setting: crossover effects in political mobilization and media usage. Inf. Soc. **27**, 209–219 (2011). doi:10.1080/01972243.2011.583812
2. Bennett, W., Segerberg, A.: The logic of connective action. Inf. Commun. Soc. **15**, 739–768 (2012). doi:10.1080/1369118X.2012.670661

3. Boyd, D., Ellison, N.: Social network sites: definition, history, and scholarship. J. Comput.-Mediated Commun. **13**, 210–230 (2008). doi:10.1111/j.1083-6101.2007.00393.x
4. Carty, V.: Wired and Mobilizing: Social Movements, New Technology, and Electoral Politics. Routledge, London and New York (2011)
5. Castells, M.: Network Society: A Cross-Cultural Perspective. Edward Elgar, Cheltenham (2004)
6. Downey, E., Jones, M.: Public Service, Governance and Web 2.0 Technologies: Future Trends in Social Media. Information Science Reference, Hershey (2012)
7. Earl, J., Kimport, K.: Digitally Enabled Social Change: Activism in the Internet Age. MIT Press, Cambridge (2011)
8. Mercea, D.: Towards a conceptualization of casual protest participation: parsing a case from the Save Roşia Montană campaign. East Eur. Polit. Soc. Cultures **2**, 386–410 (2014). doi: 10.2139/ssrn.2402744
9. Morozova, E.W., Miroshnichenko I.V.: Crowdsourcing in public policy: technologies, subjects and its socio-political role. Asian Soc. Sci. **7**, 111–121 (2015). doi:10.5539/ass.v11n7p111
10. Reddick, C.G.: Politics, Democracy, and e-government: Participation and Service Delivery. Information Science Reference, Hershey (2010). doi:10.4018/978-1-61520-933-0
11. Sokolov, A.V.: Russian Political Crowd Funding. Demokratizatsiya **2**, 117–149 (2015)
12. van Laer, J.: Activists 'online' and 'offline': the internet as an information channel for protest demonstrations. Mobilization **15**, 405–417 (2010)
13. Warnick, B., Heineman, D.S.: Rhetoric Online: The Politics of New Media. Peter land, New York (2012)
14. Yang, K., Bergrud, E.: Civic engagement in a network society. Information Age Publishing, Charlotte (2008)

The Power of ICT Towards Effective Decision Making on Public Resources Allocation: Case of Rural Areas of Uganda

Charles Karemera[1]([⊠]), Johnstone Baguma[2], and Odette Mukamuhinda[3]

[1] Mountains of the Moon University, Fort Portal, Uganda
karemecha@yahoo.fr
[2] Tooro Toro Development Network, Fort Portal, Uganda
jkbaguma@torodev.kabisa.org
[3] Kenyata University, Nairobi City, Kenya
omukamuhinda@yahoo.fr

Abstract. Many researchers have talked about the role of e - participation as a means of linking Citizens with their Leaders and also playing roles in decision making processes on public resources allocation. However, little is known about models which can cater for citizens who are in rural areas where there are limited infrastructures and other factors like low education, culture, gender, marginalization etc. This paper describes an ICT System which uses Mobile Phone SMS to accelerate citizens - leaders' democratic engagement to improve public service delivery. It builds on the Participatory Action Research (PAR) theoretical framework and aims at operationalizing the PAR e-participation model proposed by Toro Development Network in 2014. The system design develops knowledge required for joint reflection and continuous decision making during the engagement processes between citizens (civil society) and government through a participatory action research approach. The paper emphasizes the ICT convergence approach combining broadcast media specifically radio, mobile phone and ICT system to receive and request grass-roots citizens' public opinion on national strategies, policies and programs.

Keywords: e-Participation · e-Governance · Service delivery · PAR e-participation model · ICT convergence

1 Introduction

Citizens' participation in the political process is not a new phenomenon; it started in ancient Athens which was predicated when the number of citizens was small on freedom of assembly of individuals in the agora of the polis (the marketplace of the city), but after the increase in the number of citizens, governments switched to the representative democracy [8]. Public authorities started to increase citizens' participation directly; a critical aspect of democratic practices [27]. Huge investments in ICT have been taken by governments all over the world to reap public participation benefits and to involve citizens in the public policy processes.

© Springer International Publishing AG 2016
A.V. Chugunov et al. (Eds.): DTGS 2016, CCIS 674, pp. 275–289, 2016.
DOI: 10.1007/978-3-319-49700-6_26

E-government performance tends to mostly focus on the delivery and provision of online public services, and less on feedback mechanisms that allow public and stakeholders to participate in policy debates and consultations. In recent years, however, e-government has been gradually evolving into a more interactive process whereby citizen engagement through e-consultation and e-participation is now being viewed as a necessary next step towards the promotion of a more inclusive society.

In a research paper on enhancing social accountability through ICTs, Wairagala [33] emphasizes that accountability and transparency are pre-requisites of a democratic society that empowers citizens to participate in democratic governance processes of a given state. Similar concerns were previously asserted by several scholars and practitioners [6, 11, 22, 26]. It is also argued that in governance processes, ICT may increase accountability and transparency and counter corruption through more efficient administration and increase flows of information [6–8]. ICT-enhanced access to reliable and timely information and knowledge sharing platforms, whether online or offline is a key requirement, if democracy is to function in any state or economy. Strand even stresses that, for lack of this access, results in a non-participatory society in which decision making is not democratic [29].

It is observed that the use of collaborative technologies is challenging the traditional notions of democratic involvement by allowing citizens greater opportunity to express their individual political will. There are not only top-down but also bottom-up initiatives that are transforming the way governments interact with t heir citizens and vice versa. These innovative models of engagement are creating communities that are virtual and fluid, and impact policies and practices in a variety of ways and with varying degrees of success.

According to [3], ICT have played a central role in positively transforming the well-being of citizens, in particular improving their interaction with duty bears to improve essential service delivery, especially in the rural communities of the developing world. Moreover, Unwin [32] also developed further in [33] that interventions in form of technical solutions needed to ensure that they are context specific and adapted to local needs and conditions, and that the technology solutions in any circumstances needed to be informed by an understanding of a range of economic, social, political and ideological factors.

The ICT-supported system design is built on citizen engagement with duty bearers or service providers. It emphasizes active participation through an ICT tools convergence of mobile phones, online applications and broadcast technologies like FM Radios [3].

2 Background of ICT in Uganda

According to [34] by 2015, only 23% of Uganda's estimated population of 37.5 million used the Internet and there were 53 mobile phone subscriptions for every 100 inhabitants. Traffic rankings indicated that Facebook was the second most popular website in Uganda, while You Tube was the 4th most visited site. Twitter and Wikipedia were 6th and 9th respectively (Alexa, 2014). However, numerous challenges hamper the spread of ICT in Uganda. Just about 10% of the population was connected to the national electricity grid while the literacy rate was at 73%. This is an indicator that most of the People cannot access social medias for discussions and ideas sharing.

The author indicated that Uganda was the most corrupt countries in the World, ranking 142 out of 175, according to the Global Corruption Perception Index (Transparency International, 2014). It was estimated that between 2011 and 2013, the government lost more than USS 300 million due to corruption, including the creation of "Ghost" public servants and poorly monitored revenue sources and programs (Lowenstein, 2013). This has created a bigger need for fighting corruption and monitoring public services through ICT platforms which have not been extensively tested in the country but which, if found workable, could be replicated across sectors of public administration and public services provisional.

3 Some Related Existing e-Participation Models

3.1 Active Citizen E-Participation in Local Governance: Do Individual Social Capital and E-Participation Management Matter?

This model postulates that e-participation is positively affected by citizens' trust in government, their volunteer experiences, weak offline social ties, and perceived quality responsiveness during the e-participation process. This model is based on social capital and citizen participation [36].

This model reveals how active e-participation in local governance could matter for effective and transparent decision making and problem solving in local governance, showing the conditions that might be required; it is affordable in Uganda because some of the radio stations have formed groups – as such the weak offline ties as identified in the model may not be a challenge in this country – the ground formed could also be a ground for the strength of the quality responsiveness although it might be difficult to tell if such would not be influenced by other factors like the political will.

3.2 A Semantic Model for e-Participation

This model addresses the duality of e-Participation by allowing for simultaneous government led, top-down e-Participation, together with citizen-led, social media based e-Participation [30]. The model is based on the integrative e-Participation Framework. Despite the fact that the model does not give evidence of its applicability on ground, by not indicating where it has ever been applied, it nevertheless rightly brings out the need for the concerted efforts that ought to exist for the effective service delivery. The social media as medium for the citizen participation seems a feasible approach because, as experience demonstrates, most of the citizens in Uganda have mobile phones, which they can act as reliable tools for citizen interaction. As such, it is affordability and applicability seems promising. However, it remains unclear about the reliability of the information gathered through this model as it lacks a clear institutional setup.

3.3   E-Participation Modeling and Developing with Trust for Decision Making Supplement Purpose

This model is based on the synthesis of group members' preferences following an appropriate aggregation procedure [38]. The model claims to adopt the 'real life' behavior, by providing interaction and consultation between citizens in order to produce better decision's quality. Focusing on the process of making decisions on public matters with citizen participation, this model would be thought to also investigate state-of-the art models related to e-Participation. However, it does over assume that all citizens will be interested, which sometimes may not be the case; as such its affordability and applicability is highly doubted.

4   Methodology

The Research shows that the issue of the digital divide continues to be a major concern to governments worldwide. Even in technologically advanced regions such as in the European Union, the digital gap is quite significant despite a significant increase in the access to ICT equipment and services. It is estimated that about one-fourth to a third of the European Union population are still outside the pale of e-government services [10].

The main objective of this Proposed System design is to engage discourse between and among citizens and elected or appointed officials over public policy issues both those who live in urban areas where basics ICT infrastructure may be available and those who are in rural with limited infrastructures. It is intended also to operationalize the PAR e-participation model previously proposed by ToroDev in 2014 [4]. It is consequently conceptualized on the participatory action research theory [5, 15, 21]. The model clearly outlines a five-staged process in order to realize an inclusive, credible and reliable engagement between citizens and duty bearers in government.

The first stage of policy and capacity building at the bottom level of the framework is described in detail as purely a pre-requisite or building block for a successful PAR e-participation process [4, 14]. It is, therefore, implicitly considered part and parcel of the proposed e-participation system design described in this paper, even though much emphasis is explicitly devoted on the other her four stages. The system components relate and interact with each other within the framework of the four key stages of the PAR e-participation model [4]. Finally, the system design indeed aims at realizing an engagement that is objective and rigorous, systematic, valid & verifiable, empirical and critically analyzed [4, 9, 16, 18, 28].

The Proposed Model involves six actors (1) Government, (2) Government organ (Top level), (3) District level (Moderator), (4) Community/Citizens (5) Radio and (6) Office bearers/Leaders or Policy Makers. It has also media/link to enable actors to communicate. More details on how it works are under the system design.

5   Community's E-Participation in Governance and Role of ICTs in the Decision Making Process

The e-government approach grows depending on the current ICT innovations and, of course, it has an impact where ICT is still at its infancy stage. Strategic and meaningful application of ICT for the purpose of improving the efficiency, transparency, accountability and accessibility of government is possible if the ultimate objective of e-government is to promote social inclusion, or e-inclusion. The real challenge lies in not only ensuring that certain preconditions are met for *e-inclusion* such as access to ICT tools, networks and literacy, but also the degree to which e-inclusion enables an individual to participate more fully in the social, cultural and political arenas of society. Particularly in policy making, e-participation makes use of the digital communications media to allow citizens to participate through a more inclusive, open, responsive and deliberative process.

E-participation may be defined as a technology-mediated interaction that uses ICTs to engage discourse between and among citizens and elected or appointed officials over public policy issues [31]. It makes use of the digital communications media to enable citizens to participate through a more inclusive, open, responsive and deliberative process; e-participation is now being viewed as a necessary next step towards the promotion of a more inclusive society. It involves modifying community into e-communities where the participants can communicate with their leaders, observe and make comments; and respond to the input of fellow participants including commenting on the views from the leaders themselves [1, 19].

Many researchers grouped e-participation models into three broad categories: (i) information (a one-way flow of information from the government to the citizens); (ii) consultation (a two-way relationship whereby citizens are encouraged to provide feedback to the government; and (iii) active participation (a partnership arrangement with the government in which citizen engagement is actively solicited for defining and shaping policy). The proposed e-participation system is a hybrid of category of consultation and active participation, as described above. As such, the view of [19] becomes true; in their work; "*Active Citizen e-Participation in Local Governance ...*" they opine that e-participation is a means of enabling and encouraging sound citizen participation in policy decision-making processes in an economy. It is noted that through e-participation, governments will provide services and resources tailored to the actual service and resource needs of citizens and other resource users. In this way, governments will gain economies of scale and reduce costs [6]. More so, the International Association for Public Participation provides a spectrum of consultation and participation tools that range from information provision to active participation [13] and include:

(a) *Information provision::* fact sheets, Websites, open houses.
(b) *Consultation:* public *comment*, focus groups, surveys, public meetings
(c) *Involving the public:* workshops, deliberative polling.
(d) *Collaboration:* citizen advisory committees, consensus-building, participatory decision making.
(e) *Empowerment:* citizens' juries, ballots, delegated decisions.

Reference [25], under their engagement model, developed a Public Participation spectrum to demonstrate the possible types of engagement with authority stakeholders, who may include the government and agencies and communities/citizens. Key to this spectrum is that, it shows the increasing level of public impact as you progress from 'inform' through to 'empower' stages.

In a 5-tiered classification, the e-participation model culminates in 'empowerment' which allows citizens the prerogative to influence policies and laws that govern their lives. Even though to varying degrees, different countries illustrate different levels of e-participation in various parts of the world, the public participation spectrum demonstrates the ideal framework for any country that deliberately desires to realize citizens-centered development thorough a democratic process.

Table 1. IAP2's (2013) Public Participation spectrum

Inform	Consult	Involve	Collaborative	Empower
Public Participation Goal				
To provide the public with balanced and objective information to assist them in understanding the problems, alternatives and/or solutions.	To obtain public feed-back on analysis, alternatives and/or decisions	To work directly with the public throughout the process to ensure that public concerns and aspirations are consistently under-stood and considered	To partner with the public in each aspect of the decision, including the development of alternatives and the identification of the preferred solution.	To place final decision – making in the hands of the public
Promise to the Public				
We will keep you informed	We will keep you informed, listen to and acknowledge concerns and provide feedback on how public input influenced the decision	We will work with you to ensure that you concern and aspirations are directly reflected in the alternatives developed and provide feedback on how public input influenced the decision	We will look to you for direct advice and innovation in formulation solutions and incorporate your advice and recommendations into the decision to the maximum extent possible	We will implement what you decide
Example tools				
Fast sheets Web site Open houses	Public comment Focus groups Surveys Public meetings	Workshops Deliberate polling	Citizen advisory committees Consensus building Participatory decision-making	Citizen Juries Ballots Delegated decisions

The attempts in a Table 1 below demonstrate today's emphasis that decision making should involve several decision makers, also called group decision making for legitimacy purposes. Today, democratic governance requires much more citizen participation in decision making to achieve democratic ideals of democracy as the government "of the people" "by the people," and "for the people" [2, 31].

It has been observed [13] that trust as a social behavior can be used as a method to model preferences and facilitate better participation and interaction in decision making within a group of decision makers. For a successful e-participation there are some issues that have to be considered in order to develop trust and confidence in the e-Participation process including the following items.

5.1   Political Will

The success of e-government rests largely on the political will of governments, both at sub-national and national levels, to engage citizens in an inclusive process that leads to participatory decision-making. The difficulty has been, and continues to be the development of appropriate tools that can effectively measure policy outcomes as a result of e-participation. Some recent attempts however, are noteworthy, such as the Government of Canada's 'Citizens 'Citizens First' tool for measuring client expectations, priorities and satisfaction with government services at all levels of government, including tracking changes over time, and the client surveys and feedback from citizens in the UK on the quality of online services [1].

5.2   Inclusive ICTs

To achieve e-participation, alternative devices should be considered as viable means, through multi-channel strategies and solutions (ICT convergence approach), such as cell phones, community computing, traditional broadcast media including radio and television, among others. By its very nature, inclusive e-participation implies that pro-active measures should be taken by governments, agencies and non-state actors to ensure that public services are available and accessible to all and that digital exclusion is avoided at all costs. Cell phones, speech technology & wireless networking, for example, could make e-participation more accessible to those with little or no educational attainment, as well as hard-to-reach and marginalized groups in society, especially in the developing world, thereby narrowing the digital divide. A critical issue in incorporating the use of ICT in governance is to keep the gap between.

5.3   Prioritization

To promote e-participation, the implementing agency (civil society organization or government agency) should focus on:

(i) Specific target group only (e.g., the underprivileged, women, youth, the marginalized, those living in remote areas)

(ii) Targeting specific issues of greater concern to the majority of the citizens, such as social benefits, job creation, maternal and child health care, education etc. Should they be issue-based or policy-based?
(iii) Selecting a small number of priorities that require meaningful dialogue and have a high policy impact?

Policy discussions have to focus on addressing the above issues before determining any other requirements, such as technology, access and connectivity. Another critical consideration in the uptake of e-participation initiatives is the time factor. Adoption of new technology takes time to be accepted, understood and adopted. Although the accelerated pace of globalization is compelling governments to invest in internet technology and by extension, in some form of e-government, a rush to embrace ICT for use in participation could backfire unless e-participation strategies are designed and developed within the socio-cultural, economic and political context of the country. Expectations should, therefore, be realistic in terms of what is achievable given resource constraints, adequate time for adoption and implementation, and socio - political considerations [1].

5.4   The Praxis: Usability and Affordability

It goes without saying that from an accountability standpoint, more thought has to be given to understanding how best to capture the results of e-participation endeavors. The results should be assessed by specifically outlining measurable indicators and linking policy outcomes to the process, which would then be published for public review.

5.5   Validity and Reliability of the e-Participation Findings

Increasingly, the focus of e-governance through inclusive participation is shifting towards the improvement of public service delivery and, therefore, the key purpose of e-participation needs to support such government efforts. Since public services are mostly provided at the local level, it is an issue that most governments have to address head-on and e-participation is expected to provide valid information that can be relied on during this process. Moreover, with a dramatic increase in urban populations worldwide, governments increasingly have to cope with the rising expectations and demands in cities and communities. Under the circumstances, localizing the provision of public services is becoming more of a necessity than a matter of choice, challenging both national and local governments alike [1].

6   The Proposed e-Participation System Design

To improve service delivery in Uganda, with emphasis in the rural region where the infrastructures are scant, the Model of e-participation system based on a participatory action research (PAR) framework is proposed. The relationship between the system components and each of the four states of the PAR e-participation model is explained in details. The system is built on the broader concept of the ICT convergence approach [3]. The system particularly targets to exploit the opportunities provided by mobile telephony, broadcast media specifically radio and ICT technologies to generate data from citizens, who are the final public service consumers. The data is then analyzed, categorized and packaged in a prioritized way for duty bearers to discuss policy and service delivery alternatives and eventually make decisions on implementation processes.

The Proposed system also provides avenues for information dissemination, discussion platform and feedback loops for both citizens and duty bearers. The other last key functionality of the system is to provide a linkage between the e-participation process outcomes and the real public policy and service implementation (Fig. 1).

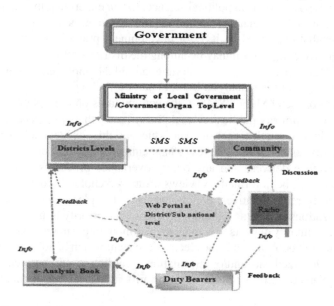

Fig. 1. The Proposed System design based on the Participatory Action Research (PAR) e-Participation.

The proposed e-participation system design proposes an interaction among moderators at District level, proposes an interaction among moderators at District level, Communities, office duties including policy makers and stakeholders charged with responsibility to provide services to the local community based on the devolved or decentralized system of governance which Uganda is embarking on these days. Different actors of the Model work as follow:

(1) Government: The government through different organs especially ministries, plan the activities to be done for or by its citizens.

(2) Government Organ/Top level: The activities from different institutions are channeled in that organ which may be for example Ministry of Local government or any other organ and takes lead of monitoring government plans.

(3) District level: The state/government plans according to the needs of the citizens after consultation or not. That is why Districts work closely with the ministries during the implementations of programs; the proposed model suggests that districts have to work with only the top organ which is in charge of gathering all plans of the state from the citizens' communities.

At the District level there will be a selected group of individuals (i.e. Moderators/actors) and other partners interested in the e -participation process. This component of the system is conceived at stage 2 (planning & content development) of the PAR e-participation framework [13, 27]. The moderators may also be particularly composed of the following: *(i)* an expert in political science, *(ii) an* expert in public administration and management, *(iii)* a social and community development actor, *(iv)* a communications/educationalist expert *(v)* an ICT for development practitioner and, *(vi)* a social analyst. The above composition may be among the district staff or pat time employees except a social analyst who must be a full time individual employed by the District and may be the manager of the e-analysis Book in part "6" below:

The moderators send Mobile SMS to the communities on their phones and request them to respond to priority public service delivery issues that are agreed on by moderators at district level through consensus. The issues should seek feedback on any positive as well as negative interventions, issues or happenings in different citizen communities on status of service delivery and any other governance processes. The selection of priority issues may be informed by views from stakeholders such as government personnel, elected representatives, policy-makers and implementers, businesses, civil society organizations as well as individual citizens. The priority issues should be translated in local community dialects or languages. The moderators may also get information from the discussion book which is the electronic system which handles the analysis and packaging of prioritized data and/or information according to sub-national and national development plans to inform consensus on priority issues for engagement through e-participation.

(4) Community/citizen: The Community should have a level of engagement which can be looked at as democratic political engagement that involves the means to be informed (Information), the mechanism to take part in the decision-making (Consultation) and the ability to contribute and influence the policy agenda (Active Participation). These concerns should particularly be addressed at stage 1 of the PAR e-Participation model [13]. When the above level of engagement is ensured, the next step to look at is how citizens are not demotivated in their interaction with the e-participation system. This is because most of the time they think that nothing will come out from the interaction. In order to motivate the respondents to participate efficiently and effectively, a level of recognition will be attached on the numbers of SMS sent to the e-analysis Book and also emphasis on trust derived from the system, in terms of ensuring privacy levels and feedback linkages targeted at addressing raised issues of concern by citizens. A legal framework is another key factor to consider protecting the respondents and feeling free to participate.

Various surveys have identified six kinds of socio-demographic factors that hinder the e-participation namely: geography, income and social status, education, gender, age and disabilities [28–30].

For this Proposed system to work, the above hindrances will not affect the usability so much because (1) basic infrastructures will be phones and the majority of people in Uganda can access the network easily, (2) the cost of SMS sent by the Communities will be free of charge and measures to sensitize them will be strengthened, (3) the model does not require a certain level of education to read or to write back and there is a belief that most of people who have phones at least know how to read a message and for those who do not know how to read and write can seek for assistance to read and reply for them. The radio media also will be used hand in hand with SMS to reach more people, (4) the model will not segregate the respondents, and, (5) some priority issues may target a certain age group. So it does not matter about the questions asked as long as they are clearly stated.

Community shall respond to the questions from the moderators through a toll free number and their responses shall be automatically captured in the web portal of the District. In order to motivate the citizens to respondent to the e-participation issues raised through the system, a mention of the participant's name on radio but not their responses could be handy. Other ways of motivating the citizens to respond to priority issues suggested by stakeholders include; giving them feedback on issues/questions asked, sensitization about the objectives of the e-participation initiative, respondents be given a token at district/sub-national level depending on participation level and radio presenters be part of sensitization and have a good approach of packaging the content. Also it is suggested in the system that citizens should send messages to the toll free numbers without necessarily being prompted by particular questions from moderators. These are intended to bring out issues happening in the community upon which moderators can deliberate on.

(5) Web Portal System: Web Portal System, which is conceived at stage 3 of the PAR e-Participation model, with all requirements, is coordinated by the district and a trusted server host to secure the database and responses of respondents. The security of the Web shall be at different levels to ensure the confidentialities of respondents. The Portal will be able to display some statistics on the responses for further discussions and also allow citizens, policy makers to access the system and see how they are participating in decision making process. In normal circumstance this interaction should be the responsibility of all citizens, but at the starting a token of motivation (incentive) will be attached to get more citizens involved in the process. Special focus on the above proposed system is the process of engaging citizens through ICTs in policy and decision-making in order to make it participatory, inclusive, and deliberative. At Top organ, there will be a server to monitor districts servers and also to show a picture of what is happening in the whole Country.

(6) e-analysis Book: From the Web Portal, a technical representative of moderators or actors will extract and analyze responses from citizens and use intuitional judgment of the emerging issues and filters them from the non-issues or those deemed not to require attention [4]. The judgment of the technical representative shall be based on the number of responses on a particular issue or the nature of the raised concern. In normal circumstances the more the responses, the more attention it deserves. Also the happenings of a public activity or phenomenon in the region shall influence the attention of the technical representative of the moderators or actor. The filtered information shall be put on the Discussion book, presented for discussion by the moderators/actors of the district and feedback sought from the responsible leader or concerned citizens. It is important that a committee of moderators/actors, which selected priority issues, should be the same to select those which need urgent attentions and be addressed. The committee may invite the responsible people to address the issues pointed out by the communities and also make sure to link them. Means or communication channel between communities and invited people the committee can decide on it.

(7) Radio/Broadcast media: Radio or any other broadcast media technology may be used as one of the main channels for reaching to the communities and leaders to seek responses about a particular issue. The radio stations in the Uganda shall be approached by the moderators and formalize contractual obligations of each party.

(8) Office Bearers/Leaders: Based on the recommendations of the moderators or actors, particulars policy makers or leaders may be invited by the committee to address the key issues raised out by citizens. A proper way of connecting community with the concerned officers has to be well planned. This shall be through a radio program or a physical interaction at a community meeting. The feedback from leaders should also be made available at the web portal of the District.

7   Requirements for the Proposed Model

7.1   Model and Its Sustainability

(a) Commitment: demonstration of leadership.

The district leadership specifically information officers and district planners must support the implementation of the proposed model in the following ways: (i) Getting list of Contacts as many as possible, (ii) The reports from the Feedbacks to be distributed to all sub-national/national departments, (iii) To help in getting to all radios/broadcast media in Districts/sub-national levels, (iv) To monitor Radios in disseminating the information, (v) Reporting how radios are managing the programs, (vi) Receiving Report about Respondents, (vii) Sensitizing people as they meet them, (viii) Mobilize the communities from Education Sector like Schools, Churches having Banners, etc. and (ix) Info Centers to be given the info to be shared obligation to secure citizens' right to access information, be consulted and participate in policy development.

(b) Rights: demonstration of how government institutions meet their obligation to secure citizens' right to access information, be consulted and participate in policy development.

(c) Clarity: demonstration of clarity of objectives and citizens' roles at each phase from the very outset of e-participation process.

(d) Time: Allowance of sufficient time allotted at each question as early as possible to ensure that all possible options are considered.

(e) Evaluation: Having an assessment mechanism after a certain period to evaluate the performance of the e-participation.

(f) Objectivity: demonstration of the objective nature of information provided its completeness and accessibility to all willing to participate in policy making.

(g) Resources: demonstration of the provision of adequate and accessible resources – technical, financial, human – needed to conduct participatory activities at every stage.

(h) Co-ordination: demonstration of effective inter-agency co-ordination activities across the government to exclude duplication of effort, prevent 'participation fatigue' on the citizens' part.

(i) Accountability: demonstration of the effective, responsible and transparent use by the government of citizen's feedback and other participation activities.

(j) Active citizenship: demonstration of efforts aimed at encouraging civic activism by increasing capacities and skills of the citizen to participate in policy making in a meaningful and informed manner.

8   Conclusion and Future Research

Both the academic research and practitioners discourse in their findings and modeling, emphasize that achieving a sustainable e-participation process is indeed a step – by – step process [3, 4, 14, 23, 24, 30]. The magnitude and relevance of this gradual process depends on the level of credibility and confidence it derives from both the citizens, who are the ultimate services consumers, and service providers which is the government.

A legitimate e-participation process is likely to highly influence decision making and resource allocations for improved service delivery, especially in developing countries and democracies. E-participation systems designed on proven approaches like the Participatory Action Research (PAR) is likely to be sustainable, resources saving and replicable. The role of citizen (civil society) initiated e-participation initiatives, especially in developing democracies is important, for it can attract investment from governments and produce even enormous citizens 'participation results for improved service delivery, not only in Uganda, but the rest of the developing world.

Future studies will also be required from the implementers of this e-participation system to provide a critical analysis of the linkages between the above proposed e-participation system results and changes in public policy decisions targeting improvements in public service delivery in Uganda and even beyond.

References

1. Ahamed, N.: An Overview of e-Participation Models. United Nations report (Division for Public Administration and Social Affairs, UNDESA) (2006)

2. Al-Dalou, R., Abu-Shanab, E.: E-Participation levels and technologies. In: The 6th International Conference on Information Technology (2013)
3. Baguma, J.: Citizens' advocate for public accountability and democratic engagement through ICT converge in Eastern Africa. In: Proceedings of the 2014 International Conference for Democracy and Open Governm (CeDEM14) (2014)
4. Baguma, J.: Is there hope in ICTs for Africa? Developing an e-Participation model to improve the status of public service delivery in Uganda. In: The Proceedings of the International Conference for e-Democracy and Open Government (CeDEM15). Danube University Krems, Austria, 20–22 May (2015)
5. Bergold, J., Thomas, S.: Participatory research methods: a methodological approach in motion. J. Qual. Soc. Res. **13**(1), 2–10 (2012). Art. 30
6. Bertot, C.J., Jaeger, T.P., Grimes, M.J.: Promoting transparency and accountability through ICTs, social media, and collaborative e-government. Transforming Gov. People Process Policy **6**(1), 78–91 (2012)
7. Bwalya, K.J.: Factors affecting e-Governance adoption in Zambia. Electron. J. Inf. Syst. Dev. Countries (EJISDC) **38**(4), 1–13 (2009). http://www.ejisdc.org
8. Clive, C.: Towards understanding e-Participation in the public sphere. Rev. Bus. Res. **12**(1), 140–146 (2012)
9. Dawson, C.: Practical Research Methods: A User-friendly Guide to Mastering Research Techniques and Projects. UBS Publishers' Distributors Limited, New Delhi (2002)
10. Europe Advisory Group – WG2 – e-inclusion: Final report (2005)
11. Grönlund, Å., in Cecilia, S.: Increasing transparency and fighting corruption through ICT empowering people and communities. In: SPIDER ICT4D, Ser. (3) (2010)
12. Guchteneire, P., Mlikota, M.: ICTs for good governance - experiences from Africa, Latin America and the Caribbean. In: IST-Africa 2008 Conference and Exhibition (2008)
13. IAP2: Public Participation Spectrum. International Association of Public Participation (2013). http://www.iap2.org. Accessed 21 Mar 2016
14. Islam, M.S.: Towards a sustainable e-participation implementation model. Eur. J. e-Pract. (2008). http://www.epracticejournal.eu. Accessed 18 Feb 2014
15. Kemmis, S., McTaggart, R.: Participatory action research: communicative action and the public sphere. In: Strategies of Qualitative Inquiry, Chap. 10 (2007)
16. Kothari, C.R.: Research Methodology Methods and Techniques. Wiley Eastern Limited, New Delhi (1985)
17. Kumar, V., et al.: Factors for successful e-government adoption: a conceptual framework. Electron. J. e-Gov. **5**(1), 63–76 (2007)
18. Kumar, R.: Research Methodology: A Step by – Step Guide for Beginners, 2nd edn. Pearson Education, Singapore (2005)
19. Lee, J., Kim, S.: Active Citizen e-Participation in Local Governance: Do Individual Social Capital and e-Participation Management Matter? University of Nebraska at O maha and University of Syracuse (2009)
20. Losindilo, E., et al.: Some factors that hinder women participation in social, political and economic activities in Tanzania. Arts Soc. Sci. J. (ASSJ) **4**, 1–10 (2010)
21. Mgwebi, G.N.: Social Accountability. A Key Element of Effective Service Delivery (2011)
22. OEDC: Citizen as Partners: OECD Handbook on Information. Consultation and Public Participation in Policy-Making. OECD, Paris (2001)
23. Phang, C.W., Kankanhalli, A.: A framework of ICT Exploitation for E-Participation Initiatives. Department of Information Systems, School of Computing, National University of Singapore, Accepted for the Publication in Communications of the ACM (2007). http://www.comp.nus.edu.sg. Accessed 18 Dec

24. Primo, N., Esterhuysen, A.: ICT for Democracy. A publication of Swedish International Development Cooperation Agency, Department of Empowerment, SIDA_I (2009). http://www.apc.org/en/system/files/. Accessed 30 Dec 2015
25. Reuben, W., Benitez, M.L.: The Role of Civic Engagement and Social Accountability in the Governance Equation. Social Development Notes. The World Bank (2003)
26. Schlosberg, D., Shulman, S., Zavestoski, S.: Democracy and e-Rulemaking: web-based technologies, participation, and the potential for deliberation. J. Inf. Technol. Polit. **4**(1), 37–55 (2007)
27. Singh Brar, G.P., et al.: Research methodology. Int. J. Humanit. Soc. Sci. Educ. (IJHSSE) **1**(8), 63–67 (2014)
28. Strand, C.: Increasing transparency and fighting corruption through ICT: *empowering communities and people*. In: SPIDER ICT4D, no. 3 (2010)
29. Tambouris, E., et al.: Framework for scoping e-Participation. In: The proceedings of the 8th Annual International Digital Government Research Conference, Philadelphia, USA (2007)
30. Tundjungsari, V., et al.: e-Participation: modeling and developing with trust for decision making supplement purpose. Int. J. Adv. Comput. Sci. Appl. (IJACSA) **3**(5), 1, 3 (2011)
31. Unwin, T.: ICT4D: Information and Communication Technology for Development. Cambridge University Press, Cambridge (2009)
32. Wairagala, W.: Enhancing social accountability through ICT: success factors and challenges. In: The Proceedings of the International Conference for e-Democracy and Open Government (CeDEM15). Danube University Krems, Austria, 20–22 May (2015)
33. Peter P., Noella E.: Proceedings of the International Conference for E – Democracy and Open Government, Edition Donau. Universitat Krems (2015)
34. UCC: The Rural Communications Development Fund (RCDF), Annual report, 2014–2015
35. Lee, J., Kim, S.: Active Citizen e-Participation in Local Governance: Do Individual Social Capital and e-Participation Management Matter? Accessed through Google web search on 18 Thursday June (2015)
36. Porwol, L., Ojo, A., Breslin, J.: A semantic model for e-Participation. Accessed through Google web search on 08 Thursday July (2015)

E-Participation Portals Automated Monitoring System for Political and Social Research

Andrei V. Chugunov[1], Yury Kabanov[2(✉)], and Ksenia Zenchenkova[1]

[1] ITMO University, Saint-Petersburg, Russia
chugunov@egov-center.ru, rabota.ks@mail.ru
[2] National Research University Higher School of Economics,
Saint-Petersburg, Russia
ykabanov@hse.ru

Abstract. This paper presents the opportunities, advantages and limitations of e-participation portals automated monitoring system (AMS) in social and political research. The system was initially developed in 2013 to analyse petitioning and voting dynamics of the Russian e-petitions portal – the Russian Public Initiative – and then was further expanded. In the paper the architecture and working principles of the system are described. It is argued and exemplified that the data collected automatically from e-petition portals can be used to advance research in several areas: media and PR effects on political participation, issue salience, as well as factors of voting behavior and online political engagement.

Keywords: E-participation · E-petitions · Automated monitoring · Online engagement · Media effects · Issue salience

1 Introduction

Electronic petitions are considered an important field of inquiry in e-government and e-democracy research [19]. They are also regarded as a useful tool of e-participation, supporting the dialogue between citizens and government [7]. The broad diffusion of e-petitions portals is hence not surprising. There are plenty of informal platforms, created by non-governmental actors, and formal ones, initiated by governments and institutionalized in the political system and decision-making process. Russia is not an exception. Although a lot of informal e-petitions portals had been functioning (like Change.org, Democrator.ru etc.), in 2013 the official portal – Russian Public Initiative (RPI, www.roi.ru) – was launched as a part of Putin's election program [4, 18].

From the beginning of RPI the question of its monitoring arose. Although e-services are created online and allow the use of a big data approach for their evaluation, automated monitoring is rarely used in Russia to assess effectiveness of governmental initiatives. The opportunity to monitor e-participation online would be a government-valued and important step towards effective resources allocation. It is not only the government's concern, but also in the interest of academia to get empirical data that helps to go deeper into the exploration of public participation and

A.V. Chugunov et al. (Eds.): DTGS 2016, CCIS 674, pp. 290–298, 2016.
DOI: 10.1007/978-3-319-49700-6_27

engagement. Hence, right after the RPI launch the system for its automated monitoring (AMS) was established by eGovernance Center at ITMO University.[1]

This paper aims at describing some features of the AMS and its capabilities for political and social research. We focus on three areas the data collected by the AMS can be applicable. First, there is the analysis of PR and media effects on petitioning and voting dynamics. Secondly, we look at how the system helps to see the issue salience from a comparative perspective. Thirdly, we exemplify the usage of big data on e-participation in understanding factors of online civic engagement.

The remainder of the paper is as follows. We first outline the key peculiarities and architecture of the AMS. Then we turn to the three-abovementioned areas of its application, providing cases for illustration. Finally we summarize advantages and limitations, as well as possible future steps in the AMS development.

2 Design and Architecture of the Automated Monitoring System

To describe the AMS we should first give an overview of the RPI portal itself. There are several distinct features of RPI. To submit a petition or vote for one, a person should be a legal adult registered in the United System of Identification and Authentication (USIA), which is also used in e-government and requires formal procedures of registration (passport data is needed). One can submit a petition to one of three levels of government: municipal, regional or federal, as well as choose a certain topic (category) it is related to. To go further to the expert commission with a chance to be considered by the State Duma, an initiative should acquire 100,000 votes within a one-year period. In the case of regional or municipal petitions, 5% of the population of the corresponding entity should vote for them (if the regional population is 2 million and more, 100,000 votes is necessary) [3].

The various data the portal contains is a valuable source for empirical research. In April 2014 RPI opened its API (Application Programming Interface) that helps to collect information on all initiatives and their status. Since that time the system for automated monitoring has been based on this API.

The architecture of the monitoring system is presented in Fig. 1. It contains the following elements: (1) database to store information; (2) PHP-scripts for parsing information on the portal; (3) the task-scheduler that launches PHP-scripts; (4) tools for chart display; (5) client-side software, supporting javaScript and CSS; (6) scripts and html-layout to display data.

The monitoring system allows a researcher to get a set of valuable data, the structure of which is presented in Fig. 2. In short, it allows parsing information on: (1) overall votes and votes for each initiative; (2) voting progress (votes in favor or against); (3) search filters (level of an initiative; region; status; categories and topics; period of voting, vote count, name, and content decryption). Inquiries to the database are made by SQL, output tables can be used for further statistic analysis or infographics.

---

[1] http://analytics.prior.nw.ru/services/roi/.

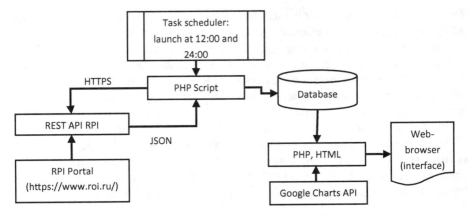

Fig. 1. Architecture of RPI module of AMS.

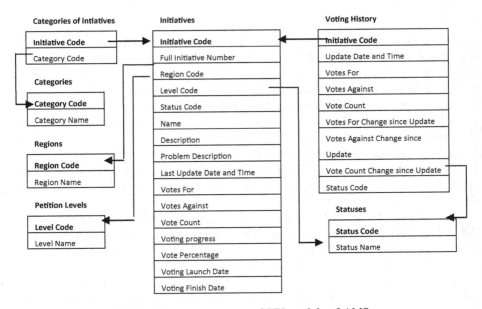

Fig. 2. Data-base structure of RPI module of AMS

3   The Application of the System to Political and Social Research

3.1   Analysing Voting Patterns and Media Effects

A big data approach seems to be a promising direction for e-participation research, e.g. in the case where we need to understand the success and failure of petitions, and the (social) media role in it. For instance, using the punctuated equilibrium concept and the data from the US portal We the People, Dumas et al. discovered patterns of political mobilisation and agenda setting in the cases of several e-petitions [5]. Hale et al. applied a big data analysis method to reveal dynamics of voting and e-petitions success in the case of the UK, having found out the signs of punctuated equilibrium, as well as social media effects on e-petitions voting [8]. Having studied the voting patterns and individuals' methods of e-petition promotions, Wright revealed strategies of different media use to attract attention to petitions [23]. The Russian RPI portal has already been analysed via the AMS by Bershadskaya et al., who found the correlation between social media use and e-participation [1].

The system under consideration can be well used for this kind of research, as it allows revealing voting dynamics, taking the minimum time intervals of one hour. By constructing a voting graph and considering it in correlation to the milieu (e.g. to an events time-line) we can test hypotheses on what actually predicts the voting patterns.

For instance, we may consider a petition submitted by a popular opposition activist Alexey Navalny as an example of media influence on voting dynamics (https://www.roi.ru/9376/). One of his initiatives submitted January 9, 2014 was intended to impose criminal responsibility for illegal enrichment of civil servants. The voting dynamics for the petition are presented in Fig. 3. Since the petitions are anonymous, the first stage of the voting process (January – September, 2014) was rather slow, since only about 3,000 votes were cast for the initiative. On September 25, 2014 Navalny posted a call for votes on his website, hence starting a PR campaign and provoking media attention to the issue. That day about 6,000 votes were attracted. Due to social media like Twitter the initiative became even more popular and by December, 2014 it received the necessary number of votes.

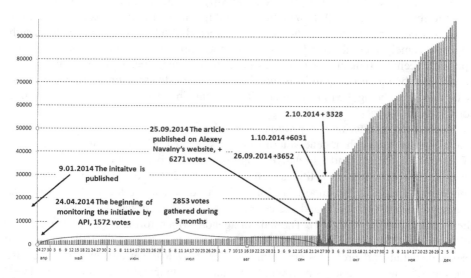

Fig. 3. Voting dynamics of Navalny's initiative (**Source**: E-Petition Portals Automated Monitoring System by eGovernance Center)

This short analysis confirms the important role the media and social networks play in e-petition success, as well as the value of the big data approach [8]. In the case of Navalny's initiative we can speak about supporters' mobilisation first that he conducted via social networks (for Twitter hash-tag #20 was used), and the personal web site. Despite the failure of the petition at the stage of expert commission review, Navalny maintains the opinion that RPI is a necessary tool for political opposition [16]. Secondly, the PR campaign provoked media attention. Media effects, like agenda setting and framing [20], containing both positive and negative judgments towards the initiative, seem to have worked for raising public awareness of the issue and RPI in general.

The automated system used for this case study, suits the purposes of comparative large-N research as well, hence more general findings can be revealed.

3.2 Measuring Issue Salience Online

Issue salience, or importance of a certain problem, is one of the crucial concepts in studies of electoral behavior, public opinion and agenda setting [22]. Information about what questions are burning at the moment may be important for decision-makers, especially at times during the electoral cycle or public discontent. However the measurement of issue salience has always been a problem for scholars. As argued by Wlezien, a widespread survey method should be carefully implemented, since the importance of an issue and its status as a problem are not the same properties [22]. Another option is to consider the agenda-setting by media (media coverage of issues) [6], but again, this technique might have some limitations to the online sphere, which is becoming larger and, as argued by Zhou and Moy, can give extra "meaning and news value to the issue" [24, p. 92]. With the rise of big data and Internet-based technology new measurements of issue salience have emerged. Mellon suggests using search engines, namely Google Trends, to evaluate the importance of problems [13]. This approach seems promising, as it regards the new – online – peculiarities of the public sphere, but, being universal in its nature, has limitations due to national characteristics, with Yandex.ru being the most popular search engine in Russia, and Baidu as a top one for China [21].

Automated monitoring of e-petition portals presents another opportunity to measure issue salience, although in general terms of the issue area. RPI data contains indicators of categories (topics), and its relative proportions may give some clues to the public agenda. The analysis of petitions submitted from 2013 to 2016 reveals several noticeable features. The importance of topics is different on federal, regional and municipal levels (Table 1), and secondly, regions of the Russian Federation vary in their issues' profiles (Table 2). The federal agenda, which forms about 95 per cent of all petitions, is dominated by Moscow as the most active region on RPI; however it seems that transport problems are of high salience by Russian citizens on all levels. Economic issues are no less important. Regional and municipal levels are more related to specific social issues like city infrastructure and ecology. Moscow and St. Petersburg, the largest Russian cities, also differ in the importance of issues. The understanding of these facts can be useful for decision-makers to adapt policies to specific regional needs.

Table 1. Top categories of petitions on RPI portal and their percentage (**source**: E-Petition Portals Automated Monitoring System by eGovernance Center)

	Federal level		Regional level		Municipal level	
	Category	%	Category	%	Category	%
1	Transport and Roads	9, 5	Transport and Roads	23, 7	Transport and Roads	28, 3
2	Economy	9, 4	City Infrastructure	16, 7	City Infrastructure	22, 7
3	Government	8, 5	Ecology	8, 3	Security	8, 4
4	Consumers and Service	8, 5	Security	6	Ecology	7, 5
5	Public Servants, Public Services	7, 4	Consumers and Service	5, 5	Houses and Yards	6, 8
6	State Support	7, 4	Houses and Yards	5, 1	Housing Facilities	3, 9

Table 2. Top categories and their percentage on RPI portal, Moscow and St. Petersburg (Source: E-Petition Portals Automated Monitoring System by eGovernance Center)

Moscow		Saint - Petersburg	
Category	%	Category	%
Transport and city	14.4	Transport and City	10.8
Consumers and services	8.9	Economy	9.8
Security	8.7	Consumers and Services	8.7
Government	7	Government	8.3
Economy	6.9	State Support	7.9
Public officials, public services	6.6	Security	7.9

Of course there are some limitations to this approach in measuring issue salience. The first one is that regions substantially differ in the quantity of petitions; hence the proportions can be distorted by too small number of initiatives. Secondly, to place a petition is not enough, as it needs to get a significant vote count for the issue to be considered really salient for the public. That is why a more elaborate technique that takes the number of petitions and votes for them will be more precise in getting the idea of what is important.

However it seems to work well enough for large and active regions with a valid number of petitions. According to the opinion-poll by the Levada Center, the key problems in Moscow in 2015 were: traffic jams, high prices on goods, problems with migrants, noise and harmful emissions produced by transport and the growth of housing rates [15]. This profile is quite similar to the one revealed by automated monitoring, which can grasp daily issue dynamics.

3.3 Exploring Disproportions in Regional Online Engagement

Attempts to explain why some people are active in political participation while others are not form a long tradition in political and social research. From one point of view, it is high social and economic status that predicts engagement, and the Internet has not changed this situation much [2, 12, 14, 17], having formed new participatory divides. Another opinion stems from the rational choice that advocates institutions, incentives, costs and efficacy as the key (de) motivators of political actions, including petitioning [9–11]. To understand, what is essential, scholars usually employ survey data, which helps to look at the individual level.

The monitoring system described can suit these goals as well, but at the moment only on the aggregate, regional, level. We have already mentioned that regions in Russia vary in terms of petitions submitted and votes cast. In order to find factors that might explain this situation we turn to the socio-economic explanation of political engagement and test whether high rates of education, income, Internet penetration and urbanization can predict a high level of petitioning and voting. The data for variables meant as dependent are gathered using the system (average votes and petitions per region, 2013–2015), other variables are calculated using statistics from the Russian Statistical Service (Rosstat, www.gks.ru). The correlation analysis (Table 3) shows significant connection between variables, indicating that this might be a promising way to analyze factors of online engagement in Russia on the aggregate level. It demonstrates that the more active are those more urbanized regions that have relatively high average education, middle income, Internet penetration and low unemployment, which is quite in accordance with the chosen theory.

Table 3. Results of Correlation Analysis (Source: Authors' Calculations)

Variables	Number of petitions	Number of votes
Level of education	,692[a]	,426[a]
Middle income	,427[a]	,273[b]
Unemployment rate	−,383[a]	−,419[a]
Share of urban population	,563[a]	,504[a]
Internet penetration	,391[a]	,347[a]

Notes: [a]Correlation is significant at the 0.01 level (2-tailed), [b]Correlation is significant at the 0.05 level (2-tailed). Source: Authors' calculations.

4 Conclusion

The paper's goal is not to advertise the system in its own right, but to show advantages of using big data approach in political and social studies, e-participation in particular. The three cases we have described present the areas of scientific inquiry, which to a larger extent depend on sociological polling data or statistics that are gathered periodically. Unlike surveys, automated monitoring has several advantages. It allows working with a large sample of cases and looking at the detailed dynamics of petitioning, voting and agenda-setting. It seems that the data can help to calculate dependent variables relevant to different research questions, with relatively low costs in comparison to surveys. Another important feature of the system is the constant and instant monitoring of e-participation effectiveness, which may be of high topicality for decision-makers. The examples of empirical research done show that the results correspond to the existing theories and previous studies, and therefore findings are plausible and can be applied in practice.

Surely there are some limitations of this approach as well. The key one is that in contrast to surveys, it is hard to collect individual data (like gender, income, education, political attitudes etc.), which is why all research tasks should be accomplished on the aggregate level (municipality, region, country). Hence dependent variables should also be found in other sources. One more problem is that the validity of data depends on the number of people who really use RPI. In the context of e-participation in Russia, when people are reluctant to use new e-tools, or use non-governmental e-petition portals instead, the picture might be distorted. The possible further steps are directed to solve these eliminations. At the moment the system has expanded to cover other portals to provide a broader perspective of e-participation in Russia.

All in all, automated monitoring seems a promising instrument to enhance political and sociological research.

References

1. Bershadskaya, L., Chugunov, A., Trutnev, D.: Evaluation of e-participation in social networks: Russian e-petitions portal. In: Janssen, M., Bannister, F., Glassey, O., Scholl, H.J., Tambouris, E., Wimmer, M.A., Macintosh, A. (eds.) Innovation and the Public Sector. IFIP EGOV 2014 and ePart 2014, vol. 21, pp. 76–83. IOS, Amsterdam (2014). doi:10.3233/978-1-61499-429-9-76
2. Best, S.J., Krueger, B.S.: Analyzing the representativeness of Internet political participation. Polit. Behav. **27**, 183–216 (2005). doi:10.1007/s11109-005-3242-y
3. Decree of President of the Russian Federation № 183 On Consideration of Public Initiatives Submitted by Citizens of the Russian Federation with the Usage of Internet – Resource "Russian Public Initiative", 4 March 2013. http://base.garant.ru/70326884/#ixzz44ErQGaGk. [in Russian]
4. Decree of President of the Russian Federation № 601 On General Directions of Public Government System Development, 7 May 2012. http://rg.ru/2012/05/09/gosupravlenie-dok.html. [in Russian]
5. Dumas, C.L., LaManna, D., Harrison, T.M., Ravi, S.S., Kotfila, C., Gervais, N., Hagen, L., Chen, F.: Examining political mobilization of online communities through e-petitioning behavior in We the People. Big Data Soc. **2**, 1–20 (2015). doi:10.1177/2053951715598170
6. Epstein, L., Segal, J.: Measuring issue salience. Am. J. Pol. Sci. **44**, 66–83 (2000)
7. Ergazakis, K., Metaxiotis, K., Tsitsanis, T.: A state-of-the-art review of applied forms and areas, tools and technologies for e-participation. Int. J. Electron. Gov. Res. **1**, 1–19 (2011). doi:10.4018/jegr.2011010101
8. Hale, S., Margetts, H., Yasseri, T.: Understanding the dynamics of Internet-based collective action using big data: analysing the growth rates of Internet-based petitions. In: Paper presented at the Annual Conference of the UK Political Studies Association (Cardiff, Wales, 25–27 March 2013). https://www.psa.ac.uk/sites/default/files/1050_571_0.pdf

9. Jho, W., Song, K.J.: Institutional and technological determinants of civil e-Participation: Solo or duet? Gov. Inf. Q. **32**, 488–495 (2015)
10. Kenski, K., Stroud, N.J.: Connections between Internet use and political efficacy, knowledge, and participation. J. Broadcast. Electron. Media **50**, 173–192 (2006). doi:10.1207/s15506878jobem5002_1
11. Kim, B.J.: Political efficacy, community collective efficacy, trust and extroversion in the information society: differences between online and offline civic/political activities. Gov. Inf. Q. **32**, 43–51 (2015). doi:10.1016/j.giq.2014.09.006
12. Lindner, R., Riehm, U.: Broadening participation through e-petitions? an empirical study of petitions to the German parliament. Policy Internet **3**, 1–23 (2011). doi:10.2202/1944-2866.1083
13. Mellon, J.: Where and when can we use Google Trends to measure issue salience? PS Polit. Sci. Polit. **46**, 280–290 (2013). doi:10.1017/S1049096513000279
14. Min, S.J.: From the digital divide to the democratic divide: Internet skills, political interest, and the second-level digital divide in political Internet use. J. Inf. Technol. Polit. **7**, 22–35 (2010). doi:10.1080/19331680903109402
15. Muscovites Call Traffic Jams and High Prices the Key Problems of Moscow. Vedomosti (2015). http://www.vedomosti.ru/politics/news/2015/08/06/603756-probki-i-dorogoviznu-moskvi. [in Russian]
16. Navalny, A.: Why to Collect Electronic Signatures for Law Drafts is Right (2014). https://navalny.com/p/3737/. [in Russian]
17. Norris, P.: Digital Divide: Civic Engagement, Information Poverty and The Internet Worldwide. Cambridge University Press, New York (2001)
18. Putin, V.V.: Democracy and Quality of Government. Kommersant, 6 February 2012. http://www.kommersant.ru/doc/1866753. [in Russian]
19. Sanford, C., Rose, J.: Characterizing e-participation. Int. J. Inf. Manag. **27**, 406–421 (2007). doi:10.1016/j.ijinfomgt.2007.08.002
20. Scheufele, D.A., Tewksbury, D.: Framing, agenda setting, and priming: the evolution of three media effects models. J. Commun. **57**, 9–20 (2007). doi:10.1111/j.1460-2466.2006.00326.x
21. Search Engine Market Share By Country. Austin Return on Now Internet Marketing (2015). http://returnonnow.com/internet-marketing-resources/2015-search-engine-market-share-by-country/
22. Wlezien, C.: On the salience of political issues: the problem with 'most important problem'. Electoral. Stud. **24**, 555–579 (2005)
23. Wright, S.: Populism and downing street e-petitions: connective action, hybridity, and the changing nature of organizing. Polit. Commun. **32**, 414–433 (2015). doi:10.1080/10584609.2014.958256
24. Zhou, Y., Moy, P.: Parsing framing processes: the interplay between online public opinion and media coverage. J. Commun. **57**, 79–98 (2007). doi:10.1111/j.0021-9916.2007.00330.x

The Right of Access to Information in Portugal and Brazil and the Challenges of Its Implementation

Marciele Berger Bernardes[1](✉), Francisco Pacheco de Andrade[1](✉), and Paulo Novais[2](✉)

[1] Law School, University of Minho, Braga, Portugal
marcieleberger@gmail.com,
franc.andrade.direito@gmail.com
[2] School of Engineering, University of Minho, Braga, Portugal
pjon@di.uminho.pt

Abstract. With the advent of Information Society and the new Technologies of information and communication (ICT) and its use through Internet, the fundamental right of access to information gets a new dimension and allows the exercise of other relevant rights such as popular participation. Thus, we think that it is worth to elaborate a comparative analysis between the Portuguese law on the access to administrative documents (LADA) and the Brazilian law on access to information (LAI). For the elaboration of such study we used the method of monographic procedure, using the technique of research based in bibliographic revision. From the analysis undertaken we will try to identify and qualify the transparency and the effectiveness of access to information in both countries.

Keywords: Access to information · Comparative law · Open government · Portugal · Brazil

1 Introduction

In a context of economic and technological changes caused by globalisation and the development of the informational society, what many could have previously considered as science fiction (although already announced by [1, 2, 3]) became reality and starts to challenge the world governments. The new informational reality poses a fundamental question: how does the emerging informational reality contribute to improve the democratic system? Does the fact that people have more access to information mean that a better democracy will arise? This is a worldwide phenomenon that has been studied and has been designated as open government, aiming to ensure more transparency in the relationship between governments and citizens, as well as the promotion of public well-being.

Having this in consideration, this work is therefore justified by the fact that it intends to analyse and understand the development of the Informational Society, the incorporation of ICT in administration and the changes arising from its use in the Brazilian and Portuguese democratic model. Furthermore, the focus of this study is also

A.V. Chugunov et al. (Eds.): DTGS 2016, CCIS 674, pp. 299–314, 2016.
DOI: 10.1007/978-3-319-49700-6_28

relevant since it intends to compare the main issues of the Portuguese 1993 Law of Access to Administrative Documents (LADA) and the Brazilian 2011 Law on Access to Information (LAI). We have chosen the methodology of comparative law because it is believed that such approach enhances the understanding of the subject besides clarifying how countries with different historical contexts concerning the implementation of democracy, popular participation, transparency and mainly right of access have been working with Internet in order to ensure the effectiveness of such rights. Besides that, it will be also possible to share experiences of both countries in the process of incorporation of ICT in Public Administration.

Concerning the relation between the Internet and the access to information, the current study was oriented towards an answer to the following questions: how does the legislation of access to information in both countries consider the use of the Internet? Do Portugal and Brazil consider the use of the Internet as a tool to ensure the access to information? Does the legislation in these countries confront the issue or does it omit it?

Therefore, the current study was divided in five different sections: the first one is an introduction, the second one focus on the evolution of informational society and the incorporation of ICT by the public administration, the third analyses the legal framework of access to information in Portugal and Brazil, the fourth encompasses a comparative study of both legislations and, finally, we shall present the challenges for the implementation of public policies of access to information and the strengthening of democracy in the analysed countries.

2 Informational Society and Modernization of Public Administration in Portugal and Brazil

The use of ICT by governmental structures is becoming popular and thus intensified on a daily basis. Public Administration is also part of this path and two main movements must be referred: first, the New Public Management[1] and second the New Public Service- NPS [4].

NGP started in the last decade of the 20 Century and had as primordial aim to make public administration as efficient as the private sector. That movement was based on "managerial principles oriented towards results, efficiency, governance and orientation of the public management to Market uses" [5]. [6] defined well the role of governments at the time: worrying more with directing than rowing[2].

Having to face the need of a wide opening to popular participation, doctrine slowly has been constructing the theory of NSP – New Public Service, which is based on the idea of public interest, valuing citizens and open dialogue [4].

NPS, proposed by Denhardt, is based on seven main basic principles: to serve the citizens; to pursue public interest; to value citizenship and public service more than

---

[1] The theory of New Public Management was proposed in 1992 by David Osborne and Ted Gaebler in their book "Reinventing Government".

[2] NPS is established "upon economic concepts such as maximization of self-interest and internal demand of modernisation of the administration" [4], p. 26.

entrepreneurship; to think strategically and to act democratically; to recognize that accountability is not simple; to serve instead of directing and to value people and not just productivity [7]. These precepts were inspired in the democratic theory, mainly on its concern with the connection between the citizens and their government, and also in approaches proceeding from a more humanistic tradition in the general theory of public administration, presented as an alternative to management and organisational design [8].

Following these NPS principles, whose focus is on the increase of popular participation mediated by ICT, it is perceived the theory of Open Government of [9].

The principles of Open Government allow the citizen, who "having access to information, is no more a passive subject but becomes co-author of public policies and a true holder of Power [4].

Based on these concepts, Open Government will be considered in this study concerning all the changes arising out of the incorporation of ICT in the democratic processes of the studied countries.

As we have already seen, the problematic of the informational society has become more notorious at the international level. In this sense, working groups were created within the United Nations Organisation in order to promote studies and debates on the governance of Internet, in which the European Union, Portugal and Brazil have been participating.

Concerning the European Union and according to the European Union Treaty (articles 179 and 180), the EU has a commitment to the development and diffusion of the Informational Society, and its strategies have been implemented in blocks of targets which began in 1993 with the edition of the White Book -COM/93 (EU, online[3]) which has been improved along the years (Action Plan eEurope 2005, i2010) and are projected to the future until 2020, whose goal is the use of ICT for an intelligent Europe, sustainable and inclusive (EUR-lex, online). Concerning the right of access to information, it is worth noting the following documents: Chart of the Fundamental Rights of the European Union (2000), Regulation of the European Commission 1049/2001, Directive 2003/98/CE (reuse of information in the public sector), and the Treaty of Lisbon (2009).

In Portugal, according to data from the Portuguese Operational Programme for Information Society (POSI, 2000) the inclusion in informational society starts late, in 1994, when the country was still at a pre-digital phase. Considering this, several governance policies have been adopted, among which (Table 1):

Following what was being done in Portugal, Brazil only started its own block of policies for the Informational Society in the end of the 90 s. In this approach, the main policies adopted by the Brazilian Government with the aim of implementing the precepts of Open Government are the following (Table 2):

As it may be noticed, the incorporation of ICT both in Portugal and in Brazil was done through a late process, with specificities depending on the State and not yet fully implemented. However, important diplomas were promulgated evidencing a commitment to the amelioration of Government and of the concept of democracy. In this sense,

---

[3] Available in: <http://europa.eu/documentation/official-docs/white-papers/index_pt.htm>. Access on 10th March 2016.

Table 1. Selected list of strategies of Open Government adopted by the Portuguese state

Year	Strategies of Open Government adopted by the Portuguese State
1996	National Initiative for the Information Society and Mission for the Information Society.
1997	Green Book for Information Society
1998	Programme for Digital Cities
1999	White Book for Portuguese Scientific and Technological Development
2000	Operational Programme for Information Society (POSI)
2000	Inter-ministries Commission for Information Society and Internet Initiative
2001	2001 Public Tender for the generalisation of the Programme for Digital Cities
2002	2002 Decree which created the Diploma of Basic Skills in Information Technologies and the Inter-ministries Commission for Information Society (public tender for the evaluation of the sites in the Internet of the organisms integrated in the direct and indirect State Administration)
2002	Unit of the Mission Innovation and Knowledge (UMIC);
2003	National Initiative for Broadband
2005	Programme Connect PT and SIMPLEX (simplification and amelioration of the provision of public services)
2007	Agency for Administrative Modernisation

Source: elaborated by the authors. Adapted from (Ligar PT, 2005; POSI, 2000; Livro Verde, 1996).

Table 2. Selected list of strategies of Open Government adopted by the Brazilian State

Year	Strategies of Open Government adopted by the Brazilian State
1995	Director Plan of the Reform of the State Bureaucracy
1999	Programme for Information Society
2000	*Government of Luíz Fernando Cardoso*
	Executive Committee for Electronic Government (CEGE).
2002	*Government of Luíz Inácio Lula da Silva*
2004	Department of Electronic Government
2009	Creation of the Transparency Portal
2010	Law of Fiscal Responsibility
2011	E-democracy portal
	Government of Dilma Roussef
	Partnership for Open Government (OGP).
	Inter-ministries Committee for Open Government (CIGA),
	National Action Plan for Open Government (PNGA).

Source: [10].

it is worth to make a study on the right of access to the information in constitutional and infra-constitutional diplomas both in Portugal and Brazil.

3 Right to Information in Portugal and Brazil: Constitutional and Legal Bases

At this point, it must be stated that the Right to Information is a fundamental right[4] of the citizens and thus it must be reflected in modern political systems. Furthermore, it is known that Technologies are not a remedy to solve all the democratic deficits [11]. However, despite all doctrinal controversies concerning the benefits and harms of ICT, this study goes in the direction proposed by Pierre Levy who stated that the network is not a pharmacon (neither medicine nor poison): it is not the place and moment to evaluate its impacts but rather of considering its irreversibility and, according to its possible uses, of deciding what to do with it [12].

Therefore, we shall synthesise some of the main policies adopted in Portugal and Brazil aimed at promoting the right of access to information.

3.1 The Right to Information in the Portuguese Legal Framework

The right to information is recognized by the Portuguese Constitution (CRP) since 1976 (principle of free access to the archives and documents of the Public Administration), and was later updated in 1982, when it was developed the right to be informed around the following principles: the right to information (articles 20 and 37), reserve of intimacy and private life (articles 26, 34, 268), right of participation in political life (arts. 48 and 268 no. 2), and secrecy of justice (article 268). Article 268 is important, since it establishes the right of citizens to be informed by the public administration and also the right of access to the archives and administrative registries.

Still concerning this subject it is important to refer the Code of Administrative Procedure (the previous code was approved by Decree of Law no. 442/91, later updated by DL 18/2008, but recently this code was replaced by a new Code approved by DL 4/2015).

Furthermore, in 1993 this subject was regulated by the Law of Access to Administrative Documents – LADA (Law no. 65/93). This law was modified in 1995 and 1996 and later on by the Directive 2003/98, and was completely revoked by the Law no. 46/2007, recently updated by the DL 214-G/2015).

It must be emphasized that the Portuguese Parliament is discussing a Law Project (PL 13/2016, 2016.02.03) that aims to modify the regime of access to the administrative documents and its reuse and also to transpose to the Portuguese legal order the Directive no. 2013/37/UE of the European Parliament and of the Council of 26th June 2013 that modified the regime of the Directive 2003/98/CE of the European Parliament and of the Council of 17th November 2013).

---

[4] The above mentioned expression was created by the Non-Governmental Organisation - NGO Article 19. Available in: <http://artigo19.org/?p=40>. Access on 28th February 2016.

The current Law of Access to Administrative Documents is divided into four chapters and has 41 articles. In the first chapter "General dispositions" are presented the principles of open administration (art. 1), its aims (art. 2), the law then establishes a difference between administrative document and nominative document (art. 3), it refers which organisms of public administration are subject to LADA (art. 4), establishes the right of citizens to require information (regardless of justification – art. 5), as well as the restrictions – information categorized by law as secret information (art. 6); the law also informs on data related to health matters (art. 7), on the persons responsible for complying with the law and for the illegitimate use of information (arts. 8 and 9) and, finally, establishes an orientation on how to make the information available and its updating (art. 10).

The second section "Exercise of the right of access and of reusing administrative documents" is divided into two sections: the first section refers to the right of access and the second one refers to the reuse of the documents.

The section concerning the right of access stipulates the different steps by which access will be granted (art. 11), its charges (reproduction taxes, art. 12), way of submitting the request (written, verbal, art. 13), as well as the time period for a reply (art. 14), as well as the eventual submission of the request to CADA (Commission of Access to Administrative Documents) that will have a time period of 30 days to clarify any doubts; besides that, CADA will be responsible for sorting any complaints concerning the non-observance of the time period or on overruled requests. It must also be mentioned that the citizen has the right of appeal to the Administrative Courts (art. 15).

On the second section (Reuse of documents) it is established the general principle on reuse of documents (art. 16), the way to formulate the request of reuse (art. 17), the documents whose reuse is not allowed (art. 18) and time period and conditions for the reuse (arts. 19 and 20) and the possibility to appeal to CADA or to the Administrative Court in case of denial of the reuse (art. 23).

The third chapter concerns CADA, explaining its nature, composition, functioning, competencies, remuneration and it is mandatory for all agents and organisms of the administration to cooperate with CADA (art. 28).

Finally, the chapter "Administrative Offence" presents the ways of violating rights, including the cases in which attempt and negligence are penalised (articles 33 and 34); and also the established fines, time period for impugnation and appeals to the Administrative Court (arts. 33 to 39). In this chapter, one can also find the dispositions revoked by LADA.

The analysis of LADA allows us to infer that the mentioned diploma omits any statement concerning the technologies that the administration must use in order to ensure the access to information. Furthermore, the referred norm is restricted to the documents' availability, without any reference either to popular consultation or the debate of public policies.

3.2   Right to Information in Brazilian Legal Framework

The Brazilian Federal Constitution of 1988 is a milestone for Brazilian law, since it restores democracy in the country and confers rights on citizens and imposes duties on the State towards the prosecution of the mentioned rights and warranties.

This Fundamental Chart states in article 5, items XIV and XXXIII, and article 37° § 3°, item II, the right of access to information. However, 23 years have elapsed and only in 2011 it was published the Brazilian Law of Access to Information (LAI).

It must be emphasised that since 2009 it had been under procedure for approval in the National Congress the Law Project no. 5528/2009, which after two years of debate was transformed and approved as Law no.12527/2011.

In this section we shall analyse the main rules, procedures and delays adopted by the Brazilian Law of Access to Information, as well as the Decree no. 7724/2012 which regulates the application of the above mentioned law in the context of the Federal Executive Power, as stated in article 1.

Following this, it is presented a brief summary of Bernardes'; Santos'; et al. (2015) study structuring the Brazilian LAI in five chapters. The first chapter (General Dispositions) informs on who is subject to the LAI (article 1st and 2nd. Next, it is presented the main rule of the law, stating that information is the rule and secrecy is the exception (article 3). Finally, article 8 brings along important guidelines, such as Active Transparency[5]; it became a duty of the State to warrant the rights of citizens to have access to information (article 5).

In Chapter II (On the Access to Information and its disclosure) article 6 focuses on the subject of transparent management and the need to allow a wide access. Article 7 deals with the kind of information embraced in the law and article 8 refers the Service of Information to the Citizen – SIC.

In Chapter III (From the Procedure of Access to Information) we may find the procedures concerning what is called Passive Transparency[6], which means, information that is not available in SIC but to which the citizen may have access through an identified request (article 10).

Chapter IV (Restrictions of the Access to Information) opens up with the restrictions on the access to information and presents the new rules concerning secrecy and classified information. It must be remembered that the main rule of the law is that access is the rule, secrecy is the exception. However, the Law itself presents some situations in which secrecy will be required, as stated in article 23.

Chapter V (Liabilities) expressly presents some situations in which the behaviour of the public agents may imply breach of rule and article 33 refers to the sanctions for the breach.

---

[5] Active Transparency refers to the minimal information that must be put, mandatorily, in the government portals, in accordance with the rule that information is the rule and secrecy is the exception [13].

[6] Passive Transparency refers to the information that is not available in the Service of Information to the Citizen, but that any interested person may get access to through an identified requirement that may be introduced via Internet; the motivation is not required [13].

Bernardes; Santos; et al., (2015) end their approach in the last section of the Brazilian LAI that focuses on the mandatory rule that all organisms and entities of the Public Administration shall designate persons/entities responsible for the compliance and monitoring of the Law, beyond the adoption of unavoidable measures for its correct functioning (article 40), especially in what concerns the need for each sphere to regulate it (article 45).

After this analysis of the main dispositions of the LAI, we shall now proceed to a comparative study of the Portuguese LADA and the Brazilian LAI.

The analysis of LAI allows us to infer that the approval of the mentioned diploma was driven by the signature by the Brazilian State of "Parceria Governo Aberto" (Partnership for Open Government) in 2011. Consequently, it incorporates the international precepts of publicity as a rule in administration. The active transparency (with a list of mandatory documents specified in the law itself, art. 8) finds a tool of implementation in the World Wide Web (art. 6 paragraph 3). It is to be noted that LAI considers the Internet as the basic tool for transparency although the details of the information remain in charge of each administrative entity.

4 Comparison Between the Portuguese and Brazilian Legislation on Access to Information and the Main Challenges to Their Implementation

This section will proceed to a comparative study of the Portuguese 1993 Law of Access to Administrative Documents (revised in 2007) and the Brazilian 2011 Law on the Access to Information.

According to data from Global Right to Information Rating (2016, online[7]) in 103 evaluated countries, Brazil ranks 18th and Portugal is the 69th. Therefore, this study is justified since it aims to find out if more recent legislation is more effective and what are the challenges for the operationalisation of the mentioned legal statutes.

But it must be underlined that the comparative study of legislation requires attention to the historical, political and social specificities of each of the analysed countries.

In this sense, Ackerman and Sandoval (2005, p. 24) explain that both contents and the way of interpreting these legislations may vary deeply, and that is why they suggest the establishing of different categories, to be followed by the comparative analysis, namely: legal coverage, exceptions, supervision, monitoring and ease of access.

Concerning "Coverage", the ideal scenario is that the law should cover "all the institutions that receive public Money, including the three powers" [14] and, as an example, the authors point to the case of South Africa that, in Sect. 32 of its 1996 Constitution, obliges even private institutions to provide information. In this sense, both Portuguese LADA (art. 4) and Brazilian LAI establish a wide coverage. That is particularly true in the Brazilian legal framework since every Power shall have to regulate the subject by Decree. The research of [15] points out that Regulation Decree

---

[7] Available in: <http://www.rti-rating.org/country-data>. Access on: 10th March 2016.

of LAI (Decree 7724/2012) only includes the Executive Power, since in the context of the Judicial Power, the subject, until now, was only regulated by Resolution 151 of the National Council of Justice, and this has generated a wide margin of freedom in the application of LAI, to the point that there was huge controversy on the issues of freedom and privacy, which led to a discussion at the Brazilian Supreme Court.

Consequently, it is important to compare the laws concerning the category "Exceptions", and for [14] this topic is complex and its wrong conduction may favour the political leaders' discretion in two main aspects: First, concerning the issue of secret information; who is to decide upon this? And what exceptions are there for secrecy? Secondly, which is very important, the issues of privacy and personal data protection.

In the comparative study we concluded that both legislations comply with the first part of this category: LAI (articles 23 and 24) and LADA (articles 5 and 6), and both possess special legislation detailing the treatment of classified information according to degrees of secrecy.

It must be said that the research on LADA found out that this Law presents what we might call over-categorisation, which means that "it is too much detailed concerning exceptions to the access, namely about national security issues and the secrecy of justice" [16]. Still, in the category of "exceptions", in the item concerning the Protection of Personal Information, we could not locate in any of the legislations a specific disposition aimed to protect personal data, both the citizens' and the civil servants'. In this respect, [14] pertinently asked: "Should we consider the information contained in CV's of civil servants as personal data or public data"?

Portuguese LADA does elaborate on this, but this subject has been widely debated since 1976, as the Portuguese Republic Constitution in articles 18, 26 and 35 mentions fundamental rights and the use of personal data. Article 35 actually underwent several changes, namely under the influence of Directive 95/46/CE (on personal data) which was transposed to the Portuguese Law by Law 67/98.

Accordingly, [17] describes a new informational reality (society of the *Homo Conectus* and big data, referring as a fundamental right in this society the right to disconnect) requiring further changes in order to better ensure personal data protection. One should add that it is already under way a new European Regulation on Data Protection[8] that should come into force in 2018. With the advent of this Regulation, it is expected that the Portuguese LADA will undergo further changes.

Brazil had to deal with similar questions when the LAI was promulgated. The issue was whether or not it should be mandatory to make it available in the net the nominal lists of civil servants, making available to the public data concerning vacancies, roles and wages.

Concerning this issue [10] inform that several judicial procedures were judged[9], in which the civil servants aimed at limiting the unrestricted access to information (making available nominal lists including civil servants wages in the sites of

---

[8] Reform of EU data protection rules. Available in: <http://ec.europa.eu/justice/data-protection/reform/index_en.htm> Access on: 10th March 2016.

[9] Among the procedures judged by the Federal Supreme Court, it should be noticed Rcl 14530, Rcl 14733, Rcl 15350, SL 689, SS 4661, SL 630, SL 623, Rcl 14739, SS 4723 e SS 3902.

Administration), on the allegation of compliance with LAI. According to these authors, the issue reached the Federal Supreme Court, and this Court suspended the actions invoking that "the wages of civil servants constitutes information of collective or general interest, in the precise terms of the first part of the item XXXIII of article 5 of the Federal Constitution"[10] [10].

The third category "Supervision and Following" may be considered as the key piece, since it influences directly the management and implementation of LAI, being suggested by [14] the creation of an autonomous and independent organism that may even be an instance of appeal; as well as the observance of a time period for providing information by governmental agencies.

On this particular aspect, Portuguese LADA excels by choosing to have a specific section about the Commission of Access to Administrative Documents (CADA), an independent national commission, to which citizens may appeal, being that, as last resource, the citizen may also appeal to the Administrative Courts. Concerning the time period, the general rule is 10 days, but there is a possibility of prorogation up to 2 months.

On the other hand, the Brazilian LAI is not characterised as an independent organism, but just determined that each institution must designate an authority responsible for the compliance with the norm, and after exhausting the administrative ways, the citizen may appeal to the judicial authorities. Here, the general time period for a reply is 20 days with a possibility of prorogation for a maximum of 10 more days.

Finally, the last category presented by [14] refers to the Ease of Access, meaning by this the effective application of the precepts of open government (referred in the 2nd item of this work). This means that it is required a pro-active demand of information on the part of the administrations, besides a constant updating and accessible language. On this aspect, LADA does not contain a disposition making it mandatory for the Administration to present the organismic structure, telephones for contact, main requirements and solicitations of the citizens; furthermore, the "charges and taxes for reproduction of information are quite expensive and totally supported by the applicants" [16].

Moreover, the studies on LADA reveal that the Portuguese legislation does not have any norm stating criteria for defining what clear, simple and precise explanations are, and this legislative silence makes it easier for the administration to exercise discretion [16].

It must also be said that the law does not require the availability of information on preliminary studies, minutes or drafts of preparatory meetings or other type of data. Another obstacle to the access to information is that the Electronic Official Journal imposes "high taxes for advanced searches (such as research in native language) and does not allow an unified research in all the series and only makes available pdf versions of the pages of the Official Journal" [16].

In the current informational context and considering the list of policies for open government adopted by Governments, the omission of the Portuguese LADA makes it

---

[10] For the full decision visit: <http://www.stf.jus.br/arquivo/cms/noticiaNoticiaStf/anexo/SL630.pdf>. Access on 1st March 2016.

difficult to supervise through the Government portals in which, according to [16], "access by the citizens, concerning the activities of the public sector, is essentially done through annual reports and activity plans of the public entities, but these are not always available online".

The above mentioned suggestions were already considered in the Law Project no. 13/2016[11], (3rd February 2016) which also suggests modifications to LADA and, among them, the incorporation of the principle of the right of access to the public administration that, in digital times, has the Internet as an important tool of optimisation. Therefore, the Law Project suggests that the Portuguese administration adopts a pro-active behaviour, making available all and any public information in the network in a complete and organised way and also in a clear and easily understandable language, regardless of a request of the citizen (Portugal, Law Project, online 2016).

The Brazilian law, because it is more recent, already encompasses the standard that, from the publication of the LAI on, "information is the rule and secrecy is the exception". Consequently, the norm is divided in two axes: active transparency (list of information mandatorily provided by the public administration) and passive transparency (list of information that must be required by the citizen through the Service of Information to the Citizen – SIC, requiring payment).

In this context, the studies developed by [4] at the moment of the promulgation of the Brazilian LAI have remarked that the decree was written in a very wide and complex approach, mainly when compared to the international concepts of open government. However, in practical terms, the evaluation of government portals in the Southern region of Brazil, led to the opposite scenario and far away from the desired goals: in 40 municipalities evaluated, none has applied the Law as a whole, and so there was neither uniformity in the governmental sites nor organisation of information, thus often not making viable its access, although they exist and are available).

It must be said that simply making the information available does not mean that there is an effective appropriation of the information by the citizens or that the citizens succeeded in getting the information in order to monitor the administration or even helping in the fulfilment of public well-being [15].

In order to understand this better, we present below the schematic table of comparison (Table 3):

From the comparison above it may be inferred that both the Portuguese and the Brazilian Laws present some interesting innovations, omissions, similarities and differences between each other, being LAI generally more detailed and more developed than LADA. However, the latest establishes important features on the organisms of control and responsibility of the agents (CADA, articles 25 to 32), as well as an important reference to health data (article 7) and obliges the periodical updating of the information.

---

[11] Law Proposal no. 13/2016 available at: <http://app.parlamento.pt/webutils/docs/doc.pdf?path= 6148523063446f764c3246795a5868774d546f334e7a67774c336470626d6c7561574e7059585270 646d467a4c31684a53556b76644756346447397a4c334277624445344c56684a53556c664d793577 5a47593d&fich=ppl18-XIII_3.pdf&Inline=true>. Access on 05th May 2016.

Table 3. Comparative study

Comparative Study Between The Acess Information Law Of Brazil And Portugal		
Name of the country	Brazil	Portugal
Influences	International Treaties	International Treaties
Constitutional Provision	CF/88, art. 5º, item XXXIII, art. 37º, item II and paragraph 3 and art. 216, paragraph 2.	CRP/1976; CRP/1982 (arts. 20, 26, 34, 37, 268) Directive EU 2003/98
Name of the law	Law of Access to Information No. 12.527/11	Law of Access to Administrative Documents - LADA (Law no. 65/93). Revoked by Law no. 46/2007, updated by DL 214-G/2015
Coverage	Wide	Wide
	Exceptions: Regulation Decree only rules Executive Power. In Judiciary context, subject is ruled by Resolution no. 151, CNJ	Exceptions: Nothing included
Exceptions:		
(a) Secrecy Information	(a) In Regulation Decree	(a) In Regulation Decree **Observation:** Many exceptions
(b) Privacy and Data Protection	(b) Nothing included **Observation:** Action: Requirement of Preliminary Injunction no. 63 (Divergences on the liberation of data of civil servants). Decision of Supreme Federal Court for a wide availability of information.	(b) Nothing included **Observation:** there is a general law on Data Protection, Law 67/98, which transposed to the Portuguese Law the European Directive no. 95/46/CE.
Supervision		
(a) Controlling Organism	(a) Nothing included **Observation:** It is required the designation of a civil servant, inside the Administration, responsible for the operationalisation of the LAI.	(a) Chapter 3 (art. 25 to 32) CADA (Commission of Access to Administrative Documents).
Ease of Access		
(a) pro-active information	(a) Active Transparency (art. 8) and Passive Transparency (art. 11)	(a) Nothing included
(b) costs	(b) supported by the applicant	See Law Project 13/2016 considering the principle of open administration in restricted sense (access to documents, data and administrative processes) and in wider sense (active divulgation and accessibility of documents, data and information as well as policies of promotion of public participation)

Source: Elaborated by the authors, adapted from [14].

Both normative dispositions specify the information that must be publicised (right of access) and LAI intends to use the Internet (without detailing the principles orienting the information in the net) while LADA omits this aspect.

It must also be said that, regardless of the fact that Brazil is better placed in the legislation of access to information (RTI, 2015) ranking, it does not mean that public entities of this country automatically have become more transparent and that its citizens get immediately information from the administration.

The Doctrine speaks of cases when the culture of secrecy endures within the Brazilian administration, even to the point of originating judicial action (Bernardes; Rover, 2014). Because of this, it can be said that, in terms of the efficacy of laws, both Brazil and Portugal are confronted with difficulties of the responsible organisms of Public Administration, thus increasing the levels of dissatisfaction of the citizens concerning public transparency.

In the study on "Portugal: public debt and the democratic deficit", [18] points out that in the past 30 years Portugal has been cyclically adopting the same strategies, signing treaties and becoming engaged, and yet the country does not believe in growth. In this sense, the author refers that one of the main problems is to align institutions with values, that is to say, it is necessary that the citizens, the State and Public Administration be aligned, otherwise the creation of new laws will not be fruitful, since these will not be complied with. Concerning the Portuguese legislation, it is still important to consider the suggestions of [16] who point out the following measures in order to reach the effectiveness of LADA:

> The adhesion to Open Government Partnership (OGP); to promote the reuse of information without costs: to implement an interactive way of showing the average time for information to be provided within all public entities; to implement a black list of public entities and public agents incurring in reiterated bad practices in the application of LADA; the inclusion of performances concerning the management of requirements of access to information in the performance evaluation systems of public entities; suspension of the transfers from the State Budget to the entities included in the mentioned black list; the legal and institutional framework must be audited by organisations of the civil society; CADA must monitor the claims and make recommendations for procedural changes whenever necessary.

Regardless of the adherence to OGP, all the above listed points may and should be followed by the Brazilian State.

Without disregarding the categories above mentioned to evaluate the legislations of access to information, in this historical and comparative approach [14] point out relevant topics to be observed in the process of research and comparison of laws of access to information.

> **Political Nature of LAI** - these dispositions are political creations and thus it is an error to believe that freedom of information will be a natural fruit of economic development;
> **Centrality of Civil Society** - it is still unusual that governments are interested in opening their internal structures of administration, so it is up to the civil society to fight for more and better information and thus it should turn to be the strength that leads the process.
> **International Actors** (ONG's - destined to evaluate the implementation of LAI, they also exercise an important role in the fight against corruption and in the pressure for more transparency on the part of governments.

According to what has been said, it may be inferred that the compilation of indicators for the implementation of the laws of access to information in any national legal order, especially in the countries that are being examined, must encompass: amelioration of the process of democratic opening; incorporation of ICT (without thinking these as mere "magic wands" that would solve all the difficulties and the democratic deficits) and, finally, the willingness of the public administration agents.

5   Final Considerations

The need for a broader openness and transparency of the Administration, as well as the use of the Internet as a mechanism to implement such principles and to allow real time monitoring by the population, becomes more and more evident within the Informational Society.

In the introduction of this study we have proposed to analyse how the precepts of the Laws ensuring the Right of Access in the Portuguese and Brazilian Legal Frameworks are being implemented. In this context, it was considered necessary to study the transformations arising out of the use of ICT (Information and Communication Technologies) and its systematic use by the public administrations of the countries observed, in the context of what is internationally referred to as open government, with the aim of transforming the mechanisms of the relationship between the citizen and government and thus ensure an wider transparency of the public administration.

From the analysis undertaken, it was observed that, regardless of the fact that Brazil has a more recent legislation and is better placed in the Global Ranking of Right to Information, it does not necessarily mean that the Brazilian State ensures more transparency and effective access to information for its citizens.

In this sense, it may be inferred that both the Portuguese and the Brazilian States are confronted with difficulties in the implementation of their laws of access to information. However, the referred laws may well be considered as paramount for the realisation of democracy and, consequently, requiring a formulation of new public policies in order to warrant an effective rapprochement between citizens and its representatives.

In the study of the Portuguese Scenario it was observed that the policies of insertion in Informational Society had various evolutionary steps, including the revision in 2007 of the first law of Access (from 1993), and a new revision of the Law in 2015. In what the Brazilian model is concerned, this appeared a bit later, since LAI was only published in 2011, 23 years after its inclusion in the Federal Constitution.

Considering this, it was thought necessary a comparative study of the main dispositions of both laws, in order to verify their limitations and the new possibilities presented by the use of ICT.

From the current study it was evidenced that although Brazil already considers Internet in its uses, and Portugal recently introduced a Law Project for the modification of LADA (to incorporate norms on Internet and the openness of the Administration) some further efforts are still required so that the mentioned precepts may be incorporated in the uses of the administration, in order to overcome the point in which the Administration just uses Internet as a "Web Portal of Messages" [19].

It was also observed that, in spite of the specificities of each legal order, both Portugal and Brazil, historically well known by their democratic deficits, have laws that comply with the international standards on Access to Information. However, both require a revision of their laws concerning the categories "coverage", "exceptions" (lack of prevision on data protection), and "supervision" (in Brazil the creation of an independent and autonomous organism; in Portugal, CADA must implement the monitoring of claims and accompany the course of procedures).

It must not be forgotten that the illnesses arising of the democratic deficits will not be solved in a short time period, even considering that the promises arising out of the current Informational Society and Open Government go in the direction of a wider public transparency.

So, to consider the political nature of laws, the change of behaviour of citizens now understood as agents of the democratic process and the cooperation of national and international organisms in monitoring and ranking, all these are indispensable factors for the analysis of this scenario, for the effectiveness of laws and for avoiding that those laws become ineffective and do not remain just as what [20] called a "sheet of paper".

Acknowledgments. Our thanks to the CAPES Foundation, Ministry of Education of Brazil, for financing this research, and also to the CIIDH-Interdisciplinary Research Centre in Human Rights, and to the Algoritimi Centre, both at University of Minho, for supporting this research. The work of Marciele Berger has been supported by CAPES under Grant N°. BEX - 1788/15-9. The work of Paulo Novais has been supported by FCT – Foundation for Science and Technology within the Project Scope UID/CEC/00319/2013.

References

1. Huxley, A.: Brave New World Perennial Classics. Perennial Classics, New York (2006)
2. Orwell, G.: 1984 Penguin Publishing Group (1950)
3. Toffler, Alvin: The Third Wave Translation John Távora, 29th edn. Record, Rio de Janeiro (2007). (in Portuguese)
4. Santos, P., Bernardes, M., Rover A.: Teoria e Prática de Governo Aberto: Lei de Acesso a Informação nos Executivos Municipais da Região Sul Funjab: Florianópolis (2012). (in Portuguese)
5. Barbosa, A.F., Faria, F.I., Pinto, S.L.: Governança eletrônica no setor público. In: Knight, P. T., Fernandes, C.C.C., Cunha, M.A.: (Org.) e-Desenvolvimento no Brasil e no mundo: subsídios para o programa e-Brasil, São Caetano do Sul, Yendis, pp. 512–537 (2007). (in Portuguese)
6. Osborn, D., Gaebler, T. Reinventando o governo: como o espírito empreendedor está transformando o setor público 7. ed. Brasília, DF, MH Comunicação (1995). (in Portuguese)

7. Denhardt, R.B.: The New Public Service: Serving, not Steering. ME Sharpe, New York (2003)
8. Denhardt, R.B.: Teorias da Administração Pública. Cengage Learning, São Paulo (2012). (in Portuguese)
9. Calderón, W., Lorenzo, S.: Open Government. Algon Editors, Jaén (2011)
10. Bernardes, M.B., Rover, J.A.: Lei de Acesso a Informação e disponibilização de dados remuneratórios pelos Tribunais de Justiça in II CongresoIberoamericano de Docentes e Investigadores em Derecho e Informática, CIIDI (2014). (in Portuguese)
11. Castells, M.: A sociedade em rede. A era da informação: economia, sociedade e cultura, vol. 1. 14ª reimp. São Paulo: Paz e Terra (2011). (in Portuguese)
12. Lévy, P. Cibercultura Traduzido por Carlos Irineu da Costa, São Paulo, Ed. 34 (1999). (in Portuguese)
13. Bernardes, M.B., Santos, M.P., Rover, A.J.: Ranking das prefeituras da região Sul do Brasil: uma avaliação a partir de critérios estabelecidos na Lei de Acesso à Informação in: Rev. Adm. Pública, Rio de Janeiro **49**(3),761–792, maio/jun. (2015). (in Portuguese)
14. Ackerman, J., Sandoval, I.: Leyes de Acceso a La Información en el Mundo in Cuadermos de transparência. IFAI, México (2005). (in Castillian)
15. Bernardes, M.B.: Democracia na Sociedade Informacional O desenvolvimento da democracia digital nos municípios brasileiros. São Paulo, Saraiva (2013). (in Portuguese)
16. Bernardo, L., Moriconi, M. Dados, conhecimento, acção: Melhorar o Acesso à Informação em Portugal. Transparência Internacional (2012). http://homepage.ufp.pt/lmbg/formacao/lvfinal.pdf (in Portuguese)
17. Andrade, F.P.: Comunicações electrónicas e direitos humanos: o perigo do "homo conectus" in Direitos Humanos e sua efetivação na era da Transnacionalidade, Debate Luso-Brasileiro, Juruá Editora, pp. 207–226 (2012). (in Portuguese)
18. Pereira, P.T.: Portugal: dívida pública e défice democrático Lisboa, Fundação Francisco Manuel dos Santos (2012). (in Portuguese)
19. Castells, M.: A galáxia da Internet: reflexões sobre a Internet, negócios e a sociedade. Jorge Zahar Edition, Rio de Janeiro (2003). Traduzido por. Maria Luiza, X.A.B. (in Portuguese)
20. Lassale, F.: Que é uma Constituição?. Edições e Publicações Brasil, São Paulo, Tradução de Walter Stönner (1933). (in Portuguese)

eKnowledge: ICTs in Learning and Education Management

Talent Management in e-Society: How Investments in Human Capital Work in the Community of World Class Programmers

Oksana Pavlova$^{(\boxtimes)}$ and Philip Kazin$^{(\boxtimes)}$

ITMO University, St. Petersburg, Russia
pavlova.ifmo@gmail.com, kazin@corp.ifmo.ru

Abstract. In this paper we describe how investments in human capital are managed in the quintessential e-Society type of community, namely among the students of programming in ITMO University (Russia) who are famous for the unprecedented achievement of 6 times absolute winning of the ACM Student International Collegiate Programming Contest Championship (ICPC) (The team of ITMO University became absolute champion of The ACM-ICPC in 2004, 2008, 2009, 2012, 2013, 2015. ACM ICPC is the oldest, largest, and most prestigious programming contest in the world and is sponsored by IBM. https://icpc.baylor.edu/). The three-stage process, described in the article, is the answer to the question of how to nurture the best programmers in the world. When reproduced exactly, this process can be applied to guarantee high quality education and research in any area of science, since the model of investments in human capital can work across different disciplines and create sustainable world-class creative environments in almost any area of science.

Keywords: e-Society · Human capital development · Change management · Computer science education · Olympiads in computer science · Advanced curriculum · Employability of ICT graduates

1 Introduction

Today, we face the inexorable rise of e-Society. This is a relatively recent phenomenon, created by ourselves and we are all simultaneously affected by its consequences. Every day we witness how more and more areas of personal and social life are influenced by information and communications technologies (ICT), usually positively, but not always exclusively so.

The students and departments of ITMO University are both archetypical representatives of e-Society, subject to it, as well as the creators and users of it. At the heart of the growth of the e-Society in Russia is the Information Technology and Programming Department at ITMO University, St Petersburg (hereinafter – IT&PD), which has become a magnet for world class programmers as a result of the Department's record

© Springer International Publishing AG 2016
A.V. Chugunov et al. (Eds.): DTGS 2016, CCIS 674, pp. 317–326, 2016.
DOI: 10.1007/978-3-319-49700-6_29

of winning the ACM ICPC. The University has graduated generations of top programmers who have become leaders in fashioning the direction and future of e-Society as they proceed to produce a lot of the new software and e-services which navigate our life.

The research question of this paper is how exactly human capital development (and investments in human capital) can be organized within the process of formal higher education to produce world-class programmers. Our hypothesis is that a three-stage process, embedded within a highly structured educational program, leads to significant changes in human capital development to produce a hard core of high-quality IT-specialists who impact on the development of the broader e-society.

This paper clarifies how the three-stage process operates: including how younger generations of programmers acquire motivation and effectiveness; how the programming labs work; what the social and psychological portrait of their community is; how this impacts on the context of e-society; which management and organizational instruments are employed by the leaders of the IT&PD to determine the positive outcomes of the study programs, including the role of the alumni association in maintaining and creating a professional community for programmers, and their networks, after graduation.

2   Theoretical Framework and Methodology

This article employs the theoretical framework of human capital; that is, the model introduced by Theodore Schultz in 'Investment in Human Capital: the Role of Education and of Research' [21]. Gary Becker, developed the microeconomic foundations of the human capital theory [2] and demonstrated that education and training are among the most important investments in human capital and pointed to the influence of positive and negative habits and allocation of time on human and intellectual development. His ideas essentially served as the basis for further development of the human capital theory by Jacob Mincer [23], Irving Fisher [9] and others.

All these works study human capital in the macro-economic context of the national economy. The notion of human capital also relates to problems of time allocation and its impact on the development of skills and abilities, leading to higher life outcomes such as education attainment, wages, employment and choice of occupation [8].

The focus of this paper is that we offer three-step human capital development process [18] which imparts continuing learning and guarantees long term development. The fundamental insights on the influence of human development on employees' qualifications were proposed in the works of Lester Thurow [24], John Stuart Mill [17] and in Fritz Machlup [16]. The empirical foundation of this research is based on the practical experience of the Computer Technologies Chair (CT) at IT&PD, ITMO University, Russia, which has been running the advanced education in programming and software engineering for more than 20 years. The paper presents the data of qualitative and quantitative research, which helps to gain an understanding of students' motivations, measure employability of the graduates of the above mentioned programs and generalize facts about the effective ways of training world class IT experts. The survey pool covered about 300 students of Bachelor and Master degree programs of CT Chair.

The article also draws on Russian research, such as the work of Sergei A. Dyatlov [7], A.I. Dobrinin [6], Leonid I. Abalkin [1], Rostislav I. Kapelyushnikov [12], Yuriy A. Korchagin [14], Sergei A. Ivanov [11]. Their work addresses to the training of graduates for professional careers in the field of science and innovation, continuing education for sustainable development and the role of higher education institutions in human resource development, individually and nationally. At national level, their work identifies which instruments in higher education contribute more effectively to the development of professional and entrepreneurial competencies in the context of the national economy. This article draws on the papers devoted to the research of advanced practice in university-based training [13], and university based mechanisms for developing the creative and collaborative potential of students [4], leading to the nurturing of elite specialists.

3   Investments in Human Capital

Since the development of human capital is based on inherent personal abilities and learning as a life-long process, we argue that human capital is created in three stages, which are equally important for the development of necessary professional and personal qualities and competences, relevant to the demands of the modern economy.

The three stages within the IT&PD at ITMO University:

We firstly identify the basic human development capacity of school students from competitions as a means of talent-spotting, develop initial skills and abilities and then recruit the most talented 'school-based' programmers.

Secondly, we stimulate the development of professional and social competencies, in particular enhance innovative capabilities through project-based learning.

Thirdly, we manage the direction of human capital development and nurture it through a career strategy and interaction with the alumni community. All these steps are closely connected with each other and mirror the rapid process of the emergence of new technologies, which require constant upskilling by professionals in the field. The following sections of this paper cover these three stages of human capital development in more detail.

3.1   The First Step - Pre-selection of Early Talent

The first stage of the human capital development is aimed to expose school students from different regions of Russia to the "Olympiads" managed by school teachers and universities and then involve students in studies of exact science as the "Olympiads" are the most important and effective instrument for identifying potential and developing early skills.

The "Olympiads" are youth competitions in Maths, Physics, Informatics and Programming and etc. The "Olympiads" are organized for school students regionally and nation-wide. They are designed to test students' ability to demonstrate maximum concentration, sense of purpose, knowledge and skills. Our University has adopted the European and US model of reviewing an individual's use of time - the notion of "quality time". Quality time is important for youth development. It is the time which is spent in the most productive way, ensuring that a person achieves the best possible and optimal results in the shortest of time. The "Olympiads" test and develop students' capacity of time employment in solving programming problems. So Olympiads contribute to positive youth development.

First of all, the "Olympiads" identify talented young people, who can take up advanced study programs. They also guide students towards selecting their future profession. The "Olympiads" contain an element of games as well. A wish to be a winner additionally motivates young people to prepare for the Olympiads carefully.

Preparation for the "Olympiads" takes a long time. This helps students to develop time management skills and self-discipline. Since the "Olympiads" use new technologies, they nurture taking the initiative and entrepreneurship, as well as the ability to be innovative. The "Olympiads" teach students to search and find information very quickly. The team section of the "Olympiads" also develops team-work in students by forcing them to work with others in a group.

They also stimulate the interest of high school students in learning Maths, Physics, Informatics and Programming. The rise in the popularity of these subjects is very important socially and economically, as recently we have been witnessing a fall in interest towards them among young people [10, 20]. The 'Olympiads' involve students in developing creativity, making them feel being closer to the world of Big Science. This way they can develop innovative skills, vision and prepare young people for working in the 'innovation economy'.

Many young people learn Maths, Physics or Programming as a hobby in their spare time, which means that they are very excited about developing their knowledge [3, 15]. This is evident from the results of our market research undertaken by the ITMO's Computer Technologies Chair into why students opt to enter the Olympiads Competition. The results are presented in Fig. 1.

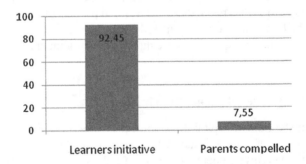

Fig. 1. Motivation structure of the students to participate in the Olympiads, (%)

The results demonstrate, that the majority of the contestants indicate personal interest as a key reason to participate. The majority of the young people participating in the "Olympiads" are doing so out of passion, which means that they are highly motivated, because they like what they do. In fact they invest in themselves, and such investments are most effective [5], being connected with self- realization.

We also see that many students take part in several "Olympiads". This proves that the game-type of motivation serves also as an instrument for bringing more and more students into studying STEM subjects (Science, Technology, Engineering and Mathematics) in general (see Table 1).

Table 1. Structure of prize winners of two and more student "Olympiads", afterwards entering Computer Technologies Chair of ITMO University

Types of Olympiads	2011	2012	2013	2014
Math+Informatics	21	6	16	17
Math+Physics	2	2	4	6
Physics+Informatics	1	-	4	5
Informatics+Informatics	1	-	1	1
Maths+Informatics+Physics	1	4	5	3
Maths+Maths+Informatics	-	-	-	1
Informatics+Physics+Russian	-	-	-	1
Total	26	12	30	34

So the first step of the human capital development focuses on revealing, developing, evaluating and selecting early talent. The University's recruitment strategy recognizes that key knowledge can be evident from the early years.

3.2 The Second Step – The Development of Human Capital at the Higher Education Institutions

The second step is the development and formation of high-quality human capital within the university so that students meet the requirements of modern economy. The main aim of this step is to train highly qualified specialists able to solve complex problems in different areas of economic activity. This aim can be achieved only with a help of innovative infrastructure of the university and specific learning environment.

Innovative infrastructure implies tight integration of science, industry, business and education, which plays a key role in training professionals, especially of interdisciplinary areas. In general, value of specialists (including graduates) is determined by the level of their professional competences and a set of useful innovative qualities which can only be achieved through training and hands-on practice in everyday usage of skills. Therefore, training is based on the practical development of knowledge – using and mastering. It is necessary to create such learning medium that is similar to real practical environment of acquiring knowledge, which helps to acquire and master skills and develop professional competences. For this purpose, the curriculum along with the core computer science subjects contains internships and R&D disciplines. Internships are carried out with leading Russian and international IT-companies which ensure the high quality of the relevant competencies' formation. Within R&D students are assigned special tasks, set in the form of mini-research projects, mostly experimental in nature and initiated in most cases by students and aimed at solving real (practical) problems via creation of new (unknown until then) results, new methods that require from learners to apply received knowledge, creative and innovative skills during the learning process, and form responsibility, independence, initiative and other necessary qualities of the "innovative person" [19]. At IT&P Department students carry out research & developments in the interdisciplinary fields such as machine learning and bioinformatics in the international research laboratories which were co-established with international partners at Computer Technology Chair.

The teachers have to have professional experience and a unique relevant knowledge in the field of information technologies (IT). IT practitioners are invited to teach. Such lectures are able to adapt the curricula, syllabuses and subjects to a rapidly-changing IT market. This allows to provide relevant training courses (subjects) and dissertation research. Such cooperation contributes to bridging the gap between the theoretical knowledge and practical area of its application as the contents of curricula are tightly related to the level of industry development. It ensures very close link between the University and IT business.

Another requirement that has to be met is intensive and advanced study program which produces highly qualified professionals, capable of dealing with complex, non-standard tasks. The high level of the learning process complexity is justified by: (a) demand for graduates both in Russia and in the USA or high-income European countries after graduation; (b) high salaries of the graduates [25].

Data from Fig. 2 confirm the effectiveness of the learning process:

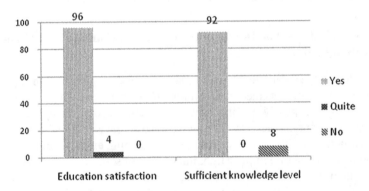

Fig. 2. Indicators of education satisfaction among MA graduate students (%), 2014

Our purpose in the context of e-Society is to create the so-called 'innovative individual'. Above mentioned approaches develop a set of essential features or characteristics for "innovative person", form high professional competences able to contribute to the development of high-tech companies and innovative technologies.

As it was mentioned earlier, e-Society essentially tends to standardize human behavior and thinking. It produces comfortable, quick and user-friendly services which are created by a tiny elite league of very smart people in order for all the rest to enjoy massive consumer society. "Innovative person" is not a typical e-Society consumer, but, on the contrary is an e-Society supplier, who always stands several steps ahead of the market needs. He/she produces ideas for the future and creates new markets. Step 2 of talent management in e-Society therefore teaches the students how to be the quickest in producing new ideas and solutions as the pace of intellectual competition in e-Society is extraordinary high.

3.3 The Third Step – Further Development of Human Cooperation with Companies

The third step - is the usage of human capital and its further development within the concept of "life-long learning". The dynamism of human creativity in e-Society, acceleration of social, economic, scientific and technological progress requires permanent improvement of acquired knowledge during the training. Continuous development and improvement of human capital can be achieved only with the help of scientific and innovative potential of the innovative companies, which can help to develop the continuous education system, including joint courses, trainings, conferences, research laboratories, alumni links and industry relations.

Young managers and leaders of innovative projects of different ICT companies come to the University to teach students. They possess cutting edge knowledge of the most recent developments in ICT industry and bring this knowledge to the classroom. Also the most talented graduates are offered to stay at university in order to work for international research laboratories and this way transfer knowledge and experience to the students. Partner companies often provide additional financial support to such teachers, who act in fact as 'entrepreneurs in residence'. These companies ensure their deep involvement in learning process and development of human capital of their further employees. As a result, a win-win situation for all is created: the university gets best teachers, highly involved in the current market agenda, students get best hands-on training, companies get knowledge and influence on educational process. An integrated system of strategic investments in talents and human capital is created, contributing both to the development of the companies, working in the target sector of the economy, as well as the university.

The graduates' wish to keep on working in IT sphere and a high rate of employability of graduates reflect the success of an integrated three-part system of human capital development. The data and interpretation of the results are presented below in Fig. 3.

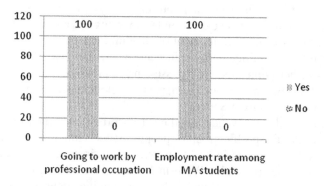

Fig. 3. Indicators of master students' employability (%), 2014

All students are sure that their education meets the needs of their future professional career, which means: (a) students made the right choice and like this kind of professional activity; (b) they will continue to develop and improve their knowledge of IT. Also, all the master degree program students have got permanent jobs before graduation from university. It implies that all the graduates within this specialty are in demand, they possess the qualities and competencies of innovative person and these qualities & competencies meet the requirements of e-Society. 100 % employment proves the high level of competitiveness of the study program and the high level of developed system of forming human capital with essential innovative qualities and professional competences.

According to the recent studies from Jena University, the European graduates from Germany and Poland are worried about their future employment and salary perspectives. They are not sure about their future [22]. In comparison, all the graduates of the Computer Technology Chair are 100 % employed by the date of their graduation, eager to continue the chosen profession (which means they are happy with it) and have salary of the level much higher than on average in the region [25]. This means that the above discussed three-step process of human capital development leads not only to high qualification, but also to well-being, social stability of the graduates and life satisfaction which is important for further development or "lifelong learning".

4   Conclusions

Our research results indicate that special attention to human capital development in the IT&PD has created a specific ecosystem that stimulates creativity and passion in achieving new kinds of employment-ready graduates. The heart and core of this ecosystem is the three-step process of development of human capital of the team:

1. Search for people with correct potential and develop it;
2. Introduction of effective contest-based education which develops human capital;
3. Launch of smart system of cooperation with former students when they enter the labor market.

Effective education is the heart and core of this system. It develops professional intellectual and creative competencies, stimulate mobility and adaptability, sparks motivation, which influences the development of such important individual characteristics as independence, responsibility, perseverance and positive life view. When like-minded people come together (simultaneously possessing impressive intellectual capital), an extremely fruitful environment for permanent development appears, which acts as "incubator" of innovation for e-Society.

Within our research we have identified most important instruments of management of human capital in this specific group of people. At the same time we argue that this management can be replicated in the other areas of business, research and education through clearly identified principles. While in the case of the ITMO Universities' IT&PD one of the key elements of this system are the programming contests ("Olympiads"), in the other areas similar competitions can be used for the same purpose of correct identification and selection of talents. After the selection, the process of quality education supported by permanent development of staff involved in research and teaching, creates the stable environment which reproduces and supports itself.

The tripartite process of human capital development is the answer to the question of how to bring up the best programmers in the world:

- accurately identify the talents;
- teach creatively and keep motivation strong;
- help students in career management.

These three processes, being reproduced correctly, can guarantee high quality education in many areas of economy (not only in IT). Since investments in human capital work this way in the community of world class programmers, who are the pioneers of newly established e-Society, it's worth adopting these experiences in developing effective talent management practices everywhere.

References

1. Abalkin, L.I.: Russian Strategic Response to the Challenge of the New Century. Exam, Moscow (2004). (in Russian)
2. Becker, G.S.: Human Capital: Theoretical and Empirical Analysis with Special Reference to Education. University of Chicago Press, New York (1993)
3. Benson, P.L., Scales, P.C., Hamilton, S.F., Sesma, A.J.: Positive Youth Development: Theory, Research, and Applications: Theoretical Models of Human Development. Wiley, Chichester (2007)
4. Bilyatdinova, A.Z., Karsakov, A.S., Bezgodov, A.A., Dukhanov, A.V.: Virtual environment for creative and collaborative learning. J. Knowl. Inf. Creativity Support Syst. **416**, 371–381 (2016)
5. Del Boca, D., Monfardini, C., Nicoletti, C.: Self-investments of Adolescents and Their Cognitive Development. NY University, New York (2014)
6. Dobrinin, A.I., Dyatlov, S.A., Tsarenova, E.D.: Human capital in transitive economy: formation, evaluation of effective usage. Science, Saint Petersburg (1999) (in Russian)
7. Dyatlov, S.A.: Fundamentals of Human Capital Theory. SPbUEF, Saint Petersburg (1994). (in Russian)
8. Fiorini, M., Keane, M.P.: How the allocation of children's time affects cognitive and non-cognitive development (2012) https://www.nuffield.ox.ac.uk/economics/papers/2012/FioriniKeaneOct2012.pdf
9. Fisher, I.: The Nature of Capital and Income. Cosimo Inc., New York (2006)
10. Gross, D.: In the nearest time there will not be Nobel Prize winners in the Russian Federation. In: Izvestia (2006) (in Russian). http://izvestia.ru/news/313734#ixzz43SFJXSiQ
11. Ivanov, S.A.: Human Capital in the Conditions of Restructuring of North-East Federal Region of the RF. SPbUUE, Saint Petersburg (2014). (in Russian)
12. Kapelyushnikov, R.I., Lukianova, A.L.: Transformation of Human Capital in Russian Society. Fund Liberal Mission, Moscow (2010). (in Russian)
13. Kartashova, A., Shirko, T., Khomenko, I., Naumova, L.: Educational activity of national research universities as a basis for integration of science, education and industry in regional research and educational complexes. J. Procedia Soc. Behav. Sci. **214**, 619–627 (2015)

14. Korchagin, Y.A.: Human capital as an intensive social and economical factor of development of personality, economy, society & state (2011) (in Russian). http://www.lerc.ru/?part=articles&art=3&page=35
15. Lerner, R.M.: Promoting positive youth development: theoretical and empirical bases. Technical report, Science of Adolescent Health and Development Workshop (2005)
16. Machlup, F.: The Economics of Information and Human Capital. Princeton University Press, Princeton (1984)
17. Mill, J.S.: The principles of political economy with some of their applications to social philosophy. The University of Adelaide Library (2014)
18. Pavlova, O.N.: Scientific & innovative potential of HEI in the context of human capital development of Russian economy. Dissertation, IRES RAS (2015). (in Russian)
19. Pavlova, O.N.: The role of Russian higher education institutions in modernization of the country's economy. J. Vestnik RAEN **20**(2), 56–62 (2016). (in Russian)
20. Prohorov, L.: Fundamental science – problems or crisis? J. New World **12**, 89–90 (1997). (in Russian)
21. Schultz, T.W.: Investment in Human Capital: The Role of Education and of Research. Free Press, New York (1971)
22. Silbereisen, R.K.: Dealing with uncertainties of life under threat of social and political change. Technical report, Positive Youth Development in the Context of the Global Recession Conference (2014)
23. Studies in Human Capital: Collected Essays of Jacob Mincer. Edward Elgar Publishing, Cambridge (1993)
24. Thurow, L.: Investment in Human Capital. Wadsworth, Belmont (1970)
25. Zarplatomer, Salary Measurer: Monthly review of salaries. Super Job **87**(03), 10–18 (2016). (in Russian)

Educational Activities in the E-learning Environment

Alexander Fedosov[✉]

Russian State Social University, Moscow, Russia
alex_fedosov@mail.ru

Abstract. The article considers the various aspects of the potential capacities of school and university E-learning environment for the organization of educational activities with students. The environment of the e-learning opens a number of new opportunities which are not only for the organization of a learning activity, but also for creation of the conditions for self-realization of the personality and socialization of the student.

Keywords: Educational activities · E-learning environment · Personal learning environment (PLE)

1 Introduction

The open educational process in it is based on others, than in traditional education, the organizational, technological, methodical principles, providing expansion and availability of education to various social groups, carrying out transition to the concept of continuous education [1, 3].

«The increasing availability of information and knowledge through technology is transforming education systems, expanding learning opportunities as well as generating demand for new skills. This is impacting on the type of competencies required of teachers, as their role is changing from that of "transmitter of knowledge" to "enabler of learning"» [7, p. 18].

Emergence of intellectual training technologies has allowed constructing such models of a learner, a process of training, a domain object in recent years which provide effective formation for each learner in an individual educational trajectory and training strategy.

However, through the specificity in the course of electronic education, also as well as, in the traditional forms of education, the main types of pedagogical activity are realized: teaching and educational work. Teaching is impossible without educational work, these are two sides of one process and the degree of efficiency depends on realization of their inter influence there it will be planned.

The success of the doctrine in many instances depends on formation of cognitive interest and the relation to the learning activity in general, in other words, on results of not only teaching, but also on the educational work. Besides, the integral components in content of education, regardless of its form along with the knowledge and abilities which a person seizes in the course of training and shows experience of creative activity

© Springer International Publishing AG 2016
A.V. Chugunov et al. (Eds.): DTGS 2016, CCIS 674, pp. 327–332, 2016.
DOI: 10.1007/978-3-319-49700-6_30

and the emotional and valuable relation to the world around (V.V. Kraevsky, I.J. Lerner, M.N. Skatkin). Without the unity of teaching and educational work, it isn't possible to realize these elements of education.

In this regard in the organizational problem of the educational environment and at realization of the e-learning with management of various types of activity of students for a purpose of solution some problems of their harmonious development is extremely actual and demands development of the corresponding methodology and applied techniques with implementation of a learning activity of a teacher in the e-learning.

2   The Possibilities of the E-learning Environment for the Solution the Student's Education Objectives

The main design objectives of the circumference of the e-learning in educational institution (particularly University) act as:

- Creation of conditions for development and the identity of a student, quality improvement of education due to development of educational motivation for a student, his educational and object competence in interacting process with personally focused components of the electronic environment in training;
- Ensuring effective use of educational process and administrative management of information the educational resources, including the distributed information of the Internet resources;
- Application on the base on the environment of the e-learning with new forms of information exchange of all subjects of the educational process.

Realization of various forms of the e-learning assumes participation of students in the network teaching community which considerably broadens the field of interaction and a joint activity of learners and teachers. A teacher can not only directly communicate with a learner, but he also can watch their activity in network and operate it. Thus, the components which are connected with a learner activity of network are added to traditional means of educational influence.

The e-learning, realizing modern pedagogical system, assumes obligatory independent activity of a learner on getting knowledge and formation of abilities. However ability of the learner to it is one of the results of training too. Therefore, any productive activity of the learner has to be planned by the teacher at the tactical or strategic level.

As a learner, obtaining knowledge and other information, builds the relations with the electronic educational environment and expands the personal learning environment (PLE), his control of the teacher continues before the management of development with the personal educational circle of the learner by means of information which influences the personal information circle of a teacher in the electronic educational environment [2]. Just in this positive effect of personal information circle of a teacher and new educational opportunities of the electronic educational environment are concluded.

According to it, the relations of students in collective can be also projected and coped in a positive aspect of information which exchanges their personal learning environments [6].

The environment of the e-learning can act as an intermediary for democratic character, friendliness, kindness, tolerance in relations between all participants of the educational process, make positive impact by the intellectual and cultural potential to create a favorable climate.

Thus, both the psychological aspect, and the educational function of electronic educational environment is expressed by formation of an interpersonal relations. Psychological compatibility of subjects in training is formed by joint in community-based efforts with cognitive and sociocultural interests, requirements, unity of moral and ethical values, on the basis of a joint activity. It is possible to speak about formation of the new educational field, uniting certain subjects of training at the e-learning platform.

3   Educational Functions of the E-learning Environment

Educational function of the e-learning environment is shown in the solution of the problems of skill formation and joint knowledge, communication skills for education, education of feeling of responsibility partnership, observance of moral ethical standards and rules of conduct in environment; a complex of legal and ethical knowledge, abilities, skills and the reflexive interaction with the information environment (information and legal culture) [5], in creation of conditions for civil formation and self-realization of the personality, in a solution of the problem of student socialization, in granting an opportunity to a student to show the civil conscious and social activity.

The realization of educational functions and the environment of the e-learning can promote:

– Use of electronic educational and methodical complexes on the disciplines, forming bases of ecological, legal and civil culture of students during unsociable hours and extracurricular activities;
– Application of methods of active training, in particular game methods;
– Use of educational potential disciplines of some professional block.

It is necessary to cancel an important component of a learning activity of a teacher who is carried out in the electronic educational environment – inclusion of students in a joint activity with surrounding society [4]. This work has to be carried out from the earliest age (perhaps within the work with a prospective student) to overcome practical problems and interaction with the social environment which they form the call of duty, responsibility, participation in affairs of the university and academic community, the city and the country.

One of the most perspective directions in realization of the developing and educational functions of the electronic educational environment is designing, in particular social design serves familiarizing the students with judgment and definition of social prospects, finding the solutions of existing social problems. Special value has a social design for their involvement in the sphere of social creativity, spiritual and civil education. The possibility of participation trained in teaching and educational projects on the basis of Internet resources of an ecological, civil and patriotic orientation, a volunteer movement promotes activation of their creative, research activity, designing of new knowledge, promotes more effective solution of education problems.

It raises possibilities of variability and individualization of a subject training process, in particular, of a choice by the student (at his desire and by means of the tutor) an individual educational trajectory [8].

Inclusion of the student in a joint activity with surrounding society promotes a solution of one more actual social task: "allows avoiding formation of subjective feeling of loneliness, rigidity, fear to be the rejected, low sense of value of active social contacts characteristic of the Internet addicted".

4   The Forms of Realization of Educational Activities in the E-learning Environment

In the environment the e-learning the solution of problems of education is possible in the following types of activity of learners:

- game activity;
- cognitive activity;
- problem and valuable communication;
- art creativity;
- social creativity;
- labor (operating) activity

Educational result of training activity is a direct spiritual and moral acquisition due to its participation in this or that kind of activity. Corresponding, educational effect of activity influences this or that spiritual and moral acquisition on development of the learner identity.

The most significant result to which educational achievement activity in the environment of the e-learning is directed to receive the independent public action by the student experience. Only in independent public action, action in open society (which includes the professional environment) a student really becomes a social figure, a citizen, a free person, lays the foundation of the professional formation. It is obvious that for achievement of this level of results the best part is that the special value of a student interaction of the social subjects not only inside, but also out of walls of university, in the open- public and professional environment.

Achievement of the given educational result increases probability of emergence of education effects and active socialization and vocational guidance of a student. A leaner can create communicative, ethical, social, civil competence, and also socio-cultural identity.

There will be given some possible achievements of educational results corresponding to types of activity of a learner (Table 1).

Table 1. Possible achievements of educational results corresponding to types of activity

Types of activity of a learner	Forms of achievement of educational results
Play activity	Modeling social games
Cognitive activity	Student's research projects, actions of a cognitive direction (remote student's conferences, intellectual marathons, etc.)
Axiological issues in communication	Axiological issues in discussion (webinar) with participation of external experts
Art creativity	Network art events (virtual exhibitions, competitions, flash mobs)
Social creativity	Social and educational network projects
Labor (operating) activity	Joint educational production of teachers and students within university science and technology parks, implementation of research projects and etc.

5   Future Work

Development and implementation of innovative forms of organization of activity of a learner in E-learning environment for the purpose of more effective implementation of its educational opportunities.

6   Conclusion

The environment of the e-learning opens a number of new opportunities which are not only for the organization of a learning activity, but also for formation of the interpersonal relations. In fact, the educational field uniting subjects of the educational process powered by the e-learning platform. Educational function of the environment of the e-learning is shown in the solution of problems in skills formation of joint knowledge, education of communicative skills, observance of complex and ethical standards and also rules of conduct in environment and in virtual space, abilities, skills and reflexive installations in interaction with the information environment.

The environment of the e-learning allows creating conditions for self-realization of the personality promotes the directed socialization of the student and it has opportunities for manifestation of civil and social activity.

Traditional forms of achievement the educational result are transformed in the environment of the e-learning, providing a student an experience of independent public action and the solution of a problem in effective professional formation.

References

1. Ally, M.: Foundations of educational theory for online learning. In: Anderson, T., Elloumi, F. (eds.) Theory and Practice of Online Learning. Athabasca University, Athabasca (2004). Creative Commons

2. Dabbagh, N., Kitsantas, A.: Personal learning environments, social media, and self-regulated learning: a natural formula for connecting formal and informal learning. Internet High. Educ. **15**(1), 3–8 (2012). doi:10.1016/j.iheduc.2011.06.002
3. Educational technology of distance learning: tutorial/E. Polat and others; under red. E. Polat. – M: Publishing Center «ACADEMIA» (2008)
4. Oztok, M., Zingaro, D., Makos, A., Brett, C., Hewitt, J.: Capitalizing on social presence: The relationship between social capital and social presence. Internet High. Educ. **26**, 19–24 (2015). doi:10.1016/j.iheduc.2015.04.002
5. Patricia, J., van Tryon, S., Bishop, M.J.: Theoretical foundations for enhancing social connectedness in online learning environments. Distance Educ. **30**(3), 291–315 (2009). doi: 10.1080/01587910903236312
6. Siragusa, L., Dixon, K.C., Dixon, R.: Designing quality e-learning environments in higher education. In: ICT: Providing Choices for Learners and Learning. Proceedings Ascilite Singapore 2007. Centre for Educational Development, Nanyang Technological University, Singapore, 2–5 December 2007. http://www.ascilite.org/conferences/singapore07/procs/
7. UNESCO's Medium-Term Strategy for 2014–2021. http://unesdoc.unesco.org/images/0022/002278/227860e.pdf
8. Vayndorf-Sysoeva, M.: Organization of virtual educational environment for preparing a teacher of new generation Athens 2013 VI International GUIDE Conference (2013). http://www.guideassociation.org/proceedings/Guide_2013_Atene

Organization of Group Classes Through an Automated System

Artem Mekhonoshin$^{(\boxtimes)}$, Anastasiia Denisova,
and Natalia Gorlushkina

ITMO University, Saint Petersburg, Russia
luckygnom@gmail.com, denisova.anastasiia@gmail.com,
nagor.spb@mail.ru

Abstract. As the title implies the article describes a way to solve a problem of automated assistance to a teacher that organize practical group classes in a higher education. It is spoken in a detail about developing automated system to help teachers in dividing students group into working subgroups. Proposed automated system should take into account student's level of concepts knowledge of studied subject as well as the personal characteristics of students.

Keywords: Expert systems · Group classes · Automated system · Education · Psychology tests · Knowledge bases · Data mining

1 Introduction

A lot of different automation technologies are widely used to improve the educational process in the recently times. Good examples of such technologies are different electronic materials, educational-methodical complexes, a big variety of computer training systems and others. However, itself they are not a sufficient condition for ensuring the effectiveness of the training: these technologies must be properly applied. Among the topical issues of automation of the educational process we can highlight following issues [1, 7, 16]:

- He determines how to maximize efficiency of the time available, he decides what is necessary to study in the classroom, and what students can learn themselves, he decides what material should be submitted the with the greatest clarity and a lot of other things of the same kind. In addition, it is necessary to allocate students with different abilities, to individualize the learning process. Ideally, we would like to achieve such process of organization where the initiator of the study and, at the same time, the performer would be a student and the teacher would perform as a counselor.
- With the introduction of competency-based approach the purpose of education has changed: now the main thing is not knowledge of the discipline material, it is an ability to apply this knowledge in real-life situations. The educational process must be built with the creation of the situations close to the real life situations and use information and communication technologies.

A.V. Chugunov et al. (Eds.): DTGS 2016, CCIS 674, pp. 333–343, 2016.
DOI: 10.1007/978-3-319-49700-6_31

- Changes in education objectives involves changing of the focusing of control measures that need to be adjusted and coordinated with competencies that should be formed by the graduates [8].
- Automation of the educational process involves an active position of students. Therefore, you must generate a positive motivation to training actions. Otherwise, there won't be any effect of automation.
- Another interesting problem is the difficulty of creating models of group work. The professional activity in almost all specialties requires teamwork and the ability to create a part of something that later becomes the unit of the whole.

List of considered problems, of course, is not exhaustive in such a complex process as the automation of the educational process, but allows us to define a number of interesting destinations, solutions of which are reviewed in this article.

Also we should take in consideration that one of the features of modern Russian education is the lack of practical application of the individual educational plan based on the student's personal features. Based on this, we have a problem associated with the lack of individual approach to each student. Whereas, if student will be applied to an individual approach, the assimilation of the material they will be much more effective. Almost all educational activities in a higher education are in the form of group sessions; individual work of the student is left under his responsibility and carried on their own during extracurricular time. Let's consider the most popular types of educational activities in higher education:

- Lecture - is a form of educational activity, where discipline's basic theory are studied;
- Along with the guide role of the teacher seminars require from a student intense individual work. Various options for solving practical problems are discussed at the seminars;
- Practical classes have a significant place in the student's preparation for professional work. A significant part of such classes is the solution of problems and doing exercises.
- The laboratory classes are held in specially equipped laboratories with equipment and instrumentation
- Consultations are held for answering the questions concerning the organization and methodology of students' individual work.

As part of our theme us we are primarily interested in practical and laboratory classes. One of the traditional ways of conducting such studies is to divide students group into small working subgroups, each of which carries some small task, usually with similar task compared to the other subgroups.

The goal of the study is to develop a prototype of an automated system that should take into account student's level of concepts knowledge of studied subject as well as the personal characteristics of students, which will improve such classes.

The hypothesis of the study is the assumption that the understanding of the personal characteristics of each individual student, as well as the accounting of these characteristics in the formation of working subgroups for the practical classes will help to increase the level of competences formation stated in the working program of discipline.

2 Theoretical Part

Transition to a competency educational model involves the development of student-centered learning, which should be constructed in such a way that students will feel themselves included in the learning process. It is necessary that students had internal motivation to be included in the learning process. It should be considered that the students do not always have internal motives related to learning content [5]. Their motives may have purely external nature, or be internal, but have little to do with an education. Formation of competency is impossible without active work of the student. However, usually the learning process is based on the activity of the teacher. This leads to a negative attitude to learning, students do not look for solution of the problem they are trying "customize" result to get the right answer. Formation of competency of students involves control system that is different from the existing. As has been said above, it is necessary to create competence-oriented tasks to control formation of the specific competences. Traditionally, control belongs to the teacher. However, there are quite a lot of educational studies which indicate that in the learning process, students should be able to form the ability to monitor and evaluate their own and their companion's activities, which should make a difference in the learning process. As a result, it is necessary to change educational process to satisfy the following conditions:

- Firstly, student right from the start should be a subject, not an object of educational process. He should seek solutions to problems, and the content of educational process should be done in a way where he has enough for this search, or for the implementation of his own, personally meaningful activities.
- Secondly, educational activity should have a real result that student can use in a future, possibly in his professional activities. Students should be confident in the usefulness of their results to have enough motivation to continue.
- Thirdly, he must have ways to be able to adequately assess the result of his own educational activities, to see what else he needs and to identify 'white' spots in his knowledge. It is also desirable to be able to compare his own results with results of his classmates, so he will be able to do a critical analysis of his achievements.

Based on the foregoing, it follows that the most effective way is the development of a certain type of practical education, in which students from the beginning will take a proactive stance to address the challenges. They should not only master the discipline related to the formation of a specific competencies, but also to be able to see the result in relation to their future specialty.

To understand what teacher exactly do at practical classes we made IDEF0 scheme of teacher's work structure from the information point of view (Fig. 1).

Usually, teachers implement such activities in the form of games. It allows students to hold positions (playing the role of) various specialists in their chosen profession, to see the holistic sense of the specific situations they play and their specialty as a whole. They are not afraid to make a mistake and this promotes experimentation and the development of a researcher position in their work. These considerations inspired the creation of an automated system to solve problems of organization of practical group classes with students [19].

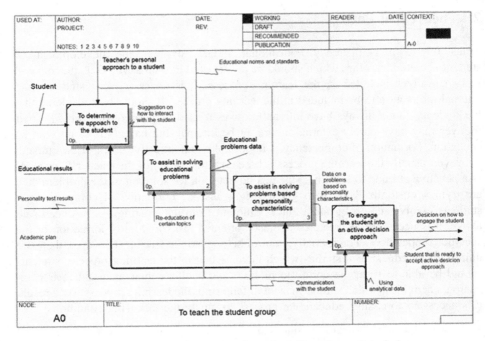

Fig. 1. Teacher's work structure from the information point of view

3 Practical Part

3.1 Scheme of the Automated System in Conducting Group Sessions

Within the framework of the given topic we are primarily interested in practical and laboratory classes. More precisely is when classes are held with a divide of a student's group into small groups, each of which carries some small task, usually kind of similar to a task of other subgroups. It is proposed an automated system to help teachers in conducting group practice sessions, which will take into account the personal characteristics of students. The system can be divided into four components (Fig. 2):

- Component of personality tests. Group work is largely complicated by the fact that people often have to interact with very different personality types, with different views on life and, therefore, work with different approaches to the work [15]. One of the most important features of practical classes in the various disciplines is the focus of these activities on the group work, with many of the problems that are simulating the process of working in the real working team.
- This component stores personality tests itself and everything related to them: the results of passed tests, the keys to decrypt the results and everything of this kind. With the help of personality tests each individual student's personal characteristics can be revealed for a teacher. Individualization of practical classes is achieved because we are able to know every student's personal characteristics [2].

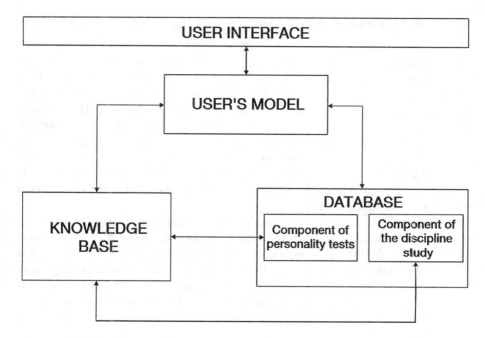

Fig. 2. Scheme of the automated system in conducting group sessions

- Component of the discipline study. This component stores all the information related to the discipline (theoretical material, exercises, etc.). First of all, it is the texts that give additional information about the knowledge received by the student on the lectures or help students recover in their mind the information received at the lectures. Secondly, it is the practical exercises for extracurricular work or work in the classroom. Third, it is materials for self-control and preparation for the exam or discipline test. Fourth, it is a variety of educational materials, tips for students which organize their work on the formation of the necessary competencies. For example, some sections of the text associated with the lectures that is worth repeating, or any additional references that should be studied.

  We can adjust student's way of learning discipline by using adaptive educational test. With the help of "question and answer system" related to the evaluation module, we can show to the student where his knowledge is insufficient, and give him a link to the information that he should learn himself in order to improve his knowledge on the subject. Student's extracurricular work thus associated with his individual characteristics, especially his knowledge. However, a problem arises when we speak about student's motivation to use an automated system.

- User's model. This component is a certain part of the system, which stores the results of a user's interaction with a component of discipline study and with a component of personality tests. User's model receives data from these two components and allows the system to interact differently with different users.

- Knowledge base [13]. Knowledge base provides the rules that are used to obtain the values of the characteristics affecting the model of the user. Knowledge base works both with component of the discipline and component of personality tests study [4, 9].

Work with the component of the discipline study is about giving advice to the student about weaknesses in his knowledge of the subject [11]. The way how knowledge base is working here is very simple [14]. After student passed tests on knowledge of the subject and done practical exercises, we have some values as a result. These figures reflect the level of student's knowledge of any part of passed theme or how well he knows the various topics of the subject as a whole [17]. Values are falling in various intervals, the system advises the student to repeat specific sections or the individual topics [20]. Due to this when preparing for the test that wasn't passed (or the next test) student is not required to repeat the whole array of information, but rather to focus on a particular material he knows badly.

Work with the component of personality study is about analyzing the results of personality tests passed by the student. In this case, the work of the knowledge base is similar to her work with the component of the discipline study [12]. Results of test passed by the student are falling to certain intervals of values. The knowledge base based on the chosen rule (rules described by the creators of these psychological tests) decrypts results into a human language and, as a result, the user gets information about his personality characteristic [3]. Further work of the knowledge base based on the mathematical model [6].

3.2 Mathematical Model for Creating Working Subgroups

Purpose of automated system is to establish several working groups roughly equal in their potential (understanding of the subject). This ensures that all groups will be in the same conditions: for all of them practical task will be equally difficult or easy [10]. Teamwork also involves the distribution of roles within the group, and this is the reason for the presence of a component of personality tests in a system. When calculating the value, which will affect the formation of the working group, mathematical model is required to take into account not only the criteria associated with the knowledge of certain concepts of discipline, but also personality characteristics of the students.

At first with using classification method mathematical model divides all students at three groups based on educational results: group with good educational results, group with decent results and group with worst results. Before using classification method we have an "ideal" example of a student – this is theoretical student that has excellent results after completing every test and exercise up to this point. Model is comparing "real" student to this "ideal" student and decides which group this "real" student deserves. It should be noted that different educational results could have different weights, for example, if student somehow has good knowledge of specific themes, but has bad knowledge of theoretical basics he still will be at group with worst results.

Second step is creating working subgroups from these three groups that mathematical model got after using classification method. Model should divide students into a subgroups with N members, and each one of them will have own role in subgroup. Every role has own requirements in terms of personality characteristics. For example, if we will talk about IT sphere: working group leader, programmer and designer all have different personality characteristics.

So the result of mathematical model work will be the value that will help to select a rule from the knowledge base on which the working subgroup will be formed to carry out practical exercises.

The main task of the practical classes is to prepare students for professional work and for better understanding the principles of operation of the staff. It seems that the most promising approach is an approach where every student will test himself in a various roles of working group. Working on whatever project involves determining ways of interaction among people working on this project, or ways of interaction between workers and the customer, which can be supported by a set of specific rules or tools. From this it follows that one of competencies that should be developed in consideration of the studying discipline is the ability to interact with customer or other people in your working group. Student should have negotiating skills and ability to anticipate the outcome of future activities considering project. He also should be able to choose the most appropriate technology for the project and be able to explain his choice. This means that system should be able to and will go through two steps every time teacher want to rotate members of a subgroups and every time teacher will do this, system will operate with new values since students will pass more tests and will do more practical exercises.

4 System at Work

For a better understanding of the system lets review the example of its work in organization of group classes of the discipline "information systems designing" that is being taught at the ITMO University. Goals and objectives of the discipline define content of the automated system, component of discipline study and lecture material. Information system designing process defines the structure of the classes, goals of the component of discipline study and formed competence. There are a lot of competencies and they described at official documents, some of them are: the graduate should be able to find creative solutions to social and professional problems; he should have the ability to develop new programs and system interfaces and to make the necessary technical documentation; he should be able the ability to participate in the development of intelligent systems architectures; he should have the ability to formulate the technical specifications, to design and use knowledge-based information systems; he should have willingness to apply the methods of options analysis, to develop and to search for compromise solution and other competencies.

The student after he starts to study "information systems designing" is being recorded in the automated system and passes personality tests, which determine his personality traits (Fig. 3). As required in the course of studying of the discipline each one of the students can study the materials available on the passed themes to pass adaptive learning tests. He receives advices from an automated system about materials that he should repeat, if he wants to deepen his knowledge in a particular subject.

In this way, system obtained the following data:

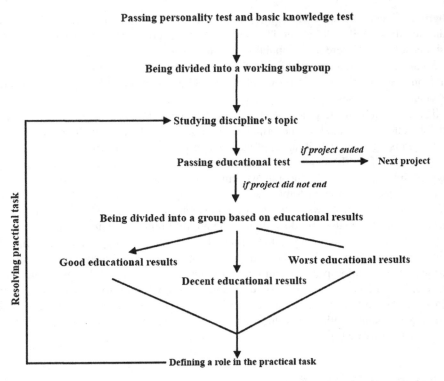

Fig. 3. Student's cycle in the system

1. personal information;
2. knowledge on the subject (knowledge of concepts);
3. student characteristics:

   - obtained characteristics - personality traits that have been gained through the personality tests;
   - output characteristics - learning outcome in different roles in the group.

These data values are used by the mathematical model to calculate the optimal distribution of students in sub-working groups, i.e. system advises teacher the best way to distribute the students. System also advises teacher what role he should give to each individual student as part of student's subgroup on the execution of practical tasks.

As a result of the passing of each topic, the system receives a new values of student's knowledge on the subject (based on the test results and practical tasks done by their subgroups) and student's characteristics (based on case studies of done by their subgroups). Because of this, after student passes each topic, the system updates her knowledge base regarding students. This leads, in theory, to a situation where each case study can be performed in different subgroups, if the optimal distribution of students, according to the results of studying the past topics, changed.

Another thing we should consider is how we want to build a development of the course discipline. "Information systems designing" discipline is being studied at seventh, eighth and ninth semesters. In the first semester students learn the basics of information systems design theory at lecture classes and doing the practical tasks at practice classes, corresponding to the first five stages of the information system design plan.

Stage 1. Formulation of the information system requirements. The following stages are highlighted at the initial stage of design:

1. examination of the object and need for the development of an information system;
2. the formation of user requirements for information system;
3. making final report and technical specifications report.

Stage 2. Development of the information system concept:

1. studying of the automation object;
2. carrying out the necessary research work;
3. developing an options for the concept of an information system that meet the users requirements;
4. making final report and concept approval.

Stage 3. Technical specifications report:

1. development and approval of the technical specifications report for the creation of information system.

Stage 4. Draft project:

1. development of preliminary design decisions of the information system and its parts;
2. development of conceptual documents of the information system and its parts.

Stage 5. Technical design:

1. development of design decisions of the information system and its parts;
2. development of documentation of the information system and its part;
3. development of the documentation of the supply of products;
4. development of the design tasks in adjacent parts of the project.

Practical tasks carried out at the level of documentation. However, the main idea is to work out the client-performer interaction through these classes. Students are divided into subgroups of 4-6 persons and do a study on the need for such development. After it, they write technical specifications report for the development of a particular type of information system that they studied. Technical specifications report prepared by one subgroup transferred to another, while other subgroup transfers her technical specifications report to the third subgroup and etc. A third part of a semester is given for this task, the other two thirds of the semester students prepare documentation according to technical specifications report they got from other subgroup [18].

5 Conclusion

System allows creating different working subgroups to perform each practical task, allowing each student to try himself in different roles. Also system allows teacher to not spend his time on the formation of subgroups. It is assumed that the correct usage of the system forms the approach to learning, in which the formation of competencies takes place by means of educational content, and use of the automated system. The result of working with the system is student's personal abilities that he can use to solve the real problems of everyday working life. Educational competencies that student gets during his education include components of his future functional literacy, but these competencies are not limited only to this purpose. It should be noted that the development of competence is a process that does not end because of its final formation. This process should not be interrupted during the entire life of a person, as the scope of his activities fall into new, more complex problems that require new approaches to solve them.

References

1. Abdalova, O.I., Isakov, O.J.: The use of e-learning technologies in educational process. Distance Virtual Learn. **12**, 50–58 (2014)
2. Arinina, G.A., Knyazev, A.M.: The Study of the Individual Within the Organization. RAGS, Moscow (2006)
3. Bruklich, A.: Expert Systems: Principles and Examples. Radio and Communications, Moscow (1987)
4. Dvoryankin, A.M., Kizim, A.V., Zhukov, I.G., Siplivaya, M.B.: Artificial Intelligence. Knowledge Bases and Expert Systems. The Ministry of Education of the Russian Federation, Volgograd State Technical University, Volgograd (2003)
5. Galanova, M.A.: Formation of is professional-subject position of the future teacher in the conditions of the information educational environment. Educ. Sci. **9**, 104–113 (2009)
6. Gavrilova, T.A., Chervinskaya, K.R.: Extraction and Structuring of Knowledge for Expert Systems. Radio and Communications, Moscow (1992)
7. Ilicheva, S.V.: Automation of educational process on discipline "Multimedia Technologies". Open Distance Educ. **2**(38), 42–47 (2010)
8. Khlopotov, M.V., Shishkin, A.R.: Diagnostic system of formation of professional competence of students specialty "Information technologies in education". Distance Virtual Learn. **2**, 59–69 (2010)
9. Kiryakova, G.S.: Knowledge Base and Expert Systems. Russian Federation Ministry of Education, Krasnoyarsk State Technical University, Krasnoyarsk (2002)
10. Kolesin, I.D.: Principles of Modeling of Social Self-organization. Lan, St. Petersburg (2013)
11. Kovalenko, V.E., Koltsov, N.E., Lobanov, Y.I., Remizov, E.A., Soloviev, A.V.: Knowledge bases for educational purposes, issue 2. Research Institute for Higher School, Moscow (1992)
12. Litvinenko, V.: Intelligent knowledge base systems. V. Litvinenko (2009)
13. Miconi, S.V.: Models and Knowledge Bases. The Ministry of Railways of the Russian Federation, Petersburg State University of Railways (LIIZhT), Saint-Petersburg (2000)
14. Nilsson, H.: Artificial Intelligence. Methods of Finding Solutions. Mir, Moscow (1973)
15. Pichot, P.: Psychological Testing, 16th edn., St. Petersburg (2003)

16. Polat, E.S., Buharkina, M.Y.: Modern Pedagogic and Information Technologies in the Educational Systems. Academy, Moscow (2007)
17. Pospelov, D.A.: Simulation Argument. Radio and Communication, Moscow (1989)
18. Rozanov, V.: Automation solutions of multi-criteria assessment of the results of productive activity of students. In: Abstracts of the Congress of Young Scientists, issue 3, p. 198. ITMO, St. Petersburg (2012)
19. Venkatesh, R., Naganathan, E.R., Uma Maheswari, N.: Intelligent tutoring system using hybrid expert system with speech model in neural networks. Int. J. Comput. Theory Eng. **2** (1) (2010), doi:10.7763/IJCTE.2010.V2.108
20. Solovyov, A.E.: Knowledge Base. Polytechnic Institute, Perm (1988)

Management of Collaboration Based on the Analysis of Social Structure

Evgeny Patarakin[1]([✉]), Roman Parfenov[1], Vasiliy Burov[2], and Igor Remorenko[2]

[1] WikiVote!, Moscow, Russia
{patarakin,parfenov}@wikivote.ru
[2] Moscow City University, Moscow, Russia
{burov,Rector}@mgpu.ru

Abstract. The paper presents a form of management and support for participants in socio-educational co-creative projects. The method is based on the use of the social network analysis. The results of the social network analysis, static and dynamic sociograms are used as materials that augment the narratives that we send to participants.

Keywords: E-governance · E-learning · Collaboration · Co-creation · Crowdsourcing · Agency · Learning analytics · GraphViz, R, NetLogo

1 Introduction

There is a need in contemporary society for citizens capable of acting as independent and self-sufficient agents under decentralized management. Contemporary education is intended to nurture citizens able to devise, create, use and share new products. Information and communication technologies support, facilitate and augment agent's activities. New economic models emphasize the importance of new knowledge, innovation, and the development of human capacity as the sources of sustainable economic growth. It is through education and human capacity development that individuals not only add value to the economy but contribute to the cultural legacy, participate in social discourse, improve the health of the family and community, conserve the natural environment, and increase their own agency and ability to continue to develop and contribute, creating a virtuous cycle of personal development and contribution.

2 Socio-educational Co-creative Projects

Governance and society needs co-creative projects with a final document as the end output of the collective activities. Education needs in a co-creative projects with a XXI skills as the learning outcomes of the collective activities. All these needs lead to the emergence of new type mixed projects socio-educational co-creative projects. Resulting from the data analysis of various spheres (science, legislation, economics, public activity, education etc.) the importance of collaborative productive activity determining

© Springer International Publishing AG 2016
A.V. Chugunov et al. (Eds.): DTGS 2016, CCIS 674, pp. 344–349, 2016.
DOI: 10.1007/978-3-319-49700-6_32

the dynamics of the modern society development emerges. The analysis of the previous research results in the sphere of computerization and society development allows to define the new strengthening social trend for integration of people via computer devices into network units for knowledge production.

We believe that socio-educational co-creative projects are not only productive environments but developmental environments also. As John Raven wrote "in developmental environments people can think about their organizations and their society and come to understand and perceive these institutions (and their operation) in new ways that have marked implications for their own behavior" [8].

We create collaborative environment for creation, improvement and promoting bills within public and legislative projects [2]. Enacting a new law means that a community devises out new rules which help it to become more efficient. In the general case, the web site contains a complete text of the document, which chapters and items were split in small segments. The project participants can create their own segment versions and vote for segments created by other participants. Public construction of a document aiming at complex cloud issues has high educational value. This collaborative practice helps not only produce a quality document and build a community of people interested in its implementation, but promote the innovative document, maintain a new level of its understanding and perception by the society. This allows not only to improve the efficiency of administrative processes, but also to receive educational and social outcomes as by-product. As John Dewey wrote « the measure of the worth of any social institution, economic, domestic, political, legal, religious, is its effect in enlarging and improving experience; yet this effect is not a part of its original motive, which is limited and more immediately practical » [4]. The learning design within the frame of the given concept structures not only the conditions for a separate learning agent activity within a limited time and space interval but also determines conditions for mid-term interrelation of the learning agents and the exchange of the activity products as well as the conditions for the development and long-term evolution of the whole collaborative activity system based on the selection of the most important objects.

We have successfully used this collaborative environment to support several socio-educational projects, where the number of participants was several thousand people. We organize collaborative work's massive projects, with the total number of members registered on the site edu.crowdexpert.ru of more than 90 thousand people. We regard this crowd of participants as a huge virtual team - group of geographically dispersed coworkers that are assembled using a combination of telecommunications and information technology.

3   Management of Collaboration

Virtual team needs ongoing scaffolding and management. One of the oldest methods of transmitting knowledge across people is storytelling. The role of narration and the meaning of the practice of narration for various fields of activity were stressed by J.S. Bruner [1]. We believe that storytelling can effectively allow teammate collaboration. Teams whose members receive a story have more similar team mental models than teams whose members do not receive a story [10]. Therefore, we weekly newsletter to all participants of the project the stories of what is happening in the project.

The point of the socio-educational co-creative projects is not only the created product of the project, but also the social structure itself. The value is in the creation process of this social structure during collaborative work and the formation history of this structure. Usually the social structure and the history of its formation are hidden for the participants. In best cases the subject for participants' discussion is the number of created objects and the number of comments and ratings. Meanwhile a social structure is a significant characteristic in many respects determining the success of collaboration. We believe that visualization of the social structure can support the process of group reflection.

Reflexivity is defined as "the extent to which group members overtly reflect upon the group's objectives, strategies, and processes, and adapt them to current or anticipated endogenous or environmental circumstances" [11]. M.A. West distinguished between task reflexivity and social reflexivity. In teams high in social reflexivity, team members often reflect and deal effectively with collaboration problems, and thus display a good quality of relationships and friendly attitudes. Social reflexivity is associated with the social functioning part of a team, deals with interpersonal relation, strengthens collaboration among team members, and therefore leads to better performance [3]. While various studies have found that social reflexivity has significant positive relationship with team outcomes [6, 9], little is known regarding the mechanisms underlying group social reflexivity in network collaborative projects. We start from the hypothesis that social reflection can be triggered by sociograms.

Learning analytics and diagrams methodology help to analyze and discuss situations that develop during a network collaboration in different domain. Analysts in this field have established Social Network Analysis (SNA) as an empirical method to study the ties between actors in the network. SNA uses various concepts to evaluate different network properties like centrality, connectivity, cliques, etc. The study of dynamic networks greatly benefits from visualizations that can illustrate ideas and concepts not immediately visible in a static sociogram. Moody and others' research illustrates the need to visualize how networks develop and change over time [7]. Among the tools developed in the complexity field, agent-based modeling and network analysis are very important in sustaining the process of bringing complexity to bear on the policy world. The combination of the two methods can increase enormously the potential of complexity-based policies [5]. Since agent-based modeling is inherently dynamic, the problems with static networks are overcome naturally. Agent-based modeling permits the desired richness of behaviors and attributes that might bridge the gap between agent-nodes and the real world.

The network environment in which the modern collaborative activity is carried out allows to follow the links which occur between the agents and objects of activity. As a rule modern socio-technical systems in which the collaborative activity is carried out, store the full history of all activities. In general terms, this history can be presented as a record of a chess or go game, consisting of many moves. Each move in the socio-educational project as a game contains three required elements:

Agent ID|Object ID|Type of an action (Writing, Editing, Voting)|

Every action of an agent towards an object leads to the formation of a link between them. If the agents perform action over one and the same object they become agents of the collaborative activity, indirectly linked with one another by the mutual object of activity. The collaborative activity network could be presented as the bipartite graph combining agents with objects of collaborative activity.

The projected system of the collaborative network activity gives extra possibilities not only for the productive activity but also for the analysis and reflection on the processes inside the system. Participants can use data analytics to monitor a network of relationships, which develops as a result of co-creation.

The tools should open the possibility to assess from the network point of view both the position of each participant and the degree of the whole system development as the learning network. The analysis of the activity of each participant inside the acting community allows to link the act of activity and the development of one participant with the development of the whole community. In order to investigate the links between the agents and the objects of the network activity within the framework of the given research special tools for visualization of links between the authors and the objects were developed which represent the relations between actors in the form of a network, the units of which are the pages and the participants creating these pages.

Usually the monitoring and the management are based on the analysis of the common quantitative data about the actions of the participants - including views, registrations, creation of objects, etc. Participant's actions on objects result in the formation of relationships and the formation of the social structure. In the frame of collaborative work the social structure matches with a social network. Social structure is a by-product of the collaborative work. At the same time the social structure affects the productivity of collaborative work.

There are a variety of software tools that has been developed to support analysis of network structures. In our work, we have chosen a tools that allows us to easily identify the stable patterns in the field of collaborative work, as well as to track and analyze the dynamics of sociograms, to select the participants among stable patterns for their targeted management.

Our first learning analytics application is based on Graphviz – open source graph visualization software. Graph visualization is a way of representing structural information as diagrams of abstract graphs and networks. The Graphviz layout programs take descriptions of graphs in a simple text language, and make diagrams in useful formats. The use of GraphViz diagrams allows to conduct express analysis of the position at the field of the collaborative network activity. With this application we have identified the typical configurations in the field of a collaborative work (single, paired figures, small groups, cliques, clusters, giant components, binder key players).

Our second learning analytics application is based on a collection of network analysis tools iGraph in R language environment. iGraph package provides a simple and flexible set of utilities for working with graphs and is a powerful tool for the study of graphs and their properties, the manipulation and visualization of graphs and the statistical analysis of networks. With this application we connected typical configurations in the field of a

collaborative work with indicators of network metrics (density, the number of components, indicators of centrality and clustering coefficients) and with planned results of a
collaborative work (studied and improved document, accumulated social capital).

Our third learning analytics application is based on Netlogo language – an effective
tool for modeling and can be successfully used by students and teachers for modeling
natural, social, and engineered complex systems [12]. The use of NetLogo allowed to
present the collaboration as a dynamic diagram in which each actor can interact with
each other tens of thousands of actors. The created model used NetLogo features such
as breeds and agentset. We have successfully used this application to support several
socio-educational projects, where the number of participants was several thousand
people. We have used various breeds of agents to separate the subjects and objects of
activity, as well as to separate the actors into different classes. Due to this we are able
to identify network characteristics that are typical for certain groups of actors. For
example, only for administrators, only for teachers of literature, only for employees of
a particular territorial office etc.

During research, we used the technique of dynamic agent-based sociograms to:

- Trace how and on what objects forming links between participants of collaborative
  production is based.
- Identify key players and stable biggest cliques, which serve as cores that support the
  operation of network communities.
- Analyze the effects of removal of the key players from the field of collaborative
  production.

With NetLogo model we have created the library of dynamic sociograms, each of which
presents the history of the development of a collaborative work in a particular project.
The library allows to compare the dynamics of the collaborative work projects from
different domains:

- Information environment of Education Management where organized crowdsourcing
  activities for discussions and improvement the local regulations of education. Participants vary by study subjects and geographical regions.
- Information environment of the company for crowdsourcing activities to improve
  internal regulations. Participants can create, evaluate and discuss proposals for
  improving the regulations. Participants vary by position and subordinations to territorial divisions.
- Information environment of the complex of schools that share Google Apps domain.
  Participants can create, view, and edit digital objects of various types. Participants
  vary by positions, teaching subjects and campuses they work in.

4   Conclusion

The methods presented in this paper are intended as a guide to the intuition when thinking
about socio-educational co-creative projects. As the experience of the projects
presented, the partial transfer of control from the organizers to the participants of the

activity helps to nurture productive agency of the participants. As a result participants use open learning analytic data to improve their collective behavior.

The received results of our research can be used for project management collaborative network development; management of network communities, in case the organization's activity is focused on the creation and improvement of user-generated content development; management of organization, in case the organization is associated with the creation and improvement of its internal documents.

References

1. Bruner, J.S.: Actual Minds, Possible Worlds. Harvard University Press, Cambridge (2009)
2. Burov, V. et al.: A crowdsourcing model for public consultations on draft laws. In: Proceedings of the 6th International Conference on Theory and Practice of Electronic Governance, pp. 450–451. ACM, New York (2012)
3. Carter, S.M., West, M.A.: Reflexivity, effectiveness, and mental health in BBC-TV production teams. Small Group Res. **29**(5), 583–601 (1998)
4. Dewey, J.: Democracy and Education. Paradigm Publishing, Boulder (2014)
5. Fontana, M., Terna, P.: From agent-based models to network analysis (and return): the policy-making perspective. University of Turin (2015)
6. Gurtner, A., et al.: Getting groups to develop good strategies: effects of reflexivity interventions on team process, team performance, and shared mental models. Organ. Behav. Hum. Decis. Process. **102**(2), 127–142 (2007)
7. Moody, J. et al.: Dynamic Network Visualization (2005)
8. Raven, J., Stephenson, J. (eds.): Competence in the Learning Society. Peter Lang International Academic Publishers, New York (2001)
9. Schippers, M.C., et al.: Reflexivity in teams: a measure and correlates. Appl. Psychol. **56**(2), 189–211 (2007)
10. Tesler, R.: The Effects of Storytelling and Reflexivity on Team Mental Models and Performance in Distributed Decision-Making Teams (2010)
11. West, M.A.: Reflexivity and work group effectiveness: a conceptual integration. In: West, M.A. (ed.) Handbook of work group psychology, pp. 555–579. Wiley, Chichester (1996)
12. Wilensky, U., Rand, W.: An Introduction to Agent-Based Modeling: Modeling Natural, Social, and Engineered Complex Systems with NetLogo. MIT Press, New York (2015)

The Study Approaches for Dissemination of Research Results in the Information Society

Dmitry Prokudin[1,2(✉)], Irina Mbogo[1,2], Lyudmila Murgulets[1], and Marina Kudryavtseva[1,2]

[1] ITMO University, Saint Petersburg, Russia
hogben.young@gmail.com, Irina.Mbogo@gmail.com,
ludmila@murgulets.ru, mvkudriavtceva@corp.ifmo.ru
[2] Saint Petersburg State University, Saint Petersburg, Russia

Abstract. This paper presents the results of the study of current trends in the quick dissemination of scientific research results based on the application of information society technologies. The paper demonstrates approaches enabling automatic integration of scientific metadata into different information systems. It also demonstrates an optimal solution for the dissemination of interdisciplinary research results published as proceedings of an annual scientific conference. Specific features of metadata dissemination in diverse information systems have been studied. An approach is presented for the optimization and automation of metadata preparation and for their presentation into diverse information systems that do not support automatic metadata exchange.

Keywords: Dissemination of scientific knowledge · Open access · Repositories · Metadata · Heterogeneous information systems

1 Current Trends of Dissemination and Popularization of Scientific Knowledge

Evolution of the information society has stimulated the creation of new initiatives in the field of scientific research based on the extensive use of information and communication technologies. The most prominent among these are the Open Archives Initiative and Open Access Initiative. They are created in accordance with the Open Science paradigm [6, 22, 24, 27, 29] and play an important role in the dissemination and popularization of scientific knowledge by recommending scientific organizations to do the following:

- to assume responsibility for archiving all their research results and requiring their staff to place electronic copies of all their published articles into open access online archives;
- to encourage their staff to publish their articles in open access scientific journals, if such journals are available, and to provide them support in such publications [26, 41].

Open access scientific journals have been created in the framework of these initiatives. These journals are essentially web-sites for the publication of scientific articles in digital form (PDF is the most popular format there). In this way, information

A.V. Chugunov et al. (Eds.): DTGS 2016, CCIS 674, pp. 350–362, 2016.
DOI: 10.1007/978-3-319-49700-6_33

becomes accessible for an unlimited audience of Internet users immediately after appearance of the corresponding journal issue, which makes research results instantly accessible. Benefits include publishers of traditional scientific journals starting to issue their versions online; on the other hand, online scientific journals appear which have no printed version. And finally, others lessen publishing costs and engage in a shorter publishing cycle [8, 22, 32, 38, 43].

There are also many other types of information systems intended for the accumulation of scientific research results and provision of free access to this information, where authors can publish their information if they want to (for example, https://www. Academia.edu, http://ORCID.org, https://www.ResearchGate.net).

Scientific research, however, is conducted not only within individual scientific institutions. Joint research initiatives are often conducted by teams of researchers from different organizations. Interdisciplinary and transdisciplinary research, which reflect the modern trends toward investigating at the interface of different sciences, are especially often conducted as joint research. [15, 31, 33, 36, 39, 40].

Furthermore, results of such research are disseminated usually through the framework of scientific conferences – through speeches at meetings and in 'collected works' publications. Research results reflected in collections of conference proceedings are spread mainly in the following ways:

- in open repositories of organizations;
- on web-sites of scientific conferences.

Such publications are usually made in the form of a single file without publishing metadata for each article, which hampers both search by article and further spreading of information into external information systems. Open repositories of organizations are confined to these organizations, so when it comes to the results of interdisciplinary studies, only those articles will be presented there which are placed there immediately by their authors. In some cases, however, materials are placed into repositories by articles as, for example, in the open repository of ITMO University (http://openbooks. ifmo.ru/ru/collections/).

2 Goals, Objectives, Methodology

The goal of our study had been defined as a result of reviewing current trends of dissemination of scientific research results. It is the identification of technical solutions that provide the most efficient, automatic and quick dissemination of scientific research results presented in collections of articles or conference proceedings.

The objectives of our study were:

- substantiation of the selection of a software platform for placement of proceedings of the scientific conference "Internet and the Modern Society" (IMS) for automated metadata exchange with external information systems;
- development of an approach for the most efficient integration of metadata of conference proceedings into diverse information systems that do not support automatic metadata exchange.

The main current approaches and trends of dissemination of scientific research results, as they are described in modern studies, have been reviewed in order to achieve these objectives. We have analyzed open registers of repositories of scientific information and the most popular free software platforms used for the construction of open repositories. Software for the creation of a core of a scientific research information space for the presentation of conference proceedings has been selected using criteria developed by us. We have also developed tools for the most effective automation of the integration of conference proceedings metadata into systems that do not support automated metadata exchange.

3   The Study Technologies of Information Society for Dissemination of Scientific Research Results

Scientific research results are mainly disseminated in the information society on the basis of the Open Access initiative [35]. This initiative is realized through different information technologies:

- Gold Route – publication of articles in open access scientific journals;
- Green Route – placement or self-archiving of scientific research results in open institution or field-oriented repositories or archives;
- Grey Route – utilization of different information technologies for getting access to so-called "grey" literature published in non-conventional ways.

The Gold Route does not ensure quick dissemination of scientific information because reviewing, editing, and proofreading processes take a lot of time. In addition to this, this procedure often requires essential costs for publication of collections by commercial publishers.

The Grey Route allows the spread of separate materials in isolated information systems, which creates fragmented presentation of research results in particular fields.

The Green Route is therefore considered to be the most effective dissemination route, which is confirmed by many studies [2, 7, 9, 13, 21, 23, 30]. In this approach, scientific conference proceedings are methodically placed in information systems of respective scientific societies and can be then quickly disseminated in the digital information space only if these processes are automated. Therefore, the use of Web 2.0 elements as scientific social networks (for example, Academia.edu, ResearchGate) [19, 42] and the personal pages of researchers [16] are not studied in our work because those are mainly used for the communication and organization of collective scientific activities [3, 34].

Main processes in this field include:

- initial creation of a scientific text in the digital form with respective metadata;
- placement of a collection of articles or conference proceedings as of a set of individual articles into a local information system of a scientific community (organization, conference, etc.);
- translation of collection metadata into external information systems.

Usually for the accumulation of information in local information systems, technologies of construction of open electronic repositories are applied. A technological solution for construction of such a repository must include automation of placing information into it, as well as of translation of metadata into external information systems.

Subject/discipline specific repositories designed to support investigations in particular scientific fields [5, 37] are mainly designed for direct placement of scientific texts by their authors. Such repositories include, for example, arXiv (http://xstructure. inr.ac.ru/) that contain scientific papers in the fields of mathematics, physics, astronomy, computer science, quantitative biology, statistics, and quantitative finance. As a result of this, such repositories usually lack automation means which enable the exchange of metadata with other information systems.

There is a wide range of open source software applicable for construction of open repositories [4]. We used the most comprehensive registers of open repositories – Directory of Open Access Repositories (OpenDOAR) (http://www.opendoar.org) and Registry of Open Access Repositories (ROAR) (http://roar.eprints.org) – in order to analyze trends in using this software.

OpenDOAR was established in 2006 (hosted by University of Nottingham, UK). It contains presently more than 3000 records. ROAR was established in 2000 (hosted by the School of Electronics and Computer Science at the University of Southampton). It contains presently more than 4000 records.

Both directories allow independent introduction of information in repositories by their owners (organizations, scientific societies, etc.), but despite this, these resources adequately reflect trends in development of open repositories.

Using a sampling analysis of both directories, we acquired data on distribution of repositories by the type of software (Tables 1 and 2). Main software platforms for construction of open access repositories are Dspace and ePrints, which present 57.15% according to OpenDOAR data and 53.63% according to ROAR data of the total number of repositories (Figs. 1 and 2). This trend is characteristic both for USA (28.63% according to OpenDOAR data and 27.81% according to ROAR data), which hosts more repositories than any other country, and for Russia (79.17% according to OpenDOAR data and 48.28% according to ROAR data). Software solutions include unidentified solutions, which are probably heterogeneous software solutions:

- according to OpenDOAR data – 9.12% of all repositories, 18.53% of USA repositories and 4.17% of Russia repositories;

Table 1. Use of the Dspace and ePrints software platforms for construction of open repositories according to OpenDOAR data (March, 2016).

Software	All countries	Russia	U.S.A.
Dspace	1326	17	112
ePrints	416	2	24
Not specified	278	1	88
Any software	3048	24	475

Table 2. Use of the Dspace and ePrints software platforms for construction of open repositories according to ROAR data (March, 2016).

Software	All countries	Russia	U.S.A.
Dspace	1652	22	151
ePrints	592	6	62
Other software (various)	531	22	70
Any software	4184	58	766

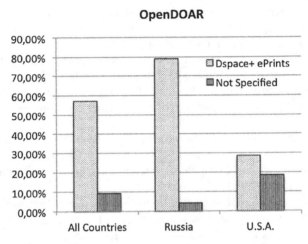

Fig. 1. The share of repositories using Dspace and ePrints of the total number of repositories according to OpenDOAR data (March, 2016).

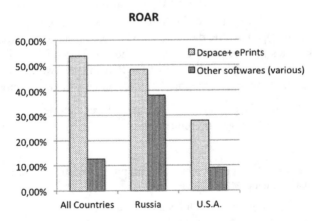

Fig. 2. The share of repositories using Dspace and ePrints of the total number of repositories according to ROAR data (March, 2016).

- according to ROAR data – 12.69% of all repositories, 9.14% of USA repositories and 37.93% of Russia repositories.

Then we analyzed only repositories working on the Dspace and ePrints platforms. The share of repositories of organizations in the total number of repositories functioning on these platforms constituted (Tables 3 and 4):

Table 3. Use of the Dspace and ePrints software platforms for construction of open repositories of organizations according to OpenDOAR data (March, 2016).

Countries	All repositories	Repositories of organizations
All countries	1742	1590
Russia	19	19
U.S.A.	136	115

Table 4. Use of the Dspace and ePrints software platforms for construction of open repositories of organizations according to ROAR data (March, 2016).

Countries	All repositories	Repositories of organizations
All countries	2244	1693
Russia	28	22
U.S.A.	213	148

- according to OpenDOAR data - 91% for all countries, 85% for USA repositories, and 100% for Russia repositories;
- according to ROAR data - 75% for all countries, 69% for USA repositories, and 79% for Russia repositories.

These data demonstrate that overwhelming majority of repositories of organizations use software platforms based on Dspace and ePrints (Figs. 3 and 4). These trends are characteristic for Russia as well.

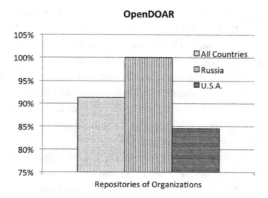

Fig. 3. The share of repositories of organizations in the total number of open repositories using Dspace and ePrints according to OpenDOAR data (March, 2016).

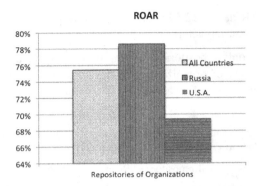

Fig. 4. The share of repositories of organizations in the total number of open repositories using Dspace and ePrints according to ROAR data (March, 2016).

These systems implement support for the OAI-PMH protocol at both the harvester level (automated acquisition of metadata from other information systems) and the provider level, which allows transfer of publication metadata into different external aggregators and repositories.

Dspace was designed for the organization of electronic libraries and is presently used mainly for the creation of different institutional repositories of diverse documents. The ePrints platform was originated in the Scholarly Communication movement and is therefore designed for the placement of scientific articles. The ePrints system has much in common with Dspace, but it is optimized for independent introduction (placement) of data(articles, reports, books, etc.) by their authors, while the Dspace system is intended for long term storage of digital data used in scholarly investigations [17, 25]. These systems, however, are not intended for fast publication of scientific research results in the form of a collection of articles and conference proceedings, so they poorly serve the complex task of fast publication of scientific research results and their automatic dissemination.

The analysis has shown that some repositories are created using the free Open Journal Systems (OJS) software: 4 repositories according to OpenDOAR data and 25 repositories according to ROAR data. OJS is an open source and free software.

In addition to realization of the OAI-PMH data exchange protocol at the provider level as it is done in Dspace and ePrints, OJS includes other means of automation of information exchange with external systems, such as an XML format article import & export module, which supports the import of native.dtd documents. It also supports the root nodes <article>, <articles>, <issue>, and <issues>, which allows the integration of imported metadata into relevant aggregators, as well as the importing of articles and whole issues from other systems that support the native.dtd metadata model (including from other information systems supporting OJS).

Unlike other systems, the OJS system is designed to support electronic versions of periodicals and issuing electronic journals. As the collections of conference proceedings have the same structure as periodicals, it is very reasonable to choose this software platform for the placement of scientific research results and their quick dissemination through automatic metadata exchange with external information systems using the OAI-PMH protocol.

4 Practical Application of the Study Results for Formation of the Integrated Information Space for Interdisciplinary Investigations

This study investigates and is designed for the scientific community of researchers, being formed currently in Russia, who work in the field of Information Society Technologies. This field includes such topics as: development of interdisciplinary investigations of information technologies, electronic libraries, methods and technologies of integration of electronic collections; interaction of information resources and formation of the information space of electronic documents of scientific research and innovations.

Communication and consolidation of the researchers is taking place (from 1998) in the framework of the annual joint scientific conference IMS, where they present their research results. Before 2014, the conference proceedings had been placed on several Internet resources. In 2014, it was decided to create an integrated information space for support to the interdisciplinary field of investigating information society technologies. The following principles were used in the concept of this space:

- support to organization and conduct of the annual conference IMS;
- automation of the presentation of scientific data of conference participants for their subsequent integration within the information space;
- accumulation of conference proceedings;
- dissemination and popularization of conference proceedings that reflect the results of essential research.

The following components have been developed and implemented within this process:

1. An information site of the scientific conference IMS (http://ims.ifmo.ru). A software and hardware platform has been developed in ITMO University. The system includes a mechanism for filing applications for participation in the conference and for loading manuscripts of articles and theses. This solution is integrated with the Management Information System (MIS) of ITMO University, which ensures display of applications and subsequent publications of ITMO staff members in their corporative profiles, which are then considered as a part of their scientific results.
2. An information space "Information Society Technology" (http://ojs.ifmo.ru), where proceedings of the conference IMS are placed (http://ojs.ifmo.ru/index.php/IMS). The Open Journal Systems (OJS) software platform was selected for this component. This choice is based on the investigation results presented in this study.

Proceedings of the conferences from 2011 to 2014 have been introduced into the OJS system manually. Integration of the OJS system with external aggregators has been performed at the of OAI-PMH protocol: OAIster (http://www.worldcat.org/search?q=on:DGCNT+http://ojs.ifmo.ru/index.php/index/oai+IMS+RUITM&qt=results_page)

and the Socionet information system (https://socionet.ru/collection.xml?h=repec:rus:ims000), which possesses semantic capabilities [28]. The system was registered in the Google Academy, so that articles from the collections are indexed also there.

Starting from 2015, ITMO University requires its staff members to place their publications into the ITMO open publication database (repository) (http://www.openbooks.ifmo.ru), which is in full accordance with the ideas of the Open Archive Initiative. Therefore, the three collections of scientific articles resulting from the 2015 conference have been introduced into this information system. In this process, the metadata table proposed by software platform developers of the ITMO University open repository has been filled manually. Information on article collections contained in the repository does not allow automation of the transfer of article metadata into external aggregators and other information systems.

In order to automatize metadata introduction into the OJS system, XML files of the corresponding format were created in cooperation with the ITMO University information technology service as a result of export from the ITMO open repository database. However, not all tags of these files were identified properly during the import into OJS (with the use of the standard XML format import module), which demanded additional manual work.

Placement of metadata of scientific publications in the unified scientometric database "Russian Science Citation Index" (RSCI), which is functioning on the platform of the Electronic Scientific Library (ESL), is an important element of informational support to scientific investigations and of the evaluation of the publication activity of scientists and researchers in Russia. The online tool "Articulus" has been used for introduction of metadata of articles and collections into ESL (http://elibrary.ru) with manual filling corresponding database fields. Automation in this process included only drag-and-drop and copy-past mechanisms.

The authors also plan to perform scientometric research aimed at the evaluation of their approach to the quick dissemination of scientific research data on the basis of the created information system containing interdisciplinary research results and using the latest trends in scientometric research [1, 8, 12, 14, 18, 20].

5   Development of Approaches for Automation of Scientific Information Integration into Heterogeneous Information Systems

During formation of the integrated information space, the researchers and developers encountered the problem of extensive manual work for metadata input during the presentation of scientific data for the conference, as well as during their introduction into the open repository of the ITMO University and into the Electronic Scientific Library. In addition to this, duplicate manual work was required from authors of articles to accompany manuscripts of their articles or theses: first filling a metadata form according to the template created by conference organizers, and then filling an extended metadata form for placement into external information systems, such as Electronic Scientific Library.

Due to these problems, the task was set to develop tools which enable obtaining all the required information from authors at the stage of filing their application and article (theses) manuscripts. So that this information will be the only source used for publication of conference proceedings collections, as well as for their placement in external information systems that do not support metadata acquisition through the OAI-PMH protocol.

Furthermore it is necessary to develop software for the package processing of article metadata and recording it in electronic formats for the subsequent import in diverse external information systems that do not support automatic metadata exchange processes.

To complete this task, a template in the form of a text file with support for MS Word macros (.docm extension) was created. The template consists of two sections: a formatted article and a table with a full set of metadata. The template includes a style set for uniform article formatting and subsequent preparation for publication. An article includes the following basic set of metadata in Russian and English: article title, authors' surnames, initials of authors' first and middle names, authors' affiliation, e-mail addresses, summary, keywords, and reference list.

Metadata in the table are of the three following types:

- data copied from the article body (with the use of a macros);
- data filled manually by the author;
- data filled by conference organizers (for example, a reference to the article electronic copy placed in the open repository of the ITMO University).

Further, it is planned to develop an application for package processing of all files with metadata in the HTML format saved in a specified folder. In addition to article metadata processing, this application will allow manual entering of the information about collections of scientific articles that will be available only after their publication – metadata and publisher's imprint. The data processing will form several files for metadata placement into diverse information systems (the open repository of ITMO University, the electronic archive of the conference IMS, and the Electronic Scientific Library).

It shall be mentioned that references to full texts of articles are entered into the table only after their placement in the open repository of ITMO University.

6   Conclusions

The following conclusions can be made on the basis of this research:

- the Green Route is among major approaches to quick dissemination of scientific research results, and the main technology of this approach is utilization of open repositories of scientific data;
- open source and free software with automatic metadata exchange with the use of the OAI-PMH protocol (Dspace, ePrints) is mainly used for construction of the (chiefly institutional) repositories;
- another software used for construction of open repositories is Open Journal Systems (OJS);

- for creation of an open topical repository of a scientific community that presents its results in proceedings of an annual conference, an Open Journal Systems (OJS) software platform was chosen, which is substantiated by the following arguments:
- the proceedings collections of the conference IMS have the same structure as issues of scientific periodicals (journals);
- OJS supports automatic metadata exchange with external information systems using the OAI-PMH protocol;
- the system includes modules of export/import of metadata into the general XML format, as well as for their presentation to popular aggregators that do not support automation.

During the research, it has been found out that there are information systems that do not support automatic metadata exchange. Preparation of metadata in some specified formats with their subsequent manual uploading into corresponding information systems is necessary. The main systems analyzed are the ITMO University open repository and Electronic Scientific Library. An effective approach is proposed in order to reduce manual work and optimize metadata preparation for their placement into diverse information systems. In the framework of this approach, it is further planned to develop an application for package processing of templates with article metadata and file formatting for importing this metadata into diverse external information systems that do not support automatic metadata exchange.

References

1. Aguillo, I.F.: Open Science, Metrics 2.0 and their impact at individual level (2015). http://hdl.handle.net/10261/131489
2. Dhiman, A.K., Sharma, H.: Accessing scholarly information in networked environment through institutional repositories. Pak. J. Inf. Manage. Libr. **9**, 97–111 (2008). http://journals.pu.edu.pk/journals/index.php/pjiml/article/viewFile/814/449
3. Ashraf, K., Haneefa, M.: Scholarly use of social media. Ann. Libr. Inf. Stud. **63**(27), 132–139 (2016). http://op.niscair.res.in/index.php/ALIS/article/view/12451
4. Bankier, J.G., Gleason, K.: Institutional Repository Software Comparison (2014). http://works.bepress.com/jean_gabriel_bankier/22/
5. Björk, B.C.: Open access subject repositories: an overview. J. Assoc. Inf. Sci. Technol. **65**, 698–706 (2014). doi:10.1002/asi.23021
6. Burgelman, J.C., Luber, S., von Schomberg, R., Lusoli, W.: Open science: public consultation on Science 2.0: Science in transition. Key results, insights and possible follow up (2015). http://www.science20-conference.eu/wp-content/uploads/2015/04/01_Jean-Claude_Burgelman_-_Open_Science__outcome_of_the_public_consultation_on__Science-20_science_in_transition.pdf
7. Calderón-Martínez, A., Ruiz-Conde, E.: Leading emerging markets: capturing and diffusing scientific knowledge through research-oriented repositories. Scientometrics **104**(3), 907–930 (2015). doi:10.1007/s11192-015-1603-9

8. DeSordi, J.O., Conejero, M.A., Meireles, M.: Bibliometric indicators in the context of regional repositories: proposing the D-index. Scientometrics **107**(1), 235–258 (2016). doi:10.1007/s11192-016-1873-x

9. Ferreras-Fernández, T., García-Peñalvo, F.J., Merlo-Vega, J.A.: Open access repositories as channel of publication scientific grey literature. In: Proceedings of the 3rd International Conference on Technological Ecosystems for Enhancing Multiculturality - TEEM 2015, pp. 419–426. ACM Press, New York (2015). doi:10.1145/2808580.2808643

10. Fisher, J.H.: Scholarly publishing re-invented: real costs and real freedoms. J. Electron. Publishing **11**(2) (2008). doi:10.3998/3336451.0011.204

11. Friesike, S., Widenmayer, B., Gassmann, O.: Opening science: towards an agenda of open science in academia and industry. J Technol. Trans. **40**, 581–601 (2015). doi:10.1007/s10961-014-9375-6

12. Gorraiz, J.: Individual Bibliometric Assessment @ University of Vienna: From Numbers to Multidimensional Profiles. Zenodo (2016). doi:10.5281/zenodo.45402

13. Griffiths, P.: Maximizing the impact of your publications in an open access environment. In: Presentation on 43rd Biennial Convention (2016). http://hdl.handle.net/10755/603401

14. Henkel, R., et al.: Bibliometrics: tracking research impact by selecting the appropriate metrics. Asian J. Androl. **18**(2), 296–309 (2016). doi:10.4103/1008-682X.171582

15. Kartashova, A.A.: Transformation and deformation of scientific knowledge in connection with expansion of scientific approaches and techniques. Rossiyskiy Gumanitarnyi Zhurnal (Russ. Hum. Sci. J.) **5**, 347–357 (2015). doi:10.15643/libartrus-2015.5.3. (in Russia)

16. Kousha, K., Thelwall, M.: Disseminating research with web CV hyperlinks. J. Assoc. Inf. Sci. Technol. **65**, 1615–1626 (2014). doi:10.1002/asi.23070

17. Kudim, K.A., Proskudina, G.Y., Reznichenko, V.A.: Comparing the EPrints 3.0 and DSpace 1.4.1 electronic libraries. In: Works of IX All-Russian Scientific Conference: Electronic Libraries: Advanced Techniques & Technologies, Electronic Collections - RCDL2007. Pereyaslavl-Zalesskyi, 15–18 October 2007 (2008). http://dspace.nsu.ru:8080/jspui/bitstream/nsu/143/1/paper_66_v2.pdf (in Russian)

18. Li, X., Thelwall, M., Kousha, K.: The role of arXiv, RePEc, SSRN and PMC informal scholarly communication. Lib J. Inf. Manage. **67**(6), 614–635 (2015). doi:10.1108/AJIM-03-2015-0049

19. Mas-Bleda, A., Thelwall, M., Kousha, K., Aguillo, I.F.: Do highly cited researchers successfully use the social web? Scientometrics **101**(1), 337–356 (2014). doi:10.1007/s11192-014-1345-0

20. Miguel, S., Tannuride, O., Cabrini, G.: Scientific production on open access: a worldwide bibliometric analysis in the academic and scientific context. Publications **4**(1), 1 (2016). doi:10.3390/publications4010001

21. Laakso, M.: Green open access policies of scholarly journal publishers: a study of what, when, and where self-archiving is allowed. Scientometrics **99**(2), 475–494 (2014). doi:10.1007/s11192-013-1205-3

22. Mukherjee, A., Stern, S.: Disclosure or secrecy? The dynamics of open science. Int. J. Ind. Organ. **27**(3), 449–462 (2009). doi:10.1016/j.ijindorg.2008.11.005

23. Nicholson, S.W., Bennett, T.B.: Dissemination and discovery of diverse data: do libraries promote their unique research data collections? Int. Inf. Libr. Rev. **48**(2), 85–93 (2016). doi:10.1080/10572317.2016.1176448

24. Nielsen, M.: Reinventing Discovery: The New Era of Networked Science. Princeton University Press, Princeton (2011)

25. Nixon, W.: DAEDALUS: Initial Experiences with ePrints and Dspace at the University of Glasgow. Ariadne (37) (2003). http://www.ariadne.ac.uk/issue37/nixon/

26. Open Access 2020. http://oa2020.org

27. Paprinov, S.I.: Development of electronic libraries is the way to the open science. In: Electronic Libraries: Advanced Techniques and Technologies, Electronic Collections: Works of the XI All-Russian Scientific Conference RCDL 2009, pp. 225–234. Karelia Scientific Center of the Russian Academy of Science, Petrozavodsk (2009). http://rcdl.ru/doc/2009/225_234_Invited-2.pdf (in Russian)

28. Parinov, S., Lyapunov, V., Puzyrev, R., Kogalovsky, M.: Semantically enrichable research information system socionet. Knowledge engineering and semantic web. In: 6th International Conference, KESW 2015, Moscow, Russia, September 30 - October 2, 2015, Proceedings. 518 of the series Communications in Computer and Information Science, pp. 147–157 (2015). doi:10.1007/978-3-319-24543-0_11

29. Parsons, J.: Welcome to Science 2.0|Open Access in Action. Library Journal, March 15 (2016). http://lj.libraryjournal.com/2016/03/oa/welcome-to-science-2-0-open-access-in-action/

30. Pinfield, S.: Making open access work: the "state-of-the-art" in providing Open Access to scholarly literature. Online Inf. Rev. 39(5), 604–636 (2015). doi:10.1108/OIR-05-2015-0167

31. Porter, A.L., Rafols, I.: Is science becoming more interdisciplinary? Measuring and mapping six research fields over time. Scientometrics 81(3), 719–745 (2009). doi:10.1007/s11192-008-2197-2

32. Prokudin, D.E.: Through an open software publishing platform for integration into the global scientific community: addressing rapid publication of research results. Sch. Commun. Rev. 6 (18), 13–18 (2013). doi:10.18334/np36109

33. Qin, J., Lancaster, F.W., Allen, B.: Types and levels of collaboration in interdisciplinary research in the sciences. J. Am. Soc. Inf. Sci. 48, 893–916 (1997). doi:10.1002/(SICI)1097-4571(199710)48:10<893:AID-ASI5>3.0.CO;2-X

34. Jamali, R., Russell, D., Nicholas, D., Watkinson, A.: Do online communities support research collaboration? Lib J. Inf. Manag. 66(6), 603–622 (2014). doi:10.1108/ajim-08-2013-0072

35. Schmidt, B., Orth, A., Franck, G., Kuchma, I., Knoth, P., Carvalho, J.: Stepping up open science training for European research. Publications 4(2), 16 (2016). doi:10.3390/publications4020016

36. Siedlok, F., Hibbert, P.: The organization of interdisciplinary research: modes, drivers and barriers. Int. J. Manag. Rev. 16, 194–210 (2014). doi:10.1111/ijmr.12016

37. Smith, I.: Open access infrastructure. UNESCO, Paris (2015). http://unesdoc.unesco.org/images/0023/002322/232204e.pdf

38. Solomon, D.J.: Strategies for developing sustainable open access scholarly journals. First Monday 11(6) (2006). doi:10.5210/fm.v11i6.1335

39. Strakhovskaya, I.G.: Culturological tools of interdisciplinarity. Vestnik Slavyanslik Kultur (Bull. Slavic Cultures) 4, 35–43 (2011). (in Russian)

40. Syrov, V.N.: Philosophy and Prospects of Interdisciplinary Researches in Russian Science. Vestnik VolgU (Bulletin of Volgograd University), Series 7, Philosophy. Sociology and Social Technologies, vol. 3, pp. 5–14 (2011)

41. Ten years on from the Budapest Open Access Initiative: setting the default to open. http://www.budapestopenaccessinitiative.org/boai-10-recommendations

42. Thelwall, M., Kousha, K.: Research gate: disseminating, communicating, and measuring scholarship? J. Assoc. Inf. Sci. Technol. 66, 876–889 (2015). doi:10.1002/asi.23236

43. Willinsky, J.: Open journal systems: an example of open source software for journal management and publishing. Libr. Hi Tech. 23(4), 504–519 (2005). doi:10.1108/07378830510636300

Digital Textbook for Vocationally-Oriented Informative Reading in the Research University

Natalia V. Semenova[✉] and Elena A. Svyatkina

National Research Nuclear University MEPhI (Moscow Engineering Physics Institute),
Kashirskoe Shosse, 31, 115409 Moscow, Russia
{nvsemenova,boumerdes198}@mail.ru

Abstract. The article characterizes a digital textbook as one of the most promising informational and learning resources that is in greatest demand now in online university education. Considering the requirements of competence-oriented approach to learning, the authors describe the advantages of up-to-date computer-based informational and educational technologies that promote effective application of new-format learning materials in local and distance learning. Theoretical points are illustrated by a pilot project of a digital textbook "Academic Skills" for vocationally-oriented foreign-language informative reading, which is aimed at the improvement of the communicative and informative competences of physics students. The textbook operates on the basis of Moodle and uses the SCORM standard. It is being developed to support English-speaking environment and is scheduled for integration in the INFOMEPHIST author system of the Online University within the National Nuclear Research University MEPhI.

Keywords: e-Learning · University transformation · Languages · Theory · Human factors

1 Introduction

Implementation of new-generation computers in the learning environment, as well as the development of various telecommunication facilities brought about transformation of the contemporary university environment: e-learning tools appeared. Currently, academic activities are increasingly supplemented by visual modeling techniques and tools for tracking and testing students' knowledge, as well as hypertext, multimedia and hypermedia techniques based on broad application of various informational resources. To provide different kinds of training, comprehensive e-learning applications are being intensively developed, and the digital textbook (DT) format is now perceived to be the most promising. It is best suited for distributing via the Internet as a networked learning resource that has software applications enabling server-to-client operation. As a rule, a DT has distance and local versions, which provide a way for using it over the Internet or independently, within local university networks.

The new textbook format has become widespread among technical communities, and the experience of the National Research Nuclear University MEPhI is the example of effective introduction of e-learning tools in academic activities. Since 2002, own tools

A.V. Chugunov et al. (Eds.): DTGS 2016, CCIS 674, pp. 363–369, 2016.
DOI: 10.1007/978-3-319-49700-6_34

have been developed here in conformity with the specialization of MEPhI as the leading nuclear university and in accordance with the requirements of its strategic partner – the Rosatom State Corporation. But the up-growth of the university's English-language environment due to its participation in the 5–100 Program has set a new goal for the university's specialists: the development of specialized courses on the basis of a foreign language DT. The purpose of this article is to demonstrate the advantages of the DT as a promising type of English textbooks in a contemporary technical university and present a pilot project of a DT in foreign-language informative reading for the students of physics. This DT may be considered as a way of arranging students' independent work on the experimental course of English "Academic Skills" designed for third-year engineering students.

2　Theoretical Background of Study

While using the "informational resources" notion, we must mention that the Federal Law "On information, informatization and information protection" dated 20.02.1995 No. 24-FZ defines them as "single documents and single document files, documents and document files in information systems (libraries, archives, funds, data banks and other information systems)." In the Federal Law dated 27.07.2006 No. 149-FZ "On information, information technologies and information protection" (with amendments and annexes, effective since 10.01.2016) this definition was to some extent revised and supplemented. However, the standards of the Institute of Electrical and Electronics Engineers (IEEE) consider an "informational resource" to be a digital or non-digital learning object that may be used for the purpose of learning. And in the IEE LOM (Learning Object Metadata) standard accepted back in 2002 an information resource was defined as a document (set of documents) that has been designed and self-formatted for distributing among an unlimited number of users, or that serves as the basis for providing informational services.

Thus, an informational resource (IR) is included in a unified model for systematization of informational entities (any kinds and forms) pertaining to education. The body of IRs becomes the very basis for creating a unified learning environment. There is a great number of ways to classify IRs: according to the type of activity, according to the topic, to the way of information arrangement, to the techniques of access restriction or protection etc. A special cluster is represented by informational learning resources (ILR) whose main goal is education, not just information (content) storage. Moreover, in accordance with its designation, an ILR has a set of special features such as scientific character, availability (a real possibility to use learning materials from any remote access point and to deliver such materials to many other remote access points), high quality and sufficiency for realization of academic subject (module), interactivity, adaptability (possibility to adapt learning materials for the needs of a particular educational institution), interoperability (ability to use learning materials regardless of the original platform) (Guseva et al. 2010).

ILRs are used as the main instrument of educational interaction in distance learning that is now becoming especially popular. Improvement of the universities' technical capabilities resulted in the development of the three basic technologies of distance learning: (1) "case technology" based on preparing the sets ("cases") of textual teaching aids that are mailed to the students for self-study; (2) educational television or direct-broadcast satellite technologies that employ the capabilities of radio, cable and satellite television systems which is widespread abroad, and (3) network technology that is becoming, according to expert opinion, a synonym of distance learning – at least, in domestic education.

In contemporary university education, the greatest demand is for network technology that is applied in the framework of "Open, or Online University". The need for such universities, as well as the technology itself, is explained not only by the ability of the country's leading universities to apply high technologies, but also by the increased demand for educational services that may be delivered parallel to the main occupation.

The National Research Nuclear University MEPhI is now effectively using a wide-spread virtual (online) university; a broad network of ILRs is functioning, with digital textbook as the preferred format. E-learning is effected in the framework of the INFO-MEPHIST author system (INFOrmation MEPHI System of Telecommunications: on the basis of Moodle (http://infomephist.ru). The system's designation is to arrange informational learning environment for unsupervised students' work and storage of teaching aids. The network education format is now being actively introduced in MEPhI, and 5 programs have been developed jointly with other universities, while another 17 – together with partner companies. In one form or another, ILRs are used in 85 programs in cooperation with Russia's leading research institutions and enterprises.

Preference was given by MEPhI to the DT format, considering that:

– unlike conventional textbooks that presuppose "linear" course completion, the architecture of the DT-format learning system is built on the basis of a specialized database enabling multilevel access from different points of ILR operation, presentation algorithms using the principles of multiwindowing and hypertext, providing data flow and free access from any point of an ILR, training and control modules;
– the DT is optimal in performing informational, communicative and controlling functions;
– individualization of educational process is not only due to variable methods of course material presentation and the use of multimedia and hypermedia techniques; it is also achieved through an individual schedule of course completion.

In addition to the above-mentioned advantages, the DT in English provides the following added benefits:

– The DT creates multidimensional stimuli for foreign language learning activity (communicative and cognitive);
– The DT furnishes a means of arranging all the components of communicative competence in a specific data bank form. These data banks serve as informational basis of the DT and include: communicative tasks data banks; data banks of speech minimums and units of communication; formal linguistic units (lexico-grammatical) data banks; data banks of printed texts, videos, pictures, tables and diagrams; drill exercises data banks; standard correct answers banks etc. Every unit of a data bank is described by

means of a particular feature set, which provides a way for a search engine (based on the user's inquiries) to move easily from one database unit to another.

The DT as a special kind of the ILRs operating within the MEPhI's INFOMEPHIST system possesses own model of digital learning elements that can be subdivided into controlling, communicative and informational elements. Informational elements are represented by the glossary and the resource. Communicative elements (i.e. those providing communication between the teacher and the student) are the forum, the e-mail and the chat. The controlling part, which is essentially a structure-forming component of digital learning, includes the following units: "data base – tasks", "quiz – test", "SCORM package – lecture", "seminar – Wiki files".

The employed SCORM standard is attractive, first of all, for the easily applied modular principle. As is known, modules are self-contained informational units reusable to achieve different learning goals. Learning objects, just like elements of a toy construction set, may be easily transferred from one course to another, they may be connected and separated regardless of their content and volume. Within the SCORM standard, such modules are represented by SCOs. The SCO (Sharable Content Objects) is a single learning object that is available for launching by the learning management system (LMS) and using Run-Time Environment for interaction with the LMS.

3 Metodology

1990s, American scientists K.L. Evelyn NG and William P. Olivier stated the proposition that computer technology in teaching foreign languages should be used to perform the functions of a tutor, text editor, consultant, partner and learning object (Evelyn Ng and Olivier 1987). This proposition is very well illustrated by the intensively developing trend of vocationally-oriented foreign language informative reading. This term came to be used by Soviet scholars in 1970, when the work of I.M. Berman was published (Berman 1970), and since the 80s of the 20th century it has become wide-spread in teaching practice, denoting a special kind of reading. Afterwards, the theory of foreign-language informative reading was elaborated in the research by T.S. Serova (Serova 1988), and now, in the framework of her concept, vocationally-oriented foreign-language informative reading is considered as verbal written communication aimed at extraction of information that is new for the reader, which is achieved by means of words, word combinations and sentences of the whole text and resulting in satisfied demand for professional information, namely: evaluation, acquisition and subsequent use of the required information and own product creation.

Vocationally-oriented foreign-language informative reading has the following advantages:

- It is a prerequisite for successful improvement of the professional culture of future engineers and technicians;
- Professional orientation for the desired occupation when teaching informative reading is achieved through the specially selected and arranged *subject-matter of*

speech activity of informative reading that acts as a means for motivating students to engage in professional activity.

Skills training for conforming to the sufficient competence level is achieved in course of informative reading on the basis of specially selected and arranged system of exercises within informative reading sub-types: evaluative-informative, acquisition-informative and creative-informative reading.

4 Results

The main result of our research is the development of a unique online course in vocationally-oriented informative reading "Academic skills" in DT format. It is designed for 72 h and includes 12 topics that broaden and enrich the knowledge of physics students: "Effective reading", "Innovative technologies", "Nuclear plant", "Nuclear technology", "Nanotechnology, nanoscience, nanosubject", "Nanotechnology in medical physics", "Astrophysics", "Energy", "Global Warming", "Laser Physics", "Physics and Cybernetics", "Research. Physics Discoveries in the Modern World". The structure of the "Academic Skills" DT includes the following components: (1) curriculum; (2) course syllabus, including the description of initial and final competences of students; (3) list of main and additional literature with notes on availability of books in the library; (4) presentations (reference outline); (5) brief lecture summaries; (6) a set of tests for each lecture (5 categories, each consisting of 4 questions); (7) a set of tasks for self-study (one task per lecture); (8) annotated index of external Internet resources; (9) glossary.

The above structure is in conformity with the ILR template applied in MEPhI's INFOMEPHIST system (Guseva and Putilov 2014), and, correspondingly, fits in the common model of digital learning elements that are divided into controlling, communicative and informational.

The "Academic skills" course is intended for students that have completed the basic training in accordance with the principal educational program and decided to continue learning English online. According to the Vocationally-Oriented Language Learning Scale (VOLL) their level is estimated as B2, threshold level of foreign language competence (Level 3, upper-Intermediate).

Twenty-nine students took part in the preliminary stage of the experiment, subdivided into three groups: one experimental group and two control groups. The experimental conditions were as follows: competence level of the students was equal; number of students in the groups was nearly the same; the students in the experimental group were taught English using the materials of the "Academic skills" DT; the latter was not used in control groups; all the groups were taught by one teacher during the term. The students were tested at the term beginning and at its end for knowledge of the main facts and the basic features of the original technical text, as well as understanding of a preselected text part (information). Text understanding was evaluated considering the following items: (1) correct interpretation of the author's communicative intention (depth); (2) accurate and complete understanding of the information contained in the text, which is adequate to the goal set before the recipient when reading the text. Testing conditions were the same for all the students: they were given a traditional printed text and equal time for completing the after-text tasks.

To attain control data, the following formula was used: $K = P/N$, where K is the coefficient of material acquisition, P is the number of correctly completed tasks (test operations), and N is the total number of tasks. The data obtained in this way were converted into percentages and transferred into a unified 100-point scale ($1 = 100\%$).

The preliminary experimental data have shown that the system of DT tasks that takes into account the peculiarities of reading type resulted in increased accuracy, completeness and depth of understanding vocationally-oriented texts by the experimental group students; it has also strengthened their cognitive motivation. The competence level in vocationally-oriented reading and text understanding of the experimental group students have grown by 9.2% during one term, whereas the competence level of control group students has grown by 6.5% only. The experimental group has demonstrated a higher motivation level (keenness on reading foreign-language vocationally-oriented literature), which was evaluated by means of a special test: 60% began to read more professional literature in a foreign language, as compared to a medium level of 30–40% in control groups.

5   Conclusion

Any textbook is an information model of one or another educational system. The new – digital – textbook format reflects the peculiar features in the transformation of conventional models and systems. Qualitative difference of the DT from traditional textbooks is best of all reflected in its new functions: individualization and differentiation of learning process, interactivity, research and creative functions, training, imitation and modeling functions, prediction, working with multimedia and hypermedia, online aid and script setting etc. For the extending DT's functional capabilities, its two versions are undoubtedly required: local and distance learning versions that will be available in local networks, independently within a given educational institution, and correspondingly, over the global Internet network.

In our opinion, the use of digital content while completing the "Academic Skills" course will effectively promote skill training in unaided application of obtained knowledge in their future professional work. The obtained data are preliminary by nature and need further experimental verification. But in any case, this course in the DT format, as we see it, fully meets the requirements of competence-oriented approach as it is aimed at development of communicative and informative competences. Students get a real opportunity to work out their own course track, while the teacher is given the chance to offer various language learning strategies. It helps achieve such teaching and learning goals as arranging unsupervised students' work, improvement of receptive and productive speech skills, providing consultations, checking the scope of text understanding by means of learning monitoring systems built in the ILR software.

References

Berman, I.M.: Metodika obuchenija anglijskomu jazyku v nejazykovom vuze (Methods of teaching English in non-linguistic higher education institution). Vysshaja shkola, Moscow (1970)

Evelyn Ng, K.L., Olivier, W.P.: Computer assisted language learning: an investigation on some design and implementation issues. System **15**(1), 1–17 (1987). doi:10.1016/0346-251X(87)90043-1

Guseva, A.I., Putilov, A.V.: Opyt ispol'zovanija informacionnyh tehnologij v oblasti inzhenernoj jekonomiki v NIJaU MIFI (Experience of using information technologies in the field of engineering economics in NRNU MEPHI). In: International Conference "New Challenges for Pedagogy and Quality Education: MOOCs, Clouds and Mobiles", IITE 2014, Moscow (2014). http://conference2014.iite.unesco.org/wp-content/uploads/2014/11/Guseva-Putilov.pdf

Guseva, A.I., Gavrilov, S.I., Tikhomirova, A.N.: Model' upravlenija kachestvom informacionno-obrazovatel'nyh resursov (Model of quality management information and educational resources). Programmnye produkty i sistemy (Softw. Syst.) **1**, 146–149 (2010)

Serova, T.S.: Psihologicheskie i lingvodidakticheskie aspekty obuchenija professional'no-orientirovannomu inojazychnomu chteniju v vuze (Psychological and linguistic-didactical aspects of teaching professionally-oriented foreign language reading in a higher educational institution). Ural State University, Sverdlovsk (1988)

The Application of Online Team Project Training in Nuclear Engineering Education

Gennady K. Baryshev[✉], Aleksandr V. Berestov, and Nadezhda A. Konashenkova

National Research Nuclear University MEPhI, Moscow, Russia
{GKBaryshev,AVBerestov}@mephi.ru, konashenkova-nadezda@yandex.ru

Abstract. We discuss the problem of the application of online team project training in nuclear engineering education in bachelor, specialist and master programs in the area of nuclear physics and technologies, nuclear reactors and materials of National Research Nuclear University MEPhI (Moscow Engineering-Physics Institute). The methodological aspects of organization of student online work in a team project, development of a "design office" and "project office" as well as application of project management practice are in focus of attention. The results of the ongoing process of the transformation of engineering education in compliance with the CDIO (Conceive-Design-Implement-Operate) international and Russian federal national educational standards are discussed.

Keywords: Nuclear engineering education · Team project training · CDIO

1 Introduction

One of the most relevant challenges in nuclear education is the training of skilled engineering workers, who, by the university graduation, have a basic training as well as possess project activities skills and teamwork experience. They are also supposed to be capable of analyzing and solving problems arising while working on a project [2, 3, 7]. To encounter this challenge, National Research Nuclear University MEPhI launched a pilot project of a bachelor program designed in accordance with the principles of the international CDIO standards [4, 6, 8].

The CDIO (Conceive - Design - Implement - Operate) is a large international project launched in 2000 and intended to reform engineering education. This project called "Worldwide CDIO Initiative" includes the technical curricula of the key engineering schools and technical universities in the USA, Canada, Europe, Russia, Africa, Asia and New Zealand. The project aims at providing students with the education that highlights the engineering basics presented in the context of the life cycle of actual systems, processes and products.

The CDIO Initiative aims at bringing the engineering educational programs content and effectiveness into compliance with the state of the art of modern technologies and employers' expectations. The 12 CDIO Standards define special requirements to the CDIO curricula [1]. These requirements could be used as guidelines for reforming and assessing educational programs in the technical and technological fields, as well as

© Springer International Publishing AG 2016
A.V. Chugunov et al. (Eds.): DTGS 2016, CCIS 674, pp. 370–379, 2016.
DOI: 10.1007/978-3-319-49700-6_35

establishing conditions for the continuous improvement and development of these programs.

The 12 CDIO Standards define the requirements to:

- the concept of engineering educational program (Standard 1);
- the formation of the curriculum (Standards 2, 3);
- practice oriented educational environment (Standards 4, 5, 6);
- the methods of the teachers'' training and level of proficiency (Standards 7, 8, 9, 10);
- the methods of the assessment of the students'' educational results and of the program in the whole (Standards 11 and 12).

Fulfillment of the requirements of these standards is based on proper methods applied to the specific educational program. One should first formulate a methodological basis to effectively organize online student team work project training.

We solved the task of organization of student work in a team project and development of student's project management skills for nuclear engineering education in compliance with the CDIO standards (see Fig. 1).

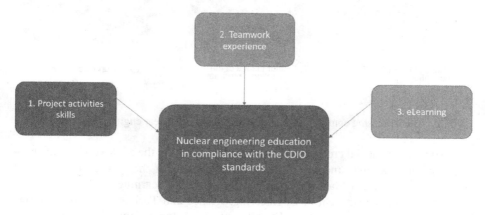

Fig. 1. The illustration of crucial components for nuclear engineering education

2   Organization of Student Work in a Team Project

Standard 5, according to which the curriculum of an educational program should include two or more projects involving the familiarization of a student with project implementation, plays a crucial role in the implementation of the CDIO concept.

A project will be understood to be a training and practical task related to the design and production of products, which are realized with the help of the engineering disciplines complex. By solving the training and practical tasks integrated in the curriculum, the students improve their skills of the design and production of new products and systems, as well as their ability to apply theoretical knowledge in the engineering practice.

The tasks on the design and creation of new products and systems could vary from basic to advanced depending on their intensity, difficulty and place in the curriculum.

For instance, the tasks related to the design and creation of less complex products and systems are offered at the early stages of the program, whereas more complex engineering and technical tasks are suggested at the later stages, which allows students to apply in practice the knowledge they acquired earlier (see Fig. 2). The tasks related to the planning, design, realization and management of the products and systems can also be included in curriculum as an extra-curricular work - for example, as course papers or practical training). A gradual increase of the difficulty of the tasks facilitates a better acquisition of the fundamental knowledge, which is the basis for clear understanding of technical disciplines.

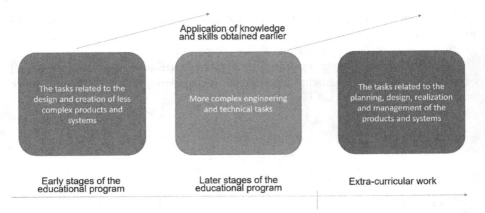

Fig. 2.   The increasing complexity of engineering tasks in nuclear engineering education

The development and creation of products and systems in the context of actual engineering practice allows students to determine the fields of their future professional interests. To implement Standard 5, a team project-based learning methodology was developed by the Department of Engineering Science and Technology. The methodology was successfully tested on the Department's bachelor students. A team project is a hands-on training that is aimed at the development of engineering, designing, technological etc. projects in the real-life environment.

The advantages of the method:

– Combination of individual and team work;
– The method stimulates the development of creative skills and critical thinking;
– The project implementation in groups requires each participant to know the projection process;
– Teamwork cultivates the skills of interpersonal communication, which is important for the solution of professional tasks.

Thus, a "Team project" was included in the bachelor student's curriculum. Each project involves both third- and fourth-year student's participation.

Third year students, starting from the fifth term, obtain knowledge in specific disciplines that require the completion of practical tasks assigned to them by fourth-year students. The solutions of the tasks are used in team projects. Fourth-year students are divided into groups in the following way (see Fig. 3):

1. Project office is a set of groups in accordance with the number of projects. Each group comprises of a chief designer and a project manager. Each group is working on a project, which includes all stages of a lifecycle, from statement of work to prototype production.
2. Design office is a set of groups. Each group includes two or three people. Each group is responsible for particular field of problems, for instance, "Electronics", "Automatic machinery", "Development", "Coding". Design office files the project office's orders, splits up the work among third-year students, controls the working process and renders assistance if necessary.

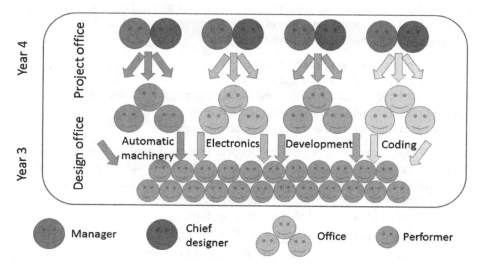

Fig. 3. The pattern of the communication of students during the implementation of a team project

A number of engineering and technical tasks was formulated so that to involve the best students with engineering skills in solving high-priority tasks for development of systems of quality control of new-type perspective nuclear fuel elements for increasing reliability and economic effectiveness of nuclear power plants – the R&D performed by National Research Nuclear University MEPhI (the Department of Engineering Science and Technology). They included:

- patent research on the problem as well as development documents for information measuring systems, ultrasonic measuring devices, software and prototypes;
- development of principal and operating schemes of the systems of control of parameters of gas environment in nuclear fuel elements during the process of their fabrication, corrosion damages of the nuclear fuel elements covers, etc.;
- choosing optimal technical characteristics of the systems of quality measurement of control of perspective nuclear fuel elements.

Thus, fourth-year students gain decision-making, team and project management experience, whereas third-year students develop their practical problem solving skills within the scope of the studied subjects.

3   Testing of "Project Management Practice" Discipline in Nuclear Education

The guidelines for "Project management practice" were developed in order to fulfil the CDIO Standards requirements, to acquire basic knowledge and skills, to gain experience of project management and participation in team project activities. The discipline is included in the Department of Engineering Science and Technology curriculum. The course intends to provide the students with the basic principles, tools and approaches in project management in order to continue the mastering of the discipline on a practical level.

The goals of the course are achieved through:

- studying of project management theory;
- studying of project documentation basics;
- solving of hands-on tasks, which involve development of project documentation, project planning and work progressing monitoring;
- implementation of a team technical engineering project.

The "Project management practice" course ensures a complex approach to the teaching of the project management basics, development of practical project management and organizational skills and improvement of personal and personal competencies. The curriculum and the guidelines are based on the project's life cycle and the project management stages list and include the following topics:

1. Introduction to project management:
   - The term "project", the distinctive features of a project, basic notions and terms of project management.
   - The notions of "project program" and "project portfolio", the classification of projects, a project's life cycle.
   - Russian and international project management standards, the policy in nuclear project management in the Russian Federation.
2. The organizational structure of a project:
   - Subjects of project management: customer, manager, supervisor etc. Main stakeholders.
   - Types of organizational structures of a project: functional, matrix, project-based, mixed. The comparison of organizational structures.
3. The functions and processes of project management:
   - Process groups.
   - Interrelations of process groups.
4. The initiation (preparation) of a project:
   - Initiating processes.
   - Project's targets, goal setting levels.
   - Project charter.

     – The criteria of project success, basic requirements to the formulation of criteria.
5. Project planning:
     – Project planning processes. Project planning algorithm.
     – Structure decomposition of works.
     – Organizational planning of a project. Organization planning (organizational chart, roles, matrix of responsibilities).
     – Schedule and resource planning (network diagram, methods of the activity duration estimation, schedule plan, critical path, resource plan, resource levelling).
     – Financial planning and budget preparation basics.
6. Project risk management:
     – The notion of "risk". Risk management processes.
     – Methods and tools of risk identification.
     – Methods of risk response.
7. The control, monitoring and implementation of a project. The management of the changes in a project:
     – The processes of the control, monitoring and implementation of a project.
     – Approaches to the creation of a project control and monitoring system.
     – The processes of the management of the changes.
     – Changes requests.
     – The basics of the requirements management.
8. Project close-out:
     – Project close-out processes.
     – Project's archive. Project accounting.

The educational process consists of three basic parts:

1. Theoretical training includes lectures and self-guided work with guidelines;
2. Student teamwork on the tasks and games offered by the teeacher. Team work and individual work on the course paper.
3. Implementation of a technical engineering project in teams.

    A course paper is of the greatest practical interest to the students as it allows them to learn new skills of project management skill and working in a team. A course paper is a virtual company's set of projects that includes R&D programs on the development of a pilot, one-of-a-kind or stock-produced items, on the preparation and mastering of production, on the enterprise computer systems development. The projects are interconnected, have resource, deadlines and work quality limitations. Implicit risks are present too. Students examine the suggested materials and choose the projects they will work on within the framework of a course project work.

    At the first stage of the course project the students prepare and defend a project charter. Within the scope of the charter they define:

– the key aims and purposes of the project;
– the organizational and functional limits of the project;
– organizational structure of project management and monitoring procedures.

    At this stage, the control over the maintaining of connection between the projects is exercised.

At the next stage, the students come up with an action plan and resolve resource conflicts between the projects through personal interaction.

While preparing the project charter and the action plan through studying the current normative documentation, a student gains an insight into the main stages and phases of engineering work from the idea to the production.

At the final stage of a course project, the students put together, explain and defend risk lists, carry out qualitative assessment of the risks and define risks response methods.

After the results of the course paper defense have been announced, students proceed to the implementation of a team technical engineering project. In 2015, for third year bachelor students of the Department of Engineering Science and Technology of MEPhI the topic of the project was "System of Measurement of Radiation Dose Fields of Medical Electron Accelerators".

The system of measurement of radiation dose fields is designated for the metrological support of beam therapy. The system under development is a part of a water phantom. A water phantom is a medical device that consists of a mechanical and measuring blocks and a reservoir with distilled water. It is used to determine the parameters of ionizing radiation and the spatial distribution of the absorbed dose. Water phantoms help to determine the way and the extent to which a human body is being exposed to radiation if various radiation sources or medical devices using such sources are used.

The system is intended to position the water phantom's measuring knot in accordance with a specified scanning program and to process the data provided by the water phantom. The results of scanning are used for the dose field calibration.

Within the scope of the project the following tasks were solved:

– the development and coordination of the project's chart, formalizing the project's aims and tasks, project management procedures, project's organizational structure, the formation of the budget, the determination of the milestones and stages of the work.
– the development of the system requirements specification, the development of design documentation and software to control the system. Production and system tests aimed at determining its characteristics while working in radiation fields, produced by the medical linear accelerators.

The control over students carrying out the project is exercised through the Planfix collective work management system designed for the management of the team project work [5].

Figures 4, 5, 6 and 7 illustrate some of the project results developed at the Project management practice" discipline and by the Design and Project student offices at the Department of Engineering Science and Technology of MEPhI for students of the 3rd academic year of the bachelor program.

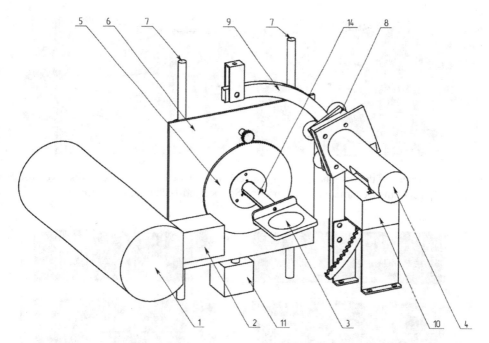

Fig. 4. Illustration of the mechanical part of the machine for quality control of uranium-oxide coating on the fission chamber electrodes developed by the students of the Department of Applied Nuclear Physics of MEPhI

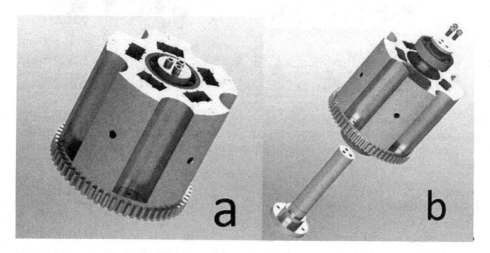

Fig. 5. Illustration of the dry chamber-type storage for radioactive isotopes developed by the students of the Department of Materials Science of MEPhI

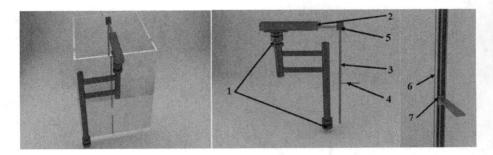

Fig. 6. Illustration of the water phantom mechanical system based on harmonic drives developed by the students of the Department of Engineering Science and Technology of MEPhI

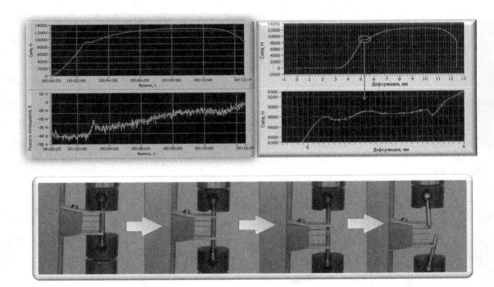

Fig. 7. Illustration of the information measuring system (the virtual device for measurement of deformation of the sample) of electrophysical non-destructive abruption testing of metallic samples developed by the students of the Department of Engineering Science and Technology of MEPhI

4   Conclusion

Thus, a project-based approach is an inherent element of the implementation of the international nuclear engineering education standards of the Worldwide CDIO Initiative. In case of pilot projects, the implementation of this approach was demonstrated on the example of the combination of management activities and online-technologies (teamwork system). Students master their project skills (including those related to the specific disciplines) working on the tasks in construction, automatics, programming and electronics within the scope of design and project offices. A further perfection of the communicative tools between the design and project offices is planned in order to allow them to complete the course projects on the "Project management practice" discipline online. It should increase the worldwide recognition and availability of the educational programs taught in the National Research Nuclear University MEPhI.

Acknowledgements. The authors of the paper send their sincere acknowledgements and regards to the Ministry of Science and Education of Russian Federation according with the agreement No. 14.578.21.0067, unique project ID RFMEFI57814X0067.

References

1. Crawley, E.F.: The CDIO syllabus: a statement of goals for undergraduate engineering education. The Department of Aeronautics and Astronautics, Massachusetts Institute of Technology (2001)
2. Fedorov, I.B., Medvedev, V.E.: Engineering education: problems and tasks. High. Educ. Russ. **12**, 54–60 (2011)
3. Saprykin, D.L.: Engineering education in Russia: history, conception, future trends. High. Educ. Russ. **1**, 125–137 (2012)
4. The CDIO Standards. http://www.cdio.org
5. The collective work management system Planfix. https://planfix.com/
6. The Educational Standard of Higher Education of National Research Nuclear University MEPhI 14.03.02 Nuclear Physics and Technologies. http://www.mephi.ru/eng
7. Vladimirov, A.I.: About Engineering-Technical Education. Nedra Publishing House, Moscow (2011)
8. Yakovlev, D., Pryakhin, A., Korolev, S., Shaltaeva, Y., Samotaev, N., Yushkov, E., Avanesyan, A.: Engineering competitive education using modern network technologies in the NRNU MEPhI. In: Proceedings of the 2015 IEEE Workshop on Environmental, Energy, and Structural Monitoring Systems, pp. 39–43. IEEE Press (2015)

Project-Implementation in Nuclear Education: Perspectives of Development via eKnowledge

Aleksandr P. Biryukov[✉], Elena P. Varyatchenko, and Elena A. Barysheva

National Research Nuclear University MEPhI, Moscow, Russia
bir.sasha@rambler.ru, epvaryatchenko@mephi.ru, tv4848@yandex.ru

Abstract. The paper describes the results of the application of project-implementation methods in nuclear education in National Research Nuclear University MEPhI (Moscow Engineering-Physics Institute). The role of information technologies and eKnowledge in the transformation of educational process is discussed as well as the brief description of future perspectives. The general description of the new methodology as well as a case scenario are provided.

Keywords: Nuclear education · Project-implementation methods · Information technologies in education

1 Introduction

The exponential growth of digital technologies and e-learning systems (eKnowledge) creates great opportunities for the modernization and transformation of nuclear education in a modern research university. They contribute to the development of a university research and innovation capacity as well as the modernization of educational programs and the quality improvement of training of specialists in the sphere of nuclear technologies, first and foremost, in accordance with the Worldwide CDIO Initiative standards of education in international engineering [1, 2, 4].

Under pilot projects, major educational programs of the specialty "Nuclear Physics and Technology" were modernized in National Research Nuclear University MEPhI (Moscow Engineering-Physics Institute) with the focus on the students' acquisition of expertise in project-implementation [5]. On the other hand, the development of digital technologies opens new possibilities for the implementation of new educational formats and technologies as well as the assessment of the learners' skills [6].

2 Testing of Project-Implementation Methodology in Nuclear Education

In the academic year of 2015–2016, on the basis of community engineering disciplines, studied by students of nuclear specialties in NRNU MEPhI, testing of a number of new methodologies corresponding to the implementation of the CDIO international standards

© Springer International Publishing AG 2016
A.V. Chugunov et al. (Eds.): DTGS 2016, CCIS 674, pp. 380–385, 2016.
DOI: 10.1007/978-3-319-49700-6_36

of education in engineering was conducted. These methodologies encompassed (see Fig. 1):

- Organization of a network format of the students' communication and joint work on engineering projects via social networking websites and SaaS-systems;
- Holding a motivation module aimed at helping students familiarize themselves with the engineering picture of the world, with a general image of the future of engineering activity and with holding business games aimed at the development of system-engineering thinking – such as "Knowledge Reactor" developed by S.B. Pereslegin and the Future Designing group [3], the "Space station" game developed by Kazan Game-practice Center and others;
- Holding a project module aimed at involving students in practicable engineering projects implemented in the Department of Engineering Science and Technology as well as holding masterclasses on development and design, developing engineering thinking with involvement of experts of the Rosatom State corporation, Skolkovo, etc.;
- Holding an engineering module related to the students' formulation of technical tasks for engineering projects, preparing design drafts, performing engineering calculations of the main construction units and elements.

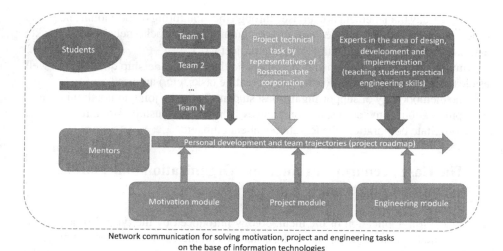

Network communication for solving motivation, project and engineering tasks
on the base of information technologies

Fig. 1. Scheme of application of new project implementation methodology in nuclear education with the aid of eKnowledge instruments

To immerse students in engineering activity, to work on practicable engineering projects and to develop their thinking, communication and teamwork skills, during seminars masterclasses of experts, group work, modified brainstorming methods, business and strategy games are actively used (100% of seminars).

The assessment of the student projects, their work on further creative tasks, as well as extra classroom work on projects, is undertaken via a course group on the social networking website VKontakte and Saas-systems of organization of group project work (see Fig. 2). The best projects are submitted as reports to international scientific conferences.

Fig. 2. Screenshot of the course group on the social networking website VKontakte

Day-to-day management is exercised through the monitoring of individual and group progress in developing a project via the community on the social network VKontakte and Saas-systems of organization of group project work.

Implicit indicators (demonstrated systematic thinking, leadership qualities) as well as clear ones (report on the project, essay, creative tasks, etc.) are used.

The methodology of supporting the best students is used – joint authorship in scientific publications, invitations to conferences, forums, internships organized by the Rosatom State corporation, the Rosatom student club, etc.

3   The Case Scenario – From Team Organization to a Youth Scientific Conference

The successful application of the methodology introduced by the typical trajectory of most talented students who passed all the tasks and completed their engineering projects.

A number of engineering and technical tasks was formulated so that to involve the best students with engineering skills in solving high-priority tasks for development of systems of quality control of new-type perspective nuclear fuel elements for increasing reliability and economic effectiveness of nuclear power plants – the R&D performed by National Research Nuclear University MEPhI (the Department of Engineering Science and Technology). They included:

- patent research on the problem as well as development documents for information measuring systems, ultrasonic measuring devices, software and prototypes;
- development of principal and operating schemes of the systems of control of parameters of gas environment in nuclear fuel elements during the process of their fabrication, corrosion damages of the nuclear fuel elements covers, etc.;

– choosing optimal technical characteristics of the systems of quality measurement of control of perspective nuclear fuel elements.

At the beginning of the 2015–2016 educational year they were organized for get-to-know each other and for future joint work via the instruments of the Russian social networking website VKontakte. A specific group was organized to provide their communication in the most effective way.

With the aid of mentors, several games of the motivation modules have been held, allowing students to formulate their personal and collective vision of the engineers of the future. As a result of these games, about 35 teams (out of 180 students) were organized. Most groups already had leaders that appeared there, in others this kind of people appeared later.

Several lectures and master-classes have been held by experts of Rosatom state corporation. During the meetings the actual problems of Russian nuclear industry were discussed (see Figs. 3, 4 and 5). There were about 10 engineering and technical tasks formulated, so that one problem was to be solved by 2–4 teams, so that at the end of the academic year the experts would choose the best engineering solution.

Fig. 3. A master-class by S. Haprov (CEO of ASTRAROSSA)

Later the ongoing process of online communication and solving the engineering tasks with the aid of the PlanFix SaaS system began. Mentors and experts in the area of design, development and implementation supported the process all the way, and communication between students and experts was not only in the classroom or laboratories of the university, but also held online. In included thorough examination of online educational materials (on Coursera etc.), discussion and solving of various particular problems.

Fig. 4. Gennady Baryshev, head of the CDIO-MEPhI Youth Project Office, performs the "Space Station" engineering game

Fig. 5. The competition of research and development projects organized by MEPhI and Rosatom State Corporation

At the end of the academic year there were lot of fruitful results – the application of new methodology allowed students to focus on solving the given engineering tasks in a better way than via traditional forms of education, and eKnowledge instruments increased the effectiveness of their work, obtaining of knowledge and skills.

The competition was organized to choose the best engineering solutions. As a result, five teams with the best developed projects were honored by Rosatom experts. Later on, their competition presentations were improved and are being transformed at the moment as reports of several youth scientific conferences.

4   Conclusion

Thus, the key factor of the project-implementation approach development in nuclear education is the wide application of interactive and telecommunication methods and techniques. It is important to note that a request for transforming educational process and increasing transparency of the education, research and innovation environment at significant extent comes from students and postgraduates. It means that the digital technologies applied in education (eKnowledge) are changing not only the technological but also the sociocultural environment of a modern research university.

The proposed model has been validated with the aid of eKnowledge instruments on the base of Nuclear Physics and Technology educational program and will be scaled for the whole MEPhI university in the nearest future.

Acknowledgements.   The authors of the paper send their sincere acknowledgements and regards to the Ministry of Science and Education of Russian Federation according with the agreement No. 14.578.21.0067, unique project ID RFMEFI57814X0067.

References

1. Crawley, E.F.: The CDIO syllabus: a statement of goals for undergraduate engineering education. The Department of Aeronautics and Astronautics, Massachusetts Institute of Technology (2001)
2. Grasso, D., Burkins, M.B. (eds.): Holistic Engineering Education: Beyond Technology. Springer Science+Business Media, New York (2010). doi:10.1007/978-1-4419-1393-7
3. Pereslegin, S.B.: A Self-teacher for Playing at the World's Chessboard. AST, Moscow (2006)
4. The CDIO Standards. http://www.cdio.org
5. The Educational Standard of Higher Education of National Research Nuclear University MEPhI 14.03.02 Nuclear Physics and Technologies. http://www.mephi.ru/eng
6. Yakovlev, D., Pryakhin, A., Korolev, S., Shaltaeva, Y., Samotaev, N., Yushkov, E., Avanesyan, A.: Engineering competitive education using modern network technologies in the NRNU MEPhI. In: Proceedings of the 2015 IEEE Workshop on Environmental, Energy, and Structural Monitoring Systems, pp. 39–43. IEEE Press (2015)

Digital Transformation as the Key to Synthesis of Educational and Innovation Process in the Research University

Yuri V. Bozhko[1], Aleksandr I. Maksimkin[1], Gennady K. Baryshev[1(✉)],
Andrey I. Voronin[2,3], and Anastasia S. Kondratyeva[4]

[1] National Research Nuclear University MEPhI, Moscow, Russia
ybozhko@gmail.com, avian4uk@gmail.com, gkbaryshev@mephi.ru
[2] National University of Science and Technology MISiS, Moscow, Russia
voronin@misis.ru
[3] South Ural State University, Chelyabinsk, Russia
[4] Peter the Great Saint-Petersburg Polytechnic University, Saint-Petersburg, Russia
A_kondrateva@spbstu.ru

Abstract. The focal point is the problem of synthesis of educational and innovation process in the contemporary research university. The main purpose of the paper is to describe motivational and methodological aspects of such transformation, necessary to increase the effectiveness of educational process with the aid of CDIO standards. The particular case of implementation of the new laboratory module on how digital transformation of educational process works as the key to development of new approaches and achievement of major results in obtaining new competences and skills for graduates of nuclear engineering educational programs is introduced.

Keywords: Digital transformation · Engineering education · Innovation in education

1 Introduction

To provide successful development and curriculum modernization in the modern research university it is important to use the tools which satisfy contemporary educational standards and methods, first of all, the tools based on digital technology [3]. The purpose of this is to gain the synthesis of educational and innovative activities in a contemporary research university through the application of international standards of CDIO engineering education as well [1, 4].

The CDIO (Conceive - Design - Implement - Operate) is a large international project launched in 2000 and intended to reform engineering education. This project called "Worldwide CDIO Initiative'' includes the technical curricula of the key engineering schools and technical universities in the USA, Canada, Europe, Russia, Africa, Asia and New Zealand. The project aims at providing students with the education that highlights

A.V. Chugunov et al. (Eds.): DTGS 2016, CCIS 674, pp. 386–391, 2016.
DOI: 10.1007/978-3-319-49700-6_37

the engineering basics presented in the context of the life cycle of actual systems, processes and products.

According with the principles of CDIO, a future engineer should care not only about the quality of knowledge he or she gets, but precisely about the quality of practical work and skills obtained.

We describe results of development and approbation of motivational and methodo-logical aspects of digital transformation, necessary to in-crease the effectiveness of educational process with the aid of CDIO standards.

2 Methodological Aspects of Digital Transformation of Educational Process to Obtain Student's Practical Skills in the Area of Analogue Electronics

An important part of transformation of a contemporary research university – for example, National Research Nuclear University MEPhI (Moscow, Russia) with the aid of the 5 top 100 competitiveness program is increasing the quality of engineering educa-tion (mostly with the methodological support of international standards, such as CDIO), and provide synthesis of educational and innovation process. The last one is also crucial for successful implementation of CDIO.

As a result of the pilot project of implementation CDIO standards in MEPhI for nuclear engineering education, new principles of education were developed and appro-bated. Some of them concerned application of new digital instruments for student's obtaining practical skills in analogue electronics – important to design contemporary information measuring systems for nuclear technologies.

An approach to teaching the disciplines related to analogue electronics and the elab-oration of analogue devices is changing now. Today not only the knowledge of the theory and several basic principles is significant, but also the knack of applying them and getting a high-quality and competitive product [6]. The essential part of staff training is practice, when a student perceives the gained theoretical knowledge firsthand through the training tasks, gets and polishes up the working skills. In our case these skills are in development, engineering and construction of electronic devices.

It is necessary to provide students with corresponding infrastructure, tools and meth-odology for developing their practical skills, in order to solve the aforementioned tasks [2, 5]. The laboratory facilities for analogue electronics have been constructed in the same way as the collection of laboratory practice has been created with special meth-odological guidelines. The Laboratory Practical Manual as a basic instrument for students to get-to-know with new instruments required special attention due to the pecu-liarities of the standards for engineering education being implemented.

The development of new digital instruments for obtaining practical skills in the area of analogue electronics, which could satisfy all claimed requirements of CDIO stand-ards, was a piece of sufficient work and was divided into several stages in compliance with the structure of laboratory facilities themselves. Laboratory facilities by definition should consist of:

1. Laboratory bench - an object of practical research;
2. Program complex;
3. Laboratory Practical Manual;
4. Collection of laboratory practice;
5. Technological digital infrastructure which provides a proper conduction of laboratory practice.

3   The Description of the Developed Analogue Electronics Laboratory Module

The National Instruments company technologies were applied for the realization of the claimed task of digital transformation of educational process to obtain student's practical skills in the area of analogue electronics to develop contemporary information measuring system for Russian nuclear industry since these hardware products had already been introduced in several departments of the National Research Nuclear University MEPhI. By their means the laboratory facilities were created on the base of a personal computer and a NI ELVIS II laboratory workstation (Educational Laboratory Virtual Instrumentation Suite). A standard breadboard (in a set together with a laboratory workstation) has been substituted by a created module with the same interface to connect to a laboratory workstation.

Such a set of elements allowed to solve a number of tasks for student's practical training at the Semi-conductor Devices and Analogue Electronics courses. The main feature of the laboratory complex is practically unlimited number of experimental circuits that can be realized on it. The outcome of this feature was the universal educational application of the complex both for beginners and more experienced student users.

One of the most important parts of laboratory facilities is the software. The peculiarities of the software determine the way how the corresponding methodological guidelines will be written and the training process will be designed in general.

The specific feature of the developed platform is that all control and measurement equipment is in a single device - the NI ELVIS II laboratory workstation. The user's interface is I/O devices of a personal computer: a monitor, a keyboard and a mouse or another manipulating device for commands input.

For this reason so-called virtual devices are applied as a program complex, i.e. an outer cover of hardware management. In this case it is a set of virtual tools.

In order to complete all laboratory practice it is enough to use all measurement equipment installed in the NI ELVIS II laboratory workstation and provided virtual tools. Their interface and product scope completely satisfy the most modern and widely applied control and measurement devices.

Such universal laboratory facilities require an advanced methodological support. For this purpose, according to the curriculum already set, special methodological guidelines were created. They consisted of 30 laboratory practical works devoted to three basic units: "passive elements", "semiconductor elements" and "operational amplifiers".

The corresponding provisions have been designed for complying with these guidelines, which meet new requirements. Their use has allowed to create the cutting-edge guidelines, which do not conflict with traditional views and accumulate long-term experience of teaching electrical disciplines in the National Research Nuclear University MEPhI.

This designed collection of practical works with the guidelines provides the connection with other disciplines related to the tracks of metrology, standardization and certification; thermophysical calculations and modelling, issues of material engineering in the electronic industry. So, a student gets a comprehensive understanding not only about the basic disciplines, but the concurrent ones. As clear cross-disciplinary connections appear the student's interest increases.

Each section of the guideline consists of several laboratory tasks, containing theoretical information, a calculation task, a practical task, a laboratory guideline and a self-check quiz. Theoretical information concerns circuits to study during the laboratory practice as well as includes calculation formulas. Each work is provided with a sample calculation task for better understanding of the work of circuits to study. Detailed description of the laboratory facility and software is provided as well for each case.

Figures 1 and 2 illustrate the educational process in one of the laboratories of the Department of Engineering Science and Technology of MEPhI supplied with the developed laboratory module.

Fig. 1. Equipment for the developed analogue electronics laboratory module

Fig. 2. Educational process for first-year students – basic laboratory tasks with the aid of the Educational Laboratory Virtual Instrumentation Suite

The outcome of the developed methodological guidelines was that the students performed mathematical calculations to prepare for the specific laboratory task in a better way. Knowledge of basics of mathematical analysis and complex variable theory is required for that. The guidelines do not replace, but are in addition for the textbooks on analogue electronics.

4   Conclusion

The outcome of application of the developed Analogue Electronics laboratory module resulted in increased effectiveness of educational process.

Students that take nuclear educational engineering programs have a possibility to obtain practical skills in analogue electronics in a better and faster way. They have contemporary hardware, universal virtual devices and proper methodological support to grow into qualified specialists that can successfully solve the task of development of contemporary information measuring systems for nuclear industry with the application of obtained skills and competences.

And this is the focal point where educational and innovation process in a contemporary research university come to a synthesis – because practical tasks of development of information systems for quality and safety control of operation of nuclear reactors and facilities are typical tasks for students graduate works for several educational programs in MEPhI. The universality of the laboratory module developed allows students not only to perform training tasks to obtain and develop practical skills in the area of analogue electronics – but also to solve real practical hi-tech industrial engineering tasks with the aid of the same methodological, hardware and software digital instruments.

The given example is just one of the cases of digital technologies implementation in the educational process when students can master practical skills by the means of modern digital equipment. Thus, subsequently, in the framework of research work and the execution of final qualifying work, as well as innovative activities in the university, a student will rely primarily on skills and competencies obtained during such laboratory practical works.

The results of implementation of the developed laboratory module showed higher effectiveness of obtaining practical knowledge and skills in electronics for students taking the Nuclear Physics and Technology educational program of National Research Nuclear University MEPhI. On the other hand, the developed equipment is actively used for purposes of practical innovation projects of the university realized by teachers and students – thus realizing the synthesis of educational and innovation process.

Acknowledgements. The authors of the paper send their sincere acknowledgements and regards to the Ministry of Science and Education of Russian Federation for funding via the State Assignment for carrying out socially significant events in the area of education, science and youth policy.

References

1. Crawley, E.F.: The CDIO syllabus: a statement of goals for undergraduate engineering education. The Department of Aeronautics and Astronautics, Massachusetts Institute of Technology (2001)
2. Saprykin, D.L.: Engineering education in Russia: history, conception, future trends. High. Educ. Russ. **1**, 125–137 (2012)
3. Fedorov, I.B., Medvedev, V.E.: Engineering education: problems and tasks. High. Educ. Russ. **12**, 54–60 (2011)
4. The CDIO Standards. http://www.cdio.org
5. Vladimirov, A.I.: About Engineering-Technical Education. Nedra Publishing House, Moscow (2011)
6. Yakovlev, D., Pryakhin, A., Korolev, S., Shaltaeva, Y., Samotaev, N., Yushkov, E., Avanesyan, A.: Engineering competitive education using modern network technologies in the NRNU MEPhI. In: Proceedings of the 2015 IEEE Workshop on Environmental, Energy, and Structural Monitoring Systems, pp. 39–43. IEEE Press (2015)

Using the Contextual Search for the Organization Scientific Research Activities

Olga Kononova[1,2(✉)] and Sergey Lyapin[3]

[1] The Sociological Institute of the RAS, ITMO University, 199034 St. Petersburg, Russia
[2] The Sociological Institute of the RAS, 190005 St. Petersburg, Russia
`kononolg@yandex.ru`
[3] Department of International and Project Activities of the Arkhangelsk Regional Museum,
163000 Arkhangelsk, Russia
`lyapins@yandex.ru`

Abstract. The article discusses an approach of coordinating university scientific activities with using contextual search and contextual knowledge extraction technologies. For the implementation of the proposed approach, the authors use an e-library «Humanitariana» with services of contextual search, different types of queries, automated extraction of knowledge from the scientific texts. The advantage of using «Humanitariana» is in the possibility of combining the resources of several organizations, which can function in a local network mode and in distributed IT environment with ability to appeal to all resources from any of the servers of participating organizations. The approach was created and tested in context of preparation of master's theses in "Applied Computer Science" (ITMO University) and scientific exploratory research (The Sociological Institute of the RAS).

Keywords: e-Libraries · Transformations of science · Open research · Scientific research activity · Contextual knowledge · Technologies of extraction contextual knowledge · Contextual search · Thematic collection of search queries · Paragraph-oriented query · Frequency-ranked query

1 Introduction

A global information society is changing its requirements for quality information including its extraction methods and analysis tools. Some of the main requirements are transparency and reliability of data, as well as ability to manage information resources independently – search, analyze, evaluate information and thereby obtain new expertise. And it is satisfying the information needs of society that increases efficiency of management of enterprises, organizations, the public sector of the economy and public institutions, certain types and aspects of human activity.

Problems of information search:

– Electronic documents discovered on queries generated by the user, are irrelevant to user's informational needs in most cases.

© Springer International Publishing AG 2016
A.V. Chugunov et al. (Eds.): DTGS 2016, CCIS 674, pp. 392–399, 2016.
DOI: 10.1007/978-3-319-49700-6_38

- There are two types of relevance-retrieved documents. Search relevance is an assessment of the extent to which documents request. The consumer relevance is a measure of the relevance of retrieved documents matching the information needs of the user.
- The human factor is not taken into account sufficiently. Search queries are determined weakly formalized or vague terms and are largely dependent on the experience and preferences of the person.

Contextual search techniques are used in most of the modern BI systems and support business analytics, provide easy search and smart data retrieval from organized information storage, enhance business resilience [1, 4, 6]. An important aspect of the contextual search application is support of the research activities in state organizations and private sector. In practice, the use of contextual search techniques requires adjustment of staff's approach as well as change in the criteria of collecting, processing, analysis and evaluation of the real value of the information.

Therefore, in order to form internal motivation, relevant competencies, acquire necessary skills for utilization of contextual search technology, Universities should implement these technologies in the educational process, primarily on graduate programs' research work. In addition contextual search technology should be used by all scientific staff in project, analysis and educational activities.

2   System Architecture and Services of the «Humanitariana»

«Humanitariana» was developed in a client-server Internet/Intranet architecture: Web-browser/Web-server – Application Server/Relational DBMS, with protocols HTTP, CGI, PIPE API, ODBC. Given the trends in the development of modern information space, a decentralized environment model was selected under the control of the user's browser, with a focus on Web services and Internet protocols. The browser accesses to a plurality of independent servers that are managed by different organizations [3]. «Humanitariana» provides reproducibility and interpretability of results, allows to prove the relevance and practical significance of the subject matter of the proposed study.
Contextual Search and Knowledge.

Full-Text Search. IP Services provide two types of paragraph-based, and four types of frequency-based contextual search, and support various forms of representation of query results.

Paragraph-oriented search – is a search carried out on a selected set of resources based on inflection search terms (for example, the plural or singular in the English language, a decline in cases in Russian). Search is designed to search for and present the text up to the individual copyright paragraphs that contain user-defined terminological structure (thus explicating "horizontal" micro context in which the search terms are part of the paragraph). Author paragraph is selected as the natural unit of semantic articulation of the text.

Information systems provide two kinds of paragraph-based contextual search, and support various forms of presentation of search results. Simple ("single-layer") thematic search – search on one complex field for entering terms and for the use of these terms is a logical grouping of operators, the compulsory exclusion or explicitly include the term in the query. The search result is a list of paragraphs that meet specified conditions. Services:

- viewing, on the same screen page, the corresponding resource (article, book, etc.) in a file formats (text documents, graphic images of the document, audio or video documents);
- expert evaluation of the found paragraph;
- automated assembly in a separate file thematically oriented paragraphs of the various documents, along with their bibliographic descriptions and originals;
- recording of the file on a portable storage medium.

Advanced ("multi-layer") thematic search – search functionality with additional thematic focus of the request. The search field "layer" (from 2 to 8 layers) is a technical tool for the isolation of a substantial "aspect" of interest to the user "threads." For example, in the first layer, the term coined is "government", in the second – the term "services", in the third – the term "region". Thus, in the structure of the query theme "government" is specialized in connection with the "services" and "region".

Frequency-based search is constructed for frequency-ranked lists of terms, and thus the explication of the various "vertical" macro context implicitly presented in a separate document, or an array of documents. «Humanitariana» provides support for two types of frequency-based search:

- absolute frequency, which results in a frequency-ranked list of nouns included in the resource search and reduced to the normal form (nominative, singular);
- relative frequency, which results in a frequency-ranked list of nouns, included only those paragraphs that contain the term predetermined by the user.

The relative frequency-based search results in a frequency-ranked list of nouns including only those paragraphs that contain user-defined term (thus, term-table constructs a "relative" of the term). The search can be carried out simultaneously on one, two or three baskets resources. All the terms appearing in the Term-table are active. Clicking on any of them, you can go to a formed paragraph-oriented query by that term, and explicate its micro context. Implemented using contextual search services:

- textual analysis of the document;
- identification and description of the documents subject area;
- drawing up a list of keywords.
- comparative analysis of subject areas, different authors or different documents;
- texts check for plagiarism, etc.

«Humanitariana » allows for not only standard features of finding the required information resources, their descriptions, cataloging, storage, retrieval, inherent in classical automated information library systems, but also provides the maximum possible automation of work with the thematic collections of requests [5]. In the structure of «Humanitariana» there is a subsystem of Personal Resources. It is designed to create and manage a set of personal repositories of information obtained through «Humanitariana» services and its resource base. It can be:

- lists of bibliographic descriptions with attached full-text resources;
- arbitrary paragraphs or a combination resulting from a full-text search;
- complete collections of material (optional collect subject in full-text search);
- term-tables (frequency-sorted list of terms);
- lists of literature, used when writing reviews of scientific reports and publications, citation of sources;
- complete structures of user requests, etc.

Query results can be used in analytical expert work and for extraction of contextual knowledge, and as a custom tool for creating and expanding thematic collections of full-text materials. Extra search capabilities and the presentation of its results:

- showing "the cluster of paragraphs", which is found in paragraph (opening few paragraphs located in the primary document found before and after);
- graphical display of the original resource page text containing the found paragraph of a text;
- the ability to save a registered user requests for the subsequent formation of "My Account" user, stored on the server.

3   Experimental Base

The three information sources form «Humanitariana» data, used for study, testing approach and library services. The first source was the archive of scientific publications e-Government Technology Centre ITMO University on the subject of "e-Government and e-Services" (70 resource consisting of 5.2 thousand news reports) for 2011-2015.

Category "Computer Games" used two sources [2]: Russian-language scientific periodicals placed in the public domain on the portal e-library – Scientific Electronic Library (http://elibrary.ru/). Total 604 files for 2005-2015 years were prepared for analysis; – English-language scientific journals: «Game Studies» (published since 2001), «Games and Culture» (published since 2006).

Organization of University Research Activities.   Among the tasks of student, professors and research associates the following problems were identified: the analysis and synthesis of the research results using modern science and technology; the analysis and development of information management methods; preparation of publications on the subject of research.

Search, analysis and selection of useful information are key for researchers, teachers and students requiring certain competencies and skills. During the search process huge amount of information is accumulated and needs to be stored for further processing and analysis. It is necessary to create a personal full-text thematic collection of scientific materials, which currently can be done using several approaches and tools:

- saving the web-page on your computer in the original format using the web-browser capabilities;
- copying URL and the text discovered and further saving it in a text format, such as MS Word document, in a folder on your computer;
- using NetSnippets type system to copy and save the documents found with the ability to proceed studies;

However, these approaches have significant drawbacks:

- diversity of formats of the data;
- inability to create a uniform bibliographic descriptions for all found on the internet as well as in stand-alone digital libraries of heterogeneous information resources;
- inability to organize an effective full-text search of the desired material in sufficiently large full-text collections;
- lack of ability to submit and index full-text documents for further use.

Increased manageability, quality and intensification of study activities can be accomplished through the use of distributed information systems with functional, transparent contextual search. The traditional study has five stages.

Stage 1. Formulation of the problem

The main result at this stage is formation of a frequency-ranked list of terms characterizing the subject area of the research (semantic macro-context). It allows to formulate topics of the subject area, which determine the dynamics of the scientific community interests and identify the most perspective scientific problems to public.

The overall study directions of their corresponding university departments and other organizations cooperating with the university, determine the area of study in graduate programs. The specific topics for a student research are selected the study leaders (Table 1).

Table 1. Problem formulation

Content	Services	The user's results
The direction of research (research subjects).	Contextual search. Personal storage of information resources.	1. Research subjects list. 2. Meaningful structuring of an arbitrary set of documents for the formation of repositories of information resources on the domain.
Identify customer requirements.	Frequency based contextual search.	1. The frequency-ranked list of the subject area terms.
		2. Unicom individual keyword list (relevant terms).

The overall study directions of their corresponding university departments and other organizations cooperating with the university, determine the area of study in graduate programs. The specific topics for a student research are selected the study leaders.

Stage 2. Nomination and support of R&D

The results of study are:

- selection and justification of the relevance of topics, determination of possible solutions of research problems (concepts isolated explication domain);
- approval of the topic and projection of Research and Development;
- bibliographies, source lists, catalogs (Table 2).

Table 2. Nomination and support of R&D

Content	Services	The user's results
The collection, examination, analysis of the results of fundamental and exploratory research. Comparative assessment of potential topics for R&D.	Paragraph-based contextual search. Categories depositary. Archive requests and search results.	1. Searches of various types in order to extract the context of knowledge based on keyword lists. 2. Saving the query and search results. 3. Analysis of requests.
Selection and justification of the relevance of the topic, way to solve research problems. Submission and development of the theme. Selection of the scientific literature on the subject.	The combination of frequency-based and paragraph-based contextual search.	1. Searches in storehouses of information resources. 2. Analysis of selected contexts (horizontal and vertical). 3. Legend meaning "vertical context" and theming material. 4. Legend "horizontal context" use of terms in the framework of copyright paragraph.
Drawing on the research report.	Personal storage of information resources.	Creating personal thematic collections of electronic documents. Formation of the bibliography, resources descriptions.

Stages 3–4. Theoretical and experimental studies

Table 3. Theoretical and experimental research

Scope of work	Services	User's results
Preparation of analytical review, abstracts, publications.	Personal storage of information resources. Paragraph-based contextual search.	1. Personal thematic documents collections. 2. "Horizontal" micro contexts. 3. The citing works list.
Drawing up a terms list.	Absolute frequency-based contextual search.	Frequency-oriented query terms list.

Main outcomes at this stage are preparation of materials for analysis (term-tables), formation of personal thematic collections, preparation of analytical reviews on research (based on explicate linearly ordered list of "horizontal" micro-context) using contexts for quoting parts of the text (Table 3).

Stage 5. Analysis and comparison of results

At this stage, any combination of «Humanitariana» services can be used (Table 4).

Table 4. Analysis and comparison of results

Scope of work	Services	User's results
Preparation of a graduation paper.	Personal repository of information resources.	Personal thematic documents collections. Bibliography resource descriptions.
Preparation of scientific publications on the study subject.	Full-text paragraph-based contextual search.	The citing works. Contexts replication for quoting parts of the text.
Delivering of a final graduate paper demonstrating a use of e-library services.		

4   Conclusions and Recommendations

Using various methods of contextual knowledge extraction and contextual search, MSIS Department of ITMO University provided enhanced reporting and analytics of Research, developed systematization and storage of department's scientific publications and materials, formed its own thematic repositories for management of state information systems and established an access to thematic repositories and collections of other organizations.

Testing «Humanitariana» in the teaching process of graduates' students showed that its features of contextual search allow:

– monitor results of work of students and their research activity;
– enhance efficiency of the preliminary stage of research, namely choosing scientific issues, considering appropriate supervisor and research topic;
– reduce complexity in processing of information resources.

The work outlines the ways of further development of the research, analytical and project activities at the department with the help of already implemented and potential services «Humanitariana» has to offer.

The further possibilities for development using information systems are a comparison arrays of texts in Russian and in English and tracing the chronological order of its dynamics. It will enhance and intensify the research, primarily analytical.

Acknowledgments. Analytical results of the reported study (an analysis of scientific journals on the subject of computer games) was funded by RFBR 16-06-00368.a and is designed for 2016–2018. Testing of library services was carried out in the framework of the project RHF № 14-03-12017 and is designed for 2014–2016.

References

1. Szetela, D: Effective . https://www.seroundtable.com/archives/018064.html
2. Kononova, O.V., Sergeeva, O.V., Krut'ko, E.A., Oreh, E.A.: Play computer experience as a subject of the scientific periodical press in focus of the automated context search. In: Proceedings of the IV International Scientific and Practical Conference «Communications in Social and Humanitarian Knowledge, Economy, Education», pp. 251–253. Minsk (2016)
3. Ljapin, S.H., Kukovjakin, A.V.: Tematicheskie kollekcii polnotekstovyh zaprosov dlja izuchenija kontekstnogo znanija (proekt Humanitariana) [Thematic collections of full-text queries for learning contextual knowledge (project Humanitariana)]. Sbornik nauchnyh trudov XVIII Ob#edinennoj nauchnoj konferencii «Internet i sovremennoe obshhestvo» [Collection of scientific papers XVIII of the scientific conference "Internet and Modern Society"], pp. 216–224. St. Petersburg (2015)
4. Melucci, M.: Contextual search: a computational framework. Found. Trends Inf. Retrieval 6(4–5), 257–405 (2012). doi:10.1561/1500000023. http://dx.doi.org/10.1561/1500000023
5. O model'nom zakone «O mezhdunarodnom informacionnom obmene»: postanovlenie Mezhparlamentskoj Assamblei gosudarstv - uchastnikov sodruzhestva nezavisimyh gosudarstv ot 26.03.2002 № 19-7 [On the model law "On international information exchange": Resolution of the Interparliamentary Assembly of States - members of the Commonwealth of Independent States on March 26, 2002 № 19-7]. http://base.consultant.ru/cons/cgi/online.cgi?req=doc;base=INT;n=13288
6. Smart, P.R., Sieck, W.R., Shadbolt, N.R.: Using web-based knowledge extraction techniques to support cultural modeling. In: Salerno, J., Yang, S.J., Nau, D., Chai, S.-K. (eds.) SBP 2011. LNCS, vol. 6589, pp. 113–120. Springer, Heidelberg (2011). doi:10.1007/978-3-642-19656-0_18

A Case Study of Open Science Concept: Linked Open Data in University

Nikolay Karmanovskiy, Dmitry Mouromtsev, Mikhail Navrotskiy,
Dmitry Pavlov, and Irina Radchenko[✉]

ITMO University, St. Petersburg, Russia
{karmanov,mouromtsev}@mail.ifmo.ru, m.navrotskiy@gmail.com,
dmitry.pavlov@vismart.biz, iradche@gmail.com

Abstract. The article gives an overview of Open Science concept to support online scientific collaborations and open science data contribution. The authors give a description of 'Linked Open Data in University' project (developed Russian universities linked open data hub, architecture of this portal, published datasets and approach to mapping data from relational database to RDF).

Keywords: Linked Open Data · Online scientific collaboration · Open data · Open Science

1 Introduction

One of the main tasks of the modern university is sustaining knowledge economy, i.e. investing into human capital and increasing the volume of accumulated knowledge provided for learning.

Scientific community and university face the same set of challenges: upholding and fostering the international scientific collaboration, provision of open access to research results and to scientific publications, promotion and popularization of project in science, attracting the students audience and general public to relevant (demanded by employers) courses, the utilization of a maximum number of acknowledged and reliable information sources: web-sites, books and guides of various kinds. Usage of Open Science concept provides an opportunities for changing of the typical approaches to these challenges.

2 Open Science

Open Science is an umbrella term for a movement whose purpose - to make research data accessible and disseminated to all levels of society concerned (from amateurs to professionals).

Open Science concept presumes the transparency of the research and observation methodology as well as the broad access to scientific data sets collections used and acquired as results of experiment, free accessibility and re-use of scientific data, availability and transparency of scientific communications, the use of virtual platforms for collaborative scientific work flow support.

A.V. Chugunov et al. (Eds.): DTGS 2016, CCIS 674, pp. 400–403, 2016.
DOI: 10.1007/978-3-319-49700-6_39

The major development and promotion trends in Open Science are:

- The development of e-infrastructure for Open science,
- Open data bases (in spreadsheet formats and in a form of linked data),
- Open platforms for collaborative scientific work flow,
- Open scientific publications,
- Open experiment methodology,
- Open source software used by researchers,
- The development of Open Notebook Science,
- Citizen Science (incl. Extreme Citizen Science),
- Open peer review of scientific papers,
- Open Educational Resources.

The movement for Open Science has been gradually spreading around the world.

Besides the importance of accessibility of research publication, there exists another problem – a problem of open access to scientific data. This particular issues is investigated in the article "Open Data in Science" by Peter Murray-Rust [3].

The online repositories could be utilized for publication of research results, they allow publication of research data together with descriptions (i.e. metadata). The article "Recommended Data Repositories" [4] printed in Scientific Data journal reviews the possible options and recommends particular repositories for datasets publication. On the other hand, the datasets can be also released on Zenodo platform[1] and on open data platforms (CKAN[2], DKAN[3], Socrata[4], Junar[5], etc.

By the beginning of 2016 more than 600 tools and innovations in scholarly communications immerged. The comprehensive list of them could be found in project "101 innovations in scholarly communication"[6].

Such tools prove to be incredibly efficient for scientists and researchers, but in reality there happens to be a large number of them who is not familiar with tools scholarly communications and research. Opens Science Labs portal[7] sees its primary goal in promotion and dissemination of these tools.

It accumulates information on Open Science and Open Education projects, which originated in Russia, and maintains a registry of up-to-date tutorials and guides related to online services and tools designed to assist the researchers and scientists (the foundation for publication of tutorials was laid at one of the International Open Data Day celebration in March, 2016).

---

[1] http://www.zenodo.org/.
[2] http://ckan.org/.
[3] https://www.drupal.org/project/dkan.
[4] https://opendata.socrata.com/.
[5] http://junar.com/.
[6] https://101innovations.wordpress.com/.
[7] http://www.opensciencelabs.ru/.

3   Linked Open Data in University

Semantic Web is a Web of machine-readable data, where each data source can be used in different applications. One of the best solutions for publishing related data is to use the technology of linked data which based on W3C standards and technologies such as RDF and OWL. Universities play a major role in the development of this research area. Today leading universities of Europe and the USA are developing projects using Semantic Web principles and Linked Open Data (LOD): LODUM, Open Data about the University of Oxford, University of Southampton Open Data Portal, Dataverse, Linked Open Aalto Data Service and others.

Its good practice in such projects to published datasets include data about: courses; publications; research projects; places, such as buildings; researches and staff; organizational structure; news and events.

On the basis of these data sets there are distinct possibilities to develop visualizations and applications that demonstrates how linked open data can be used to improve the transparency of a university, add value to both students and staff, and to help decision makers understand and track the workings of a distributed, knowledge-based organization.

Authors use kOre framework [1, 2] for mapping data from university database to RDF:

- A knowledge engineer develops an algorithm of mapping data from the relational database to RDF and writes it as a mapping file with SML language;
- The system transforms data to linked data (transform data from relational database to RDF);
- The system uploads data to Triple store (Virtuoso).

The developed data hub presents a web application: the client is HTML5 application (bootstrap, reactjs), and the server is Rails application. Data hub is developed on the basis Linked Open Data portal of ITMO University[8] which publishes data about scientific laboratories, staff, research areas.

The server consists of the following modules (see Fig. 1):

- Virtuoso LOD storage system. It implements access to datasets through SPARQL.
- Pubby – a LOD Frontend for SPARQL Endpoints.
- API (RESTful) module – a module giving access to data. It returns data in the JSON format, for example, for mobile clients.
- Web client – the module implements user interface and base functionality (visualization, semantic search, add datasets).

Publications data from different universities (data sources) allows developing a lot of applications by using this data such as: datasets publishing (with DOI), Semantic Search. Visualization, and Indoor navigation.

---

[8] http://lod.ifmo.ru.

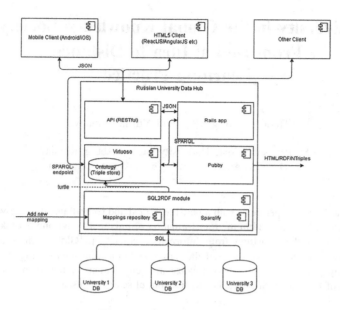

Fig. 1. Data hub architecture

4   Conclusions

The presented overview prompts us to conclusion that in the next couple of years we will witness a major breakthrough in the sphere of support and organization of scientific research carried out in the virtual space. The immense financial support allocated by European Commission for Open Science will encourage the initiation of a great number of projects and elaboration of new approaches and methodologies for research conducted with the use of Internet. Open Science approaches will contribute to the lecturing and teaching activities.

The implementation of Open Science and Linked Open Data concepts on university grounds could significantly broaden the studying audience, boost the visibility and foster the respect for teaching professions beyond the university campus, assist in checking the essence and quality of educational courses.

References

1. Ermilov, I., Höffner, K., Lehmann, J., Mouromtsev, D.: kOre: Using Linked Data for OpenScience Information Integration, iSEMANTiCS 2015 (2015)
2. Mouromtsev, D.I., Lehmann, J., Semerkhanov, I.A., Navrotskiy, M.A., Ermilov, I.S.: Study of current approaches for Web publishing of open scientific data. Sci. Tech. J. Inform. Technol. Mech. Opt. **15**(6), 1081–1087 (2015)
3. Murray-Rust, P.: Open data in science. Ser. Rev. **34**(1), 52–64 (2008). doi:10.1016/j.serrev.2008.01.001
4. Recommended Data Repositories. http://www.nature.com/sdata/data-policies/repositories

University in the Global Knowledge Society: From Digital Idea to Distance Learning Practice

Radomir Bolgov$^{(\boxtimes)}$ and Yuliia Dunaeva

St. Petersburg State University, St. Petersburg, Russia
rbolgov@yandex.ru, j.dunaeva@spbu.ru

Abstract. The paper deals with a new theoretical and technological framework of higher education within the transformation of university environment taking into account the transition from Information Society to Global Knowledge Society. The authors synthesized the new communication methodologies and teaching practices, as well problematize the achievement of the main benchmarks of Innovative Society, such as freedom of scientific research and creative activity.

Keywords: Innovative educational practices · World summit on the information society · Intellectual capital · Distance learning · e-Learning · Digital divide

1 Introduction

Knowledge society scenarios system is formulated in the UNESCO World Report 2005 [1] and consists of two stages: the information age of the global society and knowledge civilization turned information into an intellectual product of the world civilization.

One of the knowledge society purposes is the freedom of scientific research and creative activity. The reform of higher education is conducted for this purpose. The inclusion of Russian universities in the knowledge society has consistently held in two stages: national programs "Electronic Russia (2002–2010)" [2] and "Information Society (2011–2020)" [3].

The term "Information Society" appeared in the 1960s, both in the US and Japan. [4] Knowledge society claims as main purpose the equal and universal access to information. In the information society the technological parameters are crucial (the new wave of high-tech, Internet, mobile communication of the third generation, etc.) A new integrated information system is forming which merged telecommunications, computer, electronic and audiovisual equipments [5].

Information is a tool of knowledge, but it is not the actual knowledge. Additionally it requires a combination of creative and analytical principles. The process of converting information into knowledge has a place in the educational and research environments.

© Springer International Publishing AG 2016
A.V. Chugunov et al. (Eds.): DTGS 2016, CCIS 674, pp. 404–410, 2016.
DOI: 10.1007/978-3-319-49700-6_40

2 International Organizations Activities on Knowledge Society Development

At the end of the twentieth century the debate on the prospects for the information society and its development into a knowledge society was discussed in the Council of Europe, the European Commission and other international organizations. At the beginning of the 21st century a World Summit on the Information Society (WSIS) held under the auspices of the United Nations: in 2003 in Geneva and in 2005 in Tunisia. [6] UNESCO's contribution to the development of the concept of the knowledge society is the program "Information for All". UNESCO formulated key principles of knowledge societies: quality of education, universal access to knowledge and cultural diversity. UNESCO's work on developing the concept of the knowledge society is divided into two phases: Geneva (2003–2005) and Tunis (2005–2015) [7]. UNESCO argues that it is not enough to reduce the digital divide, but it is necessary to strive for equality of opportunity in all spheres of culture, i.e. to overcome the "cognitive divide" - the gap in knowledge. This task was assigned to the science and education, which required reconsider traditional approaches of high school and go to innovative educational process.

Parameters of «educated and skilled population» are one of the four pillars of knowledge economy. According to the Knowledge Economy Index of the World Bank (KEI), education parameters are closely connected with the intellectual capital.

3 International Assessment of the Intellectual Capital in Russia

The development progress in Intellectual Capital Development in CIS differs from country to country [8]. There are numerous factors influencing the progress in the region including the socio-economic situation, political instability, leadership, public administration reform, investment policies, regulation and legislation, national culture, etc [9–11].

3.1 UN Human Development Index (HDI)

Since 1990, the UN began publishing annual Global Human Development Reports based on the data received from countries. In turn, the countries publish national "Human Development Reports" [12], which gave rise to the revision of the main criteria for determining the well-being and prosperity of the country. The Report 2014 focuses on the national achievements in the field of development.

For the Russian Federation, in the ranking in 2014, she lost 2 positions compared to the previous year and finished 57th, which gives it a presence in the group of highly developed countries. [12] According to experts, the negative factors are social inequality, environmental problems, and low life expectancy. Nevertheless, Russia is ahead in the ranking in 2014 of its partners in the BRICS. However, Russia, which is on the level of literacy of the population in the 10th place, and on a completely respectable 31st place in terms of enrollment, feels the urgent need for new personnel qualifications, able to adequately respond to the challenges of the new economics. But the indicators included in the index, does not reflect this problem [12].

3.2   World Bank' Intellectual Capital Assessment

In 2014 the report by the World Bank "Diversified development: Making the Most of Natural Resources in Eurasia" was published [14], which takes note of a need for a well-balanced economic policy" [15].

Parameters "educated and skilled population" are one of four pillars of the Knowledge Economy framework. KEI contains a set of Education parameters linked with Intellectual Capital, particularly, Government expenditure on education, Government expenditure per student, Literacy rate (% of people of different social groups), Unemployment etc. A set of Science & Technology parameters contains, for example, "Researchers in R&D (per a million people)", "Patent applications", "Trademarks applications" etc.

We can see in Table 1 that, according to the World Bank' Knowledge Economy Index (KEI) 2012 Rankings [14], Russia was rated as 55 (KEI 5,78), Belarus – 59 (KEI 5,59), Kazakhstan – 73 (KEI 5,04). All this counties ranked higher than in the previous ranking 2000.

Table 1. World Bank KEI 2012

Rank 2012	Country	KEI	Education	Education rank
1	Sweden	9.43	8.92	6
2	Finland	9.33	8.77	11
3	Denmark	9.16	8.63	15
55	Russian Federation	5.78	6.79	44
59	Belarus	5.59	7.37	
73	Kazakhstan	5.04	6.91	

3.3   World Economic Forum' (WEF) Intellectual Capital Assessment

The WEF pundits scrutinized facilities in the spheres of education, healthcare, labor activity, favorable environment across 122 nations. [16] National data on the workforce share, the number of secondary school students, infant mortality, life expectancy and a series of other indices were also given consideration. [17] As a result, Russia gained only 51 marks. One of the reasons, according to experts, was the low activity of the investment policy of the Russian government in the human capital.

A set of parameters "Skills", closely linked with Intellectual Capital, is one of five pillars of the WEF Networked Readiness Index. It contains such parameters as Quality of educational system, Quality of math & science education, Secondary education gross enrollment rate, and Adult literacy rate.

We can see in Table 2 that, according to the WEF Networked Readiness Index 2015 [18], Kazakhstan was ranked as 40 (index is 4,50), and Russia – as 41 (4,50).

Table 2. World Economic Forum (WEF) Networked Readiness Index 2015

Rank 2015	Country	NRI 2015	5.01 quality of the education system, value (rank)	5.02 quality of math and science education, value (rank)	5.03 secondary enrollment rate, value (rank)	5.04 adult literacy rate, value (rank)
1	Singapore	6.0	5.8 (4)	6.3 (1)	107.1 (16)	96.8 (36)
2	Finland	6.0	5.9 (2)	6.3 (2)	107.7 (14)	n/a
3	Sweden	5.8	4.6 (26)	4.4 (49)	98.4 (38)	n/a
40	Kazakhstan	4.5	3.6 (76)	4.1 (72)	97.7 (40)	99.8 (6)
41	Russian Federation	4.5	3.5 (84)	4.3 (59)	95.3 (54)	99.7 (10)
58	Armenia	4.2	3.5 (86)	4.2 (69)	95. 9 (49)	99.7 (12)

In 2013 Kazakhstan was ranked as 38th, and Russia – as 50. Thus, Russia has improved its global rankings.

According to the WEF Global Information Technology Report 2013 [19], based on Executive opinion survey, Kazakhstan was ranked as 69th out of 144 in 2012 (as 66 in 2011). Russia was ranked as 106 in 2012 (as 99 in 2011).

Russia, Armenia, and Kazakhstan joined the Top-10 Most Improved Countries since 2012. Russia ranks 79th in the Political and regulatory environment pillar of the NRI, because of the lack of independence (109th) and inefficiency of its judicial system, as well as the poor protection of intellectual property (106th), among other issues.

4   High School in the Knowledge Society: New Educational Approaches and Issues

In the knowledge society organization is decentralized (as opposed to the vertical hierarchy of the industrial age), their structure is agile, competitive, multiparadigmatic by nature. The significance of such methods, the stimulation of the student, the ability to critically evaluate new knowledge, the ability to take risks, exchange of roles in the learning process, the development of non-formal learning, etc. [20].

Overproduction of highly qualified specialists in Russia resulted in the so-called "scissors effect" between supply and demand in the labor market. Increasing the number of students has led to the liberalization of higher education in the information society: at the turn of the century in Russia there were private universities, significantly reduced the national scientific potential. In Russia, only 2–5% of the innovation potential is involved in practice. For comparison, the figure is 85% in Japan and 60% in the United States" [21].

For a breakthrough in the field of science national innovation system (NIS), integrating the state, educational institutions, business, and non-governmental organizations are necessary. Since 2010 a set of competencies instead of disciplines and credit units instead of teaching load hours are put in university programs. Russia's recognition of foreign diplomas and academic degrees [13] demanded from the universities to meet the rankings of publication activity in Web of Science and Scopus, and enter the first hundred of the world's leading universities (5/100 program).

National program of education development (2016–2020) [22] provides design-oriented approach in contrast to the classical program-oriented approach of 2011–2015, the introduction of new structures (models) of high schools, modernization of distance education technologies, the transition to a system of effective contract with the teaching staff, the formation of applied qualifications attract employers to participate in education, etc.

The new trend of the knowledge society is an information transparency and accessibility of education. Universities are moving to create open content: open training courses of leading scientists and research teams are placed in the Internet. Michael Allen, a professor of the University of Minnesota and expert in e-learning, said a good phrase: "The terms "dull" and "effective" are mutually exclusive in the learning". [23] Electronic products LMS, Authorware visual tool and a great number of Intel training courses help to raise an interest in learning at the University. Innovative learning technologies such as e-universities, libraries, virtual "round tables", seminars and workshops are developing. [24].

The problem of "brain drain" is a type of abnormal scientific mobility between the regions of the world. According to Y. Magarshak, "today, the Russian scientific and technological abroad has the potential to disproportionately greater than the actual Russian Academy" [25]. The methods of overcoming this negative trend are the establishment of international laboratories working on a joint research program. An example of such a productive program is the international human genome project.

Model of creative learning that combines acquisition, renewal and use of knowledge, is the aim of higher education reforms.

5 Conclusion

A new type of social organization - the knowledge society - includes not only knowledge as a value, but also humanistic aspects. The danger of inequality, imbalance of information and knowledge, lack of freedom to express opinions, manipulation of information for political purposes are tasks to solve.

Science and education are basic factors in the knowledge society, so its analysis is impossible without the characteristics of the reform in education. ICT open new opportunities for global access to education. Due to the high level of education (according to the HDI) Russia has good chances of its full integration into the global information field of the Knowledge society, but at the same time, inefficient use of human capital is the cause of backwardness of Russia in the overall international ranking of post-industrial development [25].

References

1. Towards Knowledge Societies: UNESCO World Report. Paris (2005)
2. Electronic Russia (2002–2010): National Program of the Russian Federation. http://minsvyaz.ru/common/upload/Postanovlenie_k65_Eletronnaya_Rossiya[1].pdf
3. Information Society (2011–2020): National Program of the Russian Federation. http://www.kremlin.ru/events/state-council/10053
4. Masuda, Y.: The Information Society as Post-Industrial Society. Wash (1981)
5. Castells, M.: The Information Age: Economy, Society and Culture: The Power of Identity. Blackwell Publ, Oxford (1996)
6. World Summit on the Information Society, Geneva. 2003. UNESCO "Information for All", 2007. St. Petersburg (2004)
7. UNESCO Between Two Phases of the World Summit on the Information Society, Proceedings. Moscow (2005)
8. CIS Program of Long-term Cooperation for the Promotion of Information Society till 2015. http://www.iacis.ru/eng/activities/long_term_plan/
9. Bershadskaya, L., Chugunov, A., Dzhusupova, Z.: Understanding e-government development barriers in cis countries and exploring mechanisms for regional cooperation. In: Kő, A., Leitner, C., Leitold, H., Prosser, A. (eds.) EGOVIS/EDEM 2013. LNCS, vol. 8061, pp. 87–101. Springer, Heidelberg (2013). doi:10.1007/978-3-642-40160-2_8
10. Bolgov, R., Vasilyeva, N. Intellectual capital impact on evolution of information society in Russia. In: ACM International Conference Proceeding Series, 2nd International Conference on Electronic Governance and Open Society: Challenges in Eurasia, EGOSE 2015, pp. 211–215 (2015)
11. Bolgov, R., Karachay, V., Zinovieva, E.: Information society development in eurasian economic union countries: legal aspects. In: ACM International Conference Proceeding Series,. 8th International Conference on Theory and Practice of Electronic Governance, ICEGOV 2014, pp. 387–390 (2014)
12. Human Development Report "Sustainable human progress: reducing vulnerability and increasing resilience" (2014). http://hdr.undp.org/sites/default/files/hdr14-summary-ru.pdf
13. Lukichyova, L.I.: Human Capital Management. Omega-L, Moscow (2007)
14. The World Bank overview "diversified development: optimal use of natural resources in Eurasia" (2014). http://www.worldbank.org/content/dam/Worldbank/Feature%20Story/ECA/diversified-development-eurasia-overview-russian.pdf
15. The World Bank recommends the Eurasian nations to invest in human capital, 04 Feb 2014. http://www.regnum.ru/news/polit/1762393.html#ixzz3FwUe0xM4
16. KAM (2012). http://siteresources.worldbank.org/INTUNIKAM/Resources/2012.pdf
17. The Human Capital Report (2013). http://reports.weforum.org/human-capital-index-2013/
18. Bazalishvili, M.: The international experts have placed Russia to the 51 position. In: Delovoy Peterburg, 03 Oct 2013. http://www.dp.ru/a/2013/10/03/Rossija_malo_vkladivaetsja/
19. WEF Global Information Technology Report (2013). http://www.weforum.org
20. Kleiner, G.B. The formation of a knowledge society in Russia: socio-economic aspects. In: Social Studies and the Present, No. 3 (2005)
21. Kapelyushnikov, R., Gimpelson, V. Session of the expertly group No. 7 "the job market, professional education, migration policy"/"evolution of human capital in Russia" (2011). http://2020strategy.ru/data/2011/09/29/1214758802/zasedanie_22.09.pdf
22. National program of education development (2016–2020). http://www.consultant.ru/document/cons_doc_LAW_180188/2914760a9fb16ee00146b08c29c054ca2a2208a1/

23. Allen, M.W.: Creating Successful E-Learning: A Rapid System For Getting It Right First Time, Every Time. Pfeiffer/Wiley, San Francisco (2006)
24. Dunaeva, Y.: Information technologies as tools of university education [in Russian]. In: Regionalnyie problemy preobrazovaniya ekonomiki, No. 2 (2016)
25. Magarshak, Y.: Triangle civilization. Russian academic science. It needs an overhaul [in Russian]. Vremya Novostei, 4 (2007)

Automation of Knowledge Work: A Framework of Soft Computing

Alexander Ryjov[✉]

Department of Mechanics and Mathematics, Lomonosov Moscow State University,
Moscow, Russia
ryjov@intsys.msu.ru

Abstract. Modern information technologies have changed our world dramatically during last years. We see how a number of traditional professions were died, and how a number of new specialties and workplaces were born under pressure of new technologies. Technologies are moving so quickly, and in so many directions, that it becomes challenging to even keep in mind a general picture. In this article, we shortly discuss one of the most visible disruptive technologies – automation of knowledge work, and tried to formulate our vision why and how we can use soft computing framework in this area. Main ideas are illustrated on a very core activity in every society – smart learning for education.

Keywords: Automation of knowledge work · Evaluation and monitoring for complex processes · Smart learning for education

1 Introduction

Modern economy is technology-based and technology driving in many respects. Following [2], we will articulate economical impact of disruptive technologies as a transformation the way we live and work, enable new business models, and provide an opening for new players to upset the established order. Examples of such technologies could be the semiconductor microchip, the Internet, or steam power in the Industrial Revolution. We agree with the McKinsey & Company Global Institute (MGI) vision [2] that business leaders and policy makers need to identify potentially disruptive technologies, and carefully consider their potential, before these technologies begin to exert their disruptive powers in the economy and society.

General picture of modern disruptive technologies [1] is presented on Fig. 1. Top-5 technologies with estimated potential economic impact across sized applications in 2025 more than $1 trillion annually are: mobile internet ($3,7–$10,8 trillions annually), Automation of knowledge work ($5.2 trillion to $6.7 trillion per year), Internet of Things ($2.7–$6.2 trillions annually), Cloud technology ($1.7–$6.2 trillions), Advanced robotics ($1.7–$4.5 trillions annually).

Internet of Things and Automation of knowledge work seems the most interesting from points of view: (1) impact to very fundamental activities in any society – health care and education, and (2) readiness-to-use. It means a very big impact in a very near future.

© Springer International Publishing AG 2016
A.V. Chugunov et al. (Eds.): DTGS 2016, CCIS 674, pp. 411–421, 2016.
DOI: 10.1007/978-3-319-49700-6_41

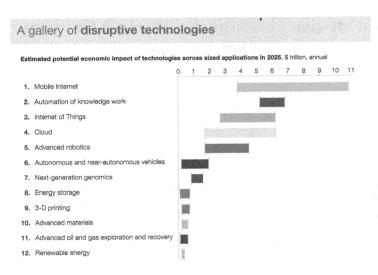

Fig. 1. A gallery of disruptive technologies [1].

The rest of this paper is organized as follows: Sect. 1 proposes the main features of Automation of knowledge work direction. Section 2 provides description of technology for evaluation and monitoring of complex processes as a framework for big class of automation of knowledge work tasks. Case study for smart learning for education from Uchi.ru is presented in Sect. 3. Section 4 is a conclusion of the work.

2   Automation of Knowledge Work

Automation of knowledge work is a new enough direction based on advances in artificial intelligence, machine learning, big data, and natural user interfaces (Fig. 2).

McKinsey & Company, who has introduced this term, defines the "automation of knowledge work" as "the use of computers to perform tasks that rely on complex analysis, subtle judgments, and creative problem solving" [2].

3   Human-Centric Systems for Evaluation the Status and Monitoring the Progress of Complex Processes

A big part of "tasks that rely on complex analysis, subtle judgments, and creative problem solving" [2] is evaluation the status and monitoring the progress of processes in society. Modelling and control for social and political processes is very different from physical and technical ones. Social processes are unique in physical sense – a series of independent experiments is not possible; we cannot measure parameters like in physics – "measuring device" is a person; we do not have adequate models like heat equation – processes are describing in natural language or in the form of parametric dependencies, etc. As a result, we can conclude that classical mathematics is not suitable for describing and modelling

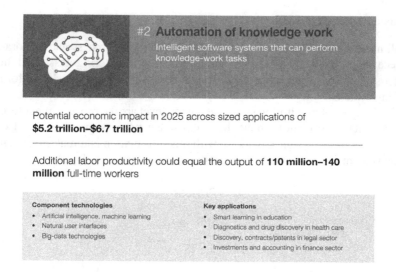

Fig. 2. Automation of knowledge work components [2].

of socio-economic processes due to huge complexity, uncertainty, vague. Only the right mix of computer intelligence and human intelligence can solve these problems.

This section describes main ideas of Information Monitoring Systems (IMS) as a technological base for automation of knowledge work domain. From systems point of view, information monitoring systems relate to a class of hierarchical fuzzy discrete dynamic systems. The theoretical base of such class of systems is made by the fuzzy sets theory, discrete mathematics, methods of the analysis of hierarchies which was developed in works of L.A. Zadeh [16, 17], M.D. Mesarovich [7], T.L. Saaty [14], and others. The analytic hierarchy process (AHP) was developed in the 1980s by Saaty [14]. It is a systematic decision making method which includes both qualitative and quantitative techniques. It is being widely used in many fields for a long time. Buckley [6] incorporated the fuzziness into the AHP, called the FAHP. Hierarchical fuzzy systems have attracted considerable attentions in recent years. Torra [15] summarized the related recent research work in this domain. Detailed FAHP literature review is also presented in [8].

IMS address to process uniformly diverse, multi-level, fragmentary, unreliable, and varying in time information about some problem/process. Based on this type of information IMS allow perform monitoring of the process' evolution and work out strategic plans of process development. These capabilities open a broad area of applications in business (for example, [4]), socio-political problems (control of bilateral and multilateral agreements [9], healthcare [3]), etc.

3.1   Basic Elements of IMS

We shall name a task of evaluation of a current state of the process and elaboration of the forecasts of its development as an information-monitoring task, and human-computer systems ensuring support of a similar sort of information tasks - information monitoring systems.

Basic elements of monitoring system at the top level are the process, the information space, in which information about the state of the process circulates, and experts (analysts, users of the system), working with this information and making conclusions about the state of the process and forecasts of its development (Fig. 3).

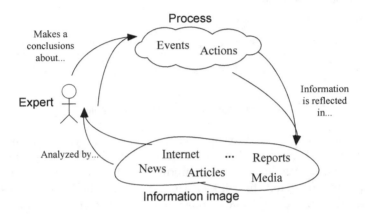

Fig. 3.   Basic elements of IMS and their interaction.

The *information image* represents a set of various information elements, which can be characterized as follows:

- diversity of the information carriers;
- fragmentariness. The information more often concerns to any fragment of the process;
- multi-levels of the information. The information can concern to the whole process, to some its parts, to a particular element of the process;
- various degree of reliability. The information can contain the particular data which has a various degree of reliability, indirect data, and results of conclusions on the basis of the reliable information or indirect conclusions;
- possible discrepancy. The information from various sources can coincide, slightly to differ or in general to contradict one another;
- varying in time. The problem develops in time; therefore the information at different moments of the time about the same element of the process may and should be differ;
- possible bias. The information reflects certain interests of the source of the information, therefore it can have tendentious character.

The *experts/analysts* are an active element of the monitoring system and, observing and studying elements of the information space, they make conclusions about the state of the process and prospects of its development taking into account listed above properties of the information space.

3.2 Basic Elements of IMS

Information monitoring systems allow:

- to process uniformly diverse, multi-level, fragmentary, unreliable, information varying in time;
- to receive evaluations of status of the whole process and/or its particular aspects;
- to simulate various situations in the subject area;
- to reveal "critical ways" of the development of the process. It means to reveal those elements of the process, the small change of which status may qualitatively change the status of the process as a whole.

Taking into account the given features of the information and specific methods of its processing, it is possible to declare the main features of the information monitoring technology as follows:

- The system makes it possible to process fragmentary and/or multi-level information. For this purpose, a considerable part of the model is represented in the form of a tree or graph (Fig. 4).

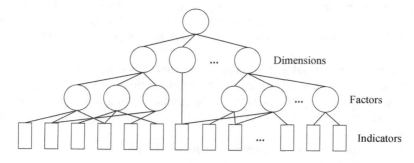

Fig. 4. Typical structure of a model for IMS

- The information with a various degree of reliability, probably, biased can be processed in the system. For this purpose the description of the influence of the information received on a status of the model of a process was done with use of fuzzy linguistic variable. It is necessary to take into account, that the evaluation of the element of model may both vary under influence of the information received and remain unchanged (i.e. be confirmed).
- Time is one of the parameters of the system. This makes it possible to have a complete picture of the variation of the status of the model with time.

Due to page limitation, we can present only high-level description of the workflow with IMS (Fig. 5). Detailed description is presented in [9].

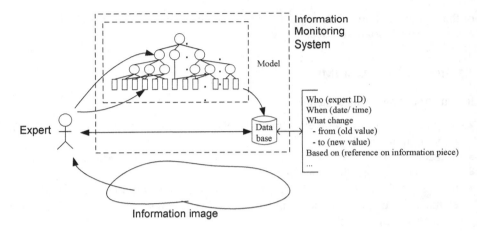

Fig. 5. IMS workflow.

3.3 Theoretical Base of IMS

For effective practical application of the proposed technological solutions it is necessary to tackle a series of theoretical problems, the results of which are given below.

It is assumed that the expert describes the degree of inconsistency of the obtained information (for example, the readiness or potential for readiness of certain processes in a country [9]) in the form of linguistic values. The subjective degree of convenience of such a description depends on the selection and the composition of such linguistic values [11].

It is assumed that the system tracks the development of the problem, i.e. its variation with time. It is also assumed that it integrates the evaluations of different experts. This means that one object may be described by different experts. Therefore, it is desirable to have assurances that the different experts describe one and the same object in the most "uniform" way.

On the basis of the above we may formulate the first problem as follows:

Problem 1. Is it possible, taking into account certain features of the man's perception of objects of the real world and their description, to formulate a rule for selection of the optimum set of values of characteristics on the basis of which these objects may be described? Two optimality criteria are possible:

Criterion 1. We regard as optimum those sets of values through whose use man experiences the minimum uncertainty in describing objects.

Criterion 2. If the object is described by a certain number of experts, then we regard as optimum those sets of values which provide the minimum degree of divergence of the descriptions.

It is shown [11] that we can formulate a method of selecting the optimum set of values of qualitative indications (scale values). Moreover, it is shown that such a method is stable, i.e. the natural small errors that may occur in constructing the membership functions do not have a significant influence on the selection of the optimum set of values. The sets, which are optimal according to criteria 1 and 2, coincide. The results obtained are described in [13]. Following this method, we may describe objects with minimum possible uncertainty, i.e. guarantee optimum operation of the information monitoring system from this point of view.

Information monitoring technology assumes the storage of information material (or references to it) and their linguistic evaluations in the system database. In this connection the following problem arises.

Problem 2. Is it possible to define the indices of quality of information retrieval in fuzzy (linguistic) databases and to formulate a rule for the selection of such a set of linguistic values, use of which would provide the maximum indices of quality of information retrieval?

It is shown [10] that it is possible to introduce indices of the quality of information retrieval in fuzzy (linguistic) databases and to formalize them. It is shown that it is possible to formulate a method of selecting the optimum set of values of qualitative indications which provides the maximum quality indices of information retrieval. More-over, it is shown that such a method is stable, i.e. the natural small errors in the construction of the membership functions do not have a significant effect on the selection of the optimum set of values. The results obtained are shown in [10]. It allows to approve that the offered methods can be used in practical tasks and to guarantee optimum work of information monitoring systems.

Because model of the process has hierarchical stricture (see Sect. 3), choice and selection (tuning) of aggregation operators for the nodes of the model is one more important issue in development IMS. We may formulate this problem as follows:

Problem 3. Is it possible to propose the procedures of information aggregation in fuzzy hierarchical dynamic systems which allow us to minimize contradictoriness in the model of problem/process in IMS?

It is shown that it is possible to propose the following approaches based on different interpretations of aggregation operators: geometrical, logical, and learning-based. The last one includes learning based on genetic algorithms and learning based on neural networks. These approaches are described in details in [12]. In this point we use all appropriate tools of Soft Computing.

3.4 IMS Analytics

Having IMS, we can solve two type of problems: direct and inverse.

The direct problem is to find all "critical ways" of the process. It means to reveal those elements of the process, the small change of which status may qualitatively change the status of the process as a whole. For big class of aggregation operators, we can calculate degree of criticality for any element of the model. It means that we can under-stand and measure a strengths and weaknesses of any element of the current process.

This understanding is a base for development a strategic plan for control of the process by optimal way.

The inverse problem is to find elements of the model, which must be changed for reaching some given status of the target element of the model. For example, we can understand how we can reach maximal effect for given budget or reach given effect for minimal budget.

Analytical capabilities of IMS are presents on Fig. 6.

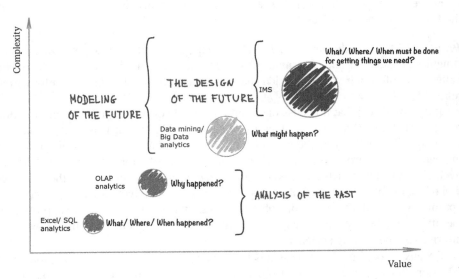

Fig. 6. Analytical capabilities of IMS.

3.5   Summary for IMS

IMS works with diverse, multi-level, fragmentary, unreliable, and varying in time information about some process and allows performing monitoring of the process evolution and working out strategic plans of the process development.

IMS are effective when we do not have (we cannot to build) a mathematical model of the process in form of equations, automats, etc., but we have experts/analysts who monitor the process on a regular base. This is a typical situation for economic, social, and political processes.

Development of IMS is possible when we can to build "semantic model" of the process (a set of factors and indicators and their interdependences) and we can use real information (we can use machine learning approach for tuning the model).

The most difficult point in development process is the elaboration of structure of the process model. Perspective way for automation of this point (development of the model) is an application of advanced technologies like data mining. Our experiments showed that data mining can be a good tool for this task especially if we have enough data on the process.

4   Smart Learning for Education: Uchi.ru Case Study

Knowledge work automation can augment teacher abilities and enhance or replace lectures with "adaptive" learning programs - dynamic instruction systems that alter the pace of teaching to match the student's progress and suggest additional drills based on student responses. The economic impact of such tools in education would come from improving instructional quality and enabling teachers to provide more one-on-one attention and coaching. New self-teaching tools could also enable fundamental changes in scheduling: courses could be tied to subject mastery, rather than semesters or quarters, allowing students to progress at their own pace.

Cloud platform Uchi.ru allows to measure all student's activities and results like time, number of right/wrong answers, behavior (for example, playing with mouse, etc.); integration with PC/tablet sensors, weather (Internet), and gadgets like health trackers, potentially allow to use a number of environment characteristics. Based on these initial measurements we can "calculate" current status of the students in terms of information processing capabilities, speed, attentiveness, endurance and others. This understanding and personal history allow system to generate content which is optimal for the student for now. General presentation of Uchi.ru architecture is given in Fig. 7.

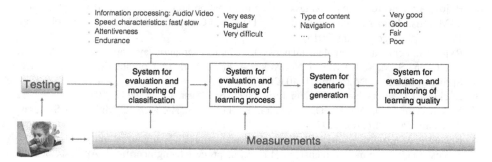

Fig. 7.   Uchi.ru architecture.

Features of initial measurements, their generalizations, fuzzy rule-based and similarity-based reasoning and adaptation, and application of personification and optimization technologies [4, 5] have been discussed in the report.

About 1 000 000 pupils, 65 000 teachers, 7 700 schools, 450 cities use Uchi.ru every day for now (more detailed information is available on www.uchi.ru, www.happynumbers.com).

5   Conclusion

Automation of knowledge work is one of the most perspective disruptive technologies (№. 2 in McKinsey Global Institute list of disruptive technologies).

This class of tasks cannot be solved by computer intelligence or by human intelligence separately – only human-computer intelligence is capable to solve this.

A big part of "tasks that rely on complex analysis, subtle judgments, and creative problem solving" [2] is evaluation the status and monitoring the progress of complex processes. System for evaluation and monitoring of complex processes could be tool for this part of automation of knowledge work tasks. Because of these systems are human-computer on their nature, only soft computing can be a technological base for these systems. Analytical capabilities of this type of systems allow us to optimize design of the future process.

References

1. A gallery of disruptive technologies. http://www.mckinsey.com/assets/dotcom/mgi/slideshows/disruptive_tech/index.html#
2. Manyika, J., Chui, M., Bughin, J., Dobbs, R., Bisson, P., Marrs. A.: Disruptive Technologies: Advances That Will Transform Life, Business, and the Global Economy, 176 p. McKinsey Global Institute (MGI), New York City (2013). http://www.mckinsey.com/insights/business_technology/disruptive_technologies
3. Ahkmedzhanov, N.M., Zhukotcky, A.V., Kudrjavtcev, V.B., Oganov, R.G., Rastorguev, V.V., Ryjov, A.P., Stogalov, A.S.: System for evaluation and monitoring of risks of cardiovascular disease. Intell. Syst. 7(1–4), 5–38 (2013). (in Russian)
4. Ryjov, A.: Towards an optimal task-driven information granulation. In: Pedrycz, W., Chen, S.-M. (eds.) Information Granularity, Big Data, and Computational Intelligence, vol. 8, pp. 191–208. Springer, Cham (2015)
5. Ryjov, A.: Personalization of social networks: adaptive semantic layer approach. In: Pedrycz, W., Chen, S.-M. (eds.) Social Networks: A Framework of Computational Intelligence. Springer, Cham, vol. 526, pp. 21–40 (2014)
6. Buckley, J.J.: Fuzzy hierarchical analysis. Fuzzy Sets Syst. 17, 233–247 (1985)
7. Mesarovich, M.D., Macko, D., Takahara, Y.: Theory of Hierarchical Multilevel Systems. Academic Press, London (1970)
8. Rostamy, A.A.A., Meysam, S., Behnam, A., Takanlou, F.B.: Using fuzzy analytical hierarchy process to evaluate main dimensions of business process reengineering. J. Appl. Oper. Res. 4(2), 69–77 (2012)
9. Ryjov, A., Belenki, A., Hooper, R., Pouchkarev, V., Fattah, A., Zadeh, L.A.: Development of an Intelligent System for Monitoring and Evaluation of Peaceful Nuclear Activities (DISNA), IAEA, STR-310, Vienna (1998)
10. Ryjov, A.: Modeling and optimization of information retrieval for perception-based information. In: Zanzotto, F., Tsumoto, S., Taatgen, N., Yao, Y.Y. (eds.) Proceedings of the International Conference on Brain Informatics 2012, Macau, China, 4–7 December 2012, pp. 140–149 (2012)
11. Ryjov, A.: Fuzzy linguistic scales: definition, properties and applications. In: Reznik, L., Kreinovich, V. (eds.) Soft Computing in Measurement and Information Acquisition, vol. 127, pp. 23–38. Springer, Heidelberg (2003)
12. Ryjov, A.: On information aggregation in fuzzy hierarchical systems. Intell. Syst. 6, 341–364 (2001). (in Russian)
13. Ryjov, A.: The Principles of Fuzzy Set Theory and Measurement of Fuzziness. Dialog-MSU Publishing, Moscow (1988). (in Russian)

14. Saaty, T.L.: The Analytic Hierarchy Process. McGraw-Hill, New York (1980)
15. Torra, V.: A review of the construction of hierarchical fuzzy systems. Int. J. Intell. Syst. **17**, 531–543 (2002)
16. Zadeh, L.A.: Fuzzy sets. Inf. Control **8**, 338–353 (1965)
17. Zadeh, L.A.: The concept of a linguistic variable and its application to approximate reasoning. Part 1, 2, 3. Inform. Sci. **8**, 199–249; **8**, 301–357; **9**, 43–80 (1975)

Use of Game Technologies for the Development of Virtual Laboratories for Physics Study

Yevgeniya Daineko[✉], Madina Ipalakova, Ravil Muhamedyev, Mariya Brodyagina, Marina Yunnikova, and Batyrkhan Omarov

International Information Technology University, Almaty, Kazakhstan
yevgeniyadaineko@gmail.com, m.ipalakova@gmail.com,
ravil.muhamedyev@gmail.com, maria.brodyagina91@gmail.com,
myunniko@gmail.com, batyahan@gmail.com

Abstract. In the article the application of Unity 3D game engine for the implementation of the virtual physical laboratory is considered. The competing platforms, program models, the development methodology and the realization of the laboratory work to study the light polarization are described. It was shown, that the Virtual physical laboratories represent one of the successful examples of introduction of information technologies in the training process.

Keywords: Virtual laboratory · Unity3D · Physics · Game engine · Virtual reality

1 Introduction

At the present time we can witness the rapid development of information technology, and how it affects all the spheres of our life and changes the processes within them. Higher education is not an exception. Introduction of new information technologies, computerization of institutions, along with innovative activities of faculty staff are the main directions of modernization of education, to which a special attention is paid currently all around the world and in Kazakhstan in particular [3, 7, 11].

The use of innovative teaching techniques and new ways of interaction between lecturers and students also lead to the renewal of educational process. In this context computer-based training systems are gaining more and more interest. According to [20] they are aimed to help to master new material, to control the performance and to prepare teaching material. Automated tutorials, library systems, multimedia training simulators are the examples of such systems.

Currently virtual laboratories gain more popularity among new teaching tools. Here are some reasons. First, it is not always possible for universities to equip real laboratories to conduct experiments in different subjects due to financial or safety factors. Besides, university laboratories allow carrying out not all experiments. In such cases virtual laboratories are perfect alternative. Using them it is possible to conduct experiments many times with minimal cost and effort and without any danger for students. And with the development of information technology the use of virtual laboratories in educational process becomes more and more accessible. Second, such training systems are

A.V. Chugunov et al. (Eds.): DTGS 2016, CCIS 674, pp. 422–428, 2016.
DOI: 10.1007/978-3-319-49700-6_42

irreplaceable in distance learning, which becomes more widespread again with the development of ICT.

It needs to be mentioned that the use of virtual experiments with models of objects and processes is very often the only way of economic verification and estimation in the problems of complex systems development. It can be said that the use of virtual experiments reflects the general trend of education and engineering development.

In the work the application of the game platform (engine) Unity 3D for the development of a virtual physical laboratory is presented.

2   Related Works

Today, ICT is widely used in various fields of science and technology. Almost in every sphere real experiments and practical tasks are possible to replace with their virtual analogues, which are safer and cheaper, and with enough quality and effectiveness. Math, physics, chemistry, biology, medicine, mechanics, robotics, nanotechnology are not the full list of fields of knowledge, where the computer modeling of real processes is justified and widely used within different virtual laboratories.

LabinApp uses modern technology for the benefit of education [12]. It is a piece of software with 3D graphics, which helps people to interact with, visualize and study the science. Currently four laboratories in physics and biology are available. All of them allow conducting experiments, studying the subjects interactively with detailed visualization.

Newton programs are virtual physical laboratories, which help to study kinematics, dynamics, thermodynamics, optics and other sections of physics using only a PC [4]. A user controls the whole process of an experiment. He (or she) assembles mechanisms himself (herself), watching the process on a sub video.

The Star virtual laboratories are a project of MIT [19]. Its main function is to develop educational and research applications in biology, genetics and hydrology.

In the Colorado University the project PhET was found. It includes lots of laboratories, which demonstrate different physical, biological and chemical phenomena [9].

The virtual laboratory teachmen.ru – is a project of Chelyabinsk State University [2]. All the material is aimed to study physics and it is more likely interactive tutorial with provided functionality to conduct experiments.

In the South-Ural State University a number of virtual laboratory works in material science were created. They provide experimental research to study crystallization of lead, antimony and their alloys [18].

The resource VirtuLab.net is a platform with lots of virtual experiments [21]. A user conducts and observes an experiment following the instructions on the screen.

Wolfram Demonstration Project demonstrates the concepts of modern science and technology [5]. It comprises 11 sections with physical, chemical and mathematical laboratory works.

Algodoo – is an application for 2D simulations. It has many tools to create various objects, mechanisms and systems in order to model their physical properties and interactions. For instance, it is possible to develop a model of clocks or an air rifle [1].

In the article [16] the chemical laboratory works are presented. A user runs the application for simulation, chooses one of the works and proceeds to the virtual environment to perform it.

The experimental psychologist and engineer of the human interface Sebastian Koenig developed a Virtual Game lab, which helps people with mental illnesses, studies cognitive abilities and human behavior [17].

The game engine Unity3D is widely used in education. There are a lot of projects that had been developed using it. Most of them are created and used in USA.

For example, NASA used Unity3D to simulate the solar system and its objects within the project Eyes on the Earth [10].

The realistic astronomical simulator Universal Sandbox allows observing the interaction between the various celestial bodies, based on the physical laws [6].

The company FX Palo Alto used Unity 3D to create a 3D model of a chocolate factory. Users can watch all the technological processes in real time [5].

MIT Media group employed the engine for the same purpose and to speed up the visual analysis of information, which was placed in a created 3D space [14].

3   Technological Background

To implement the virtual laboratory work the analysis of game engines to select the most suitable for our purpose has been made. Five most popular game engines, their advantages and disadvantages were considered.

Unity3D is an available and colorful game engine. Its main advantages are cross-platform, a lot of lessons and tutorials, easy to use, popularity among developers that allows quickly solving errors in the program itself.

Unreal Engine is one of the most popular engines among game developers. The main advantages of Unreal Engine are cross-platform, many tutorials in the Internet, and a wide range of development tools. However, lots of them are quite subjective and difficult to use in projects, which can be considered as a disadvantage of the engine.

CryEngine 3 is an engine that makes the main emphasis on the graphics. Secondly, excellent background music can be named as its advantage. The main disadvantages of this game engine are negligent support of the program free version and its novelty. Thus, not enough information about usage of the engine is available.

HeroEngine is a game engine that has been designed for the development of multi-player games. The engine is well applicable for creation of maps and locations, and has good technical support. Nevertheless, a free version of the program is not presented and not all the scripts of the game engine are convenient to use.

Rage Engine provides a wide range of opportunities to create maps and worlds, to choose a variety of gameplay styles, and to write fast network code. However, this game engine has a number of cons as inconvenient interface and lack of tutorials. Besides, the control is badly optimized for a keyboard and a mouse.

The analysis of the game engines is presented in Table 1.

Table 1. Comparative characteristics of the game engines

Engine	Advantages	Disadvantages
Unity3D	Many video tutorials	The limited set of tools
	Cross-platform	
	Easy to use	
	Developers' choice	
Unreal Engine	Many video tutorials	Difficult to use
	Multi-platform	
	A wide set of tools	
CryEngine 3	Excellent graphics	Novelty
	Good sound	Only proprietary software
HeroEngine	Good tech support	Only proprietary software
	Easy to create maps	Inconvenient scripts
Rage Engine	Easy to create maps	Not enough tutorials
	Many gameplay styles	Inconvenient interface
	Quick network code	Difficulties with the keyboard and mouse

After the analysis performed, the choice in favor of Unity3D game engine was made. The engine meets the requirements of the authors about the availability of information and graphics capabilities, and it is easy in use. It should be noted that the wide usage of this tool was an additional argument in favor of this choice.

Unity is applied not only in the gaming industry, but also in the other areas. For example, in [13] Unity3D game engine is used to develop and prototype a biological network and molecular visualization application for subsequent use in research or education. In the work [15] the usage of the game engine for the modeling of cell apoptosis is described. In the article [22] the creation of the virtual reality system based on the GIS platform and Unity3D is considered. Game technology as visual representation tool for architecture and urban design studies is discussed in [8]. The number of publications with mention of this game engine has increased from 190 in 2010 to nearly 2,000 in 2015 (Fig. 1).

The choice of the software development methodology has the same importance as the choice of the development environment.

Agile software development is a set of approaches to development of the software, which are focused on interactive development and ensuring interaction. Nowadays, there are several techniques, which are classified as agile, for example: extreme programming, DSDM, Scrum, FDD. The main objective of these methodologies is the reduction of risks, which is provided by the division of a development process into several short cycles.

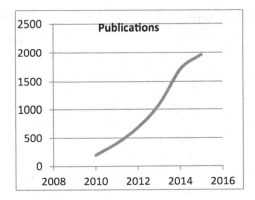

Fig. 1. The graph of the growth of publications with Unity

4   Implementation

The prototype of a 3D scene has been developed based on a real physical laboratory of the university. The prototype has been created with 3Ds Max and Google SketchUp. When a user starts the application, the laboratory with the necessary equipment on a desktop appears on the scene. To start the experiment the user must approach the desktop. To turn on the light source, «E» key must be pressed. If after this the light source is not switched on, the user should press «E» key a second time or press «Q» key. To turn off the light source, the user must press «Q» key. If the source is not switched off after that, press «E» key or again press «Q» key. The diagram of this process is shown in Fig. 2.

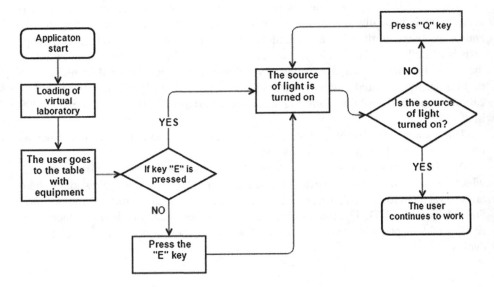

Fig. 2. The diagram, which describes the operation of the light source

The interaction between the user and the program is performed in several ways directly via the interface and via manipulators: a mouse and a keyboard. The interface provides to the user a peculiar reference point that allows interacting with the program (Fig. 3).

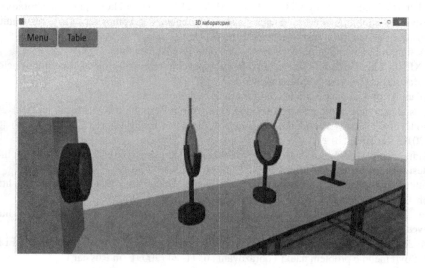

Fig. 3. The laboratory, view of installation

Using the mouse, the user can control the program, select various program modes, configure it, and control the camera of the game character. Control via the keyboard allows the user to conduct the experiment, to operate the equipment and to control the movement of the character in the virtual laboratory.

5   Conclusion

The described approach allows creating the three-dimensional visualizations of laboratory installations, necessary equipment and premises of a laboratory, which provide high extent of "penetration" into the studied process and feeling of reality.

Effective application of virtual laboratories in educational process contributes not only to improvement of quality of education, but also economy of significant financial resources. Moreover, virtual laboratories create safe and clean environment. We believe that developed virtual physical laboratory to study the polarization phenomenon is the modern innovative realization of computer-based training systems of new generation.

Acknowledgements. The work was funded by the grant No. 2622/ГФ4 of the Ministry of Education and Science of the Republic of Kazakhstan.

References

1. Algoryx Algodoo. http://www.algodoo.com
2. Chelyabinsk State University. http://www.teachmen.ru
3. Cheremisina, E.N., Antipov, O.E., Belov, M.A.: Rol' virtual'noi kompjuternoi laboratorii na osnove tekhnologii oblachnih vichislenii v sovremennom kompjuternom obrazovanii. J. Distancionnoe virtual'noe obuchenie **1**, 50–64 (2012)
4. DesignSoft Newton. http://www.newtonlab.com/English/newton
5. FXPAL The Virtual Factory. http://www.fxpal.com/research-projects/the-virtual-factory-industrial-collaboration-environments
6. Giant Army Universe Sandbox. http://universesandbox.com
7. Gosudarstvennaya programma razvitiya obrazovania Respubliki Kazakhstan na 2011-2020 godi: utv. Ukazom Prezidenta Respubliki Kazakhstan ot 7 decabrya 2010 goda, № 1118 (2010). (in Russian)
8. Indraprastha, A., Shinozaki, M.: The investigation on using Unity3D game engine in urban design study. J. ICT Res. Appl. **3**, 1–18 (2009)
9. Interactive simulations for science and math. University of Colorado Phet. http://phet.colorado.edu
10. Jet Propulsion Laboratory, California Institute of Technology NASA's Eyes. http://eyes.nasa.gov/index.html
11. Kudinov, D.N.: Perspectivi razrabotki virtual'nix rabot na baze kompleksa program T-FLEX. J. Sovremennie problem nauki i obrazovania **6**, 71–74 (2009). (in Russian)
12. LabinApp - A 3D Virtual Laboratory. Physics I, Physics II. http://labinapp.com
13. Lv, Z., Tek, A., Da Silva, F., Empereur-mot, C., Chavent, M., Baaden, M.: Game on, science - how video game technology may help biologists tackle visualization challenges. PLoS One **8**(3), 57990 (2013)
14. MIT Media Lab DoppelLab. http://doppellab.media.mit.edu
15. Muhamedyev, R.I., Gladkikh, V., Gopejenko, V.I., Daineko, Y.A., Mansharipova, A.T., Muhamedyeva, E.L., Gopejenko, A.V.: A method of three-dimensional visualization of molecular processes of apoptosis. In: De Paolis, L.T., Mongelli, A. (eds.) AVR 2014. LNCS, vol. 8853, pp. 103–112. Springer, Heidelberg (2014). doi:10.1007/978-3-319-13969-2_8
16. Romanenko, V.V., Shmoylov, V.O., Friyuk, S.I., Posdnyakov, P.P., Savitsky, V.U.: Virtualnye laboratornuye raboty po discipline "Chimiya". J. Sovremennye nauchniye issledovaniya **6**, 2–4 (2014). (in Russian)
17. Sebastian Koenig. Virtual Game Lab. http://www.virtualgamelab.com/
18. Seksyaeva, Y.A., Popenova, L.I., Lisovskiy, R.A., Radionova, L.V.: Laboratornuye raboty pri izuchenii kursa "Materialovedeniye". J. Sovremennye nauchniye issledovaniya **3**, 2786–2790 (2012). (in Russian)
19. Software Tools for Academics and Researchers. http://star.mit.edu
20. Tarasov, D.P., Sidorkin, A.F., Haustov, R.V.: O znachnimosti elektronnogo uchebnogo posobiya pri podgotovke I vypolnenii laboratornoi raboty po Fizike. J. Perspektivy nauki i obrazovaniya, 81–89 (2013). (in Russian)
21. Virtual Educational System. http://www.virtulab.net
22. Wang, S., Mao, Z., Zeng, C., Gong, H., Li, S., Chen, B.: A new method of virtual reality based on Unity3D. In: 18th International Conference on Geoinformatics, pp. 1–5. IEEE Press (2010)
23. Wolfram Demonstrations & Contributors Wolfram Demonstrations Project. http://demonstrations.wolfram.com

Methods of Student Motivation by Means of E-learning System

Anton Govorov[1](✉), Marina Govorova[1], and Anna Bulakova[2]

[1] Saint Petersburg National Research University of Information Technologies, Mechanics and Optics, St. Petersburg, Russia
antongovorov@gmail.com, maran77@mail.ru
[2] St. Petersburg State Autonomous Vocational Educational Institution «College of Tourism and Hotel Service», St. Petersburg, Russia
aniabul@mail.ru

Abstract. This study developed methods to improve student motivation by means of an e-learning system. While using e-learning systems in higher educational institutions, which train students in areas of science and technology, not enough attention is paid to the use of methods and means of motivating students. The developed technique helps to solve this problem. This paper presents the results of testing of developed methods in the educational process of ITMO University.

Keywords: E-learning · Gamification · Motivation

1 Introduction

To achieve high quality student training, which has a sufficient level of professional and social competence in accordance with the requirements of modern educational standards, it is necessary to create models in which the student becomes an active subject in the educational process. This can be done through the activation of all types of training activities, including self-cognitive activity. In this regard, the current stage of Russian educations' informatization puts a high priority on the introduction of e-learning technologies at all levels of education (school, vocational, higher education, further education).

In all educational institutions, there is constant use of e-learning tools. Every year, a large part of the training load goes into the e-learning environment. Learning tools are becoming more complex with oversaturated capabilities. At the same time, less attention is paid to the student's motivation to use e-learning tools.

Today's learning management systems focus on the formation of educational content. To create e-learning courses, in most cases, the teacher simply takes the textual representation of his lectures in electronic form, in most cases without carrying out any adaptation of the content for e-learning. Generally, in the transition to e-learning, a student's motivation for studying, which is enhanced by live contact between teacher and student, is lost. Consequently, to preserve the level of motivation, the teacher must be implement a means of stimulating internal and external motivation to learn. Not every teacher will be able to carry out such a transformation of educational content.

A.V. Chugunov et al. (Eds.): DTGS 2016, CCIS 674, pp. 429–438, 2016.
DOI: 10.1007/978-3-319-49700-6_43

The functionality of using means of motivation, which are implemented in the design of electronic educational resources, play no less an important role than the adaptation of content for e-learning.

One effective tool to enhance student interest is traditional game technologies. At present, more and more attention of developers learning management systems attracts the gamification educational process. Now it is typical and usually used for distance online learning systems [3, 7]. However, it is rarely implemented in the traditional educational process.

Thus, the problem of educational motivation in students reveals the following contradiction. On the one hand, there are ample opportunities to introduce e-learning systems and tools. On the other hand, the motivation of students is not sufficiently developed.

The purpose of this research is to develop a methodology for use in the educational process of learning management systems with elements of gamification and game technologies, providing cognitive motivation of students.

The objectives of this research are to:

1. Identify the features of gamification and game technologies in the educational process.
2. Study the characteristics of educational motivation.
3. Explore the software system.
4. Carry out testing of the system in training bachelors of technical areas.
5. Based on the results of testing, to identify the most effective means of motivating students in the learning management system and develop guidelines for the application of gamification learning management systems.

The hypothesis of the study is that, if used in the learning process, gamification and game technologies enhance the learning motivation of students. In turn, this can achieve better results in academic disciplines.

2 Gaming Technology and Gamification

In this study, to improve students' motivation, gaming technology and gamification are used in the educational process.

The organization of playing and the competitive process of studying both require a clear definition, and to identify a clear line between the game and the competition.

2.1 Games

Caillois R. describes a game as an activity that is voluntary and enjoyable, separate from the real world, uncertain and unproductive; the activity does not produce any goods of external value, and is governed by rules [2].

Bernard S. proposes the following definition of a game: "Playing a game is the voluntary attempt to overcome unnecessary obstacles" [8].

"The game is the body's activity aimed at modelling the conditional expanded activities" [1]. Antsupov A.J. and Shipilov A.I. claim is based on German scientist Gross K., who stated that game activity contributes to the acquisition of experience of resolutions in various simulated conflicts and situations.

Thus, the game can be considered a form of construction of the educational process, in which simulation of different situations is directed not only to specific competences, but also to increase the level of motivation. This may then develop students' desire to study for its own sake, for the pleasure that it brings.

2.2 Competitions

The analysis of the available definitions [1, 9] suggests that the concept of "competition" allows us to create a new definition in relation to the educational process: "Competition is a form of construction of the educational process, in which the motivation process involves the development of students' desire to outdo each other in the development of educational material."

2.3 Gaming Technology

The use of games and competitions (hereinafter these technologies will be referred to as "gaming technology") in the learning process is capable of enhancing the effectiveness of the educational process. Panfilova A.P. highlights the following features of gaming technology [6]:

- the opportunity to embrace a wide scope of issues;
- the possibility of preparing a constructive professional dialogue;
- the possibility of increasing the level of involvement of students in the learning process, encouraging them to take part in involuntary activity;
- the presence of feedback in the actions of participants in the educational process;
- the form of value orientation and installation of professional work - it is easier to overcome stereotypes and develop correct self-esteem;
- provoking the trainees, including their reflexive processes, provides an opportunity for comprehensive analysis, interpretation, interpretation of the results;
- provoking the student to the manifestation of all the qualities of his personality helps to reveal his negative and positive individual abilities.

The experience gained from the interaction with the game can be more productive than the experience gained in the actual operation. Panfilova A.P. identifies several reasons that justify this fact [6]:

- the possibility of spending any of the options to address a specific situation, clearly see the effects of the selected option, and test alternative solutions;
- Completeness of information provided during the game compared with the frequent lack of information in real life helps stimulate the process of taking responsibility for decisions taken.

In today's education process, the following types of gaming technology should be allocated, based on studies by Panfilova A.P. applicable to e-learning systems [6]:

- Group technology: in this approach students study in groups;
- Role-playing and simulation games: these games feature the model of the control system and the model of the environment. The model of the environment is a set of models of different nature.

2.4 Gamification

Gamification adds to the normal educational process a context, allowing boring routine processes to "veil by a mask", which has set not only the training goals.

Gamification as a tool attracts new users and supports involvement. It is used in the following systems: Foursquare, Red Critter Tracker, Crowdrise, Open Badges, etc. [4].

Universities and research institutions are looking for ways to attract students' attention and keep them learning. For example, studies of the University "Mediterranean" show which game elements are most relevant. The study revealed the most popular game elements in the educational process of higher educational institutions [7]:

- level system;
- scale of experience;
- the system of awards/badges;
- progress bars;
- leader board;
- availability of feedback;
- game story.

It is necessary to draw the line between gaming and gamification technologies. The introduction of gamification is not intended to change the educational content. It is subject to change control and evaluation activities of the trainees, while the introduction of gaming technology change is subject to the educational process itself.

An implementation model of gamification and game technology is shown in Fig. 1.

Bernard S. identified three characteristics of the game [8]:

- target;
- regulations;
- Voluntary.

Every game has to have a purpose. For example, any sports-based game has a purpose. The purpose of football is to get the ball into the opponents' goal. Any game should be designated with the rules of the game. Any member of the game is to voluntarily comply with these rules. Consequently, the introduction of gaming technology and gamification in the educational process should provide a set of academic and non-academic purposes. The rules to achieve these goals involve voluntarily trying to achieve their goals. It should be noted that gamification involves extra-curricular objectives, while gaming technologies are changing the learning process for the implementation of educational objectives in the game.

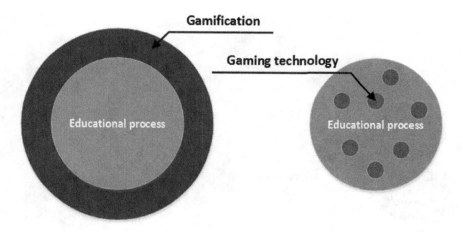

Fig. 1. Implementation model of gamification and game technology

2.5   Person, Gamification and Game Technology

In considering the question of motivation of the learner to the studying process, the overall motivation of the student should be considered as individual to any process or action. The motivational properties of the individual are entrenched and preferred methods of forming a motive.

In this work, the classification of Murray B. [5] is used, which involves the following motivational personality traits:

– the achievement motive;
– the motive of avoiding failure;
– the motive of power;
– the affiliation motive;
– the rejection of the motive;
– altruistic motives.

To be able to further substantiate the results from the point of view of psychology, it was necessary to build links to the most popular elements of gamification, game technology and motivational personality traits. The result is shown in the form of the intelligence card depicted in Fig. 2.

The generally accepted position is that games themselves are not sufficient for learning but there are elements of games that can be activated within an instructional context, which may enhance the learning process.

3   Method

A study was carried out via pedagogical supervision and pedagogical experimentation, which took place from 2013 to the present. The study included pupils and students at educational institutions of St. Petersburg, who were trained in three courses:

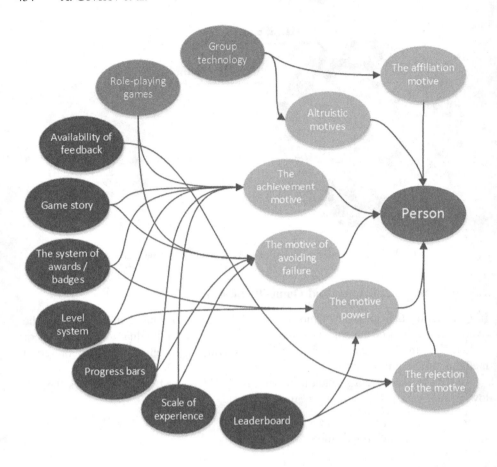

Fig. 2. Influence of gamification and game technologies on the motivation personality traits

- "Computer science" (52 pupils): The Institute of Information Technologies SEGRIS ("SEGRIS – IIT");
- "Databases" and "Database Administration" (102 students): ITMO University.

The courses follow the traditional lecture-and-lab format.

In the period from September 2013 to 2015, a simple system of completing an academic journal with the use of gamification was developed and tested. The journal was used in the educational process of training students in computer science at the "SEGRIS-IIT", a non-profit educational organization.

E-gradebook, which is open access, was developed by means of the freeware service "Google Docs". Any student or parent can go to the website of the e-gradebook and become familiar with its content. E-gradebook largely repeats the usual gradebook. The student does not receive marks, but total points for the lesson, which is made up of the points for the presence and extra points (Fig. 3).

E-gradebook was realized by means of Google sheets. The main working area of the e-gradebook was divided into 4 blocks:

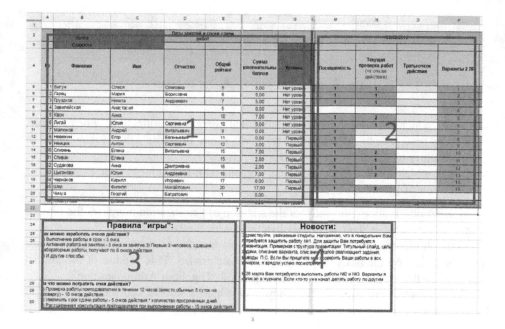

Fig. 3. E-gradebook interface

- Block № 1 - information about students.
- Block № 2 - information about sessions.
- Block № 3 - description of the rules working with the e-gradebook.
- Block № 4 - Information and news.

In developing the e-gradebook, the following elements of gamification were used:

1. Level system.
2. The system of awards/badges.
3. Leader board.
4. The system of quests.

A sum score influenced the conditional option "trainee level" or "level reflecting the degree of student awareness of the subject with respect to his classmates" (Fig. 4). This assessment was subjective, but motivated students. Students saw a performance evaluation analogy with computer games. That process was similar to the accumulation of experience points in MMORPG type games (Massively Multiplayer Online Role-Playing Games), which greatly motivates students to accumulate points for performing tasks.

The system provided a rewards system. A pupil can get bonus points for work done on time, the first performance of the group work, a high level of activity in the lesson, helping their colleagues, performing a very difficult task, and so on. Various quests were used in the system. Quests can be viewed from two perspectives:

	Фамилия	Имя	Адрес почты	Уровень	Количест	5-Sep	9/9/2013	1?
1	Веселовский	Федор	veselovskij.fedor@gm	Десятый	398.50	12	3	
2	Еремин	Артем	arteremin98@gmail.c	Восьмой	280.00	-3	-3	

Fig. 4. Statistical performance of students.

- Quests which do not modify the educational content (gamification). For example, for the performance of work the first two times in a row, the student gets an opportunity to select the next operation.
- Quests which modify the educational content (slot technology). For example, the execution of group work.

Teacher observations showed that the addition of gamification increases the interest of students to achieve their learning objectives with the best results.

In the third version of the e-gradebook, it was decided to separate the game points from the points on the basis of which students are graded. This version of the journal was used in the training courses "Databases" and "Database Administration".

Game scores were used as "currency", for which a student can trade a variety of bonuses, such as:

- express check of work;
- longer delivery work;
- Extended consultation in the carrying out of work.

Scoring of the output levels of the e-gradebook was done using MS Excel functions. This means that the use of such e-gradebooks can be available to all teachers in secondary schools.

All training content was designed in such a way that the student was playing a role in a virtual environment similar to the real scope of getting tasks. As a result, the student does not perform laboratory work, but passes a quest in the role play.

As part of the course, group work took place, which groups of students competed with each other.

4   Results and Discussion

This pedagogical experiment was carried out at the Department of Smart Technologies in the humanitarian sphere of the Natural Science Faculty of the University ITMO. This experiment involved 102 students.

During the initial examination, the data were analysed for simple quantitative indicators of the progress of the experimental and control study groups (Table 1).

The results show higher performances for the experimental group. However, it is not possible to draw a reasonable conclusion about the positive impact of gamification on the motivation of students, as the behaviours of students in the gaming system may vary significantly.

Table 1. The results of training of the experimental and control groups

Subject	Experimental group			Control group		
	Studying period	Number of students	The average total score (out of 100)	Studying period	Number of students	The average total score (out of 100)
Data-bases	2014/2015	20	74,5	2014/2015	24	65,8
					20	42,4
Database Admini-stration	2015/2016	20	83,9	2014/2015	18	71,2

To substantiate the results, further research will examine the study patterns of the behaviour of students in the gaming system on the basis of a questionnaire, which will allow assessment of the impact of game elements on motivation and learning outcomes.

Nevertheless, the results of this study have shown that technology can be used to:

- support the involvement of students in the learning process by providing continuous feedback;
- track and reinforce desired behaviour and provide a personal recognition of the achievements of students;
- increase interest in obtaining good results in tasks;
- Develop teamwork skills by using group learning activities;
- Observation during the experiment has shown that game mechanics strengthens the motivation to achieve and avoid failure, which has a positive impact on the achievement of learning objectives.

5   Conclusion

Use of the e-gradebook in the educational process of the above group's leads to the following conclusions:

- the appearance of game objectives, in addition to traditional academic tasks, encourage most students to achieve goals and avoid failure;
- The use of active learning methods, such as group tasks (the implementation of which is carried out by means of a fully developed electronic gradebook) affected the motives of power, rejection, altruistic motives and affiliations.

Based on the preliminary results, the primary principles of the motivation system using gamification resources are as follows:

1. Participation of students in the learning process, which uses a system of motivation, should be voluntary.
2. Methods of motivation should be simple and clear. In the event of a significant complication of some motivation methods, learners can quickly get bored, because it can complicate the learning process.
3. The most effective motivation of the person works in the complex.
4. Motives are constantly changing.
5. If at any point in the application of techniques, the teacher stops using motivational elements in the learning process, the teacher may have problems with the re-engagement of students.
6. Every student is different. Methods that positively influence a student could adversely affect other students. Using a complex system of motivation should be tailored to every student. If the student has negative emotions in relation to the motivation process, it can have a negative impact on the learning process.

Further development of this experiment will allow for a statistical evaluation of the degree of influence of game elements and motives of learning outcomes, and justify the possibility of introducing these techniques in the educational process.

References

1. Antsupov, A.J., Shipilov, A.I.: Conflict specialist dictionary, 2nd edn. (Slovar confliktologa, 2-e izd.). Piter, St. Petersburg (2006)
2. Callois, R., Barash, M.: Man, Play, and Games. University of Illinois Press, Urbana (1961)
3. Chang, J.W., Wei, H.Y.: Exploring engaging gamification mechanics in massive online open courses. Educ. Technol. Soc. **19**, 177–203 (2016)
4. Glover, I.: Play as you learn: gamification as a technique for motivating learners. In: Proceedings of World Conference on Educational Multimedia, Hypermedia and Telecommunications 2013, Victoria, British Columbia, pp. 1999–2008. AACE, Chesapeake (2013)
5. Iljin, E.P.: Motives and Motivation (Motivi I motivasia). Piter, Saint Petersburg (2002)
6. Panfilova, A.P.: Innovative Educational Technologies. Active Learning (Innovasionnie pedagogichskie tehnologii. Aktivnoe obuchenie). ACADEMIA, Moscow (2009)
7. Scepanovic, S., Zaric, N., Matijevic, T.: Gamification in higher education learning - state of the art challenges and opportunities. In: Proceedings of The Sixth International Conference on e-Learning (e-Learning 2015), Belgrade (2015). http://econference.metropolitan.ac.rs/files/pdf/2015/23-Snezana-Scepanovic-Nada-Zaric-Tripo-Matijevic-Gamification-in-higher-education-learning-state-of-the-art-challenges-and-opportunities.pdf
8. Suits, B., Hurka, T.: The Grasshopper: Games, Life and Utopia. Broadview Press, Orchard Park (2005)
9. Venger, A.L.: Development Psychology. Dictionary (Psihologia razvitia. Slovar.). PER SE, Moscow (2006)

eCity: ICTs for Better Urban (Rural) Planning and Living

Social Media in Identifying Threats to Ensure Safe Life in a Modern City

Aleksandr Dorofeev[1(✉)], Alexey Markov[1(✉)], and Valentin Tsirlov[2(✉)]

[1] Security Department, NPO Echelon, Moscow, Russia
{a.dorofeev,a.markov}@npo-echelon.com
[2] Information Security Department, Bauman MSTU, Moscow, Russia
v.tsirlov@bmstu.ru

Abstract. The article is devoted to the issues of identifying security threats to a citizen using Open Source Intelligence. To refine the search for information on the Internet about a person or event that poses a potential security threat it was suggested to use a structured method of collecting and analyzing information based on decomposition of data and connections between data. The method of testing alternative hypothesis was used. The article provides classification of open information sources. A conceptual model that allows experts to perform substantiated sequential information search was developed. The article gives real-life examples that confirm efficiency of the suggested methodological approach to the search and analysis of information.

Keywords: Human resources security · Structured analytic techniques · Social networks · Intelligence cycle · Internet resources · Competitive intelligence · Screening · Smart city · Safe city

1 Introduction

Life in a modern city is associated with certain threats that are posed by criminals - loners and their groups (terrorist organizations, criminal communities, sects, extremist political organizations etc.). The progress of the internet-based technologies (primarily, social media) allows for efficient identification of criminals and taking timely counteractions against them.

Nowadays, the World Wide Web - Internet is a gold mine for information about people and events. Information from the open sources gives us a chance to find out a lot about the person before we enter into any kind of relationship with the person. However, fragmentation and dynamic nature of data on the Internet, vagueness and instability of connections between the objects and events make it difficult to find accurate target result about a specific person or event. Systemic approach in certain cases may require a lot of time due to the need to process incredibly large quantities of information [1]. To eliminate these drawbacks this article suggests a structured stage-based analysis of information that is aimed at obtaining accurate information about a specific person or event directly.

A.V. Chugunov et al. (Eds.): DTGS 2016, CCIS 674, pp. 441–449, 2016.
DOI: 10.1007/978-3-319-49700-6_44

2 Structured Analysis Concept

We define structured analysis as a direct stage-based approach to collecting and processing data and connections between data that allows obtaining most exhaustive and accurate information about a specific person or event. In a sense, structured analysis transforms vague knowledge about data and data connections into accurate one by decomposing (structuring) data and relations between them. Traditionally the analysis of information includes initial stage (definition of the sources, collecting and assessment of prior data) and further iteration steps on data processing (analysis, making conclusions and hypotheses) to obtain most objective and exhaustive information.

3 Threats in a Modern City

Prior to considering a suggested approach to collecting and analyzing information, let us review current examples of security threats posed by criminals in a modern city:

- Threats to physical health (physical conflict; sexual abuse);
- Threats to psychological health (dragging into sects, terrorist groups etc.; publication of information disgracing honour; emotional extortion);
- Property threats (fraud; theft);
- Other threats (dragging into criminal or extremists activities).

4 Classification of Information Sources

To gather information about a person or event efficiently a researcher should understand where and what information he can find. In our case, a researcher may be a police officer, security officer or an ordinary citizen. It should be noted that the open source intelligence approach under consideration has been known for decades, but now it is rising to a new level thanks to the progress in information technologies [2]. Speaking about government officials we should add open government data sets (open data [3]), published in the public information systems.

Taking into account the target and its context, the initial information about a person may be represented by a tuple:

$$D = < G_n, R_l, C_n, P_h, J_b, E_d, M_l, Z_n, H_b, S_p, O_w, O_t >,$$

which includes sets of general identifying information G_n, family relations R_l, contact information C_n, physical data P_h, information about a job J_b, education E_d, military status M_l, circle of friends Z_n, hobby H_b, sports S_p, owned property O_w, other information O_t, especially, if it is related to the problem. Definition of subsets and their permissible values will provide details, for instance, for software implementation [4–8].

5   Intelligence Cycle

The above information about where and what information can technically be found is basically an initial mind map, whereas structured analysis procedures create a route of movement around it. There are several structural models for collecting and analyzing information about a person or an event (particularly, intelligence cycle of CIA and FBI [9]), which include 4–6 stages. In our opinion, the cyclic 7-process model presented below is efficient (Fig. 1).

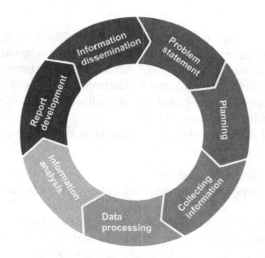

Fig. 1. Cyclic seven-process information search model

Conceptual model of the cycle may be as follows:

$$M = < S_1, S_2, S_3, S_4, S_5, S_6, S_7, R_1, R_2, R_3 >,$$

where: S_1 – set of questions, S_2 – ordered set of sources, S_3 – set of received data, S_4 – set of data retrieved as a result of decomposition, S_5 – set of answers to questions, S_6 – set of conclusions, S_7 – set of conclusions in a visual form, $R_1: S_1 \cup S_2 \rightarrow S_3$, $R_2: S_3 \rightarrow S_4$, $R_3: S_1 \cup S_3 \cup S_4 \rightarrow S_5$.

5.1   Problem Statement

Depending on the available conditions the problem may include a set of questions or tasks [10]. The following methods may be used to clarify the statements:

1. Rephrase: state problem in other words without losing the initial meaning. Example: How to prevent price increase?→How to limit price increase?
2. Reverse: state a reverse problem. Example: How to persuade staff members to go to the theatre altogether?→How to dissuade staff members from going to the theatre?

3. Expand the problem focus. Example: Should I change a car?→How to become more attractive for the fairer sex?
4. Focus on something else. Example: How to decrease expenses?→How to increase sales?
5. Ask the "Why?" question recursively and restate the problem trying to find the underlying cause. Example: A person does not feel good. Why?→Head hurts. Why? →He celebrated birthday a day before....

5.2   Planning

At the planning stage it is necessary to determine what data is being searched for and why. Due to large volumes of information about a person or event, it is not always sensible to gather all available information, i.e. it is necessary to focus on the data, which are going to help to solve the problem and find answers to the raised questions (or solve problems). For structured planning (and further analysis) we may use approach known as testing the alternative hypotheses [11, 12].

The algorithm of testing the alternative hypotheses in this case may be represented as consisting of eight stages, i.e.:

1. Register the hypotheses for analysis;
2. Prepare a list of important evidence items and arguments in favour of and against each hypothesis;
3. Prepare a matrix that correlates the hypothesis to the evidence. Analyze to what extent the evidence allows defining the relative probability of each hypothesis;
4. Revise the matrix. If necessary, change the statement of hypothesis, remove useless evidence and arguments;
5. Make preliminary conclusions about relative probability of each hypothesis. Continue analysis, trying to refute each hypothesis, not prove it;
6. Evaluate the responsiveness of the obtained solution in relation to some evidence, inter alia assess the consequences for the performed analysis, if the evidence is incorrect, or leads to misperception or incorrect interpretation;
7. Prepare a report with conclusions and discuss the relative probability of all hypotheses, not just the most probable;
8. Define the key moments for further observation, which may result in reassessment of the situation.

By registering certain hypotheses and stating questions, answers to which are going to help to identify arguments and facts that would confirm or repute the selected hypothesis, it is possible to prepare a special map for searching for the required information (Fig. 2).

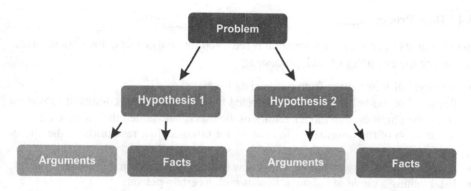

Fig. 2. Relations between statement of the problem, hypotheses, arguments and facts

After stating the hypotheses, it is possible to create a Table with the list of possible questions the answers to which will allow preparing a list of evidence items (facts) and arguments in favour of and against each of the hypotheses: $1 = \sum p(H_i)$. The principle of exhaustiveness of mutually exclusive hypotheses should be observed, when generating the table.

5.3 Collecting Information

Once we know exactly what we are looking for, we can proceed to technicalities – search of information on the Internet. As a rule, it is easy to find a person's presence on different social networks and services, knowing his nickname, i.e. some unique identifier (nickname) [13, 14]. The following typical algorithm for the initial search of information about a person may be formed:

1. Search pages that contain the person's full name. For clarifications it is necessary to use some known information;
2. Search for accounts on social networks and services;
3. Determine the persons' nickname and e-mail addresses;
4. Search pages that contain e-mails.

We should also keep in mind indirect indicators, which have been mentioned above. Indirect indicators may help to establish connections between people, which they do not want to display. For instance, the following information may be correlated: date and place of residence, study, military service, work, event these people and their close friends took part in reviews the algorithm for revealing such covert connections, which is based on hypothesis that the more indirect connections there are between the people, the more likely it is that there is a real connection. We should also remember about the deep web, which might also have information about an event or a person. Deep web, as a rule, stands for the part of the internet, which cannot be reached by the search engines. Further steps will depend on a specific search problem.

5.4 Data Processing

In the course of processing information is retrieved for analysis from the obtained data. Below are the examples of such processing:

- Retrieval of information from online data bases;
- Retrieval of hidden data from the detected files: for instance, geo-tags, information about the photo camera model, names of the users, who edited the image etc.;
- Restoration of the information in case of, for instance, low resolution of the photo-document etc.;
- Establishing identity of people, who know this person, based on the obtained photos;
- Establishing a circle of common friends with a certain person.

A good example of geo-data processing for calculating the location of the cargo can be found in article [15]. It is rational to assess facts and arguments during their analysis, for instance, "normal" – "abnormal" – "interesting" – "unique" – "accidental", as suggested in article [16]. It is also important to remember about the assurance level of the information source.

5.5 Analysis

The next logical and integral step of the obtained information processing is its analysis. At this stage the obtained data may be arranged as a Table that specifies whether a certain hypothesis is supported or not. It is essential to understand that the structured approach to the search and analysis of information will be more beneficial, in case of big volumes of information and a large assembly of hypotheses that are selected for testing.

5.6 Report Development and Dissemination

Our article is focused on possible methods of collecting and analyzing information about a person or event on the Internet, thus the authors will not dwell on report development and dissemination to the interested parties, as it is explained in detail in the reference literature [17].

6 Examples of Structured Analysis Application

We will give two real-life examples of the structured techniques use: one is from the work experience of the partner company [18]. Situation: an anonymous blogger wrote a negative article about the company. The work algorithm was as follows:

1. The task was defined as follows: to identify a person and make him apologize. We all know how the behavior of a person changes once his actions are no longer anonymous.
2. The following hypotheses were defined:
   - The blogger was related to a competitor (company) (H1);
   - The blogger was related to the customer (company) (H2).

3. We chose his blog, social networks and search engine return as the initial sources of information.
4. As a result of the blog analysis we discovered his posts with photos from a professional exhibition, which helped us to define that he was working for the competitor.

We knew the name of the company, and searched the social network pages for the users, who specified that company as their employer. On one of the pages of that company's employee there was a link to a private blog, which coincided with the web-site, which published the information. The full name of the author was established. The data interrelation is shown in Fig. 3.

5. All information that demonstrated prejudiced attitude to the company was gathered.

   As a result, the blogger apologized.

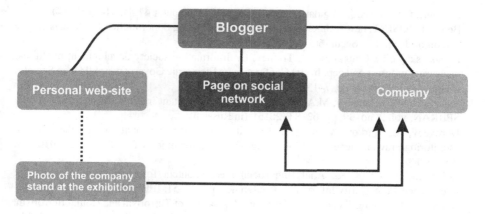

Fig. 3. An example of the mind map for establishing the identity of an anonymous blogger

7   Summary

The progress of the internet and various social media gives us an opportunity to find important information about a specific person or an event to identify potential threats posed to citizens.

At the same time the dynamic nature of the data on the Internet and dashing growth of their total volume make it necessary to use various expert optimization techniques for information collection and analysis. This work offers a methodological approach to carrying out a structured analysis that allows obtaining maximum volume of significant data about a person within reasonable time through step-by-step decomposition of data and connections between them. The method is based on so-called intelligence cycle for collecting and analyzing information and testing of alternative hypotheses technique.

One of the benefits of the structured analysis is that it does not impose limitations on the use of any expert analysis techniques and the use of any additional information sources.

The suggested method has direct applied significance and the work shows real-life examples of receiving target information both about study subjects and objects. This method may be used to implement control measures aimed at employee check within the framework of Information Security Management System subject to the requirements of ISO/IEC 27001:2013 [19].

This approach has been applied and tested on multiple occasions, and currently there is a study course on the topic. Further development of the structured method is perceived in complexing various techniques of expert and objective analysis about a specific person and event, and in formalization, to achieve maximum automation of information collecting and analysis.

References

1. Hurlburt, G.F., Voas, J.: Big data, networked worlds. Computer **47**(4), 84–87 (2014)
2. Benes, L.: OSINT, new technologies, education: expanding opportunities and threats. a new paradigm. J. Strateg. Secur. **6**(3), 22–37 (2013)
3. Bershadskaya, L., Chugunov, A., Trutnev, D.: Information society development in Russia: measuring progress and gap. In: 1st Conference on Electronic Governance and Open Society: Challenges in Eurasia, pp. 7–13. ACM, New York (2014)
4. Pilkevich, S.V., Eremeev, M.A.: Model of socially important internet resources. In: Trudy SPIIRAN, vol. 2, no. 39, pp. 62–83 (2015). (in Russian)
5. Doroveev, A., Markov, A.: Structured monitoring of open personal data on the Internet. Monitoring pravoprimeneniya [Monitoring of Law Enforcement] **1**(102), 41–53 (2016). (in Russian)
6. Colbaugh, R., Glass, K.: Analyzing social media content for security informatics. In: Intelligence and Security Informatics Conference, pp. 45–51. IEEE (2013)
7. Knoke, D.: Emerging Trends in Social Network Analysis of Terrorism and Counterterrorism. Emerging Trends in the Social and Behavioral Sciences. An Interdisciplinary, Searchable, and Linkable Resource. WOL, 1–15 May 2015
8. Bazzell, M.: Open Source Intelligence Techniques: Resources for Searching and Analyzing Online Information, 4th edn. CreateSpace Independent Publishing Platform (2015)
9. Intelligence Cycle. FBI. https://www.fbi.gov/about-us/intelligence/intelligence-cycle
10. Minto, B.: The Pyramid Principle: Logic in Writing and Thinking, 3rd edn. Prentice Hall, Upper Saddle River (2010)
11. Heuer Jr., R.J., Pherson, R.H.: Structured Analytic Techniques for Intelligence Analysis, Spi edn. CQ Press, Washington, D.C. (2014)
12. Pherson, K.H., Pherson, R.H.: Critical Thinking for Strategic Intelligence. CQ Press, Washington, D.C. (2012)
13. Layton, R., Perez, C., Birregah, B., Watters, P., Lemercier, M.: Indirect information linkage for OSINT through authorship analysis of aliases. In: Li, J., Cao, L., Wang, C., Tan, K.C., Liu, B., Pei, J., Tseng, V.S. (eds.) PAKDD 2013 Workshops. LNCS, vol. 7867, pp. 36–46. Springer, Heidelberg (2013). doi:10.1007/978-3-642-40319-4_4
14. Bowman, M., Debray, S.K., Peterson, L.L.: Reasoning about naming systems. ACM Trans. Program. Lang. Syst. **15**(5), 795–825 (1993)
15. Mazzola, L., Tsois, A., Dimitrova, T., Camossi, E.: Contextualisation of geographical scraped data to support human judgment and classification. In: Intelligence and Security Informatics Conference, pp. 151–154. IEEE (2013)

16. Skillicorn, D., Bourassa, M.A.J.: A framework for analyst focus from computed significance. In: Wiil, U.K. (ed.) Counterterrorism and Open Source Intelligence, pp. 33–47. Springer, Heidelberg (2011)
17. Clark, R.M.: Intelligence Analysis: A Target-Centric Approach, 4th edn. CQ Press, Washington, D.C. (2012)
18. Dorofeev, A., Markov, A., Tsirlov, V.: Structured approach to the social network analysis of information about a certain individual. In: 2nd International Conference on Electronic Governance and Open Society: Challenges in Eurasia, pp. 174–178. ACM, New York (2015)
19. Doroveev, A.V., Markov, A.S.: Information security management: basic concepts. Voprosy kiberbezopasnosti [Cybersecurity Issues] 1(2), 67–73 (2014). (in Russian)

Internet of Things Framework for Smart Home Building

Sylvia Ilieva, Andrey Penchev, and Dessislava Petrova-Antonova[(✉)]

Sofia University, 125, Tsarigradsko shoes Blvd., Block 2, fl. 3, Palo Alto, USA
sylvia@acad.bg, andrei.penchev@gmail.com,
d.petrova@fmi.uni-sofia.bg

Abstract. Nowadays the smart home represents the most sensible form of the Internet of Things (IoT) world. The communication protocols allowing devices to share data and respond to commands using a little power and wireless connection exist over a decade. The variety of the devices and communication protocols as well as the lack of standards for their manufacturing make building of smart homes challenging task and leads to a need for implementation of integration frameworks. The paper addresses this challenge by proposing an IoT Framework for integration of short range devices, called smartFW. The smartFW framework acts as mediator between integration platforms used by the end users to control their smart homes and the connected devices in those homes. It has a flexible architecture allowing to be enriched with new application and communication protocols to enable integration of wide range of devices. The smartFW framework is based on the OSGi standard and currently supports Zigbee, EnOcean, KNX, X10, Z-Wave device communication protocols as well as Coap, MQTT and XAMPP application protocols.

Keywords: Internet of Things integration framework · Short range devices integration · Device communication protocols · Smart homes

1 Introduction

The Internet of Things (IoT) affects all areas of everyday life of citizens and span a wide range of applications from different domains such as health, energy transportation, living, etc. [9]. IoT world considers all home devices as "smart" things that are connected in a common environment in order to deliver home automation services to the customers. The smart things allow clients to receive notifications about what is happening in their homes as well as to control devices reacting to their unique preferences. According to ABI Research more than 10 billion devices in the market are wirelessly connected until 2013 and over 30 billion devices are expected to be connected by 2020 [1]. The emergence of communication protocols for short range devices such as Zigbee, EnOcean, KNX, X10, Z-Wave and the extensive usage of hub devices like smartphones, tablets and notebooks are key enables of the IoT.

Besides the huge potential of IoT, the concept behind it faces many unsolved problems related to security, missing standards for manufacturing "smart" devices, variety and variability of communication protocols, data volumes, etc. This implies a

© Springer International Publishing AG 2016
A.V. Chugunov et al. (Eds.): DTGS 2016, CCIS 674, pp. 450–462, 2016.
DOI: 10.1007/978-3-319-49700-6_45

necessity for implementation of frameworks providing services for integration and unified control of devices over wide range of communication protocols [6].

Following the current needs of IoT, this paper proposes an IoT Framework for integration of short range devices, called smartFW. It could be use in creation ubiquitously networked societies and more especially in building smart homes for citizens.

The rest of the paper is structured as follows. The Sect. 2 provides a comparison analysis of the most popular IoT platforms and related frameworks. Section 3 gives an overview of the smartFW framework including its concept, requirements and use cases. Section 4 presents the framework's architecture, while Sect. 5 describes its implementation details. Section 6 is devoted to the deployment and testing of the smartFW. Finally, Sect. 7 concludes the paper and gives directions for future work.

2 Related Work

This section analyzes the most popular IoT platforms and related frameworks for building of smart homes. First a brief overview of the platforms is given. Next, a criteria for their comparison are identified and the results from analysis are summarized in tables.

2.1 IoT Platforms

ThinkPark is an IoT enabled platform supporting variety protocols that are available in the connected devices [8]. In order to guarantee interoperability among objects and applications, it is based on Core oneM2M - ETSI M2M standard. ThinkPark platform provides a network for sleepy sensors requiring long range indoor penetration. It uses an integration framework, called Cacoon [3] that supports Zigbee, 6LoWPAN and KNX device protocols. The M-Bus and ModBus are additionally added. ThinkPark platform is based on OSGi standard and provides possibility for implementation of applications over the Coap protocol. Thus, it could be connected to other integration platforms and frameworks.

Eclipse SmartHome is a framework for implementation of end user solutions on it [2]. Its basic version does not support protocols for communication with short range devices, but its architecture is designed to allow such protocols to be easily added. It fosters the modularity provided by OSGi standard for Java applications. Eclipse Smart Home ensures a modular rule engine than allow specification of rules for automated control of connected objects. In contrast to ThinkPark platform, it implements an abstract device representation layer.

Xively platform provides a collection of services for IoT with open access [10]. They support communication over HTTP/HTTPS, Sockets/WebSockets and MQTT. The Xively microservice APIs provide building blocks for applications to manipulate and retrieve data, create and connect to devices, organizations, users and other entities in the Xively ecosystem. The communication between devices and applications uses three cloud-based services, namely Blueprint, Messaging and Identity Management.

A drawback of the Xively platform is that it does not provide an integration framework for connection of short range devices to the cloud.

Dragrove is an open source integration framework delivered as generic gateway for the IoT [5]. It communicates directly with short range devices using XBee and Arduino protocols. The goal of Dragrove is to solve the problems related to the connectivity of devices allowing developers to integrate or develop products on top of rich interface.

Candi is a solution providing Cloud admin service, interface Toolkit, and Open IoT Server to manage, display, and integrate remote devices and data [4]. The Cloud admin service manages sites, devices, groups, users and roles. The Toolkit provides mobile and browser application templates, and APIs for integration with Cloud admin service, applications, and other services. The Open IoT Server coordinates communication between devices and protocols, user applications, third-party web services and the Cloud admin service. It supports ZigBee, Z-Wave, Wi-Fi, Ethernet, serial, powerline and other transport layers and protocols, and a range of specific manufacturer implementations.

2.2   Comparison Criteria

The comparison criteria cover the characteristics of the presented IoT platforms from two points of view: (1) as a component for building IoT ecosystem; and (2) as a single unit for building IoT solutions.

The comparison criteria are as follows:

- Availability of connection between an integration platform and IoT framework – provides connectivity of short range devices to global network;
- Possibility for connection of IoT frameworks to multiple integration platform and frameworks – reduces the data traffic to the integration platform and provides communication among devices without need of mediators;
- Implementation of variety application protocols for communication with integration platform – provides possibility for usage of different integration platforms;
- Possibility for adding new application protocols – provides an opportunity to use specific application protocols for interoperability with a given integration platform;
- Implementation of variety device protocols – provides possibility for usage of different short range devices;
- Possibility for adding new device protocols – provides an opportunity to use specific device protocols for connection to given short range devices.
- Support of OSGi standard – provides possibility for continuous work of the server without stopping for update;
- Possibility for working of the IoT framework as a single unit – the coupling of the IoT platform and underlying framework prevents working of the framework in case of missing internet connection or IoT platform failures.
- Possibility to easily add new short range device – the need for in-depth technical knowledge to add a new device to the framework reduces its flexibility.
- Implementation of abstract device layer – helps to extend the framework with new protocols' implementations;

- Open source – accessibility of provided services for more customers;
- Independence from the hardware infrastructure – opportunity to choose the hardware configuration for deployment;
- Multiplatform support – an opportunity to choose the deployment environment.

2.3 Summary of the Analysis

The analysis is performed in three main directions: (1) Connectivity with integration platforms; (2) Connectivity with short range devices; and (3) Characteristics of the framework as single unit. The results are shown accordingly in Tables 1, 2 and 3. The satisfied criteria by the corresponding frameworks are marked with the sign "+" and those that are not satisfied are marked with a sign "−".

Table 1. Connectivity with integration platform

Criterion	[8]	[2]	[10]	[5]	[3]	smartFW
Connectivity with single integration platform	+	−	−	−	+	+
Connectivity with multiple integration platforms	−	+	−	+	−	+
Supported application protocols	Coap	−	−	−	N/A	Coap, MQTT
Extensibility with new application protocols	−	+	−	+	−	+

Table 2. Connectivity with short range devices

Criterion	[8]	[2]	[10]	[5]	[3]	smartFW
Implemented open protocols	Zigbee, 6LoWPAN, KNX, M-Bus, ModBus	−	−	Xbee, Arduino	Zigbee, Z-Wave	Zigbee, EnOcean, KNX, X10, Z-Wave
Possibility for adding new protocols	−	+	−	+	−	+
Implementation of abstract device layer	−	+	−	−	−	+
Possibility for adding new device	+	+	−	+	+	+

3 Overview of the Framework

The main goal of the smartFW framework is to identify short range devices and to provide a communication channel among them. It is motivated by the variability of the communication technologies and protocols used by the vendors of such devices.

Table 3. Characteristics of the framework as single unit

Criterion	[8]	[2]	[10]	[5]	[3]	smartFW
OSGi based	+	+	−	−	N/A	+
Possibility for independent work	+	+	−	+	+	+
Independence from hardware infrastructure	+	+	−	−	+	+
Multiplatform support	+	+	−	−	+	+
Open source	+	+	−	+	−	+

Figure 1 shows the conceptual model of the smartFW framework. The framework acts as mediator among different short range devices by implementing functionality for sending commands and obtaining information about their state. At the same time, it communicates with an integration platform providing interface to the end users. The platform receives notifications for connected devices by the framework and allows users to specify commands to them. It could be integrated with several frameworks sharing their connected devices and load balancing.

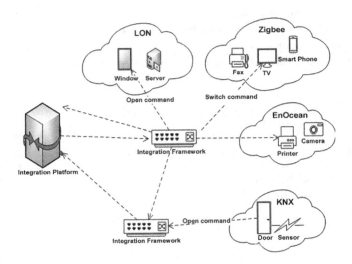

Fig. 1. Conceptual model of the smartFW framework

3.1 Requirements

The functional requirements to the smartFW framework are as follows:

- Integration of open protocols for communication with short range devices;
- Integration of application protocols for communication with the integrated platform;
- Possibility for easy configuration of new devices;
- Support of basic short range devices (lights, binary switches, sensors, measurement devices, tune up devices).
- Possibility for sending commands to short range devices;

- Possibility for sending notifications to the integrated platform;
- Possibility for receiving commands from the integrated platform;
- Possibility for obtaining information about the current state of the connected devices.

The non-functional requirements to the smartFW framework are following:

- Performance – the time for execution of single command sent by the integration platform to the smartFW framework should not exceed 500 ms;
- Fault tolerance – the smartFW framework should recover successfully in case of exceptions saving all configurations related to the current state;
- Security – encrypted data should be used for communication;
- Interoperability – several smartFW frameworks connected to the same integration platform should balance the workload and prevent execution of the same commands;
- Expandability – the smartFW framework should allow integration of arbitrary device and application protocols;
- Connectivity – the smartFW framework should allow communication with different integration platforms;
- Deployability - the smartFW framework should be easily deployed on variety hardware configurations;
- Testability – each component of the smartFW framework can be tested separately.

3.2   Use Cases

The smartFW framework can be used by end users and integration platforms. Figure 2 shows the use cases from both perspectives.

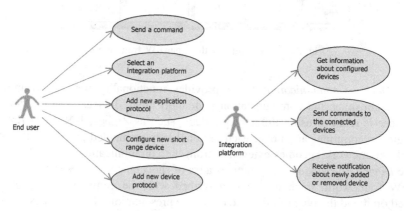

Fig. 2. End user use cases

The end user is able to control the connected short range devices and to configure a new device in the smartFW framework. He/she can select through the framework an integration platform that will be used for sending commands to and receiving notifications from the devices. His/her choice could be extended with additional integration platforms by adding new application protocols to the framework. The end user is also provided with functionality for adding new device protocols. Thus, he/she can extend the framework to support new short range devices that could be subsequently configured and controlled.

The integration platform receives notifications during initial configuration of the connected short range devices and each time when a new device is added to the smartFW framework. It is able to send and receive device data through the framework. Thus the framework acts as mediator between the integration platform and the connected short range devices.

4   Framework Architecture

The smartFW framework has a three-tier architecture, shown on Fig. 3.

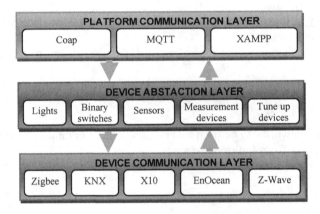

Fig. 3. Architecture of the smartFW framework

The *Device Communication Layer* provides functionality for discovering, connection establishing and communication with short range devices. The integration of the devices is realized using different protocols such as Zigbee, KNX and EnOcean. The logic for communication over each protocol is implemented in different modules. Thus, the framework becomes extensible from the communication protocols view.

The *Device Abstraction Layer* defines a set of short range devices supported by the smartFW framework. Each device is described with the commands allowed to be executed on it and the type of provided data. The presentation of the devices is abstract i.e. it does not depend on the underlying communication protocols. Thus, the framework's components are provided with a unified access to the devices that is independent from their realization and the type of the communication network (wireless, electrical, etc.).

The *Platform Communication Layer* is responsible for communication between the integration platform and smartFW framework. The supported application protocols are Coap, MQTT and XAMPP. The logic for communication over each application protocol again is implemented in different modules. The notifications for newly connected devices are passed to the platform through a method for serialization of Java object in JSON. The commands from the platform to the smartFW framework are sent through a method for deserialization of JSON to Java object. Both methods are executed by EclipseLink Moxy module.

5 Framework Implementation

This section describes the implementation of the smartFW framework. The component structure of the layers building its architecture and the processes of adding new devices and new protocols are presented.

The *Platform Communication Layer* consists of 4 components as follows: (1) *fw.-communication.api* implementing an API for communication with the integration platform that are accessible from external modules; (2) *fw.communication.coap* implementing communication over Coap protocol; (3) *fw.communication.mqtt* implementing communication over MQTT protocol; and (4) *fw.communication.xampp* implementing communication over XAMPP protocol.

The *Device Abstraction Layer* has 6 components. The *fw.device.abstraction.layer. api* component defines abstract representation of short range devices from different types. The *fw.device.lamp.gui* component implements user interface for abstract presentation of lights. The *fw.device.sensor.gui* component implements user interface for abstract presentation of sensors. The *fw.device.binaryswitch.gui* component implements user interface for abstract presentation of binary switches. The *fw.device.meter. gui.gui* component implements user interface for abstract presentation of measurement devices. The *fw.device.setvalue.gui.gui* component implements user interface for abstract presentation of tune up devices.

The *Device Communication Layer* has six components. The *fw.protocol.api* component defines interfaces for communication with shot range devices accessible from external modules. Thus, the external modules are not provided with information about the actual implementation of those interface. The *fw.protocol.impl.zigbee* component implements communication with devices over Zigbee protocol. The *fw.protocol.impl. knx* component implements communication with devices over KNX protocol. The *fw. protocol.impl.enocean* component implements communication with devices over EnOcean protocol. The *fw.protocol.impl.x10* component implements communication with devices over X10 protocol. The *fw.protocol.impl.zwave* component implements communication with devices over Z-Wave protocol.

The process of adding a new protocol implementation is shown in Fig. 4.

The workflow presented in Fig. 4 is applicable both for protocols providing device communication and application protocols used for communication between the smartFW framework and particular integration platform.

The process of integration of a new device is shown in Fig. 5. The smartFW framework provides a user interface for control of the following types of devices:

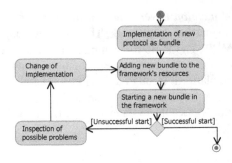

Fig. 4. Integration of new protocol

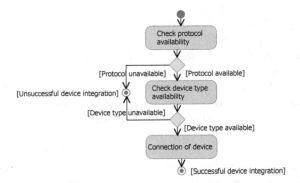

Fig. 5. Integration of new device

- Lights – ability for control of light intensity;
- Binary switches – ability to perform switch on and switch off operations;
- Sensors – ability to send notification in case of event fire (alarms);
- Measurement devices – ability to retrieve device information about time, temperature, velocity, color, etc.;
- Tune up devices – ability to send information about time, temperature, velocity, color, etc. to device.

6   Deployment and Testing

The deployment of the smartFW framework requires hardware infrastructure with limited resource, shown in Table 4.

The initial installation requires: (1) setting the integration platform that will be connected to the smartFW framework; (2) setting the short range devices that will be integrated to the smartFW framework; and (3) setting addresses of other smartFW frameworks if any. The smartFW framework works by default with Equinox implementation of the OSGi core framework specification [7]. Other OSGi implementation are also suitable for deployment.

Table 4. Minimum hardware requirements for deployment

Component	Minimum requirement
RAM	256 MB
Hard disk	100 MB
Processor	32 bit, 1 core, 512 MHz

6.1 Test Case Design

The functionality of the smartFW framework is verified through three groups of test cases. The first group tests the integration of short range devices and includes the following test cases:

- Testing of abstract representation of all devices in the *Device Abstraction Layer* of smartFW framework;
- Testing of adding a new short range device;
- Testing of commands sent from the smartFW framework to device using a given protocol (zigbee/knx/enocean/x10);
- Testing of notifications sent from a device using a given protocol (zigbee/knx/enocean/x10) to the smartFW framework;
- Testing of implementation of device protocols (zigbee/knx/enocean/x10);
- Testing of adding a new device protocol.

The second group verifies the user interface and includes the following test cases:

- Testing for availability at the user interface of all commands defined in the *Device Abstraction Layer*;
- Testing of receiving notifications in the user interface from the integrated devices;
- Testing of sending commands to integrated devices from the user interface;
- Testing of sending commands to a given device from two different user interfaces.

The third group verifies the connection with the integration platform and includes the following test cases:

- Testing of connectivity between the integration platform and the smartFW framework;
- Testing of availability at the integration platform of all integrated devices;
- Testing of sending commands from the integration platform to a given device;
- Testing of notifications sent from a given device to the integrated platform;
- Testing the implementation of the application protocols (MQTT/COAP/XAMPP);
- Testing of adding a new application protocol;
- Testing of integration of the smartFW framework with an integration platform that is different by the default one.

The non-functional characteristics of the smartFW framework are tested using the following test cases:

- Performance testing during normal work of the smartFW framework – sending a single command from the integration platform to the smartFW framework;

- Stress testing – simultaneous sending of 100 commands from the integration platform to the smartFW framework;
- Interoperability testing – checking communication of single integration platform with two different smartFW frameworks;
- Deployability testing – simultaneous sending of 20 commands from the integration platform to the smartFW framework deployed with minimum hardware requirements described in Table 4.

6.2 Performance Analysis

The results from test case execution shows that the smartFW framework works properly according to the requirements defined in Sect. 3.2. They are summarized in Table 5. According to the requirements the time for processing a command by the framework should be less than 500 ms. The test performed to check that requirement calculates the average time for sequential processing of 100 commands during normal operational work of the framework.

Table 5. Processing time

Processing time	Sequential processing [ms]	Simultaneous processing [ms]
Minimum	97.92	18287.32
Maximum	257.58	23553.16
Average	183.79	20996.56
Deviation	183.79	1569.72

Figure 6 shows the processing time during simulation of 100 commands.

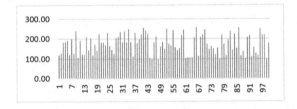

Fig. 6. Processing time during consequently sending of 100 commands [ms].

Figure 7 shows the processing time in millisecond during simultaneous execution of 100 commands. The test is repeated 100 times and the results show that the average time for execution is 20996.56 ms.

The average time for execution of single command is 183.79 ms, which obviously satisfies the requirement defined. The standard deviation of 47.78 ms is due to the different time required for processing of different commands and the different time for execution of given command using different device protocols. Two factors are calculated during testing with simultaneous sending of 100 commands: working of the smartFW framework under a high load and time for simultaneous processing of all

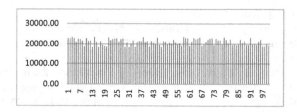

Fig. 7. Processing time during simultaneous sending of 100 commands [ms].

commands. The smartFW framework successfully processes all commands without omissions.

7   Conclusion

The paper presents an IoT framework for integration and control of short range devices. Its benefits can be summarized as follows:

- Possibility for usage different integration platforms by end users due to ability for extending with new application protocols;
- Possibility for connecting different short range devices due to extensibility with new device communication protocols and implementation of device abstraction layer;
- Provision of complete smart home solution due to provided IoT integration platform and several device communication protocols by default.

Future work includes further improvement of the framework in three directions:

- Implementation of new device communication protocols such as Insteon and BacNet that the end users could be use by default;
- Extension of the device abstraction layer in order to support more types of devices;
- Implementation of new application protocols such as DDS, STOMP and AMQP that the end users could be use by default.

The current design of the framework allows extensibility in the mentioned directions. It has flexible architecture tailored to the rapid growth of IoT technologies.

Acknowledgments. The authors acknowledge the financial support by the Scientific Fund of Sofia University under agreement no. 180/13.04.2016.

References

1. ABI   Research.   https://www.abiresearch.com/press/more-than-30-billion-devices-will-wirelessly-conne
2. Al-Fuqaha, A., Guizani, M., Mohammadi, M., Aledhari, M., Ayyash, M.: Internet of Things: a survey on enabling technologies, protocols, and applications. IEEE Commun. Surv. Tutorials **17**, 2347–2376 (2015)

3. Cacoon Project. http://cocoon.actility.com/
4. Candi. Open IoT Server. https://www.candicontrols.com/index.html
5. Dragrove - Generic gateway for Internet of Things. http://www.seeedstudio.com/wiki/Dragrove
6. Mattern, F., Floerkemeier, C.: From the internet of computers to the Internet of Things. In: Sachs, K., Petrov, I., Guerrero, P. (eds.) From Active Data Management to Event-Based Systems and More. LNCS, vol. 6462, pp. 242–259. Springer, Heidelberg (2010). doi:10.1007/978-3-642-17226-7_15
7. McAffer, J., VanderLei, P., Archer, S.: OSGi and Equinox: Creating Highly Modular Java Systems. Addison Wesley, Reading (2013)
8. ThinkPark WireLess. http://www.thingpark.com/en
9. Vermesan, O., Friess, P.: Internet of Things: Converging Technologies for Smart Environments and Integrated Ecosystems. River Publishers, Aalborg (2013)
10. Weinberger, M., Köhler, M., Wörner, D., Wortmann, F.: Platforms for the Internet of Things. An analysis of existing solutions. In: Bosch Conference on Systems and Software Engineering (2014)

Envisioning Smart Villages Through Information and Communication Technologies – A Framework for Implementation in India

Sanjeev Kumar Katara[✉]

National Informatics Centre, A-Block, CGO Complex, Lodhi Road, New Delhi, India
sanjeevkatara@nic.in

Abstract. Technology has shown its capability in different segments of development in rural and urban areas. Urban areas are more inclined to adopt and accept Information and Communication Technologies (ICTs) due to advantages of better financial and digital literacy as compared to rural areas. Urban landscapes are congenial to the success of ICTs. Most of the villages in India are agrarian based and rural economy is based on agriculture. The rural populace needs to be sensitized on the role of ICT being an enabler and gains they can make by effective utilization of the same. The driving motivation behind the idea of "Smart Village" is that technology should act as an accelerator for growth and sustainable development. It should enable education, improve local business opportunities and promote health. The "Smart Village" theory aims to realize its objective through providing decision makers with perceptive analyses of the challenges of smart village development. This paper will explore how ICTs improves quality of life in the form of Smart Village for rural citizens and a possible framework for implementation. It will also explore a few challenges and solutions. It also campaigns for use of mobile technologies to bring e-Governance services closer to rural citizens.

Keywords: Digital India · Framework · Smart Village · Unnat Bharat Abhiyan · ICTs

1 Introduction

A Smart Village comprises a group of services, which are delivered to its businesses and dwellers in an efficient and effective way. Numerous services including health care, education, sanitization, smart agriculture, road infrastructure, disaster management, water supply, construction, electricity, retail manufacturing and logistics are needed in building a smart village [1].

The initiative of Govt. of India, Unnat Bharat Abhiyan (UBA) [18] is inspired by the vision of transformational change in rural development activities by leveraging knowledge institutions to help build the framework of an inclusive India. The Mission of Unnat Bharat Abhiyan is to enable higher educational institutions to work with the

© Springer International Publishing AG 2016
A.V. Chugunov et al. (Eds.): DTGS 2016, CCIS 674, pp. 463–468, 2016.
DOI: 10.1007/978-3-319-49700-6_46

rural areas of India in identifying development challenges and emerging solutions for accelerating sustainable growth [3].

The Government's ambitious "Digital India" [7] plan aims to digitally connect all of India's village gram panchayats by broadband internet, promote electronic governance and metamorphosize into a connected knowledge economy.

By the year 2019, the 'Digital India' programme of the Government of India, visualizes that 2,50,000 Indian villages will enjoy broadband and universal phone connectivity [6]. This is a truly idealistic and praiseworthy initiative. To fully utilize the rural connectivity and the Digital India programme, well equipped infrastructure should be built at each of the village panchayats level.

Current citizen and administrative services facilities in the villages are fully insufficient on all fronts. While rolling out the ICT initiatives, the concerned government and administrative agencies need to come together to simultaneously plan, design and build the service delivery framework at the respective location.

The readiness of strong and robust broadband connectivity is most demanding for the successful execution of the crucial social sector programmes and schemes in rural areas by the government agencies on e-governance. In this each stage poses its own challenge, starting with necessary clearances. This includes many government agencies [8] and is a highly bureaucratic and slow moving process.

The connectivity from state headquarters to district headquarters may be through fibre based network, subsequently connectivity to village panchayats can be through wireless network. A wireless network will require a much lesser time for network rollout so it is a preferred choice. Post rollout, the maintenance and operations cost for a wireless network will be cheaper compared to a fibre based network [2]. Technology advancement of a wireless network is less tiresome and requires lower costs. Besides, the same wireless network can be adopted to provide high quality mobile services for the rural areas as well.

To build smart villages other basic component is electricity supply and large part of rural India lacks electricity. Most Indian villages get plenty of sunshine. Hence using solar energy along with biomass-based power can fulfill the demand of the power supply. Broadband connectivity and uninterruptible power supply will push the rural socio-economic development to the next level.

2   Design Methodologies and Components

The proposed design methodology for building a Smart Village consists of:

i. Assessment of the Investment Climate of the village
ii. Formulate the Growth Strategies for the village

Further a specially designed suitable framework "STERM" for rural areas on the grounds of Science, Technology, Engineering, Regulations and Management will play a vital role to build next generation smart villages.

Following are some generalized components for the development of Smart Villages [19]:

i. Economic Component: This component will include local administration and economic factors. It will cover governance models, bandwidth, mobility, cloud computing, entrepreneurship and agriculture [17].

ii. Environmental Component: This component will include resources and infrastructures available at local level. It may covers cleaner technologies, public and alternative transportation, green spaces, smart growth, climate change [5], bio-gas and cow dung based products.

iii. Social Component: This component may address issues related to community life, participatory democracy, social innovation, proximity services, culture, ethos and ethics.

iv. Capacity Building: This component may address issues related to personality development, community development and panchayat institutions.

3 Role of Information and Communication Technologies

Role of ICT is most important in the governance of a Smart Village. It can help in rationalizing existing processes, monitoring and communication across all levels [13]. New emerging technologies like: In memory databases, Cloud Computing and Data Analytics can be adopted to maintain huge amounts of data at village level or by clusters of villages at district level.

This can reduce operation and maintenance expenses of huge servers at the village level where not much talent is available for rigorous server operations. This can smoothen the work of the people involved in governance, giving them the opportunity to concentrate on the core governance of the village. The implementation of numerous services can be controlled and observed using remote call centers with skilled professionals. Once the governance models are in place they can be used to monitor and measure the results of the services.

Therefore making villages smart would help in reducing the digital divide, lower rural to urban migrations, increase productivity, generate employment and improve the work life balance of the individuals. A smart village will not only bring digital connectivity but will also be a major factor contributing to sustainable development.

3.1 Problems vs. Potentials

ICTs have shown tremendous potential for the benefit of mankind in different areas. They can play a key role for the fast and sustainable development of rural India.

Based on the analysis on limitations of traditional rural planning and construction, the village planning needs to be a bottom-up approach that focuses on the local community involvement. ICTs have a large potential for enhancement of rural life through its applications in various areas of the rural development.

Globally, ICTs have improved the life of people living in urban areas [14]. Rural populace has remained neglected, resulting in a virtual digital divide between the rural and the urban populace.

4   Challenges

The situations and challenges in developing urban and rural areas are different due to the constraints and opportunities. The existing technologies developed for the smart cities may not be suitable for smart village. Smart village system cannot be developed on the lines of a smart city model [15].

The components taken in to consideration will differ from region to region and would be based on the available opportunities and resources. Each village is a unique example having diverse set of problems and situations. It may be difficult to implement the same model of development for all the villages.

5   Conclusion

The driving motivation behind the concept on "Smart Village" is that technology should act as a facilitator for development, empowering education and local business opportunities [4]. It can also improve health and welfare, enhance democratic engagement of village dwellers. The "Smart Village" concept aims to realize its goal by providing policymakers with insightful, bottom–up analyses of the challenges of village development [16].

In fact, many innovative applications and services will emerge once the digital connectivity is available in the rural areas. Once connectivity is established in rural areas, corporates could utilize the same for regular information sharing with their offices located in various geographical locations. New services will emerge to strengthen the current socio-economically driven business models for the Digital India programme and will enhance its viability. This will also create ample white-collared employment opportunities for the rural populace, simultaneously decreasing the rural exodus.

In a country like India, the concept of building Smart Cities will only improve living conditions for a little over 30% of the citizens, while the idea of developing Smart Villages has the potential to cover more than 50%. This will also help in the organized development of villages and will lend greater weight to achieve the goals of an ambitious national programme like Digital India.

6   Way Forward

Mobile technology has played a significant role [9] in the economic and social empowerment of rural societies in developing areas to fill the digital divide and might be able to bring ICT services closer to rural citizens [11]. Still, rural areas often suffer from slow and untrustworthy network infrastructures. This limits access to services and content that may promote economic growth.

However, with the use of ICT, empowerment and capacity development at community and individual level can be achieved to ensure delivery, demand, reach and use of quality services. It will also help in identifying system bottlenecks and gaps, improve data analysis and monitoring. It enhances technical and entrepreneurial skills, promotes social norms and etiquette favorable to the realization of smart village development. The "Smart Village" knowledge management along with ICT will focus on strengthening both capacities and systems of the rural community [12].

With nearly 1 billion telephone subscribers and 970 million mobile users, e-governance is certainly transitioning into m-governance [10]. However, under Digital India initiative, high speed broadband connectivity at village panchayat level will be brought in through the National Optical Fibre Network (NOFN) project which is being implemented and 2.5 lakh villages will be covered under the Digital India.

References

1. Adarsh Gram (Model Village). www.swaniti.com/project/model-village
2. Broadband connectivity key to rural development. http://indianexpress.com/article/opinion/columns/broadband-connectivity-key-to-rural-development
3. Centre for Technology Alternatives for Rural Areas. http://www.ctara.iitb.ac.in/index.php/framework
4. Chapman, R., Slaymaker, T.: Overseas Development Institute, UK. ICTs and Rural Development- Review of the Literature, Current Interventions and Opportunities for Action. http://www.odi.org/sites/odi.org.uk/files/odi-assets/publications-opinion-files/2670.pdf
5. Climate Smart Villages. https://cgspace.cgiar.org/bitstream/handle/10568/33322/CCAFSClimate-SmartVillages2013.pdf
6. Digital India – Making villages 'Smart'. http://telecom.economictimes.indiatimes.com/tele-talk/Digital-India-Making-villages-Smart/719
7. Digital India Programme Ministry of Electronics and Information Technology, Govt. of India. http://www.digitalindia.gov.in
8. eGovWatch: Broadband connectivity key to rural development. http://computer.financialexpress.com/features/broadband-connectivity-key-to-rural-development/7021
9. Human Resources and Skill Requirements in the IT and ITes Sector. http://www.nsdcindia.org/sites/default/files/files/IT-and-ITeS.pdf
10. Jha, B.K.: M-Governance transforming rural India. http://www.ruralmarketing.in/industry/technology/m-governance-transforming-rural-india
11. Katara, S.K., Ilavarasan, P.V.: Mobile Technologies in e-Governance: a framework for implementation in India. In: 7th International Conference on Theory and Practice of Electronic Governance, ICEGOV 2013. ACM Press, New York (2013). doi:http://dx.doi.org/10.1145/2591888.2591955
12. Mobile-Enabled Delay Tolerant Networking in Rural Developing Regions. https://www.disneyresearch.com/publication/mobile-enabled-delay-tolerant-networking-in-rural-developing-regions
13. Ranade, P., Londhe, S., Mishra, A.: Smart villages through information technology – need of emerging India. Int. J. Inf. Technol. 3(7) (2015)
14. Rao, T.P.R.: ICT and e-Governance for rural development. Center for electronic governance, Indian Institute of Management, Ahmedabad. In: Symposium on "Governance in Development: Issues, Challenges and Strategies". Institute of Rural Management, Anand, Gujarat (2004)
15. Smart Villages Must for Smart Cities | eGov Magazine. http://egov.eletsonline.com/2015/08/smart-villages-must-for-smart-cities
16. Smart Villages, New Thinking for Off-grid Communities Worldwide. http://e4sv.org/wp-content/uploads/2014/07/Cambridge-Workshop-Report-130514.pdf

17. Somwanshi, R., Shindepatil, U., Tule, D., Mankar, A., Ingle, N.: Study and development of village as a smart village. Int. J. Sci. Eng. Res. **7**(6) (2016)
18. Unnat Bharat Abhiyan. http://unnat.iitd.ac.in
19. Viswanadham, N.: Centre for Contemporary Studies, Indian Institute of Science. Design of Smart Villages. http://drona.csa.iisc.ernet.in/~nv/95DesignofSmartVillages-IISc.pdf

Multi-model Approach to City Governance in the Face of Uncertainty

Mikhail Ignatyev[1], Vladimir Marley[2], Vladimir Mikhailov[3]($\boxtimes$),
and Alexandr Spesivtsev[4]

[1] Saint-Petersburg State University Aerospace Instrumentation (SUAI),
Bolshaya Morskaya Str., 67, St. Petersburg 190000, Russia
ignatmb@mail.ru
[2] State University of Marine and River Flit (SUMRF),
Dvinskaja 5/7, St. Petersburg 198035, Russia
marley@mail.ru
[3] St. Petersburg Institute for Informatics and Automation of the Russian
Academy of Sciences (SPIIRAS), 14th line 39, St. Petersburg 199178, Russia
mwwcari@gmail.com
[4] Military Space Academy A.F. Mozhaisky, Saint-Petersburg (MSA),
Zhdanovskaya Str., 13, St. Petersburg 197082, Russia
Sav2050@gmail.com

Abstract. In this paper we describe a multi-model approach used for modeling cities as a complex poorly formalized system, based on three modeling methods: linguistic-combinatorial, logical-linguistic and algorithmic ones, which provide a holistic view of the object from different perspectives to solve fundamentally different problems to support managerial decisions.

Keywords: City · Poorly formalized system · Expert knowledge · Multi-model approach · Linguistic-combinatorial method · Logical-linguistic modeling · Algorithmic modeling

1 Introduction

Ever since Plato a city has been seen as a complex system and vast literature is devoted to its study. A great number of agglomerated forms of cities which change over time are investigated in [6, 9]. Cities that have arisen as monocentric structures are in crisis and traffic jams and gradually transformed into polycentric structures [1, 3, 7].

The poly-modeling approach is based on three successive according to the degree of abstraction levels of description of systems for which a modeling methodology is designed in order to make it possible to represent the studied system from different perspectives, to assess its condition and to manage its behavior.

The first level is the level of description in natural language with the methodology of the linguo-combinatorial modeling. Natural language is a universal sign system that allows to consider the whole class of systems for which a verbal description can be made. By doing so we are immediately confronted with the main feature of natural language – vagueness and ambiguity of the meaning of words. We denote words and

A.V. Chugunov et al. (Eds.): DTGS 2016, CCIS 674, pp. 469–477, 2016.
DOI: 10.1007/978-3-319-49700-6_47

meanings are implied. Methodology of linguo-combinatorial modeling is that key-words are allocated, determine the meaning of words, the words are combined into phrases as linguistic equation, based on which are built the equivalent system of equations with random coefficients [4, 5]. Thus, with the help of the linguo-combinatorial modeling the task of analyzing complex systems is reduced to the study of equivalent equations with arbitrary coefficients which can be used to control the behavior of the system, the solutions of optimization and other tasks.

The second level corresponds to the presentation of expert systems in the state space, implying that there is a finite set of factors with each set corresponding to a particular state of the system. Moreover, a mathematical structure of the system is unknown, and variables can be numeric as well as linguistic. A huge amount of expertise, on the one hand, and the urgent need for the use of this knowledge, on the other, are inconsistent due to the absence of effective methods of extraction and con-volution of expertise, and this, in turn, does not allow wide dissemination and the use of "implicit preserved expert knowledge" to manage complex systems.

The solution to this problem is through the use of technologies of construction of logical-linguistic models as a synthesis of fuzzy set theory and the theory of planning of experiments. A detailed description of this modeling technology is given in the articles [10, 11].

At the third level it is assumed that the expert possesses the knowledge required to represent the simulated process as an algorithmic description, the structure of which corresponds to the structure of the causal relationships in the scenario of a modeling process, and determines the sequence of transitions of the system in state space. However, experts due to their professional specialization are unable to overcome their knowledge in a classical mathematical form, allowing to implement a computer pro-gram. The algorithmic modeling technology is used to formalize expert knowledge and to represent its model in the form of algorithmic networks [2, 3]. Algorithmic nets are dual objects according to their properties. On the one hand, this tool is an ideographic representation of a complex system or object, reflecting expert knowledge about the structural characteristics of the object and algorithmic ones – about the composition of operations and causal-effect relationships between them, based on their intuitive ideas, methods, guides and other information known to the expert. On the other hand, algorithmic nets are generalized maximally parallelized algorithm allowing automatic preparation of calculation programs.

Suitable tools automatically establish a computer program based on the received descriptions and provide support to the user during the design of the model and while conducting computer experiments [3, 8].

2   The Linguo-Combinatorial Model of the City

If the keywords are "population", "passionarity", "territory", "production", "ecology and safety", "finance", "external relations", in this case in accordance with the linguo-combinatorial approach [4, 5] the equation of the city is as follows

$$A1 * E1 + A2 * E2 + \ldots + A7 * E7 = 0 \tag{1}$$

and the equivalent of the equation takes the form

$$E1 = U1 * A2 + U2 * A3 + U3 * A4 + U4 * A5 + U5 * A6 + U6 * A7$$

$$E2 = -U1 * A1 + U7 * A3 + U8 * A4 + U9 * A5 + U10 * A6 + U11 * A7$$

$$E3 = -U2 * A1 - U7 * A2 + U12 * A4 + U13 * A5 + U14 * A6 + U15 * A7$$

$$E4 = -U3 * A1 - U8 * A2 - U12 * A3 + U16 * A5 + U17 * A6 + U18 * A7$$

$$E5 = -U4 * A1 - U9 * A2 - U13 * A3 - U16 * A4 + U19 * A6 + U20 * A7$$

$$E6 = -U5 * A1 - U10 * A2 - U14 * A3 - U17 * A4 - U19 * A5 + U21 * A7$$

$$E7 = -U6 * A1 - U11 * A2 - U15 * A3 - U18 * A4 - U20 * A5 - U21 * A6$$

where A1 – a characteristic of the population which includes such characteristics as health, education, employment; A2 – a characteristic of passionarity, people's ambitions, people have freedom of choice in decision-making, which is important and evaluated by sociological analysis; A3 – a description of the territory including surface and underground constructions, this part can be a geographic information system; A4 – a description of production, including the assessment of different types of activities - scientific, industrial, transport, commercial and others, A5 – a characteristic of the environment and security; A6 – a characteristic of finance, financial flows and stocks in the city; A7 – a characteristic of the external relations of the city, including the assessment of the incoming and outgoing flows of people, energy, materials, information, finance; Ei – a variation of characteristics Ai; U1, U2, …, U21 – arbitrary coefficients which determine the adaptive capacity of the system and that can be used to manage and solve various problems on the manifold (1). The model is used in systems to support decision-making by the city authorities [4, 5].

An important issue for St. Petersburg has been a transition from a monocentric to a polycentric model, which is shown in Fig. 1. Preliminary data indicate that this structure will ensure its further development, while preserving the historic centre (1). The business center with skyscrapers is proposed to be placed in the vicinity of Gorskaja (2) close to Levashovsky airport, which should become a business airport. Vsevolozhsk (3) and Shlisserburg (4) must become part of the city and provide an outlet to Ladoga - the major freshwater reservoir of the city. In the area of Shlisserburg at the source of the Neva and the Ivanovsky rapids there should be built hydro dams to curb the flow of water in the Neva River during flood surges the dam can not cope with. The industrial center should be located in the area of Kolpino (5). Gatchina (6) with its museums and institutions closely associated with the city should become its part. The seventh center (7) is a new port of Bronka near the dam on the southern bank of the Gulf of Finland. In accordance with the linguistic and combinatorial approach we have assessed adaptive capabilities of the polycentric structure. If we denote the number of arbitrary coefficients of the first center as $S1 = C_{n1}^{m1+1}$, the second center as $S2 = C_{n2}^{m2+1}$, …, the seventh center $S7 = C_{n7}^{m7+1}$, then we can choose constraint parameters m_i the number of variables n_i, so that the adaptive capabilities of St. Petersburg Scol were greater than the sum of

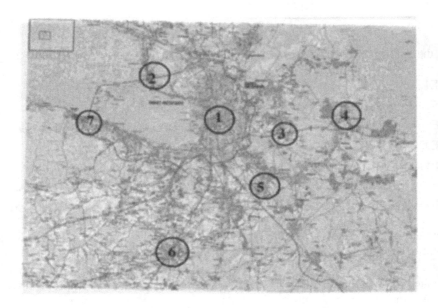

Fig. 1. Large Petersburg with a polycentric structure.

the adaptive capabilities of its parts. Scol > S1 + S2 + ... + S7, which is important in the era of change [4, 5, 7].

The number of blocks in the linguo-combinatorial model of the city can be different. In terms of modeling accuracy the more blocks are activated, the better, but it deteriorates model visibility, its perception by decision makers. For example, if the population is divided into three blocks - "children and adolescents", "adults" and "seniors", the number of variables will increase to nine, the equation of the city will contain nine variables.

$$A1 * E1 + A2 * E2 + \ldots + A9 * E9 = 0$$

While modeling the city it is important to consider the entire hierarchy of social systems of which the city is composed (family, genus, teip, domain and others). This systems also may be modeled with the help of a seven-block model by changing the content of individual units. In general, statistical offices of cities, regions and countries have all the data needed to run the model. The data for the evaluation of passionarity can be obtained from the polls. The development of information and computer technology allows you to raise the issue of mandatory preliminary modeling of the effects of decisions to avoid a great number of wrong decisions.

3 The Logical-Linguistic Model of the City

There are often problems of evaluation of large-scale objects in general terms when you need to get a general idea of the state of the city and the whole region so as to compare them with similar objects. In accordance with the procedure of the logical-linguistic modeling [10, 11] in the first stage a factor space of the linguistic variables proposed by Zadeh is formed [12]. The choice of factors is carried out on the basis of special studies with the participation of leading experts who act as experts for the task. To determine the level of the city state the following factor space was formed as is presented in Table 1. Let us take a dimensionless variable Y (the city state) as a dependent variable. Verbal characteristics are low: a towns located away from main roads, its production is mainly agricultural, although its ecology and livelihoods are quite normal, a lack of material production and rather low qualitative level of the population cause considerable demographic problems. Verbal characteristics are high: a city with a well-developed logistics infrastructure and a high material component of production makes it possible to attract qualified specialists in various fields of science and production and increase the level of innovation of the population, stabilize sufficiently high level of indicators of demography. At the same time life support is maintained at an acceptable level.

Table 1. A fragment of the polling table with the expert's estimates transferred to a quantitative form and calculated values of the polynomial model

	the material conditions of production	logistic component	the level of innovation	demography	the quality of the population	environment	livelihoods	level city status	
	x_1	x_2	x_3	x_4	x_5	x_6	x_7	Yexp	Ycal
1	-1	-1	-1	-1	-1	-1	1	0,30	0,270
2	1	-1	-1	-1	-1	-1	-1	0,35	0,342
...	...	...	...	...	...	...	...	...	...
62	1	-1	1	1	1	1	-1	0,65	0,684
63	-1	1	1	1	1	1	-1	0,50	0,523
64	1	1	1	1	1	1	1	0,70	0,673

Table 1 the polynomial expression has been obtained by data processing according to the theory of experiment planning:

$$Y = 0,469 + 0,101x_1 + 0,0291x_2 + 0,0153x_3 + 0,0195x_4 + 0,0508x_5 + 0,0164x_6$$
$$+ 0,0195x_1x_5 - 0,0093x_2x_5 - 0,0086x_4x_5 - 0,0074x_5x_7 - 0,0117x_1x_4x_5 - 0,0148x_1x_5x_6$$
$$+ 0,0072x_2x_3x_7 + 0,00859x_3x_4x_6 + 0,0074x_4x_5x_6 - 0,0074x_5x_6x_7.$$

The model includes only significant values of polynomial coefficients, the independent variables xi are presented on a standardized scale within the interval [−1, +1].

The availability and necessity of the data about a particular city or several cities which correspond to a factor space enable you to get a first approximation of a generalized integrated express assessment on the basis of the polynomial model.

Figure 2 shows graphs of the influence of individual variables on the total variation of Y, when the others are fixed at the average level. Noteworthy is the fact that with all the averages for the original factor space the generalized city condition is not up to the expected average, and is in the zone between the terms "below average" - "average". Moreover, even the maximum increase in the material component of production is not able to significantly improve the overall level of the city condition.

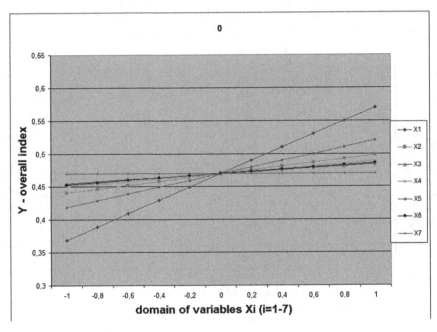

Fig. 2. The results of the numerical experiment at a fixed average level of variables

The example is purely illustrative, but it demonstrates the advantage of the method over the whole range of diverse problems in their relationship. Thus it is possible to see and quantify those alleged relationships between the variables which the expert can only guess at.

4 The Algorithmic Model of the City

In almost any scenario of the economic model of the city there is an interaction between flows of material resources, finance, human resources, information. At the macro level we can distinguish the following basic processes of urban performance: production, distribution, demographics, financial flows, people's livelihoods. Production describes the process of motion, the transformation of material resources, the relationship of the selected types of material resources, the interaction of material and human resources necessary for the creation of new material resources and services.

Distribution describes the process of motion of material assets to their consumers, their storage and interaction with financial flows and the population, which is a two-way exchange of material resources and money. Demography describes the process of changing population size, its structure, the generation of labor forces, takes into account the impact on the size and structure of livelihoods and material resource allocation results, considers the required and actual standards of life-support. Financial flows describe the process of handling cash and non-cash money, including the population and the banking sector. Life support of the population describes the motion and transformation of material resources intended to ensure the specified conditions of their life, their interaction with the population and finances.

As an example, Fig. 3 shows the model developed for the administration of the city of Ivanovo. The main purpose of the model is the evaluation of financial activities of the city at the given nature of changes in commodity prices and credits and export-import volumes.

The model (Fig. 3) includes the following blocks. Block 1 describes the reproduction of the labor force. Block 2 is the reproduction of the fixed production assets (FPA) of the sphere of material production (SMP). Block 3 is the formation and distribution ofcapital expenditure (DCE). Block 4 is the reproduction of circulating assets of SMP. Block 5 describes actual production. Block 6 gives information on the distribution of the manufactured product and the balance of the production industries and the region as a whole. Block 7 describes the process of production of financial flows. Block 8 and 9 describe the movement of consumer goods in the retail industry. Block 10 is financial flows in retail trade. Blocks 11, 12, 13 are the flows of finance in the bank and with the population, the balance of cash. Block 14 is the formation of the regional budget and its balance. Block 15, 16, 17 describe the processes of formation of unproductive capital investment (UCI), the reproduction of fixed non-productive assets (FNA) and the formation of NA costs.

An algorithmic model in the form of AN operators of algorithmic basis should be built for each unit. The screen form of the 'COGNITRON' system [8] with a fragment of the algorithmic network model is shown in Fig. 4. It shows a window with a graphical representation of the model, a calculation analysis form, a schedule of production decline of Ivanovo in 90-th years.

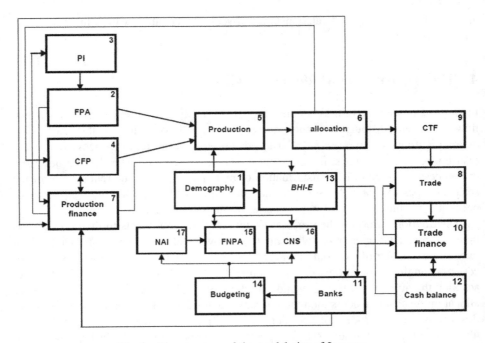

Fig. 3. The structure of the model city of Ivanovo.

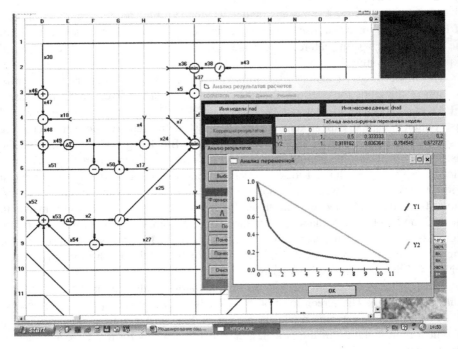

Fig. 4. The forecast of decline according to the administration of production (Y2 - line) and the model (Y1- curve).

5 Conclusion

A special feature of the presented multi-model approach is that it allows approaching the study of a complex, poorly formalized system from fundamentally different positions. Thus, the findings complement each other, but do not intersect. The linguo-combinatorial approach enables us to investigate the adaptive properties of the system based on its fundamental combinatorial properties. The logical-linguistic model built on the basis of fuzzy verbal expertise makes it possible to quantify the state of a complex system in the selected factor space. The algorithmic model allows calculating the string of states, that characterize the development of the system in time depending on the internal structure and external control actions can be calculated.

References

1. Alonso, W.: Location and Land Use. Harward University Press, Cambridge (1964)
2. Ivanishchev, V.V., Marley, V.E.: Fundamentals of Algorithmic Network Theory. SPbGTU, St. Petersburg (2000). 180 p.
3. Ivanishchev, V.V., Mikhailov, V.V.: The Automation of Modeling of Ecological Systems. SPbGTU, St. Petersburg (2000). 171 p.
4. Ignatyev, M.B.: A linguistic and combinatorial method for complex system modeling. In: Proceedings of the 6th World Multi Conference on Systemics, Cybernetics and Informatics, Computer science II, Orlando, USA, vol. XI, pp. 224–227 (2002)
5. Ignatiev, M.: A Cybernetical Picture of the World, Sophisticated Cyberphysical Systems. Palmarium Academic Publishing, Saarbrucken (2014). 472 p.
6. Fujita, M.: Urban Economic Theory: Land Use and City Size. Cambridge University Press, Cambridge (1989). 367 p.
7. Kloosterman, R., Musterd, S.: The polycentric urban region: towards a research agenda. Urban Stud. **38**(4), 623–634 (2001)
8. Mikhaylov, V.V., Marley, V.E., Korolev, O.F.: Algorithmic networks and their applications. Tutorial, 2-revised edn., 136 p. SPbSUAI, St. Petersburg (2012)
9. Pertsik, E.N.: Cities. International Relation, Geography of world urbanization. Moscow (1999). 282 p.
10. Spesivtsev, A.V., Domshenko, N.G.: Expert as an "intelligent measuring and diagnostic system." In: Collection of reports, XIII International Conference on Soft Computing and Measurements SCM, 23–25 July 2010, St. Petersburg, vol. 2, pp. 28–34 (2010)
11. Spesivtsev, A.V:. The method of extraction and formalization of expert information. In: Prokopchina, S.V. (ed.) Management Under Uncertainty: A Monograph Under the General. Publishing house of the ETU "LETI", St. Petersburg, Chap. VI, pp. 217–264 (2014)
12. ZadehL, A.: Fuzzy logic, neural network and soft computing. Commun. ACM **37**, 77–84 (1994)

Application of the Universal Decision Support System SVIR to Solving Urban Problems

Stanislav Mikoni[✉]

St. Petersburg Institute for Informatics and Automation of the Russian Academy
of Sciences (SPIIRAS), 39, 14-th Line V.O., St. Petersburg, Russia
smikoni@mail.ru

Abstract. Many problems of cities and their inhabitants can be presented as a
choice of the preferred embodiment on a finite set of alternatives. The emphasis
in the paper is not to discuss various urban problems, but to give methods for
their solution. In this paper we describe the universal Decision Support System
(DSS) SVIR and its application to solving urban problems. This system
implements most of the known methods of multiattribute choice. It is argued that
versatility of the system allows us to not only solve various problems of choice,
but also to solve a single problem by different methods. This helps to debug the
model of choice and increases the objectivity of the evaluation. The considered
system is a promising tool for solving complex social and humanitarian problems, which consist of many aspects.

Keywords: Decision making · Object · Attribute · Criterion · Utility function ·
Evaluation model · Multiattribute evaluation · Selection · Ranking ·
Classification

1 Introduction

Evaluation of different objects in many aspects plays an important role in solving urban
problems. The objects of evaluation are all parties of urban life: construction, communal facilities, ecology, transport, trade, culture, leisure, etc. From citizens' point of
view the objects of evaluation are housing, work, shopping and children's recreation
and so on. Generally, the city authorities and inhabitants of the city are interested in
making rational decisions.

Within the framework of decision theory the rational choice methods have been
developed based on different paradigms. These include [3, 4]: dominance analysis
based on Pareto-relation, multi objective optimization with constraints, multi-objective
optimization by weighted deviations, utility-based multiattribute optimization, pairwise
prioritization, multicriteria classification. These methods are included in the DSS for
different purposes.

As each method has its preferred area of application, the first task is to combine
them into a united system. This system, called the Choice and Ranking System (SVIR
in Russian abbreviation), has been developed in St. Petersburg State Transport
University under the author's supervision (http://www.mcd-svir.ru).

© Springer International Publishing AG 2016
A.V. Chugunov et al. (Eds.): DTGS 2016, CCIS 674, pp. 478–491, 2016.
DOI: 10.1007/978-3-319-49700-6_48

The DSS SVIR is a universal program tool for system analysts and decision makers (DM) to solve various management tasks.

The paper examines the main characteristics of the system SVIR. Its application is demonstrated by the example of evaluation of city apartments.

2 Background

The theoretical basis for combining different methods of multiattribute evaluation in a single system is the axiomatic proposed in [9]. Of the seven proposed axioms we will consider the two axioms directly related to the unification of methods.

Axiom of Goal. Target value c_j on the jth attribute's scale[1], $j = 1, \ldots, n$, can be arbitrary $y_{j,\min} \leq c_j \leq y_{j,\max}$. It does not necessarily coincide with one of the boundaries of the scale $[y_{j\min}, y_{j,\max}]$. Value $c_j = y_{j,\min}$ ($c_j = y_{j,\max}$) is treated as an ideal goal and an intermediate value $y_{j,\min} < c_j < y_{j,\max}$ is treated as a reasonable goal or a target [8].

From this axiom, all methods of objects ordering can be divided into two groups. The first group consists of methods of achieving the goal, and the second group consists of methods of deviation from the target. If we consider the ideal goal as a special case of the reasonable goal, the method of achieving the goal can be considered as a special case of the method of deviation from the target.

These groups of methods are referred to as Multi Objective Optimization and Target-Based Decision Analysis [1]. The first approach is used when the target value is set at one of the boundaries of the attribute's scale. The second approach allows a target value of the attributes at any scale's point.

Axiom of Mapping from Attribute's Scale to Common Scale. To aggregate attributes values measured in different scales, we must bring them to a common scale. As a common scale the bipolar range $[-1, 0, 1]$ or its parts $[0, 1]$ and $[-1, 0]$ are adopted.

To map from the attribute's domain to the common scale, two kinds of the specified function are used: a function of achieving the goal and function of the deviation from the target. Any function of achieving the goal regardless of the manner of its creation is treated as a utility function [9] $u_j: Y_j \rightarrow [-1, 0, 1]$.

There Y_j – the set of values (domain) of jth attribute.

The whole usefulness of the object x in the jth attribute $u_j(x) = 1$ holds for the full goal achievement: $f_j(x) = c_j$. Partial goal achievement occurs when $u_j(x) < 1$. Zero usefulness of the jth attribute of object x occurs when $u_j(x) = 0$. The negative half-axis $[-1, 0]$ is used when possible damage occurs.

Function of deviation from the target $\gamma_j: \Delta C_j \rightarrow [-1, 0, +1]$ is mapping deviation from the target c_j from the scale $[y_{j\min}, y_{j,\max}]$ to the scale $[-1, 0, +1]$.

There $\Delta C_j \subseteq Y_j$ – domain of deviations from the target c_j on the jth attribute's scale $[y_{j\min}, y_{j,\max}]$. A value of $\gamma_j(y_j(x)) = 0$ denotes the coincidence of the jth attribute value of the object x with a target value of c_j. One of the semi-axes of the scale $[-1, 0, 1]$ is used to measure a relative penalty for failure to achieve the target and the other

---

[1] Under attribute's scale we mean the range of attribute's values.

half-axis – to measure a relative rewards for target exceeding. In the case of non-monotonic utility function deviation from the target on either side is assessed as just penalty.

From this axiom, methods that do not use scale $[-1, 0, +1]$, form a group of *criterion-based methods* and all methods of mapping from attribute's scale to scale $[-1, 0, +1]$ form a group of *function-based methods*. First group includes the methods of dominant analysis and lexicographic optimization. Second group includes methods: multi-objective optimization, utility-based multiattribute optimization, target-based decision analysis, pairwise prioritization, multicriteria classification.

We will take these two proposed axioms as a basis for unification function-based methods in a unified system.

3   System of Function-Based Methods

Based on the similarities and differences in function-based methods (FBM), we consider the relationship between them [9]. System of the methods is shown in Fig. 1.

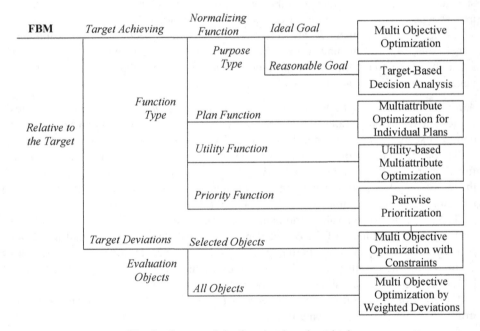

Fig. 1. System of the function-based methods

Applying the classification tree method, the identification of test relevant aspects gives the classification *Relative to the Target*. For the *Relative to the Target*, two classes can be identified: *Target Achieving* (or *Achieving of the goal*) and *Target Deviations*.

The *Target Achieving* class is further refined with the test aspect *Function Type*, four possible classes are included here: *Normalizing Function, Plan Function, Utility Function* and *Priority Function*.

The *Normalizing Function* class is further refined with the test aspect *Purpose Type*, two possible classes are included here: *Ideal Goal, Reasonable Goal.*

The *Target Deviations* class is further refined with the test aspect *Evaluation Objects*, two possible classes are included here: *Selected Objects, All Objects.*

Seven groups of function-based methods correspond to the seven terminal nodes of the tree. Each of the methods of this system is implemented in DSS SVIR and described in detail in the textbook [8]. In the section below we consider briefly the properties of these methods.

4 Methods of Multiattribute Evaluation

4.1 Methods of Objects Ordering

Both criterion-based and function-based methods are used in DSS SVIR to order and rank objects being evaluated.

4.1.1 The Dominant Analysis

The Dominant Analysis (vector optimization) is performed using the ratio of Pareto dominance. An object x_i is not dominated by an object x_j, if at least one component of its vector of attribute values $\mathbf{y}(x_j)$ is not worse than the corresponding component of the vector of attribute values $\mathbf{y}(x_j)$. In the system SVIR two methods of the dominant analysis are implemented:

- One without conversion of vectors of attribute values;
- One with ordering of components of each vector by quality.

Second method is called leksimin optimization and is characterized by indifference of criteria. For example, this method can be applied to rank students who passed the exams independent of the subjects (for which marks were obtained).

Both methods do not guarantee the linear order of objects. The presence of the same rank in the ordered set of objects is determined by the order's severity factor:

$$k_{so} = (l-1)/(N-1).$$

Here $N = |X|$ – number of evaluated objects; l – number of levels of an ordered dominance graph.

Linearly ordered set of objects corresponds to the $k_{so} = 1$, when all objects are distinguishable, i.e. each level of the dominance graph consists of a single object: $l = N$.

The partial order of objects is characterized by three parameters:

- Dominance factor $k_d = m_a/M$;
- Indistinguishability factor $k_{id} = m_e/M$;
- Incomparability factor $k_{ic} = 1 - (k_d + k_{id})$.

Here m_a – number of arcs, m_e – number of edges of an ordered dominance graph, M – number of edges in complete graph, $M = N(N-1)/2$.

All objects are ordered when $k_{ic} = 0$, and for $k_{ic} > 0$ there is a partial order.

The extreme ranks $r_{max}(x_i)$ and $r_{min}(x_i)$, which the object x_i can get as a result of ordering by any method, are determined by the ratio of indegree and outdegree of dominance graph vertices:

$$r_{max}(x_i) = \rho_i^+ + 1, \; r_{min}(x_i) = N - \rho_i^-.$$

Here $r_{max}(x_i)$ – the best rank of vertex x_i;

$r_{min}(x_i)$ – the worst rank of vertex x_i;

ρ_i^+ – the number of objects that dominate the object x_i (indegree of vertex x_i);

ρ_i^- – the number of objects on which the object is dominated by x_i (outdegree of vertex x_i).

4.1.2   Lexicographic Optimization

Lexicographic optimization method is a sequential ordering of objects in the direction of decreasing importance of the criteria.

Application of this method depends on the ratio of the domain's dimension of attributes and the number of evaluated objects.

The minimum number of criteria n_{min}, needed to ensure a linearly ordered set of objects, is determined by the formula:

$$\prod_{j=1}^{n_{min}} m_j \geq N. \tag{1}$$

Here m_i – the domain's dimension of jth attribute.

In a particular case, if all criteria are binary values, the formula (1) is converted to the following relationship:

$$2^{n_{min}} \geq N. \tag{2}$$

Hence, the minimum number of binary criteria n_{min}, required to obtain a linearly ordered set of objects, is defined by the formula:

$$n_{min} \geq \log_2 N. \tag{3}$$

4.1.3   Multi Objective Optimization

Multi objective optimization is based on the conversion of estimation vector into a scalar. For this purpose, the following Aggregate Functions are usually used:

- The weighted sum of normalized parameters;
- The multiplicative function with additional cofactors;
- The multiplicative function with factors in the degree of criteria importance.

To aggregate attribute values measured in different scales they are subjected to normalization. Normalizing function maps the value of criterion from the scale $[y_{j\min}, y_{j,\max}]$ to the scale $[0, 1]$.

Function of deviation from the target, used by the method of Multi Objective optimization by weighted deviations, maps the value of the criterion from the scale $[y_{j\min}, y_{j,\max}]$ to the scale $[-1, 0, +1]$. All deviations from target values can be characterized by the following weighted sum:

- Penalties (to account for only all failures to reach the target values);
- Rewards (to account for only all the exceedances of the target values);
- Algebraic sum of penalties and rewards (to account both penalties and rewards).

Method of Multi objective optimization by weighted deviations transforms to the Method of Multiattribute optimization for Individual Plans at the transition from scale $[-1, 0, +1]$ to percentage scale $[0\%, 100\%, 200\%]$. Failure to plan's fulfillment (<100%) corresponds to attribute's penalties and the over fulfillment of plan (>100%) corresponds to its rewards.

4.1.4   Utility-Based Multiattribute Optimization

According to [7] methods of this group use the greatest amount of information about the preferences of the Decision Maker. An expert fulfils assessments for creation of each utility function. These functions can be piecewise or continuous ones. From the second axiom linear normalizing function is taken as a simple utility function. This assumption allows DM to set in the DSS SVIR own preference both as criterion either as utility function. To aggregate all single utility functions any aggregate function can be used.

4.1.5   Pairwise Prioritization

Preferences of DM are formed in a matrix of pairwise comparisons. In the DSS SVIR ordinal preferences and three types of quantitative preferences are implemented [8]. Priorities of objects are calculated on the basis of preferences. Consistency of expert preferences is estimated by coefficients of ordinal and quantitative consistency.

In the DSS SVIR the matrices of pairwise comparisons are used to calculate the weighting factors of aggregate functions and discrete utility functions based on the expert's preferences [6]. Priority function is converted to an utility function by rationing priorities: $w_i/w_{\max}$, $i = 1, \ldots, N$. This priority values are converted from the scale $[w_{\min}, w_{\max}]$ to the scale $[0, 1]$. Matrices with any type of preference can be used to implement the analytic hierarchy process (AHP).

A special case is the tournament matrix of pairwise comparisons. Its content represents the outcome of sports competitions or results of interaction of economic agents. Content of a tournament matrix is used to determine the rating of interacting entities. The degree of rivalry in the tournament matrix is estimated by the generalized preference factor [8].

4.2   Methods of Multicriteria Classification

4.2.1   Selection of Objects that Satisfy Specified Requirements

Selection of Non-dominated Alternatives. The set of non-dominated alternatives (Pareto) is based on the ratio of Pareto dominance. Alternatives included in the Pareto set are used to find the best one.

Selection with Constraints. Feasible set of alternatives is formed on the system constraints:

- The selection of all constraints;
- The selection on the part of constraints (at least one).

Alternatives included in the feasible set are useful with respect to specified requirements.

When incompatible requirements feasible set is empty. To get non-empty set a phased reduction of requirements is fulfilled. This problem may be solved by trial and error method. The method of deviation from the target (method of pattern approximation) solves these problem even if unattainable requirements. It allows us to find the object the most satisfying goal, even if the pattern is an unattainable goal for a set of objects analyzed.

4.2.2   Multicriteria Fuzzy Classification

The problem of fuzzy classification by many criteria is to assign an object to one of the classes, ordered by quality. Classes are defined by a range of values on the scale for each attribute. The condition of fuzzy membership in the class is a non-empty intersection adjacent range. Class membership function is defined by the expert.

To define a class for many attributes generalized membership function is calculated for each class. The class with the highest value of generalized membership function is selected. For a final decision value of generalized membership function is compared with a threshold of minimum membership in the class.

Classes of membership functions can be interpreted as fragments of the utility function of attribute. It can be calculated by the membership function classes [8]. This property allows us to order objects by two ways. The order of objects, calculated based on the results of the classification, should coincide with the order obtained by the utility functions calculated on the basis of membership functions [5].

5   Multiattribute Evaluation Model

Multi-Attribute Evaluation model (MAE model) consists of two parts: Input Data (ID) model and Evaluation Conditions (EC) model. ID model is a table "Objects/Attributes". ID model is invariant with respect to any method of evaluation of a finite set of objects.

Object's performance can be measured both in natural and in subjective scales. To solve the problem of ordering of objects values of attributes are replaced by scores.

Attributes with quantitative estimations can be used as arguments of derived indicators. For example, based on the cost a liter of petrol and its consumption per 100 km is possible to calculate cost of travel of the journey distance.

To divide attributes into groups the hierarchical MAE model is formed. The interdependence of the attributes is defined by the correlation matrix. The created ID model is saved in a Domain file.

EC model is created for each specific task. To implement the methods of dominant analysis it is enough to set the direction of attribute optimization (max or min). Lexicographic optimization method requires the assignment of importance of criteria, measured by an ordinal scale. In order to aggregate vector of partial estimates of an object the following additional information is used:

1. On the scale of each attribute to be evaluated a preference value in the form of a criterion or a utility function is specified in terminal hierarchy tables. In a two-stage decision ordering problem (pre-selection), the same attribute can participate in the selection and ordering.
2. Boundaries of each attribute's scale are defined on the basis of sampling the evaluated objects or provided by an expert.
3. Importance of each attribute is set on the scale $[0, 1]$.
4. Expert chooses an aggregate function corresponding to its authority by averaging over partial estimates of an object.

To solve the fuzzy classification expert defines the following tasks: the order of the classes on the scale of each attribute; the border between the neighboring classes; membership function for each class. EC Model is stored in the configuration file.

6 Implementation of the System

DSS SVIR developed in C++ and occupies 4 MB of memory on the hard drive. It runs under Windows 2000 operating systems and later. DSS SVIR is the autonomous system and is associated with the Microsoft Office Information System. Its distinctive features are: focus on experimental debugging of multiattribute evaluation model and implementation of many methods of multiattribute evaluation. The system includes a subsystem of calculating priorities, which is implemented as a dynamic link library. This subsystem implements the functions of the matrices of pairwise comparisons, described in Sect. 4.1.5.

DSS SVIR is a reconfigurable system. To solve the mass evaluation task a part of the system is allocated for solving this task. In terms of preferences specified by the Decision Maker (DM) DSS SVIR is comparable to the system which realizes multi-attribute utility theory methods [2]. Execution of utility theory methods requires for DM to have a deep knowledge about the subject domain. In contrast to this approach DSS SVIR allows DM to choose any optimization methods depending on the depth of knowledge about the evaluated domain, for instance, methods of multi-objective optimization or dominant analysis. In addition, DSS SVIR implements methods of multicriteria classification and calculation of the priorities on the basis of pairwise comparisons matrices.

The System's User Interface has three sections: Objects properties, Task setting and Task solution (Fig. 2).

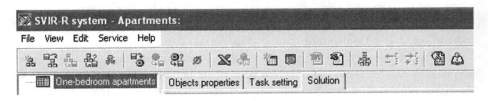

Fig. 2. The SVIR System's User Interface

In the section "Objects properties" hierarchical multiattribute evaluation model is created and edited. All operations for creating and editing models are made with the mouse. Attributes moving from one table to another one carry out with the help of "drag-and-drop" technology. This technology is also used to modify the subordination of tables in the hierarchy.

To carry out the methods of aggregation the qualitative values of attribute are converted to the scores. It is possible to reverse the conversion. The problem of objects comparability is solved by the creation relative and specific auxiliary attributes. Their values are calculated using the built-in calculator. Besides its standard functions aggregate functions (min, max, average, sum of the number of objects) are used. The numbers are the same for all attributes that are formed in the constant editor. DSS SVIR has the means to perform correlation analyses of attributes. It has means to carry out expert's assessment and to calculate priorities of criteria based for these preferences.

Input data can be imported from tabular processor MS Excel and all components of the Multi-Attribute Evaluation Model and solution can be exported to it.

The section "Task setting" has the context depended interface for each task setting. It is based on the classification of multiattribute evaluation methods, described at Sect. 3. The initial task setting menu includes 2 options: Optimization or Classification. Optimization methods, in turn, are divided into two classes: criterion-based or function-based methods and so on.

In the "Task solution" section the solution is displayed in the table form and Cognitive graphics. It includes: Schedule of a generalized function; Contribution of attributes to the general estimations of objects; Table and the schedule of comparison of two ratings. Cognitive graphics facilitates the interpretation of the results of solving the problem. Due to its properties the DSS SVIR may be considered as the universal tools for optimization and classification tasks solving.

7   Application of DSS SVIR

Methods implemented in DSS SVIR allow us to solve a variety of problems of rational choice. For example, the method of multicriteria classification can be used for determining professional inclination of pupils and students. Multi-objective optimization methods are applicable to a wide range of urban problems related to the options of development and ranking of existing objects. The model of utility theory, composed by experienced professionals, best reflects the essential properties of the subject area. To obtain objective assessments DSS SVIR implements methods of group selection.

We show the feasibility of the joint use of several optimization methods on many criteria by comparing the market value of a St. Petersburg apartment with their consumer characteristics.

50 one-bedroom apartments were selected from the city database for the experiment. These apartments are characterized by six attributes: "Square" (Area), "Bathroom", "Floor", "Building", "Status", "Zone". Of these, only the square (area) of the apartments has a physical unit. The remaining five attributes are measured by nominal and quality units. A fragment of ID model which includes 8 apartments of fifty is shown in Fig. 3. To compare different methods we select apartment 8 (82680).

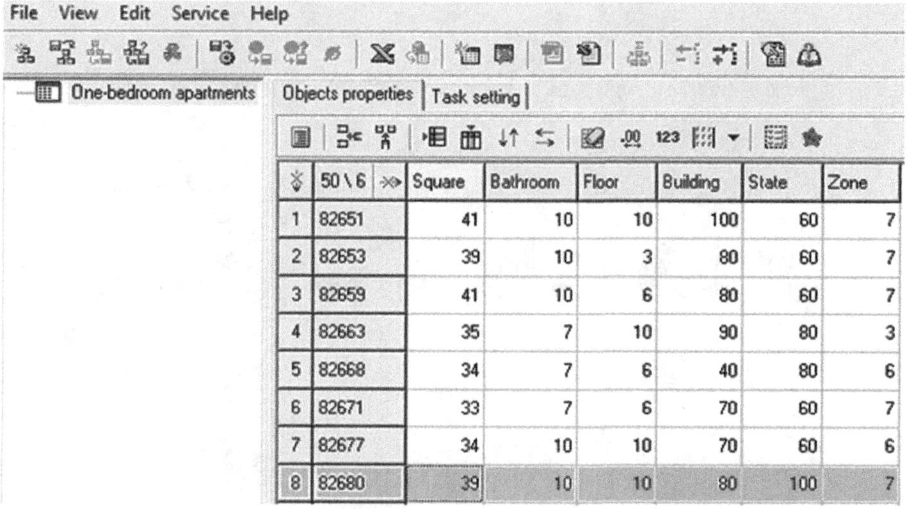

	50\6		Square	Bathroom	Floor	Building	State	Zone
1	82651		41	10	10	100	60	7
2	82653		39	10	3	80	60	7
3	82659		41	10	6	80	60	7
4	82663		35	7	10	90	80	3
5	82668		34	7	6	40	80	6
6	82671		33	7	6	70	60	7
7	82677		34	10	10	70	60	6
8	82680		39	10	10	80	100	7

Fig. 3. Computer's input data model for the domain "One-bedroom apartments"

The values, shown on the quality scale, were coded by experts in scores. To determine the relationship of superiority on the set of qualitative values of an attribute, experts used the matrix of pairwise comparisons. Priorities calculated on the basis of the matrix were measured in the scale of $[0, 1]$. Values of the quality attribute "Zone" does not require coding, as these have already been expressed in scores. This attribute characterizes the attractiveness of the location of the block of flats in the city.

To determine the candidates for the best apartment we apply Pareto dominance relationship. The EC model Interface to solve the problem of partial ordering of apartments by Pareto dominance method is shown in Fig. 4.

Pareto-dominance Graph for 50 Apartments is shown in Fig. 5.

The vertex (apartment) 8 belongs to the Pareto set. Therefore, it may claim the 1st place. It dominates the 26 vertices of the graph. Consequently, it will take place no less than 24 at any method of evaluation.

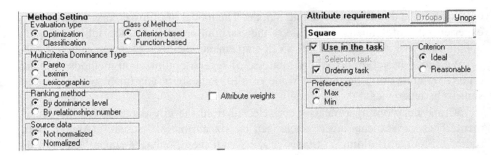

Fig. 4. Interface set to solve the problem of Pareto dominance

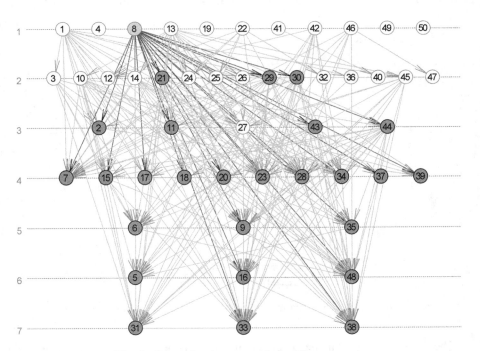

Fig. 5. Pareto-dominance graph for 50 apartments

To get the linear order of apartments we use the method of Multi Objective optimization with the additive aggregate objective function (AOF) for equal attribute's weights. EC model Interface for this method is shown in Fig. 6.

Overall Ratings Schedule obtained by Multi Objective optimization method is shown in Fig. 7.

In this Schedule apartment 8 (82680) occupies the 3rd place among the five best apartments.

As the market value and the price per square meter of apartments are known, we rank them according to these characteristics, starting with the most expensive

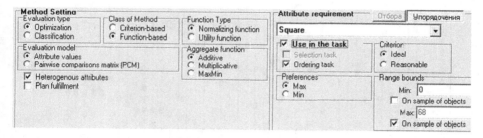

Fig. 6. Interface for method of multi objective optimization with the additive AOF

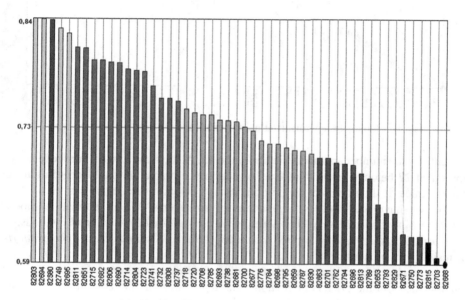

Fig. 7. Overall ratings schedule of apartments.

apartment. Ratings of the apartments based on market value and the cost per square meter are shown in Fig. 8.

The monotonous line of points corresponds to the estimates of apartments by market value and scattered points on the "market value" line correspond to estimates of apartments at a price per square meter. But the difference in the order of apartment's places, ordered by their market cost, with a dominance graph levels was found to be 45.66%. This demonstrates the practical independence of the market cost of the apartments on their level of quality on Fig. 5. As a linear relationship between these ratings is virtually non-existent (9.5%), the difference between these ratings can be explained by the fact that comforts of residing in a certain apartment were taken into account when its market value was defined.

By market value apartment 8 (82680) took 17th place, and by the price of a square meter it took 22nd place. If using six attributes it would be sufficient to represent the quality of the apartments, the apartment 8 should have to take place no worse than

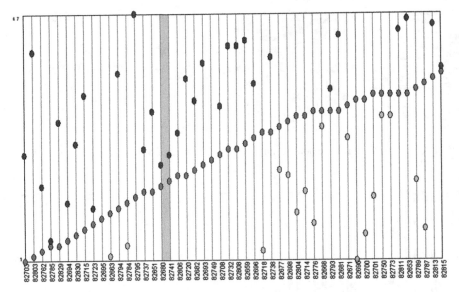

Fig. 8. Ratings of apartments at market value and the cost per square meter

eleventh by the number apartments in the Pareto set. At the same time the most expensive apartment 27 belongs to the third level of dominance graph, although according to its market value, it should reflect the best quality and belong to the Pareto set.

So, we have four *different estimations* of apartments. Which estimation should Decision Maker *trust*? Everything depends on *the validity* of models and methods.

Cost per square meter is verified more easily. But it *does not reflect all the comforts* of residing in an apartment.

The market value of the apartment should reflect *all aspects of residence*. But their relationship with the price *is ambiguous* and *depends on market conditions*.

MAE model allows to explicitly taking into account all aspects that characterize the convenience of living in the apartment. Its creation requires the participation of experts. But it is only the selected attributes that affect the results of the evaluation. The results also depend on the assigned scales and weights of attributes, as well as on the selected aggregate objective function. Therefore, the disadvantage of the MAE model is subjectivity of expert assessment in assigning bounds of scales and the weights of criteria.

Let is assume that the decision maker *is convinced* of the validity of *market value*. Then he has to offer *to improve the MAE model* by system analyst.

If the decision maker *trusts MAE model*, he may be suspected of market value appraisers *in corruption*.

In this example, the decision maker must give preference rating of flats, a definite on their market value, since it covers the convenience of living. Lower trust of MAE model is explained by the fact that the 6 attributes do not reflect all aspects of the quality of accommodation. Therefore, by using results of experiments we conclude the need to refine the ID model.

Thus, the implementation of the SVIR system different estimation methods allows decision-makers make an informed decision in tasks of rational choice.

8 Conclusion

It seems obvious that each method has its own area of effective application. Often, however, those who follow a certain approach are trying to expand its scope. An alternative to this is to combine the different methods in a single system. This approach has been applied in the development of DSS SVIR. Its implementation required the development of theoretical foundations of multiattribute evaluation of objects. Based on this theoretical base DSS SVIR shows to be effective in solving various problems of rational choice. This allows us to recommend this system for the solution of urban problems.

Acknowledgments. This research is supported by ONITRAS (project № 0073-2015-0007) within budgetary themes № 0073–2014–0009, the Russian Foundation for Basic Research (grants 15-07-08391, 15-08-08459, 16-07-00779, 16-08-00510, 16-08-01277), grant 074-U01 (ITMO University), project 6.1.1 (Peter the Great St. Petersburg Polytechnic University) supported by Government of Russian Federation, Program STC of Union State "Monitoring-SG" (project 1.4.1-1).

The author would like to thank my colleagues Dr. Dmitry Burakov, Dr. Marina Garina and Dr. Igor Kisilev whose efforts contributed to the presented research. I also thank anonymous referees for their helpful suggestions.

References

1. Bordley, R., LiCalzi, M.: Decision analysis using targets instead of utility functions. J. Decis. Econ. Finan. **23**, 53–74 (2000)
2. Jimenez, A., Rios-Insua, S., Mateos, A.: A decision support system for multiattribute utility evaluation based on imprecise assignments. J. Decis. Support Syst. **36**, 65–79 (2003)
3. Keeney, R.L., Hammond, J.S., Raiffa, H.: Smart Choices: A Guide to Making Better Decisions. Harvard University Press, Boston (1999)
4. Koksalan, M., Wallenius, J., Zionts, S.: Multiple Criteria Decision Making: From Early History to the 21st Century. World Scientific, Singapore (2011)
5. Mikoni, S.V., Garina, M.I.: Study relationship between utility function and membership function in the problem of object ranking. In: Artificial Intelligence Driven Solutions to Business and Engineering Problems, pp. 41–45. ITHEA, Rzeszow, Sofia (2012)
6. Mikoni, S.V.: Utility function design on the base of the pairwise comparison matrix. In: Artificial Intelligence Methods and Techniques for Business and Engineering Applications, pp. 325–333. ITHEA, Rzeszow, Sofia. (2012)
7. Mikoni, S.V.: Ordering multiattribute optimization methods from the utility point of view. Int. J. Inf Technol. Knowl. **7**(1), 94–99 (2013)
8. Mikoni, S.V.: Teoriya prinyatiya upravlencheskih reshenij: Uchebnoe posobie (Theory of administrative decision making: A Tutorial). Lan', St. Petersburg (2015). (in Russian)
9. Mikoni, S.V.: Aksiomatika metodov mnogokriterial'noi optimizacii na konechnom mnozhestve al'ternativ (Axioms of multicriteria optimization methods on a finite set of alternatives). J. Trudy SPIIRAN. **44**, 198–214 (2016). Proceedings of the SPIIRAS

Groups and Collectivities in Crowd Modeling: Critical Evaluation of the State-of-the-Art and Suggestions for Further Studies

Daniil Voloshin[1]([✉]), Kseniia Puzyreva[2], Ivan Derevitsky[1],
and Vladislav Karbovskii[1]

[1] ITMO University, Saint Petersburg, Russia
achoched@gmail.com, iderevitskiy@gmail.com,
vladislav.k.work@gmail.com
[2] Graduate School of Social Sciences, University of Amsterdam,
Amsterdam, Netherlands
kseniiapuzyreva@gmail.com

Abstract. It is known that crowds as spontaneous aggregations of people have been studied from as early as XIX century. Today these investigations have advanced to the point where scholars are trying to not only observe and analyze crowds, but also simulate those using computational methods. As a result, a distinct area of research emerged that draws expertise from various subject fields – crowd modeling. Though the applicability of crowd modeling is widely acknowledged, the conceptual development of the area received rather scarce attention. It seems that it has so far been developing as an area predominantly driven by the aim of informing the practice of planners and decision makers. In this paper, we examine the current state of affairs in a distinct branch of crowd modeling that focuses on groups of people other than individuals as key actors within the crowd. We argue that crowd modeling can be effectively used to facilitate not only for prediction, but also allows to deepen theoretical understanding of the crowds as collectives of people that are complex, contextually embedded and consist of dynamic entities that impose certain logics of behavior.

Keywords: Crowd modeling · Social simulation · Computational social science · Collective behavior · Social groups

1 Introduction

Nowadays crowd modeling can be understood as an area that brings expertise from a large variety of domains [17]. The primary aim of crowd modeling is to use computational tools to reconstruct crowds to study, to prevent issues that they may be associated with or even to realistically generate them for artistic or entertainment purposes. Though it has been assumed for some time already that crowd modeling can benefit from extending the scope to aggregate agents (groups, collectivities) [19], only recently have scholars started to incorporate the notions of collective behavior into modeling on a significant scale. Crowd modeling is an area preoccupied with simulating predominantly the material and physical properties of crowds, such as: velocities,

© Springer International Publishing AG 2016
A.V. Chugunov et al. (Eds.): DTGS 2016, CCIS 674, pp. 492–497, 2016.
DOI: 10.1007/978-3-319-49700-6_49

densities and collisions. Thus, collectives in crowd models can be labeled by the term "groupings", reflecting the explicit role of proxemics, as opposed to shared norms and identities. Moreover, another feature of the field is methodological individualism [1]. These two considerations can partially explain the fact that crowd modeling has somewhat detached at a certain point from the empirical studies of crowds.

The research question this paper seeks to reflect upon is "what are the issues that currently hinder the development of simulation of group behavior in crowds?" Hence, the primary goal of the study is to present the critical analysis of the state-of-the-art in the relevant field and propose the recommendations for further development. These recommendations can be understood as supporting and extending the call to grounding crowd models in empirical and theoretical advancements in social science made by Templeton, Drury and Philippides in [19] and Aguirre et al. in [1]. We claim that though up-to-date pedestrian modeling methodologies and approaches are effective in reproducing local short-term interactions between people, they yet have not gained enough explanatory power to reproduce effectively the complexity of crowds. There are cases, where assumptions and conceptualizations that are suitable for small-scale aggregations may fail - for instance, when reproducing large gatherings dedicated to religious, sport and other events [10, 14], where crowds are highly heterogeneous and are comprised of associations of different nature.

2 Modeling Collective Behavior in Crowds: State-of-the-Art

In this paper a scope of research has been limited in accordance with the typology proposed in the elaborate review by Templeton, Drury and Phillipides [19] who have analyzed and classified existing crowd modeling papers in relation to the way they treat group behavior. Authors came up with two broad groups of papers – those following the "mass approach" (neglecting the role of groups and associations in crowd modeling) and "small groups" approach. In this paper, works attributed to the first group have been excluded from consideration. Studies identified as following "small groups approach" in Templeton et al., as well as newer articles on modeling collective behavior in crowds have been analyzed in more details. It is worth noting that unlike in Templeton et al. [19], literature focused on developing models of crowds ("synthesis" as referred to in [2]) is distinguished herein from papers dedicated to proposing methods for automated detection and tracking of pedestrians in crowds ("analysis" as in [2]). Conceptualization of groups in visual analysis of crowds is an interesting topic itself; however, tasks that are being solved under this rubric are excessively different from the ones approached in the area of modeling crowds. Moreover, the former area bears its distinct technical limitations on reproducing group behavior – namely, it is restricted to purely proxemics or behavioral observations in analyzing group structures in crowds.

Since crowd modeling is being developed, discussed and applied in many domains, there is a need to estimate spheres of practice and research where the major part of the effort in collective behavior modeling is made. That may help understand the research dispositions that prevail in the field. In order to do so, it is proposed to refer to the subject areas of the papers included into the selection of works that can be found in the SCImago

Journal Ranking [24]. It has been found that some of the journals have multiple equivalent affiliations with research fields – as an effect from multidisciplinary nature and application of crowd modeling. The analysis shows that the majority of papers covering the topic of group behavior in crowds have been published in the journals labelled as completely or partially dedicated to the sphere of computer science, almost three times less frequent is affiliation with engineering and social sciences. Journals with medical affiliation attract even less group behavior-themed papers. Such a distribution of subject area affiliations partially speaks in favor of "mechanicistic reductionism" [7] in crowd modeling, and partially – of gradual diffusion between the listed domains.

The third step of analysis was aimed at identifying empirical grounding of the papers under revisions. The analysis has shown that not all the papers contain the validation section, due to a lack of appropriate real-world data or technical limitations. In other studies, researchers either prefer to use the data collected for a specific case [2, 15] or use publically available datasets found in open access [5, 22]. In the field of automated visual analysis and tracking of pedestrian movement, researchers tend to go for the second option, as it facilitates fast, free and generalizable validation of techniques as well as easy reproducibility. Scenarios that are reproduced in the observed cases can be both "natural" (derived from real-world crowds) or artificial (compiled in the form of controlled experiment in the lab). The majority of observed papers seem to compromise on the following accounts: (a) the choice of a particular case is rarely justified (instead of the detailed description of the case, the logics of the space, the composition of the observed crowd, authors predominantly list the characteristics of the footages themselves) in a proper manner and presented "as is"; (b) datasets (in a form of video recordings) are limited both in spatial coverage (for the most part footages capturing a small square or a corridor are used [2, 6, 9, 23]) and capacities to cover longitudinal phenomena (the max length of the footage capturing pedestrian movements among the reviewed papers is two hours); (c) if experimental results are used, no account is made as to what extent the constructed conditions, isolated from the social context of real-world situations can produce plausible representation of interactions between people, as opposed to collision avoidance and lane formation phenomena. Though the listed observations do not question the effectiveness of models labelled as "crowd models" to reproduce small-scale dynamics of interaction, the quality of the ground-truth used now to validate these can hardly allow scholars to reproduce the "big picture" of crowds (e.g. inter- and intra- group dynamics, logics of transition) in a longer temporal perspective.

Apart from technical limitations of crowd modelling (such as lack of real-life based simulations) this domain of inquiry clearly lacks a profound conceptual work. The analysis showed that to times it is not clear if the described case can be classified as "crowd" or just a voluntary aggregation of pedestrians. In this sense, there is little reasonable distinction made in the literature as to define crowds other than "a large group of individuals in the same physical environment, sharing a common goal" [16]. As it has been asserted in [18], "one of the more remarkable features of traditional crowd psychology is that it has tended to constitute a theory without a referent", meaning that superficial. Today crowd modeling seems to drift to the other side of the scale, when an extensive amount of fragmentary research is being conducted without visible results on the side of epistemological and theoretical work.

3   Suggestions for Further Studies

The research on group dynamics has long tradition in the various domains of scientific inquiry. The long scholarly interest towards social groups has resulted in many categorizations and conceptualizations of what can be accounted as a group. Thus for instance, some scholars identify shared identity [4] and shared tasks and goals [11] as the basis for defining collectivity as a group, while the others stress relations [8], interdependence [13] and interaction [21] as the core markers of a group. We propose to trace relations between the definition of a group (the way group members define the groups they belong to) and group dynamics/group action as a potential relief from the emergent epistemological confusion. This proposition stands close to the theory of collective action, more precisely, to the idea of collective efficacy [3], which claims that the way the group members understand the group they belong to would substantially influence the group goals, the way resources are managed, the type of strategic plans that are made and vulnerability to discouragement. It also goes in line with the socio-psychological theory of self-categorization [19].

The second proposition that we intend to make stems from the paradox of computer modelling of group behavior. Computational modelling is regarded as one able to investigate the dynamics of complex social processes. In this stance, group behavior seems an ideal object for examination. The paradox stems from the fact that computational models of group behavior rarely consider group dynamics, regarding groups as stable and homogenous entities. Taking this into account, we propose to look at collective behavior as a dynamic structure that has its internal dynamics and transformations. We suggest looking at crowd as an entity composed of smaller groups, which interact with each other and thus constitute mob dynamics. We assume that inter-crowd dynamics can be characterized by such processes as group/sub-group emergence, re-emergence and disappearance, splitting and merging, transformation of one groups into others, etc. These internal dynamics can be accounted as some of the core facilitators/drivers of crowd behavior, along with spatio-temporal context where crowd simulation unfolds. Following this logic, we propose to take a group as a unit of analysis. This is not to claim that groups can exist independently from their members, but to assume that groups possess internal capacities that cannot be reduced to the individual capacities of their members. This proposition goes in line with a Lewin's field theory claiming that groups are more than the sum of their parts [12]. So far there is no evidence to support the assumption that it is not true in the context of crowds as bigger and higher organized entities.

The third proposition is to see whether each form of collective behavior can be accounted as a group behavior. In order to make a distinction between a group and mere collectivity we propose to introduce the notion of communitas [20] into the analysis. We assume that communitas is a property of a group or a mob (if we assume that mob is a composition of groups) that is often associated with intense experiences and emotional character, is collective in nature, has temporary existence (it can emerge and vanish and usually bears immediate or spontaneous character) and may have revitalizing (e.g. create new norms, rules and ways of being) as well as destructive function.

The fourth suggestion is to account for the context of the event or the process that facilitates the emergence of crowd that is so far has not been widely investigated in the crowd modeling literature. This fact has been previously mentioned in [1] and gets even more relevant in the research aimed at reproducing group and collective behavior. However, very often context plays a role of a "stage director" guiding and arranging people's behavior with formal and informal rules. Thus, it is necessary to distinguish between the cases and circumstances where spatial and social context can play minor role or serve as a determinant for crowd dynamics. By context one may understand the physical and symbolic space of the venue that hosts the crowd or its composition (primarily – the groups that are brought together in a crowd) and logics of the event. In order to achieve this goal, we suggest the extension of the methodology used in crowd modeling. So far it has been built almost exclusively around pursuing the goal of grasping the visible, behavioral characteristics of groups in crowds. It can be developed beyond this state with an in-depth analysis of scenarios and events that are being modeled through addressing the features of collective entities and perceptions of people that constitute them with interviews and observations.

4   Conclusion

In this paper we have proposed a number of considerations that shall be done in the field of crowd modeling as to deepen the understanding of not only simplified, mechanic local interactions between the members of the crowds, but crowds as a whole. So far, this ambition has been widely proclaimed but not much has been done so far to approach it. A number of scholars [1, 19] suggested conceptualizations of groups and collective behavior in crowds that go beyond individual reductionism. Here, we are advocating for a more complex approach – that goes beyond the behavior or emergence of the group, accounting for its complex multi-dimensional structure and longer-term transformations, as opposed to emergentist perspective on conceptualizing crowds. We suggest that it would allow to understand the crowds that emerge during long-term mass events in greater details: both for the sake of computational modeling and social science.

Acknowledgments. This paper is financially supported by Russian Foundation for Basic Research, research project No. 16-36-00367 mol_a, project ID: 116021210004

References

1. Aguirre, B.E., et al.: Contributions of social science to agent-based models of building evacuation. Contemp. Soc. Sci. **6**(3), 415–432 (2011)
2. Bandini, S., et al.: Towards an integrated approach to crowd analysis and crowd synthesis: a case study and first results. Pattern Recogn. Lett. **44**, 16–29 (2014)
3. Benight, C.C.: Collective efficacy following a series of natural disasters. Anxiety Stress Coping **17**(4), 401–420 (2004)

4. Brown, R.: Group Processes: Dynamics Within and Between Groups. Basil Blackwell, Oxford (1988)

5. Cho, S.-H., Kang, H.-B.: Abnormal behavior detection using hybrid agents in crowded scenes. Pattern Recogn. Lett. **44**, 64–70 (2013)

6. Fang, J., et al.: Leader-follower model for agent based simulation of social collective behavior during egress. Saf. Sci. **83**, 40–47 (2016)

7. Gawroński, P., Kułakowski, K.: Crowd dynamics - being stuck. Comput. Phys. Commun. **182**(9), 1924–1927 (2011)

8. Gould, L.J., et al.: Experiential learning in organizations: applications of the Tavistock group relations approach. Karnac Books, London (2004)

9. He, L. et al.: Dynamic Group Behaviors for Interactive Crowd Simulation (2016)

10. Illiyas, F.T., et al.: Human stampedes during religious festivals: a comparative review of mass gathering emergencies in India. Int. J. Disaster Risk Reduct. **5**, 10–18 (2013)

11. Keyton, J., Stallworth, V.: On the verge of collaboration: identifying group structure and process. In: Frey, L.R. (ed.) Group Communication in Context: Studies of Bonafide Groups, 2nd edn, pp. 235–260. Erlbaum, Mahwah (2002)

12. Lewin, K.: Field Theory in Social Science: Selected Theoretical Papers. Harper & Brothers, New York (1951)

13. Lewin, K.: Frontiers in group dynamics II. Channels of group life; social planning and action research. Hum. Relat. **1**(2), 143–153 (1947)

14. Molloy, M., et al.: Management of mass gatherings. In: Koenig, K.L. (ed.) Koenig Schultz's Disaster Medicine: Comprehensive Principles and Practices, pp. 228–253. Cambridge University Press, Cambridge (2009)

15. Moussaïd, M., et al.: The walking behaviour of pedestrian social groups and its impact on crowd dynamics. PLoS ONE **5**(4), 1–7 (2010)

16. Musse, S.R., Thalmann, D.: A model of human crowd behavior: group inter-relationship and collision detection analysis. In: Thalmann, D., van de Panne, M. (eds.) Computer Animation and Simulation '97. Springer, Heidelberg (1997)

17. Radianti, J. et al.: Crowd models for emergency evacuation: a review targeting human-centered sensing. In: 2013 46th Hawaii International Conference on System Sciences (HICSS), pp. 156–165 (2013)

18. Reicher, S.: The psychology of crowd dynamics. In: Hogg, M.A., Tindale, R.S. (eds.) Blackwell Handbook of Social Psychology: Group Processes, pp. 182–208. Blackwell Publishing, Malden (2001)

19. Templeton, A. et al.: From Mindless Masses to Small Groups: Conceptualizing Collective Behavior in Crowd Modeling (2015)

20. Turner, E.: Communitas: The Anthropology of Collective Joy. Palgrave Macmillan, New York (2012)

21. VandenBos, G.R.: APA Dictionary of Psychology. American Psychological Association, Washington (2007)

22. Yücel, Z., et al.: Deciphering the crowd: modeling and identification of pedestrian group motion. Sensors (Switz.) **13**(1), 875–897 (2013)

23. Zhao, M.: A role-dependent data-driven approach for high density crowd behavior modeling, pp. 89–97

24. Scimagojr.com, http://www.scimagojr.com/

eHealth: ICTs in Healthcare

Reproducibility of Two Innate Immune System Models

Alva Presbitero[1,2(✉)], Valeria Krzhizhanovskaya[1,2,3],
Emiliano Mancini[2], Ruud Brands[4], and Peter Sloot[1,2,4]

[1] ITMO University, St. Petersburg, Russia
avpresbitero@gmail.com,
{V.Krzhizhanovskaya,p.m.a.sloot}@uva.nl
[2] University of Amsterdam, Amsterdam, The Netherlands
avpresbitero@gmail.com, mancini.emiliano76@gmail.com
[3] Saint Petersburg Polytechnic University, Saint Petersburg, Russia
[4] Nanyang Technological University, Singapore, Singapore
rbrands@ntu.edu.sg

Abstract. In this paper we present the first step towards the development of a mathematical model of human immune system for advanced individualized healthcare, where medication plan is fine-tuned for each patient to fit his conditions. We reproduce two representative models of the innate immune system. The first model by Rocha et al. describes the dynamics of the innate immune response by ordinary differential equations, focusing on LPS, neutrophils, resting macrophages, and activated macrophages. The second model by Pigozzo et al. describes the spatial dynamics of LPS, neutrophils, and pro-inflammatory cytokines by partial differential equations. We found that the results of the first model are fully reproducible. However, the second model is only partially reproducible. Several parameters had to be adjusted in order to reproduce the dynamics of the immune response: diffusion coefficients and the rates of LPS phagocytosis, cytokine production, neutrophils chemotaxis and apoptosis.

Keywords: Immune system model · Innate immune system · Scientific reproducibility · ODE · PDE · Finite difference method

1 Introduction

Science progresses by predicating on new knowledge and marked advancements in research that build on top of published results that are well-grounded, robust, and could stand the test of time. Corroboration is hence deemed essential for further research especially now that majority of published academic papers are irreproducible [1]. The reproducibility of published results allows scientists to build upon each other's ideas – such is the essence of the scientific method [2]. The publication process is ideally built over a foundation of readily reproducible data. This, however, is far from what happens in the scientific community. For decades, the issue of irreproducible data has been a topic of discussion among scientists, especially in the field of medicine. The costs of discovery, research, and development of drugs are immense; and late-stage failures in

© Springer International Publishing AG 2016
A.V. Chugunov et al. (Eds.): DTGS 2016, CCIS 674, pp. 501–514, 2016.
DOI: 10.1007/978-3-319-49700-6_50

clinical trials instantly drain invested capital. Researchers at Amgen Corporation found that only 11% of academic research was reproducible [3].

This practice also persists in the field of immunology. The human immune system is a complex network of highly specialized agents that work together to protect the organism against foreign substances, either in the form of pathogens, such as bacteria and viruses, or physical stresses such as hemorrhage and trauma that could be detrimental, or worse, fatal to the human body. This complexity calls for deep understanding and rigorous research through various methods, which include, but are not limited to, mathematical and computational modeling using ordinary and partial differential equations [4, 5], agent-based modeling [6] and cellular automata [7]. The goal of this research is to fine-tune the medical parameters necessary to understand, mimic, analyze, and potentially predict the behaviors of key players in the immune system. In this paper, we focus on two models of the innate immune system that made use of ordinary differential equations [4] and partial differential equations [5] with the aim to validate key parameters of the innate immune response.

Reproducing published results is only the first step geared towards modeling the human immune system and its functional responses to external or internal molecular signals. Further research in this area would allow us to model a customizable and personalized version of each individual's healthcare needs based on the said individual's immune system profile.

The article is structured as follows: The mathematical models are presented in Sect. 2. The numerical methods are given in Sect. 3. This is followed by the presentation and discussion of our results in Sect. 4. Finally, our conclusions are presented in Sect. 5.

2   Innate Immune System Mathematical Models

Mathematical modeling provides a valuable tool in analyzing and predicting the innate immune response. In this section we discuss two approaches to modeling the innate immune system through the use of differential equations.

2.1   A Simplified Model of Innate Immune System Using ODEs by Rocha et al.

A set of five ordinary differential equations developed by Rocha et al. [4] describes the dynamics of LipoPolySaccharides (LPS) denoted by variable (A), neutrophils (N), resting macrophages (RM), activated macrophages (AM) and pro-inflammatory cytokines (CH).

The LPS dynamics is described by Eq. (1). The term $-\mu_A A$ models the decay of LPS, and term $-\left(\lambda_{N|A} + \lambda_{AM|A} AM + \lambda_{RM|A} RM\right)A$ models the phagocytosis of LPS by macrophages.

$$\begin{cases} \frac{dA}{dt} = -\mu_A A - \left(\lambda_{N|A} + \lambda_{AM|A}AM + \lambda_{RM|A}RM\right) \cdot A \\ A(0) = 20 \end{cases} \tag{1}$$

The neutrophils dynamics is shown in Eq. (2). The term $-\mu_N N$ models the decay of neutrophils, $permeability_N$ models how blood vessel endothelium permeability depends on local cytokine concentration. The term $-\lambda_{A|N}A \cdot N$ pertains to the neutrophil apoptosis induced by phagocytosis, and $source_N$ describes the source of neutrophils.

$$\begin{cases} \frac{dN}{dt} = -\mu_N N - \lambda_{A|N}A \cdot N + source_N \\ permeability_N = \left(P_N^{max} - P_N^{min}\right)\frac{CH}{CH + keqch} + P_N^{min} \\ source_N = permeability_N(N^{max} - N) \\ N(0) = 0 \end{cases} \tag{2}$$

Resting macrophage dynamics is represented in Eq. (3). The term $permeability_{RM}$ shows how the permeability of blood vessel endothelium is dependent on local cytokine concentration, and $-\mu_{RM}RM$ models the apoptosis of resting macrophage.

$$\begin{cases} \frac{dRM}{dt} = -\mu_{RM}RM - \lambda_{RM|A}RM \cdot A + source_{RM} \\ permeability_{RM} = \left(P_{RM}^{max} - P_{RM}^{min}\right)\frac{CH}{CH + keqch} + P_N^{min} \\ source_{RM} = permeability_{RM}(M^{max} - (RM + AM)) \\ RM(0) = 1 \end{cases} \tag{3}$$

Equation (4) describes the dynamics of activated macrophage. The term $-\mu_{AM}AM$ models the apoptosis of activated macrophage.

$$\begin{cases} \frac{dAM}{dt} = -\mu_{AM}AM + \lambda_{RM|A}RM \cdot A \\ AM(0) = 0 \end{cases} \tag{4}$$

Cytokine dynamics is represented by Eq. (5). The term $-\mu_{CH}CH$ models the decay of cytokines, $\left(\beta_{CH|N}N + \beta_{CH|N}N + \beta_{CH|AM}AM\right) \cdot A$ models the pro-inflammatory cytokine production by neutrophils and activated macrophages.

$$\begin{cases} \frac{dCH}{dt} = -\mu_{CH}CH + \left(\beta_{CH|N}N + \beta_{CH|AM}AM\right) \cdot A \cdot \left(1 - \frac{CH}{chInf}\right) \\ CH(0) = 0 \end{cases} \tag{5}$$

2.2 A Reduced Model of Immune System Using PDEs by Pigozzo et al.

Pigozzo et al. [5] focused on three key players to model the simplified dynamics of the innate immune system: LPS, neutrophils, and cytokines. LPS, a bacterial toxin, is a potent immunostimulant that triggers an acute inflammatory response. Neutrophils are one of the main responders that mount a competent defense against local or systemic inflammation brought about by foreign agents like LPS or endogenous agents like extracellular nucleotides. Lastly, pro-inflammatory cytokines are produced by e.g. macrophages (and later on neutrophils) residing in the inflamed tissue after the interaction with LPS and/or extracellular nucleotides. Pro-inflammatory cytokines then induce an increase in endothelial permeability thereby allowing more neutrophils to get into the tissue [5].

In order to study the behavior of the population of LPS (A), neutrophils (N), and pro-inflammatory cytokines (CH) in space and time, Pigozzo et al. used three partial differential Eqs. (6)–(8).

The dynamics of LPS is described by Eq. (6) with initial and boundary conditions. The term $-\mu_A A$ corresponds to the decay of LPS over time, $-\lambda_{N|A} A.N$ models phagocytosis (the process of engulfing LPS by neutrophils), and $D_A \Delta A$ models diffusion of LPS into the tissue. A one-dimensional case is considered.

$$
\begin{cases}
\frac{\partial A}{\partial t} = -\mu_A A - \lambda_{N|A} A \cdot N + D_A \Delta A \\
A(x,0) = A_0 \left| 0 \le x < 1, \frac{\partial A(.,t)}{\partial n} \right| \partial\Omega = 0
\end{cases}
\tag{6}
$$

The dynamics of the neutrophils is modeled by Eq. (7). In this equation, the term *permeability*$_N$ refers to the dependency of the permeability of the endothelium of blood vessels on the local concentration of cytokines. The term $-\mu_N N$ corresponds to the neutrophils apoptosis (a programmed cell death), $-\lambda_{A|N} A \cdot N$ is the neutrophil apoptosis induced by phagocytosis, $D_N \Delta N$ refers to neutrophil diffusion, *source*$_N$ is the number of neutrophils entering the tissue from the blood vessels, and $-\nabla \cdot (\chi_N N \nabla CH)$ corresponds to chemotaxis (the movement of neutrophils via chemical stimulus of pro-inflammatory cytokines).

$$
\begin{cases}
\frac{dN}{dt} = -\mu_N N - \lambda_{A|N} A \cdot N + D_N \Delta N + source_N - \nabla \cdot (\chi_N N \nabla CH) \\
permeability_N = \left(P_N^{max} - P_N^{min} \right) \frac{CH}{CH + keqch} + P_N^{min} \\
source_N = permeability_N (N^{max} - N) \\
N(x,0) = N_0, \frac{\partial N}{\partial n} \big| \partial\Omega = 0
\end{cases}
\tag{7}
$$

The dynamics of cytokine is represented by Eq. (8). The term $-\mu_{CH} CH$ corresponds to the decay of cytokines, $\beta_{CH|N} N \cdot A$ refers to the production of cytokines by neutrophils, and $D_{CH} \cdot CH$ models the diffusion of cytokines.

$$
\begin{cases}
\frac{dCH}{dt} = -\mu_{CH} CH + \beta_{CH|N} N \cdot A + D_{CH} \Delta CH \\
CH(x,0) = 0, \frac{\partial CH}{\partial n} \big| \partial\Omega = 0
\end{cases}
\tag{8}
$$

Numerical simulations were divided into five cases of increasing complexity:

Case 1: Only LPS is considered in the system.

Case 2: Dynamics of LPS and neutrophils are observed. Cytokines are not considered. Source term is zero.

Case 3: Dynamics of LPS and neutrophils are observed. A source term is added to the system, but *permeability*$_N$ is set constant.

Case 4: Dynamics of LPS, neutrophils, and cytokines without chemotaxis ($\chi_N = 0$).
Case 5: Dynamics of LPS, neutrophils, and cytokines are observed with chemotaxis.

3   Implementation and Code Verification

The equations were solved by the finite difference method implemented in Python 3.5.1. The numerical method is described in the next subsections. The results were rendered using Python Matplotlib library. We used a 3.30 GHz Intel® Core™ i7-5820 K CPU with 16.0 GB RAM in all our simulations.

To verify the developed program code, the same equations were solved also in Wolfram Mathematica. Simulation results proved to be identical for identical model parameters and initial conditions.

3.1   Implementation of the ODE Model by Rocha et al.

The finite difference method provides an efficient approach to solve differential equations. For convenience purposes, we used Python *integrate.odeint* module under the *scipy* library in order to solve ordinary differential Eqs. (1)–(5). This module integrates a system of ODEs using LSODA from the FORTRAN library *odepack*. LSODA solves ordinary differential equations by automatically selecting between non-stiff (Adams' method) and stiff (Backward Differentiation Formula) methods for solving differential equations [8].

3.2   Implementation of the PDE Model by Pigozzo et al.

Similar to the numerical method used by Pigozzo et al. [5], we also employed the finite difference method for solving Eqs. (6)–(8), with the second-order accuracy in space and first-order in time. The second-order derivatives were discretized by the upwind scheme [5]:

$$f''(x) = \frac{f(x+2h) - 2f(x+h) + f(x)}{h^2} \tag{9}$$

For temporal integration, the first-order explicit numerical scheme was used:

$$f^{n+1} = f^n + \Delta t \, F(f^n) \tag{10}$$

where $F(f^n)$ is the right-hand-side of the ODE at the previous time step. To ensure convergence of a numerical scheme, the Courant-Friedrichs-Lewy (CFL) condition should be satisfied. For our explicit scheme solving three coupled one-dimensional diffusion-based Eqs. (6)–(8), it limits the time step to:

$$\Delta t \leq \min_{i} \left\{ \frac{1}{2} \frac{h^2}{D_i} \right\} \tag{11}$$

where h is a spatial step and D_i is diffusion coefficient of the i-th equation. We used $h = 0.1$ mm and $\Delta t = 0.01$ h to ensure that Eq. (11) is satisfied.

4   Results and Discussion

4.1   Studying the Dynamics of Cytokines, Neutrophils, Resting Macrophages, and Active Macrophages Using ODEs by Rocha et al.

The ODEs by Rocha et al. [4] model the acute inflammatory response, a phenomenon that is central to the innate immune system behavior. The authors focused on the temporal behavior of four agents: pro-inflammatory cytokines, neutrophils, resting macrophages, active macrophages.

In the presence of a biological or physical stress, the human immune system relies on the action of macrophages to guard the tissues for any sign of infection or inflammation. Once signals pertaining to infection or inflammation are detected, the macrophages alert the neutrophils and together they combat infectious agents that cause the inflammation in the body.

With the original model parameters, our simulation results perfectly match the results presented in [4], see Figs. 1, 2, 3, 4 and 5. The concentration dynamics of cytokines, neutrophils, resting macrophages and active macrophages is shown for varying values of the maximum number of neutrophils (Nmax) ranging from 0 to 16.

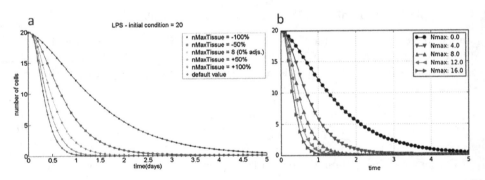

Fig. 1. Temporal evolution of LPS (A, Eq. 1). (a) Results by Rocha et al. (b) Our simulation results.

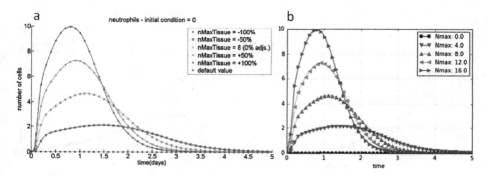

Fig. 2. Temporal evolution of neutrophils (N, Eq. 2). (a) Results by Rocha et al. (b) Our simulation results.

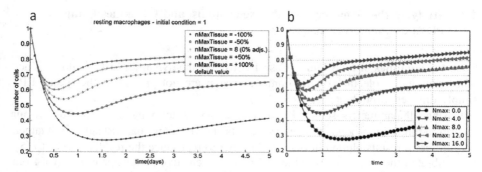

Fig. 3. Temporal evolution of resting macrophages (RM, Eq. 3). (a) Results by Rocha et al. (b) Our simulation results.

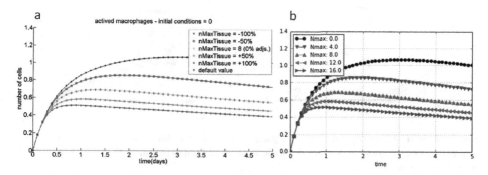

Fig. 4. Temporal evolution of active macrophages (AM, Eq. 4). (a) Results by Rocha et al. (b) Our simulation results.

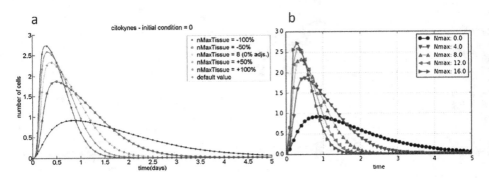

Fig. 5. Temporal evolution of cytokines (*CH*, Eq. 5). (a) Results by Rocha et al. (b) Our simulation results.

4.2 Studying the Dynamics of LPS, Neutrophils, and Cytokines Using PDEs by Pigozzo et al.

Case 1: Dynamics of LPS Only. Case 1 considers the dynamics of LPS alone. Since other cells and molecules of the immune system are not present in the tissue, LPS simply diffuses through space.

Using all parameters set by Pigozzo et al. and employing them directly in our algorithm did not reproduce the desired results shown in Fig. 6a. Instead, we obtained very different results plotted in Fig. 6b. In order to reproduce the results similar to [5], we calibrated the value of D_A, which is the most sensitive parameter in Eq. (6), from 0.002 to 2.5 mm²/day. Our calibrated simulation results are shown in Fig. 6c.

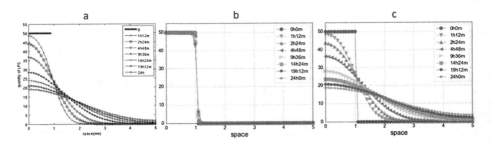

Fig. 6. Case 1: LPS only. (a) Results by Pigozzo et al. (b) Our simulation results using the parameters by Pigozzo et al. (c) Our simulations using calibrated parameters. LPS simply diffuses throughout the tissue.

Note that this is only an approximation and no form of optimization has been implemented yet. What we aim to show here is that a direct substitution of the parameters published in [5] into our algorithm did not reproduce the results shown in that paper.

LPS is a massive molecule that has molecular weight of 10–20 kDa. Based on the principle behind the Stokes-Einstein equation, the more massive a molecule is, the slower it moves. As a consequence, diffusion coefficient is also smaller. We then searched existing literature for molecules, specifically proteins, of similar molecular weights and assumed that their diffusion coefficients should approximately represent that of LPS. Proteins with molecular weights 10–17 kDa have diffusion coefficients ranging from 2.592–7.059 mm^2/day [9], which is closer to the value of D_A we have found after calibration.

Case 2: Dynamics of LPS and Neutrophils Without Source of Neutrophils. In addition to the presence of LPS in the tissue, Case 2 now deals with the dynamics of neutrophils as well. Neutrophils diffuse through space in search for LPS to phagocytose – after which they undergo apoptosis.

Once again, parameter values taken from [5] did not reproduce the results shown in Fig. 7a. For consistency, we fixed the parameter calibrated in the previous case (D_A) and proceeded inspecting the equations considered in Case 2. This provides a systematic approach in pinpointing the most sensitive parameters in every set of equations and calibrating parameters one case at a time.

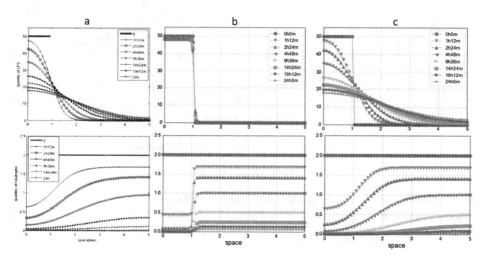

Fig. 7. Case 2: Dynamics of LPS and Neutrophils without source of Neutrophils. (a) Results by Pigozzo et al. (b) Our simulation results using the parameters by Pigozzo et al. (c) Our simulations using calibrated parameters. LPS and Neutrophils without Source.

Maintaining the previous calibration of D_A from 0.002 to 2.5 mm^2/day (Case 1), we then proceeded with calibrating D_N from 1.012096 to 2.34 mm^2/day, and both $\lambda_{N|A}$ and $\lambda_{A|N}$ from 0.55 to 0.40 (cell · day)$^{-1}$, which produced results that are close to what we are aiming for, see Fig. 7c.

According to [10], neutrophils have a diffusion coefficient of 0.1728 mm^2/day. Our calibrated value of 2.34 mm^2/day for the diffusion of neutrophils, therefore, is not biologically sound. However, it is important to note that neutrophils undergo directed movement governed by chemokines through chemotaxis. The discrepancy that we observe between the calibrated and expected values of D_N could be explained by non-incorporation of chemotaxis in the dynamics. Uptake parameters $\lambda_{N|A}$ and $\lambda_{A|N}$, on the other hand can have values from 0.25 to 1.50 $(\text{cell} \cdot \text{day})^{-1}$ [10]. Hence, our approximation of 0.40 $(\text{cell} \cdot \text{day})^{-1}$ is acceptable in this case.

Case 3: Dynamics of LPS and Neutrophils with Source of Neutrophils. Case 3 looks at the dynamics between LPS and neutrophils. The source term in this case involves a constant endothelium permeability which is just equal to P_N^{min} or the minimum permeability for neutrophils to move through the tissue. Using all the parameters indicated in the paper of Pigozzo et al. produced Fig. 8b, very different from their results (Fig. 8a).

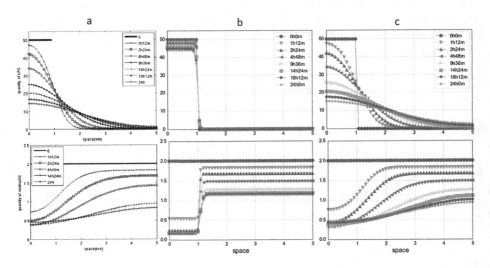

Fig. 8. Case 3: LPS and Neutrophils with source. (a) Results by Pigozzo et al. (b) Our simulation results using the parameters by Pigozzo et al. (c) Our simulations using calibrated parameters.

Case 3 explores the effect of adding a source of neutrophils to the system but maintains it at a constant. Hence, there is no need to calibrate more parameters in this case. Maintaining the calibrated values for D_A, D_N, $\lambda_{N|A}$, and $\lambda_{A|N}$, we were able to render the graphs close to what Pigozzo et al. showed in their paper (Fig. 8c). The addition of source of neutrophils allowed a nonzero concentration for neutrophils even at $t = 24$ h.

Case 4: Dynamics of LPS, Neutrophils, and Cytokines Without Chemotaxis. Case 4 looks at the dynamics between LPS, neutrophils, and cytokines without the chemotaxis term. Maintaining the calibrated values for D_A, D_N, $\lambda_{N|A}$, and $\lambda_{A|N}$, we then proceeded with adjusting the value of D_{CH}, which is the most sensitive parameter in this case since the source of neutrophils is dependent to cytokine concentrations. Cytokines, after all, are moderators for the movement of neutrophils in the tissue.

The diffusion coefficient of pro-inflammatory cytokines (D_{CH}) models the movement of cytokine in the tissue. Hence, a bigger value of D_{CH} corresponds to quicker motility. The parameter $\beta_{CH|N}$ models the rate of secretion of cytokines by neutrophils. Increasing the value for $\beta_{CH|N}$ increases the concentration of cytokines, which in turn causes a higher recruitment of neutrophils from the bloodstream into the tissue, unless neutrophils have reached the maximum concentration in the tissue. We found that calibrating D_{CH} from 0.0090216 to 4.5 mm^2/day and $\beta_{CH|N}$ from 0.4 to 0.31 (cell · day)$^{-1}$ rendered Fig. 9c, close to [5]. The value for D_{CH} tells us that chemokines are more mobile than both LPS and neutrophils, which corresponds to their biological behavior.

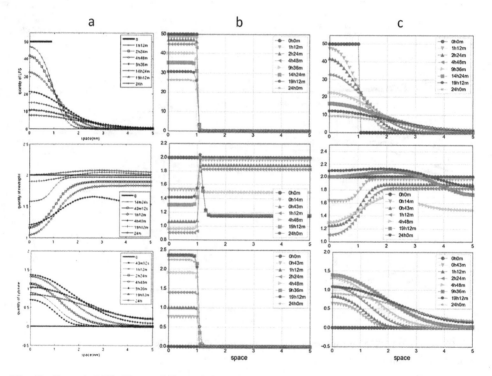

Fig. 9. Case 4: LPS, Neutrophils, and Cytokines without Chemotaxis. (a) Results by Pigozzo et al. (b) Our simulation results.

Diffusion coefficients for pro-inflammatory cytokines, which weigh 3–26 kDa, lie in the range of 2.33–4.32 mm^2/day [9]. Since the calibrated value of D_{CH} from 0.0090216 to 4.5 mm^2/day is closer to the range specified in literature, it is biologically sound. Also, note that the rate of secretion of pro-inflammatory cytokines ($\beta_{CH|N}$) is estimated to be between 0.1–0.4 (Cell·day)$^{-1}$ [10]. Hence, $\beta_{CH|N} = 0.31$ (cell · day)$^{-1}$ is an acceptable value.

Case 5: Dynamics of LPS, Neutrophils, and Cytokines with Chemotaxis. Case 5 looks at the dynamics of LPS, neutrophils, and cytokines with chemotaxis. Chemotaxis directly affects the concentration of neutrophils by causing their movement from the blood into the tissue by varying concentrations of pro-inflammatory cytokines.

Using all the parameters indicated by the authors produced the graphs shown in Fig. 10b. Like in the previous cases, maintaining the calibrated values for D_A, D_N, D_{CH}, $\beta_{CH|N}$, $\lambda_{N|A}$, and $\lambda_{A|N}$, we then proceeded with calibrating the chemotaxis coefficient χ_N, which is the only added parameter in this case. We know that increasing the value of χ_N means an increase in neutrophil motility towards LPS sites of higher concentrations. This movement is of course mediated by the cytokines.

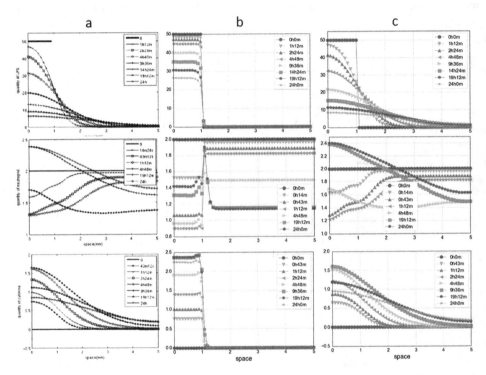

Fig. 10. Case 5: LPS, Neutrophils, and Cytokines with Chemotaxis. (a) Results by Pigozzo et al. (b) Our simulation results.

We calibrate the value of the chemotaxis coefficient χ_N from 0.0144 to 7 mm^2/day in order to achieve a configuration close to that presented by the authors. This value, however, is slightly beyond the acceptable range of $2.592 \cdot 10^{-5}$–4.6224 mm^2/day [10], but given the very wide range of accepted values, this discrepancy is acceptable.

A summary of all the parameter values we calibrated in order to reproduce the results of Pigozzo et al. and their corresponding acceptable ranges (either fine-tuned or biologically accepted) are shown in Table 1.

Table 1. Summary of calibrated parameters and feasible range of values to reproduce the results of Pigozzo et al.

Parameter	Units	Pigozzo et al.	Calibrated value	Acceptable range	Reference
D_A	$\mathrm{mm}^2/\mathrm{day}$	0.002	2.5	2.592–7.059	[9]
D_N	$\mathrm{mm}^2/\mathrm{day}$	0.012096	2.34	0.0372–0.1728	[11]
D_{CH}	$\mathrm{mm}^2/\mathrm{day}$	0.0090216	4.5	2.33–4.32	[9]
$\beta_{CH|N}$	$(\mathrm{cell}\cdot\mathrm{day})^{-1}$	0.4	0.31	0.1–0.4	[10]
χ_N	$\mathrm{mm}^2/\mathrm{day}$	0.0144	7.0	$2.592\cdot10^{-5}$–4.622	[11]
$\lambda_{A|N}$	$(\mathrm{cell}\cdot\mathrm{day})^{-1}$	0.55	0.4	0.25–1.50	[10]
$\lambda_{N|A}$	$(\mathrm{cell}\cdot\mathrm{day})^{-1}$	0.55	0.4	0.25–1.50	[10]

5 Conclusions and Future Work

Reproducibility of published results is a crucial step in the scientific process. Irreproducible results make building hypotheses on top of published ideas a waste of time and money mainly attributed to misguided research based on false results. In this paper, we attempted to reproduce the results of two models of the innate immune response by Rocha et al. [4] and Pigozzo et al. [5].

We found that the results by Rocha et al. were reproducible upon use of all parameters indicated in their paper. The parameters used in the model of Pigozzo et al. needed calibration to achieve results similar to [5]. We found approximate values of diffusion coefficients, LPS phagocytosis rate, cytokine production rate, neutrophils chemotaxis and apoptosis rate that were within the acceptable range of values in literature, except for D_N. We propose that the value for D_N should be adjusted within the biologically feasible range, even if the resulting dynamics is slightly different from [5]. The non-reproducibility of these results could be attributed to the lack of specificity of numerical parameters used in their numerical simulations. Also, it seems that their values for diffusion coefficients D_A and D_{CH} are not within the feasible range found in literature.

Our future work includes further fine-tuning model parameters by a genetic algorithm and developing a new advanced model for individualized healthcare.

Acknowledgements. This work is supported by the Russian Science Foundation project #14-11-00826.

References

1. Baker, M.: Is there a reproducibility crisis? Nature **533**, 452–454 (2016)
2. Vasilevsky, N., Brush, M., Paddock, H., Ponting, L., Tripathy, S., LaRocca, G., Haendel, M.: On the reproducibility of science: unique identification of research resources in the biomedical literature. Peer J. **1**, e148 (2013)

3. Begley, C., Ellis, L.: Drug development: raise standards for preclinical cancer research. Nature **483**, 531–533 (2012)
4. Rocha, P., Pigozzo, A., Quintela, B., Macedo, G., Santos, R., Lobosco, M.: Modelling the innate immune system. In: Gao, S. (ed.) Bio-inspired Computational Algorithms and Their Applications, pp. 351–370. InTech (2012)
5. Pigozzo, A.B., Macedo, G.C., dos Santos, R.W., Lobosco, M.: Implementation of a computational model of the innate immune system. In: Liò, P., Nicosia, G., Stibor, T. (eds.) ICARIS 2011. LNCS, vol. 6825, pp. 95–107. Springer, Heidelberg (2011)
6. Chiacchio, F., Pennisi, M., Russo, G., Motta, S., Pappalardo, F.: Agent-based modeling of the immune system: netLogo, a promising framework. In: BioMed Research International (2014)
7. Celada, F., Seiden, P.: A computer model of cellular interactions in the immune system. Immunol. Today **13**(2), 56–62 (1992)
8. Brown, P., Hindmarsh, A.: Reduced storage matrix methods in stiff ODE systems. Appl. Math. Comput. **31**, 40–91 (1989)
9. Goodhill, G.: Diffusion in axon guidance. Eur. J. Neurosci. **9**, 1414–1421 (1997)
10. Su, B., Zhou, W., Dorman, K.S., Jones, D.E.: Mathematical modelling of immune response in tissues. Comput. Math. Methods Med. **10**, 9–38 (2009)
11. Saltzman, W.: Tissue Engineering: Engineering Principles for the Design of Replacement Organs and Tissues. Oxford University Press, Oxford (2004)

Pollen Recognition for Allergy and Asthma Management Using GIST Features

Natalia Khanzhina$^{(\boxtimes)}$ and Evgeny Putin

Computer Technologies Lab, ITMO University,
49 Kronverksky Pr, 197101 St. Petersburg, Russia
nehanzhina@gmail.com, putin.evgeny@gmail.com

Abstract. In this paper we propose a way of managing allergy and asthma based on pollen recognition using images from an optical microscope. GIST descriptors are extracted as features. Our research can help to automate a time-consuming process of pollen grains classification, which is usually performed by highly qualified palynologists, and to create a real-time system of immediate notification about high atmospheric allergenic pollen concentration. Standard machine learning methods are applied and results are compared on different pollen datasets. The best model is support vector machine with 95.2% of accuracy on 9 pollen species and 98.3% on 5 pollen species.

Keywords: Allergy management · Asthma management · Image recognition · GIST · Machine learning · Dimension reduction · Pollen grains · Image preprocessing

1 Introduction

Today almost 30% of people have allergies, 8% have asthma. The most frequent origin of allergies and one of the causes of asthma is pollen. The number of people suffering of pollinosis varies between 10–15% among different countries, this number increased by 34% over last ten years because of urbanization, environmental effects of human, and also because pollen can cover long distances by air [24].

In order to manage allergies and asthma symptoms it is necessary to determine the start of the pollen dispersion. Accurate knowledge of prevalent aeroallergens can improve the diagnosis and treatment of patients. Pollen information is the key as it enables a timely start of the preventive and symptomatic treatment of seasonal allergy problems. Thus, a great need exists to catch airborne pollen and to determine immediately whether it is an allergy-causing plant species pollen or not. For these goals there exist more than 600 pollen counting stations all over Europe and only about 20 stations in Russia, where palynologists and volunteers spend much time for manual pollen operation using microscopes [24]. However, manual operation cannot provide information relevant enough for patients. For instance, 24% of adults and 40% of children in Europe cannot

© Springer International Publishing AG 2016
A.V. Chugunov et al. (Eds.): DTGS 2016, CCIS 674, pp. 515–525, 2016.
DOI: 10.1007/978-3-319-49700-6_51

travel freely due to the lack of information on atmospheric pollen concentrations in different regions in Europe [11,19].

Thus, a near real-time system, which can automate the recognition of pollen species, is required. Development of such a system can be achieved on the basis of the usage of digital images from a microscope. Recently machine learning and, particularly, deep learning have proven their effectiveness in a variety of applications such as image classification [21,32], natural language processing [7,33], speech recognition [10,16].

The need to automate pollen recognition was mentioned by Flenley for the first time in 1968 [12]. Since that time many attempts of such system development have been made, however, the problem is not completely solved yet. Proper classification of pollen grains allows to draw the appropriate conclusions and to solve problems faced by experts in other areas, not only aeropalynology [6,29,31].

Image recognition-based solution for this task consists of the following steps: pollen extraction, counting, and classification. Initially the image can include from 1 to about 50 pollen grains depending on their size and shape. Pollen extraction is the search of areas on image containing only one pollen grain per area and following pollen grain contouring. It can be obtained after preprocessing steps, described in Sect. 3.2. Counting is the quantitation of such extracted pollen grains. And classification is the determination of each pollen grain species. The final result can be presented as the percent composition of pollen species.

All researchers in this area extracted specific pollen features such as shape, brightness, texture features, and aperture [3–5,27]. Some used a scanning electron microscope (their results vary between 77% and 97% of accuracy) [1,3,31], other used stacks of images of one pollen, a kind of three dimensional representation (resulting accuracy is between 93.8% and 97.5%) [3,30,31]. Most researchers used standard machine learning methods: support vector machine, linear discriminant analysis, random forest, artificial neural networks, k-nearest neighbors and others. Many authors are members of currently existing or past global research projects, aimed to develop an automated pollen recognition tool. For instance, the European project ASTHMA specifically dealt with allergic pollen [28].

Review of pollen recognition techniques [17] revealed, that some simple and local issues within pollen recognition might be carried out, but there were still many tasks related to deformed, clumped pollen, which were not resolved. The interest to the problem is still high. Recently published papers declared results obtained with an optical microscope to be between 87% and 99% of accuracy [6, 9,23,27,29,30]. However, only few works considered the steps of extraction and pollen counting, although they are very important parts of the problem, because manual image cropping could be tedious and automatic counting is the main goal of recognition in some cases. Our research bypasses these disadvantages. Also we use images from an optical microscope, which is much cheaper than scanning electron microscope and is widely used.

Extracted features are described in Sect. 2.1. Applied dimension reduction techniques are described in Sect. 2.2. To achieve the goals of extraction and counting we use a preprocessing algorithm, which is described in Sect. 3.2. Applied classifiers are described in Sect. 3.3. The experiments are described in Sect. 3.4. Results are discussed in Sect. 4.

2 Proposed Approach

2.1 GIST Features

We choose GIST descriptors [8,26] as image features, which allows to avoid specific-purpose feature extraction. GIST is a low-dimensional scene representation. In other words, it is a kind of edges distribution histogram. An image is divided into equal parts using a grid (4×4 in our case). Edge distributions are computed on 3 scales of the image separately for every part. Edge distribution corresponds to the response of the part to every edge orientation (which has 8 or 4 values). We use color images, so this is applied to every color channel. As a result of GIST extraction, 960 descriptors were obtained. In general, the number of GIST features can be arbitrary.

2.2 Dimension Reduction

Due to the high number of GIST descriptors, dimension reduction (DR) is required. The following methods were used.

ReliefF. ReliefF is a member of the Relief algorithm family, which is a filtering feature selection technique, extended on M-classes classification. Relief is based on near-hit and near-miss measures, values of which form the weight for each feature. If the value of the weight is smaller than some threshold, this feature is rejected [34]. Weights vector is computed according the following formula:

$$w_i = \sum_{k=1}^{p} \left(\delta \left(x_k^i, near\_miss \left(x_k \right)^i \right)^2 - \delta \left(x_k^i, near\_hit \left(x_k \right)^i \right)^2 \right) \qquad (1)$$

where $i = 1 \ldots n$; n is the number of features; p is the number of objects; and $\delta(a, b)$ is the Kronecker delta.

The number of features selected by applying ReliefF is 300.

Mutual Information. Mutual information (MI) implies feature relative importance. It relies on entropy of a feature and its conditional entropy related to every class of objects [20]:

$$I(x, y) = H(x) - H(x|y) \qquad (2)$$

where I is the relative importance; $H(x)$ is the entropy of a feature; $H(x|y)$ is the conditional entropy.

The number of features selected by applying MI is 300.

Principal Component Analysis. Principal Component Analysis (PCA) is a feature extraction method. It finds a projection to a linear manifold minimizing distance of the points to the manifold [22]. 95% of origin variance of the data were used.

3   Experiments

3.1   Materials

Current research is carried out not only on allergenic plant, but also on honey plant pollen. The approach can be easily generalized to be applied to any plants dataset. The dataset includes 9 species, almost 1800 images in total. The dataset is original, never used before, made using optical microscope Olympus BX51 with Olympus DP71 image viewing system. All the pollen types were collected mostly from Russia, Perm Krai. In the Perm region, the aeropalynological profile is typical for central Russia. On average, the concentration of allergenic pollen grains in the air of Perm is lower than in other European geographical regions. Since 2010, the aeropalynological data of the Perm region have been included in the Russian pollen monitoring program. Pollen traps are located in the city center [24].

An example of an image from the dataset is presented in Fig. 1. The example shows that an image can contain stains, or debris, which are cause of wrong segmentation.

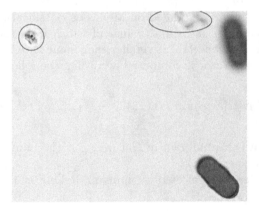

Fig. 1. Input image example

Some examples of each pollen species are presented in Table 1.

We used two versions of the dataset: full, which contains similar shape species, and partial, which contains mostly different shape species (top 5 rows of the table).

Table 1. Preprocessed images examples

Species	Images	Total
Trifolium hybridum		200
Archangelica officinalis		200
Dianthus deltoides		199
Fagopyrum esculentum		200
Chamerion angustifolium		198
Dianthus deltoides		110
Bunias orientalis		198
Salix alba		199
Tilia cordata		60

All images were normalized by RGB-values, according to the following formula:

$$I_N = (I - Min)\frac{newMax - newMin}{Max - Min} + newMin \tag{3}$$

where I stands for old pixel color value and I_N is a new value.

Cross-validation was used to evaluate the results. Its idea is to divide the dataset into disjoint training and validation subsets K different ways, the accuracy is evaluated as the mean accuracy.

We used 10-fold cross-validation and the experiments were conducted on a computer with an Intel Core i7-3770 CPU with 16 GB of RAM.

3.2 Preprocessing

We performed three preprocessing steps:

1. The first step of preprocessing is noise reduction, including Gaussian blur, dilation and erosion functions.
2. The next step is image double- and low-thresholding applied to hue and saturation channels. Such combination shows high result on images with color gradient or hotspots.
3. The last step is the segmentation and localization provided by Canny edge detector and Hu-moments [18].

The resulting sequence of preprocessing steps is presented in Fig. 2.

The extraction (segmentation) accuracy is 73%. The result is not great, the main cause of that is clumped pollen grains (Fig. 3). This is a separate complicated issue and an object of further research.

Fig. 2. Image modifications during preprocessing

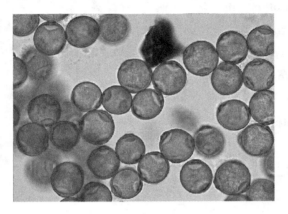

Fig. 3. Clumped pollen example

From here we will call the dataset which passed the preprocessing steps as the preprocessed dataset.

3.3   Models

The following 6 machine learning techniques were used in the research for classification [2, 13–15, 25].

1. Logistic regression (LR). A simple machine learning technique of linear classification.
2. K-nearest neighbors (kNN). This is a metric classification technique, which defines object class by its k nearest neighbors.
3. Support vector machine (SVM). It solves the problem of nonlinearly separable input vectors by projection of the low-dimensional training data into a higher dimensional feature space where they can be easily separated. The projection is achieved using kernel functions.
4. Decision trees (DT). The main idea is to recursively set up a tree over the feature space. The feature space is split with a feature value and then both subsets are split the same way recursively until the tree leaf has the minimum number of class targets for making a decision.
5. Random forest (RF). A classifier ensemble method based on bagging. Several independent models make decisions, then the common decision is determined by voting in case of classification problem and by averaging in case of regression problem.

Table 2. The results on partial dataset

Model	Origin features	PCA	ReliefF	MI
LR	$75.2 \pm 4.7\%$	$52.6 \pm 4.8\%$	$63.2 \pm 2.9\%$	$69.5 \pm 4.6\%$
kNN	$82.6 \pm 3.4\%$	$\mathbf{80.6 \pm 3.3\%}$	$81.5 \pm 3.6\%$	$82.1 \pm 2.5\%$
SVM	$73.3 \pm 4.7\%$	$78.1 \pm 3.8\%$	$69.4 \pm 3.5\%$	$73.1 \pm 4.9\%$
DT	$79.5 \pm 3.0\%$	$73.7 \pm 3.0\%$	$79.1 \pm 3.0\%$	$78.4 \pm 2.2\%$
RF	$\mathbf{84.7 \pm 3.8\%}$	$77.9 \pm 3.1\%$	$\mathbf{85.6 \pm 3.5\%}$	$\mathbf{83.9 \pm 3.0\%}$
GB	$83.1 \pm 3.2\%$	$76.2 \pm 2.9\%$	$84.3 \pm 3.7\%$	$82.4 \pm 3.1\%$

6. Gradient boosting (GB). This is a modern machine learning technique of classifiers ensemble. It minimizes the training error of classifiers linear composition by gradient descent.

3.4 Results for Different Feature Sets and Different Machine Learning Models

Each table shows combinations of dimension reduction and classification methods. Each cell in the resulting tables contains the mean accuracy of 10-fold cross-validation and its standard deviation, which follows after the plus/minus sign. The each DR method best accuracy is highlighted in bold.

Table 2 shows results comparison on the partial dataset. The best accuracy is provided by the RF model with ReliefF DR method, it is $85.6 \pm 3.5\%$.

Table 3 shows results comparison on the partial preprocessed dataset. The best accuracy is provided by the SVM model with MI DR method, the accuracy is $98.3 \pm 2.1\%$.

Table 4 shows results comparison on the full dataset. The best result is provided by the RF model with no DR, the accuracy is $78.5 \pm 3.8\%$.

Table 5 shows results comparison on the full preprocessed dataset. The best accuracy is provided by the SVM model with PCA DR method, the accuracy is $95.2 \pm 1.7\%$.

Table 3. The results on partial preprocessed dataset

Model	Origin features	PCA	ReliefF	MI
LR	$94.8 \pm 2.2\%$	$91.7 \pm 2.0\%$	$93.0 \pm 3.2\%$	$93.8 \pm 2.9\%$
kNN	$92.8 \pm 2.2\%$	$93.2 \pm 2.7\%$	$94.5 \pm 2.9\%$	$95.1 \pm 3.1\%$
SVM	$\mathbf{95.3 \pm 1.9\%}$	$\mathbf{97.0 \pm 1.2\%}$	$\mathbf{97.7 \pm 2.0\%}$	$\mathbf{98.3 \pm 2.1\%}$
DT	$79.4 \pm 3.5\%$	$81.9 \pm 3.6\%$	$84.2 \pm 4.3\%$	$84.9 \pm 3.8\%$
RF	$91.6 \pm 3.2\%$	$93.4 \pm 3.0\%$	$95.7 \pm 3.4\%$	$96.2 \pm 3.6\%$
GB	$92.7 \pm 4.0\%$	$94.6 \pm 3.9\%$	$97.1 \pm 4.8\%$	$97.9 \pm 4.2\%$

Table 4. The results on full dataset

Model	Origin features	PCA	ReliefF	MI
LR	67.1 ± 3.2%	44.9 ± 3.2%	60.5 ± 2.9%	61.2 ± 3.0%
kNN	73.6 ± 3.5%	69.1 ± 3.0%	74.6 ± 3.3%	74.3 ± 2.8%
SVM	69.9 ± 3.4%	68.8 ± 3.0%	61.8 ± 2.5%	64.4 ± 2.4%
DT	67.7 ± 5.4%	64.8 ± 2.7%	67.6 ± 3.3%	67.3 ± 3.0%
RF	**78.5 ± 3.8%**	**72.4 ± 2.6%**	**76.7 ± 3.5%**	76.6 ± 2.7%
GB	78.0 ± 2.1%	71.8 ± 1.9%	76.6 ± 2.8%	**77.1 ± 3.6%**

Table 5. The results on full preprocessed dataset

Model	Origin features	PCA	ReliefF	MI
LR	93.4 ± 2.1%	89.6 ± 2.2%	89.8 ± 2.0%	91.5 ± 1.5%
kNN	92.6 ± 2.0%	91.8 ± 1.5%	92.8 ± 1.8%	88.2 ± 2.5%
SVM	**93.9 ± 2.6%**	**95.2 ± 1.7%**	91.2 ± 1.4%	**91.7 ± 2.4%**
DT	71.9 ± 2.7%	77.5 ± 3.1%	72.6 ± 4.1%	64.8 ± 4.1%
RF	91.9 ± 1.8%	87.9 ± 2.6%	91.5 ± 2.0%	86.2 ± 2.7%
GB	93.3 ± 2.2%	90.2 ± 2.3%	**92.9 ± 1.8%**	89.7 ± 2.4%

One can see from the tables that models trained on the partial 5-classes dataset achieve much better accuracies than on the full dataset. Models trained on preprocessed datasets are significantly better than models trained on non-preprocessed datasets in terms of accuracy. Thus, preprocessing is one of the most important steps of the approach.

4   Discussion and Conclusion

In this paper we made an attempt to use machine learning to solve the problem of automated pollen grains images recognition. This is a very important problem due to the allergy and asthma management, the key cause of these diseases is pollen. To prevent allergy and asthma symptoms it is necessary to know the concentration of allergenic plants pollen in the air in real time. Existing pollen counting stations cannot provide rapid enough information because of manual processing. To automatize the recognition of pollen species we processed its images from optical microscope. We used GIST descriptors as the feature vector and applied several dimension reduction methods (PCA, MI, ReliefF). This approach gave 98.3% of maximum accuracy on the partial preprocessed dataset, which contains only 5 pollen species. The best classification model is SVM with a polynomial kernel.

That is a new approach relating to this problem, because other authors mostly used specific-purpose features focused on pollen grains nature. Usage of GIST allows to generalize our solution minimizing the accuracy loss. GIST descriptors are a kind of universal features.

We studied four versions of the dataset to see if pollen grains shape strictly assigns GIST values and to compare preprocessed and initial dataset GIST results.

We found out that the GIST-based approach works much better with the preprocessed dataset, which contains only one pollen grain per image.

We used three dimension reduction techniques and compared their results pairwise with machine learning models.

In future research we will make an attempt to use a convolutional neural network, which is a very promising technique [21], never used by other researchers within this problem. Also we plan to improve pollen the extraction stage, especially in order to resolve the issue of clumped pollen.

The final goal of this research is to develop a program for pollen recognition and bring it to the state of a real-time system, which will cut the cost on pollen operations in half.

Acknowledgments. Authors thank Andrey Filchenkov and Daniil Chivilikhin for suggestions and useful comments. This work was financially supported by the Government of Russian Federation, Grant 074-U01.

References

1. Allen, G.: An automated pollen recognition system. Masters thesis, Institute of information Sciences and Technology, Massey University (2006)
2. Bishop, C.M.: Pattern Recognition and Machine Learning, 1st edn. Springer, New York (2006)
3. Boucher, A., Hidalgo, P.J., Thonnat, M., Belmonte, J., Galan, C., Bonton, P., Tomczak, R.: Development of a semi-automatic system for pollen recognition. Aerobiologia **18**(3–4), 195–201 (2002). http://dx.doi.org/10.1023/A:1021322813565
4. Chen, C., Hendriks, E.A., Duin, R.P., Reiber, J.H.C., Hiemstra, P.S., Deweger, L.A., Stoel, B.C.: Feasibility study on automated recognition of allergenic pollen: grass, birch and mugwort. Aerobiologia **22**(4), 275–284 (2006). http://dx.doi.org/10.1007/s10453-006-9040-0
5. Chica, M.: Authentication of bee pollen grains in bright-field microscopy by combining one-class classification techniques and image processing. Microsc. Res. Tech. **75**, 1475–1485 (2012). http://dx.doi.org/10.1016/j.jfoodeng.2012.03.028
6. Chudyk, C., Castaneda, H., Leger, R., Yahiaoui, I., Boochs, F.: Development of an automatic pollen classification system using shape, texture and aperture features. In: Proceedings of the LWA 2015 Workshops: KDML, FGWM, IR, and FGDB, pp. 65–74 (2015)
7. Collobert, R., Weston, J., Bottou, L., Karlen, M., Kavukcuoglu, K., Kuksa, P.: Natural language processing (almost) from scratch. J. Mach. Learn. Res. **12**, 2493–2537 (2011)
8. Computer graphics laboratory courses. https://courses.graphics.cs.msu.ru/pluginfile.php/81/mod_resource/content/1/cv2013_09_cbir.pdf

9. del Pozo-Baños, M., Ticay-Rivas, J.R., Alonso, J.B., Travieso, C.M.: Features extraction techniques for pollen grain classification. Neurocomputing **150**, 377–391 (2015). http://dx.doi.org/10.1016/j.neucom.2014.05.085

10. Deng, L., Li, X.: Machine learning paradigms for speech recognition: an overview. IEEE Trans. Audio Speech Lang. Process. **21**(5), 1060–1089 (2013). http://dx.doi.org/10.1109/TASL.2013.2244083

11. European federation of asthma report. http://www.efanet.org/air-quality/pollen

12. Flenley, J.R.: The problem of pollen recognition, problems of picture Interpretation. In: CSIRO Workshop, pp. 141–145 (1968)

13. Friedman, H.J. Greedy Function Approximation: A Gradient Boosting Machine. IMS Reitz Lecture (1999)

14. Guggenberger, A.: Another Introduction to Support Vector Machines (2008). https://scribd.com/document/153294663/Another-Introduction-Svm

15. Hastie, T., Tibshirani, R., Friedman, J.: The Elements of Statistical Learning, 2nd edn. Springer, New York (2009). 533 pages

16. Hinton, G., Yu, D., Dahl, G.E., Mohamed, A.R., Jaitly, N., Senior, A., Vanhoucke, V., Nguyen, P., Sainath, T.N., Kingsbury, B.: Deep neural networks for acoustic modeling in speech recognition: the shared views of four research groups. IEEE Sig. Process. Mag. **29**(6), 82–97 (2012). http://dx.doi.org/10.1109/MSP.2012.2205597

17. Holt, K.A., Bennett, K.D.: Principles and methods for automated palynology. New Phytol. **203**(3), 735–742 (2014). http://dx.doi.org/10.1111/nph.12848

18. Hu, M.K.: Visual pattern recognition by moment invariants. IRE Trans. Inf. Theor. **8**(2), 179–187 (1962). http://dx.doi.org/10.1109/TIT.1962.1057692

19. International ragweed day press release. http://www.pollens.fr/docs/CP-IRD-2015.pdf

20. Kira, K., Rendell, L.: A practical approach to feature selection. In: Proceedings of the 9th International Conference on Machine Learning, pp. 249–256 (1992)

21. Krizhevsky, A., Sutskever, I., Hinton, G.E.: Imagenet classification with deep convolutional neural networks. In: Advances in Neural Information Processing Systems, vol. 25, pp. 1097–1105 (2012)

22. Manning, C., Raghavan, P., Schütze, H.: Introduction to Information Retrieval. Cambridge University Press, Cambridge (2008)

23. Marcos, J.V., Nava, R., Cristobal, G., Redondo, R., Escalante-Ramrez, B., Bueno, G., Dèniz, O., Gonzalez-Porto, A., Pardo, C., Chung, F., Rodríguez, T.: Automated pollen identification using microscopic imaging and texture analysis. Micron **68**, 36–46 (2015). http://dx.doi.org/10.1016/j.micron.2014.09.002

24. Minayeva, N.V., Novoselova, L.V.: Pollen monitoring in Perm Krai (Russia) experience of 6 years. Acta Agrobotanica **68**(4), 343–348 (2015). http://dx.doi.org/10.5586/aa.2015.042

25. Mitchell, T.M.: Machine Learning. McGraw-Hill Science/Engineering/Math, Boston (1997)

26. Oliva, A., Torralba, A.: Modeling the shape of the scene: a holistic representation of the spatial envelope. Int. J. Comput. Vis. **42**(3), 145–175 (2001). http://dx.doi.org/10.1023/A:1011139631724

27. Oteros, J., Pusch, G., Weichenmeier, I., Heimann, U., Möller, R., Röseler, S., Traidl-Hoffmann, C., Schmidt-Weber, C., Buters, J.T.M.: Automatic and online pollen monitoring. Int. Arch. Allergy Immunol. **167**, 158–166 (2015). http://dx.doi.org/10.1159/000436968

28. Projects home page. http://www-sop.inria.fr/orion/ASTHMA/asthma/asthma.html

29. Redondo, R., Bueno, G., Chung, F., Nava, R., Marcos, J.V., Cristóbal, G., Rodrìguez, T., Gonzalez-Porto, A., Pardo, C., Déniz, O., Escalante-Ramírez, B.: Pollen segmentation and feature evaluation for automatic classification in bright-field microscopy. Comput. Electron. Agric. **110**, 56–69 (2015). http://dx.doi.org/10.1016/j.compag.2014.09.020

30. Riley, K.C., Woodarda, J.P., Hwanga, G.M., Punyasenac, S.W.: Progress towards establishing collection standards for semi-automated pollen classification in forensic geohistorical location applications. Rev. Palaeobot. Palynol. **221**, 117–127 (2015). http://dx.doi.org/10.1016/j.revpalbo.2015.06.005

31. Ronneberger, O., Burkhardt, H., Schultz, E.: General-purpose object recognition in 3D volume data sets using gray-scale invariants - classification of airborne pollen-grains recorded with a confocal laser scanning microscope. In: Proceedings of the International Conference on Pattern Recognition, vol. 2, pp. 290–295 (2002). http://dx.doi.org/10.1109/ICPR.2002.1048297

32. Rosten, E., Drummond, T.: Machine learning for high-speed corner detection. In: Leonardis, A., Bischof, H., Pinz, A. (eds.) ECCV 2006. LNCS, vol. 3951, pp. 430–443. Springer, Heidelberg (2006). doi:10.1007/11744023_34

33. Sidorov, G., Velasquez, F., Stamatatos, E., Gelbukh, A., Chanona-Hernández, L.: Syntactic n-grams as machine learning features for natural language processing. Expert Syst. Appl. **41**(3), 853–860 (2014). http://dx.doi.org/10.1016/j.eswa.2013.08.015

34. Yang, Y., Pedersen, J.O.: A comparative study on dimension reduction in text categorization. In: Proceedings of the 14th International Conference on Machine Learning, pp. 412–420 (1997)

Analysis of the Classification Methods of Cancer Types by Computer Tomography Images

Galina Artemova[✉], Natalia Gusarova, Natalia Dobrenko, Vladislav Trofimov, and Aleksandra Vatian

ITMO University, Saint Petersburg 197101, Russian Federation
g.o.artemova@gmail.com, natfed@list.ru, graziokisa@ya.ru,
vladisl.trofimov@gmail.com, alexvatyan@gmail.com

Abstract. The present work is aimed at improving the efficiency of selection of traits in order to increase the information value of the checked pulmonary node, as well as the comparative evaluation of machine learning algorithms for classification in CT images.

Keywords: Machine learning · Computer tomography · Classification methods

1 Introduction

According to data of the International agency for research on cancer (IARC) [19] lung cancer is in the first place among the revealed cases and lethal outcomes among men and one of the five most common and deadly among women. In this regard, the high-quality diagnostics of lung cancer at early stages of the disease has crucial importance. Computer tomography is one of the most effective methods of diagnosis of cancer diseases. Feature extraction and classification of the type of tumors allows prescribing the timely and correct treatment.

The visual analysis of the images received by computer tomography is rather difficult, so this can often lead to diagnostic mistakes. The research allows choosing the most suitable method of machine training for segmentation, feature extraction, and classification of computer tomography results in lung cancer.

2 Related Works

Systems of computer diagnostics (CAD) offer the automated methods for assessing changes in tissues at all stages of work with the image, including [5]: segmentation for the purpose of allocation of pathological knots, classification and quantitative assessment of the allocated pathological knots to determine the type of neoplasm, search of similar fragments in the available base of images.

There is a large number of researches devoted to the automated detection of neoplasms, segmentation and analysis, both CT-images in general [2, 3], and specific areas or types of diseases, in particular lungs [6]. In scientific literature both methods of

© Springer International Publishing AG 2016
A.V. Chugunov et al. (Eds.): DTGS 2016, CCIS 674, pp. 526–531, 2016.
DOI: 10.1007/978-3-319-49700-6_52

detection of nodules in lungs on CT [5] and methods of the automatic and automated segmentation of images are presented rather widely [18]. Parameters of segmentation of images, including delimitation, volumes of pulmonary knots, etc. are quite deeply reviewed [9, 15]. Some methods of classification of the allocated and segmented pulmonary knots are studied rather well [5]. The comparison of various methods of classification of a wide range of diseases of an abdominal cavity was carried out [20]. The research of double viewing of CT-images by CAD-system and the doctor-radiologist that allows finding 72.6% of pulmonary knots was conducted, at the same time 4% of the found knots were revealed only by the system [20]. Data on the number of positive, negative, false positive and false and negative identifications of pulmonary knots and sensitivity of CAD-system were obtained [13].

Various computing methods, including methods of machine training are used for classification of pulmonary knots [16]: neural networks [10], deep belief network [8], decision trees [11], support vector machine [16].

In this work the contrastive analysis of methods of machine training is carried out, which allows to compare and choose the most productive technologies of classification of CT-images of pulmonary knots for more accurate diagnosis of a disease.

3   Materials and Methods

The disease data from LIDC-IDRI are used for the research on methods of machine training (for training and testing of algorithms) [1]. This data set is in open access in TCIA, now it contains 1010 CT-images and appropriate metadata with the results of biopsy on each sample, and also the borders of knots designated by the certified doctors-radiologists [1].

181 samples containing 31 copies of a malignant mesothelioma of pleura and 150 copies of adenocarcinoma have been selected for research, also the set has included 149 samples without malignant knots [7]. Each sample describes 12533 genes.

We randomly divided the samples into two subsets for analysis of algorithms: the training sample and the test sample. They also involve the comparison between the results obtained with the use of computational algorithms, and evaluations by doctors-radiologists with biopsy results.

The group of methods of binary classification and the problem of finding the difference of adenocarcinoma from mesothelioma have been chosen for the assessment of computing methods. The following methods of machine training have been selected: Bayesian logistic regression, Conjunctive rule, Discrimination polynomial naive Bayesian classification, Decision Stump, Propositional rule learner, Local weighing method, Radial-basis neural network, Gradient tree boosting, Random forest, Logistic regression, Simple neural network, Nearest Neighbors method, Adaptive boosting over Decision Stump.

On the basis of the obtained data ROC curves were created (dependence of positively classified results which are truly positively from those which are falsely positively [17]). The ROC curve is plotted in coordinates FPR – TPR. The TPR variable is called sensitivity (Oy axis). The (1 – FPR) variable is called specificity (Ox axis). The area under the ROC curve (AUC) has been chosen as one of the evaluation criteria. As the range of admissible values on both axes lies in the closed interval [0; 1], the maximum value of the area under the ROC curve can be 1, that corresponds to "ideal" classification. At the same time the value less than 0,5 is unacceptable (the value 0,5 signs that wrong classifications are prevailing).

The second method of the assessment is the correlation coefficient of Matthews which is also based on comparing the quantity of truly – positive, false – positive, true – negative and false – negative classifications. It shows the quality of classification of the chosen method by a scale from −1 to 1 where 1 corresponds to an "ideal" method, 0 – to casual guessing and −1 - to constant errors of classification.

4 Classification

In our work the division according to the types of knots is carried out as well as the classification by existence or lack of knots.

The package of the machine training Weka in the Java language is used for automatic processing of the data set. We have also written an application which reads information from the data set, analyzes it with the use of the chosen algorithms, and draws ROC (Fig. 1).

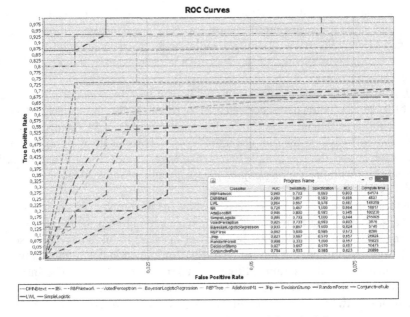

Fig. 1. Example of increase in part of the schedule

The calculation of ROC curves characteristic and coefficient of Matthews were received (Table 1).

Table 1. Characteristics of the studied methods

Method	Area under curve	Sensitivity	Specification	MCC
LWL	0,864	0,667	0,978	0,687
IBk	0,726	0,467	1,000	0,664
DMNBtext	0,999	0,867	0,993	0,886
AdaBoostM1	0,946	0,800	0,993	0,845
ConjunctiveRule	0,794	0,533	0,985	0,623
RandomForest	0,998	0,333	1,000	0,557
VotedPerceptron	0,925	0,733	0,993	0,803
BayesianLogistic Regression	0,933	0,867	1,000	0,924
DecisionStump	0,827	0,667	0,970	0,657
RBFNetwork	0,940	0,733	0,993	0,803
SimpleLogistic	0,996	0,733	1,000	0,844
REPTree	0,862	0,600	0,985	0,673
JRip	0,823	0,667	0,970	0,657

5 Features

The analysis of the image requires the extraction of allocation of pathogenic knots and the definition of their characteristics in the segmented areas. The main aim of the qualifier is the definition of classes with the use of characteristic vectors. The position of the sample in a certain class allows to carry out the selection of similar fragments from the base of images (the search of analogs in space of features). On the basis of the results of classification the ontology model has been constructed. The classification was carried out in the following directions: disease types, the list of the preparations used for treatment, symptoms and methods of diagnostics.

Use of the ontology structure in a CAD-system allows to classify the truly disease type with the accuracy more than 93% and accelerates finding of the necessary information in similar cases and treatment.

6 Results and Discussion

Comparing the results received in the article [18] to the results we received by practical consideration on the same set of methods, we can notice that the AUC and the MCC values received by practical consideration are better than the values of these parameters in the article (Table 2).

After analyzing all chosen methods with the two chosen evaluation criteria, the following methods can be considered as a good result: AdaBoostM1 (0,946 AUC and 0.845 MCC), BayesianLogisticRegression (0.933 AUC and 0.924 MCC), DMNBtext (0.999 AUC and 0.886 MCC), VotedPerceptron (0.925 AUC and 0.803 MCC), RBFNetwork (0.940 AUC and 0.803 MCC), SimpleLogistic (0.996 AUC and 0.844 MCC).

Table 2. The comparison of characteristics of the crossed methods

Method	Area under curve	Sensitivity	Specification	MCC
Boosting (article)	0,860	0,860	0,860	0,720
AdaBoostM1	0,946	0,800	0,993	0,845
Decision trees (article)	0,730	0,820	0,660	0,480
REPTree	0,862	0,600	0,985	0,673
k-nearest neighbor (article)	0,720	0,750	0,620	0,370
IBk	0,726	0,467	1,000	0,664
LASSO (article)	0,910	0,930	0,830	0,750
SimpleLogistic	0,996	0,733	1,000	0,844
RandomForest (article)	0,850	0,860	0,830	0,680
RandomForest	0,998	0,333	1,000	0,557

References

1. Armato III, S.G., McLennan, G., Bidaut, L., McNitt-Gray, M.F., Meyer, C.R., Reeves, A.P., Zhao, B., Aberle, D.R., Henschke, C.I., Hoffman, E.A.: The Lung Image Database Consortium (LIDC) and Image Database Resource Initiative (IDRI): a completed reference database of lung nodules on CT scans. Med. Phys. **38**, 915–931 (2011)
2. Bankmann, N.: Handbook of Medical Imaging. Academic, New York (2000)
3. Kononenk, I.: Machine learning for medical diagnosis. History, state of the art and perspective. Artif. Intell. Med. **23**, 89–109 (2001)
4. Dettori, L., Semler, L.: A comparison of wavelet, ridgelet, and curvelet based texture classification algorithm in computed tomography. Comput. Biol. Med. **37**, 486–498 (2007)
5. Doi, K.: Computer-aided diagnosis in medical imaging: historical review, current status and future potential. Comput. Med. Imaging Graph. **31**(4–5), 198–211 (2007)
6. Ferlay, J., Shin, H.R., Bray, F., Forman, D., Mathers, C., Parkin, D.M.: GLOBOCAN 2012: estimated cancer incidence, mortality and prevalence worldwide (2012). http://globocan.iarc.fr
7. Gordon, G.J.: Translation of microarray data into clinically relevant cancer diagnostic tests using Gege expression ratios in lung cancer and mesothelioma. Cancer Res. **62**, 4963–4967 (2002)
8. Hua, K.-L., Hsu, C.-H., Hidayati, S.C., Cheng, W.-H., Chen, Y.-J.: Computer-aided classification of lung nodules on computed tomography images via deep learning technique. OncoTargets Ther. **8**, 2015–2022 (2015)
9. Ko, J.P., Rusinek, H., Jacobs, E.L., Babb, J.S., Betke, M., McGuinness, G., Naidich, D.P.: Small pulmonary nodules: volume measurement at chest CT-phantom study. Radiology **228**, 864–870 (2003)
10. Kohad, R., Ahire, V.: Application of machine learning techniques for the diagnosis of lung cancer with ANT colony optimization. Int. J. Comput. Appl. **113**(18), 34–41 (2015)
11. Kumar, D., Wong, A., Clausi, D.: Lung nodule classification using deep features in CT images. In: 12th Conference on Computer and Robot Vision (CRV), Halifax, NS, June 2015

12. Kumar, S., Moni, R., Rajeesh, J.: An automatic computer-aided diagnosis system for liver tumours on computed tomography images. Comput. Electr. Eng. **39**, 1516–1526 (2013)
13. Li, F.: Computer-aided detection of peripheral lung cancers missed at CT: ROC analyses without and with localization. Radiology **237**(2), 684–690 (2005)
14. Orozco, H.M., et al.: Automated system for lung nodules classification based on wavelet feature descriptor and support vector machine. Biomed. Eng. **14**(1), 9–17 (2015)
15. Reeves, A.P., Chan, A.B., Yankelevitz, D.F., Henschke, C.I., Kressler, B., Kostis, W.J.: On measuring the change in size of pulmonary nodules. IEEE Trans. Med. Imaging **25**, 435–450 (2006)
16. Sergeeva, M., Ryabchikov, I., Glaznev, M., Gusarova, N.: Classification of pulmonary nodules on computed tomography scans. Evaluation of the effectiveness of application of textural features extracted using wavelet transform of image. In: FRUCT 2016, 18–22 April 2016 (in print)
17. Valente, I.R.S., et al.: Automatic 3D pulmonary nodule detection in CT images: a survey. Comput. Meth. Prog. Biomed. **124**, 91–107 (2015)
18. Wiemker, R., Zwartkruis, A.: Optimal thresholding for 3d segmentation of pulmonary nodules in high resolution CT. In: Lemke, H.U., Vannier, M.W., Inamura, K., Farman, A.G., Doi, K. (eds.) Proceedings of the 15th International Congress and Exhibition on Computer Assisted Radiology and Surgery, CARS 2001, 27–30 June, pp. 653–658. Elsevier, Berlin (2001)
19. Wormanns, D., Diederich, S.: Characterization of small pulmonary nodules by CT. Eur. Radiol. **14**, 1380–1391 (2004)
20. Yuan, R., Vos, P.M., Cooperberg, P.L.: Computer-aided detection in screening CT for pulmonary nodules. Am. J. Roentgenol. **186**(5), 1280–1287 (2006)

Mobile Telephone Technology for Better Healthcare Service Provision in Lagos Metropolis, Nigeria

Femi Ola Aiyegbajeje[✉] and Dickson 'Dare Ajayi

Faculty of the Social Sciences, Department of Geography,
University of Ibadan, Ibadan, Nigeria
femidavid2002@yahoo.com, ajayidd@yahoo.com

Abstract. This paper examined the effect of mobile telephone technology on physical distance separating out-patients from healthcare centres. A structured questionnaire which focused on socio-demographic characteristics (gender, age, income) and mobile telephone usage for healthcare services was randomly administered on 711 out-patients in Lagos University Teaching Hospital (LUTH) and Lagos State University Teaching Hospital (LASUTH). Mobile telephone ownership among out-patients was 98.9%. About 33% used mobile telephone to access healthcare services. Mobile telephone technology deployment in the health domain negates the distance decay function given a correlation value of $r = 0.86$ between distance travelled and mobile telephone usage. This suggests that mobile telephone could enhance better healthcare provision for out-patients in Lagos metropolis, Nigeria.

Keywords: Mobile telephone usage · Healthcare service provision · Distance decay effect · Lagos metropolis · Nigeria

1 Background

Physical accessibility to healthcare services is one of the aspects of measuring healthcare service provision and this is not without barriers. Barriers to healthcare services are numerous [11] identified such barriers as physical in nature. These include: patient's distance from health centres, transport cost, travel time and waiting time. Also, barrier to healthcare services is regarded as the distance between the service location and the household's/patient's location [31]. Barriers to healthcare services have been categorized into five; accessibility, availability, affordability, acceptability and accommodation [30]. The first two barriers are generally spatial in nature, while the last three are spatial and reveal socio-economic factors. Physical accessibility or spatial accessibility is the suitability of the location of the service in relation to the location and mobility of the patient (geographical or physical barrier).

However, one important technology that has now been highly deployed globally is the use of Information and Communications Technologies (ICT) to address the problem posed by physical accessibility (distance). It is obvious that the countries of the world where the life expectancy is higher are the countries where the use of ICTs is becoming more effectively mainstreamed in the different areas of national life,

© Springer International Publishing AG 2016
A.V. Chugunov et al. (Eds.): DTGS 2016, CCIS 674, pp. 532–543, 2016.
DOI: 10.1007/978-3-319-49700-6_53

including the health sector. Obviously, there exist a significant correlation between the level of the use of ICT and the level of performance in their health sector [27]. The perceived importance of ICT/mobile telephone technology to all human endeavours has been shown as a possible way of addressing problems hindering accessibility to healthcare services [20: pp. 69–76; 27; 29: pp. 11–22].

1.1 Research Problem

Physical accessibility to healthcare services has been a major concern to healthcare seekers, especially in developing countries [1: pp. 115–142; 2; 28: pp. 661–666]. Although, mobile telephone technology has been found to be a way of addressing the problem of physical accessibility to health care services [5: pp. 125–134]. This claim may be supported with the arguments of the proponents of substitution and complementary hypotheses. Studies have suggested that mobile telephone is capable of moderating the challenges posed by physical accessibility [17: pp. 87–121; 23: pp. 98–104; 24: pp. 341–353]. The work of [35] focused on within-work travels and observed that mobile telephone helps more in rescheduling trips than eliminating them. However, despite all efforts to ascertain the importance of mobile telephone in the healthcare domain, the extent of its importance in dealing with the problem of patients' physical distance to healthcare centre in Nigeria has not been fully established. This study, therefore examined the effects of mobile telephone usage on physical accessibility (distance) to healthcare services in Lagos metropolis, Nigeria.

1.2 Research Question

Can the use of mobile telephone technology address the problem of distance in healthcare provision?

1.3 Hypothesis

The only hypothesis tested in this study is that, there is a significant relationship between mobile telephone usage and distance of patients from the hospital. The basis for this hypothesis is based on the distance decay effect (DDE) postulations.

1.4 Study Area

Lagos State is located between longitudes 3° 5′E and 3° 30′E, and latitudes 6° 25′N and 6° 40′N. The Southern part is bordered by the 180 km Atlantic coastline, the Northern and Eastern parts are bordered with Ogun State. On the Western side, the state shared the same boundary with the Republic of Benin. In terms of size, Lagos State is the smallest state in Nigeria with an area of 356,861 ha. The Lagos University Teaching Hospital (LUTH) and Lagos State University teaching Hospital (LASUTH) are located in the state (see Figs. 1 and 2).

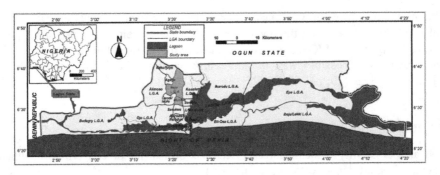

Fig. 1. Political map of Lagos state (Source: Ministry of Land and Housing, Lagos State Secretariat, Ikeja, Lagos)

Fig. 2. Location of LUTH and LASUTH within Lagos metropolis (Source: Ministry of Land and Housing, Lagos State Secretariat, Ikeja, Lagos).

Table 1 showed that the metropolis accounted for about 7,937,932 (88.1%) of the state's population (9,019,534). The metropolis comprises of sixteen local government areas (LGAs) of the state's twenty LGAs.

The state is the commercial nerve centre of the country; it hosts over half of the total industrial investments and the commercial activities in Nigeria. Some 60% to 70% of all commercial transactions in Nigeria are carried out or finalized in Lagos state. Also, about 70% of the total value of industrial investments in Nigeria is in the Lagos region with over 65% of the country's industrial employment concentrated in this region [3: p. 228; 4: pp. 265–277].

1.5   Scope of Study

The study focused on the out-patients of both Lagos University Teaching Hospital (LUTH) and Lagos State University Teaching Hospital (LASUTH). The out-patients are thereafter referred to as patients in our subsequent discussion.

Table 1. Metropolitan Lagos (Source: National Population Census, 2006)

Local government areas	Land area (Km²)	Population	Density (Pop/km²)
Agege	11.2	459,939	41,071
Ajeromi-Ifelodun	12.3	684,105	55,474
Alimosho	185.2	1,277,714	6,899
Amuwo-Odofin	134.6	318,166	2,364
Apapa	26.7	217,362	8,153
Eti-Osa	192.3	287,785	1,496
Ifako-Ijaiye	26.6	427,878	16,078
Ikeja	46.2	313,196	6,785
Kosofe	81.4	665,393	8,174
Lagos Island	8.7	209,437	24,182
Lagos Mainland	19.5	317,720	16,322
Mushin	17.5	633,009	36,213
Ojo	158.2	598,071	3,781
Oshodi-Isolo	44.8	621,509	13,886
Somolu	11.6	402,673	34,862
Surulere	23.0	503,975	21,912
Metropolitan Lagos	999.6	7,937,932	7,941

2 Literature Review and Conceptual Framework

2.1 Contributions of Mobile Telephone to Healthcare Service Delivery

The infusion of mobile telephone technology in healthcare service delivery, according to [16], dates back to a decade. Also, as shown in [5: pp. 125–134; 8: pp. 1–21; 10; 20: pp. 69–76; 21: pp. 421–427; 22; 34], mobile telephone has brought great contribution to healthcare service delivery. The work of [20] examined various ICTs used in selected tertiary hospitals and identified mobile telephone as the most used technology among health workers.

Also, [21] examined how patients' case notes (which encompass symptom, diagnosis and medication with clinical number) were transmitted referral hospital within few seconds using mobile telephone. The study noted that the system has the potential to increase medical personnel's productivity, reduce pre-natal and neo-natal mortality rates, improve medical care and minimize the cost of referral since GSM facilities are available and some mobile operators offer free text services. A study by [5] found that telecommunication has had tangible impacts on intra-hospital communication among various units and personnel. However, the study failed to evaluate the tangible impacts it may have on patients as regards physical accessibility to healthcare centres. On the use of mobile telephone as a mobile-based alert system for out-patients' adherence in Nigeria [12] noted that despite these efforts, none of these studies have adequately examined the contribution of mobile telephone usage in ameliorating access to healthcare services in Nigeria.

In a broader perspective, several studies have shown that mobile telephone/ICT usage could either substitute or complement travel in practically every human endeavour. For the substitution hypothesis, [23: pp. 98–104] found that the frequency of commuting decreases among telecommuters while no increase in non-commute travel was noticed. Furthermore, [18: pp. 229–248] investigated the importance of multi-purpose journey to work and concluded that many trips are chained to 'work trip' so that an attempt to eliminate it will automatically affect other trips chained to it. The effect of telecommuting on trip generation, trip distribution and assignment, modal choice and trip reduction was the focus of [17: pp. 87–121; 19; 26: pp. 20–25; 32].

The uniqueness of mobile telephone was further explained by [6, 9, 14]. They asserted that mobile telephone is not only changing aspects of social life, but also alters even the framework that society functions under. The use of mobile telephones for patients' follow-up has been shown to improve the care of patients discharged from the emergency department [7: pp. 745–754; 25: pp. 942–948]. In addition, the work of [33] established that investment in emerging information technology, including information systems, can lead to productivity gains only if they are accepted and effectively used by respective stakeholders.

2.2 Distance Decay Effect

Distance decay functions can be identified with spatial monopolies when the choice of a particular phenomenon or location is not possible or allowed. Distance decay simply relates to a popular term 'as distance increases, interaction between two places decreases [36: pp. 221–238]. Overtime, the development of distance decay in spatial discourse is particularly interesting. The technological advances in transport and more recently the proliferation of mobile telephone technology, have led to the view that distance is rapidly becoming less important. This has given rise to metaphors such as the 'global village' and the 'death of distance' to describe the economic development into the 21st century.

3 Methods

3.1 Data Collection

Both primary and secondary data were used for this study. A cross-sectional technique was adopted for the collection of primary data. The collection of data from the primary source was done through the administration of structured questionnaire on patients. The questionnaire on patients focused on intensity of mobile telephone usage in accessing healthcare services – preventive, medical advice and follow-up healthcare services and demographic data such as age, sex, education, occupation and income status. Others include data on determinants of mobile telephone usage, information on the effects of mobile telephone usage on waiting time at physician's office, distance (patient's residence/location and hospital), travel time, frequency of trips/visits to healthcare centres, locational distance of patients, and average number of trip reduction in a month were also collected.

Secondary data were obtained from the Records Department of Lagos University Teaching Hospital, the Lagos State University Teaching Hospital, and the Lagos State Ministry of Health. Secondary data from the selected hospitals included information on the number of doctors and the number of out-patients registered with the hospital obtained at the Records Departments. It also provided information on the number of clinics, the day and time the clinics operate. The political map of Lagos State was collected from the Lagos State Ministry of Land and Housing. The sample size for questionnaire survey was determined using Taro Yamane's formula based on the number of patients provided by the Records office. The Yamane's technique is given as:

$$n = N/1 + N\ (e)^2 \tag{1}$$

Where, n = sample size, N = sampled population and (e) = significant level or level of precision 0.05^2

Patients

$$LUTH : 1 + 26,400 \times 0.0025 = 66.0025$$
$$26,400 \div 66.0025 = 399.984849$$
$$N = 399.98$$

A total of 400 patients were therefore sampled in LUTH

$$LASUTH : 1 + 22,800 \times 0.0025 = 57.0025$$
$$22,800 \div 57.0025 = 399.982457$$
$$N = 399.98$$

A total of 400 patients were also sampled in LASUTH.
Overall, a total of 800 patients were sampled.

3.2   Data Analysis

Frequency distribution and charts were used for data analysis and presentation. Also, Pearson's correlation analysis was used to test the stated hypothesis. A total of 711 (88.9%) patients and 314 (71.3%) doctors completed the questionnaire. In all, 370 (52.1%) patients participated in LUTH and 341 (47.9%) patients in LASUTH. Similarly, 167 (53.2%) doctors participated in LUTH and 147 (46.8%) doctors in LASUTH. The relationship between patients' mobile telephone usage and distance of patients from the hospital was tested using Pearson's correlation analysis. The dependent variable was measured as (the average number of mobile telephone calls by patients to doctors in a month e.g. <4 times = 1; >4 times = 2). The independent variable is the distance of patients from the hospital measured in kilometres (distance of patients' location from the hospital (0 km – 10 km = 1; 11 km – 20 km = 2; >20 km = 3). The hypothesis that mobile telephone usage significantly predicts the reduction in the average number of patients' trips to the hospital was tested using the bivariate regression analysis. The dependent variable is the numbers of patients' eliminated trips to the hospital in a month (e.g. <5 times = 1; >5 times = 2). The independent variable is the frequency of mobile telephone usage (e.g. <5 times = 1; >5 times = 2).

The model is given as:

$$Y = a + b_1 X_1 \qquad (2)$$

Where; Y = Trip reduction; a = Y intercept; b_1 = regression coefficient; X_1 = mobile telephone usage.

4   Discussions

4.1   Demographic Profile

The demographic profiles of the patients indicated a total of 711 patients comprising 370 (52.1%) and 341 (47.9%) in Lagos University Teaching Hospital (LUTH) and Lagos State University Teaching Hospital (LASUTH). The patients consist of 275 (38.7%) males and 436 (61.3%) females while 703 (98.9%) own mobile telephone. However, a total of 236 (33.2%) patients were found using mobile telephone to seek healthcare services from the doctors.

4.2   Distance Covered by Patients to the Hospital

A total of 8 (3.4%) of the patients covered between 0 km and 5 km, among these, 5 (3.7%) and 3 (2.9%) of the patients in LUTH and LASUTH, respectively, covered distances within 0–5 km from the hospital. A total of 18 (7.6%) travelled across a distance between 6 km and 10 km from the hospital. This consists of 8 (6.0%) patients in LUTH and 10 (9.8%) patients in LASUTH, respectively. Patients covering a distance between 11 km and 15 km from the hospital were 21 (8.9%), consisting of 9 (6.7%) in LUTH and 12 (11.8%) in LASUTH. Patients who travelled across distances between 16 km and 20 km were 16 (6.8%), consisting of 7 (5.2%) in LUTH and 9 (8.9%) in LASUTH. Furthermore, there were 30 (12.7%) patients who covered distances between 21 km and 25 km comprising 20 (14.9%) patients in LUTH and 10 (9.8%) in LASUTH. A total of 35 (14.8%) patients travelled across distances between 26 km and 30 km, consisting of 19 (14.2%) in LUTH and 16 (15.7%) in LASUTH. Moreover, 34 (14.4%) patients covered between 31 km and 35 km to the hospital, comprising 22 (16.4%) patients in LUTH and 12 (11.8%) in LASUTH. In addition, 27 (11.4%) patients travelled across a distance between 36 km and 40 km. This consist of 16 (11.9%) patients in LUTH and 11 (10.8%) in LASUTH.

Similarly, 47 (19.9%) patients covered above 40 km to the hospital. This category consists of 28 (20.9%) patients in LUTH and 19 (18.6%) in LASUTH. By implication, the patients travelling across over 35 kilometres to the hospital are likely to reside outside Lagos metropolis because distances over 35 km from either LUTH or LASUTH are considered to be outside Lagos metropolis. A total of 74 (31.4%) patients

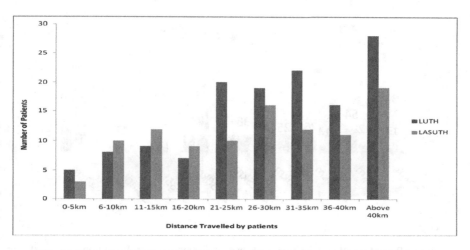

Fig. 3. Distance travelled by patients to the hospital (Source: Authors Analysis)

were in this category while 162 (68.6%) patients travelled across distances within the metropolis (see Fig. 3).

4.3 Patients' Mobile Telephone Usage Across Distances

An average of 708 mobile telephone calls was made to the doctors by the patients in a month (see Fig. 4). Out of this, 21 (3.0%) of the calls were made by patients' located between a distance of 0 km and 5 km from the hospital. These consist of 4 (1.0%) of such calls made to LUTH and 17 (5.6%) to LASUTH. A total of 76 (10.7%) calls were made by patients located within 6 km to 10 km from the hospital. This represents 22 (5.5%) mobile telephone calls in LUTH and 54 (17.7%) in LASUTH. Also, 40 (5.7%) mobile telephone calls were made from between a distance of 11 km and 15 km, consisting of 14 (3.5%) in LUTH and 26 (8.5%) in LASUTH. Furthermore, 48 (6.7%) mobile telephone calls were made among patients located between 16 km and 20 km from the hospital. This represents 25 (6.2%) mobile telephone calls in LUTH and 23 (7.5%) in LASUTH. Among patients located within 21–25 km from the hospital, a total of 79 (11.2%) mobile telephone calls were made, comprising 38 (9.4%) in LUTH and 40 (13.1%) in LASUTH.

In sharp contrast, 138 (19.5%) mobile telephone calls were made among patients located between 26 km and 30 km from the hospital. Out of this, 98 (24.3%) mobile telephone calls were made to LUTH and 66 (24.5%) to LASUTH. A sharp decrease from the above proportion to 36 (5.1%) mobile telephone calls were recorded among patients located between 31 km and 35 km from the hospital. These consists of 21 (5.2%) mobile telephone calls to LUTH and 15 (4.9%) to LASUTH. Similarly, 17 (2.4%) mobile telephone calls were made to the hospital by patients located between 36 km and 40 km with all coming from LUTH. For patients located above 40 km from the hospital, 253 (35.7%) mobile telephone calls were made comprising 164 (40.7%) in LUTH and 89 (29.2%) in LASUTH. This implies that 38.1% of the total calls were

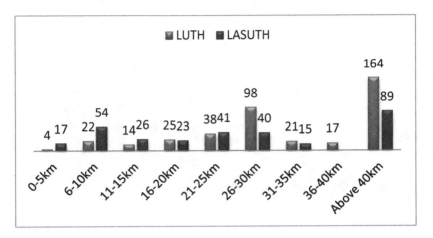

Fig. 4. Patients' mobile telephone calls across distances (Source: Authors Analysis)

from outside Lagos metropolis, with the highest number of calls coming from a distance of above 40 km from the hospital. This, therefore, suggests that mobile telephone usage to access healthcare services is an activity that increases with increasing distance.

5   Results

5.1   Relationships Between Mobile Telephone Usage and Distance from Hospital

The Pearson's correlation analysis in Table 2 shows a strong positive significant relationship between patients' mobile telephone usage and patients' distance from hospital ($r = 0.857$, $p < 0.05$). The strong positive relationship indicates that as distance of patients from the hospital increases, mobile telephone use also increases. The result shows that the variation in patients' distance from the hospital is responsible for 0.857 (85.7%) of mobile telephone usage. This implies that as patients' distance from the hospital increases, patients' frequency of mobile telephone usage to seek healthcare services also increases. This shows that patients residing far away from the hospital engage in frequent use of mobile telephone than their counterparts living around the hospital.

Table 2. Mobile telephone usage and distance of patients from hospital (Source: Authors Analysis)

	Mean	N	Df	Pearson r	Sig
Number of calls in a Month	0.995	236	234	0.857**	<0.05
Locational distance of Patient	1.215				

**Correlation is significant at 0.05 level (2-tailed) N = 236

5.2   Findings and Conclusions

The advent of mobile telephone technology and other information and communication technology (ICT) indicators have altered many theoretical and practical postulations such as the distance decay theory which states that 'human activities decreases with increasing distance from city centre'. As observed, healthcare service provision via mobile telephone is seen as an activity that increases with increasing distance (see Fig. 3 above) however, this observation negates the postulation of distance decay effect theory as explained in [13; 41: pp. 221–238; 37]. The development over time of distance decay in spatial discourse is particularly interesting. Technological advances in transport and more recently the proliferation of mobile technology, together with the advent of globalization, have led to the view that distance is rapidly becoming less important in man's travel behaviour. Furthermore, the study indicated that mobile telephone technology has served as a platform to offer better healthcare management. This is so, because, healthcare services are still being offered to out-patients despite the fact that they are far away from the hospital. Therefore, the use of mobile telephone technology was found useful in providing better healthcare services and timely management of health challenges of patients from far away distances to the hospital in Lagos metropolis, Nigeria.

References

1. Adejuyigbe, O.: Location of social science centre in Western Nigeria, the case of medical facilities. Man Soc. **1**, 115–142 (1973)
2. Adejuyigbe, O.: The location of rural basic health facilities in Ife-Ijesha area of South Western Nigeria. Research Report, University of Ife (Obafemi Awolowo University) Ile-Ife. (1977)
3. Ajayi, D.D.: Spatial Patterns of Production Subcontracting in Nigeria: a case study of the Lagos Region. Unpublished Ph.D. thesis, Department of Geography, University of Ibadan. 221 Pages (1998)
4. Ajayi, D.D.: Industrial subcontracting linkages in the Lagos region. Niger. J. Econ. Soc. Stud. (NJESS) **43**, 265–277 (2001)
5. Akadiri, O.A., Olusanya, A.A., Omitola, O.O.: Impact of improved telecommunication services on healthcare delivery in Nigerian teaching hospitals - a survey of opinions. J. Inf. Technol. Impact **9**, 125–134 (2009)
6. Amosa, B.M.G., Longe, O.L., Akinbode, O.P.: Mobile-phone based patient compliance system for chronic illness care in Nigeria. JCS&T **12**, 22–26 (2012)
7. Azam, S., Yang, Y.: Mobile Health Services for Patients with Chronic Diseases: A Systematic Literature Review. Nursing Bachelor's Thesis, Laurea University of Applied Sciences, Otaniemi, Espoo 1–48 (2013)
8. Beedasy, J.: Rural designations and geographic access to tertiary healthcare in Idaho. Online J. Rural Res. Policy **5**(2), 1–21 (2010)
9. Caffery, L., Manthey, K.: Automatic message handling for a national counselling service. In: The Success and Failure in Telehealth, Brisbane, Australia (2004)
10. Cox, P., Scott, R.: The Official Report of the 1st Asia Pacific Forum on Quality Improvement in Health Care (2002). http://www.adc.bmjjournals.com

11. Enson, T., Cooper, S.: Overcoming barriers to healthcare service access: influencing the demand side. Health Policy Plann. **19**, 69–79 (2004)
12. Eyesan, O.L., Okuboyejo, S.R.: Design and implementation of a voice-based medical alert system for medication adherence. Procedia Technol. **9**, 1033 (2013)
13. Farhaan, M., Norris, T., Stockdale, R.: Mobile technologies and the holistic management of chronic diseases. Health Inform. J. **14**, 309–321 (2008)
14. Fortunati, L.: The mobile phone: new social categories and relationships. In: Seminar 'Sosiale Konsekvenser av Mobiltelefoni', Organised by Telenor, Oslo, 16th June (2000)
15. Franklin, V.L., Waller, A., Pagliari, C., Greene, S.A.: A randomized controlled trial of sweet talk, a text messaging system to support young people with diabetes. Diabet. Med. **23**, 1332–1338 (2006)
16. Gillette, B.: Wireless Technology Serves as Next Step in Care Service, Managed Healthcare Executive, pp. 54–55 (2004)
17. Golob, T.F., Reagan, A.C.: Impacts of information technology on personal travels and commercial vehicle operations: research challenges and opportunities. Transp. Res. C. **9**, 87–121 (2001)
18. Hanson, S.: The importance of the multipurpose journey to work in urban travel behaviour. Transportation **9**, 229–248 (1980)
19. Harkness, R.C.: Telecommunications Substitutes for Travel: A Preliminary Assessment. Longman Publishing Inc., Boston (1973)
20. Idowu, B., Ogunbodede, E., Idowu, B.: Information and communication technology in Nigeria: the health sector experience. J. Inf. Technol. Impact **3**, 69–76 (2003)
21. Idowu, P.A., Ajayi, S.A.: GSM based referral system for primary health care centres in Nigeria. Int. J. Soft Comput. Medwell J. **3**, 421–427 (2008)
22. Isola, S.: The Use of Mobile Telephone in Reducing Pre-Natal Maternal Mortality: Case Study of Abiye (Safe Motherhood) Project in Ondo State, South-West Nigeria (2012). http://www.ifranigeria.org/IMG/pdf/solaisola-case-study-abiye-project-repor.pdf
23. Kitamura, R., Nilles, J., Flemming, D., Conroy, P.: Telecommunication as a transportation planning measure: initial results of state California pilot project. Transp. Res. Rec. **1285**, 98–104 (1990)
24. Kwan, M.P., Weber, J.: Individual accessibility revisited: implications for geographical analysis in the twenty-first century. Geogr. Anal. **35**, 341–353 (2003)
25. Logan, A.G., McIsaac, W.J., Tisler, A.: Mobile phone-based remote patient monitoring system for management of hypertension in diabetic patients. Am. J. Hypertens. **20**, 942–948 (2007)
26. Memott, F.M.: The substitutability of communications for transportation. Traffic Eng. **33**, 20–25 (1963)
27. Odusote, A.O.: ICT for Public Health Care Delivery in Nigeria: Challenges, Opportunities and Milestones. In: The e-Nigeria Conference (2010)
28. Okafor, F.C.: Accessibility to general hospital in rural Bendel State. Nigeria. Soc. Sci. Med. **8**, 661–666 (1984)
29. Oritz, E., Clancy, C.M.: Use of information technology to improve the quality of health care in the United States. Health Serv. Res. **38**, 11–22 (2003)
30. Penchansky, R., Thomas, J.W.: The concept of access: definition and relationship to consumer satisfaction. Med. Care **19**, 127–140 (1981)
31. Peters, D.H., Garg, A., Bloom, G.: Poverty and access to healthcare in developing countries. Ann. New York Acad. Sci. **1136**, 161–171 (2008)
32. Pool, I.: Telecommunications/transportation trade-off. In: Atshuler, A. (ed.) Lexington Books, Lexington (1979)
33. Rogoski, R.R.: Wireless by design. Health Manag. Technol. J. **26**, 1–7 (2005)

34. Rudowski, R.: Impact of Information and Communication Technologies (ICT) on Health Care. Department of Medical Informatics and Telemedicine, Medical University of Warsaw, Poland (2008)
35. Samuel, J.K.: Can mobile telecommunication reduce intra-city work travels? empirical evidence from a third world city. Ibadan J. Soc. Sci. **6**, 1 (2008)
36. Taylor, P.J.: Distance transformation and distance decay function. Geogr. Anal. **3**, 221–238 (1971)
37. Taylor, P.J.: Distance Decay in Spatial Interactions. CATMOG 2. Geo Books, Norwich (1983)

Quality of Hypertensive Patients' Electronic Health Records in Specialized Cardiological Centre: 6-Year Trends

Anna Semakova[1]([✉]), Nadezhda Zvartau[2], Ekaterina Bolgova[1], and Aleksandra Konradi[2]

[1] ITMO University, Saint Petersburg, Russia
a.a.semakova@gmail.com, katerina.bolgova@gmail.com
[2] Almazov Federal North-West Medical Research Center, Saint Petersburg, Russia
{zvartau,konradi}@almazovcentre.ru

Abstract. Electronic health records (EHRs) have the potential to form the basis for a personalized approach to patient management, deliver high-quality care, and make the healthcare system more efficient and safer. Finding and studying the possible trends and long term changes of individual results in stored medical data may facilitate selection of an optimal treatment plan. Moreover, guidelines on disease management usually include only shifted results of clinical trials that are poorly generalized to routine clinical practice. In numerous EHR-related errors have been described, such as unstructured data, missing data, and incorrectly entered data. This study aims to assess the quality of hypertensive patients' EHRs during 6 years after the implementation of EHRs in the specialized cardiological centre. The quality of patients' EHRs was estimated by the completeness and consistency of stored data. We compared information entered into EHRs with diagnostic algorithms recommended by hypertension management guidelines. The results demonstrated the incompleteness and inconsistency of information in EHRs on risk factors, diabetes mellitus (DM), and subclinical organ damage. An assessment of six-year trends showed that the quality of data decreased in parallel with increase of workload of the clinic (estimated by the number of primary visits). Results indicate the urgent need for an action plan to resolve the problem of data incompleteness and inconsistency. Integration of specially designed clinical decision support system (CDSS) considered as a possible decision promoting an increase of EHRs quality. This study is part of a larger project aimed to develop of complex CDSS on cardiovascular disorders for medical research centre.

Keywords: Electronic health records · Risk factors · Diabetes mellitus · Subclinical organ damage · Completeness and consistency of information · Learning curves · Statistical data analysis

1   Introduction

Electronic health records (EHRs) may promote the introduction of a personalized approach to patient management and make the healthcare system more efficient. Finding and studying the possible trends and long term changes of stored patient medical information

© Springer International Publishing AG 2016
A.V. Chugunov et al. (Eds.): DTGS 2016, CCIS 674, pp. 544–552, 2016.
DOI: 10.1007/978-3-319-49700-6_54

facilitates the selection of an individualized optimal diagnostic treatment plan. EHR in its ideal form for patient care is a longitudinal record of patient health information generated by multiple encounters in any care delivery setting [2, 9]. If an EHR is fully implemented, reuse of EHR data may be extremely helpful in supporting clinical research [5, 12, 15]. Integration of clinical research data with patient clinical data may provide a better understanding of true individual health status, clinical trials feasibility, etc. [6].

However, there are many obstacles to be overcome in using EHRs for clinical research [7, 14, 16]. Data quality (completeness, consistency) is another challenge for the reuse of EHR data [3, 4, 8]. A number of EHR-related errors, such as unstructured data, missing data, and incorrectly entered data, lead information incompleteness and inconsistency. These limitations currently prevent the optimal use of EHR patient data and information, and impede the advancement of medical research, the improvement of healthcare, and the enhancement of patient safety [1, 17].

In our research, we used a methodology for estimating the quality of patient EHRs, based on an assessment of the completeness and consistency of stored data. We assessed the completeness and consistency of data according to predefined in hypertension guideline risk factors and subclinical organ damage [13]. These data should be present in all hypertension patients as they are necessary for evaluation of prognosis and choice of optimal treatment strategy.

2   Current Study

2.1   Data Description

In our study, we used the depersonalized EHRs of patients referred to a specialized cardiological centre due to uncontrolled arterial hypertension (AH) during 6 years period (from 2010 to 2015). EHR represents the case history of a patient and contain information about all patient visits to the cardiological centre, complaints, results of examination, and prescribed investigations and treatment. We included only patients with an initial diagnosis of AH, which means that high blood pressure was the main reason for referral to the cardiological centre and a hypertension management algorithm had to be applied to develop a diagnostic and treatment plan.

In the current study, we focused on information filled by the treating physician during primary outpatient visit. The information in EHRs for outpatient visits contains following data:

- *general information about patient* such as age, gender, etc.;
- *anamnesis vitae and anamnesis morbid, medical examination by a doctor:* anamnesis vitae with family history of premature cardiovascular diseases (CVD), information about bad habits (smoking and drinking), complete history of the development of current condition, blood pressure level, height, weight, results of medical examination by a doctor, etc.;
- *recommendations:* diagnosis and prescriptions;
- *various medical events or procedures:* test results, instrumental investigations and other procedures.

2.2   Current Hypertension Guideline Criteria

According to current guidelines, 10-year risk of cardiovascular death should be estimated in each hypertensive patient and reassessed regularly. The risk is predicted by the severity of hypertension (the increase of blood pressure level), presence of risk factors, subclinical organ damage or clinically manifest cardiovascular and other diseases (DM, end-stage renal disease). Risk factors include blood pressure level (>140/90 mm Hg or intake of antihypertensive medications), male sex, age (men $\geq$ 55 years; women $\geq$ 65 years), dyslipidemia (lipids disorder), high glucose level, obesity (body mass index (BMI) $\geq$ 30 kg/m^2), smoking and family history of premature CVD (men aged < 55 years; women aged < 65 years); subclinical organ damage – left ventricular hypertrophy (LVH) by ECG and ECHO data, estimated Glomerular filtration rate (eGFR), microalbuminuria (30–300 mg/24 h) or albumin–creatinine ratio (30–300 mg/g; 3.4–34 mg/mmol), DM – glucose and glycated haemoglobin (HbA1c) [11].

2.3   Quality of Hypertensive Patients' EHRs Definition

In our study we assessed the quality of information in hypertensive patients' EHRs. *Quality of information* was estimated only by completeness and consistency of information about risk factors (age and gender are not included as they are automatically entered in demographic part of case history), DM and subclinical organ damage. We assessed *completeness* as compliance of data about risk factors and subclinical organ damage with current guidelines. This means that EHRs contained any information about *all* required risk factors, subclinical organ damage or both (in the history of the disease, diagnosis or test results). The term *consistency* was used for evaluation of the *logic* and the *lack of contradiction* with current guidelines of data about specific factors. For instance, for dyslipidemia, or DM confirmatory test results were required, or appropriate referrals for analysis recommended in the prescription field.

The risk factors or subclinical organ damage were defined as evaluated if the results of previous examinations were provided in the case history, or when the physician referred the patient to appropriate investigation (for instance, creatinine level for eGFR estimation). DM and risk factors such as dyslipidemia, and glucose tolerance disorder were extracted by automated data mining from the field 'Diagnosis'. Data about statins therapy was extracted from prescriptions and compared with guideline recommendations.

2.4   EHR Mistakes

For the analysis we used only initial reception records. We analyzed 32 158 records (first year: 5862, second year: 5160, third year: 4705; fourth year: 4731, fifth year: 5368, sixth year: 6332). We determined nine classes of the most common mistakes in the assessment of risk factors, DM, subclinical organ damage:

1. Information about dyslipidemia was recorded in the diagnosis field in 49.9% (16037) of primary visits and in 94.2% (15106) it was not confirmed by test results. Moreover,

among all patients diagnosed with dyslipidemia, only 58.5% (9389) received statin treatment.

2. Information about dyslipidemia was absent (in diagnosis field, previous test results data) in 46.8% (15039) of the patients. Furthermore, 67.1% (10084) of them were not further referred for lipid profile evaluation and in 14.8% (1491) statins were prescribed to patients without disclosing information about indications for lipid-lowering therapy. Assessment of only cholesterol level was recommended in 6.4% (644) of cases.

3. In 2.4% (787) of the cases the test results revealed abnormal lipid profiles, but dyslipidemia was not registered in the diagnosis field. Statins were not prescribed to 79.3% (624) of these patients, though they were recommended according to current guidelines.

4. Information about glucose tolerance disorder was present in 4.5% (1432) of records, but in 92.8% (1329) of cases was not confirmed by the information about abnormal test results.

5. Information about glucose metabolism was absent (in diagnosis field, previous tests results data) in 90.2% (29011) of the patients. Moreover, 99.7% (28920) of them were not further referred for glucose and HbA1c evaluation. Assessment of only glucose level and only HbA1c level was recommended in 5.4% (1551) and 1.7% (483) of cases, respectively.

6. Information about BMI was present in 87.6% (28179) of records.

7. Information about LVH, eGFR and microalbuminuria was absent in 42.4% (13640), 76.5% (24590) and 99.2% (31916) of the patients, respectively. This means that previous test results were not provided in the case history, and referral to appropriate investigation was not recommended.

8. Information about DM was present in 15% (4818) of records, but in 94.5% (4555) of cases were not confirmed by the abnormal test results.

9. In DM patients, assessment of only glucose level and only HbA1c level was recommended in 5.6% (1446) and 1.3% (380) of cases, respectively.

Risk factors such as smoking and family history of premature CVD were evaluated in all patients.

2.5   Statistical Data Analysis

Completeness and consistency of data may increase with time and experience of EHR system usage (learning curves). We assessed 6-year trends in the proportion of patients without complete assessment of risk factors (dyslipidemia, increased glucose level, BMI). Results are presented in Fig. 1.

There were no statistically significant changes in the proportion of patients without complete assessment of risk factors from 2010 till 2013. While during 2013-2015 there was a statistically significant at accepted level = 0.05 increase by 108% ($R^2 = 0.99$; $p = 0.05$) of cases with incomplete risk factors assessment. This indicates that the quality of patient EHRs estimated by the completeness and consistency of information about risk factors significantly decreased since 2013.

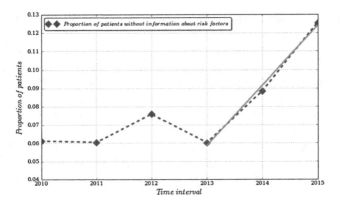

Fig. 1. Six-year trends in proportion of patients with incomplete assessment of risk factors

Six-year trends in the proportion of patients with dyslipidemia, but without recommendations for treatment with statins (for lowering of lipids level and improving of prognosis) in the prescription field are presented in Fig. 2.

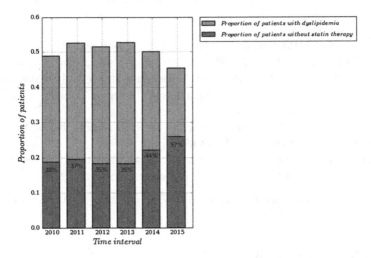

Fig. 2. Six-year trends in proportion of patients with dyslipidemia but without recommended statin therapy

During 2010–2013 the proportion of patients with dyslipidemia not on statin therapy was statistically significant at accepted level = 0.05 reduced by 9% ($R^2 = 0.97$; $p = 0.01$). While during 2013–2015 there was a statistically significant at accepted level = 0.05 growth by 64% ($R^2 = 0.99$; $p = 0.05$). So again, the completeness of data about dyslipidemia and statin therapy significantly decreased since 2013.

We assessed 6-year trends in the proportion of patients without complete assessment of subclinical organ damage. Results are presented in Fig. 3.

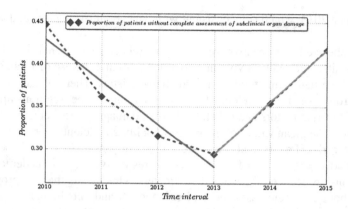

Fig. 3. Six-year trends in proportion of patients with incomplete assessment of subclinical organ damage

From 2010 to 2013 there was a statistically significant at accepted level = 0.05 descent in patients with incomplete assessment of subclinical organ damage by 34% ($R^2 = 0.93$; $p = 0.04$). But again, since 2013 there was a statistically significant at accepted level = 0.05 increase by 42% ($R^2 = 0.99$; $p = 0.01$). This means that the quality of patient EHRs estimated by the completeness and consistency of information about subclinical organ damage significantly decreased since 2013 compared to 2012–2013 time interval.

We assessed 6-year trends in the proportion of patients with DM without appropriate assessment or confirmatory test data (results of evaluation of fasting glucose level, HbA1c level or referrals to laboratory). Results are presented in Fig. 4.

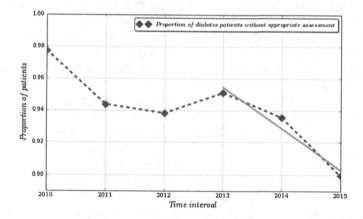

Fig. 4. Six-year trends in proportion of diabetes patients without appropriate assessment of glucose metabolism

There were no statistically significant changes in 2010–2013, while during 2013–2015 there was a statistically significant at accepted level = 0.15 reduction by 6% ($R^2 = 0.95$; $p = 0.14$). This means that the quality of patient EHRs about DM significantly increased since 2013, which is inconsistent with data about risk factors and subclinical organ damage.

We hypothesized that negative trends may be related to an increase in the number of primary visits. The samples volume was very small and the use of probability laws may lead to a shifted estimate of statistical characteristics. Therefore, we used coefficients of proportionality of elements for estimation of the relationship between completeness of risk factors and subclinical organ damage assessment, and number of primary visits. The mean values of the proportionality coefficients were approximately equivalent for risk factors and subclinical organ damage ($k_1 = 1.02$; $k_2 = 1.18$; $\Delta = \pm0.16$ and $k_1 = 1.02$; $k_2 = 1.00$; $\Delta = \pm0.02$, respectively). Results demonstrated a direct relationship between the studied parameters. This means that the proportion of patients without complete assessment of risk factors and subclinical organ damage increased in parallel with the workload of the clinic (estimated by the number of primary visits due to uncontrolled hypertension).

3   Discussion and Future Works

Results demonstrated that the EHRs without CDSS provides only incomplete and inconsistent information on risk factors, subclinical organ damage and DM. Interestingly, during first three years after implementation of EHRs there was increase in the completeness and consistency of entered data, indicating the existence of learning curves with experience of usage. While after 2013 there was a dramatic progressive drop in the completeness and consistence of stored data. One of the possible explanations is the increase in workload. This theory is confirmed by direct relationships between quality of assessment of risk factors and subclinical organ damage, and number of primary visits. Although we failed to find more factors explaining this phenomenon, we will continue our efforts in defining other regulatory, social or economic reasons for such dramatic deterioration of quality of EHR information after 2013. We will continue research on the quality of hypertensive patients EHRs data on treatment and drug therapy. It is of interest to establish whether the negative trends after 2013 will also affect the quality of drug treatment data.

The collection of detailed clinical information about reported cases, which is necessary for confirmation of the diagnosis and determinations of disease-related risk factors and subclinical organ damage, is still heavily dependent on manual processes implemented by a physician. In order to improve of the quality of data entered in EHRs, we are developing CDSS. This CDSS will be integrated with EHRs system. The CDSS will be able to integrate the heterogeneous data sources implementing semantic description and unification of reporting data (data/information fusion). The architecture of data-driven CDSS was developed on the basis of the approach proposed earlier in [10]. The main three parts of the CDSS are decisions support module, rule base, and knowledge base. Decisions support module, which will be the core of the CDSS, will provide the functional of pre-processing, filtering, and expansion data, stored in EHRs. These functions provides assessment completeness and consistent of information by means of rule base. Rule base will be filled on the basis of current hypertension guidelines. In addition, decisions support module should provide formation of knowledge base, focused on completeness and consistent of clinical data, and medical records similar precedents. Using EHRs for clinical research requires the completeness and consistency of data in EHRs, so a properly designed CDSS may be a key success factor.

4   Conclusion

In summary, results demonstrated that the quality of information about risk factors, subclinical organ damage and DM, stored hypertensive patients' EHRs, is mostly incomplete and inconsistent. Six-year trends revealed that the quality of hypertensive patients' EHRs has a tendency to deteriorate with an increase in workload (estimated by the number of primary visits). Experience with working in EHRs system has some positive impact, but it disappears with an increase in workload. We assume the CDSS, which we are developing, implementing rule-based, data-driven, knowledge-based, and hybrid approaches, will be able to improve the quality of hypertensive patients' EHRs in the cardiological medical research centre. The learning curves could be used to validate the quality of hypertensive patients' EHRs after the introduction of CDSS.

Acknowledgments.   This paper is financially supported by The Russian Scientific Foundation, Agreement #14-11-00826 (10.07.2014).

References

1. Birkhead, G.S., et al.: Uses of electronic health records for public health surveillance to advance public health. Annu. Rev. Public Health **36**, 345–359 (2015). doi:10.1146/annurev-publhealth-031914-122747
2. Coorevits, P., Sundgren, M., Klein, G.O., Bahr, A., Claerhout, B., Daniel, C., et al.: Electronic health records: new opportunities for clinical research. J. Intern. Med. **274**(6), 547–560 (2013). doi:10.1111/joim.12119
3. Cruz-Correia, R., Rodrigues, P., Freitas, A., Almeida, F., Chen, R., Costa-Pereira, A.: Data quality and integration issues in electronic health records. In: Hristidis, V. (ed.) Information Discovery on Electronic Health Records, pp. 55–95. CRC Press, London (2009)
4. De Moor, G., et al.: Using electronic health records for clinical research: the case of the EHR4CR project. J. Biomed. Inform. **53**, 162–173 (2015). doi:10.1016/j.jbi.2014.10.006
5. Dugas, M., Lange, M., Muller-Tidow, C., Kirchhof, P., Prokosch, H.-U.: Routine data from hospital information systems can support patient recruitment for clinical studies. Clin. Trials **7**(2), 183–189 (2010). doi:10.1177/1740774510363013
6. Embi, P.J., Jain, A., Clark, J., Harris, C.M.: Development of an electronic health record-based clinical trial alert system to enhance recruitment at the point of care. In: AMIA Annual Symposium Proceedings, pp. 231–235 (2005)
7. Geissbuhler, A., Safran, C., Buchan, I., Bellazzi, R., Labkoff, S., Eilenberg, K., et al.: Trustworthy reuse of health data: a transnational perspective. Int. J. Med. Inform. **82**(1), 1–9 (2013). doi:10.1016/j.ijmedinf.2012.11.003
8. Holzer, K., Gall, W.: Utilizing IHE-based electronic health record systems for secondary use. Meth. Inf. Med. **50**(4), 319–325 (2011). doi:10.3414/ME10-01-0060

9. Jensen, P.B., Jensen, L.J., Brunak, S.: Mining electronic health records: towards better research applications and clinical care. Nat. Rev. Genet. **13**(6), 395–405 (2012). doi:10.1038/nrg3208

10. Kovalchuk, S.V., Knyazkov, K.V., Syomov, I.I., Yakovlev, A.N., Boukhanovsky, A.V.: Personalized clinical decision support with complex hospital-level modelling. Procedia Comput. Sci. **66**, 392–401 (2015). doi:10.1016/j.procs.2015.11.045

11. Mancia, G., et al.: 2013 ESH/ESC guidelines for the management of arterial hypertension: the task force for the management of arterial hypertension of the European Society of Hypertension (ESH) and of the European Society of Cardiology (ESC). Eur. Heart J. **34**(28), 2159–2219 (2013). doi:10.1093/eurheartj/eht151

12. Prokosch, H.-U., Ganslandt, T.: Perspectives for medical informatics - reusing the electronic medical record for clinical research. Meth. Inf. Med. **48**(1), 38–44 (2009). doi:10.3414/ME9132

13. Sittig, D.F., Singh, H.: Defining health information technology-related errors: new developments since to err is human. Arch. Intern. Med. **171**(14), 1281–1284 (2011). doi:10.1001/archinternmed.2011.327

14. Sundgren, M., Wilson, P., De Zegher, I.: Making the most of the electronic age. Eur. Pharm. Contractor **3**, 18–21 (2009)

15. Turisco, F., Keogh, D., Stubbs, C., Glaser, J., Crowley Jr., W.F.: Current status of integrating information technologies into the clinical research enterprise within US Academic Health Centers: Strategic value and opportunities for investment. J. Investig. Med. **53**(8), 425–433 (2005). doi:10.2310/6650.2005.53806

16. Weiskopf, N.G., Weng, C.: Methods and dimensions of electronic health record data quality assessment: Enabling reuse for clinical research. J. Am. Med. Inform. Assoc. **20**(1), 144–151 (2013). doi:10.1136/amiajnl-2011-000681

17. Zhou, L., et al.: The relationship between electronic health record use and quality of care over time. J. Am. Med. Inform. Assoc. **16**(4), 457–464 (2009). doi:10.1197/jamia.M3128

Adaptive Knowledge Representation in Online Health Communication

Svetlana Mishlanova, Eugenia Bogatikova, and Yaroslav Mishlanov[✉]

Perm State National Research University, Perm, Russia
mishlanovas@mail.ru, bogatikova.eugene@gmail.com,
sconymare@gmail.com

Abstract. Newer methods of communication have largely contributed to the transformations of contemporary health service delivery. Interactive online health resources, which have profoundly affected the way in which healthcare is delivered, and with this, have brought changes in the relationship between doctor and patient. In this study, we try to find out what the characteristics of electronic doctor-patient health communication are and how we can identify features of electronic doctor's advice that increase patient's confidence and understanding. By using online medical counseling discourse analysis to find out how patients talk about health-related topics and how doctors response them we describe adaptive discursive models the doctors use to provide them with information the patients can trust.

Keywords: Discourse · Health communication · Special knowledge · Knowledge transfer · Language modeling

1 Introduction

In the 70s, health communication became an exciting area to study, one which has continued to grow and diversify, due to a constantly increasing interest in attempts to improve the efficiency of doctor-patient communication, developing organizational and strategic procedures, studying intercultural features, and interpersonal perspectives [5, 10, 28–30]. Moreover, health communication regarded as a process of an individual acquiring and converting event data into meaningful or consumable information contributes greatly to diagnosis, cooperation, council, and education [7, 8, 23, 28, 35, 37].

Despite the fact that heath communication standards are improving every day, it has become almost automated and impersonal, and there are even special decision making systems that quite effectively help to provide medical aid [2, 6, 16, 17, 27], verbal modeling of knowledge transfer is regarded to be a central issue in doctor-patient communication. It is the knowledge transfer modeling that is defined as a mechanism by which health messages are communicated from experts in the medical and public health fields to the people who can be helped by these messages.

A cognitive-discursive approach served as a methodological basis of this study. It allows modeling the cognitive mechanism of verbalization of knowledge that is involved

© Springer International Publishing AG 2016
A.V. Chugunov et al. (Eds.): DTGS 2016, CCIS 674, pp. 553–562, 2016.
DOI: 10.1007/978-3-319-49700-6_55

in the process of transfer and accumulation. Performing research in the cognitive-discursive paradigm of modern linguistics means to use complex methods to describe mental representations of special or non-special knowledge through the study of its conceptual framework and verbal form [1].

We also used methods of computational linguistics to carry out discourse analysis. Corpora analysis was accomplished on the basis of the platform "Semograph"[1], which provides a set of variables describing the context including metadata, semantic component analysis, compiling semantic fields, and a set of tools to present the results in frequency tables, semantic maps, and semantic graphs [3]. Processing the received information provides us with material for building speech models, which allow us to talk about differences in the communication participants' knowledge, the differences in its verbalization and possible ways of its decoding and encoding.

Discourse is an object of quite a number of interpretations exploring it in diverse ways. In the current study it is presented as a unity of language activity and its result, that is the text. Discourse is viewed as a complex phenomenon, realized in semiotic, conceptual and pragmatic communicative aspects of verbally mediated special activities [26, 34].

Medical discourse is a speech-and-cognitive activity in a special field where different types of knowledge are formed, accumulated and represented. Specialized discourse is a complex communicative formation, one of the types of institutional discourse, by which we mean a specialized kind of communication between people who may not know each other, but need to communicate in accordance with the norms of the society [11, 21, 22, 24, 25, 31, 33, 36]. The core of the institutional discourse is communication base pairs of participants of communication, in this case, a doctor and a patient [4, 38].

Since health communication is a kind of institutional type of discourse, it is characterized by the following features:

- Status-role relationships between participants of communication (patient, doctor)
- The purpose of communication (medical assistance: the definition of the optimal way of solving medical problems)
- Prototypical place of communication (a medical institution)
- Frame of medical reception (communication is carried out within a virtual consulting room, where the doctor and patient are in a relationship of communicative asymmetry: patients seek medical help, because doctors are more competent (they are experts), in advising a physician is guided by the standards of healthcare (Cambridge Calgary Guide, medical and economic standards, and others) [9].

It is common knowledge that a patient realizes his social role in personal and institutional spheres, speaking in the latter case as a client of a social institution. Types of situations in institutional communication are determined by the tasks of relevant institutions and in most cases are specifically stipulated in various regulations, laws, regulations, guidelines and so on. Personal communication is characterized by a fundamental openness of its borders. Within its framework there are stereotyped discursive rules based on the practical experience of the participants to communicate which determine

---

[1] http://semograph.com.

the specificity of the organization of a speech form. At the same time participants' experience of institutional communication is a polydiscoursive experience including experience in institutional discursive activities (visiting clinics, reading literature on any medical problem, access to pharmacists and so on for the patient/health counseling, training for doctors). As a result in the texts of health communication there can be detected speech patterns, roughly produced by both institutional (institutional speech models) and non-institutional discourses (personal speech models) [14, 15, 18, 19, 39].

2 Research Description

The aim of the current research is to determine speech and language models in the online health communication.

It should be noted that a speech model is a communicative and situational language model in the implementation of a specific situation of communication. Speech models differ from language models by lexical content, communication objectives and content of statements, logical stress and rhythmic intonation pattern determined by specific situation.

As communication is a two-way process, which presupposes knowledge transfer and knowledge acquisition, knowledge transfer is carried out in the discourse, it is a system of concepts that are in categorical relations. Knowledge is generated in the neurological system of the brain by means of extracting information from everyday experience of the individual interaction with the surrounding reality. The particular relevance of sharing and learning occurs when communication between an expert and non-expert takes place.

Special knowledge is a system of categorized concepts in human's brain, which are formed in professional activity. Special knowledge is mostly conscious, systemized, and shared by the members of an epistemic community; it is justified with the epistemic criteria or standards of the knowledge community, institutions or experts. Imparting special knowledge begins at the moment when an expert has to convey it to a non-expert in order to delegate his/her experience, skills, and insights effectively. It also emerges when a patient has to ask a doctor for this very special knowledge to get good advice and make his life better.

Knowledge asymmetry leads to ambiguity and this is exactly that problem which has to be resolved within the process of knowledge communication. Methods to study knowledge and experience verbalization deal with conceptualization and categorization processes. Since differences in experience lead to differences in knowledge and further to differences in its representation, the study of so-called translation mechanisms is of particular interest. Thus, representation of special/nonspecial knowledge in the discourse occurs in symbolic form at the surface level of the text and conceptual form at a deep level and it happens according to communicative-pragmatic purposes, which define solutions of the necessary communicative tasks.

The study is based on the material of interactive complexes that represent the communication between doctors and patients, taken from the US sites of medical counseling[2]. For the collection of the data there has been created a Python script, its functions are to parse the above-mentioned web pages, to search target elements (i.e. the title and the date of the patient's question, text of the question, the doctor's response etc.) and to save the collected data in the format which is suitable for its processing in Apache Sorl[3]. The total number of dialogues was 671[4].

In order to mobilize the material processing, we used the information system of graphosemantic modeling "Semograf", which is designed to extract the domain knowledge of the information files, including text samples, metadata, semantic components and semantic fields, frequency, language and thesaurus dictionaries.

3   Results

In the English language, the concept of pain is represented by three conventional versions: pain(s), ache(s), and headache.

The choice of language material was determined by the following factors. Pain is an existential concept of contradictory nature. On the one hand, pain is a universal object of human perception: any person at least once in his life has had this feeling. On the other hand, pain is highly an individual and introspective feeling inseparable from experiencing it and excluding any access to study it in a proper way. The only way to verify the pain for linguistics is its verbal description [12, 13].

---

[2] http://doctorspring.com/, http://evaidya.com/, http://onlineusadoctors.com/.

[3] http://lucene.apache.org/solr/.

[4] The typical example of an electronic doctor-patient health communication looks as following: **Question.** I've had a bad cold for several days, so I began drinking orange juice on Saturday. By Saturday night, my arms and hand were itching really bad. I took 2 Benadryl so I could sleep. I had a raspberry freezer pop for my throat as well. Sunday morning, I was still itching. I thought it was the raspberry freezer pop, so took more Benadryl. Long story short, I just realized that the only thing I've been eating or drinking since the itching began has been orange juice. I stopped the orange juice last night around 6 pm. Today, my hands arms and shoulders are still itching but it's not as bad. Before my legs and feet were itchy. Today my body still feels like my skin is crawling. Did I have an allergic reaction to orange juice and what should I do to make this stop? Do I continue with Benadryl? I'm at work and Benadryl makes me drowsy. How long does this last? Please help! **Answer.** Thank you for asking your query at DoctorSpring. Yes, this itching which you are experiencing can be a part of the allergic reaction to some of the ingredients in the orange juice. Since you have this history of allergy to food items and seasonal allergies it is quite possible that this is an allergic reaction. Orange juice can contain slight amount of salicylates (naturally). This component may be the culprit here. It is a good thing that you have stopped the orange juice consumption. I recommend you to take a balanced nutritious meal, which is allergy-safe from your experience. Go for the safes, non-allergic food as per you experience. Just take Benadryl for 1 more day (since when you stopped the orange juice). You can stop it and see how your body responds. If the itching still persists for more than 48 h, we need to look into other possible allergens. You may want to visit a Doctor too, in person. Hope this helps.

In our sample of the material, there were 193 dialogs on pain description that is 1/3 of the total material[5]. This phenomenon is explained by the fact that "a special place among the complaints takes the pain, as it is the most frequent complaint. Soreness disturbs the patient most of all and it is the direct cause for seeking medical attention right at the moment, it clearly characterizes the underlying disease and definitely belongs to his clinical picture" [20]. So, pain as the main symptom or as the main reason for going to the doctor is presented in 55 interactive complexes.

The discourse analysis reveals particular frameworks of the interactive complexes (Table 1).

Table 1. Frameworks of patient-doctor interactive complexes

Patients	Doctors
Greetings	Formal greetings
Background to the problem	*Agreement/disagreement*
Problem	*Possible options*
Guesses	*Additional questions*
'Please, help'	*Advice*
	'Consult with your GP'
	Formal goodbye

Usually the patients' discourse includes such fields as greetings, background to the problem, problem, guesses, recourse 'please, help'. Doctors' discourse is composed of more fields such as formal greeting, agreement/disagreement, possible options, additional questions, advice, compulsory recommendation 'consult with your GP', formal goodbye. The Italic type fields are the fields where the description of the medical problem can be found.

---

[5] There is an example of pain related dialog:

Question. I have pain under my lower left rib cage und back. I have had these symptoms for nearly a year and have recently had my gallstone removed, but the symptoms persist. The pain seems to peak in the early hours of the morning and wakes me up. **Answer.** Hello, Thank you for asking your query. Form your question I understand that you are having a rather troubling pain in the lower left rib cage und back. There are many possibilities for this pain but the ones I would like to consider are the following: 1. Musculoskeletal pain at ribs and intercostal muscles; 2. Lung/Pleural irritation; 3. Diaphragmatic irritation; 4. A splenic involvement; 5. Peptic Ulcer; 6. A pancreatic involvement; 7. A spine problem, with pain radiating. Now there is no need for any alarm. The way we go about finding the cause is a step by step approach and to rule out most common and not to miss causes. For that you will need to get few tests done with the help of your Physician. This will be a Chest Xray, Xray of spine AP and later, a Ultrasound of Abdomen, Complete Cholesterol study, S. Amilase, S. Lipase. This will rule out many possibilities and if needed further tests can be done. I am sure you many options for pain relief. Now I would recommend you to use an anti Ulcer drug (Pantoprazol/Omeprazol) in consultation with your Physician. This has to be taken just before sleep. If the pain has an ulcer component in it, this will help. Hope this helps. Please feel free to ask any follow-up questions.

Further analysis was carried out on the symptom descriptions of the given both by patients and the doctors. Language models of symptom representations of patients and doctors in interactive complexes as well as specialized knowledge transcoding models have been revealed in the study (Table 2).

Table 2. Language models of symptom representations in patient-doctor interactive complexes

Patient's discourse	Doctor's discourse	Transcoding model
Pain in neck	Neck pain	noun/noun + prep - > noun
Pain in chest	Chest pain	adjunct + noun
My neck	Your neck	1st PP + noun – > 2nd PP + noun
My chest	Your chest	
Chest pain	Gastro esophageal reflux/ Esophageal reflux + explanation	adjunct + noun – > term
Chest pain	Burning chest pain	adjunct + noun – > term
Chest pain	Repeated attacks of chest pain, especially burning type	adjunct + noun – > participle + noun + specification
Neck pain	It	adjunct + noun – > demonstrative pronoun

Among marked in the texts of the patient and doctor language patterns there were identified analogues, which we will consider the language patterns of the patient and doctor, respectively. This slide presents the text of the patient and the physician with the text selected in order to show their language patterns. According to the theory, the patient's words are regarded as a primary text, while text of the physician, in this case, is viewed as a secondary one (i.e., doctor, as an interpreter retells patient narrative, introducing some new logical sense and innovation). Thus, we deal with the semantic or grammatical shift, which results in the transcoding from one discourse to another within a single communicative situation.

As a result of the study we have identified six basic patterns of speech that have analogues in the speech of the patient and the doctor. Moreover, it should be noted that the shift can be performed in one direction, and in reverse one, so the data patterns are interchangeable for this type of communication. The next step was to combine the data to analyze the patterns of their composition and the study of language shift to create multiple models of speech activity in medical communications. Models are schematically indicated in the last column of the table on the slide.

There are several applications of these models; we call them "Models in Use". First of all, they project to develop natural language processing, multi-purpose speech recognition systems, machine translation, corpora annotation, etc. [32]. Disadvantages of traditional models (the language model based on the corpora date, for instance) lead to the need to develop alternatives, including statistical approaches to modeling languages, and, most importantly, speech, i.e. the main task is the ability to build models that simulate the communication, but not just recreate or decode standard language patterns. In modern English, in contrast, for example, from the Slavic languages, there are more opportunities to find and fix the analog speech patterns in communication, both manually and automatically. This is due, primarily, with a significantly smaller quantity of word forms for each word, as well as the presence of the correct word order. These features open new possibilities for researchers in creating, tracking and marking up language models based on statistical approaches, such as, for example, n-grams and their variations [32].

As our study was carried out manually and on the rather limited material, we had a possibility to consider not only grammar model (which can be useful for learning systems for automatically recognition of them on huge language corpora), but also models based on semantics, which always requires the intervention of an expert in the process of their recognition or assisting machine learning systems.

N-gram model from a semantic point of view is a sequence of sounds, syllables, words or letters. In practice, more commonly, N-gram as a series of words, including sustained phrases called collocation. Taking into account the existing data models in internet-mediated medical communication, it would be appropriate to use the n-gram model for the work of decision-making systems that could decode the speech of a patient and then generate a secondary text on its basis in order to optimize communication between doctors and patients.

In drawing up the language model of n-grams for this type of communication, several types of connections between objects, the subjects and their characteristics in the model should be taken into account. First, the unit should be morphologically consistent. Therefore, in this example, it corresponds to the form of the verb and the form of the noun/pronoun (chest burns, it aches, arms ache). Thus, it is obvious that the morphological information should be a very important part of the language model. Evidently, in such models the homonyms should consider: ache can be both a noun and a verb. Lexical aspect also has to be taken into account in the models: in spite of the fact that almost all the models can be interchanged on a bilateral basis (pain – it, and vice versa), the replacement of personal pronouns must occur due to the characteristics of the subject and object of communication ('my pain' may belong only for patient discourse while 'your pain' only for doctor discourse).

Among all selected models we only have one, decoding/recreation of which will be quite problematic. This applies to a model with a term. The fact that the appearance of the term in the discourse of the doctor/patient is connected with not only the language/speech factors, but, first of all, the peculiarities of conceptualization and categorization of reality. A doctor due to his/her professional experience and special knowledge, can bind non-specific information (burning type of pain in chest), which can be a complaint of a patient with any disease, i.e. medical problem, expressed in the language of the special vocabulary, which has, as a rule, the Greek or Latin origin (gastroesophageal reflux).

To work with the model of the conversion of one discourse type to another, we must specify all the necessary information on the form and content of a model taking into account all the data gathered from the communicants' speech patterns. For example, some researchers introduced the concept of categorical language model to determine all the properties of the model. This is applied, in particular, to attributes. Each attribute can have one of several features (e.g., features for the attribute "part of speech" are "noun", "adjective", "verb" and so on). In case when an attribute is meaningless for a given word, for example, an attribute "tense" for a noun, it gets special sign "undefined". This classification makes it possible to reproduce the desired pattern in the model without any errors.

For a doctor as a communicant, the choice of strategy of generating text in the framework of this activity is determined, on the one hand, by his individual experience, on the other – by his knowledge about the types of functioning in a given society at a given historical period, discourses, and a separate component of this knowledge is an idea of what kind of speech patterns in these discourses should be used, as well as possession of communicative norms which he must adhere to the standards when communicating with the patient.

4   Conclusion

On the bases of the obtained results, it can be said that different types of knowledge are explicated in discourse in a different way. As we have seen throughout this paper, specialized knowledge presents a higher level of abstraction, it presupposes taking into account the generic-specific relationships in the process of re-encoding the info and using the mechanisms of substitution naive data by scientific. While taking over the same events by different participants of medical communications there is dissimilitude in the representation of the concept of pain. Language modeling of knowledge transfer in medical communications can be carried out according to an n-gram model, where N corresponds to the number of language units in the model. Such a model should be built with taking into account the peculiarities that make the process more automated. We are confident that such knowledge transfer modeling will be enhanced in patient-centered health communication and that it is likely to prove its usefulness beyond the subject field of medicine.

Acknowledgements.   The research is funded by the Russian Foundation for Humanities (RFH) (projects № 16-13-59006 and № 16-16-59009).

References

1. Alekseeva, L.M., Mishlanova, S.L.: Medical discourse: theory and analyzing principles. Perm University Press, Perm (2002). (in Russian)
2. Barsalou, L.W.: Situated simulation in the human conceptual system. Lang. Cogn. Process. **18**, 513–562 (2003)
3. Belousov, K.I., Mishlanova, S.L., Zassedateleva, M.G.: Thesaurus modeling of the subject area «Competence-based approach»: research design and program realization on the IS «Semograph» base. Innovative Projects Programs Educ. **4**, 3–11 (2013). (in Russian)
4. Bigi, S.: Analyzing doctor-patient communication: methodological issues. Bull. suisse de linguistique appliquée **2**, 133–145 (2010)
5. Bigi, S.: Evaluating argumentative moves in medical consultations. J. Argumentation Context **1**(1), 51–65 (2012)
6. Boldyrev, N.N.: Knowledge representation in language system. Issues Cogn. Linguist. **4**, 17–27 (2007). (in Russian)

7. Brédart, A., Bouleuc, C., Dolbeault, S.: Doctor-patient communication and satisfaction with care in oncology. Curr. Opin. Oncol. **17**(14), 351–354 (2005)
8. Burt, J., Abel, G., Elmore, N., et al.: Assessing communication quality of consultations in primary care: initial reliability of the global consultation rating scale, based on the Calgary-Cambridge Guide to the medical interview. BMJ Open **4**, e004339 (2014). doi:10.1136/bmjopen-2013-004339
9. Calgary-Cambridge guides communication process skills (2013). http://communication4 integration.ca/wp-content/uploads/2013/05/CambridgeGuideHandout_Numbered_C4Iweb. pdf. Accessed 15 Nov 2015
10. Daud, A., Li, J., Zhou, L., Muhammad, F.: Knowledge discovery through directed probabilistic topic models: a survey. In: Proceedings of Frontiers of Computer Science in China, pp. 280–301 (2010)
11. van Dijk, T.A.: Discourse and Knowledge: A Sociocognitive Approach. Cambridge University Press, Cambridge (2014)
12. Ehlig, K.: The language of pain. Theoret. Med. **6**, 177–187 (1985)
13. Fiehler, R.: Erleben und Emotionalitä als Problem der Arzt-Patienten-Interaktion. In: Ehlich, K. (Hrsg.). Medizinische und therapeutische Kommunikation. Diskursanalytische Untersuchungen, pp. 41–45. Westdeutscher Verl, Opladen (1990)
14. Gagarina, E.Y.: Communicative behavior of virtual doctor's personality in medical internet-forum. Ph.D. thesis, Astrakhan (2015). (in Russian)
15. Geyer, M.: Das ärztliche Gespräch. Allgemein-psychotherapeutische Strategien und Techniken. Volk und Gesundheit, Berlin, Verl (1985)
16. Golovanova, E.I.: Introduction to Cognitive Terminology. Encyclopedia, Tchelyabinsk (2008). (in Russian)
17. Ha, J.F., Longnecker, N.: Doctor-patient communication: a review. Ochsner J. **10**, 38–43 (2010)
18. Hagihara, A., Tarumi, K.: Doctor and patient perceptions of the level of doctor explanation and quality of patient-doctor communication. Scand. J. Caring Sci. **20**(2), 143–150 (2006)
19. Harvey, K., Koteyko, N.: Exploring Health Communication: Language in Action. Routledge, NY (2013)
20. Kurtz, S.M., Silverman, J.D.: The Calgary-Cambridge referenced observation guides: an aid to defining the curriculum and organising teaching in communication training programmes. Med. Educ. **30**, 83–89 (1996)
21. Kurtz, S., Silverman, J., Draper, J.: Teaching and learning communication skills in medicine, 2nd edn. Radcliffe Medical, Oxford, San Francisco (2005)
22. Lee, R.G., Garvin, T.: Moving from information transfer to information exchange in health and health care. Soc. Sci. Med. **56**(3), 449–464 (2003)
23. Little, P., Everitt, H., Williamson, I., et al.: Observational study of effect of patient centredness and positive approach on outcomes of general practice consultations. BMJ **323**(7318), 908–911 (2001)
24. Maguire, P., Pitceathly, C.: Key communication skills and how to acquire them. BMJ **325**(7366), 697–700 (2002)
25. Makoul, G.: The interplay between education and research about patient-provider communication. Patient Educ. Couns. **50**, 79–84 (2003)
26. Mishlanova, S.L.: Metaphor in Medical Discourse. Perm University Press, Perm (2002). (in Russian)
27. Novodranova, V.F.: Cognitive analysis methods in LSP studies. Terminology Knowl. **3**, 11–19 (2013). (in Russian)

28. Parrott, R.: Emphasizing "communication" in health communication. J. Commun. **54**, 751–787 (2004)
29. Pleasant, A., Cabe, J., Patel, K., Cosenza, J., Carmona, R.: Health literacy research and practice: a needed paradigm shift. Health Commun. **15**(12), 1176–1180 (2015)
30. Rimal, R.N., Lapinski, M.K.: Why health communication is important in public health. Bull. World Health Organ. **87**, 247 (2009)
31. Roter, D.L.: Physician/patient communication: transmission of information and patient effects. Md State Med. J. **32**(4), 260–265 (1983)
32. Sheremetyeva, S.O., Osminin, P.G.: On methods and models of keyword automatic extraction. Bull. South Ural State Univ.: Ser. Linguist. **12**(1), 76–81 (2015). (in Russian)
33. Silverman, J., Kurtz, S., Draper, J.: Skills for Communicating with Patients, 3rd edn. Radcliffe, Oxford (2013)
34. Spranz-Fogasy, T.: Äztliche Kommunikation – Transfer diskursanalytischen Wissens in die Praxis In: Ehlich, K. (Hrsg.) Medizinische und therapeutische Kommunikation. Diskursanalytische Untersuchungen, pp. 143–55. Westdeutscher Verl, Opladen (1990)
35. Stewart, M.A.: Effective physician-patient communication and health outcomes: a review. CMAJ **152**(9), 1423–1433 (1995)
36. Thistlethwaite, J., Spencer, J.: Professionalism in Medicine. Radcliffe, Oxford (2008)
37. Thompson, T., Robinson, J., Anderson, D., Fedorovicz, M.: Health Communication: Where We Been and Where Can We Go? Applied Health Communication. Hampton Press Inc., Cresskill (2008)
38. Tongue, J.R., Epps, H.R., Forese, L.L.: Communication skills for patient-centered care: research-based, easily learned techniques for medical interviews that benefit orthopaedic surgeons and their patients. J. Bone Joint Surg. Am. **87**, 652–658 (2005)
39. Weinhold, C.: Kommunikation in Krankenhäsern. Ein Forschungsbericht über deutschsprachige Analysen der Gespräche zwischen Arzt und Patient und das Gesprächsverhalten des Pflegepersonals. Zs. f. Germanistik **3**, 674–684 (1991)

eScience: Big Data and Complex Calculations

Chunking in Dependency Model and Spelling Correction in Russian

Ivan Anisimov[1], Elena Makarova[2], and Vladimir Polyakov[3(✉)]

[1] Yandex, Moscow, Russia
ivananisimov2010@gmail.com
[2] Institute of Linguistics of Russian Academy of Sciences, Moscow, Russia
antaresselen@mail.ru
[3] NUST "MISIS", Moscow, Russia
pvn-65@mail.ru

Abstract. The present paper presents an overview of the syntactic model used for automated spelling correction. We chose chunking in dependency model as Russian syntax for several reasons, as we consider it having a great potential. First, it does not require a complete description of the syntactic model. Second, it is closer to the logical description than traditional syntax, Chomsky's model and Tesnière's syntax. Spelling correction in Russian texts became the pilot task for chunking in the dependency model suggested in the present paper. We tested the work of the program on a mini-collection based on 20 Twitter messages, which allowed us to demonstrate the advantages of the program as well as define the frames of future improvement.

Keywords: Chunking · Spelling correction · Tesnière's dependencies · Syntax · UIMA · JAVA · Russian

1 Introduction

Spelling correction, one of the most popular problems of natural language processing, has existed for over fifty years [5]. Nowadays, there are two main directions of work on automated spelling correction: (a) effective search for possible corrections of the word that is not found in the dictionary, and (b) selection of the best correction alternative using context [10].

Despite numerous studies dedicated to the automated spelling correction problem, some issues still remain unsolved, including, first of all:

- Choice of the best candidate in situations when a program finds several alternative corrections and fails to make a decision in the batch mode;
- Ungrammaticalness (neologisms, first names, surnames, company names, etc.) that does not present any difficulty for a human, but can considerably hinder the work of an automated corrector;
- Multilingual mode when a sentence contains words in two different languages.

The present research is aimed at building an automated spelling corrector supported by a syntactic model. Potentially, it will give an opportunity to make a decision in a batch

© Springer International Publishing AG 2016
A.V. Chugunov et al. (Eds.): DTGS 2016, CCIS 674, pp. 565–575, 2016.
DOI: 10.1007/978-3-319-49700-6_56

mode in case the program generates several variants of correction. In such situations a syntactic model can provide an indispensable context, which is also used by a human corrector.

Using chunking for automated spelling correction seems especially promising for inflectional languages, where the number of potential corrections is usually high due to the appearance of numerous inflectional forms of the same word as candidates for the correction.

2 Syntactic Model

The most popular syntactic models are Chomsky's model [3, 4] and Tesnière's model [11, 12] (or the so-called dependencies). The program of chunking suggested in the present paper is based on the latter, as, firstly, Tesnière's model is intuitively closer to native speakers of languages with free word order, such as Russian [7, 8]. Secondly, the model of dependency trees is close to a logical notation.

The suggested chunking model contains description of each syntactic situation, which, unlike [6], is quite modest and includes only the most important data. The work on the model began with [1, 2], but, considering its years-long application, we introduced new heuristics into the chunking models aiming to improve the productivity of the program.

3 Chunking Pipeline

The program of spelling correction is written in Java in UIMA framework using the NLP@CLOUD library. Despite the shortcomings of the chosen tools (Java is slower than C/C++, and the UIMA library works slower than the library described in [13, 22]), it has a great advantage: the opportunities of portability and scaling in UIMA and JAVA are much wider. Thus, they seem much more perspective in future applications.

The input of the pipeline is a text in Russian. Its processing is implemented in eleven stages basing on Apache UIMA library [17]. The format of the output XML is described in [16].

Pre-processing. The pre-processing is performed with help of Apache Tika library [15]. This first stage of the algorithm includes text extraction ignoring all meta-information and identification of the language of the document.

Tokenization. The tokenization stage uses a finite-state machine generated with help of the JFlex analyzer [19]. It creates annotations RussianWord (sequence of letters of the Russian alphabet) and ComplexWord (sequence of letters of the Russian alphabet separated by a hyphen). The stage also includes text normalization.

Segmentation. Among all punctuation marks found at the stage of tokenization, the program searches for those indicating the end of a sentence (full stop, dots, exclamation marks, etc.) and divides the text into segments according to them detecting annotations Clause (one simple sentence).

The polysemy of comas is a stumbling block of many segmentation programs, because a coma in Russian can separate:

- clauses within compound and complex sentences,
- direct and indirect speech,
- homogeneous parts of the sentence,
- participles and participial phrases,
- parenthesis and addresses,
- some attributes and adverbials.

The segmentation stage was not realized in the current version of the program, which led to the following results: 72% of the collection cannot be properly processed without segmentation (cf. the Discussion Section). Thus, this stage is crucial for the chunking algorithm for Russian.

Morphologic Analysis. Morphological analysis is performed on the basis of OpenCorpora dictionary [21]. The program creates annotations Wordform (an inflectional grammar form of a word) and Word (a set of potential Wordforms).

The stage of morphological analysis is included in the pipeline, as Russian, being an inflectional and synthetic language, is very rich in inflectional morphology [14].

Synthesis of Potential Corrections. The synthesis of potential corrections is performed with help of Levenshtein automaton based on the morphological dictionary using Liblevenshtein program library [20]. The program detects all words that were not found in the morphological dictionary and generates all possible corrections with Levenshtein distance [6] equaling one step, or with a group of identical symbols being replaced by one such symbol (a phenomenon popular in Internet societies used to mimic the intonation of a word, e.g. *I'm soooooooo tired.*)

The program creates annotations CorrectedWord (a set of potential Words) that include all synthesized corrections.

Building an Expanded Grammar Tuple of Words. In order to facilitate the algorithmic processing of chunk lists and maintain the homogeneity of the syntactic structure of chunk trees we suggest a set of heuristics introduced at the stage of building of an expanded grammar tuple of words.

The program searches the whole text looking for: (a) prepositions, (b) particles *бы*, *ли*, *не*, *ни*, (c) conjunctions, (d) adverbs denoting quality and action intensification[1], and marks their presence in the grammar characteristics of the words they are attributed to. The above-listed auxiliary parts of speech and adverbs are further excluded from the lexical contents of the sentence and shifted to its grammar structure.

Search for the Subject and Predicate[2] of the Sentence. For each possible correction or combination of corrections generated at the stage of synthesis of potential correction, the program finds all possible pairs "subject-predicate" using the decision scheme. Each of these pairs forms a chunk which necessarily becomes the top in a potential

---

[1] We shall further call all the remaining words notional.

[2] Should not be confused with grammar subject in typology.

chunk tree. Noteworthy, any chunk tree can include only one chunk representing the probable subject and the predicate of a clause.

Forming a Set of Potential Chunks. Inside every clause the program builds connections between different Wordforms by adding them to the database with a description of all possible types of chunks and characteristics of their main and dependent word. All notional words in a clause are successively joined pairwise; and those pairs that meet the requirements of one of the possible chunk types from the database form a set of potential chunks. Due to the high homonymy of words and inflectional forms of Russian words, a lot of false chunk are likely to arise at this stage, but they will be eliminated at the stage of choosing the best chunk tree.

The result of this stage, realized using DBMS H2 [18], are annotations CorrectedChunk that include all possible combinations with the generated corrections.

Building a Set of Potential Chunk Trees. The program builds a graph that includes all chunks from the set generated at the previous stage[3]. Each potential chunk "subject-predicate" is the top of a tree, and each tree generated at this stage is a unique set of graph nodes.

Choice of the Best Chunk Tree. Among the set of all potential chunk trees the program choses the best – one, which includes most words from the clause. This tree becomes the annotation CorrectedChunkTree - a tree consisting of references to CorrectedChunk annotations.

Output of Results. All received corrections are sorted according to their place in the sentence forming sequential corrected intervals. The program joins them with intervals of uncorrected text (i.e. text that did not contain errors) and outputs the whole text into a resulting file in XML format.

Example of the Pipeline Work. Below is a fragment of the chunking program log for one simple sentence.

Input text: *Спортсмен *получиль удовольствие от *чемпионатат России*[4]
Levenshtein algorithm execution (the information in square brackets reflects the grammar characteristics of each generated correction):

---

[3] The work with graphs is executed by the means of the Java library.

[4] Here and further: Asterisk marks words with a spelling error.

Word missing in morph dictionary: получиль
Replacements: [

получил [[masc, sing, perf, tran, past, indc]]
получмиль [[inan, femn, plur, gent]]
получила [[femn, sing, perf, tran, past, indc]]
получили [[plur, perf, tran, past, indc]]
получило [[neut, sing, perf, tran, past, indc]]
получись [[sing, perf, intr, impr, excl]]
получить [[perf, tran]]
получишь [[sing, perf, tran, 2per, futr, indc]]
]
Word missing in morph dictionary: чемпионатат
Replacements: [

чемпионата [[inan, masc, sing, gent]]
чемпионатам [[inan, masc, plur, datv]]
чемпионатах [[inan, masc, plur, loct]]

]

Choice of the best chunk tree (the number in round brackets denoted the ID of the type of chunk from the "Type_of_chunks" Table from the database):

Спортсмен получил (15)
  получил удовольствие (37)
    удовольствие от чемпионата (128)
      от чемпионата России (138)

Output text: *Спортсмен получил удовольствие от чемпионата России* (The sportsman enjoyed Russian championship).

4   Decision Scheme

The decision scheme, designed for search for the subject and the predicate of the clause, presents a certain innovation. The scheme contains word pairs that can form potential main chunks of future trees. Thus, the program traverses the chunk graph (which includes both correct and false chunks) and marks several potential chunk trees according to the number of pairs "subject-predicate" found at the corresponding stage. Figure 1 illustrates the first fragment of the decision scheme. The phrases in square frames show what the program looks for in the clause. Circled are the potential subject and predicate, and an example of such pair.

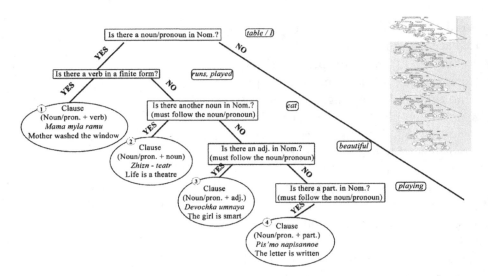

Fig. 1. Fragment of the decision scheme designed for search for potential subject and predicate of the clause

5   Structure of the Database "Chunking"

The database "Chunking" was created especially for the program described in the present paper. It contains a number of innovations and heuristics. First, as already mentioned above, the program realization of the database was executed in DBMS H2, which is characterized by its ability to store the database completely in the random-access memory. And this can considerably increase the execution speed of chunking program.

Second, we suggested a set of heuristics concerning the shift of grammar features of certain words and chunks (that are expressed lexically) to the feature space of the database. These heuristics are described in Sect. 3: Building an expanded grammar tuple of words. Thus, the chunk became two-member (consisting of the main and the dependent part). It allowed excluding the nodes, which perform an auxiliary function, from the graph. And the structure of the chunk tree became closer to the logic form.

6   Test Mini-Collection

Originally we planned to test the chunking program on a set of 3232 twits, which were manually collected for this purpose. We extracted sentences with spelling errors (they made some 30% from the initial set). As at the present time our pipeline does not have a segmentation stage, we excluded all sentences that necessarily require it, keeping about 16% of the original collection. Finally, we eliminated all sentences with offensive language and political issues, including politicians' names. As the result, there remained only 409 (13%) of all twitter messages.

The analysis of 100 sentences failed to give any examples of spelling errors that can be corrected using only one single-character edit. Thus, we decided to form an artificial mini-collection of 20 sentences in order to demonstrate the work of the program. Twenty Twitter-messages from the original collection were abridged so that they became simple sentences not requiring segmentation. We replaced proper names with nouns and personal pronouns and made 1–3 spelling mistakes that need one single-character edit. The resulting mini-collection is presented in Table 1.

Table 1. Collection of 20 test sentences

#	Twitter message from mini-collection
1	*Поруга *пасоветовала написать в администрацию школы.
2	Сколько сейчас *стит лицензионный *дсик Windows.
3	Где можно купить *меховый наушники в *Москв?
4	Кто *знат средства хорошие для *комбинированой кожи?
5	Какими *программаи вы чаще всего *пользуитесь сидя за компьютером?
6	На *деньк рождения подарили *детскйи конструктор.
7	Я *просыпаюс с мыслью *побрють кота *налысо.
8	Посоветуйте *мно профессиональный монитор для *ииииигр.
9	Сегодня нет *праздничноо настроения.
10	Хочу *сделаль наращивание *рестниц.
11	Коленка *чешится к *ольшой любви.
12	Что вам *нравиься в *вашх телефонах.
13	Меня дома застать невозможно *ыбло в воскресенье.
14	Спортсмен *получиль удовольствие от *чемпионатат России.
15	Взгляд много значит в *наший *жизн.
16	Мы *слушам сейчас *записи со времен *шоклы.
17	Где в Питере найти *стонку экскурсионного *автобусэ?
18	Я нашел это *пасхальнае яйцо.
19	*Мй ребенок очень *любь прогулки по лужам весной.
20	*Ништо не *смогет отнять меня у меня.

Processing of this collection by the chunking program showed the following results.

Four sentences (20%) underwent the right correction, for example[5]:

Input text: *На *деньк рождения подарили *детскйи конструктор.*

Levenshtein algorithm execution:

---

[5] The complete log of the mini-collection processing is available online at https://cloud.mail.ru/public/3dEL/shZZiwcKt.

Word missing in morph dictionary: деньк

Replacements: [

день [[inan, masc, sing, nomn], [inan, masc, sing, accs], [sing, perf, tran, impr, excl]]

денек [[inan, masc, sing, nomn], [inan, masc, sing, accs]]

денька [[inan, masc, sing, gent]]

деньке [[inan, masc, sing, loct]]

деньки [[inan, masc, plur, nomn], [inan, masc, plur, accs]]

деньку [[inan, masc, sing, datv]]]

Word missing in morph dictionary: детскйи

Replacements: [

детски [[]]

детский [[masc, sing, nomn], [inan, masc, sing, accs]]]

Choice of the best chunk tree:

Best tree:

На день рождения (37)

  рождения подарили (15)

    подарили конструктор (37)

      конструктор детский (1)

Output text: *На день рождения подарили детский конструктор* (They gave [me] a children's construction set on [my] birthday)[6].

Five sentences (25%) were corrected wrongly, as at the stage of building the chunk tree the program failed to resolve the polysemy of corrected words. Editorial correction suggested more than one variant, and all these variants met the requirements of syntactic agreement (see example below).

Input text: *Посоветуйте *мно профессиональный монитор для *ишшигр.*

Fragment of program log with morphological analysis of generated corrections:

ано [anim, masc, sing, Sgtm, Fixd, datv, Name]

мне [sing, datv, 1per]

Best tree:

Посоветуйте ано (37)

  ано профессиональный (12)

    профессиональный монитор (219)

      монитор для игр (128)

Output text: *Посоветуйте ано профессиональный монитор для игр* (Recommend Ano a professional computer monitor for games).

---

[6] Despite a mistake in chunk (15) of the tree, the program chose the right corrections.

Ten sentences (50%) were corrected wrongly, because the program chose false chunks, and, as a result, the final chunk tree was incorrect. As the rule, the reason for this situation is contained in the database "Chunking", and in further work this bug will be fixed. An example of the wrong correction is presented below.

Input text: *Я нашел это *пасхальнае яйцо.*

Word missing in morph dictionary: пасхальнае
Replacements: [
  пасхальна [[femn, sing, Qual]]
  пасхальная [[femn, sing, nomn, Qual]]
  пасхальнее [[Qual]]
  пасхальное [[neut, sing, nomn, Qual], [neut, sing, accs, Qual]]
  пасхальные [[plur, nomn, Qual], [inan, plur, accs, Qual]]

Best tree:
Я нашел (15)
  нашел яйцо (37)
    яйцо это (1)
      это пасхальная (233)

Output text: *Я нашел это пасхальная яйцо* (I found this: SING, NEUT, Easter: ADJ, SING, FEM egg: NOUN, SING, NEUT).

One sentence (5%) were corrected wrongly due to both errors described above. The program failed to make the right decision between two correction variants with the same grammar characteristics, and built a false resulting tree.

7 Discussion

About 70% of 3232 sentences from the initial collection of Twitter messages require the stage of segmentation, which was not realized in the current version of the pipeline. Such percentage testifies to the high importance of segmentation in the algorithm of chunking.

As a result, we were forced to reject this collection and create another mini-collection basing on some sentences from the original Twitter messages in order to test the suggested pipeline. The processing of this mini-collection showed that syntax can play an important role in spelling correction, but only under certain circumstances.

Spelling mistakes were corrected right in 20% of the sentences, which means that the suggested method does work.

The analysis of the errors in the execution of spelling correction program showed that the reason for the big number of mistakes (50%) is shortcomings of the database "Chunking", which will be eliminated in further work. As for the inability of the program to resolve syntactic polysemy (20% of mistakes), this can be fixed only by adding semantic context, i.e. there is little hope for the progress in the near future.

8   Conclusion

The suggested chunking model uses Tesnière's syntactic theory [11, 12] (theory on dependency trees). As opposed to Melchuk's syntax [7, 9], we introduced a number of heuristics into chunk description. Particularly, we suggested creating an expanding tuple of the word: lexically expressed grammar features (prepositions as case markers, particles бы, не, ни, ли, some adverbs serving as action or quality intensifiers, homogeneous parts of the sentence and compound verbs) are shifted from dependency trees to a word or chunk tuple. Thus, the chunk becomes two-member (main part and dependent part), and the chunk tree becomes more homogeneous, which increases the opportunities of its algorithmic processing.

Another innovation consists in the creation of a decision scheme designed for search for the subject and the predicate of a clause, basing on which the program builds a set of competitive trees. The description of 244 chunk types in the suggested notation is included in the database "Chunking".

Spelling mistakes are corrected by Levenshtein method. The program builds a sole graph consisting of all possible chunks from the sentence (both correct and false chunks) and forms a set of uncontroversial trees. Finally, it defines the tree, which includes most words from the original sentence, as the best chunk tree. In order to fasten the execution of the chunking program, we used DBMS H2, whose main advantage is ability to store the complete data in random-access memory.

The algorithm of the suggested program is created using NLP@CLOUD library, which has a number of advantages such as high portability and scalability due to the Java language. Realization of chunking in the dependency model in Russian offers a new view over the task of spelling correction. It allows, in particular, eliminating the possible alternatives generated by the system according to the morphological dictionary. As soon as we include the segmentation stage into the pipeline, we will be able to test the work of the program on a collection of real Twitter messages.

The chunking model suggested and described in the present paper is maximally close to a logic formula, i.e. it will integrate well with semantic ontologies.

In future we are planning to realize a similar chunking model for English and French.

Acknowledgement. The idea of the study and the heuristics belong to V. Polyakov. The database "Chunking" and the decision scheme for search for the subject and the predicate were developed by V. Polyakov and E. Makarova. The program was realized by I. Anisimov.

The research was supported by RSF grant # 15-11-10019.

References

1. Bushtedt, V.: Model of decision making based on syntactic analysis in tasks of patent information procession. Ph.D. paper, Specialty 05.13.01, "System analysis, information management and processing (in production)", defended in 2011 (2011). (in Russian)
2. Bushtedt, V., Polyakov, V.: Heuristics for Improvement of Partial Syntactic Analyzer Work. Scientific Notes of Kazan State University, vol. 151, no. 3, pp. 214–228 (2009). (in Russian)
3. Chomsky, N.: Syntactic Structures. Mouton, The Hague (1957). (Reprint: Chomsky N. Syntactic Structures. De Gruyter Mouton (2002). ISBN 3-11-017279-8)
4. Chomsky, N.: Three models for description of language. IRE Trans. Inf. Theor. **IT-2**, 113–124 (1956)
5. Damerau, F.J.: A technique for computer detection and correction of spelling errors. Commun. ACM **7**(3), 171–176 (1964)
6. Levenshtein, V.I.: Binary codes capable of correcting deletions, insertions, and reversals. Sov. Phys. Doklady **10**(8), 707–710 (1966)
7. Melchuk, I.: Levels of dependency in linguistic description: concepts and problems. In: Ágel, et al. (ed.) Dependenz und Valenz, vol. I, pp. 170–187. Walter de Gruyter, New York (2003)
8. Melchuk, I., Pertsov, N.: Surface Syntax of English: A Formal Model Within the Meaning-Text Framework. Benjamins, Amsterdam (1987). ISBN 90-272-1515-4
9. Sannikov, V., Boguslavky, I., Iomdin, L., Yu, A.: Theoretic Problems of Russian Syntax. Languages of Slavic Cultures (Yazyki Slavyanskih Kultur) (2010). 408 pages. (in Russian)
10. Sorokin, A.A., Baytin, A.V., Galinskaya, I.E., Shavrina, T.O.: Spellrueval: the first competition on automatic spelling correction for Russian. In: Proceedings of the Annual International Conference "Dialogue", Issue 15 (2016)
11. Tesnière, L.: Dependency Syntax: Theory and Practice. SUNY Press, Albany (1988). 428 pages
12. Tesnière, L.: Elements of Structural Syntax, 2nd edn. Klincksieck, Paris (1959). Reviewed and Corrected. ISBN 2-252-02620-0. (in French). Re-edition of: Tesnière, L.: Éléments de syntaxe structurale, Klincksieck, Paris (1959). ISBN 2-252-01861-5
13. Vydrin, D., Polyakov, V.: Realization of electronic dictionary based on N-Grams. In: Proceedings of III International Scientific-Practical Conference "Artificial Intelligence – 2002", vol. 2, pp. 79–84. Institute of Problems of Artificial Intelligence, Kacevelli (2002). (In Russian)
14. Zaliznyak, A.A.: Grammar Dictionary of Russian. Inflection. Russky Yazyk, Moscow (1977). (in Russian)
15. Apache Tika: The Apache Software Foundation. https://tika.apache.org
16. Apache UIMA Documentation: The Apache Software Foundation. https://uima.apache.org/uimafit.html#Documentation
17. Apache UIMA Project. http://uima.apache.org/
18. H2, the Java SQL Database. http://www.h2database.com/html/main.html
19. JFlex Lexical Analyzer. http://jflex.de/
20. Liblevenshtein program library. https://github.com/universal-automata/liblevenshtein-java
21. OpenCorpora dictionary. (in Russian). http://opencorpora.org/dict.php
22. Vydrinm, D.: Programs for morphological analysis. http://macrocosm.narod.ru/madown.html

The Process of Personal Identification and Data Gathering Based on Big Data Technologies for Social Profiles

Alexey Y. Timonin[✉], Alexander S. Bozhday, and Alexander M. Bershadsky

Penza State University, Krasnaya Street, 40, 440026 Penza, Russia
c013s017b301f018@mail.ru, bozhday@yandex.ru, bam@pnzgu.ru

Abstract. Currently, the problem of efficient gathering and analysis of hetero-geneous data from public Internet sources is relevant to many companies working with social issues. Also it applies to the task of building a social profile for the subsequent person identification. This paper addresses the issues of direct and indirect identification a person on the Internet as well as data structure development to store the static and dynamic information of a personal social profile. The article considers the basic options of personal network identification such as an identification by profiling data, IDs, personal websites and blogs, accounts in social networks, e-mail addresses and links from other resources. After identifying it is necessary to collect and structure the detected data about a person. For this purpose, the authors proposed a basic data structure divided into static and dynamic parts. The static part is represented in the form of a relational database and contains immutable data that uniquely identify a specific human (for example, name and surname, completed educational institutions, career, curriculum vitae etc.). The dynamic part is organized as a NoSQL store and accumulates all the information about the current human activity in the network (for examples, accounts in social networks, network friends, current preferences when buying products, preferences when visiting network resources, political and social beliefs etc.).

Keywords: Personal social profile · Public data sources · Social media · Unstructured data · Data analysis · Data gathering · Big data · Data mining

1 Introduction

Building a personal social profile is an important interdisciplinary task which can find its application in many spheres of human activity, such as a management of social processes, issues of artificial intelligence, searching and using contextual information, a human network activity research. The use of social profiles can be of great benefit for marketing and social researches, as well as searching for vacancies, and thematic communities' development (e.g. scientific conferences), or even detecting anti-terrorism activities. The task of constructing and analyzing a human social profile is achieved through the use of software systems for Big Data collection and analysis, tools for sharing NoSQL data stores and relational databases, methods of monitoring and analysis of social media.

© Springer International Publishing AG 2016
A.V. Chugunov et al. (Eds.): DTGS 2016, CCIS 674, pp. 576–584, 2016.
DOI: 10.1007/978-3-319-49700-6_57

2 Background

Researches in the field of social media analytics and Big Data technologies were carried out by many scientists.

Paul Eskesa, Marco Spruit and others are considering the usage of data from smartphones for social analysis in their publication called "The sociability score: App-based social profiling from a healthcare perspective" [3]. In the new article "A picture tells a thousand words-About you! User interest profiling from user generated visual content" [19] Quanzeng Youa, Sumit Bhatiab and Jiebo Luo engaged in studying user profiling based on non-textual data, but graphical content. "Using Social Network Analysis to profile people based on their e-communication and travel balance" [9] of P. Roy, A.J. Martinez, G. Miscione, M.H.P. Zuidgeest, M.F.A.M. van Maarseveen devoted to revealing the relationship between a personal interaction in social networks and a travel activity. Aaron C. Weidmana and Cheri A. Levinson consider a social anxiety appearance in their work "I'm still socially anxious online: Offline relationship impairment characterizing social anxiety manifests and is accurately perceived in online social networking profiles" [16].

Issues of social analytics based on Big Data, particularly linguistic features in the object description by different peoples, discussed in the works "New perspectives on gathering, vetting and employing Big Data from online social media: An interdisciplinary approach" of Teri Schamp-Bjerede, Carita Paradis, Kostiantyn Kucher, Andreas Kerren and Magnus Sahlgren [10], as well as "Big Questions for Social Media Big Data: Representativeness, Validity and Other Methodological Pitfalls" of Zeynep Tufekci [15]. It is also worth noting the publication "Big data privacy issues in public social media" of M. Smith, C. Szongott, B. Henne, G. von Voigt [12] and "The danger of big data: Social media as computational social science" of Andre Oboler, Kristopher Welsh, Lito Cruz [8].

Wenjie Wu and Jianghao Wang explore the interactions within the urban network [18], based on information obtained with use of Big Data technology. Rob Kitchin holds quite a similar study, presenting its' results in the publication "The real-time city? Big data and smart urbanism" [6].

In the article named "Does Social Media Big Data Make the World Smaller? An Exploratory Analysis of Keyword-Hashtag Networks" [4] A. A. Hamed and X. Wu describes the results of Milgram's experiment implementation on Facebook and Twitter networks. Work "Big Social Data and Social Media Analytics: Tools for exploring Social Media Engagement Behaviour" of R. Dolan, J. Conduit, J. Fahy, S. Goodman [2] demonstrate how social media data can be manipulated and analyzed by Facebook Insights and NCapture applications.

The analysis of similar works in this area has revealed insufficient study of the mathematical and technical formalization details of a personal social profile. This paper suggests a possible approach to the such formalization. It also discusses important issues related to specific areas of social networks analysis and Web mining.

3   The Problem of a Person Identification in the Internet

A social profile is an information set which could describe the social properties of a person in any way. This information must be clearly structured for ease of a human perception and subsequent automated processing.

The application area of social profiles derived from public information sources is quite broad. As already mentioned, it affects anti-terrorist activities, social analytics and forecasting, promotion of goods and services, personal search for social and scientific communities, development of artificial intelligence methods, individual adjustment of environment using the "Internet of things", etc.

A personal social profile is based on data from the Internet open sources. Identifying a person in the network is carried out through defining an occurrence points such as registration records (accounts) on Web resources which provide a range of opportunities for its use (e.g., write comments, receive newsletters, download files) and allocate a specific person from the mass of other network users. Furthermore, a social profile information can be retrieved from external Web resources, where the person may be referred to in any context without having a personal account.

Usually, a person may have many different web accounts. The search of links between them is a quite difficult task. In the best case, accounts have a binding to each other via special tokens, like Facebook, Twitter, LinkedIn, Google+ . This makes it much easier to search, because, firstly, there is a clear relationship and free transition between the accounts in this case, and secondly, a large part of the connected accounts' profile data (name, e-mail, ICQ, time zone, settings…) is the same.

Account binding to a specific e-mail address or phone number is the most common. Then accounts search is quite simple and will be produced by occurrences of the specified mail/phone on account profile pages.

But what will you do if the identified person has multiple e-mail addresses? In this case, these logins and aggregate profile data are checked for matching information, such as a list of contacts or friends. Upon such matches' detection it can also be useful to check the dates and locations of the entry points (e.g., repetitive access from single IP address). Many popular online services use this approach to search for multi- and fake accounts [7].

After the procedure of finding accounts, the obtained results need to be sorted by the use frequency to optimize the subsequent search of the actual social profile information. Then it is necessary to analyze the user activity and collect relevant information from the profile data. Typically, many online resources provide date marks registration and visitor counter for these purposes.

The common steps for the personal identification on the Internet are presented in Fig. 1.

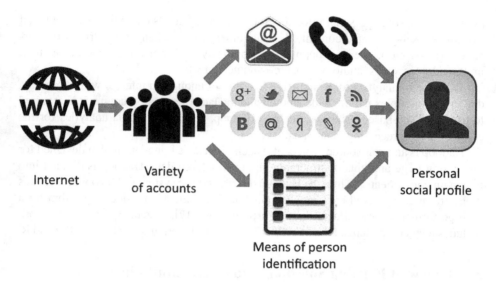

Fig. 1. The scheme of a person identification algorithm

In the future, such methods can also be used for identifying the implicit relations between people and for searching hidden dependencies in social data trends.

4   Differentiation of Collected Social Profile Data

To achieve an acceptable level of storage and usability, all social profile data varieties should be divided into static and dynamic parts.

The static part of a social profile data includes information that uniquely identifies the person and does not change with time. It is contained in the description of identified person accounts and therefore forms a frame linking all other isolated profile data. Social profile static data are collected in a table and represent the so-called information card. Its' detection is a priority for creating a specific social profile.

In most cases, the search for a person on the Internet starts with entering one or more unique criteria such as name, e-mail address, age, account ID. Although in some cases (for example, due to incomplete or conflicting criteria) the search is conducted by circumstantial signs: activity, popular posts, exclusive user-generated content. Therefore, it is necessary to add a separate field for most fully identifying signs into the information card, where the reference to the table with signs will be located. At the same time these signs will be foreign keys to the database with dynamic social profile information.

This type of data is easy to detect by traditional means, without resorting to Big Data solutions, due to their small number, availability, consistency and continued relevance. The information card provides a basic personal portrait to the analyst and becomes a foundation for the further social profile development.

The dynamic content exists in addition to the static one and depends on time and other factors. As a part of the social profile the following list can be represented: posts/comments, contacts/friends, subscriptions/preferences, ratings/marks, spatial data, avatars, nicks, some personal info, etc. Some of the list items can only be incremental (locations, user-generated content…), while others can be changed arbitrarily (preferences, friends, etc.). The most popular types of the dynamic content on Internet are text, multimedia (graphics, audio, video, etc.) and geodata.

Traditional analytics tools and RDBMS are not enough to interact with these data due to their complex nature, wide amount and the lack of a clear structure. It is required to use Big Data-based solutions, such as Hadoop, and social media analytics for the collection and processing of such data.

Hadoop is an open-source project of Apache Software Foundation, that designed for processing large amounts of structured and unstructured data. Hadoop is divided into two main components such as the Hadoop distributed file system (HDFS) which makes it easy to manage linked files between machines; and the MapReduce algorithm for a high-performance parallel/distributed data processing [17]. Also the Hadoop framework includes next components: Hive, YARN, Zookeeper, the program languages Pig and R.

5   Review of Existing Solutions and Their Limitations

Web analytics is the measurement, collection, analysis, presentation and interpretation of web data for purposes of understanding and optimizing web usage. There is a wide amount of specialized web analytics tools. Here are some of them [1, 5]:

1. Social Bakers is the most popular analytical tools provider of social media, statistics and indicators for Facebook, Twitter, Google Plus, YouTube and LinkedIn. It provides a mobile application analysis.
2. Hootsite is the platform with an intuitive interface and ability. Service schedule posts simultaneously for several channels and keep track all social pages. It allows to communicate with the Google Analytics system.
3. IQBuzz is a Russian toolkit for online reputation management. It provides the studies cases and the widgets to brand awareness and consumer attitudes analytics in social networks. The official site consist of relevant marketing information for researches.
4. The JagaJam service platform enables the community analysis in social networks such as VKontakte, Classmates, Facebook, Twitter and Instagram. The objects of analysis are audience, its activity and involvement, the published content. The platform provides a dynamic comparison of communities, benchmarking, crossing of community audiences.
5. Klout covers a wide range of social media platforms. Analysis is based on data from Twitter, Facebook, Google + , LinkedIn, Foursquare, YouTube, Instagram, Tumblr, Blogger, WordPress, Last.fm and Flickr, measures a personal network size and published content number.
6. Service SocialMention monitors about 100 sources (including Twitter, Facebook, FriendFeed, YouTube, Google…) in real time. It gives the possibilities of RSS-channels setting, e-mail notifications or widgets on the site. Results of analytical service operations can be exported into simple CSV/xls format for further processing tasks.
7. Wobot is a Russian service, that includes Wobot Monitor tool - an instrument for social media monitoring. It accesses to such statistics as the number of authors,

resources, indicators of coverage and involvement, calculates opinion leaders, etc. Also Wobot works with VKontakte social network's data.

8. The FacebookInsights service allows you to analyze Facebook pages metrics. All particular page administrators can get access to Facebook Insights data at any time that will allow its owners to track the number of active users, to determine their behavioral patterns, and to evaluate the efficiency of this page and inbound marketing SMM strategy.

9. Twitter Analytics provides free tools for integrated monitoring of user activity on a separate page of social network or blog (TweetReach, TwentyFeet, Twitter Counter, Social Bro and Twitalyzer).

Currently such tools are widely used in electronic marketing and social analytics but not appropriate for current problem. These services can be used only as a secondary element for gathering dynamic content and identify patterns in the popular social networks. Many web analytics tools are ineffective in a person identification within the network because specialized social bot trackers often can't distinguish a fake and a real person account [7]. Therefore it is necessary to process Big Data volumes manually. To avoid such problems, it makes sense to implement enhanced distributed storages and automated search methods of data retrieved through Big Data implementations.

6   Proposed Solutions and Their Advantages

Initial information search on the Internet provides by analyst, but entire process will be automated after finding one or several unique criteria. The general information and links for all person accounts is supplied to the search robot and stored in the information card. Additionally, the script is created to specifies the templates of accounts binding tokens, the typical fields and the page names containing the social profile data. Also, the search of multi- and fake accounts is performed using the set of specialized services (for example, AntiDogs and VKfake for VKontakte social network) and a custom algorithm that takes the common patterns of such accounts (no user-generated content with many reposts, massive friend list, the explicit relationship between the activity of some accounts, matched nick/avatar, etc.).

Filling the information card is most easily done using a simple web crawler with complex query capability and build-in results filter (e.g. VisualWebSpider [13] or Teleport VLX). Due to the small number and the uniqueness, data can be successfully stored in a traditional relational database or JSON/CSV spreadsheet formats. You should use a special identifier field for communication with other entities (e.g., dynamic data). Approximate data representation shown in Table 1.

Table 1. Example of Information Card structure.

Id	Name (primary)	Date of birth	Place of birth	Main "root" account	Most famous signs	...
1	John Doe	01.01.1990	Earth	Acc_example @mail	List1.db	...

The next stage is the dynamic content search with distribution on the data type. The search will be carried out in information fields and attached cards. Then the results processed by means of social media analytics (ready-made solutions or custom Hadoop software modules) for compliance with the considered person. After, information distributed by type: accumulating and editable.

Database without data modification capabilities (for example, HBase) is the most rational way to storage accumulating data. Second datatype requires more sophisticated NoSQL solution, for example, MongoDB or CouchDB. Graph databases (Neo4 J) provides convenience of further social data analysis and presentation (such as contact lists). Geodata storage needs to apply a set of PostGIS/OpenGeo, or Neo4 J Spatial module.

IBM InfoSphere BigInsights and i2 software systems from Big Data solutions can be stand out there [14]. They are provided as a means of collecting unstructured data from different sources (BoardReader, DataExplorer), storage (BigSheets, iBase), analysis (BigSQL, ContentAnalytics, TextChart) and presentation (Analytic's Notebook).

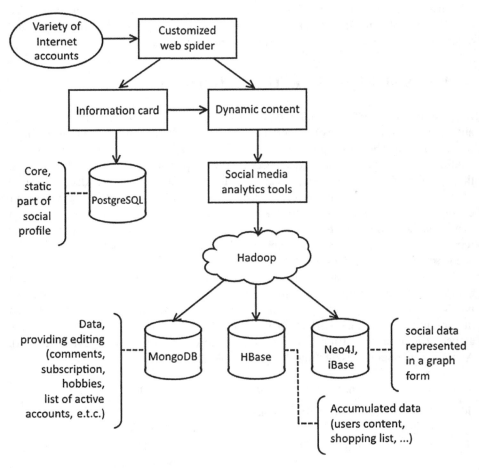

Fig. 2. The structure of identification and data collection system for building a social profile

Initial data is firstly placed in HBase-like storage, then the primary filtering carry out and information exports to CSV-table. Then these spreadsheets are input iBase database and will be analyzed.

Deployment system of a build social profile can be based on the Hortonworks Data Platform, in addition to the IBM Big Data implementation. HDP advantages are open source, flexible configuration, latest technology innovations and cooperation with many Big Data communities. It can be fast deployed on a usual stationary PC or inexpensive server hardware. The desired data separation and general structure of solution for human identification are presented in Fig. 2.

Also it's possible to create dashboards in Google Analytics for collecting and tracking dynamic content. Dashboard concisely presents statistical data, reports, often with infographics elements [11]. It helps to easy detect changes in user preferences, his activity and popularity in a single Internet resource. Definitely the block of Social media analytics tools must be able to connect dashboards.

7 Conclusion

The problem of a personal identification in the Internet is being addressed through an integrated approach consisting of his accounts detection by the unique account identifiers, email address, bind tokens and matching profile data. These social profile data divided into an information card and dynamic content storage. This approach ensures the efficient use of system resources to collect and analyze the social profile data, as well as the presentation convenience for analysts and end users.

References

1. 10 services for social media analytics and monitoring and evaluating your SMM strategy efficiency (2014). https://vk.com/topic-72178837_30130622
2. Dolan, R., Conduit, J., Fahy, J., Goodman, S.: Big social data and social media analytics: tools for exploring social media engagement behaviour. In: ANZMAC 2015 Proceedings, pp. 370 – 370 (2015). http://hdl.handle.net/2292/28321
3. Eskesa, P., Spruita, M., Brinkkempera, S., Vorstmanb, J., Kas, M.J.: The sociability score: app-based social profiling from a healthcare perspective. Comput. Hum. Behav. **59**, 39–48 (2016). doi:10.1016/j.chb.2016.01.024
4. Hamed, A.A., Wu, X.: Does social media big data make the world smaller? An exploratory analysis of keyword-hashtag networks. In: 2014 IEEE International Congress on Big Data (BigData Congress), pp. 454–461. IEEE, Anchorage, AK (2014). doi:10.1109/BigData.Congress.2014.72
5. Izmestyeva, E.: 12 tools for social media monitoring and analytics (2014). https://te-st.ru/tools/tools-monitoring-and-analysis-of-social-media/
6. Kitchin, R.: The real-time city? Big data and smart urbanism. GeoJournal **79**(1), 1–14 (2014). doi:10.1007/S10708-013-9516-8
7. Mikoyan, A.: Bots in social networks - how to recognize "dead souls"? (2015). http://mediastancia.com/articles/3811/
8. Oboler, A., Welsh, K., Cruz, L.: The danger of big data: social media as computational social science. First Monday, **17**(7) (2012). doi:10.5210/fm.v17i7.3993

9. Roy, P., Martнnez, A.J., Miscione, G., Zuidgeest, M.H.P., van Maarseveen, M.F.A.M.: Using social network analysis to profile people based on their e-communication and travel balance. J. Transp. Geogr. **24**, 111–122 (2012). doi:10.1016/j.jtrangeo.2011.09.005

10. Schamp-Bjerede, T., Paradis, C., Kucher, K., Kerren, A., Sahlgren, M.: New perspectives on gathering, vetting and employing big data from online social media: an interdisciplinary approach. In: International Computer Archive of Modern and Medieval English - ICAME Conference. Trier, Germany (2015). http://lup.lub.lu.se/luur/download?func=downloadFile&recordOId=5146832&fileOId=5146847

11. Sletova, E.: Google Analytics: How to configure and use dashboards to monitor and analyze site content (2014). https://vc.ru/p/ga-dashboard

12. Smith, M., Szongott, C., Henne, B., von Voigt, G.: Big data privacy issues in public social media. In: 2012 6th IEEE International Conference on Digital Ecosystems Technologies (DEST), pp. 1–6, Publisher: IEEE, Campione d'Italia (2012). doi:10.1109/DEST.2012.6227909

13. Timonin, A.Y.: Development of social profile on the basis of available tools. In: New Information Technologies and Systems: digest of scientific articles XII International Scientific and Technical Conference, pp. 221–224, Penza: PSU Publisher, Penza (2015)

14. Timonin, A.Y., Bozhday, A.S.: The use of big data technologies to build a human social profile on the basis of public data sources. Bull. Penza State Univ. **2**(10), 140–144 (2015)

15. Tufekci, Z.: Big questions for social media big data: representativeness, validity and other methodological pitfalls. In: ICWSM 2014: Proceedings of the 8th International AAAI Conference on Weblogs and Social Media, Ann Arbor, MI (2014). http://arxiv.org/abs/1403.7400v2

16. Weidmana, A.C., Levinson, C.A.: I'm still socially anxious online: offline relationship impairment characterizing social anxiety manifests and is accurately perceived in online social networking profiles. Comput. Hum. Behav. **49**, 12–19 (2015). doi:10.1016/j.chb.2014.12.045

17. Working with unstructured data in Hadoop Distributed File System. Competence Center for Technology IBM Big Data, p. 30, Moscow (2014)

18. Wu, W., Wang, J.: Exploring city social interaction ties in the big data era: evidence based on location-based social media data from China. In: 55th Congress of the European Regional Science Association: "World Renaissance: Changing roles for People and Places", pp. 25–28, Lisbon, Portugal (2015) http://www.econstor.eu/handle/10419/124698

19. Youa, Q., Bhatiab, S., Luo, J.: A picture tells a thousand words—about you! User interest profiling from user generated visual content. In: Signal Processing, vol. 124, pp. 45–53 (2016). doi:10.1016/j.sigpro.2015.10.032

An Automated System for Gravimetric Monitoring of Oil and Gas Deposits

Assem Nazirova[1(✉)], Farida Abdoldina[1], Murat Aymahanov[1],
Gulzada Umirova[1], and Ravil Muhamedyev[2,3]

[1] Kazakh National Research Technical University After K.I.Satpayev,
Almaty 050013, Republic of Kazakhstan
assem.berlibayeva@gmail.com, aymahanov@gmail.com,
{farida_mail, gulmuha}@mail.ru
[2] Institute of Information and Computational Technologies,
Almaty 050010, Republic of Kazakhstan
ravil.muhamedyev@gmail.com
[3] ISMA University, Riga LV 1019, Latvia

Abstract. This work describes an automated system for preprocessing gravimetric data from an oil and gas deposit located in the southeastern part of the Caspian Depression. The functional modelling of the company's gravimetric monitoring was accomplished. The modelling allowed us to define the functionality and models of the system data. The executive part and database of the system are compiled by using Oracle APEX. A specialized geographic information system (GIS) was developed as part of the visualization subsystem. The GIS uses Google Maps API as a basis for the visualization of layers and as a provider of maps. The functionality and user interface of the system are described.

Keywords: GIS · Gravimetric monitoring · Oil and gas deposit · Process model · Functional modelling · Information system · Google maps API Oracle APEX

1 Introduction

In recent years in the Republic of Kazakhstan, much attention has been paid to questions of the geodynamic and ecological safety of oil and gas development. Such activities are carried out in order to predict changes in subsoil conditions on the developed deposit. The production induced influences caused by deposit development can bring about events of geodynamic character caused by geodynamic processes (extensive sags of the terrestrial surface and activation of fault zones). Such activities are carried out in order to predict changes in the status of the subsoil producing field. In order to avoid such geodynamic processes it is necessary to perform in a timely fashion high-quality monitoring which includes gravimetric monitoring in measurements of gravity variations. It is also important to know the location and types of wells, volumes of pumped water, production volumes, reservoir pressures, profiles, and well statuses. Geodynamic research includes measurements conducted using a gravimeter.

© Springer International Publishing AG 2016
A.V. Chugunov et al. (Eds.): DTGS 2016, CCIS 674, pp. 585–595, 2016.
DOI: 10.1007/978-3-319-49700-6_58

The gravimetric monitoring of oil and gas deposits is done to study opportunities of complex measurements located in a difficult horizontally non-uniform environment and to research of abnormal variations communications of gravity in time with processes of deposit development [1].

The processing of considerable volumes of primary data involves using graphic, visual and interactive technologies. By means of geographic information systems (GIS) it is possible to considerably simplify the work of experts.

A review of geographic information systems and technologies used in exploration geophysics and demonstrates that there is no ready, fully-fledged GIS which focused on the solution of actual geological tasks for any region, in particular the geologic-geophysical information providing processing, interpretation and storage of gravimetric shooting results and accompanying geological and geophysical information [2].

Thus, the development of in-house software using the proposed technique of processing and data presentation is of the utmost significance.

2 The Functional Model of Gravimetric Monitoring in the Development of an Oil and Gas Deposit

The creation of an information system can be divided into analysis, design, coding, testing and maintenance stages. It is known that the correction of mistakes made at an early stage may cost approximately 10 times more than at later stages, therefore the first stages are the most critical of IS creation. It is extremely important to have effective remedies for automation at the early stages of IS creation [3, 4].

One of the most important stages in the design of an information system involves the modelling of automated business processes. A qualitatively executed design of the software is an indicator of its functionality and reliability [5].

Figure 1 shows a context diagram that presents a general description of a business system and its interaction with the environment. Using the IDEF0 methodology allows us to create a functional model that displays the structure and functions of the system and the information flows of material objects linking these functions.

The context diagram shows the allocation of the main flow of input information in the system. This includes area data, gravimeter data, profile and supervision station data, and primary data obtained during gravimetric research. The control interface is divided into two logical blocks: the gravimetric research procedure and the raw data processing of the gravimetric monitoring procedure. The mechanisms are presented by the chief engineer-geophysicist, chief geophysicist, operating geophysicist, and inter-preting geophysicist. Output information comprises reporting documents such as tables and schedules necessary for carrying out the analysis of gravitational measurements in the field. Work [6] describes the business processes of a company in the data pro-cessing of gravimetric shootings on the deposit.

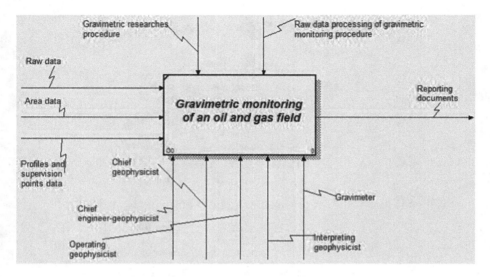

Fig. 1. A context diagram of company activity (IDEF0).

3   Automation of Data Processing in Gravimetric Research

The primary data processing system of gravimetric monitoring is based on the declarative Oracle Application Express programming language (Oracle APEX). Using only a web browser in this system makes it more effective and flexible for the development and expansion of appendices within the minimum time. In addition, there is the possibility to create both simple and difficult reports on the basis of the existing objects from the Oracle database. Moreover, schedules can also be created for analysis in the field.

Figure 2 presents an example of a chosen development environment for the processing of primary data of gravimetric monitoring. As primary data are submitted in a. txt format from the file of the gravimeter, the processing of every line of the file and their entering into the corresponding table of the database is necessary.

After loading and processing the gravimeter file on the following page of the system it is possible to see the relevant data from the file in a system format. In Fig. 3, the necessary condition before an exception of improper lines is an indication of the number of supervision times (cycles). After the distribution of data in the database tables, the system starts to exclude inappropriate lines (see Fig. 4).

The calculation of average Grav, SD, Temp, Tide, and Time values and also the determination of the average sizes of increment values of gravitational fields (dG) on each point (see Fig. 5) is an important stage in the system development.

Figure 6 presents the calculation of the measured increments of gravitational deposits by means of two gravimeters within several days on each point of supervision.

All operations performed are based on calculating the sum of squared deviations by the method of the smallest squares. If we can reach an acceptable value of the sum of squared deviations of no more than 0.007, it is possible to draw a conclusion on the correctness of the calculations made.

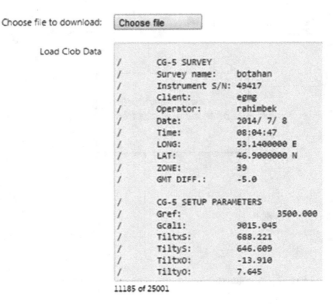

Choose file to download: Choose file

Load Clob Data

```
/      CG-5 SURVEY
/      Survey name:    botahan
/      Instrument S/N: 49417
/      Client:         egmg
/      Operator:       rahimbek
/      Date:           2014/ 7/ 8
/      Time:           08:04:47
/      LONG:           53.1400000 E
/      LAT:            46.9000000 N
/      ZONE:           39
/      GMT DIFF.:      -5.0
/
/      CG-5 SETUP PARAMETERS
/      Gref:                    3500.000
/      Gcal1:          9015.045
/      TiltxS:         688.221
/      TiltyS:         646.609
/      Tiltx0:         -13.910
/      Tilty0:         7.645
11185 of 25001
```

Fig. 2. Loading of primary data in the system.

Survey Name	Client	Operator	Line	Stat	Alt	Grav	Sd	Tiltx	Tilty	Temp	Tide	Dur	Rej	Time	Dectime Date
BOTAHAN	EGMG	RAHIMBEK	0	1000	0	1,369.4080	0.0330	-6.1000	2.8000	-0.9500	0.0530	40	0	08:18:05	41797.34534
BOTAHAN	EGMG	RAHIMBEK	0	1000	0	1,369.4130	0.0440	2.0000	2.1000	-0.9500	0.0530	40	5	08:18:51	41797.34587
BOTAHAN	EGMG	RAHIMBEK	0	1000	0	1,369.4150	0.0440	1.1000	2.6000	-0.9500	0.0530	40	0	08:19:35	41797.34638

Fig. 3. Loading data into system database.

Station	Grav	Time	Insert Date	Group In Station	Excluded
1000	1369.422	11:11:39	16-MAR-16	2	0
1000	1369.423	11:10:55	16-MAR-16	2	0
1000	1369.425	11:10:11	16-MAR-16	2	0
1000	1369.427	11:09:27	16-MAR-16	2	0
1000	1369.431	11:08:43	16-MAR-16	2	1

Fig. 4. Rejection of inappropriate lines.

The automation of data processing has excluded mistakes arising during data migration from files of the gravimeter at the selection (rejection) of the measured data on points of supervision and when calculating increments of a gravitational deposit. Therefore, the accuracy of the calculations is increased.

Station	Grav	Time	Dg	Sd	Temp	Tide	T Type Point Id
1000	1.369.4150	0.3470	-1.1020	0.0460	-0.9500	0.0530	1
2	1.370.5360	0.3370	0.0170	0.0610	-0.9800	0.0590	2
2	1.370.5220	0.3660	0.0000	0.0530	-0.9400	0.0650	2
12.1000004	1.370.2730	0.3740	-0.2500	0.0160	-0.9600	0.0690	0
22	1.374.5460	0.3890	4.0200	0.0240	-0.9800	0.0760	0

Fig. 5. Increment calculation of gravitational field (dG).

Result

Survey name

BOTAHAN ◆

Cycle List

7 ◆

M	N	M/N	Sum Dg Dev From Avg	Cko
83	25	3.32	0.0027	0.0038

Q ∨ | | Go | 1. Primary Report ◆ | Actions ∨

Station	Date	DG	Instrument	Cnt Duplicat	Avg Dg To Station	Dg Dev From Avg	Is Reject
1	24-APR-13	-0.1167	40680	1.0000	-0.1454	0.0287	1
1	24-APR-13	-0.1492	40827	1.0000	-0.1454	-0.0038	0
1	26-APR-13	-0.1582	40680	1.0000	-0.1454	-0.0128	1

Fig. 6. Calculation of the sum of squared deviations by the method of the smallest squares.

Thus, at this stage it is already possible to draw a conclusion as to the importance of automating data processing of gravimetric monitoring on oil and gas deposits.

The system allows the calculated data to be displayed in the form of schedules that substantially help geophysicists carry out the analysis of change in a gravitational deposit (Fig. 7). The parameters of schedule creation are set by the user. These include the names of the deposit, number of profiles on which points of supervision are located, and number of cycles in which the schedule of an increment of a gravitational deposit will be under construction.

4 GIS for the Visualization of Data

For data analysis by a human, it is convenient to represent data in the form of a spatial system, often tied to geographic coordinates, using GIS.

Several multifunctional GIS, including web-based systems (MapServer, MapFish, Geo Mixer, ArcGIS, Google Maps API, qGIS), have been developed. Each system has advantages and specific characteristics [7–9] (Table 1).

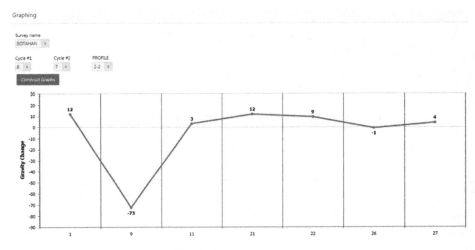

Fig. 7. Charting windows.

One of the most popular GIS services is Google Maps. Google Maps provides a cartographic service and an application programming interface (API) working in the web mode.

The main advantages of working with the service are:

1. Simplicity and availability of data:

   – the service requires only a web browser;
   – the simplest interface for working with data allows the user to have elementary geographical knowledge in order to find necessary places on a map;
   – switching the card to a space picture and also shifting around axes is possible (up and down, to the right and to the left);
   – in version 6.9 of Google Maps, maps of certain regions can be kept in the offline mode;
   – no special software for viewing the data is required.

2. Development by means of Google Maps:

   – to use this service on the web page, one must register on http://www.google.com/apis/maps/. Then it is necessary to enter a unique code into the web page text;
   – possibility of free use for development;
   – using AJAX technology allows the user to update page contents without needing to reset, thus, change the scale and movement according to the card without any delays;
   – the name of settlements and territories should be entered in Russian, which is important for Russian-speaking users.

3. Thematic data. There is the possibility that users can add data on the map. Simple commands allow contours, markers, interactive hints and pop-up windows to be

Table 1. GIS comparison table.

Parameters	MapServer	GeoMixer	ArcGIS	Google Maps API	QGIS
License type	Freeware	Shareware	Proprietary	Freeware	Freeware
Country of origin	USA	Russian Federation	USA	USA	Volunteer community
Developer	University of Minnesota	RDC ScanEx	ESRI	Google	Volunteer community
Documentation	English: user and developer level	Russian: user and developer level	English, Russian: user and developer level	English, Russian: user and developer level	English, Russian: user and developer level
Development language	C/C++	.NET, Flash	C#, Visual Basic, Python	JavaScript; Python	C++, Python
API language	Java, .NET, Perl, PHP, Python, Ruby	JavaScript	JavaScript; Flex; Silverlight	JavaScript	QT, Python
Available OGC services	WMS; WFS	WMS	WMS, WCS, WFS, WPS и WMTS	OGC KML, WMS, WFS	WMS, WFS, WCS, WFS, WFS
Work with tiles	No	Yes	Yes	Yes	Yes
Current version	6.4.1 from 02.01.2014	2.0 from 16.03.2014	10.2 from 30.07.2013	Version 3 from 01.02.2013	2.12 «Lyon»
Official address	http://www.mapserver.org	http://geomixer.ru/	http://www.esri.com	https://developers.google.com/maps/	http://www.qgis.org
Screenshot					

added on the card. Data can be displayed both directly in the web code of pages and in external files. The behaviour control system of the card provides standard opportunities for navigation and animation. There is the opportunity to create thematic layers directly in the browse mode of the web page.

4. Popularity and reliability. Millions of developers use Google Maps APIs. The system provides functionality for browsers, Android, iOS.

Such advantages make Google Maps very attractive for the development of specific GIS.

5   Application of GIS-Technologies in the Automated System

Google Maps cartographical technology has been chosen as a monitoring GIS-system for data visualization as a simplified service working in the web mode. The special program module written for this service visualizes a set of additional layers on the territory fragment of an oil production district map. To visualize the data on the deposit information on wells coordinates, a field contour, points of supervision, profiles and also the GPS data is needed.

The end result of the program is the visualization of the available data in the oil and gas deposit district map. Figure 8 shows a fragment of the system work on the

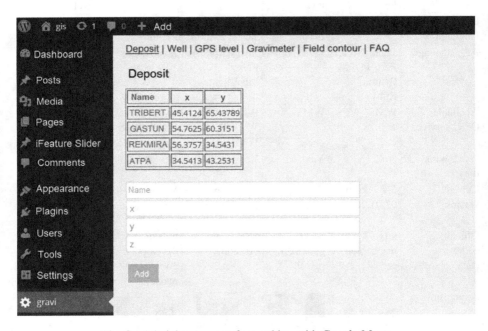

Fig. 8. Administrator part for working with Google Maps.

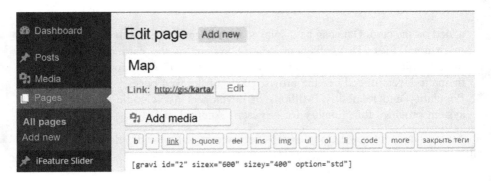

Fig. 9. Adding short-code in the client part.

administrator's part for viewing and adding new data on Google Maps. The creation of layers requires filling in data.

To display the client's part of the map it is necessary to add a short-code on the corresponding page. Figure 9 clearly demonstrates this process.

Using GIS-technology has allowed creating a picture of data with geo-referencing about the deposit. The map shows data on intake and production well deposits, deposit contours, profiles and points of gravimetric shootings, and GPS points. Figure 10 presents wells location. Information regarding well location when aiming at a certain well is also included.

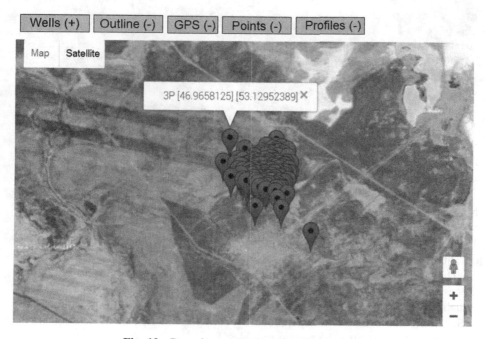

Fig. 10. Deposit map displaying wells location.

The convenience of the system is related to its ability of switching between layers. Figure 11 shows the parallel connection of several layers.

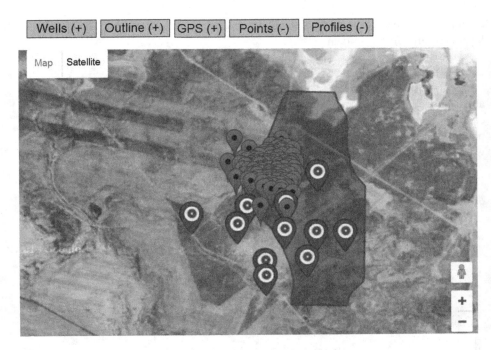

Fig. 11. Example of switching between layers.

6   Conclusions

The automated system for gravimetric monitoring of an oil and gas deposit was described briefly.

The system automates the processing of gravimetric data and allows us to not only process the gathered information, but to carry out analyses and forecasts, and to visualize the results of gravimetric research on oil and gas deposits by using special GIS. The system realizes a full operational cycle of gravimetric data processing and the representation of results. The system provides:

– automation of data input;
– calculations of the observed gravity values to obtain abnormal values;
– calculation of gravity transformations;
– graphic representation of calculations;
– well location and status; card of isobars;
– profiles;

The oil and gas deposit monitoring system allows the quality of processing and interpretation of gravimetric data to be improved. The developed information system will be useful to companies engaged in the prospecting and monitoring of subsoil and other works that are carried out in gravimetric research.

Acknowledgments. The work was partly funded by grant No. 0168/GF4 by the Ministry of Education and Science of the Republic of Kazakhstan.

References

1. Saparbekova, M.A., Umirova, G.K., and Akhmetov, E.M.: Results of geodynamic monitoring of subsoil on the Northern Buzachi field. In: Works of the International Satpayev Readings "The Role and the Place of Young Scientists in the Realization of New Economic Policy of Kazakhstan". KazNTU: Almaty, vol. III, pp. 49–54 (2015). http://portal.kazntu.kz/files/publicate/2015-10-20-elbib_33.pdf. (in Russian)
2. Abdoldina, F.N., Aymahanov, M.A.: Study of GIS technology opportunities for presenting the results of gravimetric works. In: Joint Release on Materials of the International Satpayev Readings "The Role and Place of Young Scientists in the Implementation of the New Economic Policy of Kazakhstan" KazNTU: Almaty, vol. IV, pp. 663–668 (2015). http://portal.kazntu.kz/files/publicate/2015-08-26-10974_2.pdf. (in Russian)
3. Maklakov, S.V.: Development of information systems with AllFusion Modeling. Suite Dialog-MIFI: Moscow (2003). http://bwbooks.net/index.php?id1=4&category=comp-lit&author=maklakov-sv&book=2003. (in Russian)
4. Maklakov, S.V.: BPwin ERwin. CASE development tools of information systems Dialog-MIFI: Moscow (2001). http://dit.isuct.ru/ivt/books/CASE/case5/ (in Russian)
5. Leszek, A., Maciaszek, L.A.: Requirement Analysis and System Design. Developing Information Systems with UML. Williams, England (2002). https://www.researchgate.net/publication/247394031_Requirements_Analysis_and_system_design-Developing_Information_Systems_with_UML
6. Abdoldina, F.N., Berlibayeva, A. B., Umirova, G.K.: Data processing automation of geodynamic monitoring on an oil and gas field. In: Joint Release on Materials of the International Scientific Conference "Computing and Information Technologies in Science, Equipment and Education", pp. 73–82 (2015). http://portal.kazntu.kz/files/publicate/2015-09-30-elbib_1.pdf (in Russian)
7. Muhamedyev, R., Ishmanov, A., Andreev, A., Muhamadijeva, J., Alikhodzhayev, I.: Technological preconditions of monitoring of renewable energy sources of the Republic of Kazakhstan. In: Proceedings of the 2015 Twelve International Conference on Electronics Computer and Computation (ICECCO), pp. 101–107. IEEE (2015). ISBN 978-1-5090-0199-6
8. Muhamedyev, R., Alihodzhaev, I., Ishmanov, A., and Muhamedijeva, J.: Monitoring of renewable energy sources in RK: technological preconditions, architecture of system and market volume. In: Proceedings of 16th International Symposium on Advanced Intelligent Systems, pp. 777–791. ISIS (2015)
9. Muhamedyev, R., Giyenko, A., Pyagai, V., and Bostanbekov, K.: Premises for the creation of renewable energy sources GIS monitoring. In: 2014 IEEE 8th International Conference on Application of Information and Communication Technologies (AICT), pp. 1–5. IEEE (2014). http://ieeexplore.ieee.org/xpl/articleDetails.jsp?arnumber=7035989

The Impact of Network Topology on Banking System Dynamics

Valentina Y. Guleva$^{(\boxtimes)}$, Abdulmalik Amuda, and Klavdiya Bochenina

ITMO University, Kronverkskii 49, 197101 Saint Petersburg, Russia
valentina.gul.va@gmail.com, amuda.ab@gmail.com, k.bochenina@gmail.com

Abstract. A topology of a banking network influences systemic stability under fixed banks' and customers' policy. Dynamical processes in a network affect topological changes at each iteration, so differences in initial topologies may result in different stability dynamics. Taking into account the influence of both nodes' states dynamics and topology dynamics on the network fragility, the following ways of initial topology impact can be distinguished: (i) states of nodes after initialization (as a state of a node is influenced by its degree); (ii) nodes' states dynamics; (iii) systemic risk at the fixed iteration. It seems that coevolution of network topology and states of nodes leads to the significant and unpredictable changes of initial conditions. We study the interrelations between initial and resulting system's states for different types of initial topology. Our results confirm that the dynamics of a borrowing process is significantly influenced by topological features of the underlying interbank network.

Keywords: Banking system · Adaptive network · Network topology · Complex systems

1 Introduction

Studying the influence of network topology on systemic risk in banking ecosystems was mostly focused on expected losses estimation for arbitrary shock propagation on a fixed topology. Dynamics in such networks is more likely to be represented by a contagion and knock-on effects [4], than by a network evolution. However, banking systems often demonstrate non-linear behavior [7] so it may be difficult to find a cause of a financial crisis or to determine critical values of system's parameters on the edge between its stable and unstable states. The emergence of a complex behavior, as a result of interbank interactions, can be considered in the context of multi-agent modeling, e.g. in a dynamic model of a banking system, which has an algorithm for updating bank states according to changing conditions [6]. However, there is a lack of studies clarifying the interplay between the changes of network structure and iterative adaptation of banks and householders activity.

© Springer International Publishing AG 2016
A.V. Chugunov et al. (Eds.): DTGS 2016, CCIS 674, pp. 596–599, 2016.
DOI: 10.1007/978-3-319-49700-6_59

2   Banking System Model

The model is a dynamic network with nodes representing banks and edges representing interbank lending. A network evolution is formed by (i) an interbank link formation algorithm and (ii) an algorithm of improvement of a bank state, when it is near insolvency or it can not satisfy customer requests. The algorithms are identical for all the banks in a network. Despite the similarity of rules, a system as a whole demonstrates emergent behavior, which can be quite different for various types of interbank network topologies. To study how the system evolves over time, we fix bank and customer policies and let them modify a network topology step by step, providing different simulation results.

2.1   Network Model

The interbank network is a dynamic oriented multi-graph $G^t = (V^t, E^t)$, where (V^t) is set of nodes, and E^t is set of edges, which are in a system at the moment t. Each edge is attributed by source and target vertices, the size of debt (edge weight) and deposits maturity. Thus, $E^t = \{e = (v_1, v_2, w, m)|v_1, v_2 \in V^t, w \in \mathbb{R}^+, m \in \mathbb{N}\}$. Maturity corresponds to edge life time, consequently, it is decremented at each iteration of a dynamic network evolution: $\forall e = (v_1, v_2, w, m) \in E^t \Rightarrow (v_1, v_2, w, m - 1) \in E^{t+1}$. Weighted sums of interbank edges form interbank assets and liabilities of bank balance sheets. To represent the external ones we introduce a bank-to-customer network $G_*^t = (V^t, V_*^t, E_*^t)$, where $E_*^t = \{e = (v_1, v_2, w, m)|v_1 \in V^t, v_2 \in V_*^t, w \in \mathbb{R}^+, m \in \mathbb{N}\} \cup \{e = (v_1, v_2, w, m)|v_1 \in V_*^t, v_2 \in V^t, w \in \mathbb{R}^+, m \in N\}$, V^t is a set of nodes-banks, and V_*^t is a set of nodes-households. Thus, weighted sums of bank-to-customer edges correspond to external assets and liabilities of a bank.

2.2   Metrics for Changes Evaluation

To evaluate topological changes we use the average degree, average clustering coefficient, average shortest path, the number of edges, and the invariant for Laplacian spectrum [8], since isospectral graphs have similar topology [5]. In addition, we use the node state-oriented features, described in [2].

3   Experiments

A network contain $N = 100$ banks and several thousands of customers. We use Erdos-Renyi (ER), Barabasi-Albert (BA), and Watts-Strogats (WS) models [1]. ER is used with probability of edge creation $P \in \{0.1, 0.25, 0.3, 0.35, 0.4, 0.45, 0.6\}$; BA is run with percentage of attached edges $A \in \{10, 20, 35, 50, 65, 80, 90\}$; WS has the share of attached neighbors $K \in \{4, 15, 30, 45, 60, 75, 90\}$, and the probability of edge rewiring $P \in \{0.2, 0.4, 0.6, 0.8\}$.

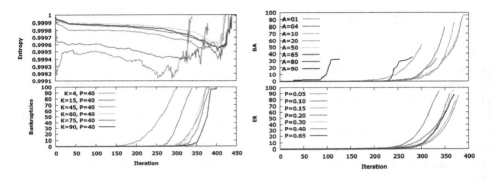

Fig. 1. Entropy and bankruptcies dynamics for WS model (on the left); bankruptcies dynamics for ER and BA models (on the right)

Watts-Strogatz. A system is destroyed quicker for sparse networks. For $K = 4$, the first bankruptcy occurs near the 150th iteration for $P = 20$ and $P = 40$, and it is near about the 100th iteration for $P = 60$ and $P = 80$. The entropy of Laplacian spectrum, as well as average clustering and shortest path, reflects changes in network structure, which are more significant for $K = 4$ for $P = 20$, and less significant for $P = 80$. The value reached with *violet graph* can not be reached by other network configurations, since they are not modified so seriously, despite the similarity of bank policy parameters. The amplitudes of entropy increase with the growth of P for both sparse and dense networks. Configurations with high initial clustering coefficient have it decreased during the network evolution; on the contrary, an initially low clustering coefficient grows with the evolution of a network. The dynamics of topological characteristics is more attributable to the processes of addition and deletion of edges (which change a number of links) than to simple edge rewiring. The values of parameters for networks with $K \in \{60; 70; 90\}$ converge at some point near the 300th iteration, and further show similar dynamics, while graphs with $K \in \{4; 15\}$ show fluctuations. The peaks of $DynamicsOfNodeStates$ plots have varying amplitude for different densities of networks, and the numbers of iterations when first peaks occur increase with the value of K.

Barabasi-Albert. For BA initial configuration we oppositely get more robust systems for sparse networks and more fragile systems for the dense ones. As well as the number of bankruptcies, the $PotentialOfInteraction$ [2] plots showed, that for $A = 90$ there is the high possibility of edges negative impact near the 50th iteration, while for $A = 10$ this occurs only about the 350th iteration. Thus, we can summarize that the systemic risk increases with increase in a number of attached edges in a Barabasi-Albert generative model.

Erdos-Renyi. As opposed to BA, all graphs for ER initial configuration show bankruptcies near the same values, nevertheless, a system with $P = 0.1$ is destroyed earlier. It can be explained by the fact that for an ErdosRenyi network with 100 nodes a threshold probability for the appearance of a giant component is $1/N = 0.1$, so $P = 0.1$ is border-line value in terms of network connectivity. Figure 1 also shows that the system is the most fragile for this value. Systems with $20 < P < 60$ show similar dynamics in bankruptcies, and converge to some value near the 350th iteration.

4   Conclusions

The results illustrate sparse networks are more robust for BA and more fragile for WS models. For particular ranges of parameters, different initial topologies were shown to have invariants converging to some similar values during simulation. As for WS, amplitudes of entropy increase with a growth of P for both sparse and dense networks. It could be explained by the fact that the disturbances in more ordered networks usually fade quicker than in chaotic ones. For the ER model our experiments show that sparse networks are more fragile for fixed bank policies.

Acknowledgements. This work was partly performed by the Master student of the Masters Programme in Computational Science [3]. This paper is financially supported by The Russian Scientific Foundation, Agreement #14–21–00137 (15.08.2014).

References

1. Chung, F.R.K., Lu, L.: Complex graphs and networks. Am. Math. Soc. Providence **107** (2006). doi:10.1090/cbms/107
2. Guleva, V.Y.: The combination of topology and nodes' states dynamics as an early-warning signal of critical transition in a banking network model. Procedia Computer Science (2016). doi:10.1016/j.procs.2016.05.436
3. Krzhizhanovskaya, V.V., et. al.: Russian-Dutch double-degree Masters programme in computational science in the age of global education. J. Comput. Sci. 10, pp. 288–298 (2015). doi:10.1016/j.jocs.2015.05.001
4. May, R.M., Arinaminpathy, N.: Systemic risk: the dynamics of model banking systems. J. R. Soc. Interface **7**(46), 823–838 (2010). doi:10.1098/rsif.2009.0359
5. Van Dam, E.R., Haemers, W.H.: Which graphs are determined by their spectrum? Linear Algebra Appl. **373**, 241–272 (2003). doi:10.1016/S0024-3795(03)00483-X
6. Montagna, M., Kok, C.: Multi-layered interbank model for assessing systemic risk. Kiel Working Paper, no. 1873 (2013). https://econstor.eu/bitstream/10419/83493/1/76900203X.pdf
7. Purica, I.: Nonlinear Dynamics of Financial Crises: How to Predict Discontinuous Decisions. Academic Press, ISBN: 978-0-12-803275-6 (2015)
8. Ye, C., Torsello, A., Wilson, R.C., Hancock, E.R.: Thermodynamics of time evolving networks. In: Liu, C.-L., Luo, B., Kropatsch, W.G., Cheng, J. (eds.) GbRPR 2015. LNCS, vol. 9069, pp. 315–324. Springer, Heidelberg (2015). doi:10.1007/978-3-319-18224-7_31

An Adaptive and Dynamic Simulation Framework for Incremental, Collaborative Classifier Fusion

Gernot Bahle[1]([✉]), Andreas Poxrucker[1], George Kampis[1,2,3],
and Paul Lukowicz[1]

[1] DFKI German Research Centre for Artificial Intelligence,
Trippstadter Str. 122, 67663 Kaiserslautern, Germany
{gernot.bahle,andreas.poxrucker,george.kampis,paul.lukowicz}@dfki.de
[2] Eötvös University, Budapest, Hungary
[3] ITMO University, St. Petersburg, Russia
http://ei.dfki.de

Abstract. To investigate incremental collaborative classifier fusion techniques, we have developed a comprehensive simulation framework. It is highly flexible and customizable, and can be adapted to various settings and scenarios. The toolbox is realized as an extension to the NetLogo multi-agent based simulation environment using its comprehensive Java-API. The toolbox has been integrated in two different environments, one for demonstration purposes and another, modeled on persons using realistic motion data from Zurich, who are communicating in an ad hoc fashion using mobile devices.

Keywords: Ad hoc communication · Incremental classifier fusion · Collaborative computing

1 Introduction

We consider an environment in which agents can classify observations they make. The nature of this environment as well as the concept represented by an agent is thereby not fixed to a certain setting, but can be adapted to different scenarios (see applications). To classify testing data agents encounter during a simulation, every agent is associated with a certain knowledge, which essentially encapsulates an instance of a certain type of classifier.

In machine learning and statistics, classification is the problem of identifying an item to which an observation belongs, taken from a set of categories (sub-populations). Classification learning is the development of classifications by machine learning techniques. Classification learning is performed on the basis of a training set, that is, data containing observations (or instances) whose category membership is known. This known membership is used a feedback to direct a convergent learning processes to the right outcomes. Trained classifiers are statistical functions that use pattern matching to determine a closest match.

© Springer International Publishing AG 2016
A.V. Chugunov et al. (Eds.): DTGS 2016, CCIS 674, pp. 600–609, 2016.
DOI: 10.1007/978-3-319-49700-6_60

Every knowledge instance is initially trained using a set of training data. The latter may contain an equal amount of data for each class or may be biased towards certain classes with more training data initially available for certain classes than for others. The quality of classification can be described by e.g. the global average of true positive rates for every class.

During our simulations, agents move around in the world either randomly or following special movement patterns. Whenever two agents meet, they merge their classifiers based on a certain classifier fusion technique and update their classification output. The concepts of movement and meeting are thereby purely abstract and can be realized according to the specific needs of a certain scenario or research interests. Keeping track of the global average true-positive rate for every class, it is possible to observe how the classification quality changes in dependence of the chosen fusion method.

We note that knowledge fusion in general and classifier fusion as a special example are well studied in Artificial Intelligence (REF) and off-the-shelf methods exist with optimal properties [7]. By contrast, collaborative (incremental) classifier fusion is a new idea. The difference is that in the former, the entire set of knowledge instances (trained classifiers) must be simultaneously available; in the latter, this condition is relaxed. Collaborative fusion is that is a natural generalization to situations where access to knowledge items is limited by temporal, geographic or other constraints.

We have developed a simulation framework realized as an extension to the NetLogo multi-agent based simulation environment [8] using a comprehensive Java-API. We have applied it in three different settings to demonstrate the flexibility and adaptivity of our approach. In all three cases, we used classifiers from the WEKA library. For fusing classifiers, we experimented with the baseline case of simply exchanging training data as well as advanced classifier aggregation functions offered by WEKA. As data basis, we used a real-world environmental audio data set, based on a public dataset from the university of Rouen, France. Recordings have been performed using a Galaxy S3 smartphone equipped with Android by means of the Hi-Q MP3 recorder application. The dataset is composed of 19 classes and audio scenes forming a given class have been recorded at different locations. The classifier task is to approximate the original classification, and our populational learning algorithms aim to achieve that by incremental fusion [3,4]. The current work belongs to a series of studies that started with simple collaborative tasks such as localization [2,5] and developed through the study of fully distributed ad-hoc communication systems [1].

2 Different Motion Models

2.1 Adaptive, Personalized Multi-modal Urban Mobility in the Allow Ensembles Simulator

First we used the movement model from the Allow Ensembles simulator [6] for multi-modal urban mobility (Fig. 1). In this scenario, we assume an urban area (show on the example of Trento, Italy) where people can use various means of

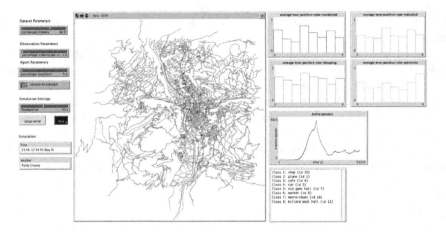

Fig. 1. Collaborative fusion based on the Allow Ensembles simulator

transportation to travel. These means include walking, cycling, going by car or taxi, or using public transportation like buses or trains. Whenever persons physically meet in the streets or share the same bus, classifier fusion is triggered by the meeting and the persons exchange classification information. What information is exchanged and how, it is determined by the respective fusion strategy tested.

We examined two different cases. In the first case, the agent population is divided into groups based on the region (such as residential, industrial, university, shopping) from where they come. Every member of a group is in turn assigned an initial training set, which is similarly biased within the same group providing different levels of expertise for the considered classes. In the second scenario, we divided the population based on the respective role of the person in the city population, e.g. worker, student, homemaker, or child. Results are discussed in a separate section.

2.2   Using a Real-World Movement Model from Zürich

In a second case study we have been using a dataset obtained in the 2013 Zurich festival. The dataset contained GPS positions of users of a smart phone app. On this basis we estimated pedestrians' key walking parameters. We obtained data for average walking speed and average walking/standing times, together with the respective error terms. The current approach uses these numbers as averages over the various crowd densities experienced in the dataset, referring to the fact that in the interesting range (3–4,000 pedestrians using the app) these parameters do not change dramatically over the time.

In this application, we use GIS shape files of the city (the simulation is thus ready to work for any city, but we only have validated the motion data for the Zurich example). We represent streets by their segments, and our motion model consists of navigation along the network defined by the resulting segments.

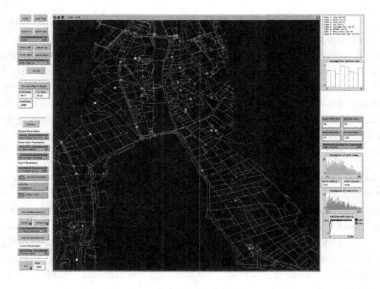

Fig. 2. Using the Zurich motion dataset

```
Class 1: shop (id 16)
Class 2: plane (id 1)
Class 3: cafe (id 4)
Class 4: car (id 5)
Class 5: kid game hall (id 7)
Class 6: market (id 8)
Class 7: metro-rouen (id 10)
Class 8: billard pool hall (id 11)
```

Fig. 3. The artificial classes used in the collaborative classifier fusion experiments

Pedestrians share a common average walking speed but have individual walking and staying times, taken from two normal distributions, which are characterized by the average walking/standing times and their standard errors, respectively. Pedestrians are always heading towards an adjacent segment and upon reaching it select next a new adjacent destination segment, but never turn back in a single step (Fig. 2).

In each of the two case studies, we applied 8 artificial classes (Fig. 3).

3   Classifier Fusion Strategies

Based on the simulation tools above, many different settings for classifier fusion can be tested. The following section gives an overview of different initial settings and strategies for action when two agents meet.

At the start of each simulation, there is a choice on how to initialize the training data each agent has available. Currently, there are two options: a random subset of all training data, or the first k% of the training data for each class. A random selection can, after enough knowledge exchange, potentially lead to a complete training set for agents, while the second alternative provides better control about what information is available at all. Also, the second option provides a natural hierarchy of experts (i.e. the training data of all agents knowing less than 70% are subsets of the experts data).

For the actual classifier fusion, we consider the following strategies:

- fusion based on exchange of training data. This strategy can serve as a baseline for other algorithms. Whenever agents meet, they exchange their set of training data. Depending on the initialization, this will eventually lead to either a complete set of training data (for the random method) or a convergence towards the level of the best informed expert (for the first k% method). Once the data has been exchanged, classifiers are retrained using the new set.
- fusion based on classifier models. This strategy involves fusing classifiers themselves, without resorting to the training data. In the case of the NaiveBayes classifier, which specifies a standard deviation and mean for each class, this involves aggregating those two values. In the simplest case, this could be done via averaging. More elaborate schemes incorporate weighting to incorporate the reliability of a given classifier (e.g. because of a larger set of training data). In more general terms, given two classifiers C and D fully described by a set of parameters P and Q, the aim is to provide a function $f : P \times Q \to R$, so that the new classifier E incorporates the knowledge of C and D. Note that this general principal can be applied both to classifiers of the same type (e.g. two trees, two neural networks) as well as to heterogeneous ones. In the latter case, concrete strategies will have to be tailored to each specific pairing (e.g. Bayes and Tree).
- fusion based on artificial training data. In order to provide a more general way to fuse two different types of classifiers while at the same time not relying on storage or exchange of training data, we are proposing yet another strategy. Based on the trained classifier an agent already has, it is possible to create random points of the feature space (or guided by some heuristic), label them via the known classifier and provide those to another agent. The agent can then incorporate them into its own classifier, either by some incremental learning algorithm or by simply retraining. This method abstracts from the specific type of classifier, has however the drawback of transmitting incorrectly labeled data some of the time.

4   Implementation

Classifiers. Classifiers are represented by an instance of the Knowledge class which offers an interface for training the classifier, obtaining classification results given some test data, and fusing it with another classifier instance. With this approach the actual implementation of the classifier is hidden from the simulation itself making it easily possible to experiment with different types of classifiers and classifier fusion methods. Even different types of classifiers are possible within the same simulation run. In our current implementation (see application scenarios below), we use the WEKA library which offers a wide range of different classifiers.

Classifier Fusion. The implementation of the fusion mechanism can be done in different ways. In the simplest case, the agents simply exchange their training data sets and retrain their classifier instances based on the merged training data. Although this approach does not involve an algorithm fusing the actual instances of the classifier can be used as a baseline. For some classifiers like the Naive Bayes for example, the WEKA library already defines methods for merging. For other classifiers or classifier combinations, it will be necessary to develop merging algorithms.

Data Basis. Just like the classifiers, the implementation of our toolbox does not impose any restrictions on the data basis to be used for training and testing. In our current implementation for example, we use a database of audio files for which we computed a set of features and stored them in the WEKA ARFF format in order to be compatible with the WEKA classifiers. It would, however, be easily possible to experiment with different data sets instead (provided they are converted to the ARFF format in case WEKA is used). In case of a completely different classification framework the simulation can be easily adapted to the necessary file formats.

5   Results

5.1   The Trento Case Study

In the Trento urban scenario, we are comparing two different scenarios:

1. agents have initial knowledge based on their role (worker, student, etc.)
2. agents have initial knowledge based on their geographic position

Furthermore, for each of those cases, we look at the exchange of training data vs. the parameter based fusion of the classifiers themselves. In both cases, data has been classified using a NaiveBayes classifier provided by WEKA, and training data has been assigned randomly. However, for the two different fusion methods, the same random seed has been used, so the initial distribution is the same for both fusion algorithms. The following results have been obtained.

Role Based Knowledge. Figure 4 shows the initial distribution for scenario 1 (role based); Fig. 5 left and right, respectively, show the true positive rate of classifiers for each class after a virtual day has elapsed for fusion based on training data and parameter based classifier fusion. As can be seen, the exchange of training data works better for all classes in general. This is to be expected,

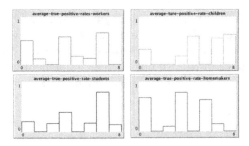

Fig. 4. Knowledge by role, random initial distrubution for each role (worker, children, students, homemakers). Figures show the average positive classification rate.

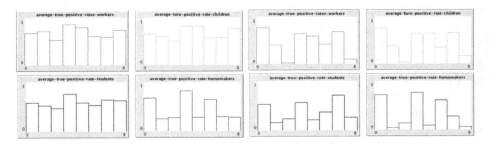

Fig. 5. Knowledge by role after 1 day. Left: training data exchange. Right: parameter fusion. While perfect classification is never achieved, in some categories and some roles the ideal situation is well approximated (especially on the left panel).

because this method grows the training data set for all agents, resulting in a more and more complete set as the day moves on. However, parameter based classifier fusion performs reasonably well if there already is some initial useful knowledge to build on (see for example classes one, four and seven). A second interesting effect: the number of interactions matters a lot more in the case of parameter based fusion. In both scenarios, the class of agents least interacting are homemakers (based on their profile, they leave their home to bring children to school or go shopping). As visible from Fig. 5 (left side), the exchange of training data is less sensitive to a small number of interactions; this is probably the case because of the cumulative effect of size increases in training data sets.

Geography Based Knowledge. Figure 6 shows the initial distribution for scenario 2, where initial training data is based on geographic information. Figure 7 left and right, respectively, once again show final true positive rates after a virtual day has elapsed.

Once again, the baseline fusion of training data outperforms the classifier fusion approach. However, other than in the role-based scenario discussed above, a strong initial knowledge of classes does not automatically yield a better performance for parameter based classifier fusion here. This is due to the reduced

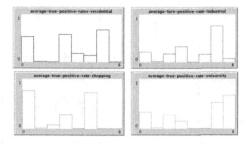

Fig. 6. Knowledge by region, random initial distribution for each region (residential, industrial, shopping, university).

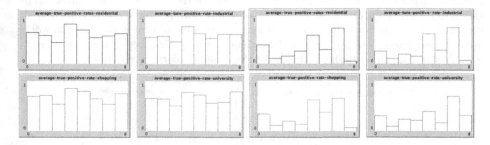

Fig. 7. Knowledge by region after 1 day. Left: training data exchange. Right: parameter fusion. Again, while perfect classification is never achieved, in some categories and some regions this ideal situation is approximated (especially on the left panel).

"mingling" of agents in this scenario. While role based agents (workers, students, etc.) can come from many different areas of origin and have many different destinations, in the geography based scenario, such diversity is reduced. For instance, workers tend to live close to their area of work, and thus many interactions will actually draw from the same set of training data.

5.2   The Zurich Case Study

The Zurich case study uses real motion data in a statistical simulation. Its basis is the daily recording of pedestrian's motion speed and its variance during the 2013 Zurich city festival.

Sample walking data are presented on Fig. 8. The motion model is based on a "mean field" approximation of the pedestrian population, hence we use the averages for walking speed 0,5 m/s, standing length 55 s (std 100) and time between standing 40 s (std 65), respectively. We take these as fixed external parameters in our simulations to test the internal parameters of the fusion algorithm. Simulated pedestrian motion is generated from a Gaussian distribution with a mean and variance as above.

With the motion model realized, we find that about half of all agents are immobile at any given time, about 20 % never move, and another 20 % never

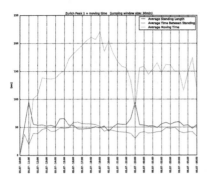
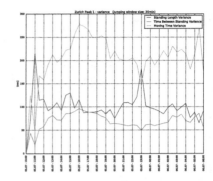

Fig. 8. Moving time (left) and its variance (right) in the Zurich motion dataset. The simulation uses the average values; note that the actual motion speed of the crowd is uneven and motion comes to a full halt at a given point of time (when the fireworks are on). Left: green - average moving time; blue - average time between standing; red - average standing time. Right: variances of the same. (Color figure online)

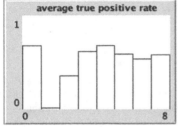
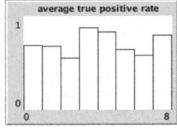

Fig. 9. Initial random (left) and evolved (right) classifications in the Zurich example. Figures show the average positive classification rate. Evolved classifications shown after 2,000 time steps (scaled for 200 min).

stand still (those values seem intuitive for anyone having visited a street festival). These facts will be significant when evaluating simulation results.

On Fig. 9, the available classifications are shown in the same histogram as above; the histogram comes from the top panel of the Zurich simulation interface.

In a comparison of the Trento and Zurich models, that is, the original large-scale collaborative learning simulation model with the merged "super model" of Zurich shows that learning and convergence take place in both but in the Zurich case in an understandably slower rate as there are pedestrians that never meet and therefore do not enter (or can be improved) by knowledge fusion.

Acknowledgements. This work is supported by the European Community (FP7/2007-2013) under grant agreement #600854 "Smart Society" as well as the H2020 Program under "FET Proactive: Global Systems Sciences" (GSS), grant agreement #641191 (CIMPLEX, https://www.cimplex-project.eu). The paper is partially supported by the Russian Scientific Foundation, grant #14-21-00137.

References

1. Franke, T., Kampis, G., Lukowicz, P.: Leveraging human mobility in smartphone based ad-hoc information distribution in crowd management scenarios. Submitted to MobiSys 2015. http://www.sigmobile.org/mobisys/2015/
2. Kampis, G., Kantelhardt, J.W., Kloch, K., Lukowicz, P.: Analytical and simulation models for collaborative localization. J. Comput. Sci. **6**(1), 1–10 (2015)
3. Kampis, G., Lukowicz, P.: Collaborative knowledge fusion by ad-hoc information distribution in crowds. In: International Conference on Computational Science, ICCS 2015, Reyjavik
4. Kampis, G., Lukowicz, P.: Collaborative localization as a paradigm for incremental knowledgefusion. In: 5th IEEE CogInfoCom 2014 Conference (2014). http://coginfocom.hu/conference/CogInfoCom14/downloads/Program_CogInfoCom_2014_final.pdf
5. Kloch, K., Lukowicz, P., Fischer, C.: Collaborative PDR localisation with mobile phones. In: Proceedings of the 2011 15th Annual International Symposiumon Wearable Computers, ISWC 11, pp. 37–40. IEEE Computer Society, Washington, DC, USA (2011)
6. Poxrucker, A., Bahle, G., Lukowicz, P.: Towards a real-world simulator for collaborative distributed learning in the scenario of urban mobility. In: 2014 IEEE Eighth International Conference on Self-Adaptive and Self-Organizing Systems Workshops (SASOW), pp. 44–48 (2014)
7. Ruta, D., Gabrys, B.: An overview of classifier fusion methods. Comput. Inf. Syst. **7**(1), 1–10 (2000)
8. Tisue, S., Wilensky, U.: Netlogo: a simple environment for modeling complexity. In: International Conference on Complex Systems, pp. 16–21 (2004)

Methodological Basis of Socio-Cyber-Physical Systems Structure-Dynamics Control and Management

Boris Sokolov[1,2(✉)], Rafael Yusupov[1], Dmitry Verzilin[3], Irina Sokolova[4], and Mikhail Ignatjev[5]

[1] St. Petersburg Institute for Informatics and Automation of the Russian Academy of Sciences (SPIIRAS), 14th line 39, St. Petersburg 199178, Russia
sokolov_boris@inbox.ru, spiiran@iias.spb.su
[2] ITMO University, 249 Kronversky Pr., St. Petersburg 197101, Russia
[3] Lesgaft National State University of Physical Education, Sport and Health, Dekabristov 35, St. Petersburg 190121, Russia
modusponens@mail.ru
[4] St. Petersburg University, Universitetskayz emb., 7-9, St. Petersburg 199034, Russia
i_sokolova@bk.ru
[5] Saint-Petersburg State University of Aerospace Instrumentation (SUAI), Bolshaya Morskaya str., 67, St. Petersburg 190000, Russia
ignatmb@mail.ru

Abstract. The main objects of our investigation are socio-cyber-physical systems (SCPS). The SCPS is the fusion of the socio, the cyber, the physical space and structures. In this case, the problems of SCPS complexity management and control are actual modern problems. The solving of these problems involve interdisciplinary researches in mathematics, cybernetics, economics, biology, physics, and computer technologies. Therefore, the paper presents new results of inter-displinary research in the field of SCPS structure-dynamics control and management theory. Our investigations have shown that this theory can be regarded as branch of neocybernetics.

Keywords: Interdisciplinary research · Cyber-physical-socio space and systems · Cybernetics · Control and management · Informational processes

1 Introduction

Today the technologies for control and management of transformation from industrial society to informational society need regulation and structuring at macro and micro level. This inspires a renewed interest to theoretical background of control and management problems. Unfortunately, logically relevant chain of fundamental notions: Cybernetics – Control – Informational processes – Universal transformer of information (computer, cybernetic machine) was split [2, 4, 23]. An expansion of computer technologies caused an illusion of their ability to solve any problem. Imperfection of these technologies has already caused catastrophes that let American and European scientists to proclaim establishing "Risk society" rather than "Informational" one [5].

© Springer International Publishing AG 2016
A.V. Chugunov et al. (Eds.): DTGS 2016, CCIS 674, pp. 610–617, 2016.
DOI: 10.1007/978-3-319-49700-6_61

Now the problems of analysis and synthesis of SCPS are closely associated with problems of complexity, which have various applications and aspects (structural complexity, complexity of functioning, complexity of decision-making, complexity of modelling and simulation, etc.) [4, 5, 15, 18, 19, 24].

So, one of the main features of SCPS is the changeability of their parameters and structures due to objective and subjective causes at different stages of the SCPS life cycle. In other words, we always come across the SCPS structure dynamics in practice. Under these conditions to increase (stabilize) SCPS potentialities and capacity for work structure control is to be performed [7–9, 15].

There are many possible variants of SCPS structure dynamics control and management. For example, they are: alteration of SCPS functioning means and objectives; alteration of the order of observation tasks and control tasks solving; redistribution of functions, of problems and of control algorithms between SCPS levels; reserve resources control; control of motion of SCPS elements and subsystems; reconfiguration of SCPS different structures [7, 8]. According to the contents of the structure-dynamics control and management problems they belong under the class of the SCPS structure – functional synthesis problems and the problems of program construction, providing for control of the SCPS development.

The main feature and the difficulty of the problems, belonging under the above class is as follows: optimal programs, providing for the SCPS main elements and subsystems control can be implemented only when the lists of functions and of control and information-processing algorithms for these elements and subsystems are known. In its turn, the distribution of the functions and algorithms among the SCPS elements and subsystems depends upon the structure and parameters of the control rules, actual for these elements and subsystems. The described contradictory situation is complicated by the changes of SCPS parameters and structures, occurring due to different causes during the SCPS life cycle [15].

At present, the class of problems under review is not examined quite thoroughly. The new theoretical and practical results were obtained on the following lines of the investigation [4, 7–10, 12, 15, 18]: the synthesis of the SCPS technical structure for the known laws of SCPS functioning (the first direction); the synthesis of the SCPS functional structure, in other words the synthesis of the control programs for the SCPS main elements and subsystems under the condition that the SCPS technical structure is known (the second direction); the synthesis of programs for SCPS construction and development without taking into account the periods of parallel functioning of the actual and the new SCPS (the third direction); the parallel synthesis of the SCPS technical structure and the functional one (the forth direction).

Several iterative procedures for solving of the joint problems, concerning the first and the second directions, are known at present. Some particular results were obtained within the third and the forth directions of investigations. All the existing models and methods for the SCPS structure – functional synthesis and for the construction of the SCPS development programs can be applied during the period of the internal and external design when the time factor is not very essential.

Therefore, the development of new theoretical base for SCPS structure-dynamics control and management is very important now. Our investigations have shown this theoretical base can be regarded as branch of neocybernetics [7–9, 15].

2   Methodological and Technical Basis of Neocybernetics

Analysis of the neocybernetic fields showed that this theory is an inter-disciplinary science oriented at analysis and synthesis of intellectual control systems for complex arbitrary objects [4–6, 10–12, 14, 22, 24]. These systems operate with both deviation-counteracting and amplifying mutual casual relationships and are able to model the environment and themselves in the environment (the cybernetics of the observer enclosed in the system). The subject of neocybernetic investigation is scientific basics of structure-functional analysis, monitoring, and synthesis of self-organizing intellectual control and management technologies and systems (SOICM TS) for SCPS.

Some words about neocybernetic history. The renovation of cybernetics has two sources. The first source lies in the attempts to revise methodological backgrounds of cybernetics [23]. As already as in 1963, Magorah Maruyama paid attention to the systems in which the mutual causal effects are deviation-amplifying [13]. Economic, social and biological examples were considered [2, 5, 10–12, 23].

In contrast to Weiner's cybernetics with deviation-counteracting systems, the studies of deviation-amplifying mutual casual relationships were called "the second cybernetics" [3]. In 1974, Heinz von Foester defined "the second-order cybernetics" with awareness that an observer is an element of the system. The studies considered processes resulting in increase of biological and social complexity [5, 10–12]. Stafford Beer in his works since 1974 emphasized that investigation on complexity problems should evolve Ashby's law of requisite variety [2].

Analysis of modern cybernetics has shown several directions for realizing this law and establishing concepts of neocybernetics [7, 8, 14, 15, 24] (see Fig. 1).

Now social aspects of neocybernetics become actual. So, for example, the authors of [4] review the social aspects of cyber-physical systems and introduce socio-cyber-physical systems, where human stakeholders play a prominent role. Particularly, context-dependent logistic operations, related to cultural, institutional, geographic and economic environment, are the foundation of socio-cyber-physical systems in production networks.

The author of [10–12] introduces a basic framework for cybernetic analysis of social systems within the third-order and fourth-order cybernetics. While the second-order cybernetics deals with autopoetic machines, the third-order cybernetics investigates the emergence of a common domain of interaction between living systems, and the fourth-order self-observing systems are comprised of cognitive subjects. The papers [1, 14] consider contribution of the theory of dynamic systems and the complex system theory to an analysis framework of social processes.

The paper [22] considers cyber-physical systems operating in social spaces, e.g. transportation systems and the smart grid, where so-called crowd-sensing information about the evolving system can be collected from humans. Furthermore, the authors

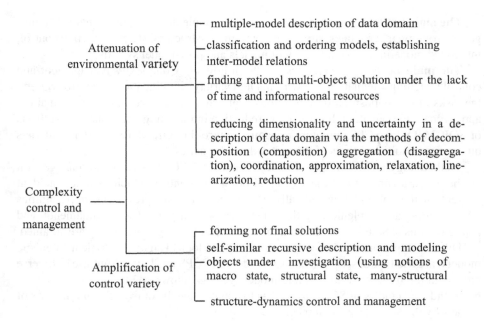

Fig. 1. Directions for realizing the law of requisite variety.

develop a mathematical approach to evaluation of the data correctness when observations are reported from sources with an unknown reliability.

We can reveal three groups of characteristics distinguishing social systems as targets of cybernetic researches. These groups of characteristics correspond to the system's elements, to the control, and to the use of a cyber space. System's elements can change their behavior according to a reflection without a strict relation to the current environment. Communication of the elements can result in nonlinear processes with positive feedbacks (the mutual causal effects are deviation-amplifying), when state variables are bounded due to limitations of resources. Communication of the elements usually results in self-organization leading to dynamic equilibriums. The system does not have a centralized control. It may exhibit an unpredictable reaction to a control impact, moreover different variants of the reaction may lead to different dynamic equilibriums. The system can change the external environment, particularly it can modify control inputs. Social media dramatically rise the intensity and scope of inter-elements communication accelerating self-organizing processes. We can denote abilities of cyber-systems using social media and global computer applications. First, such systems can and should use big data collected from the users. Second, they can produce impacts upon the real world through the users. The enumerated characteristics give a support to new concepts enriching cybernetics.

Goals of neocybernetics lie in a creation of cybernetic systems of new generation with the following features: proactive control; ability to self-actualization, self-reconfiguration, self-perfection, self-optimizing, self-treatment, and self-preservation; public behavior; sociability; kindness; honesty.

The main notions of neocybernetics include complexity, structure dynamics, emergence property, macro states, structural states, many-structural states, proactive control, integrated modeling, and qualimetry of models and poly-model systems.

The main tasks neocybernetics are the following. Complexity management and control including attenuation of environmental variety; amplification of control variety; the tasks of decomposition (composition) aggregation (disaggregation), coordination, approximation, relaxation, linearization, reduction in modeling, analysis and synthesis of SOICM TS for SCPS; structure-dynamics control in SOICM TS for SCPS; models qualimetry; traditional tasks of the first-order cybernetics.

Methodology and technique of neocybernetics for SCPS control and management are based on a concept of proactive monitoring and control, which assumes incident prevention through creating radically new forecasting and preventing opportunities when forming and implementing the control actions. At present new fundamental and applied results of SCPS structure dynamics control and management theory are obtained.

Different types of models (analytical-simulation, logical algebraic, logical-linguistic models) are used for description and study of main SCPS attributes. Joint use of diverse models in the framework of multiple-model systems, allows one to improve the flexibility and adaptability of SCPS, as well as to compensate the drawbacks of one class of models by the advantages of another one.

Modeling cyber systems with social elements (SCPS) involves integration of statistical data, obtained through observation of mass inter-element interaction, with theoretical patterns describing processes with positive and negative feedbacks [18].

Modeling of the mutual influences of the objectives, structural characteristics and mass events associated with the social and economic systems let to predict their behavior in a changing environment.

Adaptive planning and management of regulatory influences upon social systems require an analysis of three aspects: (1) objectives, which are formed through balancing goals of the subsystems and through self-organization of the target behavior of systems' elements; (2) structures of the systems; and (3) mass events associated with the change of state of systems' elements [17, 21].

Methods for integrating network models describing the structure of systems with social elements, dynamic models of coherent and self-organizing behavior of the systems' elements and models of mass events were developed to implement the modeling [18]. The interrelations between endogenous variables describing the state of social actors were presented in the terms of a signed graph notion. An approach to establishing quantitative inter-variable dependence via regression and factor analysis of statistical data was proposed. The integration of graph and quantitative models was fulfilled. The combined structural – quantitative models let forecast social actors' reactions on external impact and analyze cyclic uncontrolled changes in social medium. An algorithm for establishing the most informative characteristics of external impacts and reactions was worked out. A synthesis of classical linear dynamic models of cybernetic systems and models of optimal statistical decisions was fulfilled for the process of restructuring and evolution of systems with social elements in contrast to conventional world-class approaches to modeling of adaptation and self-organization via dynamic modeling and optimal control theory.

Decision-making supports for public and corporate policy necessitates analysis of statistical data obtained in social and economic systems. However, the data usually has mosaic nature and needs reconstruction [19].

The relationship between time distributions in systems with social elements was considered concerning the following time spaces: an unconditional dwelling time (state duration regardless of elements' state at the moment of observation); a space of time from the given state occurrence to the observation moment; a space of time from the observation moment to transition from the given state; dwelling time (under the condition that the given state was present at the moment of observation). The procedures for distributions reconstruction through the sample data of durations from state occurrence to observation moment were presented. The accuracy of the reconstruction was analyzed [19, 20].

Data of reconstruction procedures, robust to small distortions of the data and to model assumptions, were developed for three levels of conclusions based on statistical data. The levels of measuring, induction and theorizing were considered. The influence of errors and assumptions for all levels was evaluated.

Models and a general algorithm for evaluating systems' states prevalence, a state-to-state transition intensity and a state duration with the aid of mosaic data were developed [19, 20].

Density estimation technique for reconstruction of state duration distributions was worked out for the case of time data being registered for elements of social medium that were in a given state at some fixed moment of observation [19, 20].

3   Conclusion

Methodological and methodical basis of the theory of SCPS structure dynamics control and management as part of neocybernetics is developed by now. This theory can be widely used in practice. It has an interdisciplinary basis provided by classic control theory, operations research, artificial intelligence, systems theory and systems analysis. The dynamic interpretation of SCPS process provides strict mathematical base for complex socio-technical-organizational problems that were never formalized before and had high practical importance.

Acknowledgments. The research described in this paper is partially supported by the Russian Foundation for Basic Research (grants 15-07-08391, 15-08-08459, 16-07-00779, 16-08-00510, 16-08-01277, 16-29-09482-ofi-i), Russian Humanitarian Found (grants 15-04-00400), grant 074-U01 (ITMO University), project 6.1.1 (Peter the Great St. Petersburg Polytechnic University) supported by Government of Russian Federation, Program STC of Union State "Monitoring-SG" (project 1.4.1-1), State research 0073–2014–0009, 0073–2015–0007.

References

1. Becerra, G., Amozurrutia, J.A.: Rolando García's "Complex Systems Theory" and its relevance to sociocybernetics. J. Sociocybernetics **13**(15), 18–30 (2015)
2. Bir, T.: Cybernetics and Production Control. Fizmatlit, Moscow (1963)
3. Foerster, von H.: Cybernetics: Encyclopedia of Artificial Intelligence. Wiley, New York (1987)
4. Frazzon, E.M., Hartmann, J., Makuschewitz, T., Scholz-Reiter, B.: Towards socio-cyber-physical systems in production networks. Procedia CIRP **7**, 49–54 (2013)
5. Heikki, H.: Neocybernetics in biological systems. In: Helsinki University of Technology, Control Engineering Laboratory, report 151 (August 2006), 273 p. (2006)
6. Ignatyev, M.B.: Semantics and selforganization in nanoscale physics. Int. J. Comput. Anticipatory Syst. **22**, 17–23 (2008). D.M. Dubois (ed.). CHAOS, Liege, Belgium
7. Ivanov, D., Sokolov, B., Pavlov, A.: Optimal distribution (re)planning in a centralized multi-stage network under conditions of ripple effect and structure dynamics. Euro. J. Oper. Res. **237**(2), 758–770 (2014)
8. Ivanov, D., Sokolov, B.: Control and system-theoretic identification of the supply chain dynamics domain for planning, analysis, and adaptation of performance under uncertainty. Eur. J. Oper. Res. **224**, 313–323 (2013)
9. Kalinin, V.N., Sokolov, B.V.: Multi-model description of control processes for space facilities. J. Comput. Syst. Sci. Int. **1**, 149–156 (1995)
10. Mancilla, R.G.: Introduction to sociocybernetics (Part 1): third order cybernetics and a basic framework for society. J. Sociocybernetics **9**(1/2), 35–56 (2011)
11. Mancilla, R.G.: Introduction to sociocybernetics (Part 2): power, culture and institutions. J. Sociocybernetics **10**(1/2), 45–71 (2012)
12. Mancilla, R.G.: Introduction to sociocybernetics (Part 3): fourth order cybernetics. J. Sociocybernetics **11**(1/2), 47–73 (2013)
13. Maruyama, M.: The second cybernetics: deviation amplifying mutual causal process. Am. Sci. **51**(2), 164–179 (1963)
14. Nebbitt, V.E., Tyuse, S.W., Vaughn, M.G., Perron, B.E.: Conceptual tools for research on race and social problems: an overview of dynamic theory and model development. J. Hum. Behav. Soc. Env. **20**(7), 909–923 (2010)
15. Sokolov, B.V., Zelentsov, V.A., Yusupov, R.M., Merkuryev, Y.A.: Multiple models of information fusion process: quality definition and estimation. J. Comput. Sci. **13**(15), 18–30 (2014)
16. Skurihin, V.I., Zabrodsky, V.A., Kopeychenko, Y.: Adaptive Control Systems in Machine-Building Industry. Mashinostroenie, Moscow (1989). (in Russian)
17. Verzilin, D.N., Mamonov, S.A., Corbunova, I.R.: Modelling coherent and self-organization behaviour of social and economic system. In: XVI International Conference "Dynamical System Modeling and Stability Investigations" (DSMSI-2013), Taras Shevchenko National University of Kiev, Ukraine, 29–31 May 2013, 422 p. (2013). (in Russian)
18. Verzilin, D.N., Maximova, T.G.: Models of social actors' reaction on external impacts. St. Petersburg State Polytechnical Univ. J. Comput. Sci. Telecommun. Control Syst. **2**(120), 140–145 (2011). (in Russian)
19. Verzilin, D.N., Maximova, T.G.: Time attributes reconstruction for processes of states changing in social medium. St. Petersburg State Polytechnical Univ. J. Comput. Sci. Telecommun. Control Syst. **3**(126), 97–105 (2011). (in Russian)

20. Verzilin, D.N., Potapychev, S.N., Ryzhkov, N.A.: The use of simulation to evaluate the response of social and economic systems to external influences. In: V Conference "Simulation. Theory and Practice", IMMOD 2011, St. Petersburg, 19–21 October 2011, pp. 115–119 (2011). (in Russian)
21. Verzilin, D.N., Shanygin, S.I., Chereshneva A.V.: Conceptual bases of modelling of social systems and estimation of stability of social processes. St. Petersburg State Polytechnical Univ. J. Comput. Sci. Telecommun. Control Syst. **5**(133), 123–128 (2011)
22. Wang, S., Wang, D., Su, L., Kaplan, L., Abdelzaher, T.F.: Towards cyber-physical systems in social spaces: the data reliability challenge. In: Real-Time Systems Symposium (RTSS), 2–5 December 2014, pp. 74–85. IEEE (2014)
23. Wiener, N.: The Human Use of Human Beings: Cybernetics and Society. Da Capo Press, Boston (1950)
24. Zhuge, H.: Semantic linking through spaces for cyber-physical-socio intelligence: a methodology. Artif. Intell. **175**, 988–1019 (2011)

Author Index

Printed in the United States
By Bookmasters